Praise for earlier editions of

Guide to the National Park Areas: WESTERN STATES

"Will tell you how to get there, what to see, and what camping and recreational facilities are available. Like our national parks themselves, a bargain for motorhomers!"

—*Motorhome Life* magazine

"The Scotts did a lot of traveling, and their first-hand research has paid off."

—*Kliatt Paperback Book Guides*

"Offers excellent encouragement for leaving the beaten paths of overcrowded tourist areas and getting back to America's treasures."

—*Hudson Valley* magazine

"The information the authors pass on in their book will help many travelers prepare a wonderful vacation."

—*Camp-orama*

"The Scotts have a winner here . . . good basic information."

—*Pike County* (PA) *Dispatch*

A Special Message from The Globe Pequot Press

The Globe Pequot Press is proud to present the sixth edition of *Guide to the National Park Areas: Western States*. This book provides detailed information about 190 areas west of the Mississippi, and it is written by our intrepid park experts, David and Kay Scott, who have been our park authors for more than twenty years.

But this book is special to us for another reason. Globe Pequot has been publishing books on the national parks for many years. We have helped thousands and thousands of people discover our nation's most sacred treasures. And while we are very proud of our part in this, we are also well aware that with park attendance at an all-time high, the parks themselves have suffered from excessive wear and tear. We feel that if we are going to contribute to the damage to parks by directing visitors to them, we also want to help offset that damage by directing funds to the parks.

The Globe Pequot Press therefore will donate $1.00 from the sale of each copy of this book directly to the National Parks and Conservation Association, a nonprofit organization. This money will help NPCA protect parks from damaging development; monitor and inventory natural and historic resources; develop financial and transportation plans; and keep destructive and disruptive activities out of the parks.

If you would like to donate to the National Parks and Conservation Association, please send a check or money order to:

National Parks and Conservation Association
1776 Massachusetts Avenue, N.W.
Washington, D.C. 20036

The Globe Pequot Press is committed to helping preserve our national parks and ensuring that they will remain wonderful places to visit for generations to come.

The Staff of The Globe Pequot Press

Guide to the National Park Areas: WESTERN STATES

Sixth Edition

by

DAVID L. SCOTT *and*
KAY W. SCOTT

Guilford, Connecticut

Also by David L. Scott and Kay W. Scott

Guide to the National Park Areas: Eastern States

The Complete Guide to the National Park Lodges

Text photographs and Facilities and Activities Chart
reprinted courtesy of the National Park Service (unless otherwise noted).

Cover photo © Keith Walklet/Quietworks
Cover design by Adam Schwartzman
Text and map design by Nancy Freeborn

Library of Congress Cataloging-in-Publication Data

Scott, David Logan.
Guide to the national park areas. Western states / by David L. Scott and Kay W. Scott. — 6th ed.
p. cm.
ISBN 0-7627-0507-8
1. National parks and reserves—West (U.S.) Guidebooks. 2. West (U.S.) Guidebooks. I. Scott, Kay Woelfel. II. Title.
E160.S45 1999b
917.804'33—dc21 99-38953
CIP

Manufactured in the United States of America
Sixth Edition/First Printing

CONTENTS

*Map reference numbers correspond with locations on the map on pp. viii–ix.

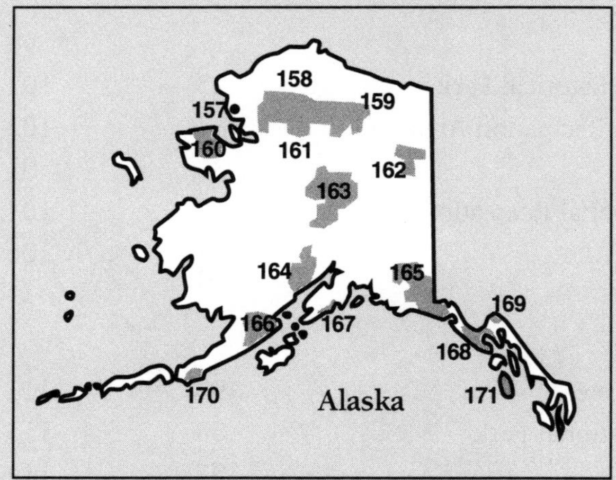
Alaska
157
158
159
160
161
162
163
164
165
166
167
168
169
170
171

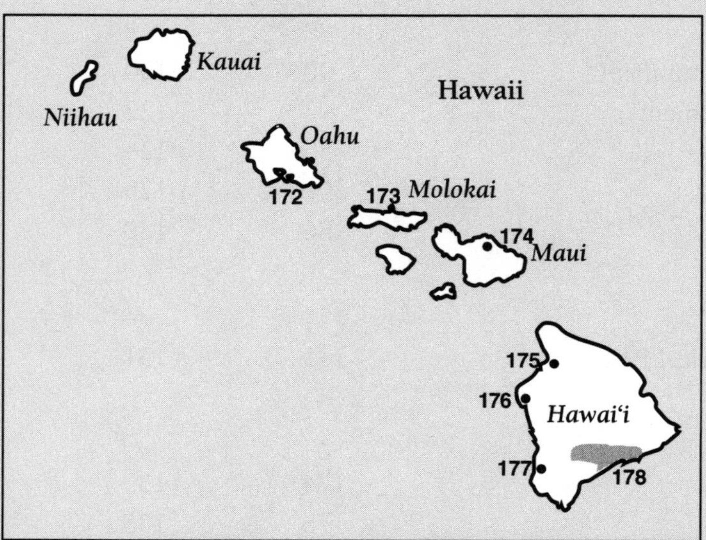
Hawaii
Kauai
Niihau
Oahu
172
173
Molokai
174
Maui
175
176
Hawai'i
177
178

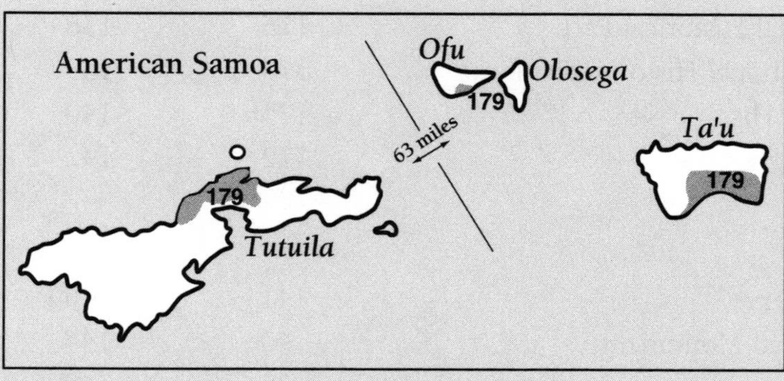
American Samoa
Ofu
Olosega
179
63 miles
Ta'u
179
179
Tutuila

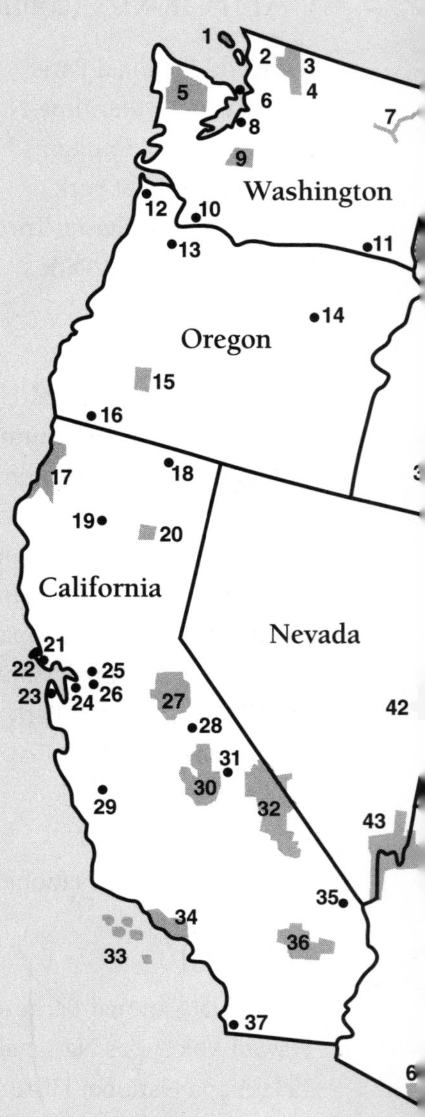
Washington
Oregon
California
Nevada
1
2
3
4
5
6
7
8
9
10
11
12
13
14
15
16
17
18
19
20
21
22
23
24
25
26
27
28
29
30
31
32
33
34
35
36
37
42
43

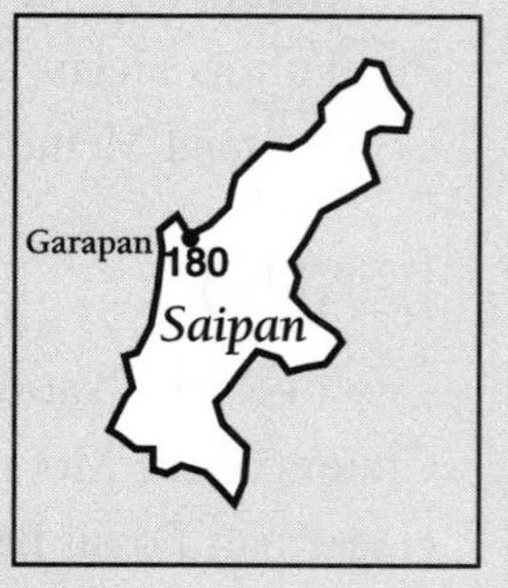
Garapan
180
Saipan

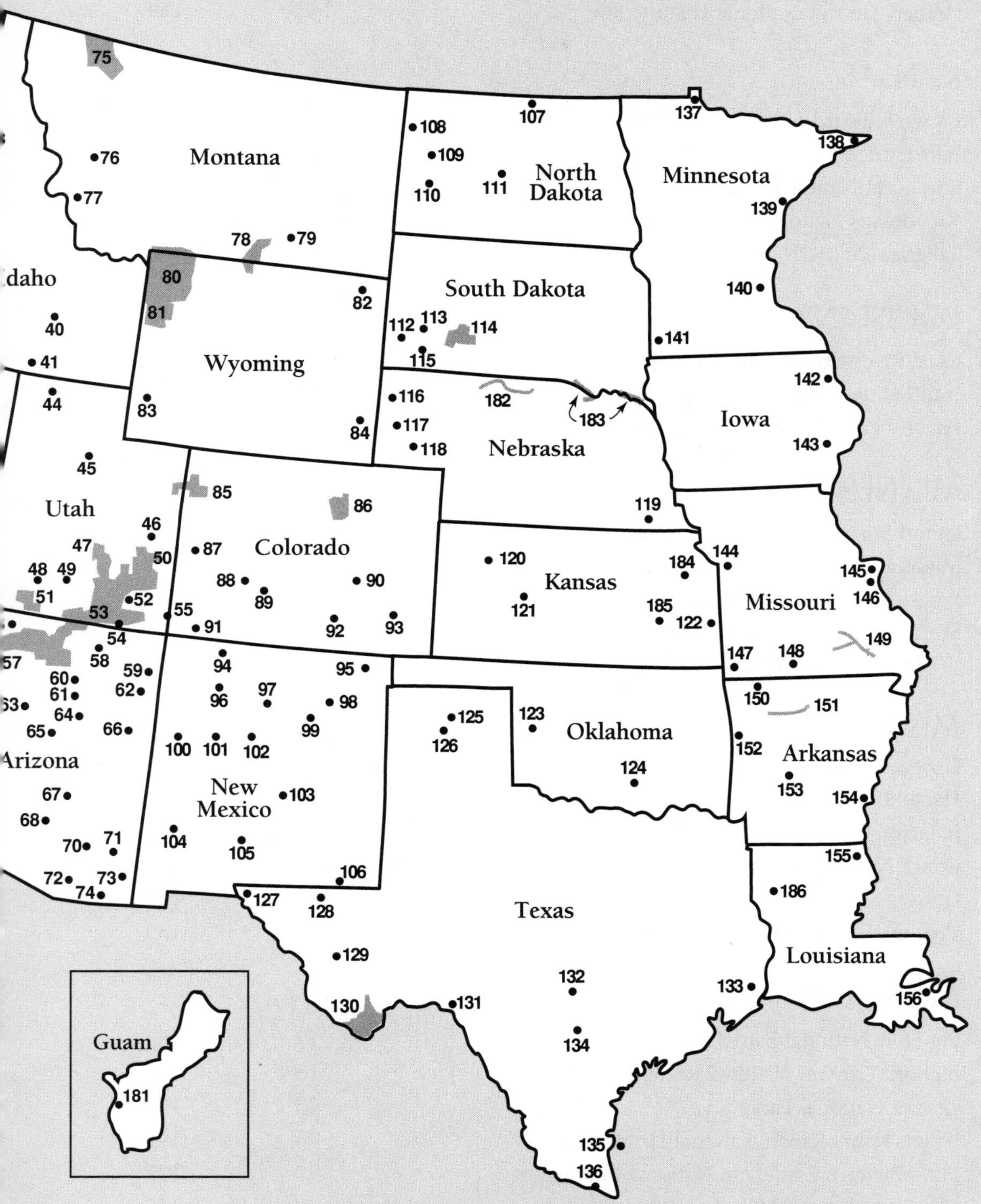

75
76
77
Montana
78
79
108
107
109
111
110
North Dakota
137
138
Minnesota
139
daho
80
81
82
South Dakota
112
113
114
115
140
141
40
41
Wyoming
44
83
84
116
117
118
182
183
Nebraska
142
Iowa
143
45
85
86
Utah
46
47
50
87
Colorado
48
49
51
88
89
90
119
120
Kansas
121
184
185
122
144
145
146
Missouri
52
53
54
55
91
92
93
57
58
59
60
61
62
63
64
65
66
94
95
96
97
98
99
100
101
102
rizona
New Mexico
103
67
68
70
71
72
73
74
104
105
106
125
126
123
Oklahoma
124
147
148
149
150
151
152
Arkansas
153
154
155
186
127
128
Texas
129
130
131
132
133
134
135
136
Louisiana
156
Guam
181

PREFACE

Any discussion of America's national parks is likely to cause most people to think instinctively of one or more well-known national parks such as Acadia, Grand Canyon, Grand Teton, Olympic, Rocky Mountain, Great Smoky Mountains (by far the most visited NPS area), Yellowstone, and Yosemite. These are eight of our most spectacular and frequently visited and photographed national parks. Literally hundreds of other beautiful and interesting areas are included in the National Park System, however, even though they are not all officially designated as national parks. The system of parks also includes national monuments, historical parks, military parks, historic sites, reserves, lakeshores, battlefields, and recreation areas. The National Park Service (NPS) administers areas that include seashores to walk, parkways to drive, rivers to float, and majestic redwoods to admire. Each area offers something special that is worth seeking out. How about a visit to a restored fort on the historic Oregon Trail? Have you tried camping in the midst of a field of cinders and volcanic rock? Perhaps you would enjoy a visit to the reconstructed fort in Oregon where Lewis and Clark camped during the winter of 1805–6 following their epic journey to the Pacific Ocean. How about a stroll around the Missouri birthplace and home of educator George Washington Carver?

Of the 378 areas administered by the National Park Service, only about 15 percent are officially designated as national parks. Most national parks are relatively large and contain a variety of resources. Other areas administered by the National Park Service, designated as national monuments, battlefields, historic sites, and historical parks, are more limited in size and scope. The different designation doesn't make these areas any less rewarding to visit. In fact, you are likely to discover that these other areas are less well known and less crowded and offer much to see and do. Several times we were the only members on ranger-guided walks, and we once experienced a wonderful campfire program with only six other visitors. These experiences frequently become a trip's most memorable events.

As these books are written we have spent twenty-six summers touring the national parks. We have visited all the states and have seen nearly all of the park areas administered by the National Park Service. We have spent a week hiking Canyonlands National Park and a day strolling through Fort Laramie National Historic Site. We took a ferry to Klondike Gold Rush National Historical Park in Skagway, Alaska, and a plane to Hawaii Volcanoes National Park on the Big Island of Hawaii; and we drove the Alaska Highway to spend a week at Denali National Park. We have seen the sights, walked the trails, talked with the park rangers, and visited with other campers. We have loved it all and in virtually every case would like to be able to go back and visit the same places again. In many instances that is exactly what we have done.

The idea for this series of books occurred to us about the fifth summer of our travels. Each time we headed in a new direction, we found ourselves trying to decide which areas of the National Park Service to visit and, once there, attempting to determine which particular points of interest and activities held the most promise for our limited time. We discovered that we often delayed trips to areas we should have visited earlier and spent time driving to parks that held less interest for us. In addition, after arriving at a park, we were often unsure of which campgrounds to use or what activities and facilities were available.

Our hope is that the contents of these books will assist others in avoiding these same pitfalls. We have tried to include enough information to allow readers to decide which parks to visit as well as how long to allow to adequately discover the major features of each park. For most areas we have tried to provide information on why the area was set aside, a summary of the history and/or geology of the area, activities for visitors, facilities such as availability of food service and overnight accommodations, campgrounds and their facilities, and possibilities for those who fish. In the limited space allotted to each area, we believe that this information is most useful to the majority of visitors.

The material in these books is believed to be accurate. The Park Service is constantly altering the areas under its jurisdiction, however, and no doubt there will be changes before you buy this book. Budget limitations have resulted in the closing of certain facilities as funds for maintenance and personnel have been cut or at least have not kept up with visitation growth. In some cases, the closings are temporary; in other instances, they appear permanent. Regardless of the changes, we can assure you that you will enjoy yourself. The people are nice, the scenery is breathtaking, and the history is real.

Swiftcurrent Lake and Mt. Wilbur, Glacier National Park

We want to express our thanks to park personnel who took the time to read and correct the written material we sent. In addition, we appreciate the time that rangers have spent with us on our annual tours. We hope these books can help you have some of the wonderful times in our national parks that we have enjoyed.

David L. Scott
Kay W. Scott
Valdosta, Georgia

The information in this guidebook was confirmed at press time. We recommend, however, that you call establishments before traveling to obtain current information.

INTRODUCTION

SOME BASICS FOR VISITING AMERICA'S NATIONAL PARKS

Preparation

Each of the 378 areas administered by the National Park Service offers something special. Learning as much as possible about what is special before you visit a park helps you appreciate what you are likely to experience. You will also waste less of your limited time after arrival. Why wait until you arrive to find out what you will be seeing? Most park officials are good about responding to requests for information.

Each of the park writeups in this book provides a telephone number, address, and, in some cases, an e-mail address to use in requesting information. You will also find park web addresses that allow access to basic information including opening and closing times, facilities, and activities. If you plan to drive thousands of miles on a vacation of several weeks, take some time to bone up on what you are likely to see, both along the way and at your destination.

What to do when you arrive

The first order of business should be to stop at the park visitor center, especially when you are planning to spend a half day or less in a park area. With a short stay you need to make every minute count. Ask someone at the visitor center information desk about the activities and sights he or she recommends for the time you have available. Most visitor centers offer exhibits and an orientation film or slide presentation to introduce you to the park. The video presentations are generally excellent at providing a better appreciation of what you will experience in the park. Visitor centers generally operate sales areas with pamphlets and paperback guides relevant to the park and nearby areas. You may want to ask someone at the information desk which publications are likely to prove most helpful. Also check for a listing of the day's ranger-led interpretive programs. Guided walks, living history programs, and ranger presentations are nearly always worthwhile.

It is our opinion that with a limited amount of time, you are better off taking time to really experience a few park areas than trying to visit as many park areas as possible. Why miss some of the worthwhile things a park has to offer when you are already there and may not return?

Fees

Most areas operated by the National Park Service levy entrance fees that range from $3.00 to $5.00 per vehicle at the low end to $20.00 per vehicle at very popular parks such as Yosemite, Grand Canyon, and Yellowstone. Separate fees apply to bikers and hikers. The initial entrance fee is generally good for several days, although this varies by park. Many individual parks also offer annual entrance passes at a higher charge. You may discover that certain activities inside a park such as a cave tour or a guided tour of a building will require a separate charge. Fees for entrance and activities have increased in both size and frequency in recent years. Many park areas that once offered free entrance now impose a fee. In addition, nearly a hundred park areas, including most of the national recreation areas, are participating in a new program for fee demonstration areas. Most of the fees collected under this program are retained by the parks that collect them.

For those who qualify, lifetime passes are available for seniors ($10) and handicapped (no charge). These two passes are good for free entrance to all the parks and a 50 percent discount on federal use fees for facilities and services such as camping, swimming, parking, boat launching, and cave tours. The passes do not cover special permit fees or fees charged by private concessioners. The passes entitle the holder to a 50 percent discount at all national park and U.S. Forest Service campgrounds. An annual Golden Eagle Passport ($50), which is available to anyone, allows free entrance but no discount on facilities or tours. It also does not normally cover recreation user fees imposed by some park areas. The Golden Eagle Passport is a worthwhile purchase when you are likely to visit a number of parks during a twelve-month period. Each of these passes is available at most entrance stations and visitor centers. A Golden Eagle Passport (but not a Golden Age or Golden Access pass) can be purchased via mail by sending a $50 check or money order to: National Park Service, 1100 Ohio Drive, SW, Room 138, Washington, D.C. 20242. Each of the passes admits the passholder and any accompanying passengers in a private vehicle. Where entry is not by private vehicle, the passport admits the passholder, spouse, children, and parents.

Entrance Fees for National Park Areas, Western States

PARK	PER VEHICLE	PER PERSON
Arches NP (UT)	$10.00	$5.00
Aztec Ruins NM (NM)	— —	4.00
Badlands NP (SD)	10.00	5.00
Bandelier NM (NM)	10.00	5.00
Bent's Old Fort NHS (CO)	— —	2.00
Big Bend NP (TX)	10.00	— —
Big Hole NB (MT)	4.00	2.00
Black Canyon of the Gunnison NM (CO)	7.00	4.00
Bryce Canyon NP (UT)	10.00	5.00
Cabrillo NM (CA)	5.00	2.00
Canyonlands NP (UT)	10.00	5.00
Capitol Reef NP (UT)	4.00	2.00
Capulin Volcano NM (NM)	4.00	2.00
Casa Grande NM (AZ)	4.00	2.00
Cedar Breaks NM (UT)	4.00	2.00
Chaco Culture NHP (NM)	8.00	4.00
Crater Lake NP (OR)	10.00	5.00
Craters of the Moon NM (ID)	4.00	2.00
Death Valley NP (CA)	10.00	5.00
Denali NP (AK)	10.00	5.00
Devils Tower NM (WY)	8.00	5.00
Dinosaur NM (CO/UT)	10.00	5.00

PARK	PER VEHICLE	PER PERSON
Effigy Mounds NM (IA)	4.00	2.00
El Morro NM (NM)	4.00	2.00
Florissant Fossil Beds NM (CO)	——	2.00
Fort Clatsop NMEM (OR)	——	2.00
Fort Davis NHS (TX)	——	2.00
Fort Laramie NHS (WY)	——	2.00
Fort Larned NHS (KS)	——	2.00
Fort Scott NHS (KS)	——	2.00
Fort Smith NHS (AR)	——	2.00
Fort Union (NM)	4.00	2.00
Fort Vancouver NHS (WA)	——	2.00
Glacier NP (MT)	10.00	5.00
Glen Canyon NRA (AZ/UT)	5.00	3.00
Golden Spike NHS (UT)	7.00	3.50
Grand Canyon NP (AZ)	20.00	10.00
Grand Portage NM (MN)	——	2.00
Grand Teton NP (WY)	20.00	10.00
Grant-Kohrs Ranch NHS (MT)	4.00	2.00
Great Sand Dunes NM (CO)	——	3.00
Haleakalā NP (HI)	10.00	5.00
Harry S Truman NHS (MO)	——	2.00
Hawaii Volcanoes NP (HI)	10.00	5.00
Herbert Hoover NHS (IA)	——	2.00
Hovenweep NM (CO/UT)	6.00	3.00
Jefferson National Expansion MEM (MO)	——	2.00
John Muir NHS (CA)	——	2.00
Joshua Tree NP (CA)	10.00	5.00
Kenai Fjords NP (AK)	5.00	3.00
Kings Canyon/Sequoia NP (CA)	10.00	5.00
Lassen Volcanic NP (CA)	10.00	5.00
Lava Beds NM (CA)	4.00	2.00
Little Bighorn NM (MT)	6.00	3.00
Mesa Verde NP (CO)	10.00	5.00
Montezuma Castle NM (AZ)	——	2.00
Mount Rainier NP (WA)	10.00	5.00
Muir Woods NM (CA)	——	2.00
Natural Bridges NM (UT)	6.00	3.00
Olympic NP (WA)	10.00	5.00
Organ Pipe Cactus NM (AZ)	4.00	2.00

PARK	PER VEHICLE	PER PERSON
Padre Island NS (TX)	10.00	5.00
Pea Ridge NMP (AR)	4.00	2.00
Pecos NHP (NM)	4.00	2.00
Petrified Forest NP (AZ)	10.00	5.00
Pinnacles NM (CA)	5.00	2.00
Pipe Spring NM (AZ)		2.00
Pipestone NM (NM)		2.00
Pu'uhonua o Hōnaunau NHP (HI)		2.00
Rocky Mountain NP (CO)	10.00	5.00
Saguaro NP (AZ)	4.00	2.00
Scotts Bluff NM (NE)	5.00	2.00
Sequoia/Kings Canyon NM (CA)	10.00	5.00
Sunset Crater NP (AZ)		3.00
Theodore Roosevelt NP (ND)	10.00	5.00
Tonto NM (AZ)	4.00	2.00
Tumacacori NHP (AZ)		2.00
Tuzigoot NM (AZ)		2.00
Walnut Canyon NM (AZ)		3.00
White Sands NM (NM)		3.00
Whitman Mission NHS (WA)		2.00
Wilson's Creek NB (MO)	4.00	2.00
Wupatki NM (AZ)		3.00
Yellowstone NP (WY)	20.00	10.00
Yosemite NP (CA)	20.00	10.00
Zion NP (UT)	10.00	5.00

Note: Vehicle rate applies to all persons in a noncommercial vehicle. Per-person rate applies to visitors walking through the entrance station. Some sites, particularly forts, collect from individuals walking in rather than vehicles driving in.

Crowds

Most of America's national park areas are heavily visited, especially during summer months when the weather is good and children are out of school. If possible, try to plan your trip during the spring or fall when crowds are smaller, prices are sometimes reduced, and the weather is still enjoyable. In fact, the weather at many of the western parks is delightful during the spring when flowers are blooming and in the fall when leaves are turning. We had an enjoyable visit to Yosemite National Park just after Christmas when the air was crisp, the valley was covered with snow, and visitors were a fraction of the normal crowds this busy park experiences during June, July, and August.

Crowds are less of a problem at some of the smaller parks, especially in early mornings and late afternoons. Parks near urban areas are nearly always less crowded during weekdays when nearby residents are working and children are in school. Try to plan trips to eating establishments before or after the most popular hours.

Campgrounds

Although many National Park Service areas, especially those with primarily a historical theme, do not have campgrounds, a number of areas in the western states administered by the National Park Service do provide camping facilities. Multiple campgrounds are in the bigger national parks, such as Yosemite, Sequoia, Olympic, Mount Rainier, Glacier, Yellowstone, Big Bend, Rocky Mountain, and Grand Teton, which serve as popular vacation destinations. Campgrounds are also at some less-heavily visited areas including Lava Beds National Monument, Natural Bridges National Monument, Devils Tower National Monument, and Theodore Roosevelt National Park.

Most National Park Service campgrounds offer similar facilities including picnic tables, fire grates, water, a dump station, and rest rooms with flush toilets. Hookups for water, electricity, and waste disposal are generally unavailable except for a few instances when a campground is operated by a private concessioner rather than the Park Service itself. Likewise, showers are not offered at most of Park Service campgrounds. Concessioners sometimes provide pay showers near a visitor center or store, but this is the exception rather than the rule.

National parks with and without campgrounds are often surrounded by national forests that offer numerous camping opportunities. U.S. Forest Service campgrounds often provide relatively rustic facilities including pit toilets although this is certainly not always the case and many U.S. Forest Service campgrounds are quite nice with paved parking pads and modern rest rooms. Because National Park Service campgrounds tend to be heavily used, you may wish to settle in at a Forest Service campground the night before entering one of the busy parks, especially if you arrive in the late afternoon.

Most National Park Service campgrounds are operated on a first-come, first-served basis, so the earlier in the day you arrive, the more likely you are to locate a vacant campsite. Approximately two dozen park areas managed by the National Park Service have campgrounds with sites that can be reserved. Campgrounds at each of the parks listed to the right can be reserved through National Park Reservation Service operated by Biospherics, a publicly held firm. Reservations (except for Yosemite, which has a separate reservation service) can be made via the Internet (reservations.nps.gov), by phone (800–365–2267), or through the mail (National Park Reservation Service, P.O. Box 1600, Cumberland, MD 21501). Reservations can be made beginning on the 5th of each month (the 15th for Yosemite), up to five months in advance. Not all campgrounds in each of the listed parks are always subject to reservation.

NPS Areas, Western States, with Campgrounds that Accept Reservations

Channel Islands National Park (CA)
Chickasaw National Recreation Area (OK)
Death Valley National Park (CA)
Glacier National Park (MT)
Grand Canyon National Park (AZ)
Joshua Tree National Park (CA)
Katmai National Park (AK)
Mount Rainier National Park (WA)
Rocky Mountain National Park (CO)
Sequoia/Kings Canyon National Parks
Whiskeytown National Recreation Area (CA)
Yosemite National Park (CA) (800–436–7275)
Zion National Park (UT)

Lodging

A limited number of national park areas (most of which are in the western states) offer overnight lodging facilities. Private accommodations are often available outside or near a park's entrance. Most national park lodges are owned by the federal government but operated under long-term lease by private concessioners who must have their charges approved by park superintendents. A limited number of park lodges are privately owned, including Furnace Creek Inn and Panamint Springs Resort in Death Valley National Park. Park lodging is subject to wide variation in both price and quality from Yosemite's luxurious Ahwahnee, which charges approximately $250 per night to tent cabins and dorm-style buildings at Grand Teton that rent for $30 to $40 per night. Most lodging facilities with a private bath are in the $90 to $120 range. Despite the relatively steep cost, park accommodations are often fully booked months in advance, so you should seek a reservation early if you plan to stay overnight at a park facility during a busy period. Reservations are easier to obtain in the off-season.

NPS Areas, Western States, with Lodging Facilities

Badlands National Park (SD)
Big Bend National Park (TX)
Bryce Canyon National Park (UT)
Canyon de Chelly National Monument (AZ)
Crater Lake National Park (OR)
Death Valley National Park (CA/NV)
Denali National Park (AK)
Glacier Bay National Park (AK)
Glacier National Park (MT)
Glen Canyon National Recreation Area (AZ/UT)
Grand Canyon National Park (AZ)
Grand Teton National Park (WY)
Hawaii Volcanoes National Park (HI)
Kings Canyon National Park (CA)
Lake Mead National Recreation Area (NV)
Lassen Volcanic National Park (CA)
Mesa Verde National Park (CA)
Mount Rainier National Park (WA)
North Cascades National Park (WA)
Olympic National Park (WA)
Oregon Caves National Monument (OR)
Ozark National Scenic Riverway (MO)
Sequoia National Park (CA)
Voyageurs National Park (MN)
Yellowstone National Park (WY)
Yosemite National Park (CA)
Zion National Park (UT)

Facilities

Facilities available in national park service areas vary widely. A large and busy park such as Yosemite or Yellowstone offers nearly anything you can find in a small town, including groceries, museums, restaurants, snack bars, medical centers, service stations, and hotels. Smaller park areas may offer little other than a visitor center and a picnic area, one of which will generally have drinking water and rest rooms. The visitor center may even have a soft drink machine, but don't count on it. Most of these smaller park areas don't have a small store, place to eat, or vending machines. They certainly don't have a place to stay the night, except, perhaps, a campground. Plan to pick up the fixings for a picnic before you enter one of the smaller parks.

KEY FOR MAP SYMBOLS

Roads

Dirt Roads

Trails

State Border

Park Area

Rivers / Water

Visitor Center

Camping

Lodge

Building

Locator / Town

Picnic Area

Ruins / Historic Site
(as noted on individual maps)

Parking

Overlook

STATE TOURIST INFORMATION

(907) 465–2010

The national parks of Alaska are immense. With a cumulative total of more than 50 million acres, or more than twenty times the area of Yellowstone, the fifteen Alaska parks include ten units authorized in 1978 that actually doubled the size of the National Park System. Many of the parks are so remote that it is necessary to charter transportation to reach them. Even for more developed and accessible parks such as Denali (formerly Mount McKinley), it is difficult to do much more than scratch the surface. Regardless, the parks of Alaska are superb, unspoiled areas and true national treasures.

Alaska may seem rather remote for most travelers, but transportation to the state is not difficult to arrange. For first-time visitors, tours involving air or a combination of air, bus, and ship are probably desirable, especially for those individuals with limited time. For visitors with more time who plan to drive, it is best to take the Alaska Marine Highway on one leg of the trip and drive the Alaska Highway on the other leg. The trip along the inland passage is spectacular. In addition, it is the only way to visit cities in the panhandle (as well as Sitka National Historical Park). Ferries leave Seattle, Washington, and Prince Rupert, British Columbia, regularly. For information on the ferry system, write Alaska Marine Highway, Pouch R, Juneau, AK 99811.

Another method of visiting Alaska is to drive the Alaska Highway from Dawson Creek, British Columbia, to Fairbanks, Alaska. Most of the highway is now paved, so the drive is not nearly as difficult and hard on a car or camper as it once was. In fact, any adventure-seeking traveler should try the drive at least once. Anyone attempting the drive should pick up a copy of *Milepost* at a local bookstore (or write to Alaska Northwest Publishing Company, Box 4-EEE, Anchorage, AK 99509).

Because of the difficulty of reaching the ten parks brought into the system in 1978, we have allotted less space to each of these new undeveloped areas. Individuals contemplating a trip to one or more of these parks will need more information than we can hope to provide in a book such as this. Readers will find a brief description of each park and an address to write to for more detailed information. Descriptions of the five older parks are more complete.

Aniakchak National Monument and Preserve (opposite page)

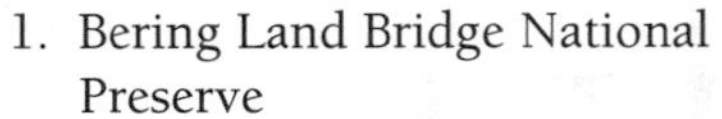

1. Bering Land Bridge National Preserve
2. Cape Krusenstern National Monument
3. Noatak National Preserve
4. Kobuk Valley National Park
5. Gates of the Arctic National Park and Preserve
6. Yukon–Charley Rivers National Preserve
7. Denali National Park and Preserve
8. Lake Clark National Park and Preserve
9. Kenai Fjords National Park
10. Katmai National Park and Preserve
11. Aniakchak National Monument and Preserve
12. Wrangell–St. Elias National Park and Preserve
13. Glacier Bay National Park and Preserve
14. Sitka National Historical Park
15. Klondike Gold Rush National Historical Park

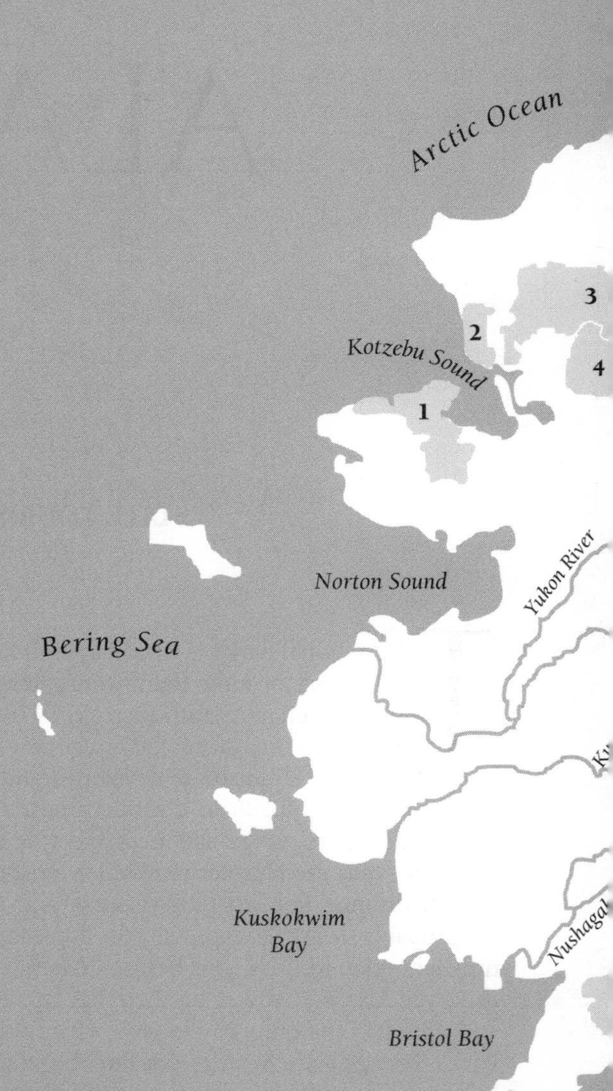

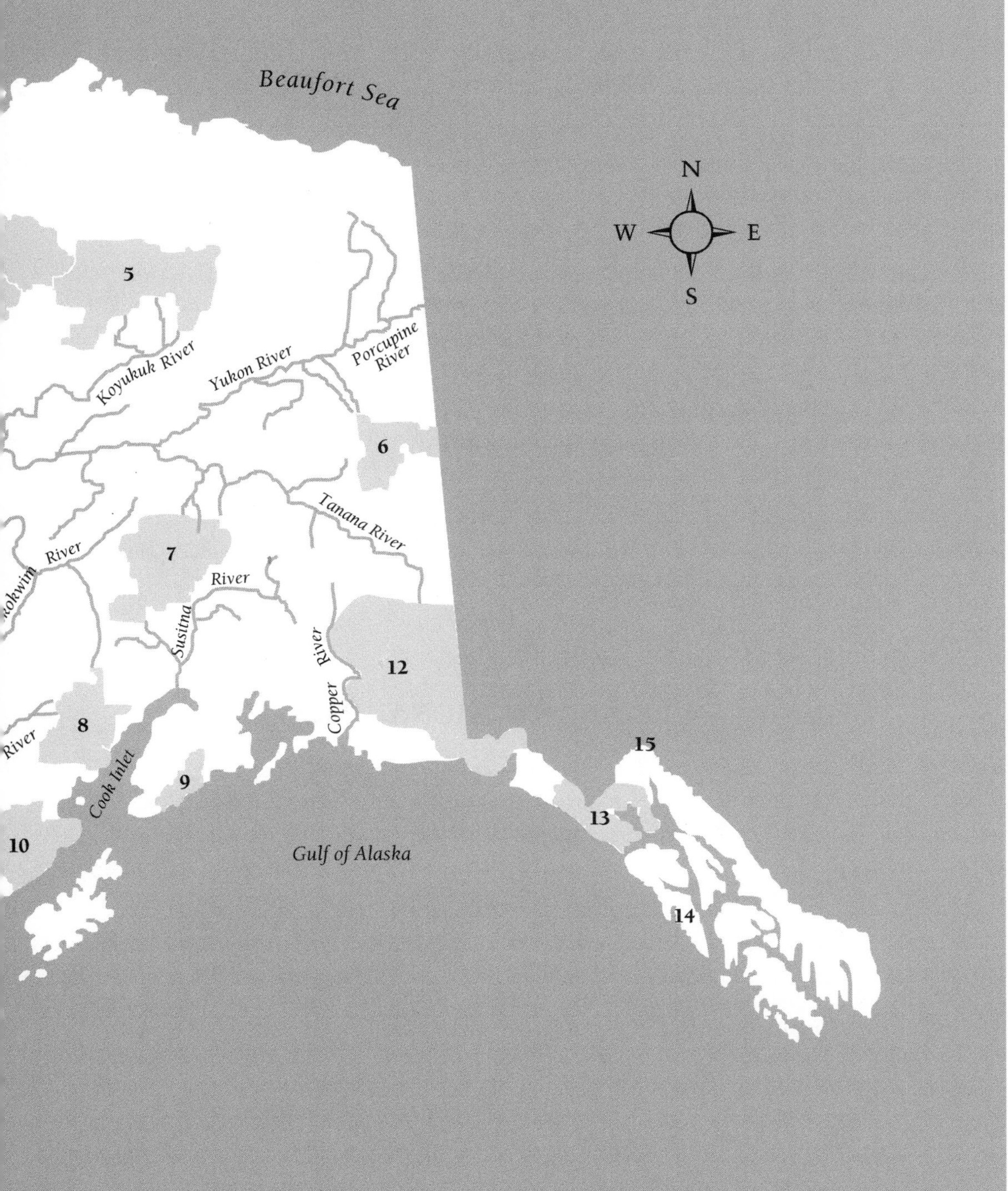

Beaufort Sea
N
W
E
S
5
Koyukuk River
Yukon River
Porcupine River
6
Tanana River
River
7
River
Susitna
Copper River
12
River
8
Cook Inlet
9
10
15
13
Gulf of Alaska
14

ANIAKCHAK NATIONAL MONUMENT AND PRESERVE

P.O. Box 7
King Salmon, AK 99613-0007
(907) 246–3305
www.nps.gov/ania/

Aniakchak comprises slightly more than 600,000 acres, including the Aniakchak Caldera, which covers thirty square miles and is one of the great dry calderas of the world. The caldera, which remained undiscovered until 1922, has a floor of cinder cones, debris, and formations formed by volcanic activity, all surrounded by 2,000-foot walls. The volcano last erupted in 1933.

The Aniakchak National Wild River begins at Surprise Lake in the caldera, passes through The Gates in the caldera wall, and then flows 32 miles to Aniakchak Bay on the south coast of the peninsula. Over the first 15 miles, the river drops 60 feet per mile as it runs through the tundra- and shrub-covered foothills. This rock-strewn section contains class 2 through class 4 whitewater. The final 17 miles are a much more gentle class 1. It is not uncommon for river runners to see brown bears, caribou, bald eagles, and, on the coast, sea otters.

Access to the park is difficult and expensive. Inclement weather often makes it impossible. Reeve Aleutian Airways (800–544–2248) flies between Anchorage and Port Heiden. From Port Heiden, a very difficult 10-mile hike is necessary to reach the monument. Access is also possible by charter plane from King Salmon or one of the towns in the lower Alaska Peninsula. The nearest lodging is in King Salmon. The King Salmon Visitor Center (907–246–4250) at the King Salmon Airport provides information about the monument and other locations and services in southwest Alaska.

BERING LAND BRIDGE NATIONAL PRESERVE

P.O. Box 220
Nome, AK 99762-0220
(907) 443–2522
www.nps.gov/bela/

Bering Land Bridge, on the Seward Peninsula of northwest Alaska, is a remnant of a land bridge that connected North America with Asia more than 10,000 years ago. The bridge was once a migration route for people, animals, and plants, but is now covered by the Chukchi and Bering seas.

Most visitors arrive during milder summer months (40 to 60 degrees Fahrenheit) when plants burst into color and wildlife becomes active. Unfortunately, insects are also bad during this period. Fishing for char, grayling, and salmon is excellent. It is also possible to observe Inupiat Eskimo subsistence activities such as hunting, fishing, and gathering.

Access to the isolated preserve is difficult. Airplanes may be chartered at Nome and Kotzebue. Nearest lodging and meals are in the same two towns.

CAPE KRUSENSTERN NATIONAL MONUMENT

P.O. Box 1029
Kotzebue, AK 99752
(907) 442–3890
www.nps.gov/noaa/

Cape Krusenstern National Monument, located in northwest Alaska, comprises 560,000 acres and has been the site of seasonal marine mammal hunting by Eskimo peoples for more than 5,000 years. Eskimos continue to hunt seals along Cape Krusenstern's outermost beach.

The monument has no facilities of any kind, and visitors generally come only to camp and backpack in this very primitive area. Insect repellent is recommended for summer months. A variety of wildlife inhabits the monument, including black and grizzly bears, caribou, lynx, moose, musk ox, and wolves. Offshore, polar bears, seals, walrus, and whales may be seen on occasion.

Access to Cape Krusenstern is by chartered boat or plane from Kotzebue. The monument, at its nearest point, is approximately 10 miles from the town, where lodging is available. Kotzebue also has small stores. The best areas for visiting are along the monument's west coast and in the hills running north to south through the park.

DENALI NATIONAL PARK AND PRESERVE

P.O. Box 9
Denali National Park, AK 99755-0009
(907) 683–2294
www.nps.gov/dena/

Denali (formerly Mount McKinley) National Park and Preserve comprises million acres of mountains, alpine glaciers, and rolling lowlands with wide rivers. The park can be reached via Parks Highway, which connects Fairbanks and Anchorage. This road is open all year. Denali may also be reached during the summer from Paxson via the gravel Denali Highway. The Alaska Railroad provides daily service from late May to mid-September and reduced service during the remainder of the year. The ride from Anchorage (234 miles) requires five hours; the ride from Fairbanks (122 miles), two and a half hours. For information write Alaska Railroad Corporation Passenger Services, P.O. Box 107500, Anchorage, AK 99510 (Continental U.S. and Hawaii 800–544–0552; Anchorage 907–265–2494; Fairbanks 907–465–4155). Several companies provide transportation service in summer, including Alaska-Denali Transit (907–276–6443); Alaska Sightseeing Tours (Anchorage 907–276–1305, Fairbanks 907–452–8518); and Grey Line of Alaska/Westours (Anchorage 907–277–5581, Fairbanks 907–456– 7741). A 3,000-foot airstrip is maintained at the park for light aircraft.

Most of Denali is covered with alpine tundra, rock, and ice. Wet tundra contains dense brush and shrubs, while dry tundra along slopes and hills is characterized by small plants and wildflowers. The park contains a wide variety of wildlife, including more than 157 species of birds. Caribou, Dall sheep, moose, and grizzly bears are commonly seen in open spaces around the park.

Detailed information on the park and its visitor activities is available at the visitor center near the park entrance. During summer months, park personnel conduct sled-dog demonstrations at park headquarters, evening slide talks and conservation movies at the Denali National Park Hotel, walks from Denali National Park Hotel and Eielson Visitor Center, and campfire programs at major campgrounds.

An 87-mile park road parallels the Alaska Range from the park entrance to Wonder Lake. Only the first 14 miles are paved, and the road is generally open from early June until mid-September. Driving beyond Savage River (mile 14) is restricted. At the closest point, the 20,320-foot summit of Mount McKinley is 27 miles from the road. Buses run regularly from the Denali Visitor Center to Eielson Visitor Center and Wonder Lake. Scheduled stops are at Teklanika River, Polychrome Pass, Toklat River, Eielson Visitor Center, and Wonder Lake. A wildlife scenic tour leaves in the early morning and mid-afternoon from the hotel and goes to the central area of the park. The driver interprets park features, and tickets are sold at Denali National Park Hotel (907–683–2215). The park shuttle is operated for the National Park Service under a concession contract. The shuttle provides visitors with access to backcountry units, campgrounds, and day-trip excursion areas. Reservations are generally required for seats on all west bound buses (907–272–7275 in the Anchorage area and outside the United States, 800–622–7275 outside Anchorage). Fees vary depending on age and destination. Full details on the shuttle service are available at park headquarters. Air tours are available through Denali Air (907–683–2261).

FACILITIES: A service station, located just outside the park entrance, has gasoline and oil. Pay showers are located nearby. Groceries and supplies are available at the adjacent store, but no vehicle or food services are available after leaving the headquarters area. (Check your gas.) Denali National Park Hotel provides lodging and dining. Reservations should be made early and may be obtained by writing ARA Denali Park Resorts, 241 West Ship Creek Avenue, Anchorage, AK 99501 (907–683–2215 summer, 907–276–7234 winter). National Park Service plans call for removal of the Denali National Park Hotel in 2001. Other lodging is available immediately outside the park.

CAMPING: Improved campgrounds with flush toilets, tap water, tables, and grills are available at Riley Creek (102 spaces, dump station), Savage River (thirty-four spaces), and Wonder Lake (twenty spaces, tents only). Campgrounds with pit toilets are located at Igloo Creek (seven spaces), Morino (sixty spaces, walk-in), Sanctuary River (seven spaces), and Teklanika River (fifty spaces). Only Riley Creek is open year-round, but no services are available in winter.

FISHING: Fishing is generally poor because rivers are silty and ponds are shallow. Arctic grayling are caught in a few mountain streams and lake trout in Wonder Lake.

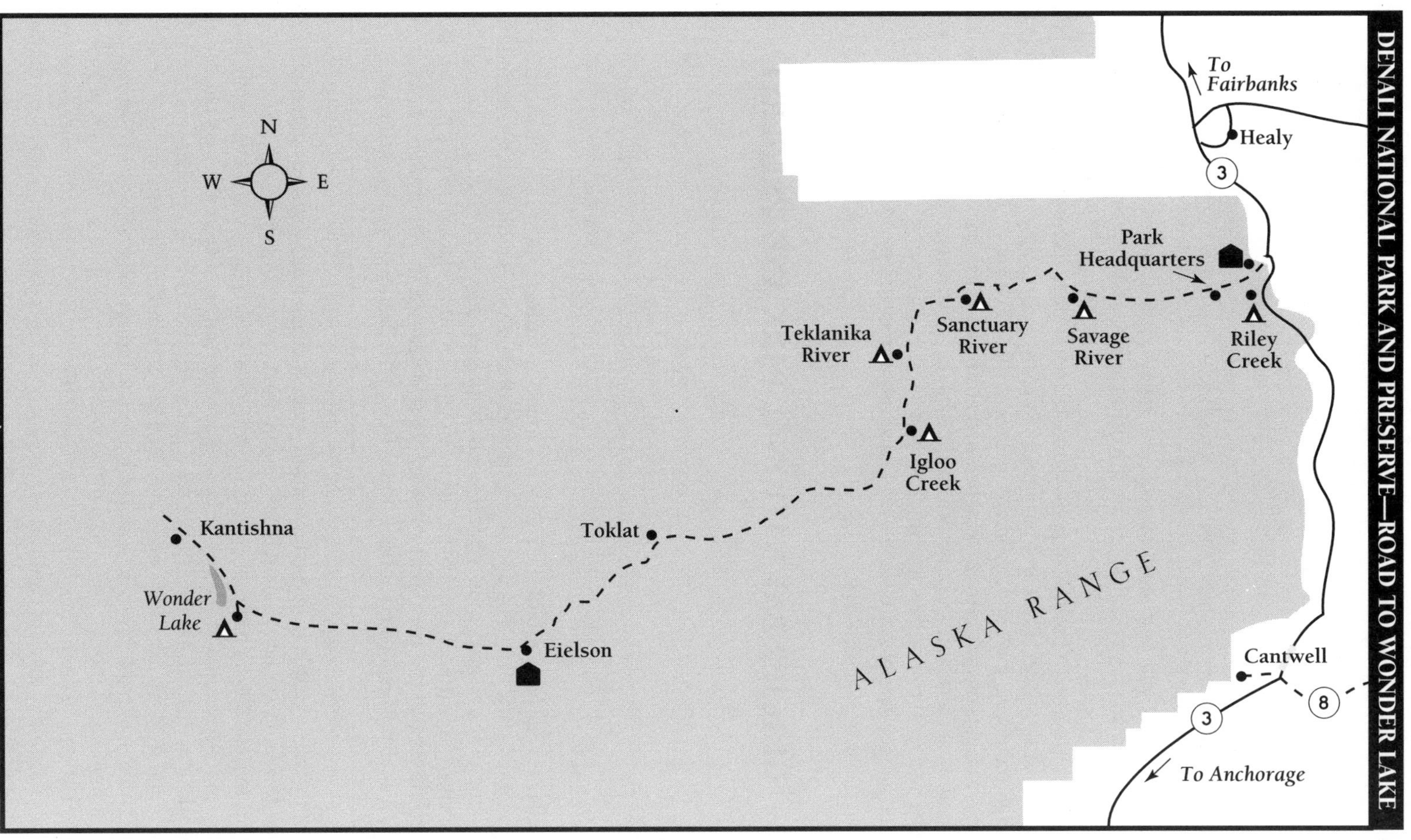

DENALI NATIONAL PARK AND PRESERVE—ROAD TO WONDER LAKE
N
W
E
S
To Fairbanks
Healy
3
Park Headquarters
Teklanika River
Sanctuary River
Savage River
Riley Creek
Igloo Creek
Kantishna
Toklat
Wonder Lake
Eielson
ALASKA RANGE
Cantwell
8
3
To Anchorage

GATES OF THE ARCTIC NATIONAL PARK AND PRESERVE

201 First Avenue, Doyon Building
Fairbanks, AK 99726
(907) 456–0281
GAAR_Visitor_Information@nps.gov

Gates of the Arctic comprises 8.2 million acres, including the heart of the spectacular Brooks Range. The entire park lies north of the Arctic Circle, where shrubs and tundra but few trees are found. Visitors will find long, magnificent valleys, rivers, lakes, and a few glaciers. Black bears, caribou, Dall sheep, eagles, grizzlies, marmots, moose, wolverines, and wolves are found in the park.

This wilderness park has no facilities, roads, or trails. Most visitors to the park backpack the valleys or float the rivers. Rock and mountain climbing are available in the Arrigetch Peaks and Mount Igikpak areas. Fish include grayling, lake trout, and char.

Access to Gates of the Arctic is via scheduled airline from Fairbanks to Bettles or Anaktuvuk Pass. Charters are available from Bettles and Fairbanks. The nearest facilities are a general store in Bettles and Anaktuvuk Pass and a lodge in Bettles. Rangers may be contacted in Fairbanks or Bettles; ranger stations in Coldfoot and Anaktuvuk Pass are periodically staffed.

GLACIER BAY NATIONAL PARK AND PRESERVE

P.O. Box 140
Gustavus, AK 99826-0140
(907) 697–2230
glba_administration@nps.gov
www.nps.gov/glba/

Glacier Bay was established as a national monument in 1925 (changed to a national park in 1980) and is comprised of nearly 3.3 million acres, including some of the world's most impressive examples of tidewater glaciers. The park is located in southeastern Alaska, approximately 65 miles northwest of Juneau. No roads lead to the park, and entrance must be gained by either plane or boat. A small airport is located about 9 miles from park headquarters in Gustavus.

Much of the snow that falls in the mountains around Glacier Bay does not completely melt. As it grows deeper, lower layers change into small grains of ice and gradually fuses into solid ice. When an icefield fills its basin, it begins flowing downhill. The glaciers eventually flow to the sea and are called tidewater glaciers. Glaciers advance and retreat as an area's climate changes.

The glaciers that can be seen in the park today are the remains of what was formed during the "little Ice Age" about 4,000 years ago. The glaciers reached maximum size around 1750, before a milder climate brought about a general melting. When Captain George Vancouver sailed through Icy Strait in 1794, Glacier Bay was little more than a huge wall of ice extending more than 100 miles to the north. By 1916, Grand Pacific Glacier was 65 miles from the mouth of Glacier Bay. Today glaciers continue to retreat on the bay's east side. Glaciers on the west side, however, stabilized by 1929, and many are even growing again. The bay includes twelve tidewater glaciers, including nine that calve icebergs into Glacier Bay.

Glacier Bay National Park is rich in both plant and animal life. Brown and black bears, mountain goats, seals, humpback whales, and porpoises are frequently seen. More than 200 species of birds are found here.

Park rangers are in the park year-round, with headquarters at Bartlett Cove. In summer, naturalists lead hikes, and a concessioner-operated tour boat (eight to nine hours) leaves from the lodge. Overnight boat trips are also available. The park is best seen by boat. A permit is required for entry (via private boat) into the park during June, July, and August. Applications are available from the park superintendent. Navigating the bay presents special problems, and appropriate precautions should be observed. One-day tours by boat are available from Glacier Bay Lodge at Bartlett Cove.

FACILITIES: Glacier Bay Lodge provides rooms and meals from mid-May to mid-September. For reservations write Glacier Bay Lodge, P.O. Box 199, Gustavus, AK 99826 in summer and 520 Pike Street, Suite 1610, Seattle, WA 98101 in winter (800–451–5952 for reservations). Temporary docking facilities, gasoline, and #2 diesel fuel are available at Bartlett Cove. No other public facilities for boats are located within the park.

CAMPING: A campground (thirty-five spaces) at Bartlett Cove has bear-resistant food caches, a fire pit, and firewood. Limited camping supplies and food are available in nearby Gustavus, while Juneau offers many shopping possibilities.

FISHING: Silver, pink, chum, sockeye, and king salmon can be caught in the park. Halibut are found nearly everywhere in the park's salt water. Cutthroat and Steelhead trout and Dolly Varden char are in lakes and streams. An Alaska fishing license is required.

KATMAI NATIONAL PARK AND PRESERVE

P.O. Box 7
King Salmon, AK 99613-0007
(907) 246–3305
www.nps.gov/katm/

Katmai National Park and Preserve occupies 4.1 million acres of rugged wilderness on the Alaska Peninsula. The interior wilderness of forests and lakes is bounded on the east by 100 miles of ocean bays, fjords, and lagoons. Katmai has no rail or road approaches, and there is no commercial boat service to any part of the park. Scheduled jets fly to King Salmon Airport on the Bristol Bay side of the peninsula. Daily commercial flights connect King Salmon and Brooks Lodge from June through Labor Day. Private float planes can be chartered for flights to scenic lakes within Katmai.

In 1912, the area that is now contained within the park was the site of one of the greatest volcanic eruptions in history. Novarupta Volcano sent forth an explosion of pumice and white-hot ash. Within a few hours two and a half cubic miles of ash flowed into the Ukak River valley, and forty square miles of the valley floor were covered to depths as great as 700 feet. Hot gases and water vapor percolating up through the ash as it settled gave rise to the name Valley of Ten Thousand Smokes. At the same time or soon after Novarupta was erupting, Mount Katmai, 6 miles to the east, was collapsing. A conduit under Mount Katmai allowed a transfer of magma and resulted in a loss of support for the mountain's top.

Katmai National Park and Preserve contains a wide variety of plant and animal life. Woodlands of spruce, poplar, and birch are interspersed with alder thickets, marshes, and grassland on the southern and western parts of the mountains. At higher elevations only plants typical of the Arctic tundra can survive the cold, high winds and short growing season. Brown bears and moose are fairly common, and bald eagles are seen frequently. The Steller sea lion and the hair seal are commonly observed on rock outcroppings. Much of the wildlife in the park at any one time depends on the runs of migrating salmon.

Park rangers give illustrated evening talks at Brooks Camp, and guided nature walks are conducted from the same location. A 3/4-mile trail leads to Brooks Falls, where there is an elevated platform from which visitors can, at certain times of the summer, watch brown bears try to catch salmon as the fish jump the falls. A concessioner-operated scenic bus tour (23 miles one way) to the Valley of Ten Thousand Smokes begins at the lodge. Good views of the valley and surrounding mountains may be enjoyed from the shelter located at the end of the trip. In addition, a short trail from the Brooks River Ranger Station leads to the site of a prehistoric dwelling. A pit house built around A.D. 1300 has been excavated and restored for public inspection.

FACILITIES: A concessioner provides accommodations and services at four points in the park. Brooks Camp has modern cabins with plumbing and family-type meals. Fishing equipment and canoes may be rented, and limited camping and food supplies are sold. Guide service is available. Overnight packages are also available for Grosvernor Camp, Kulik Lodge, and Nonvianuk Camp. A privately owned lodge is operated at Enchanted Lake. In addition, there are a number of lodges outside of the park that cater to park visitors. Information may be obtained by writing to park headquarters.

CAMPING: A single campground (twenty-one spaces) at Brooks River is open year-round. Piped-in treated water is provided from early June through early September. The camp contains pit toilets, weather shelters, and elevated food caches. It is a park regulation that campers' food must be stored in the elevated caches to secure it from the bears. Meals and showers can be purchased at Brooks Lodge. Visitors may camp anywhere in the park and preserve upon receiving a backcountry permit from a park ranger.

FISHING: Rainbow and lake trout, Dolly Varden, grayling, northern pike, and sockeye salmon are plentiful. An Alaska fishing license is required, and fishing in any way other than with hook and line (with rod or line held in hand) is not allowed. Coho, chinook, and pink salmon are occasionally seen in the streams, and one of the most magnificent sights is that of the sockeye salmon fighting upstream to their spawning ground. Brooks River is a fly-fishing-only river (catch-and-release for rainbow trout). Any salmon-spawning stream is likely to have a number of brown bears in attendance. Park rangers can provide information on how to minimize conflicts with bears while fishing.

KENAI FJORDS NATIONAL PARK

P.O. Box 1727
Seward, AK 99664-1727
(907) 224–3175
www.nps.gov/kefj/

Kenai Fjords' 650,000 acres on the Kenai Peninsula include the 300-square-mile Harding Icefield, a Quaternary icefield that radiates thirty-six named glacial arms. In addition to long glaciated valleys and mountain peaks, the peninsulas support rain forests. Wildlife includes bald eagles, sea lions, seals, whales, sea otters, moose, bear, mountain goats, and puffins.

Park headquarters and a visitor center are located in Seward, which can be reached by car or train from Anchorage. Three public-use cabins at Exit Glacier are available for rental (three-day maximum with reservations required). One winter public-use cabin is available. Commercial air and bus services are available between Anchorage and Seward. Just north of Seward is Exit Glacier, the most accessible section of the park, which is reached by a paved and gravel road and short walk. Ranger-conducted activities take place here during the summer. Boat and air charters to the fjords are available.

KLONDIKE GOLD RUSH NATIONAL HISTORICAL PARK

P.O. Box 517
Skagway, AK 99840
(907) 983–2921
KLGO_Ranger_Activities@nps.gov
www.nps.gov/klgo/

Klondike Gold Rush National Historical Park comprises more than 13,000 acres and was established in 1976 to commemorate the 1898 Klondike gold rush. The park's main unit is located in the Skagway area of the Alaska panhandle. Access is via the Alaska Marine Highway from Bellingham, Washington, or Prince Rupert, British Columbia, or by driving south from Whitehorse, Yukon, approximately 100 miles on State Highways 2 and 8. Other Alaska units include the White Pass and the Dyea–Chilkoot Trail. A separate unit of this park is in Seattle and is listed under the Washington section of this book.

The Klondike gold rush went into high gear after the arrival of the steamer *Portland* in Seattle with two tons of gold aboard. The event that started this flood of people into the wilderness area of Canada's Yukon River was a large gold strike in August 1896 on Rabbit Creek by two Indians and a white man. When other prospectors saw the gold these three brought to the settlement of Fortymile, they headed into the same area to make their own claims. It was this group that arrived in Seattle during the summer of 1897. Later that year the infusion of people created the town of Dawson at the confluence of the Yukon and Klondike rivers.

As word of the riches spread, people began a mass migration to the area. One entry to Dawson was by way of the White Pass route through the Coastal Range. Here, the city of Skagway quickly grew to a population of 10,000. A second route was to sail to Dyea and then use the less-swampy Chilkoot Pass. This popular route included three aerial tramways that helped Dyea's permanent residents number 3,500 in the summer of 1898. About this same time, construction of a narrow-gauge railroad began over the White Pass route. This route eventually captured most of the traffic, so that Dyea soon turned into a ghost town. The two other routes to Dawson were by ship to St. Michael, then by steamboat up the Yukon River; and the all-Canadian overland route from Edmonton. The first of these was very expensive, and the second was virtually impossible.

The park's visitor center in the old White Pass and Yukon Railway depot at Broadway and Second Avenue contains displays and artifacts from the gold rush. The Park Service provides an orientation, a film, talks, and guided walks through the town. The historical district, with boardwalks and false-front buildings, retains much of the flavor of the gold-rush days. In 1998, this park was combined with Canadian park units commemorating the Klondike Gold Rush to create the first international historical park.

Dyea, the gateway to the Chilkoot Pass, is about 9 miles from Skagway via a dirt road. The drive is beautiful. Most of the Dyea buildings were torn down for use as firewood or as materials for buildings in Skagway. All that is left now are scattered remains of foundations and a half-mile row of piling stubs from the old wharf. The town fell into disuse after an 1898 avalanche and the completion of the railroad from Skagway to the White Pass Summit in February 1899. Visitors may hike the old 33-mile Chilkoot Trail (three to five days) to Lake Bennett. The trail offers historic ruins and artifacts along the way. These are not to be disturbed.

FACILITIES: Lodging and food services are not provided by the Park Service, but both are available in downtown Skagway. No facilities are in Dyea.

CAMPING: A Park Service campground with tables and pit toilets (no water) is located in Dyea. Skagway has several campgrounds. The Dyea site is much nicer.

FISHING: Fishing is available at both Skagway and Dyea.

KOBUK VALLEY NATIONAL PARK

P.O. Box 1029
Kotzebue, AK 99752
(907) 442–3890
www.nps.gov/noaa/

Kobuk Valley National Park comprises approximately 1.75 million acres in northwestern Alaska above the Arctic Circle. The park lies along the valley surrounding the Kobuk River and includes a boreal forest, sand dunes, and archaeological sites from 10,000 years of human occupation. Wildlife includes caribou, grizzly and black bears, lynx, moose, and wolves. Fishing can yield arctic char, grayling, salmon, and sheepfish.

Access to the park is via chartered aircraft from Ambler, Kiana, and Kotzebue or by chartered boat from Ambler or Kiana. A few visitors backpack in from these two villages. There are no facilities within the park. Lodging is available in Kiana, Ambler, and Kotzebue. All three towns have small stores with staples.

LAKE CLARK NATIONAL PARK AND PRESERVE

4230 University Drive, Suite 331
Anchorage, AK 99508
(907) 271–3751
www.nps.gov/lacl/

Lake Clark National Park and Preserve comprises more than 4.5 million acres in the heart of the Chigmit Mountains, where the Alaska and Aleutian ranges join. The park lies along the western shore of Cook Inlet and contains mountain peaks, glaciers, two active volcanoes, and more than twenty glacially carved lakes. Three wild rivers are located here. Activities center around backpacking, river running, and fishing. Rainbow trout, northern pike, arctic grayling, Dolly Varden, and five species of salmon inhabit streams in the park.

Access to Lake Clark National Park is by chartered aircraft from Anchorage, Kenai, or Homer. The trip takes one to two hours.

NOATAK NATIONAL PRESERVE

P.O. Box 1029
Kotzebue, AK 99752
(907) 442–3890
www.nps.gov/noaa/

Noatak National Preserve comprises more than 6.5 million acres including the largest untouched river basin in the United States. The Noatak River flows more than 425 miles, carrying Mount Igikpak's glacial melt to Kotzebue Sound through boreal forest and treeless tundra.

There are no Park Service facilities within the preserve. Most visitors enter to canoe or kayak the Noatak or to backpack in the foothills. A variety of wildlife, including bears, caribou, and wolves, inhabit the park. Fish include arctic char, grayling, whitefish, and several species of salmon.

Access is by chartered plane or boat from Kotzebue or by air charter from Bettles. Kotzebue may be reached by commercial flights from either Anchorage or Fairbanks.

SITKA NATIONAL HISTORICAL PARK

P.O. Box 738
Sitka, AK 99835
(907) 747–6281
www.nps.gov/sitk/

Sitka National Historical Park comprises 107 acres. It was set aside as a federal reserve in 1890 and designated a national monument in 1910 to commemorate the site of the last major Tlingit Indian resistance to Russian colonization. The park is located in the town of Sitka in Alaska's southeastern panhandle. Sitka is reached by scheduled airline or by boat. The town is a stop on the Alaska Marine Highway, but the park is 7 miles from the ferry terminal.

An 1804 battle between the Russians and the Tlingit Indians resulted in an important "victory" for the Russians (the Tlingit claim the Russians won by default because of a Tlingit withdrawal caused by a lack of ammunition), who strengthened their hold on the northwest coast of the American continent. The Russians were able to continue using the area as an important source for furs and established Sitka as the busiest port in the North Pacific. Although the Tlingit lost the battle and their homes, they returned to trade after several years and settled just outside the Russian stockade. In 1806, Sitka became the headquarters of the Russian American Company. In 1867, the Russians sold their overseas empire for $7.2 million, and Alaska became an American possession.

The park's visitor center includes exhibits, native craft workshops, and an audiovisual room for slide presentations and movies. Exhibits include displays of Tlingit history and culture. A self-guiding trail begins behind the visitor center and leads into the rain forest to the 1804 battleground and fort site. Fourteen totem poles are located in the park. The visitor center can supply visitors with a map of a walking tour of Sitka. The town is especially interesting, and the tour is a must.

A second section of the park, the 1842 Russian Bishop's house (entrance fee charged), is 1/4 mile from the visitor center on Lincoln Street. The Park Service completed a restoration of this historically important building in 1988. The first floor contains exhibits about Russian America, the Russian American Company, and the efforts of the Russian Orthodox Church in Alaska. The second floor is restored to its 1842–53 appearance with many of the original furnishings. The Chapel of the Annunciation contains the original icons given to Bishop Innocent.

FACILITIES: A picnic area with tables and a shelter is located near the impressive visitor center. Rest rooms and drinking water are available in the building. The park is within walking distance of the town of Sitka, where complete facilities are available.

CAMPING: No camping is available at the park, but a U.S. Forest Service campground with tables and pit toilets is a short distance north of the ferry terminal on Halibut Point Road.

FISHING: The park is surrounded by the Indian River and Sitka Sound, where saltwater fishing is available with an Alaska fishing license. Salmon fishing is not permitted in the Indian River.

WRANGELL–ST. ELIAS NATIONAL PARK AND PRESERVE

P.O. Box 439
Mile 105.5 Old Richardson Highway
Copper Center, AK 99573
(907) 822–5234
wrst_interpretation@nps.gov
www.nps.gov/wrst/

Wrangell–St. Elias is the largest park area in the National Park System, with 13 million acres of mountains, remote valleys, wild rivers, and coastal beaches. The park has America's second-highest mountain, 18,000-foot Mount St. Elias, and North America's largest collection of peaks above 16,000 feet in an area where three mountain ranges converge. More than one hundred glaciers exist in a landscape dominated by mountains and snowfields.

Visitors to the park engage in backpacking, camping, cross-country skiing, mountain climbing, and river running. The park can provide a list of licensed operators for air taxis, river trips, backpacking, big game hunting, and mountaineering. Summers are often cloudy with rain, although clear, relatively hot days occur in July.

No lodging within the park is provided by the park service. Lodging on private property within park boundaries is available. Modern motels and cabins are found in Glenallen and along the Richardson Highway and Tok cutoff. Private and state campgrounds are located near the park. A small National Park Service campground is located near the end of McCarthy Road between Chitina and McCarthy.

Wrangell–St. Elias is one of the few new Alaska parks with road access. A 61-mile road follows an old railroad route from the community of Chitina to McCarthy. In the northern section of the park, a secondary road extends from Slana to the privately owned mining community of Nabesna.

YUKON–CHARLEY RIVERS NATIONAL PRESERVE

Box 167
Eagle, AK 99738-0167
(907) 547–2233
www.nps.gov/yuch/

Yukon–Charley comprises 2.5 million acres along the Canadian border in central Alaska. The park incorporates all of the 120-mile Charley River and 135 miles of the 1,800-mile Yukon River, including old cabins and relics of the gold rush.

The primary activity in the preserve is floating the rivers. The Yukon is most popular and provides particularly good floating from June through September. It takes approximately a week to float between Eagle at the preserve's upper end, and Circle, at the lower end. The towns of Eagle and Circle both provide interesting sights for visitors. The Charley, a particularly scenic clear water river, is class 2 water that requires river experience. The best time to float this river is June and July. It is common to see Dall sheep, caribou, moose, bears, peregrine falcons, eagles, and water fowl along both rivers. Fishing for grayling, northern pike, and whitefish is available on side tributaries. Grayling fishing is excellent on the Charley.

Access to the preserve is by way of Eagle and Circle. Both are served by scheduled air taxis, and both may be reached via a gravel road from the Alaska Highway. Air access is also available from Tok and Fairbanks. Call the preserve for air taxi information. There are no roads within the park. Both Eagle and Circle offer food service, gas, groceries, campgrounds, and limited lodging. The preserve maintains an information center in Eagle.

Mt. Drum, Wrangell–St. Elias National Park and Preserve (Cynthia Jones)

AMERICAN SAMOA

TOURIST INFORMATION
(684) 633–1092

NATIONAL PARK OF AMERICAN SAMOA

Pago Pago
American Samoa 96799
(684) 633–7082
NPSA_Administration@nps.gov
www.nps.gov/npsa/

National Park of American Samoa comprises nearly 9,000 acres and was established in 1988 to protect wild and scenic Old World rain forests, coral reefs, and white sand beaches on three volcanic islands in the South Pacific. American Samoa is approximately 2,300 miles southwest of Hawaii.

American Samoa is comprised of five islands and two coral atolls in the Samoan chain of islands that stretches for 300 miles in the South Pacific. The National Park of American Samoa protects cultural and natural resources on three of these islands. All the lands making up the park are village or communally owned. The federal government has a fifty-year lease agreement that permits the public to visit village lands.

Pago Pago on the main island of Tutuila is the arrival point for park visitors. This island has a major expanse of undisturbed mixed-species rain forest. Visitors can take a scenic drive to the island's northern coast with its sheer cliffs and sheltered coves. Either park headquarters or the American Samoa Office of Tourism (684–633–1092) can help make arrangements for

National Park of American Samoa (opposite page)

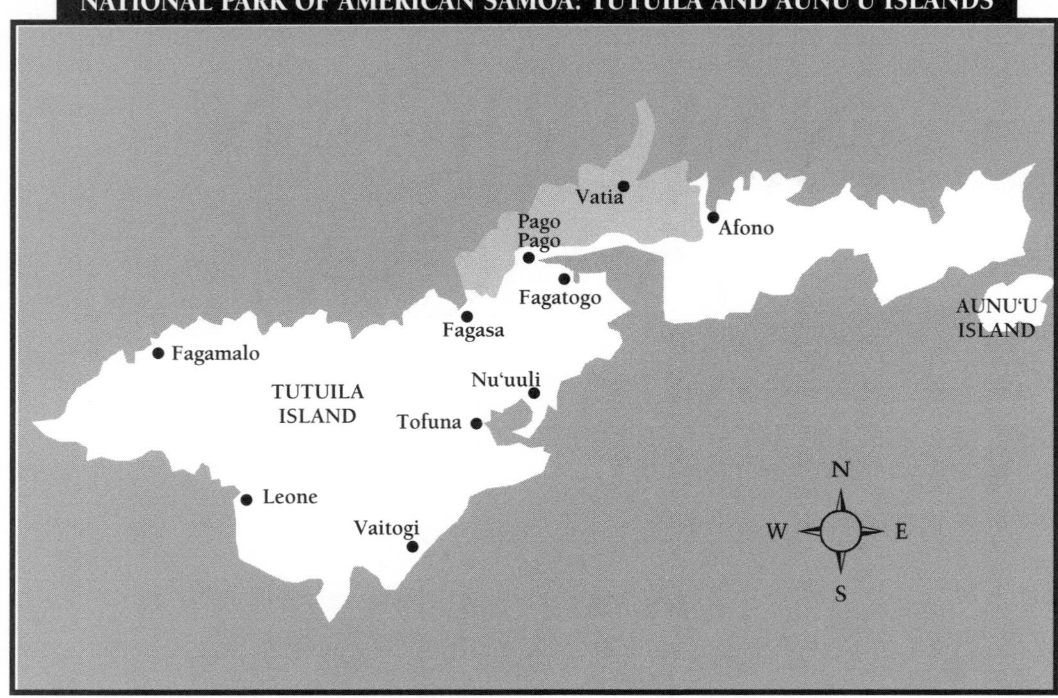
NATIONAL PARK OF AMERICAN SAMOA: TUTUILA AND AUNU'U ISLANDS
Vatia
Pago
Pago
Afono
Fagatogo
Fagasa
AUNU'U
ISLAND
Fagamalo
TUTUILA
ISLAND
Nu'uuli
Tofuna
Leone
Vaitogi
N
W
E
S

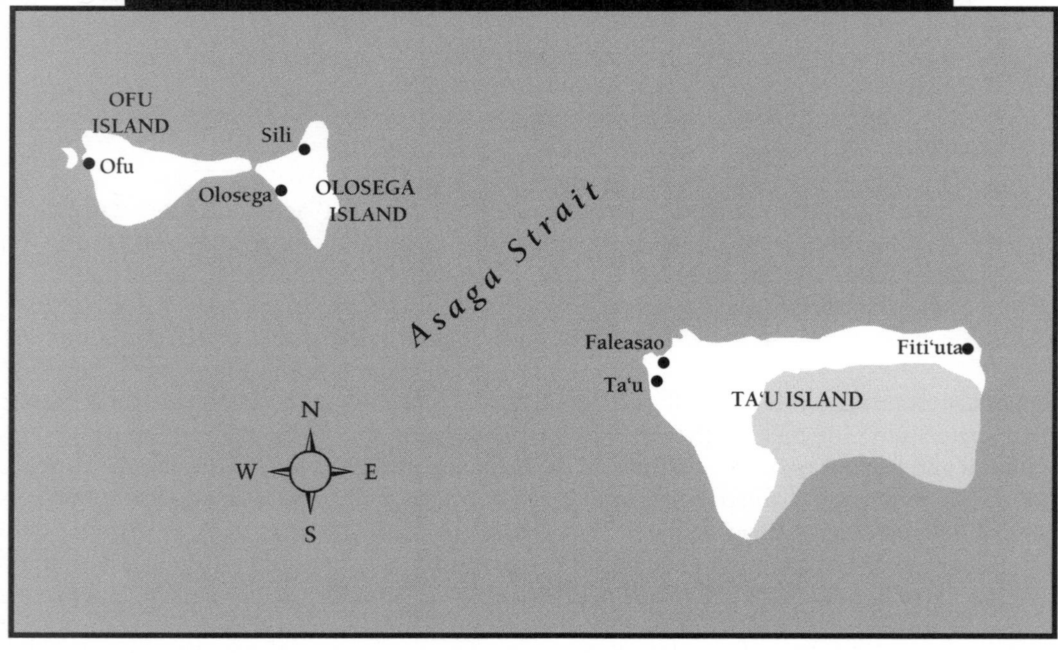
NATIONAL PARK OF AMERICAN SAMOA: MANU'A ISLANDS
OFU
ISLAND
Sili
Ofu
Olosega
OLOSEGA
ISLAND
Asaga Strait
Faleasao
Fiti'uta
Ta'u
TA'U ISLAND
N
W
E
S

overnight stays in a Samoan home. Another activity is hiking to the top of 1,610-foot Mount Alava for a view of the harbor.

The islands of Ta'u and Ofu, which contain the other two units of the park, are 60 miles east of Tutuila and are reached via a 30-minute plane ride. Ta'u, with the largest of the three park units, is mostly rain forest. It is also the home island of Saua, the Samoan legendary birthplace of Polynesia. Tufu Point on the island's south coast provides a spectacular view of steep cliffs that drop from the top of Lata Mountain to the rugged coastline. The island of Ofu, 9 miles from Ta'u, provides white sand beaches and a magnificent coral reef. This unit offers the park's best snorkeling.

FACILITIES: No lodging is available in the park. Lodging and food are available in Pago Pago on Tutuila. Medical treatment is available only on Tutuila.

CAMPING: Camping is available but requires the permission of landowners.

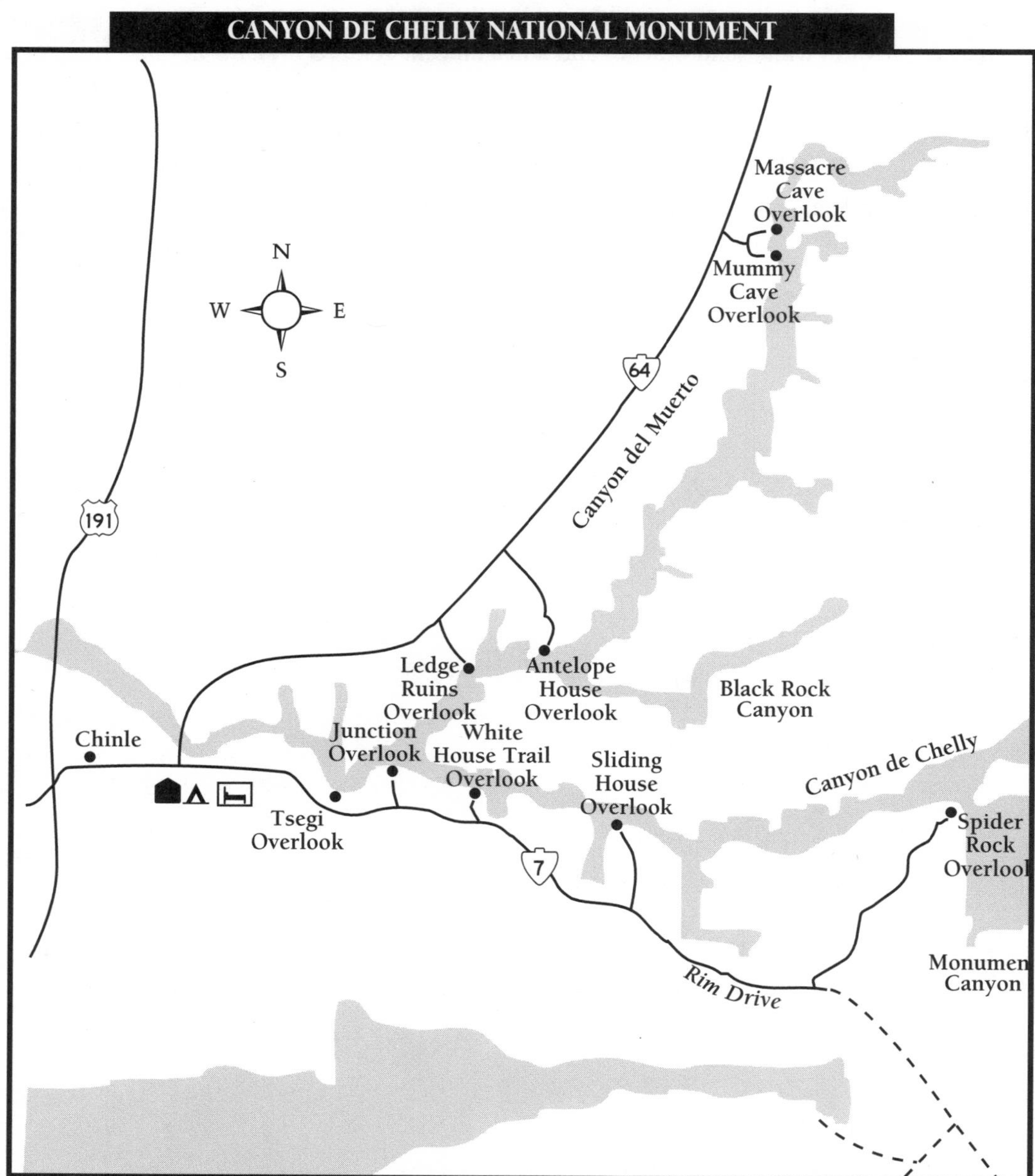
CANYON DE CHELLY NATIONAL MONUMENT
N
W
E
S
191
64
Canyon del Muerto
Massacre Cave Overlook
Mummy Cave Overlook
Ledge Ruins Overlook
Antelope House Overlook
Black Rock Canyon
Chinle
Junction Overlook
White House Trail Overlook
Sliding House Overlook
Canyon de Chelly
Tsegi Overlook
7
Spider Rock Overloo
Monumen Canyon
Rim Drive

STATE TOURIST INFORMATION
(888) 520–3434

CANYON DE CHELLY NATIONAL MONUMENT

P.O. Box 588
Chinle, AZ 86503
(520) 674–5500
www.nps.gov/cach/

Canyon de Chelly (pronounced "d' Shay") National Monument comprises 83,840 acres. It was authorized as part of the National Park System in 1931 to preserve ruins of Indian villages built in steep-walled canyons between A.D. 350 and 1300. The monument is located in northeastern Arizona, approximately 85 miles northwest of Gallup, New Mexico, near Chinle, Arizona. Monument headquarters is 2 miles east of U.S. 191. Highway 7, connecting South Rim Drive with Fort Defiance, is dirt between the monument boundary and the town of Sawmill. It is virtually impassable during bad weather.

Following an uplift of the Defiance Plateau, Rio de Chelly cut through sandstone and left canyon walls in Canyon de Chelly 30 to 1,000 feet high. Typically, the streams of this region are dry except during the rainy seasons and the spring thaw of mountain snow.

The canyons contain the ruins of several hundred prehistoric Anasazi villages, most of which were built between A.D. 350 and 1300. The earliest known Indians lived in pithouses, grew crops of corn and squash, and made intricate baskets. Centuries later, the Anasazi began making pottery and constructed rectangular houses of stone masonry above the canyon walls. The canyon dwellers (now known as Pueblos) built most of the large cliff houses between A.D. 1100 and 1300.

During the 1200s, occupants of the Four Corners region left their homes and scattered throughout the Southwest. In later years, the canyons were occupied sporadically by the Hopi, a Pueblo group culturally related to the Anasazi, and later the Navajo, who continue to inhabit Canyon de Chelly today. The Navajo began to move into this area around 1700. They brought domesticated animals acquired from the Spanish and used the canyons to grow corn and raise peaches.

Except for a trail to White House Ruin, travel in the canyons is permitted only with a park ranger or other authorized guide. The park ranger on duty at the visitor center will help to arrange guides for those interested in hikes or four-wheel-drive vehicle trips. Horseback-riding tours are also available. Thunderbird Lodge near monument headquarters offers group trips to the canyon floors.

The first order of business upon entering the monument should be to stop at the visitor center, where exhibits help explain the history of the canyon and the cultures of its inhabitants. A Navajo silversmith is sometimes in the center demonstrating crafts. Here you may also obtain guidebooks for driving both the north and south rims. These books are quite helpful in interpreting the drives. From Memorial Day through Labor Day, talks are presented at the visitor center, and guided walks begin at various places around the monument. During the summer season, nightly campfire programs are provided in the National Park Service campground.

Twenty-two-mile Rim Drive, along the south rim of Canyon de Chelly, provides access to six scenic overlook points and the trailhead of White House Trail. Even though the 500-foot climb back up the trail from White House Ruin (2½ miles, one and a half to two hours, round-trip) will leave you breathless, the hike is worthwhile. Not only does it afford a close viewpoint of the impressive ruin and some pictographs, but unless you take a guided trip, this will be your only chance to see this beautiful canyon from its floor. Spider Rock, an 800-foot sandstone spire, can be viewed from an overlook at the junction of Canyon de Chelly and Monument Canyon. Mummy Cave Ruin, in Canyon del Muerto, is one of the larger ruins and includes a three-story tower house. Pictographs may be seen at many places in the canyons, with some dating from prehistoric Basketmaker and Pueblo periods.

FACILITIES: Food, lodging, gifts, and tours are available at the Thunderbird Lodge near the monument entrance. Reservations and information may be obtained by writing Thunderbird Lodge, Box 548, Chinle, AZ 86503 (520–674–5841). Two other restaurants, lodging, and a supermarket are within 3 miles of the visitor center.

CAMPING: Cottonwood Campground (104 spaces), set in a grove of cottonwood trees, is located near the park entrance. The campground is open year-round and contains grills, tables, and, during the summer season, water and flush toilets. Individuals are limited to a five-day stay. Three group camps are available by reservation only. Recreational vehicles and trailers are not permitted in the group camping sites. No camping is permitted in the canyons without a guide.

FISHING: No fishing is available in Canyon de Chelly National Monument. Fishing for trout is permitted in Wheatfields Lake, near where the North Rim Drive intersects Highway 12. A tribal fishing license is required.

CASA GRANDE RUINS NATIONAL MONUMENT

1100 Ruins Drive
Coolidge, AZ 85228-3200
(520) 723–3172
www.nps.gov/cagr/

Casa Grande Ruins National Monument comprises 472 acres. The land was set aside in 1892 as Casa Grande Reservation (changed to a national monument in 1918) to preserve ruins of a massive four-story building constructed by Indian farmers more than 650 years ago. The monument is about midway between Phoenix and Tucson, in the town of Coolidge on Arizona Highway 87.

Hohokam Indians farmed the Gila Valley for more than a thousand years, eventually utilizing up to 1,000 miles of irrigation canals, many measuring from 8 to 10 feet in width and 7 to 10 feet in depth. Crops of cotton, corn, beans, and squash were grown with the use of these canals.

Approximately 650 years ago Indian farmers in the valley constructed the four-story Casa Grande. The building was given its Spanish name (meaning "Big House") by the Jesuit priest Father Kino when he discovered it in 1694. The purpose of the structure is uncertain. Casa Grande was probably built around the early 1300s and used for a relatively short period. This type of village in the Gila Valley had generally been abandoned by the mid-1400s.

The monument is open from 8:00 A.M. to 5:00 P.M. throughout the year (closed Christmas), although summer temperatures are very high. The visitor center contains a collection of artifacts made and used by the Hohokam. Park rangers in the visitor center answer questions and conduct periodic tours from Thanksgiving to early spring. In addition, a self-guiding trail leads visitors through the ruins. Heaviest visitation occurs between Thanksgiving and Easter.

FACILITIES: Lodging and food service are not available in the monument, but several restaurants and motels are located in Coolidge. A picnic area with tables, water, and shade is available at the monument. Flush toilets and drinking water are located in the visitor center.

CAMPING: No camping is permitted at the monument. Two mobile home parks in Coolidge accept overnighters.

FISHING: No fishing is available at Casa Grande Ruins National Monument.

CHIRICAHUA NATIONAL MONUMENT

HCR 2, Box 6500
Willcox, AZ 85643-9737
(520) 824–3560, ext. 104
www.nps.gov/chir/

Chiricahua National Monument comprises 11,985 acres (including 10,290 acres of wilderness) and was established in 1924 to preserve varied rock formations created by volcanic activity millions of years ago. The monument is located in southeastern Arizona, 36 miles southeast of Willcox, Arizona, off State Highway 186.

An area of pinnacles and balanced rocks, Chiricahua stands out from the surrounding dry grasslands. The monument's range in elevation from 5,124 to 7,563 feet results in many species of shrubs and trees. The shady glens are alive with various types of birds. Arizona white-tailed deer are frequently seen, and dense vegetation grows in the shaded canyon bottoms and on the north slopes at higher elevations. Temperatures are generally moderate, ranging from summer highs of more than 90 degrees in May and June to freezing temperatures from November

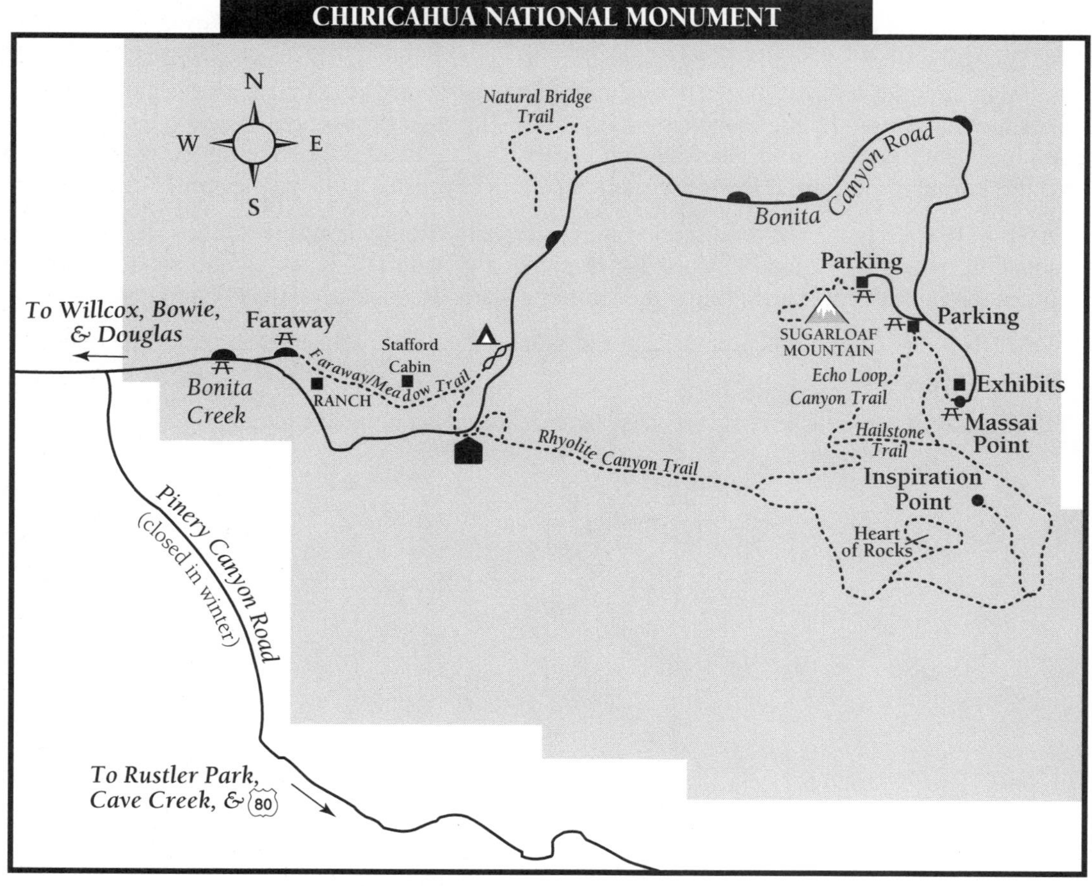

Chiricahua National Monument (opposite page)

through March. Annual precipitation is 18 inches and falls mostly in July and August when afternoon thunderstorms are common. Light snows fall during winter months.

The area's present geologic features began forming millions of years ago when the region was subject to extensive volcanic activity. Explosions covered the area with many layers of volcanic ash. Later, the earth's crust was slowly lifted, and cracks developed in the land. These gradually grew larger as water and winds used the openings to work at erosion.

A visitor center is located 2 miles inside the park's west entrance. It contains exhibits describing the area's history and geography. Rangers are present to answer visitors' questions. A single 6-mile paved road winds through the monument, ending at Massai Point. The turn at the road's end provides an excellent view of the monument. Faraway Ranch is a pioneer homestead that once served as a working cattle ranch and guest ranch. Tours of the main house are conducted daily.

More than 17 miles of trails are provided for hikers. A self-guided loop trail, located at Massai Point, takes about thirty minutes to walk. Features along the trail include a balanced rock and a lookout point with view finder. One of the highest points in the monument can be reached via the 1-mile Sugarloaf Trail, which begins at the end of a side road. Round-trip walking time is 1⅓ hours. Fire and Flood Trail is a self-guided loop that begins at the visitor center parking area. Walking time is approximately twenty minutes. One of the most scenic hikes is a 3½-mile loop trail through Echo Canyon and Echo Park. Round-trip time is two hours. A longer hike (four to five hours round-trip) leads to Big Balanced Rock and Punch and Judy.

FACILITIES: No overnight accommodations or food services are available within the monument. Motels, restaurants, groceries, and gasoline are available at Willcox. Modern rest rooms and drinking water are located at the visitor center and the campground. Picnic facilities are also available at designated areas.

CAMPING: A single campground (twenty-four spaces) is located ½ mile from monument headquarters in Bonita Canyon. Flush toilets, drinking water, tables, and grills are available, and the campground is open all year. The monument is nearly surrounded by Coronado National Forest, where a dozen U.S. Forest Service campgrounds are located.

FISHING: No fishing is available within the monument.

CORONADO NATIONAL MEMORIAL

4101 East Montezuma Canyon Road
Hereford, AZ 85615
(520) 366–5515
www.nps.gov/coro/

Coronado National Memorial comprises 4,750 acres. It was established as a national memorial in 1952 to commemorate the Hispanic heritage and initial European exploration of the American Southwest. The memorial is located in southeastern Arizona on the Mexican border. It is 26 miles west of Bisbee, Arizona, and 21 miles south of Sierra Vista, Arizona, on State Highway 92.

Coronado National Memorial overlooks the valley through which Francisco Vásquez de Coronado first entered the present United States. The Coronado expedition was viewed as a failure at the time it was completed because no riches were discovered. Perhaps more important, however, the explorers brought back information about both the land and the people and opened the way for subsequent Spanish explorations and colonization.

The Coronado expedition began from Compostela, Mexico, in February 1540, with a party of approximately 1,100 Spanish soldiers and Mexican-Indian allies. The expedition moved north and east before crossing New Mexico through present-day Albuquerque. By spring 1541, the group had crossed through northern Texas, the Oklahoma panhandle, and into central Kansas. Disillusioned with the discoveries, Coronado returned to Mexico in the spring of 1542.

Memorial headquarters contains a visitor center and museum and is located near the east entrance, 5 miles west of Arizona 92. It is open daily from 8:00 A.M. to 5:00 P.M. Montezuma Pass, a 3-mile scenic drive from the visitor center, provides access to viewpoints and to the beginning of a foot trail that leads to Coronado Peak. From this point the visitor has a panoramic view of the country through which Coronado and his party marched. The 3-mile Joe's Canyon Trail leads from Montezuma Pass to the headquarters and picnic area. One-mile-long Yaqui Ridge Trail leads from Joe's Canyon Trail to the United States–Mexico boundary. This is the southern terminus of the Arizona trail, which, when completed, will run the length of the state from Mexico to Utah.

Visitors may tour Coronado Cave, which is ¾ mile from the visitor center. The 600-foot-long cave contains stalactites, stalagmites, and flowstones. The Park Service recommends that visitors bring water, hiking shoes, and a flashlight (two when traveling alone). Permits are required and may be obtained free at the visitor center. The park's climate is relatively warm (high 80s) and rainy during summer months and mild during winter (low 30s).

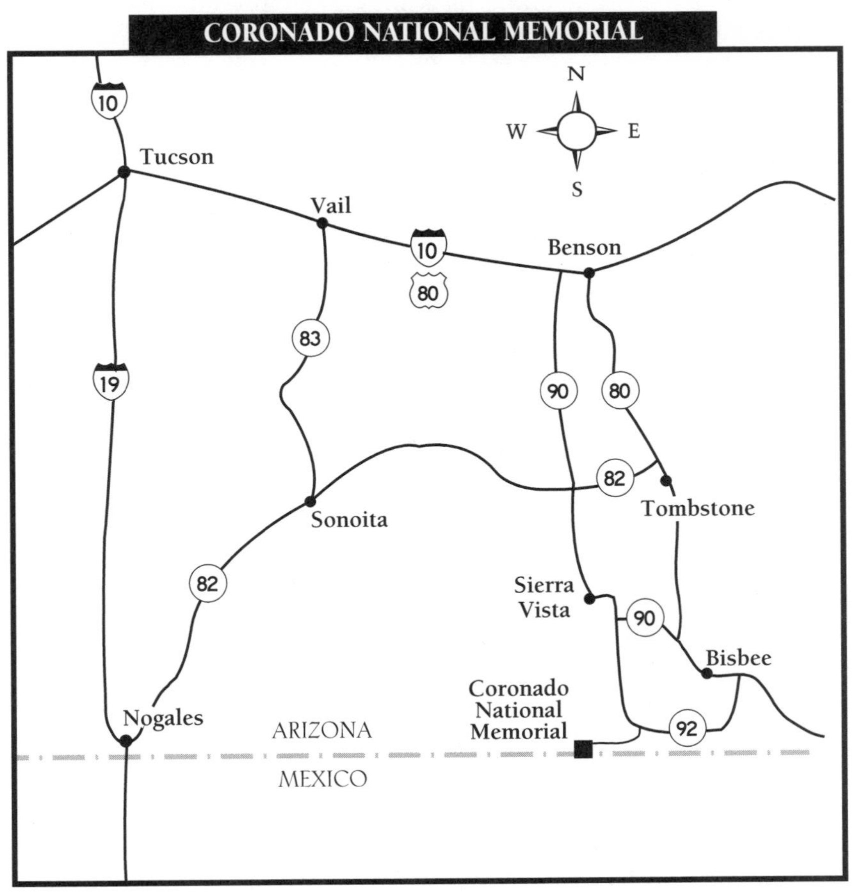

FACILITIES: No food service or lodging is available in the memorial. The nearest places for meals and overnight accommodations are Bisbee, 26 miles to the east, and Sierra Vista, 21 miles north. A picnic area near the visitor center contains tables and grills. Rest rooms and water are also available at the visitor center.

CAMPING: No camping is available within the park. A U.S. Forest Service campground is located at Parker Canyon Lake, 18 miles west of the memorial. In addition, open camping is permitted in Coronado National Forest, which abuts the memorial to the north and west.

FISHING: No fishing is available at Coronado National Memorial.

FORT BOWIE NATIONAL HISTORIC SITE

P.O. Box 158
Bowie, AZ 85605-0158
(520) 847–2500
www.nps.gov/fobo/

Fort Bowie National Historic Site was authorized by Congress in 1964 to preserve the Apache Pass Stage Station, Apache Spring, the Fort Bowie complex, and a portion of the Butterfield Overland Mail Route. The 1,000-acre park is 12 miles south of Interstate 10 at Bowie on a mostly paved road. From Willcox, on Interstate 10, Fort Bowie is 22 miles southeast on Arizona Highway 186 and then east on a graded dirt road to Apache Pass. The major portion of the historic site can be reached only by a 1½-mile foot trail that begins at a parking area on Apache Pass Road.

The spring located at Apache Pass has drawn a procession of Indians, immigrants, prospectors, and soldiers. Apaches made this their homeland sometime around the sixteenth century but were unable to protect it during the westward expansion of the nineteenth century. In 1857, the postmaster general awarded an overland mail contract to John Butterfield, and the Apache Pass Station was constructed in 1858 as a stop along the St. Louis–to–San Francisco route.

After years of relative peace between Apaches and the white man, the early 1860s saw sporadic fighting between the Indians and the settlers and military. In 1862, Fort Bowie was built in order to keep Apache Pass open to Union troops coming from and going to New Mexico during the Civil War. Peace was made by Cochise and his people in 1872. The Apaches were given a reservation of about 3,000 square miles, but two years later Cochise died, and soon hostilities resumed under the leadership of Geronimo and others. After years of intense fighting, a final surrender in 1886 resulted in the remaining Indians being shipped to forts in Florida and later Alabama. Fort Bowie was officially abandoned on October 17, 1894.

The ruins and historic trail are open to the public from sunrise to sunset. A moderately strenuous, 1½-mile foot trail to the fort ruins begins at the parking lot. The trail passes a number of historic features. Access to the fort ruins is by the trail only. Handicap access is available by appointment, by phone or mail. A park ranger is normally on duty at the small ranger station–museum from 8 A.M. to 5 P.M. daily, except Christmas.

FACILITIES: There are no lodging or eating facilities within the park. Overnight accommodations and food are available in Willcox. Drinking water and rest rooms are located at the ranger station near the ruins of the fort.

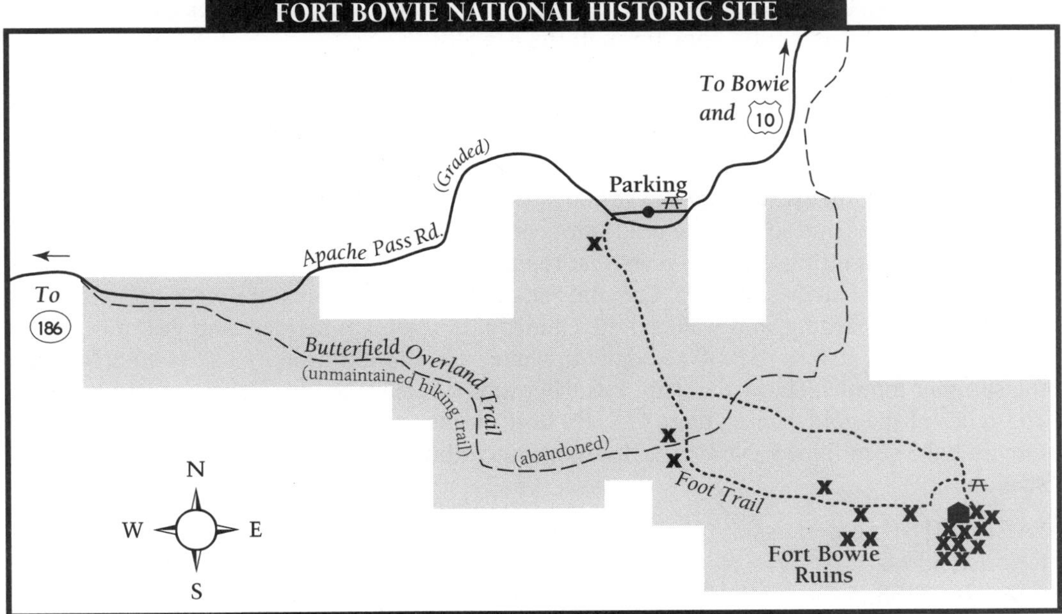

CAMPING: No camping is permitted within the park, but a campground is located at Chiricahua National Monument, 25 miles southwest of Fort Bowie. Private campgrounds are located in Bowie and Willcox.

FISHING: No fishing is available at Fort Bowie National Historic Site.

GLEN CANYON NATIONAL RECREATION AREA

P.O. Box 1507
Page, AZ 86040-1507
(520) 608–6200
GLCA_CHVC@nps.gov
www.nps.gov/glca

Glen Canyon National Recreation Area comprises 1.25 million acres (most of which are in Utah). It is the result of the Glen Canyon Dam built by the Bureau of Reclamation between 1956 and 1964. Lake Powell, formed from the Colorado River in back of the dam, is 186 miles long with nearly 2,000 miles of shoreline. The southern portion of the park—the most accessible part—is intersected by U.S. 89 through Page, Arizona. Page is 129 miles east of Zion National Park and 132 miles north of Flagstaff. The park also may be crossed at Hite Crossing via Utah Highway 95, and via Utah Highway 276, which is connected by a ferry (cars and people) that runs from Halls Crossing to Bullfrog and back six times per day during the summer season and four times per day during the winter except for one month in winter when the ferry is serviced.

The name Glen Canyon was given to a long stretch of the Colorado River by John Wesley Powell, who led exploration trips through the canyons in 1869 and 1871. Around 1900, the area attracted prospectors looking for gold, but the particles were too fine to be economically recovered. The Navajo Nation borders Glen Canyon to the south. According to anthropologists, Navajos were latecomers to the area, arriving in the 1860s. Prior to that time, prehistoric Anasazi Indians lived in the region. Ruins of these Indians exist throughout the park.

The canyons themselves are the result of a general uplifting of the region that occurred about 60 million years ago. As the uplift progressed, streams of the ancient, low-lying Colorado Basin ran faster, cutting the deep scars that remain today.

Most of the activities at Glen Canyon National Recreation Area are water-related. These include boating, fishing, and waterskiing. Guided tours through the dam and visitor center are available from 8:30 A.M. to 3:30 P.M. daily in winter months, and from 8:30 A.M. to 5:30 P.M. in the summer months. Below the dam, U.S. Highway 89A leads to Lees Ferry, roadside exhibits, and relics of the gold mining days. U.S. 89 north leads to Kanab, Utah, where many western movies have been filmed. Numerous locations, including the beach at Wahweap, are good for swimming.

FACILITIES: All concession facilities listed are available through ARAMARK Lake Powell Resorts and Marinas, 2916 North 35th Avenue, Suite 8, Phoenix, AZ 85017 (800–528–6154; 602–278–8888 in Phoenix). The main lodging facility is at Wahweap.

Bullfrog: Visitor center, launching ramp, and picnic area. Concessioner-operated campground lodging, service station, restaurant, camp store, marina, and trailer village with hookups. Write Bullfrog Resort and Marina, P.O. Box 4055, Bullfrog, Lake Powell, UT 84533 (801–684–2233).

Dangling Rope Floating Marina: Ranger station,water, rest rooms, emergency communications,. fuel service, and camp supplies. Reached only by boat.

Halls Crossing: Ranger station and launching ramp, concessioner-operated campground, lodging, boat rental, marina, boat excursions, boating and camping supplies, and trailer village with hookups. Write Halls Crossing Marina, P.O. Box 5101-Halls, Lake Powell, UT 84533 (801–684–2261).

Hite: Ranger station, concessioner-operated boat rental, marina, camp store, service station, and small primitive camping facilities. Write Hite Marina, Inc., Box 1, Hanksville, UT 84734 (800–528–6154 outside Arizona; 602–278–8888 in Arizona).

Lees Ferry: Ranger station, launching ramp, and campground. A store, motel, restaurant, and service station are 3½ miles away at Marble Canyon.

Page: Motels, restaurants, and stores. Scenic flights are available from Page airport. Carl Hayden Visitor Center is at Glen Canyon Dam. Write Chamber of Commerce, Box 727, Page, AZ 86040.

Wahweap: Ranger station, campground (see camping section), picnic shelters, and launching ramp. Concessioner-operated boat rental, boat tours,.boating supplies and repairs, marina, restaurant, motel, lodge, trailer village with hookups, and service station. Write Wahweap Lodge and Marina, P.O. Box 1597, Page, AZ 86040 (520–645–2433).

CAMPING: The major camping area is at Wahweap, 7 miles northwest of Page. A concessioner-operated campground (178 spaces) offers water, a dump station, flush toilets, tables, and grills, but no hookups. A concessioner-operated trailer park (123 spaces) has hookups and pay showers. Campgrounds are also located at Hite (six spaces with pit toilets), Lees Ferry (fifty-eight

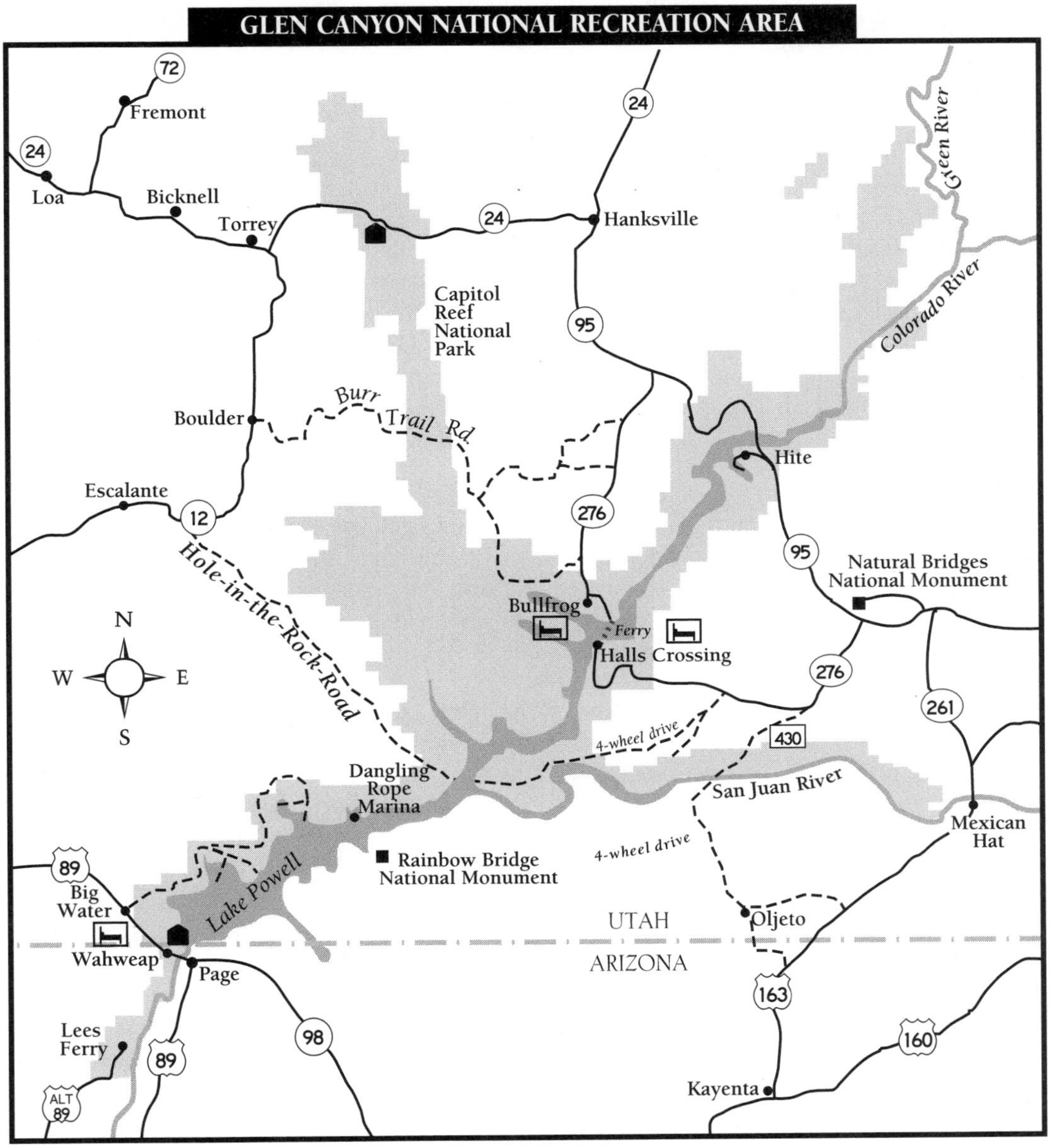

GLEN CANYON NATIONAL RECREATION AREA

spaces with flush toilets), Halls Crossing (sixty-five spaces with flush toilets), and Bullfrog (eighty-six spaces with flush toilets). Concessioner-operated trailer parks are at the latter two locations as well as at Wahweap.

FISHING: Striped bass, largemouth bass, and black crappie have been planted in Lake Powell. Catches of striped bass frequently include specimens of up to ten pounds. Native catfish are also plentiful. Below the dam, the clear cold river makes Lees Ferry famous for trout fishing. An appropriate state fishing license (Arizona or Utah) is required.

GRAND CANYON NATIONAL PARK

P.O. Box 129
Grand Canyon, AZ 86023-0129
(520) 638–7888
www.thecanyon.com/nps

Grand Canyon National Park contains nearly 1.2 million acres of land where the forces of erosion have unveiled a variety of spectacular formations that illustrate vast periods of geological history. The park is located in northwestern Arizona. The South Rim is approached from Flagstaff via U.S. 180 (80 miles to Grand Canyon Village) or by U.S. 89 and Arizona Highway 64 (82 miles to Desert View). The North Rim is 45 miles south of Jacob Lake via Arizona Highway 67.

About 1,700 million years ago, volcanic islands were pushed against the North American continent's edge. After these island-based layers were eroded away, movements within the earth created a basin in which sediments and volcanic rocks collected. About 800 million years ago, these layers were pushed upward to form a new, uplifted plateau that, in turn, eroded away. Between 225 and 570 million years ago, the region was an intercontinental sea similar to today's Gulf of Mexico. The sandstones, shales, and limestones that collected in the basin make up today's upper three-fourths of the canyon walls. About 65 million years ago the region began to rise above sea level, and moisture falling on the newly created Rocky Mountains created the Colorado River, which began cutting the canyon some six million years ago.

The park is divided into two separate sections—the North Rim and the South Rim—with the inner canyon accessible from either side. There are fifteen concessioners licensed by the National Park Service offering three- to nineteen-day trips along the Colorado River. Information may be obtained at the South Rim Visitor Center or by mail from the park. (Write Trip Planner, Grand Canyon National Park, P.O. Box 129, Grand Canyon, AZ 86023.)

Although an average of 10 miles separates the developed areas of the North and South Rims, the distance by road is 220 miles. By foot, the Kaibab Trail (20½ miles) leads from Yaki Point on the South Rim down to the river, across to Phantom Ranch, and then up to the North Rim, ending 2 miles from Grand Canyon Lodge. Campgrounds in the canyon require reservations. Phantom Ranch, north of the river on Kaibab Trail, offers meals and accommodations. Reservations (303–297–2757) are required.

NORTH RIM

The road to the less-developed North Rim winds through forests of pine, spruce, and aspen on the Kaibab Plateau. This area of the park is at elevations of 7,800 to 8,800 feet and has a cooler and wetter climate than the South Rim. The North Rim is closed by heavy snowfall from mid-November to mid-May. Facilities close by mid- to late October.

The main information station is located beside the Bright Angel Point parking area. Park rangers are available to answer questions, and publications concerning the park are for sale. The entrance station is located 13 miles north of Bright Angel Point. A U.S. Forest Service information station is located at Jacob Lake, 32 miles north of the North Rim Entrance Station.

A 23-mile paved road connects Grand Canyon Lodge to Cape Royal. This latter point provides an eastward view of the canyon toward the Painted Desert. Point Imperial, on a 3-mile spur off the Cape Royal Road, offers the best eastward view across the canyon. Point Sublime is 17 miles south of the park entrance via a four-wheel-drive dirt road. Ask at the NPS Information Desk for directions.

GRAND CANYON NATIONAL PARK

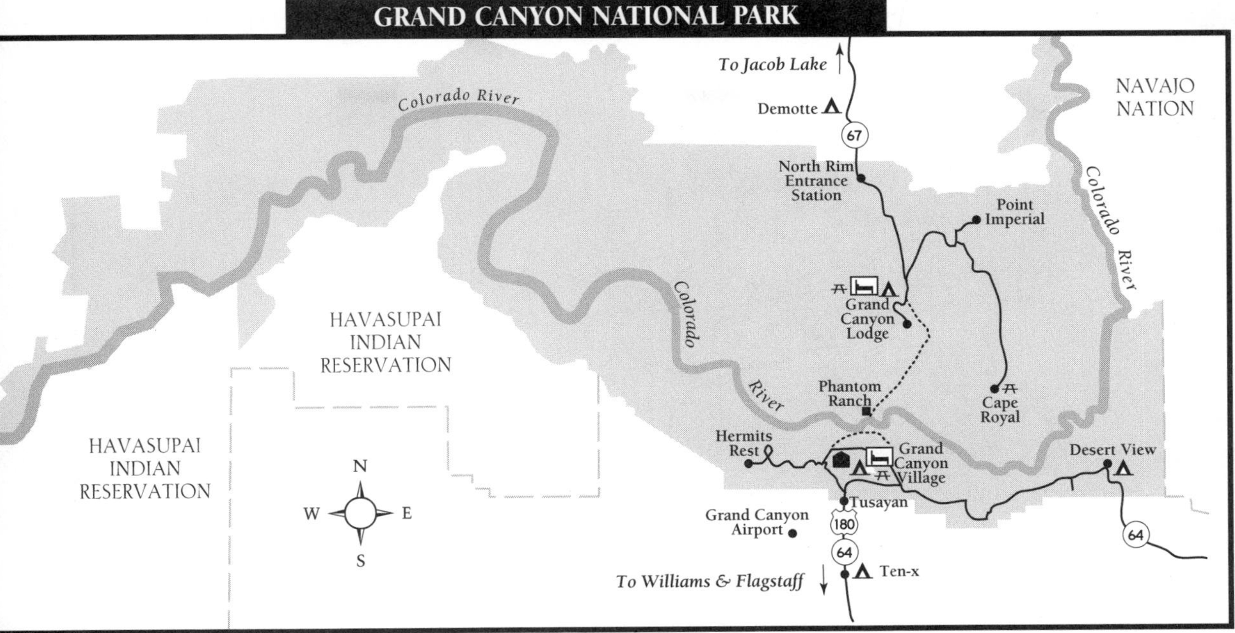

Various ranger-guided walks are scheduled during summer months. Bright Angel Point Trail is a 1/3-mile self-guided nature trail that begins near the lodge. Transept Trail (1 1/2 miles) provides a leisurely walk along the canyon rim from Grand Canyon Lodge to North Rim store and campground. Uncle Jim Trail (2 1/2 miles) starts at the Kaibab trailhead and winds through the forest, ending at a point overlooking the canyon. Cape Royal Trail is a 1/3-mile self-guided nature trail from the Cape Royal parking lot. The inner canyon is reached via the North Kaibab Trail (9 miles round-trip to Roaring Springs) by foot or mule. Information on mule trips may be obtained by writing Grand Canyon Trail Rides, P.O. Box 1638, Cedar City, UT 84720.

FACILITIES: Meals and lodging are available from mid-May to mid-October at Grand Canyon Lodge, which provides cabins and motel-type units. For information or reservations write Grand Canyon National Park Lodges, Amfac Park and Resorts, 14001 East Iliff Avenue, Suite 300, Denver, CO 80014. Call (303) 297–2757; fax (303) 297–3175. A general store, service station, post office, showers, and laundry are also located near the campground, 1 mile north of Bright Angel Point. Additional food services and accommodations are located at Kaibab Lodge (5 miles north of the entrance station) and at Jacob Lake.

CAMPING: North Rim Campground (eighty-two spaces) provides tables, grills, water, flush toilets, and a dump station. It is located 1 mile north of Bright Angel Point, 12 miles south of the entrance station. Reservations may be made by calling Biospherics, Inc., (800–365–2267). De Motte Campground (5 miles north of the entrance station) and Jacob Lake Campground (32 miles north of the entrance station) are operated by the U.S. Forest Service and provide water and rest rooms.

FISHING: Access to fishing is very difficult, and catches are generally poor. Brown and rainbow trout live in the bottom of the canyon in Bright Angel Creek near Phantom Ranch. Channel catfish are very rarely taken from the nearby Colorado River and rainbows from Thunder River and Tapeats Creek. An Arizona fishing license is required.

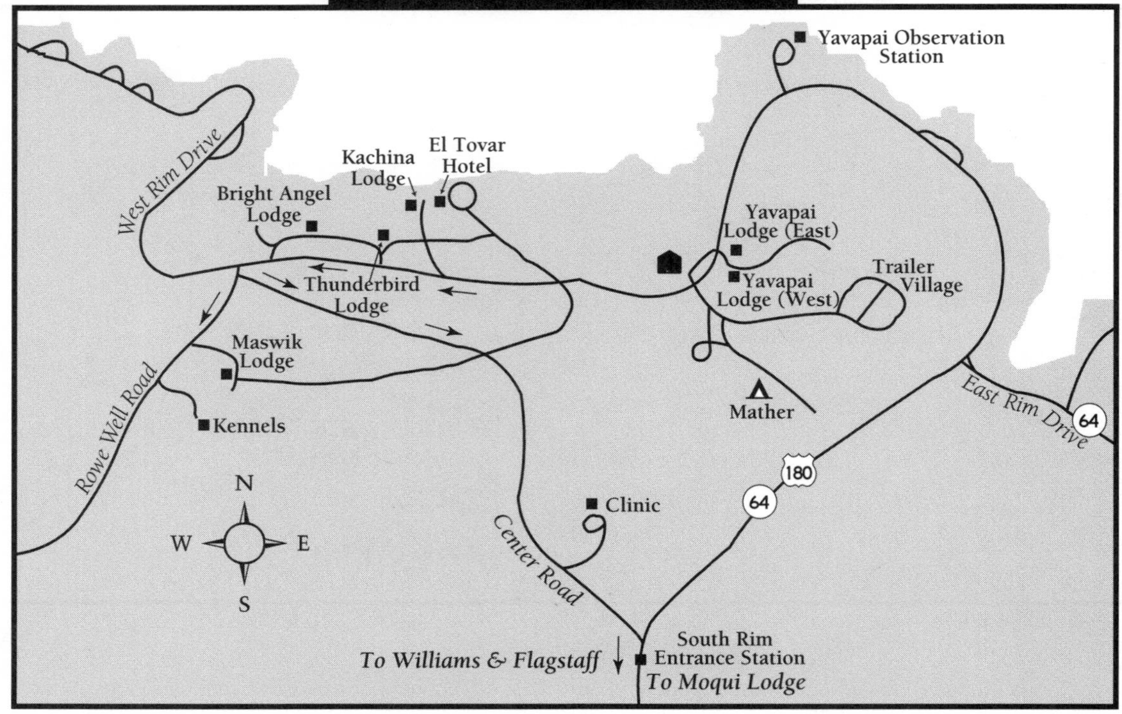

SOUTH RIM

The South Rim is open year-round, and temperatures during summer months range from the mid-forties at night to the mid-eighties in daytime. The visitor center is located in Grand Canyon Village, 7 miles north of the South Entrance Station. Rangers are available to answer questions, and a schedule of activities is posted. The visitor-center museum contains exhibits explaining the human and natural history of the park. Additional museums are the Yavapai Observation Station (1/2 mile east of the visitor center) and Tusayan Museum (3 miles west of Desert View), with displays describing prehistoric inhabitants of the area.

From mid-March through mid-October, a shuttle bus provides free transportation throughout Grand Canyon Village. In addition, it goes to ranger activities, visitor facilities, and along West Rim Drive. This latter road (8 miles) offers several scenic viewpoints of the canyon on the way from Grand Canyon Village to Hermits Rest. East Rim Drive to Desert View (26 miles) offers an excellent view of the canyon at several viewpoints. The Watchtower at Desert View overlooks the canyon and the Painted Desert.

A number of self-guided nature trails, paths, and undeveloped trails lie along the rim between Yavapai Museum and Hermits Rest. Canyon Rim Nature Trail (1 1/2 miles) leads from the hotel to the visitor center and Yavapai Observation Station. Ranger-guided walks are presented on a scheduled basis at Grand Canyon Village throughout the year and at Desert View and Tusayan Ruins in summer.

LODGING: The South Rim of the Grand Canyon has six lodges within the park boundaries. Accommodations range from the historic El Tovar (completed in 1905), which sits near the edge of the South Rim, to motel-type units at Yavapai, Maswik, Thunderbird, and Kachina, to rustic cabins at Bright Angel Lodge. Reservations for all six lodging units are available by writing Grand Canyon National Park Lodges, Amfac Parks and Resorts, 14001 East Iliff Avenue, Suite 300, Aurora, CO 80014. Call (303) 297–2757; fax (303) 297–3175. The same firm operates Moqui Lodge, another motel-type unit that is a short distance outside the South Entrance. Other private lodging is near the South Entrance.

FACILITIES: Nearly anything the heart desires can be found in Grand Canyon Village. This includes a bank, general store, post office, service station, laundry, restaurants, gift shops, showers, pet kennel, and lost-and-found facility. A general store, snack bar, and service station are located at Desert View.

CAMPING: The park's most developed campground is Mather Campground (310 spaces and seven group camps) at Grand Canyon Village. It provides tables, grills, water, flush toilets, pay showers, laundry facilities, and a dump station. Reservations for Mather are available by calling Biospherics, Inc. (800–365–2267). Nearby, Trailer Village (eighty-two spaces) is operated by Grand Canyon National Park Lodges and provides hookups. Write Amfac Parks and Resorts, 14001 East Iliff, Suite 600, Aurora, CO 80014; (303) 297–2757. Desert View Campground (fifty spaces) is located ½ mile west of the east entrance station and has tables, grills, water, and flush toilets. Ten X Campground (seventy sites, pit toilets), operated by the U.S. Forest Service, is located 10 miles south of Grand Canyon Village, outside the park. Ten X is a pleasant campground with lots of shade.

FISHING: Access to fishing is difficult, and catches are generally poor. See fishing section under the North Rim section for details.

HUBBELL TRADING POST NATIONAL HISTORIC SITE

P.O. Box 150
Ganado, AZ 86505-0150
(520) 755–3475
www.nps.gov/hutr/

Hubbell Trading Post was authorized as a national historic site in 1965 to preserve an active Navajo trading post. The site is on the Navajo Nation, one-half mile west of Ganado, Arizona, and 55 miles from Gallup, New Mexico.

Hubbell Trading Post is the oldest continuously operating trading post on the Navajo Nation. The post was established in 1871. The trader John Lorenzo Hubbell purchased the post from William Leonard in 1878. Hubbell eventually established a network of trading posts, a wholesale house in Winslow, and a stage and freight line. A personal friend of men such as Theodore Roosevelt and General Lew Wallace, Hubbell was instrumental in early Arizona history and statehood. His death in 1930 was mourned by the Navajos, and his body lies overlooking the trading post on Hubbell Hill. The Hubbell family operated the post for eighty-nine years, until it became a national historic site.

Visitors may participate in the experience of a living, active post. Here, members of the Navajo, Hopi, Zuni, and other tribes still come to sell and trade such crafts as hand-woven rugs, jewelry, baskets, and pottery. Ranger-led interpretive programs are available. Weaving demonstrations are offered in the visitor center. A booklet for a self-guided tour of the site may be borrowed at the visitor center.

The site is open daily except Christmas, New Year's Day, and Thanksgiving. Hours are 8:00 A.M. to 5:00 P.M. October through April, and 8:00 A.M. to 6:00 P.M. the rest of the year. Daylight savings time is observed.

FACILITIES: The trading post continues traditional operation under the direction of the Southwest Parks and Monuments Association, a nonprofit organization operating the post for the National Park Service. Many fine Navajo, Hopi, Zuni, Apache, and other Indian arts are offered for sale in the trading post. Groceries and snacks may also be purchased here. A half-mile east, in the town of Ganado, visitors will find three cafes, gas station, and market. Rest rooms and drinking water are available in the visitor center.

CAMPING: No camping is allowed at the site. Canyon de Chelly National Monument, 40 miles north on Highway 191, offers 104 sites at Cottonwood Campground (flush toilets).

FISHING: No fishing is available at Hubbell Trading Post National Historic Site.

MONTEZUMA CASTLE NATIONAL MONUMENT

P.O. Box 219
Camp Verde, AZ 86322
(520) 567–3322
nps.gov/moca/

Montezuma Castle National Monument was established in 1906. It contains one of the best-preserved prehistoric cliff dwellings in the Southwest. The five-story, twenty-room castle is 90 percent intact. The monument is located in central Arizona, just off Interstate 17, 55 miles south of Flagstaff and 4 miles northeast of the town of Camp Verde. The monument is approximately 90 miles north of Phoenix.

Several million years ago the Verde River was dammed by lava, forming a lake 35 miles long and 18 miles wide. Later, after tributaries had deposited large quantities of limy mud in the lake, overflows wore down the lava dam and the lake drained. The Verde River and its tributaries then cut deep channels through the sediments, and further erosion caused a broadening of the valleys.

Although there is little evidence of the earliest inhabitants of the Verde Valley, Indians are known to have lived in the Southwest for several thousand years. About A.D. 700, the Hohokam Indians came into the valley from the south. About 350 years later, these farming Indians moved north to the fertile lands created by the eruption that created Sunset Crater in the mid-1060s. Around 1100, a group of dry-farming Indians entered the valley from the north. About 1250, they began erecting large dwellings on hilltops or in cliffs. The limestone cliff along the north bank of Beaver Creek was an ideal place to build house clusters, because it had good cropland on the creek terrace nearby. Two of the clusters (including Montezuma Castle) eventually became five-story apartment houses that were occupied for about two centuries. By about 1450, Montezuma Castle appears to have been abandoned.

Montezuma Castle National Monument (opposite page)

The visitor center is in the Montezuma Castle section of the park. It contains exhibits describing the culture of the people who lived here. Examples of weaving, basketry, jewelry, and pottery-making tools are on display.

Additional prehistoric Indian work can be seen at Montezuma Well, 11 miles northeast of Montezuma Castle. This part of the monument contains a limestone sink 470 feet in diameter with water 55 feet deep. Indians diverted the well water into irrigation ditches that are still visible today. This section also contains the remains of a Hohokam pithouse and Sinagua dwellings.

FACILITIES: No food or lodging is available within the monument's boundaries, but both can be found nearby. Limited picnic facilities are located in each of the two sections of the park. Drinking water and modern rest rooms are available in the visitor center. There is easy handicapped access to rest rooms, the visitor center, and the trail at the Montezuma Castle section.

CAMPING: No camping is permitted in the monument. Forest service campgrounds are located in Coconino National Forest, and other private campgrounds are located nearby.

FISHING: No fishing is available in the monument, but the nearby Verde River offers fishing with an Arizona fishing license.

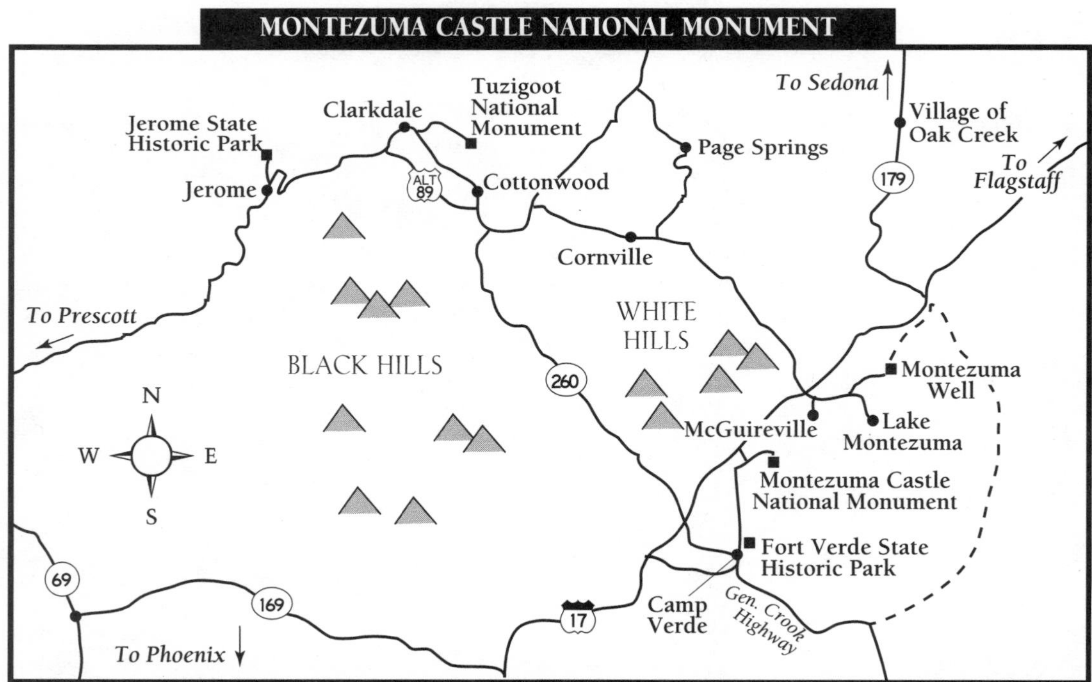

NAVAJO NATIONAL MONUMENT

HC 71 Box 3
Tonalea, AZ 86044-9704
(520) 672–2366
www.nps.gov/nava/

Navajo National Monument comprises 360 acres, surrounded by Navajo Nation land. It was established in 1909 to preserve the spectacular cliff dwellings built by the ancestral Pueblo Indian farmers who lived in the canyons more than 700 years ago. Park headquarters, located on the Navajo Nation in northeastern Arizona, can be reached by following U.S. 160 east 50 miles from Tuba City or west 29 miles from Kayenta. At Black Mesa, a 9-mile paved road (Highway 564) leads to the monument.

For about 2,000 years the San Juan Basin of the Four Corners region was occupied by the ancestral Pueblo Indians. Archaeologists adopted a Navajo word, *Anasazi* ("alien ancestors"), to describe these people. They were originally hunters and gatherers but began to rely on agriculture, which came into the region on ancient trade routes. Archaeologists divide the people into three cultural divisions: Mesa Verde in southwestern Colorado, Chaco in northwest New Mexico, and Kayenta in northeastern Arizona.

The cliff dwellings of Betatakin and Keet Seel were inhabited during the late thirteenth century, prior to a time of great change and population movements. The people farmed corn, beans, and squash in the fertile canyon bottoms. They supplemented these crops with gathered plants, seeds, and some hunting. Vivid multicolored pottery was created for use by the people and for trade. By 1300, the people of these villages joined their neighbors in slow migrations from their homelands to new areas. Today's Hopi Indians claim close ties with the area. Tribal elders consider these villages temporary stops in their clans' migrations, and they return annually to visit sacred shrines nearby. In the early 1800s, an unrelated group of people, the Navajo, began to settle in the area.

The monument is located within the vast Navajo Nation. Keet Seel is the largest village, with more than 160 well-preserved rooms. An 8½-mile (one way) primitive trail leads to the village. Keet Seel may be visited from Memorial Day weekend until Labor Day by backpacking. Visits are limited to twenty people per day. Reservations may be obtained (starting two months prior to the date of the visit) by writing or calling the monument. Demand is great, so call early. A primitive campground is available at Keet Seel for hikers.

Betatakin, with 135 rooms, may be visited on five-hour-long ranger-led tours, usually available from May through September. Tours are limited to twenty-five people (first-come, first-served daily). Betatakin may be seen from the view point at the end of the Sandal Trail, a 1-mile round-trip from the Visitor Center. The Sandal Trail is open year-round. Allow forty-five minutes to view the site and return. The Aspen Forest Overlook Trail is a 4/10 mile (one-way) trail into Betatakin Canyon and provides visitors with a close-up look at the aspen growth at the bottom of the canyon. Visitors hike to a view point, then return the same route. Inscription House Ruin is a major cliff dwelling in Navajo National Monument. Unfortunately, Inscription House Ruin is closed to the public indefinitely.

At the visitor center, which is open daily except Thanksgiving, Christmas, and New Year's, you may view museum exhibits on the ancestral Pueblo people and the Navajo people, purchase books, and view a film, slide show, and video. An Indian arts-and-crafts shop is located next door.

FACILITIES: Food, gas, and lodging are not available at the monument but can be found nearby. Rest rooms and water are available at the visitor center and at the campground. A picnic area is located near the visitor center.

CAMPING: A campground (thirty spaces, limited to vehicles 25 feet in length or less) is open year-round. Stays are limited to seven days. Picnic tables, flush toilets, and a dump station are provided. No open fires, including charcoal, are allowed.

FISHING: No fishing is available at Navajo National Monument.

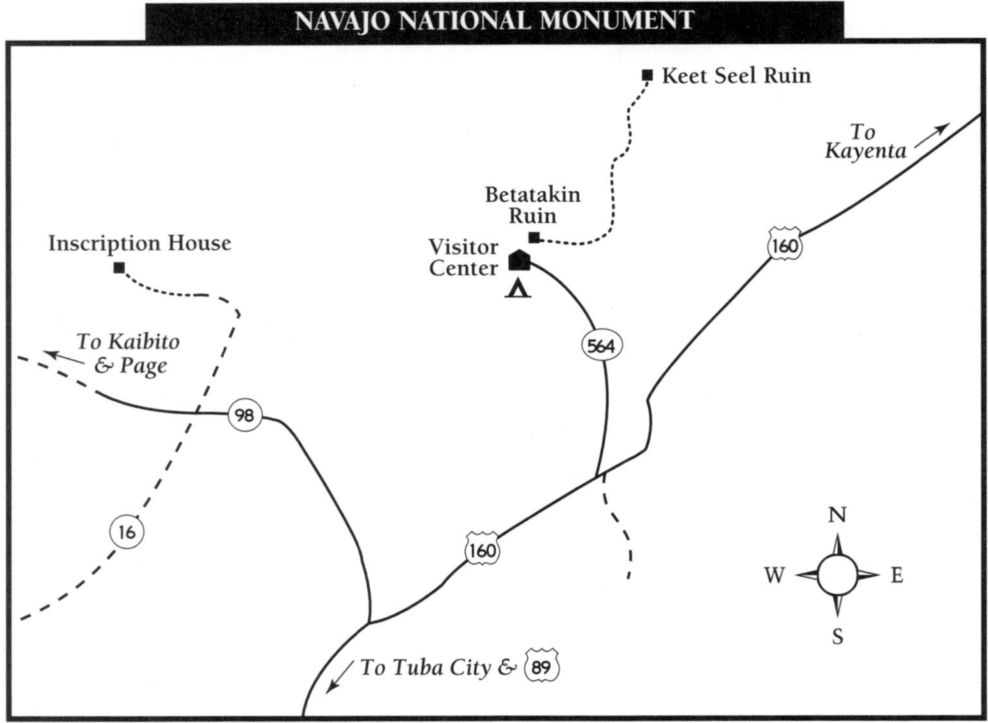

ORGAN PIPE CACTUS NATIONAL MONUMENT

Route 1, Box 100
Ajo, AZ 85321-9626
(520) 387–6849
orpi_information@nps.gov
www.nps.gov/orpi/

Organ Pipe Cactus National Monument comprises 330,689 acres. This park was established as a national monument in 1937 to preserve and protect unique Sonoran Desert plants and animals, including the rare cactus for which the park is named. The monument is located in southwestern Arizona on the Mexican border, 141 miles south of Phoenix and 144 miles west of Tucson. From Phoenix, take Interstate 10 to Arizona 85 south. From Tucson, take Arizona 86 (Ajo Way) west and then Arizona 85 south. The monument visitor center is 34 miles south of Ajo.

Organ Pipe Cactus National Monument was designated to protect the natural features and life contained in this segment of the Sonoran Desert. The stark and rough landscape of the monument includes mountains, plains, canyons, and dry washes. Summer days can be quite warm—temperatures of 95 to 105 degrees Fahrenheit are most common. Of the 9¼ inches of annual rainfall, nearly two-thirds results from summer thunderstorms. Winter weather is generally mild, with sunny days. Temperatures can hover just above freezing during winter nights with occasional dips below that mark.

A visitor center containing exhibits explaining the monument and desert is located 17 miles south of the northern entrance. The visitor center is open year-round (except Christmas) from 8:00 A.M. to 5:00 P.M. Evening campfire programs are presented in the campground amphitheater during the busy winter months from mid-December through mid-April.

A single paved road (Arizona 85) through the park connects Why, Arizona, with Sonoyta, Mexico. Two graded loop drives through remote areas begin at the visitor center, where guide booklets are available. Puerto Blanco Drive is 40 miles long and takes approximately one-half day to drive. This route circles the Puerto Blanco Mountains and parallels the Mexican border. Side roads lead to a stand of senita cactus at Senita Basin and to a human-made oasis at Quitobaquito Springs. Ajo Mountain Drive is a 21-mile road that takes approximately three hours to drive and provides outstanding views of the desert. Various species of cactus can be seen as the road circles the Ajo Mountains.

A number of trails are located in the park. A 1½-mile trail connects the campground and visitor center, and a 1½-mile self-guided Desert View Nature Trail leads from the group campground to a nearby ridge overlooking the desert. Victoria Mine Trail (5 miles round-trip) leads to what was once one of the area's most productive silver and gold mines. O'Odham Day, a celebration of native culture, is celebrated on the third Saturday of March. Demonstrations include pottery, dancing, story-telling, native plant use, and dry farming.

FACILITIES: Lodging and food service are not available within the monument. A motel, post office, grocery store, cafe, and service station are located in Lukeville, 5 miles south of the visitor center. Motels and restaurants are located in Ajo, Gila Bend, and Sonoyta. A cafe, grocery store, motel, and service stations are located in Why, near the park's northern entrance. Modern rest rooms and drinking water are available at both the visitor center and campground.

CAMPING: A single campground (208 spaces) is open all year and is located 1½ miles southwest of the visitor center. The campground contains tables, grills, flush toilets, and a dump station. There is a 35-foot limit on trailers and motorhomes. A drive-in primitive campground with four sites is at Alamo Canyon. A permit from the visitor center is required. No motorhomes are allowed.

FISHING: No fishing is available in Organ Pipe Cactus National Monument.

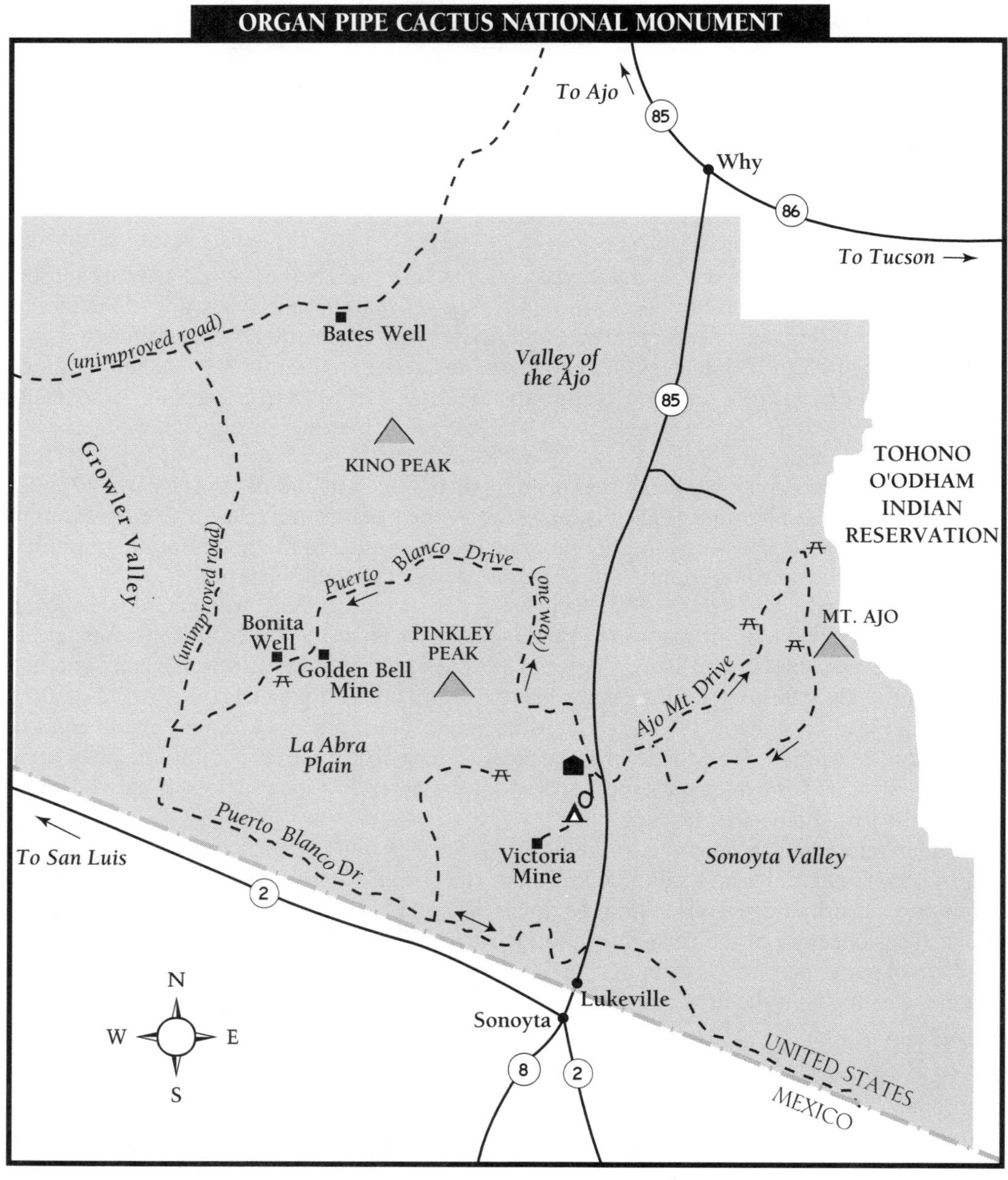

PETRIFIED FOREST NATIONAL PARK

Petrified Forest National Park, AZ 86028-2217
(520) 524–6228
www.nps.gov/pefo/

Petrified Forest National Park was proclaimed a national monument by President Theodore Roosevelt in 1906, and was legislated as a national park by Congress in 1962. The park protects 93,533 acres of late Triassic Period plants, animals, and trees that fossilized to multicolored stone. Early Puebloan dwelling sites, petroglyphs (pictures and designs chiseled in rock faces), and a portion of the Painted Desert are also found within the park. The park is located in northeastern Arizona, 46 miles from the New Mexico border on Interstate 40. It is 119 miles east of Flagstaff, Arizona.

The Painted Desert of northern Arizona is a landscape of various colors and shapes. Within the eroded badlands of Petrified Forest National Park, visitors will find a multitude of logs brilliant with jasper and agate. Long before modern visitors came to the park, early Native Americans used the fossilized wood for tools and as building material for some of their pueblos. Some dwellings and petroglyphs can still be seen at Agate House, Puerco Pueblo, and Newspaper Rock.

The fossils of Petrified Forest tell of a very different place and time. This region was crossed by many streams as part of a vast tropical floodplain 225 million years ago. On drier upland areas and near the streams' headwaters, large coniferous trees grew. As trees fell, many were carried downstream and buried by mud. While buried, the lack of oxygen slowed the decaying process. The overlying sediment was rich in silica from volcanic ash. Silica, carried by groundwater, was absorbed by the waterlogged trees. The silica gradually crystallized into quartz. Today these hardened remains of the Triassic are found among the badlands in the sedimentary layers of mudstone, silts, clays, and sandstones known as the Chinle Formation.

The Painted Desert Visitor Center (just off Interstate 40) provides information about the park and offers a free 20-minute film every half-hour. At the park's south entrance (off Highway 180), the Rainbow Forest Museum contains specimens of petrified wood, fossils of plants and animals, and exhibits about the Triassic Period. A short, paved trail behind the museum provides access to some of the largest and most colorful fossilized logs. A 28-mile paved road connecting these two locations contains wayside exhibits and scenic overlooks at points of interest. Ranger programs are available throughout the summer, and program locations and times are posted at the Painted Desert Visitor Center and Rainbow Forest Museum. The park is open year-round; however, hours vary with the season. For park hours and information, call (520) 524–6228. The park is closed on Christmas Day. Be aware that winter storms may close the park or delay the opening. Use yellow phones to report emergencies or threats to park resources.

Nearly thirteen tons of petrified wood are stolen from this park each year. The collection or destruction of any natural or cultural resource is prohibited. Violators may be fined, imprisoned, or both. Do your part to protect your park.

Some of the major points (numbers keyed to those found on map) are:

1. Painted Desert Visitor Center—The first stop upon entering the park from Interstate 40. A free, 20-minute park film *Timeless Impressions* is shown every half-hour. A restaurant, gift shop,

Jasper Forest, Petrified Forest National Park (courtesy Petrified Forest Museum Association)

gas station, and travel store are located next to the visitor center; rest room facilities are available year-round.

2. The Painted Desert—Eight overlooks provide views of the Painted Desert. Rest rooms are available year-round at the Painted Desert Inn, a National Historic Landmark located at Kachina Point, with rest rooms during summer months only. A picnic area is available at Chinde Point.

3. Puerco Pueblo—The remains of a 1,000-year-old pueblo and some outstanding petroglyphs are a short walk from the parking area. Rest rooms are available year-round. An emergency phone also is available.

4. Newspaper Rock—Excellent petroglyphs may be viewed on the surface of a massive sandstone block at the base of the overlook. Free spotting scopes are on the viewing platform.

5. The Tepees—Colorful mounds that resemble tepees or haystacks are examples of erosion of the soft-layered clay deposits of the Chinle Formation.

6. Blue Mesa—A 3-mile loop road leads travelers to several excellent viewpoints. A 1-mile self-guiding trail meanders through an area of badlands and petrified logs. An emergency phone is available.

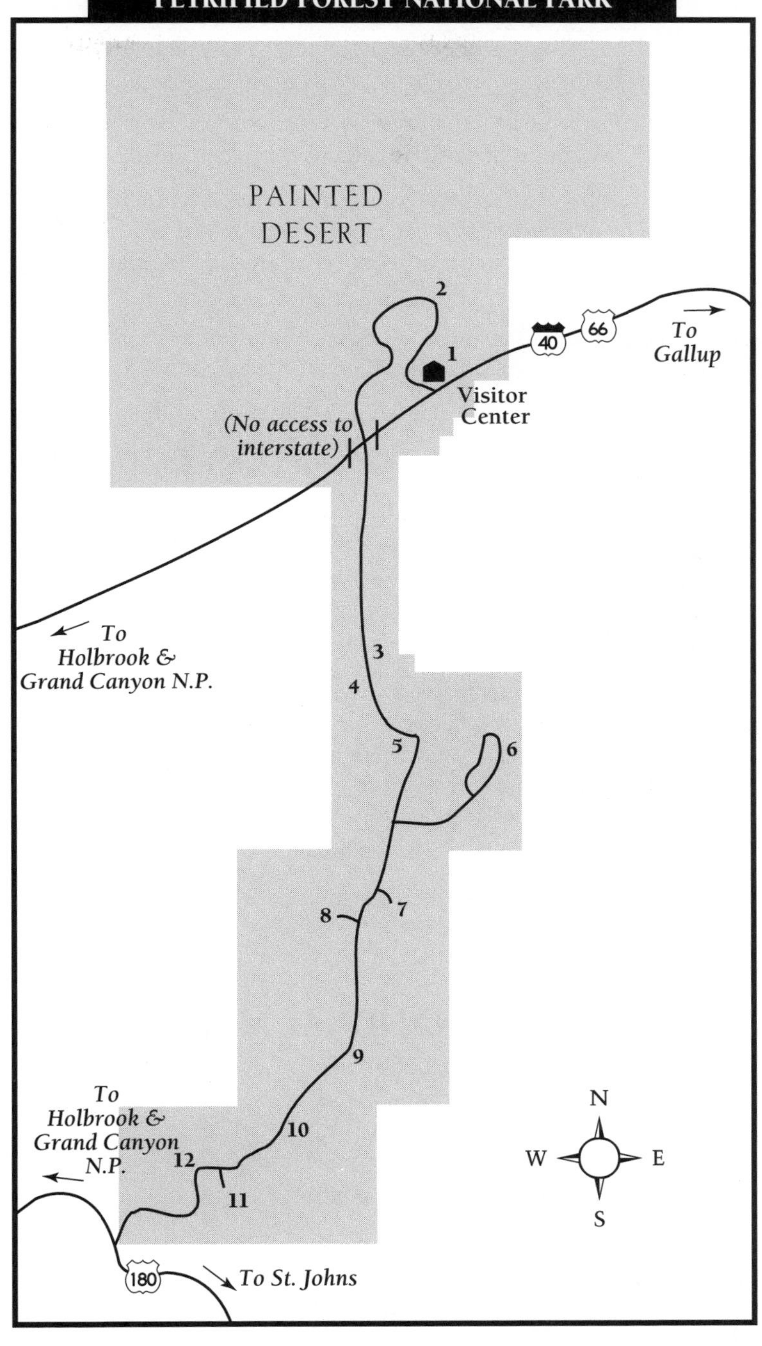
PETRIFIED FOREST NATIONAL PARK
PAINTED DESERT
1
2
3
4
5
6
7
8
9
10
11
12
Visitor Center
(No access to interstate)
40
66
To Gallup
To Holbrook & Grand Canyon N.P.
To Holbrook & Grand Canyon N.P.
180
To St. Johns
N
W
E
S

7. Agate Bridge—A huge petrified log lies partially exposed across a gully. Both ends of the log are encased in sandstone, with a 40-foot ravine beneath that has been carved by erosion. This unusual feature was reinforced by concrete in 1917. Rest rooms are available only during summer months.

8. Jasper Forest Overlook—Masses of log sections litter the valley floor below.

9. Crystal Forest—These fossil logs were once filled with clear and amethyst quartz crystals. Before the turn of the century, most of the crystals were removed by souvenir hunters and gem collectors. A trail leads through an impressive area of large fossil logs.

10. Flattops—Massive remnants of a once-continuous layer of durable sandstone form a large mesa above the softer layered deposits of the Chinle Formation. Once widespread, this sandstone layer has been removed by erosion in most other areas of the park.

11. Long Logs and Agate House—The ½-mile Long Logs loop trail is an area of exceptionally long logs that are only partially uncovered. Another ¾-mile trail leads to Agate House, a partially restored eight-room pueblo made of petrified wood sections.

12. Rainbow Forest Museum and Giant Logs Trail—The museum displays sections of petrified wood, and geology and paleontology exhibits. The ½-mile self-guiding Giant Logs Trail begins behind the museum. Rest room facilities are available year-round.

FACILITIES: No overnight lodging is available in the park, but accommodations can be found in nearby communities. Food, gifts, and gasoline can be obtained all year at the Painted Desert Oasis next to the Painted Desert Visitor Center at the north entrance. Rainbow Forest Curios, near the south entrance, has refreshments and gifts. Picnic areas are located at Chinde Point and near the Rainbow Forest Museum.

CAMPING: No campgrounds are available in the park. Backcountry camping is allowed by wilderness permit only and requires backpacking into the Painted Desert Wilderness Area (43,020 acres). Travel is cross-country, and there are no trails, facilities, or water. The nearest public campgrounds are in national forests to the southeast and west, nearly 100 miles away. Private campgrounds are located at both Holbrook and Winslow. A county park near Joseph City has limited camping. Two state parks in the area are Lyman Lake and Homolovi Ruins.

FISHING: No fishing is available in Petrified Forest National Park.

PIPE SPRING NATIONAL MONUMENT

HC 65, Box 5
Fredonia, AZ 86022
(520) 643–7105
pisp_interpretation@nps.gov
www.nps.gov/pisp/

Pipe Spring National Monument comprises forty acres. It was established in 1923 to preserve a historic fort and other structures built by Mormon pioneers. Pipe Spring is located in northwestern Arizona near the Utah border. The monument is 15 miles southwest of Fredonia, Arizona, on Arizona Highway 389. It is located 66 miles from Zion National Park, 89 miles from the North Rim of the Grand Canyon, and 45 miles from Hurricane, Utah.

Located on the Arizona Strip (the northern part of Arizona separated from the rest of the state by the Grand Canyon), the water of Pipe Spring has allowed plants and animals to thrive in this dry, desert region. Humans have also taken advantage of this water for at least 1,000 years. Ancestral Puebloans (Anasazi) grew crops near the springs. Paiute Indians gathered seed from abundant grasses, hunted animals that used the springs, and raised crops in the area. In the late 1850s Mormon missionaries en route to the Hopi lands camped at the spring. The name of Pipe Spring supposedly originated when one of the men shot the bottom out of a smoking pipe to demonstrate his marksmanship.

James Whitmore followed trails pioneered by the missionaries and established a claim at Pipe Spring in 1863. Because of the abundant forage, in 1865 he built a dugout, fenced an area, and started a livestock ranch. At the same time that Mormons were migrating into the region, the U.S. Army was waging a war south of the Colorado River with the Navajo. No one is certain who killed Whitmore on January 8, 1866. Pipe Spring was subsequently abandoned until the area found use by the Utah Territorial Militia as a base of operations against the Navajo. By 1868 a peace treaty was signed with the Navajos, and pioneers began to return to the Arizona Strip area.

In 1870 Brigham Young bought the Pipe Spring claim from Whitmore's widow. A fortifed ranch house, called Winsor Castle (after the first ranch superintendent), was constructed directly over the main spring to protect the water supply and provide protection from the Indians. Winsor Castle was never attacked and became the headquarters of a large tithing ranch for the Mormon church. In the early days a dairy was operated from Pipe Spring. It always served as a way station for travelers, and in the 1880s and 1890s, Pipe Spring was a refuge for the wives and children of polygamists sought by the federal marshals. In the mid-1890s Pipe Spring passed into private hands but continued to serve as a ranch until its purchase by the National Park Service in 1923.

The climate at Pipe Spring is fairly temperate because the area is nearly 1 mile above sea level. Plant and animal life are typical for a semidesert area. Small rodents live among the cactus and sagebrush, and coyotes are occasionally seen. Water from the spring provides a perfect habitat for the flora and fauna of this oasis. Birds are abundant in this monument.

The monument is open from 8:00 A.M. to 5:00 P.M. (Mountain Standard Time), year-round, with the historic buildings open from 8:30 A.M. to 4:30 P.M. The monument is closed Thanksgiving, Christmas, and New Year's Day. Guided tours are offered on the hour and half-hour year-round. Ranger talks and living history programs, representative of pioneer and Paiute life, are offered during the summer months. The monument grounds include a re-created historic orchard and garden, Winsor Castle, the East Cabin (lived in during the building of the castle), the West Cabin (used by John Wesley Powell's survey crew in the early 1870s), a juniper-log corral, the site of the dugout (the first dwelling at Pipe Spring), and a ½-mile loop trail, with markers discussing the natural and cultural history of the area. The visitor center contains displays and an introductory video.

FACILITIES: A gift shop/bookstore is operated by the Zion Natural History Association. A small cafe next to the gift shop is operated by the Kaibab-Paiute Indian Tribe.The nearest town with accommodations is Fredonia, 15 miles to the northeast. Similar facilities are also available in Hurricane and Kanab, Utah.

CAMPING: No camping is permitted at Pipe Spring. A campground operated by the Kaibab-Paiute Indian tribe is located ¼ mile north of the monument. Full hook ups and tent sites are available. Zion National Park (66 miles) and Utah's Coral Pink Sand Dune State Park (45 miles) both have complete camping facilities.

FISHING: No fishing is available in the monument.

SAGUARO NATIONAL PARK

3693 South Old Spanish Trail
Tucson, AZ 85730-5699
(520) 733–5100
www.nps.gov/sagu/

Saguaro National Park comprises 91,000 acres in two sections near Tucson, Arizona. It was established as a national monument in 1933 to preserve giant saguaro cacti. The park's largest part, Saguaro East, is about 4 miles east of the Tucson city limits on Old Spanish Trail. A smaller part, Saguaro West, is approximately 7 miles west of the city limits. This part can be reached by driving west to Kinney Road on either Gates Pass Road or Ajo Way.

Saguaro National Park was named after a large cactus in the Sonoran Desert that averages a height of 30 feet and lives up to 150 years. The seed of the saguaro sprouts and survives in the shade of another desert plant. After five years it has grown only a few inches, and at thirty years is only a few feet tall. At seventy-five years the plant may reach 15 or 20 feet and begin developing its first branch.

The saguaro is well suited to the area's dry climate. The root system is widespread and lies just below the ground surface so as to absorb as much of the infrequent rain as possible. A mature plant weighing six to ten tons may absorb as much as a ton of water. During long dry periods, the saguaro consumes its stored moisture and shrinks in girth. During May and early June, clusters of white flowers appear on the saguaro's branch ends. These are Arizona's state flower.

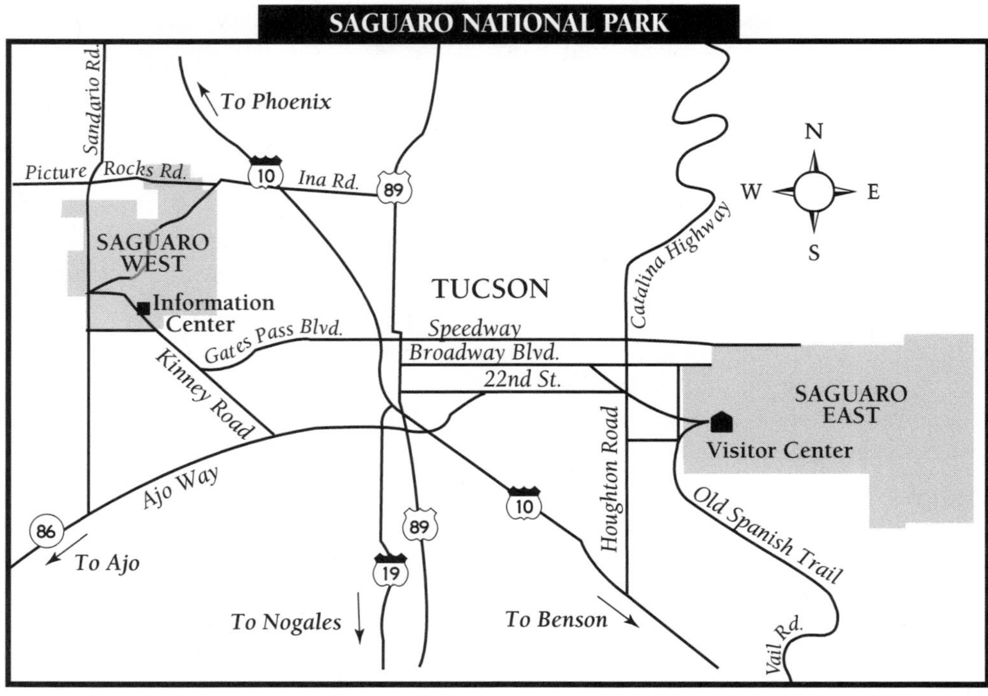

Variations in elevation from 2,800 to 8,700 feet within the park make it the home of numerous types of plant and animal life. The saguaro cactus itself serves as home for several species of birds. Woodpeckers and flickers bore holes that are later used by owls, martins, and flycatchers.

A visitor center, located at the west entrance of Saguaro East, contains exhibits describing the history and geology of this area of the country. Ranger-guided walks are conducted from here during winter months. An 8-mile paved road that begins near the visitor center takes the motorist on a scenic drive through the stands of large, old saguaros found in the eastern section of the park. Pullouts are located along the drive so visitors can walk along some short trails.

Saguaro West contains stands of young saguaros. The main road through this section leads to hiking trails and scenic overlooks. Ranger-guided hikes are also conducted here during winter months. A modern visitor center is located at the south entrance, and the nearby Arizona-Sonora Desert Museum contains exhibits of living plants and animals of the Sonoran Desert. Mild temperatures from fall through spring turn uncomfortably hot (over 100 degrees Fahrenheit) during summer months.

FACILITIES: Modern rest rooms and drinking water are available at the visitor centers of both the East and West units. Four picnic areas with tables, shelters, and rest rooms (but no water) are located in Saguaro West. Two picnic areas are also located on Cactus Forest Drive in Saguaro East. Other facilities can be found in nearby Tucson.

CAMPING: No developed campgrounds are in the park. Walk-in camps are along backcountry trails. Permits are required.

FISHING: No fishing is available in Saguaro National Park.

SUNSET CRATER VOLCANO NATIONAL MONUMENT

Route 3, Box 149
Flagstaff, AZ 86004
(520) 526–0502
www.nps.gov/sucr/

Sunset Crater Volcano National Monument was created in 1930 to preserve 3,040 acres containing a magnificent volcanic cinder cone formed around A.D. 1064. The monument is located 15 miles north of Flagstaff, Arizona, off U.S. 89 on FS 545. It is a convenient stop for motorists traveling from Flagstaff to the South Rim of Grand Canyon National Park (approximately two hours away). Wupatki National Monument is a short drive north of Sunset Crater.

North-central Arizona is covered with cinder cones, volcanic peaks, and lava flows representing about 10 million years of volcanic activity. The 200-year eruptive phase that started in A.D. 1064–65 resulted in the symmetrical cinder cone and black lava and cinder area of Sunset Crater. Lava, cinders, and ash were blown from a volcanic vent, creating a 1,000-foot-high cone-shaped volcano. Prevailing southwesterly winds caused most of the material to fall on the northeast side. As eruptions slackened, lava outpourings occurred from vents near the cinder cone's base. Later, hot springs and vapors seeped out from fumaroles near the vent. Minerals from these vapors stained the cinders and make the summit seem to glow with the hues of a perpetual sunset.

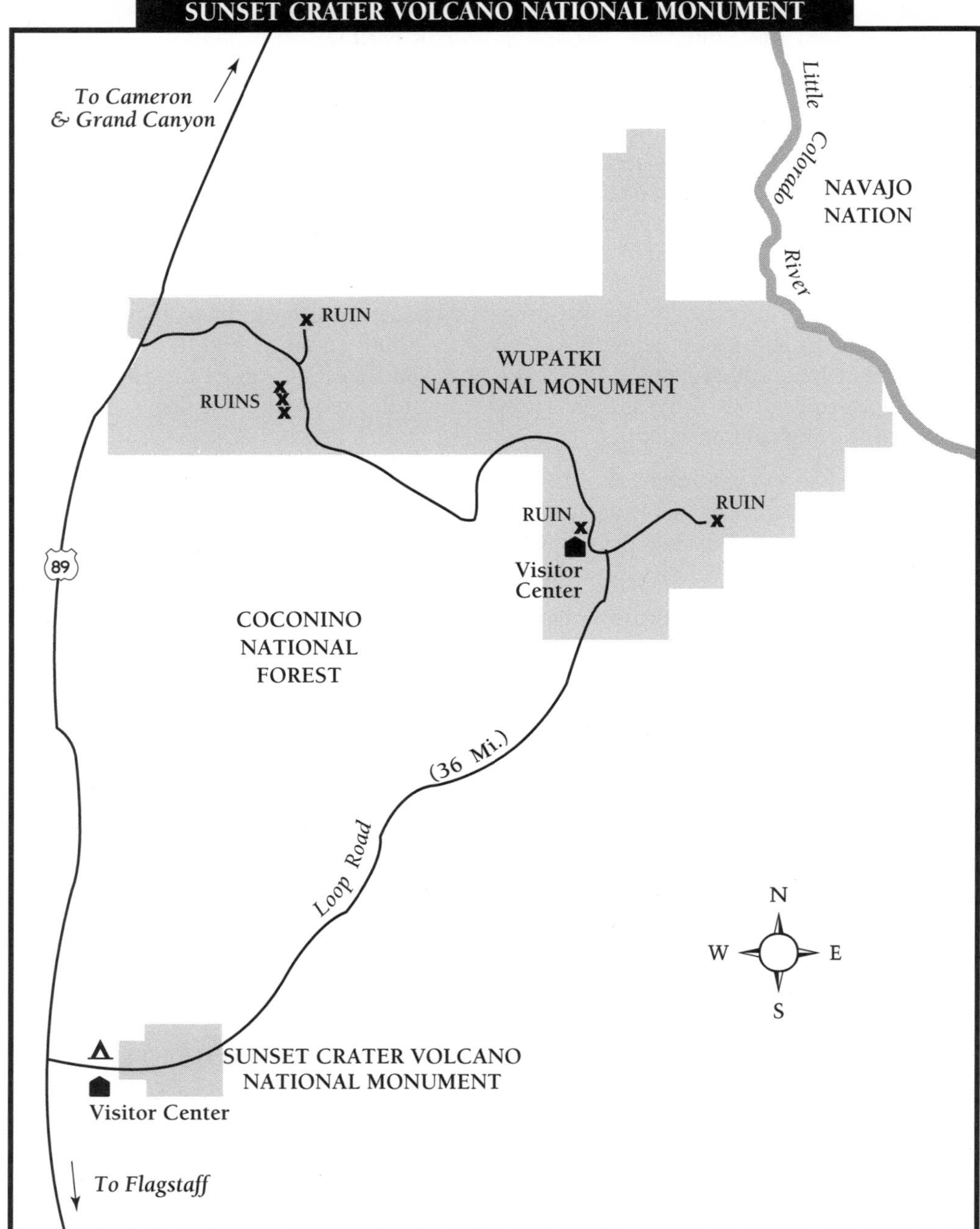

A visitor center is located along the 35-mile Sunset Crater–Wupatki Loop Road, 2 miles east of Highway 89. The center contains exhibits and other information concerning the monument and should be your initial stop. Rangers are on duty year-round (except Christmas) to answer questions. During summer months a variety of activities are available, including evening programs (in the campground) and guided walks.

Lava Flow Nature Trail begins 1½ miles east of the Sunset Crater Visitor Center. This leisurely forty- to fifty-minute walk wanders across some of the lava flow, around part of the volcano base, and by the opening to an ice cave. The hike is made more enjoyable by trail markers along the way.

Roads are kept open year-round, although the summer tourist season is most popular. Daytime temperatures during the summer are generally pleasant, and evenings can be quite cool because the monument is located at an elevation of 7,000 feet. July and August can also be quite damp.

FACILITIES: No facilities are available within the monument. Drinking water and modern rest rooms are located at the visitor center. Gas stations, motels, and food service are located along Highway 89 toward Flagstaff.

CAMPING: The U.S. Forest Service's Bonito Campground (forty-four spaces) is across from the visitor center. Grills, tables, water, and flush toilets are available during the camping season of May until September. Campsites are widely spaced on a field of volcanic cinders, with scattered pine trees providing some shade.

FISHING: No fishing is available within Sunset Crater Volcano National Monument.

TONTO NATIONAL MONUMENT

HCO2, Box 4602
Roosevelt, AZ 85545
(520) 467–2241
www.nps.gov/tont/

Tonto National Monument comprises 1,120 acres. It was established in 1907 to preserve prehistoric cliff dwellings. The monument is located just off Arizona 88, 28 miles northwest of Globe. From Phoenix, take U.S. 60 east approximately 70 miles and turn left on Arizona 88 toward Roosevelt.

The area occupied by Tonto National Monument was once the home of the Salado (Spanish for "salty") Indians. The newest archaeology in the area suggests that the earliest identifiable Salado sites date from approximately 1100. No one really knows for sure where the Salado came from, but by 1100 they were here. They lived in small villages along the river edges until the 1200s, when they began moving to ridgetops. In the early 1300s, a move to caves commenced, and cliff dwellings built in natural caves remain preserved in the monument. The Upper Cliff Dwelling contains about forty rooms, and the Lower Cliff Dwelling has nineteen rooms. The villages are constructed of stone and mud, and some sections are two stories high. As was the case with most Pueblo cultures in the Southwest, the Salado abandoned the Tonto Basin around 1450. Where they went and why they left is uncertain.

The monument's visitor center, 1 mile from the park turnoff, is open from 8:00 A.M. until 5:00 P.M. daily. The building contains items made and used by the Salado. A ranger is on duty to answer visitors' questions. A self-guided trail to the Lower Cliff Dwelling that begins at the visitor center closes to uphill travel each day at 4:00 P.M. Along the trail, the hiker will see many of the same species of desert plants that were used by the Salado—barrel cactus, saguaro, jojoba, sotol, cholla, yucca, and others. The strenuous 3-mile, three-hour round-trip hike to the Upper Cliff Dwelling is by guided tour only. Advance reservations are required, and space is limited.

FACILITIES: Picnic facilities, drinking water, and modern rest rooms are available in the monument. Food and lodging are not provided in the park, but both can be found in Roosevelt, at Roosevelt Lake Resort, and in the Globe-Miami area.

CAMPING: No camping is permitted in the monument, but several campgrounds with modern rest rooms and dump stations are located along Highway 88 in Tonto National Forest.

FISHING: No fishing is available in Tonto National Monument.

TUMACACORI NATIONAL HISTORICAL PARK

Box 67
Tumacacori, AZ 85640-0067
(520) 398–2341
tuma_interpretation@nps.gov
www.nps.gov/tuma/

The forty-seven-acre Tumacacori National Historical Park was established in 1908 to commemorate the introduction of European civilization into present-day Arizona. The ruins of three typical frontier mission churches illustrate Spanish colonial endeavor. The park is located in extreme south-central Arizona, just off Interstate 19, approximately 45 miles directly south of Tucson.

More than 500 years ago, Spain sent soldiers and missionary priests into Central America and Mexico to bring Christian civilization to the Indian tribes of the frontier areas. Missions were established among friendly tribes and military posts (presidios) were constructed in areas inhabited by hostile Indians. These missions served as both churches and centers of European culture. The churches at Los Santos Angeles de Guevavi, San Jose de Tumacacori, and San Cayetano de Calabasas were northern outposts of a mission chain constructed by Franciscan priests in the late 1700s on sites previously established by Jesuits in what was then the Mexican province of Sonora. The Jesuits had been expelled from all Spanish dominions in 1767.

After Mexico won independence from Spain in 1821, many frontier missions were abandoned because the new government was unable to provide a defense against hostile Indians. In addition, Mexican law tended to weaken the power of the church, and missions were required to become parish churches. In 1844, Mexico sold some of the Tumacacori mission lands to a private citizen. The mission community was abandoned in December 1848.

The park office and museum (open from 8:00 A.M. to 5:00 P.M.) are next to the parking area. Exhibits in the museum depict early Indian and Spanish history. Craft demonstrations take place on weekends. A self-guided walk leads through the church, and a park employee is on duty to help visitors. In addition to the church, which still stands, a cemetery and unfinished mortuary chapel are just north of the church. A special two-day fiesta takes place on the first weekend in December. Weather at the monument favors winter visits because of high summer temperatures.

FACILITIES: No food service or accommodations are available in the park. Both can be found in nearby communities. Drinking water and rest rooms are located at the museum, and picnic grounds are nearby.

CAMPING: No camping is permitted in the park, but private campgrounds are in close proximity on the Tucson-Nogales Highway. Patagonia Lake State Park provides more than 200 camping sites (with flush toilets) 15 miles northeast of Nogales on Highway 82. Coronado National Forest, 13 miles off Interstate 19, approximately 18 miles north of Tumacacori, has campsites (pit toilets).

FISHING: No fishing is available in the park.

TUZIGOOT NATIONAL MONUMENT

P.O. Box 219
Camp Verde, AZ 86322
(520) 634–5564
www.nps.gov/tuzi/

Tuzigoot National Monument comprises forty-three acres and was established in 1939 to protect a prehistoric Indian town built between A.D. 1000 and 1400. Tuzigoot is located in north-central Arizona, 55 miles south of Flagstaff via U.S. 89A (an exceptionally beautiful drive). The monument is approximately 25 miles off Interstate 17 connecting Flagstaff and Phoenix. See the area map under Montezuma Castle National Monument in this section.

The Verde Valley's first permanent settlers were the Hohokam Indians, a farming people, who moved into this area around A.D. 600. The Hohokam, who used irrigation techniques to grow a variety of crops, were later joined by the Sinagua, who had inhabited and dry farmed the foothills and the plateau beyond the valley. The Sinagua borrowed the agricultural techniques of the Hohokam and began constructing aboveground masonry dwellings that eventually evolved into large pueblos constructed on hilltops and cliffs. By the early 1400s, the Sinagua had abandoned the Verde Valley. In the 1500s, Spanish soldiers entered the valley and found the pueblos, which then lay undisturbed for nearly four centuries.

Tuzigoot is a remnant of a Sinaguan village that began as a small cluster of rooms inhabited by about fifty persons. More than a century later, the village population expanded as farmers surrendered the drought-parched land and moved to the irrigated valley.

The monument and visitor center are open daily from 8:00 A.M. to 5:00 P.M., with a ranger on duty. The visitor center contains exhibits, and a short self-guided trail to the ruins begins near the center.

FACILITIES: There are no accommodations or food service available in the monument. Both can be found 2 miles away in either Clarkdale or Cottonwood. Water and rest rooms are located at the visitor center.

CAMPING: No camping is permitted in the monument, but Dead Horse Ranch State Park (45 sites), with flush toilets, showers, hookups, and a dump station, is located north of nearby Cottonwood.

FISHING: No fishing is available in the monument. Nearby Dead Horse Ranch State Park offers fishing.

WALNUT CANYON NATIONAL MONUMENT

Walnut Canyon Road, #3
Flagstaff, AZ 86004
(520) 526–3367
www.nps.gov/waca/

Walnut Canyon is a 3,541-acre monument established in 1915 to protect the remains of Sinagua Indian cliff dwellings that were constructed nearly 800 years ago. The park is located at the end of a 3-mile paved road that begins 7½ miles east of Flagstaff on Interstate 40. (Take exit 204.)

More than 800 years ago the inhabitants of Walnut Canyon made their homes in the natural recesses of the limestone cliff faces. These creative people, who are known today as the *Sinagua* (Spanish for "without water"), existed in this relatively dry region through a combination of gathering, hunting, and farming. The Sinagua occupied the cliff dwellings at Walnut Canyon for approximately one hundred years before departing and buiding new villages a few miles to the southeast. Most historians believe the Sinagua were eventually assimilated into the Hopi culture. The homes in Walnut Canyon remained relatively undisturbed until the late nineteeth century, when souvenir hunters arrived on the railroad.

The visitor center contains exhibits detailing the history of the Walnut Canyon area. Park employees are present to answer visitors' questions. A paved footpath at the rear of the center leads to Island Trail, which provides a close view of twenty-five cliff dwelling rooms and allows observation of one hundred others across the canyon. Interpretive signs are located along the trail, which closes an hour before the park. The round-trip of slightly less than a mile requires climbing that is fairly strenuous (309 descending steps and 240 ascending steps). Another walk along Rim Trail begins just outside the front of the visitor center. This ¾-mile paved trail is relatively flat and provides views of cliff dwellings across the canyon. A cutoff from this trail to the parking lot takes visitors past some surface ruins. Allow at least two hours to visit the museum, hike down to see the cliff dwellings, and walk the Rim Trail.

FACILITIES: No accommodations or food services are available in the monument, but full facilities are available a short distance away in Flagstaff. Water and modern rest rooms are located at the visitor center. A shaded picnic area is located near the parking lot. Three smaller picnic areas are on the entrance road. A Flagstaff visitor center is at 101 West Santa Fe Avenue. Phone (520) 774–9541 or (800) 842–7293.

CAMPING: No camping is permitted in the monument, but a number of private facilities are found near Flagstaff, and Forest Service campgrounds are located to the south, near Lake Mary and Oak Creek Canyon. Another Forest Service campground (with flush toilets) is located at Sunset Crater Volcano National Monument, 15 miles north of Flagstaff and about 21 miles from Walnut Canyon. It is open from late spring through early fall. For additional information on camping, write: Supervisor's Office, Coconino National Forest, 2323 Greenlaw Lane, Flagstaff, AZ 86004. Phone (520) 527–3491.

FISHING: No fishing is available in the monument.

WUPATKI NATIONAL MONUMENT

HC 33 Box 444A
Flagstaff, AZ 86004
(520) 679–2365
www.nps.gov/wupa/

Wupatki National Monument is comprised of 35,000 acres. It was established in 1924 to preserve ruins of red sandstone pueblos built by farming Indians about A.D. 1100. The monument is located in north-central Arizona, approximately 35 miles north of Flagstaff via U.S. 89. It may also be reached by exiting U.S. 89 at Sunset Crater Volcano National Monument (15 miles north of Flagstaff) and driving over a good 35-mile paved loop road. See the map of both areas under Sunset Crater in this section.

After the eruptions of Sunset Crater Volcano to the south of Wupatki ceased about 900 years ago, the land was covered with black ash. The improved farmland drew farming Indians into the area, which became a melting pot of Indian cultures as word of the rich farmland spread.

Of the villages that were established in the area, one of the longest inhabited is now called *Wupatki,* the Hopi word for "tall house." From its location near one of the region's few springs, Wupatki grew to three stories and contained one hundred rooms during the 1100s. Near the pueblo are the remains of an open-air amphitheater and a stone-masonry ball court. By 1225, after a decade of drought, all of the Indians had left the area, perhaps because continuous farming and winds had stripped the land of volcanic ash.

The Wupatki visitor center, which contains exhibits of the area's cultures, is located near the south entrance to the monument, 14 miles from U.S. 89 and 18 miles north of Sunset Crater. Self-guided trails to Nalakihu-Citadel Pueblos and to the Wupatki Pueblo begin from the main road. The latter is just behind the visitor center. The Wupatki Pueblo trail has guidebooks at the trailhead. Paved roads will take you to pueblos at Wukoki and Lomaki. Wayside exhibits are located on both the Citadel and the Lomaki trails. If time in the monument is limited, visitors should at least stop at the visitor center and walk through Wupatki Pueblo.

FACILITIES: Rest rooms and drinking water are available at the visitor center. Picnic areas are located about 5 miles north of the visitor center and on the road between Sunset Crater and Wupatki. All other facilities are available along U.S. 89 and in Flagstaff.

CAMPING: No camping is available at Wupatki. A U.S. Forest Service campground (with modern rest rooms) is located near the visitor center at Sunset Crater Volcano National Monument. Contact the Peaks Ranger Station of the Coconino National Forest (520–526–0866) for more information.

FISHING: No fishing. Although the Little Colorado River borders the northeast corner of the monument, it is generally dry.

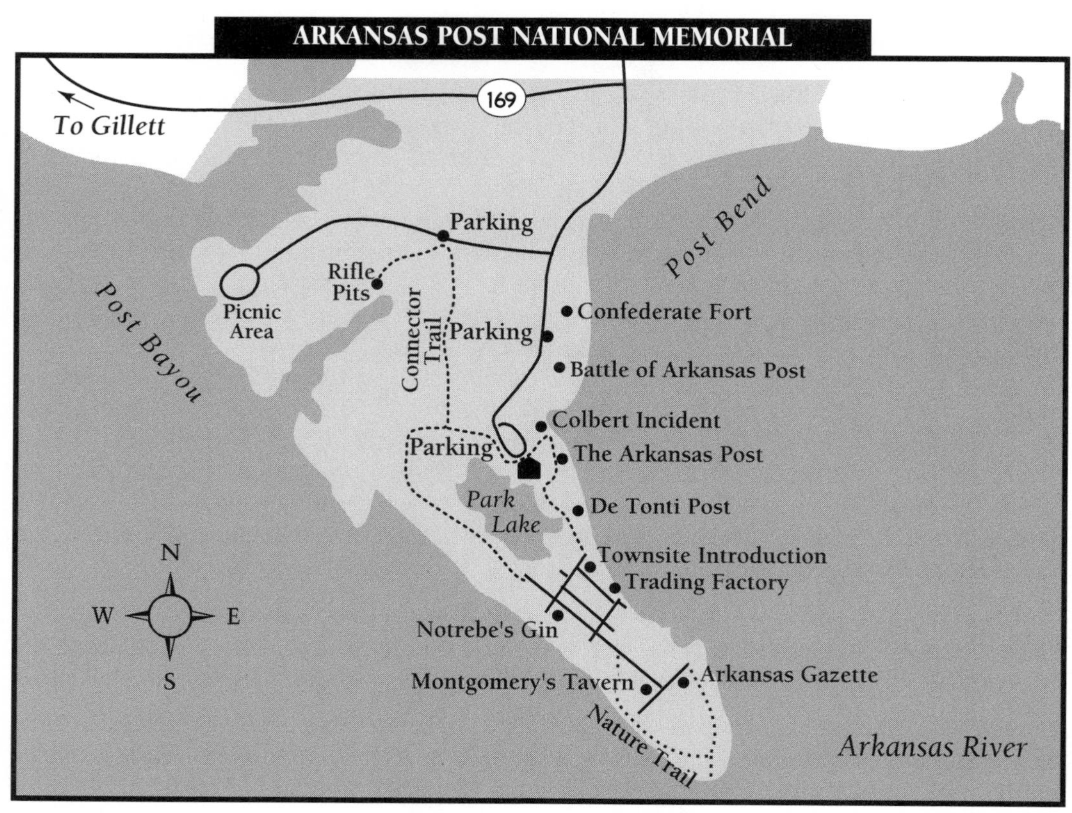
ARKANSAS POST NATIONAL MEMORIAL
169
To Gillett
Parking
Post Bend
Rifle Pits
Picnic Area
Post Bayou
Connector Trail
Confederate Fort
Parking
Battle of Arkansas Post
Colbert Incident
Parking
The Arkansas Post
Park Lake
De Tonti Post
Townsite Introduction
Trading Factory
N
W
E
S
Notrebe's Gin
Montgomery's Tavern
Arkansas Gazette
Nature Trail
Arkansas River

STATE TOURIST INFORMATION
(800) 628–8725

ARKANSAS POST NATIONAL MEMORIAL

1741 Old Post Road
Gillett, AR 72055
(870) 548–2207
www.nps.gov/arpo/

Arkansas Post is comprised of 389 acres that were incorporated into the National Park System in 1960 to commemorate the site of the first permanent French settlement in the Lower Mississippi Valley. The site is located in eastern Arkansas on the banks of the Arkansas River between Gillett and Dumas. It is on Arkansas Highway 169, 7 miles south of Gillett via U.S. 165 (Great River Road) and about 20 miles northeast of Dumas via U.S. 165.

While the French were the first white settlers in this area in 1673, Arkansas Post passed through a number of hands as a strategic military and commercial center on the frontier. The reason for its importance is its location near the confluence of the Arkansas and Mississippi rivers. In 1763, France ceded Louisiana (which included the Arkansas Territory) to Spain following the British victory in the French and Indian War. The Spanish recognized the area's value in controlling British influence and Indian trade in the region. The Quapaw Indian tribe played an important role in the history of this area by offering trade and protection to the French and, later, the Spanish. The Quapaw were forced to leave their traditional homeland in 1824 by the U.S. government.

Following the American Revolution, frontiersmen moved into the Mississippi Valley and settled on the rich river-bottom land. In addition to provoking more Indian raids, this also caused Spain to strengthen the post. In 1800, the Spanish ceded Louisiana back to France after Napoleon Bonaparte rose to power. Pressed for money, Napoleon sold Louisiana to the United States in 1803.

As the first capital of the territorial government for Arkansas, Arkansas Post became a typical frontier village. In 1821, however, the capital was moved to Little Rock, and Arkansas Post began its downhill slide. The area was temporarily revived when Confederate forces constructed a fort here during the Civil War.

Today, this post, which has contained at least five different forts and settlements, has few visible remains. The park contains 2 miles of trails, including a 3/4-mile trail near Park Lake that permits visitors to get a sense of the post's history. A visitor center is open daily (except Thanksgiving, Christmas, and New Year's Day) from 8:00 A.M. to 5:00 P.M. and offers exhibits and an audiovisual program to help explain the events that occurred here.

FACILITIES: No food or lodging is available in the park, but both can be found in nearby Gillett. Rest rooms with flush toilets are located in the visitor center and near the shaded picnic area, which has tables and grills. The visitor center, rest rooms, and picnic facilities are accessible to wheelchairs.

CAMPING: No camping is permitted in the park. The nearest camping facilities are at Pendleton Bend, 20 miles southwest of the park off Highway 165, and Merrisach Lake Park, 25 miles northwest of the park off Highway 44. Both facilities are operated by the U.S. Army Corps of Engineers.

FISHING: Fishing is permitted with an Arkansas license. Catches are best in spring and fall and include largemouth bass, channel catfish, bream, crappie, and shad. No boat launching is allowed at the park, but a ramp is available at Moore Bayou, a short distance outside the Arkansas Post entrance.

BUFFALO NATIONAL RIVER

P.O. Box 1173
Harrison, AR 72602-1173
(870) 741–5443
www.nps.gov/buff/

The Buffalo River, which winds 135 miles through 95,700 acres, was authorized as part of the National Park Service in 1972. It is one of the most scenic, unpolluted, and undeveloped free-flowing rivers remaining in the lower forty-eight states. The park is located in northwestern Arkansas in the Ozarks, across a three-county area. The nearest sizable community is Harrison, population 10,000, located 13 miles away.

Buffalo National River flows eastward through forested hill country dominated by oaks and hickories. Along its course, the river has cut through limestone and sandstone, leaving bluffs as tall as 400 feet. The area boasts a wide variety of fish, plants, and wildlife along the river, which drops from a level of 2,300 feet in the Boston Mountains to 400 feet at its confluence with the White River. A side canyon at Hemmed-In Hollow contains a 204-foot waterfall, one of the highest between the Rockies and the southern Appalachians.

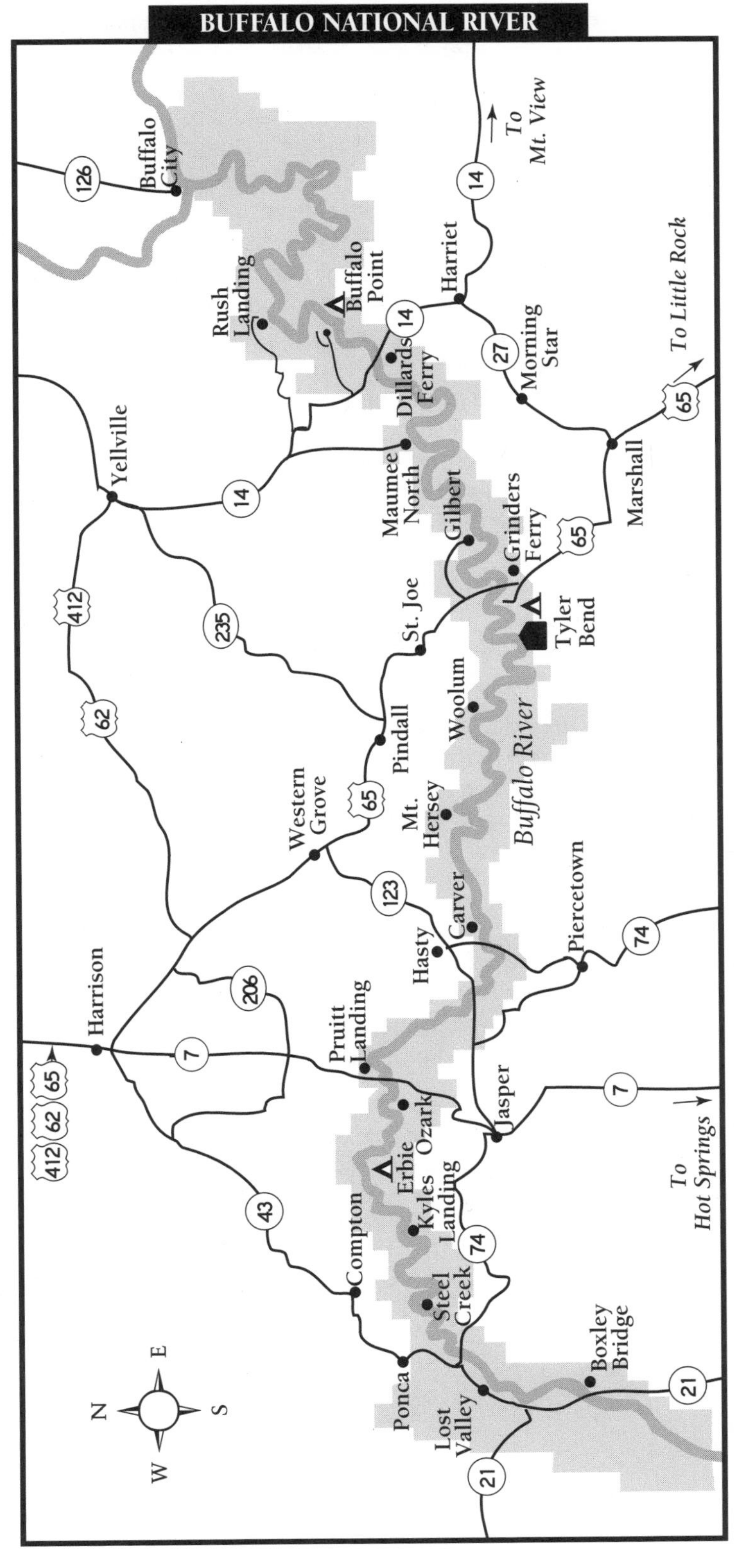

BUFFALO NATIONAL RIVER
Buffalo City
126
Rush Landing
Buffalo Point
14
To Mt. View
Harriet
Dillards Ferry
Morning Star
27
To Little Rock
65
Marshall
Yellville
Maumee North
Gilbert
Grinders Ferry
412
235
St. Joe
Tyler Bend
Woolum
Buffalo River
62
Pindall
Western Grove
Mt. Hersey
Piercetown
123
Carver
Hasty
74
Harrison
206
Pruitt Landing
7
Jasper
Ozark
Erbie
To Hot Springs
43
Kyles Landing
Compton
Steel Creek
Boxley Bridge
Ponca
Lost Valley
21
N
E
S
W

Information may be obtained at Tyler Bend Visitor Center, the park's main visitor center, at Buffalo Point Ranger Station, at Pruitt Ranger Station, and at park headquarters in Harrison. Centrally located in the park is Tyler Bend Visitor Center, where exhibits and auditorium programs help to tell the park story. Guided walks and campfire programs are offered at or near all three contact stations between Memorial Day and Labor Day. At Tyler Bend and Buffalo Point, interpretive programs about the history and flora and fauna of the area are presented daily throughout the summer, with more extensive program offerings on weekends. Interpretive programs at Buffalo Point are the most extensive in the park.

On the west side, several primitive campgrounds (vault toilets and drinking water only) offer spectacular scenery. These sites are extremely popular in spring, when higher water flows allow for canoeing in the area. The Tyler Bend campground has hiking trails, a boat launch, and swimming and picnic areas. On the east side, Buffalo Point is a popular destination area, with hiking trails, a canoe-launch area, swimming areas, a picnic area, and the most developed campground, including hookups and showers.

One of the most popular activities in the park is canoeing or floating the river. Visitors may enjoy anywhere from a half-day to a ten-day, 120-mile trip. Environments vary along the river, with wildernesslike areas between Carver and Woolum and a developed setting around Buffalo Point. Sixteen concessionaires along the river rent canoes and related items and provide shuttle services to various points along the river. A list of concessionaires may be obtained by writing to the park superintendent.

There are three congressionally designated wilderness areas within the park. Two of the three, the Ponca Wilderness and the Lower Buffalo Wilderness, have maintained trails.

FACILITIES: Books and theme-related items may be purchased at all three contact stations and at park headquarters. The only food service or lodging provided in the park is at Buffalo Point. At Buffalo Point, eight modern and five rustic concession-operated cottages are available for rent from April 1 to November 30. A restaurant, open Memorial Day through Labor Day, is also available. For information, write to Buffalo Point Concession, HCR 66, Box 388, Yellville, AR 72687 (870–449–6206).

CAMPING: A total of fourteen campgrounds are scattered along the river. All have vault toilets. All but Hasty, Mt. Hersey, Woolum, Maumee, and Dillards Ferry have drinking water. The most developed campgrounds are Tyler Bend (thirty-eight spaces, five group camps) and Buffalo Point (103 spaces, five group camps), which offer tables, grills, a dump station, flush toilets, and showers. Both Tyler Bend and Buffalo Point charge a camping fee; the other campgrounds do not.

FISHING: Smallmouth and other varieties of bass, perch, suckers, and gar are the most common fish caught. An Arkansas fishing license is required. Keeper bass are limited to 14 inches, two per day. Hunting is permitted in the park, in accordance with Arkansas Game and Fish regulations.

FORT SMITH NATIONAL HISTORIC SITE

P.O. Box 1406
Fort Smith, AR 72902
(501) 783–3961
www.nps.gov/fosm/

Fort Smith, which comprises thirty-five acres, was incorporated into the National Park System in 1961 to preserve the site of two highly significant United States military posts west of the Mississippi. Fort Smith later became a center of territorial law and order as the frontier moved westward. The park is located on Rogers Avenue in downtown Fort Smith, Arkansas. The parking lot is reached from U.S. 64 (Garrison Avenue) by turning south on Fourth Street and then west on Garland Avenue..

On orders of the U.S. Army, construction on the first Fort Smith commenced in 1817. The purpose was to house troops that could help put an end to the Indian wars taking place on the frontier. The fort was abandoned in 1824, and construction began on a second Fort Smith in 1838, 100 yards east of the first site. As the frontier continued to move westward, Fort Smith became an important supply depot for forts in Indian Territory, military expeditions, and settlers and travelers throughout the Southwest. It was abandoned by the U.S. Army in 1871.

Within a year of the army's departure, Fort Smith's former soldiers' barracks was converted to the courtroom and jail for the federal court for the Western District of Arkansas. This federal court held jurisdiction over thirteen counties in western Arkansas and the vast Indian Territory, a haven for bands of outlaws and desperadoes in the aftermath of the Civil War. Judge Isaac C. Parker arrived in 1875 as the youngest member of the federal judicial bench. During his twenty-one years on the bench, more than 9,000 defendants were convicted or pleaded guilty and 160 were sentenced to hang (yet only 79 were actually hanged). During this same period, more than one hundred deputy marshals were murdered. Parker gradually brought law to the Indian Territory, but as more settlers moved into the region, additional federal courts took much of his jurisdiction. Parker died in 1896 and is buried in Fort Smith National Cemetery.

A visitor center containing exhibits of the area's history is located in the former courtroom/jail building, which also contains a reconstructed courtroom. The center is open daily except Christmas and New Year's Day. Visitors can also view the reconstructed gallows, the restored commissary building, and the first Fort Smith location. A ½-mile paved walking trail follows the Arkansas River. An overlook has exhibits on the Trail of Tears. Ranger-led activities and demonstrations are regularly scheduled during summer months.

FACILITIES: Food and lodging are available a few blocks from the site. Rest rooms and drinking water are available in the visitor center.

CAMPING: No camping is permitted at the site. A U.S. Army Corps of Engineers' campground with tables, grills, water, and flush toilets is 2 miles north of Barling.

FISHING: Fishing in the Arkansas River is permitted with an Arkansas license.

HOT SPRINGS NATIONAL PARK

P.O. Box 1860
Hot Springs National Park, AR 71901-1860
(501) 624–3383, ext. 640
(501) 624–2308 TDD
hosp_interpretation@nps.gov
www.nps.gov/hosp/

Hot Springs National Park, which was designated a reservation in 1832 and added to the park system in 1916, comprises 5,500 acres. It is famous for the forty-seven hot springs that provide nearly a million gallons of water a day for thermal bathing. The park is located in central Arkansas, approximately 50 miles southwest of Little Rock via Interstate 30 and U.S. 70. It may also be reached on Arkansas Highway 7 and U.S. 270.

The hot springs of Arkansas were used by local Indians long before white people came into the region. Permanent settlement began after the United States purchased the Louisiana Territory from France in 1803. In 1832, the springs were made into a federal reservation.

The rainwater that soaks through fractured rocks northwest of the springs is heated as it comes into contact with hot rock deep beneath the earth's crust. Each day, approximately 850,000 gallons of water heated to 143 degrees Fahrenheit flow from the park's forty-seven springs. The water—which is colorless and entirely free of bad odors and taste—is collected, cooled, and piped to central reservoirs for bathhouse use. Two springs, accessible from Bathhouse Row or the Grand Promenade, are open for display to visitors, in addition to a larger display at the Tufa Terrace, where the flow of the upper springs built up a thick mineral deposit. The remainder have been covered to prevent contamination.

The park's visitor center, in the restored Fordyce Bathhouse, provides exhibits of the history and geology of the area and is open for touring. A seventeen-minute movie program is presented in the auditorium. Nearby—on Reserve Avenue, Bathhouse Row, and the Grand Promenade—drinking fountains provide free thermal water. Water from natural cold-water springs is available on Fountain Street and on Whittington Avenue.

Visitors may take baths, sit in a whirlpool, or have a massage at a number of bathhouses operated by concessioners and permittees in accordance with National Park Service regulations. A list of facilities and locations is available at the visitor center.

Numerous trails wander around the park's mountains and through its dense oak-hickory forests. Many of these begin from the scenic paved road that climbs Hot Springs Mountain and North Mountain. Conducted walks and campfire programs take place in the summer. The Fordyce Bathhouse Visitor Center is open year-round, except for Thanksgiving, Christmas, and New Year's Day.

FACILITIES: No food service or lodging is provided in the park, but nearly any type of facility can be found in the city of Hot Springs, which adjoins the park. Modern rest rooms are provided in the visitor center, on Bathhouse Row and the Grand Promenade, and at the campground.

CAMPING: A single campground (forty-three spaces) is located at Gulpha Gorge in the northeast corner of the park. Although the sites are fairly close together, the campground is quite nice. Tables, pedestal grills, water, flush toilets, and a dump station are provided. The campground is open year-round.

FISHING: No fishing is available in the park, but nearby Lakes Catherine, Hamilton, and Ouachita provide good possibilities. Boats and sporting supplies are available at the lakes.

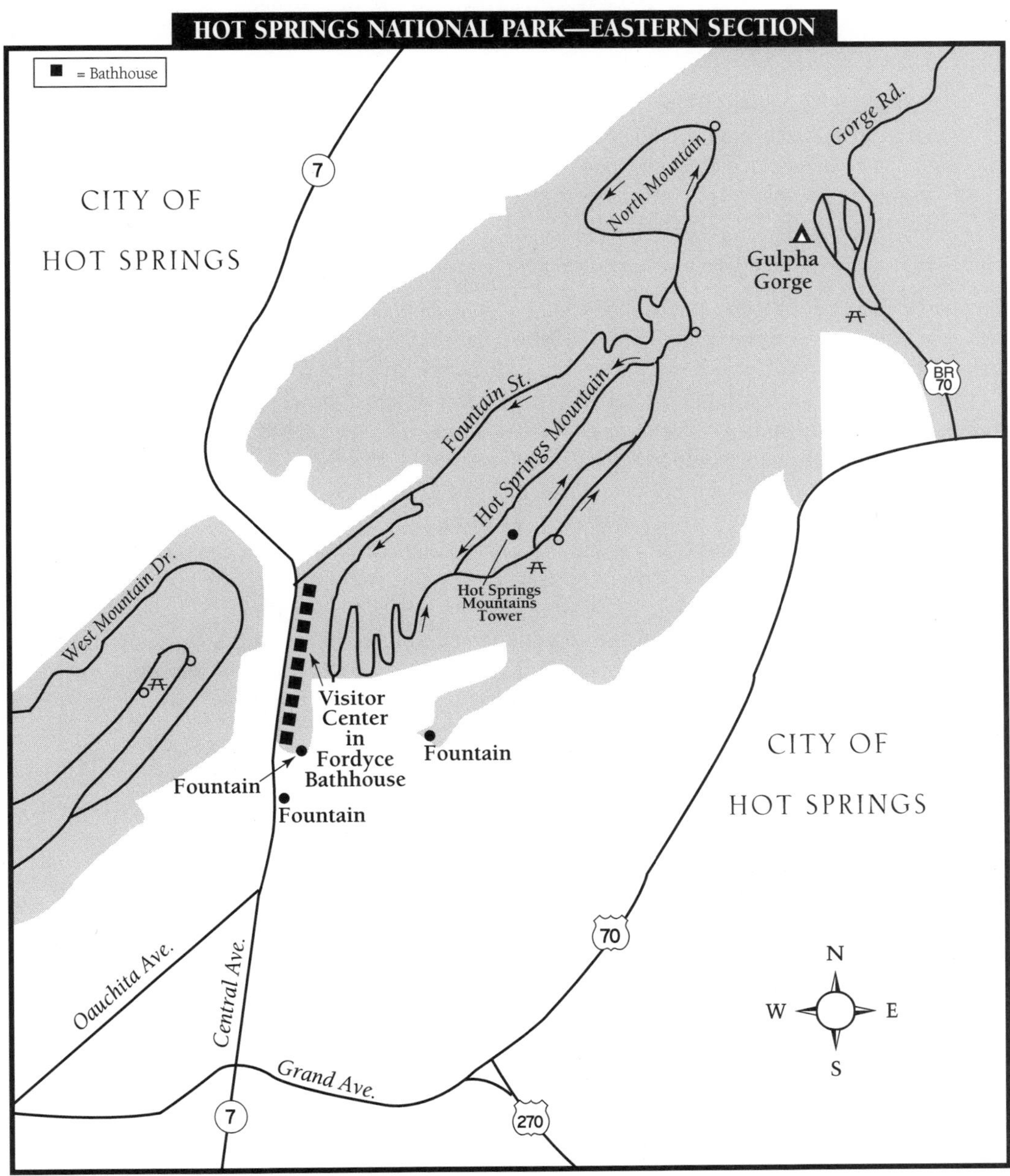

PEA RIDGE NATIONAL MILITARY PARK

P.O. Box 700
Pea Ridge, AR 72751
(501) 451–8122
PERI_Interpretation@nps.gov
www.nps.gov/peri/

Pea Ridge National Military Park, which is comprised of 4,300 acres, was authorized in 1956 to memorialize the site of one of the major Civil War military battles that took place west of the Mississippi River. The park is located in northwestern Arkansas, 10 miles northeast of Rogers and 30 miles northeast of Fayetteville via U.S. Highway 62.

The battle of Pea Ridge was fought during a two-day period in March 1862. Late in the previous year, the new commander of federal forces in southwest Missouri initiated an aggressive policy of pushing pro-Confederate forces out of the state. Many of these men moved south near Fayetteville and joined a large force of Confederate soldiers. The combined group of 16,000 marched northward with an eventual goal of St. Louis. Between their position and St. Louis, the new federal commander stood with 10,500 soldiers at Pea Ridge.

The Confederate commander decided to circle the area and attack from the north. After two days of fighting, the Confederates ran short of ammunition while located near the Elkhorn Tavern and retreated eastward down the Old Huntsville Road. By noon, the battle was ended with an overall federal victory. Reported casualties were 203 Union troops and an estimated 250 Confederates killed. The state of Missouri was saved for the Union.

A visitor center near the park entrance contains exhibits to help visitors interpret the park. Personnel are on duty from 8:00 A.M. until 5:00 P.M. to answer questions. A terrace at the back of the building affords visitors a sweeping view of the battlefield. Near the visitor center is a short (7-mile) self-guiding auto road to significant battlefield sites.

FACILITIES: No lodging or food service is available at the park, but both can be found in Rogers. Water and rest rooms are located in the visitor center. A picnic area with tables is located nearby.

CAMPING: No camping is permitted in the park, but public campgrounds are available at Beaver Reservoir, 20 miles away.

FISHING: No fishing is available at Pea Ridge National Military Park.

STATE TOURIST INFORMATION

(800) 862–2543

AIDS MEMORIAL GROVE NATIONAL MEMORIAL

856 Stanyan Street
San Francisco, CA 94117
(415) 750–8340
aidsmemgrv@aol.com
www.aidsmemorial.org

AIDS Memorial Grove National Memorial is an affiliated area of the National Park Service that was authorized in 1996 to memorialize individuals who have died as a result of acquired immune deficiency syndrome (AIDS) and to support caregivers and those living with AIDS. The memorial is located in the eastern end of San Francisco's Golden Gate Park.

The AIDS Memorial Grove National Memorial is dedicated to the creation and long-term maintenance of the first living memorial to those lost to AIDS and in support of the individuals living with HIV. This memorial is designed as a place for the living to mourn, remember, and begin the process of healing. The memorial grove is a fifteen-acre wooded area located in the eastern section of Golden Gate Park. The grove includes a woodland path, a valley floor of wildflowers and grasses, and a fern grotto. Monthly workdays for maintaining vegetation at the memorial grove have occurred since 1991.

FACILITIES: Food and lodging are available in the city of San Francisco. See the Facilities section of Golden Gate National Recreation Area for more information.

CABRILLO NATIONAL MONUMENT

1800 Cabrillo Memorial Drive
San Diego, CA 92106–3601
(619) 557–5450
www.nps.gov/cabr/

Cabrillo is a 144-acre monument established in 1913 to commemorate Juan Rodriguez Cabrillo, the explorer who claimed the West Coast of the United States for Spain in 1542. The monument is located on Point Loma in the city of San Diego. It can be reached by following Rosecrans Street (California 209) to Canon Street, following Canon to Catalina Boulevard, and driving south on Catalina to the end of Point Loma.

The Cabrillo expedition sailed from Navidad, Mexico, on June 27, 1542, to explore the unknown lands along the Pacific Coast. After frequent stops for bad-weather refuge, supplies, and information from Indians, present-day San Diego was reached on September 28. The expedition left on October 3 to explore farther north, and on January 3, 1543, Cabrillo died from injuries sustained in a fall several weeks earlier. The expedition eventually reached the southern boundary of Oregon before returning to Navidad in the spring of 1543. The voyage helped open the way for later expeditions that gained Spain a foothold in what later became the West Coast of the United States.

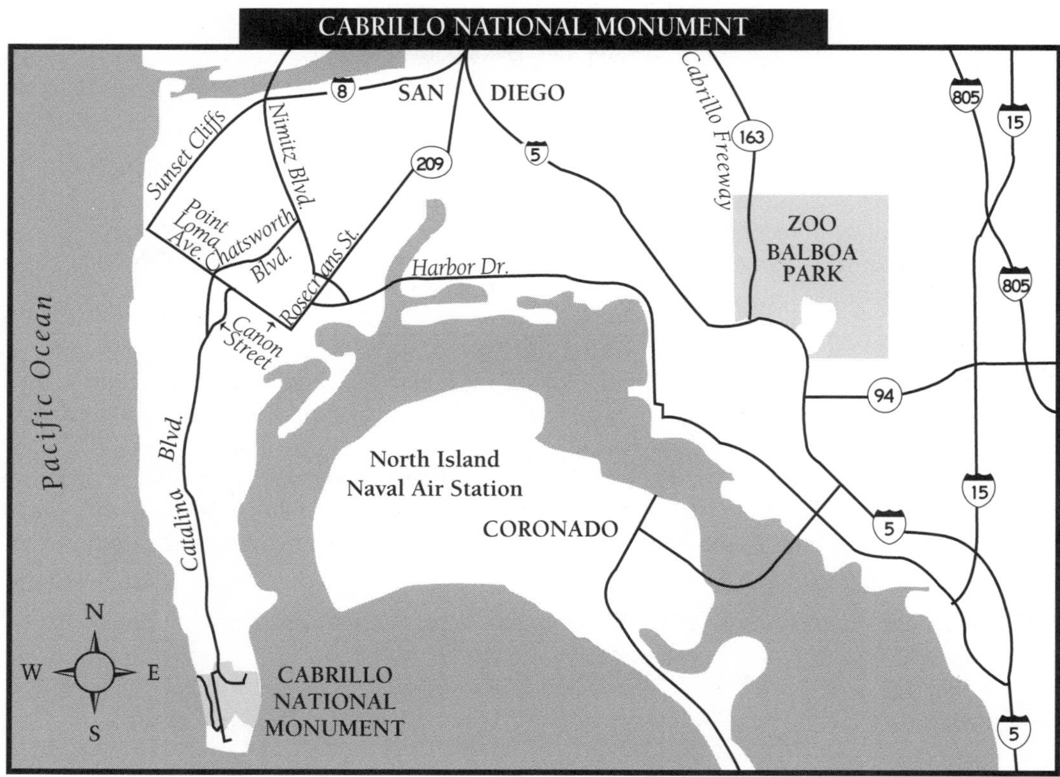

The monument is open daily from 9:00 A.M. to 5:15 P.M., with extended hours during summer months. A visitor center near the park entrance contains exhibits and interpretative programs and offers an exceptional view of San Diego and San Diego Harbor. Make this your initial stop. An old lighthouse, constructed in 1854 and abandoned in 1891, is open to the public. Ranger-led programs bring to life the history of the monument.

Overlooks and walkways at the monument present views of Mexico and the Pacific coastline. Tidepools on the coastal side of Point Loma contain sealife such as sea anemones, crabs, and sea hares. Bayside Trail presents the hiker with views of wildlife, splendid vistas, and remnants of a coastal artillery system dating from World Wars I and II. From December through February, thousands of gray whales migrate from the Arctic Ocean to the lagoons of Baja California. Ten- to fifteen-foot spouts may be seen from the whale-watching station, where a tape-recorded message explains the migration.

FACILITIES: No food or lodging is available at the monument, but both are located nearby. Water and modern rest rooms are provided at the visitor center.

CAMPING: No camping is permitted in the monument. Private campgrounds can be found on Mission Bay north of the monument.

FISHING: Surf fishing is available on the west side of the monument off Gatchell Road. A California fishing license is required, and bait must be brought to the monument. Fishing is fair, with catches of bass, halibut, opaleye, and shark. A bit of scrambling is required to reach the shoreline. Extreme care is necessary because of unstable sandstone cliffs.

CHANNEL ISLANDS NATIONAL PARK

1901 Spinnaker Drive
Ventura, CA 93001-4354
(805) 658–5730
chis_interpretation@nps.gov
www.nps.gov/chis/

Channel Islands National Park was established in 1980. It now comprises more than 249,000 acres of land and water, with large rookeries of sea lions, nesting seabirds, and unique plants and animals. The Channel Islands extend about 150 miles from the latitude of San Diego to that of Santa Barbara and from 10 to 70 miles offshore. Access to the islands is by private boat or public transportation.

Millions of years ago, mountains rose from the sea and large areas along the continent cracked. Land masses rose above the ocean and then slowly sank back beneath the water. A great land mass along the western edge of North America eventually submerged, leaving only the mountaintops now known as the Channel Islands.

For many thousands of years, the islands were inhabited by the Chumash and other tribes of Indians. These people were skilled in making ornaments out of shells inlaid by means of asphalt. They also built large seagoing canoes of planks lashed together with thongs and caulked with native asphalt. The ancient Indian burial and village sites on some of the Channel Islands possess considerable archaeological information covering the past 10,000 years.

Anacapa Island, at the eastern end of Santa Barbara Channel, is 11 miles from the mainland. It is actually a chain of three closely linked islets combining to a length of approximately 5 miles. Anacapa's rocky shoreline is highlighted by sheer cliffs, and the only beach not submerged at high tide is at Frenchy's Cove. Here, a day-use area is located near tide pools containing a variety of marine life. On East Anacapa Island are found the ranger station, the campground, nature trails, and a small visitor center, all within the setting of an old Coast Guard station. In neither location are there docking facilities, and a small craft is required to go ashore. There is no safe anchorage at East Island, and public transportation is advised for those wishing to visit this portion of Anacapa.

Santa Barbara Island (630 acres), 42 miles off the coast, is surrounded by kelp beds abounding in marine life. The island is composed of rolling, grass-covered hills that are edged by high cliffs from the sea. Anchorage is rough, and landing in the rocky cove is hazardous. A Park Service ranger is stationed throughout the year on both Anacapa and Santa Barbara islands.

Santa Cruz is the largest island in the park and is especially important for its diversity of habitat. The National Park Service owns east Santa Cruz. The western part is owned by The Nature Conservancy. Landing on the western portion of the island requires a permit from the landowners. The island's western portion may be reached by day trips provided by The Nature Conservancy. Write Santa Cruz Island Project Office, 213 Sterns Wharf, Santa Barbara, CA 93101 (805–962–9111). The National Park Service portion of the island is accessible by boat at Scorpion Harbor.

Santa Rosa is the park's second largest island and exhibits a variety of natural features, including cliffs, high mountains, fossil beds, grasslands, rolling hills, beaches, and a marsh. Harbor seals breed on the island's beaches. No permit is required for landing at Bechers Bay or Johnson's Lee (day-use only).

San Miguel has outstanding natural and cultural features, including the best examples of caliche (a mineral sandcasting). The island hosts large numbers and varieties of seals and sea lions, and the island's largest mammal, the island fox, can be seen here. San Miguel contains

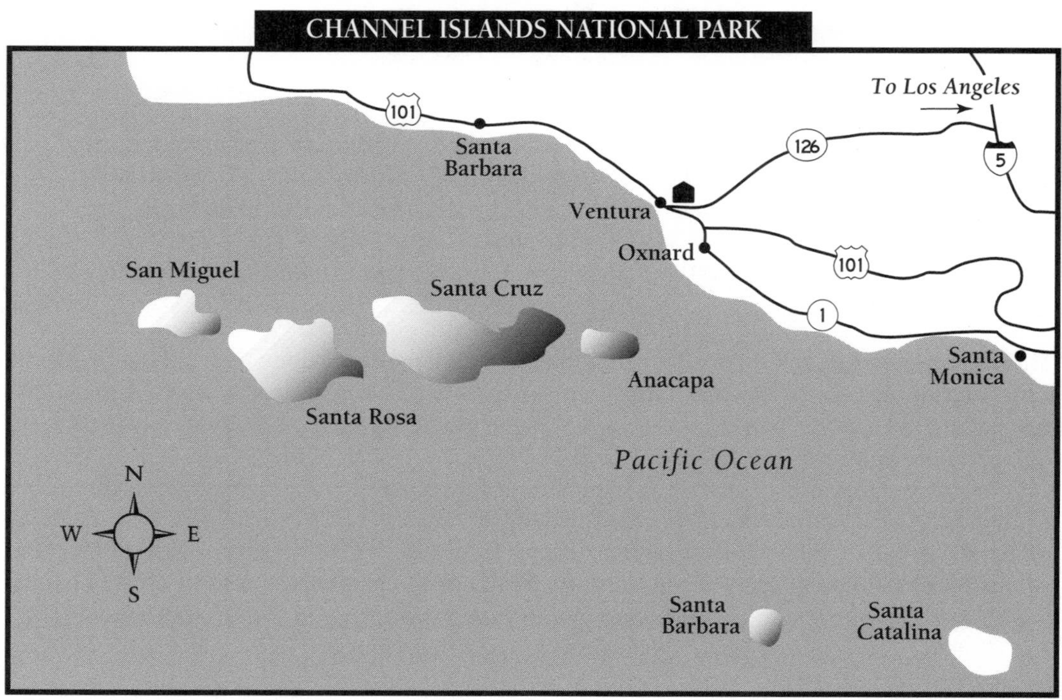

more than 500 relatively undisturbed archaeological sites, some dating back thousands of years. Visitors may land on the beach at Cuyler Harbor without a permit for day-use only. Contact park headquarters for information on guided hikes.

FACILITIES: No accommodations, concessioner facilities, fuel, or other services are available on the islands managed by the National Park Service. Pit toilets, but no drinking water, are located at the primitive campgrounds on Anacapa, Santa Barbara, Santa Cruz, and San Miguel islands. Santa Rosa Island has water available in the campground.

CAMPING: Five campgrounds, one each on Anacapa, Santa Barbara, Santa Cruz, San Miguel, and Santa Rosa islands, are very primitive. Maximum capacity at each site varies. Reservations are required. Campers need to take water, camping gear, food, cooking equipment, and fuel for cooking. No campfires are permitted. Pit toilets and picnic tables are available on the islands.

FISHING: Fishing is permitted in accordance with California regulations, unless further restricted by federal law. Sea bass, barracuda, bonito, and yellowtail are among the varieties of fish living in the surrounding Pacific waters.

DEATH VALLEY NATIONAL PARK

Death Valley, CA 92328-0579
(760) 786–2331
www.nps.gov/deva/

Death Valley National Park, which comprises 3.3 million acres, was established as a national monument in 1933 to preserve a large desert containing the lowest point in the Western Hemisphere. The major part of the park is located in southeastern California, with the remaining portion in southern Nevada. Four paved roads enter the park from the east and two enter from the west. The major road through the park is California Highway 190. The visitor center is approximately 135 miles from Las Vegas.

Death Valley is a special place. The harsh environment, with an average annual rainfall of as little as 2 inches, requires hardy varieties of plants, animals, and humans. Most life revolves around permanent water sources such as springs. Higher elevations have cooler temperatures and more moisture, resulting in a greater variety of plants and animals. In spite of hordes of prospectors seeking precious metals over the years, even humans have been unable to establish much of a life in this area.

The focal point of the park is the Furnace Creek Visitor Center. Here visitors may view exhibits and obtain information on self-guided auto tours and trails. An illustrated slide program is available, and programs are presented by rangers during winter months. Ranger-conducted programs are scheduled daily during winter months. Activity schedules are posted.

Seeing the park requires a considerable amount of driving. Some of the more interesting places (with numbers keyed to the map) are:

1. Scotty's Castle, a desert mansion built by Albert Johnson and enjoyed by Death Valley Scotty (the area's most famous resident). A fifty-minute tour of the castle is provided frequently during the day.
2. Ubehebe Crater, 1/2 mile across and 500 feet deep.

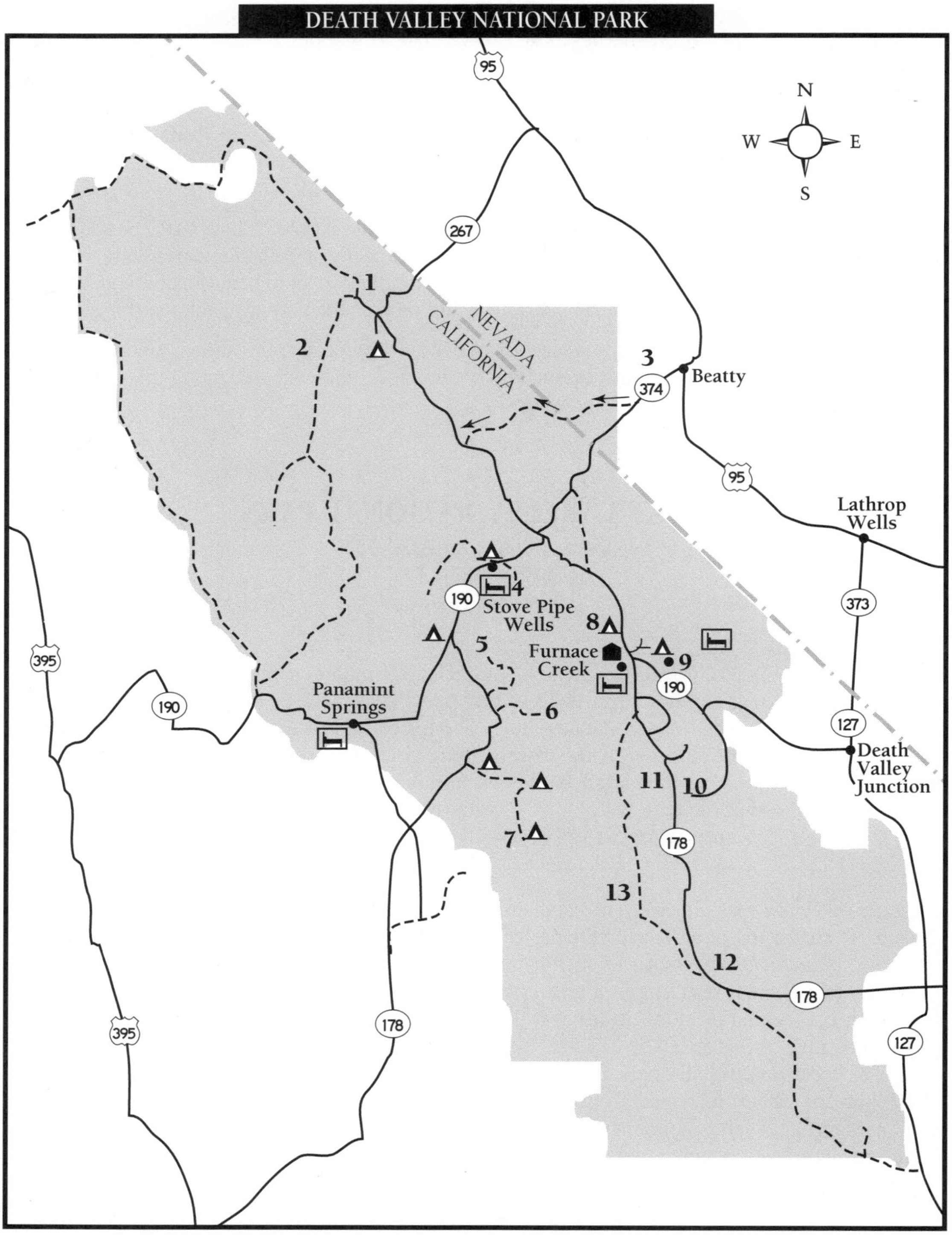

DEATH VALLEY NATIONAL PARK

95
N
W
E
S
267
1
2
NEVADA
CALIFORNIA
3
374
Beatty
95
Lathrop Wells
4
190
Stove Pipe Wells
8
Furnace Creek
9
190
373
395
5
190
Panamint Springs
6
127
Death Valley Junction
11
10
7
178
13
12
178
395
178
127

3. The ruins of Rhyolite, an old mining town, are a short distance outside the park boundary.
4. Mosaic Canyon, a small canyon containing interesting rock formations.
5. The site of Skidoo, an old mining town. High-clearance vehicles are recommended for the dirt road.
6. Aguereberry Point, which provides a grand view of the valley and the east mountains. High-clearance vehicles are recommended for the dirt road.
7. A 7⅗-mile trail from the Mahogany Flat Campground that leads to Telescope Peak, which at 11,049 feet is the park's highest point.
8. Harmony Borax Works, an old borax-processing plant.
9. Zabriskie Point, which presents a view of colorful and dramatically eroded hills.
10. Dantes View, which provides views of the Panamint Range and the Western Hemisphere's lowest point.
11. Badwater, which at 280 feet below sea level is the lowest point to which a motorist can drive in the Western Hemisphere.
12. Ashford Mill, the ruins of an old gold mill.
13. Westside Road, which provides a scenic trip along the valley floor. This is the historic route of the twenty-mule-team borax wagons. High-clearance vehicles are recommended for the dirt road.

FACILITIES: Furnace Creek Inn and Ranch Resort provides rooms, food service, a store, service station, and swimming year-round. Horseback riding is available from early November through Easter. The inn is an unusual and wonderful (and expensive) hotel, while the ranch is comprised of motel-type accommodations. For information or reservations write Furnace Creek Inn and Ranch Resort, P.O. Box 1, Death Valley, CA 92328. Call (800) 236–7916. Stove Pipe Wells Village provides motel rooms, food, a store, service station, and swimming pool access year-round. For information or reservations write Stove Pipe Wells Village, Death Valley, CA 92328. Call (760) 786–2387. Scotty's Castle offers food service, gasoline, and souvenirs, but not lodging. Panamint Springs Resort on the western edge of the park provides motel-type rooms and meals. Write P.O. Box 395, Ridgecrest, CA 93556 for information and reservations. Call (775) 482–7680

CAMPING: Nine NPS-operated campgrounds are located within the park. Furnace Creek (136 spaces), Mesquite Spring (thirty spaces), and Texas Spring (ninety-two spaces, October–April) each offers tables, grills, water, flush toilets, and a dump station. Campsites at Furnace Creek and two group campsites in Texas Spring may be reserved. Call (800) 365–2267. Emigrant (ten sites, tent only) offers tables, grills, water, and flush toilets. Sunset (1,000 sites, October–April) and Stovepipe Wells (200 sites, November–April) offer water and flush toilets. Wildrose (thirty sites) offers tables, grills, and pit toilets. Thorndike (ten sites) and Mahogany Flat (ten sites) are open from March to November and offer tables, grills, and pit toilets. The roads to these last three are not passable for trailers, campers, or motor homes. Private or concession-operated campgrounds are at Stovepipe Wells and Panamint Springs.

FISHING: No fishing is available in Death Valley National Park.

DEVILS POSTPILE NATIONAL MONUMENT

P.O. Box 501
Mammoth Lakes, CA 93546
(760) 934–2289
www.nps.gov/depo/

Devils Postpile National Monument is nearly 800 acres in size and was established in 1911 to preserve two natural features: the formation of columnar basalt known as Devils Postpile and 101-foot Rainbow Falls. The monument is located on the east side of the Sierra in east-central California. From Bishop, drive 39 miles north to the junction of U.S. 395 and S.R. 203, and then west 17 miles on S.R. 203. A shuttle bus (fee charged) operates over the last 8 miles of the narrow mountain road that connects Minaret Summit with the monument. Day-use visitors are required to use the shuttle from early morning to late afternoon.

Less than 100,000 years ago, basalt lava, which was to become Devils Postpile, erupted in the already-glaciated valley of the Middle Fork San Joaquin River. The cooling lava cracked horizontally and vertically in a specialized way forming the columns. About 10,000 years ago, a glacier flowed through the area and overrode the solidified lava. The moving ice removed much of the fractured lava mass, leaving the more-resistant parts, such as Devils Postpile. The glacier also quarried away one side of the Postpile, exposing a sheer wall of columns 40 to 60 feet high.

A ranger station by the parking area and shuttle stop has booklets about the monument. A short, steep hike along a well-used trail leads visitors to the top surface of the Postpile. Here the columns have been worn level and polished by the grinding of the glacier. Exposed cross-sections of the three- to seven-sided columns have the appearance of a mosaic.

Devils Postpile National Monument has numerous short trails and is one of the key points on the 211-mile John Muir Trail that stretches between Yosemite and Sequoia national parks. Two miles down the river trail from the Postpile, Rainbow Falls makes a drop of 101 feet into

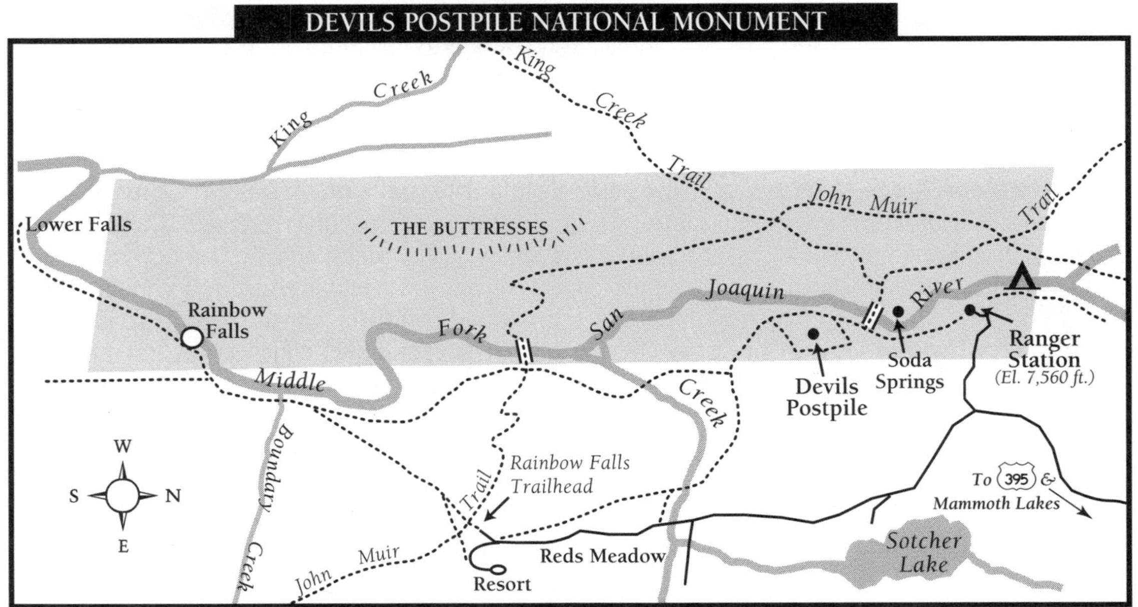

a deep green pool. During the middle of the day, a rainbow forms to add to the beauty. A short, steep trail leads to the bottom of the falls, where a garden of trees, flowers, and grasses is found. A bubbling hot spring at Reds Meadow is evidence of the lava that still exists underground in this area.

The shuttle bus stops at a number of locations in addition to the Postpile, including Reds Meadow and Sotcher Lake. Visitors are free to ride the shuttle as much as they desire so long as they don't leave the valley. The narrow access road combined with the valley's traffic congestion make the shuttle an excellent way to see the monument and the surrounding scenery.

FACILITIES: Outside monument boundaries, about 2 miles from the campground, are the Reds Meadow Resort and Store, where groceries, meals, cabins, a telephone, and saddle and pack horses are available. Water and flush toilets are provided at the monument's campground. Full services are available 13 miles away in the town of Mammoth.

CAMPING: A campground (twenty-one sites) with tables and flush toilets is open from July 1 to October 15. Campers may ride the shuttle to Reds Meadow for supplies or meals. A number of U.S. Forest Service campgrounds are located outside the monument in Inyo National Forest. Additional Forest Service campgrounds are located at Mammoth Lakes.

FISHING: The Middle Fork San Joaquin River contains rainbow, brook, and brown trout. Fishing is only a short walk from the campground and from several of the shuttle stops. A California license is required for persons over sixteen years of age.

EUGENE O'NEILL NATIONAL HISTORIC SITE

P.O. Box 280
Danville, CA 94526-0280
(925) 838–0249
www.nps.gov/euon/

Eugene O'Neill National Historic Site was established in 1976 to commemorate the contribution of Eugene O'Neill to American literature and drama. The park is located in Danville, California, 30 miles east of San Francisco. Tours are by reservation only.

Nestled in the Corduroy Hills above the San Ramon Valley is an unusual house and courtyard of Chinese design elements combined with California Monterey–style architecture. The site at one time provided this country's only Nobel Prize–winning playwright with a sanctuary in which to create masterpieces of American drama.

Built in 1937, the home today serves as a memorial to Eugene O'Neill's contribution to our country's vast cultural heritage. Named Tao House (referring to the Chinese philosophy) by O'Neill and his wife, Carlotta, it served as their home for six years. While residing at Tao House, Eugene O'Neill completed the last five plays of his successful career. Today his best-known work is *Long Day's Journey into Night.*

Free guided tours of the historic home and grounds are offered Wednesday through Sunday, at 10:00 A.M. and 12:30 P.M. Reservations are required, and the Park Service recommends making reservations about two weeks prior to the desired date (925–838–0249). Access to the site is by Park Service van. The two-and-one-half-hour tours allow visitors a glimpse into the personal and professional life of an internationally famous playwright. The tour of Tao House focuses on O'Neill's work and life. A visitor center provides displays, and a self-guided grounds tour is available. Comfortable walking shoes are recommended.

FACILITIES: No overnight accommodations are available within the park, but food and lodging are available in nearby communities. Rest rooms and drinking water are available in the visitor center.

CAMPING: No camping is permitted at the site.

FISHING: No fishing is available.

FORT POINT NATIONAL HISTORIC SITE

P.O. Box 29333
Presidio of San Francisco, CA 94129
(415) 556–1693
goga_wr_information@nps.gov
www.nps.gov/fopo/

Fort Point comprises twenty-nine acres and was established as a national historic site in 1970 to preserve a classic brick-and-granite mid-nineteenth-century coastal fortification. The fort sits just under the south end of the Golden Gate Bridge. From U.S. 101 going south, take the 25th Avenue exit at the tollgate. Northbound on 101, take the exit marked VIEW AREA, PRESIDIO, GOLDEN GATE NRA. From there, turn right to Lincoln, go left on Lincoln, and turn left again at Long Avenue.

Fort Point was constructed during an eight-year period beginning in 1853 to bar the entrance of hostile ships into San Francisco Bay. The three-story brick structure was designed for 126 cannons and 600 soldiers. Guns with ranges of up to 2 miles fired cannon balls weighing from 24 to 128 pounds. The fort's walls average 5 to 12 feet in thickness. Fort Point was the only fort of its kind on the West Coast and one of the last built in the country.

In 1886 the fort was abandoned because more powerful guns made a brick structure such as this obsolete. From 1933 to 1937 it was used as a base of operations for building the Golden Gate Bridge, and during World War II the fort served as protection for a submarine net stretched across the entrance to San Francisco Bay.

The fort contains a visitor center and exhibits. Park personnel present historical demonstrations such as cannon loading and conduct half-hour guided tours of the fort throughout the day. Visitors may also take a self-guided tour. For guided tours and information, contact the information center in the fort. Fort Point NHS is open Wednesday through Sunday, 10:00 A.M. to 5:00 P.M.

FACILITIES: A drinking fountain and pit toilets are located just outside the fort. Modern toilet facilities are available 800 yards east of the fort, near the Administrative Office.

CAMPING: No camping is permitted at Fort Point National Historic Site. Campsites are at Marin Headlands (hike-in only) and China Camp in San Rafael.

FISHING: Fishing is permitted from the seawall surrounding Fort Point. Catches include perch, flounder, and an occasional bass. A California fishing license is required to fish from the seawall but not from the nearby pier.

GOLDEN GATE NATIONAL RECREATION AREA

Fort Mason
San Francisco, CA 94123-1308
(415) 556–0560
(415) 556–2766 TDD
goga_wr_information@nps.gov
www.nps.gov/goga/

Golden Gate NRA was established in 1972 and is comprised of more than 76,000 acres of ocean beaches, redwood forests, lagoons, marshes, and historical places of interest. The park is located along the western and northern perimeters of the city of San Francisco as well as south of the Golden Gate Bridge to San Mateo County and north of the bridge in Marin County.

Golden Gate National Recreation Area is a large, diverse, and spectacularly beautiful park that comprises numerous individual areas. The park headquarters in Building 201 of Fort Mason in north San Francisco is a must stop for anyone intending to explore the park or sightsee in the city, and it is open from 9:30 A.M. to 4:30 P.M. on weekdays, with personnel available to answer questions. Picnic tables and fishing piers are available here for relaxation.

Transportation around the San Francisco section is available on the Municipal Railway (MUNI) system (415–673–MUNI), and access to areas across the Golden Gate is provided by Golden Gate Transportation (415–332–6600). Ferries from San Francisco Terminal provide access to Alcatraz (415–705–5555) and Angel Island (415–435–2131).

Because of the great diversity within Golden Gate National Recreation Area, it is not possible to cover each area and every activity available to visitors. Two of the more popular portions of the park follow.

SAN FRANCISCO AREA

Alcatraz: A 1½-mile guided tour of this former prison takes approximately two hours. A Blue and Gold ferry leaves from Pier 41 at Fisherman's Wharf every forty-five minutes beginning at 9:00 A.M. Call (415) 705–5555 for reservations.

Fort Mason: Headquarters of this park offers a wide variety of cultural, educational, and recreational programs (415–556–0560).

The Presidio: A new part of Golden Gate NRA (1994) provides access to a variety of recreational activities. Plans include a community of institutions that address social, cultural, and environmental challenges. The Presidio Visitor Information Center contains exhibits and provides information. It is open from 9:00 A.M. to 5:00 P.M. daily (415–561–4323).

Crissy Field: Part of the Presidio, it provides a quiet stretch of shoreline for hiking, fishing, or picnicking. Plans include a spectacular shoreline park with restored wetlands, recreational facilities, and a historic military airfield (415–561–4323).

Fort Point: See information under Fort Point National Historic Site on page 74.

Baker Beach: A sandy shoreline for hiking, swimming, or sunbathing.

China Beach: A small beach nestled in a steep shoreline, providing one of the best swimming areas in the city.

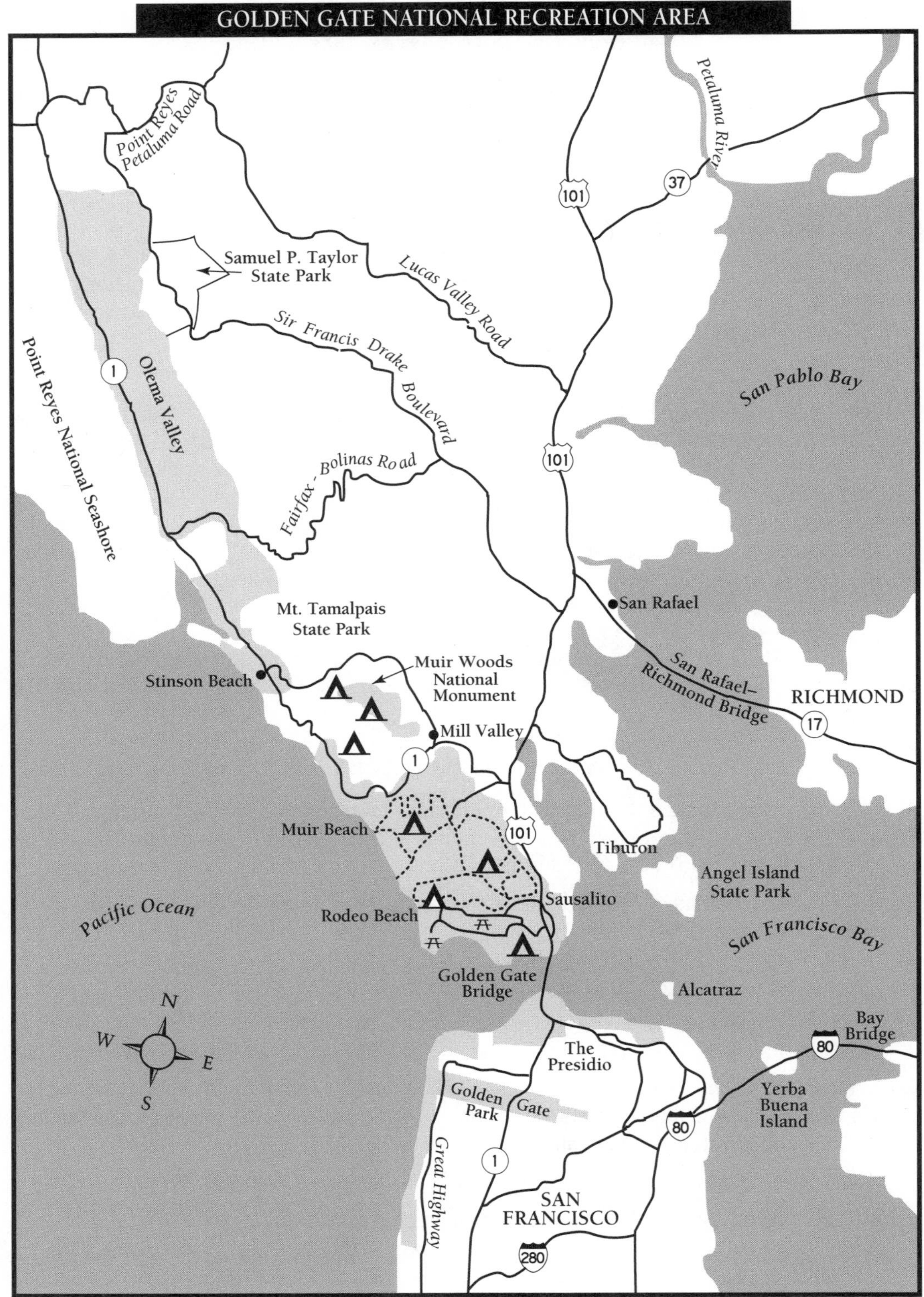
GOLDEN GATE NATIONAL RECREATION AREA
Point Reyes Petaluma Road
Petaluma River
101
37
Samuel P. Taylor State Park
Lucas Valley Road
Sir Francis Drake Boulevard
Point Reyes National Seashore
1
Olema Valley
San Pablo Bay
101
Fairfax - Bolinas Road
San Rafael
Mt. Tamalpais State Park
Muir Woods National Monument
Stinson Beach
San Rafael–Richmond Bridge
RICHMOND
17
Mill Valley
1
Muir Beach
101
Tiburon
Angel Island State Park
Sausalito
Pacific Ocean
Rodeo Beach
San Francisco Bay
Golden Gate Bridge
Alcatraz
N
W
E
S
Bay Bridge
80
The Presidio
Golden Gate Park
Yerba Buena Island
80
Great Highway
1
SAN FRANCISCO
280

Land's End: A beautiful natural area with trees, birds, and vistas. Contains the route of an abandoned train to Cliff House and defense batteries of West Fort Miley.

Cliff House: Excellent viewpoints of the coast with offshore Seal Rocks serving as home for sea lions and marine birds (415–556–8642).

Fort Funston: A loop trail with picnic areas provides vistas of coastal scenery. Hang gliders often use the cliffs and strong winds (415–239–2366).

NORTH OF THE GOLDEN GATE

Marin Headlands: Wind-swept ridges, beaches, and protected valleys offer a major change from San Francisco's urban setting (415–331–1540).

Tennessee Valley: A narrow, secluded valley with a winding 2-mile trail ending at a small beach (415–331–1540).

Muir Woods: See information under Muir Woods National Monument on page 91.

Muir Beach and Stinson Beach: Vistas of the ocean and surrounding hills (415–388–2596).

Angel Island: A state park with picnicking, hiking, and beautiful scenery (415–435–1915).

FACILITIES: Lodging is available in San Francisco and surrounding communities. Food can be found at numerous locations near the park. Youth hostels are at Fort Mason and Fort Berry.

CAMPING: Camping is available in the Marin Headlands (415–331–1540) and at Mt. Tamalpais State Park (415–388–2070). Private campgrounds are located along State Route 1. For additional information, see the camping section under Point Reyes National Seashore.

FISHING: Surf fishing is possible at two piers and numerous locations along the beaches.

JOHN MUIR NATIONAL HISTORIC SITE

4202 Alhambra Avenue
Martinez, CA 94553-3883
(925) 228–8860
JOMU_Interpretations@nps.gov
www.nps.gov/jomu/

John Muir National Historic Site was established in 1964 to preserve the home of John Muir and to commemorate his contributions to conservation and literature. The park is located in Martinez, California, approximately 25 miles northeast of Oakland.

John Muir immigrated to the United States from Scotland in 1849, when he was eleven years of age. After living in Wisconsin and acquiring an interest in both mechanics and biology, he started on his now-famous walks in 1867. Over the years his treks took him through much of the American wilderness, and to Alaska, South America, Africa, India, the Orient, and Australia. His special place of interest was the Sierra Nevada.

Muir began writing in the 1870s and continued until his death in 1914. A great deal of the writing was undertaken at the house that is preserved at the site where Muir lived from 1890

until 1914. Muir had resolved to do what he could to make the wilderness better loved and preserved for future generations. He was an important influence in President Theodore Roosevelt's decisions to add 148 million acres of forests, twenty-three national monuments, and five national parks to our nation's forest and park system.

The National Park Service has restored the buildings and grounds to their appearance at the time John Muir lived here. The site is open Wednesday through Sunday, from 10:00 A.M. to 4:30 P.M., except on Thanksgiving, Christmas, and New Year's Day. Park Service personnel are available to provide information, and a movie dealing with Muir's life is presented in the visitor center. Guided tours of the house are offered daily at 2:00 P.M. Tours at other times are self-guided, and a booklet is available in the visitor center. Four tours are offered on weekends.

FACILITIES: No facilities other than a small picnic area and bookstore are available at the site, but food and lodging can be found nearby. Drinking water and rest rooms are provided in the visitor center. A picnic area is located at Nancy Boyd Park, south of the historic site on Pleasant Hill Road.

CAMPING: No camping is permitted at the site, and no campgrounds are in the immediate vicinity.

FISHING: No fishing is available at John Muir National Historic Site.

JOSHUA TREE NATIONAL PARK

74485 National Park Drive
Twentynine Palms, CA 92277-3597
(760) 367–5500
www.nps.gov/jotr/

Joshua Tree is a 793,000-acre national park that was established in 1936 to preserve a section of California desert containing a notable variety of richness of vegetation. The park is 140 miles east of Los Angeles. From the west it is approached via Interstate 10 to a point 15 miles east of Banning, where Highway 62 to Joshua Tree and Twentynine Palms fronts the north entrances. The south entrance is 35 miles east of Indio via Interstate 10.

At Joshua Tree National Park, two desert ecosystems determined by different elevations converge. Desert plants in both systems have to be able to adapt to survive in a harsh environment. They must be able to go for prolonged periods without water and yet be able to absorb large amounts of moisture during brief rainstorms. Some plants spread roots close to the surface, while others have roots growing deep into the earth.

One of the park's features is the Joshua tree. It grows to heights of 40 feet and during March and April bears white blossoms in clusters 8 to 14 inches long. The tree is usually found at elevations above 3,000 feet in the central part of the park.

The visitor will find five oases of California fan palms within the park. The largest, in Lost Palms Canyon, contains more than one hundred palms. It is 4 miles by trail from the visitor center at Cottonwood Spring. The oasis at Fortynine Palms Canyon, just inside the northern boundary, is reached by a 1½-mile trail (one way).

John Muir National Historic Site (opposite page)

The main visitor center is just outside the north entrance, near Twentynine Palms. Exhibits and a self-guided nature trail are located here. A new visitor center is also located at Cottonwood Spring. Other points of interest (keyed with numbers corresponding to those found on the map) are:

1. A moderately strenuous trail (3 miles round-trip) to Fortynine Palms Oasis, where water-loving plants thrive.
2. A ½-mile loop nature trail, accessible from Indian Cove Campground.
3. A trail system that winds between massive boulders and leads through a legendary cattle rustler's hideout.
4. Barker Dam, which forms a small reservoir. At one time the dam provided water for cattle and for mining use.
5. Lost Horse Mine, accessible via trail (4 miles round-trip).
6. Keys View, at 5,185 feet, provides a panoramic view.
7. A moderately strenuous trail (3 miles round-trip) to the Ryan Mountain summit, which provides several outstanding viewpoints.
8. An 18-mile self-guided motor nature tour that winds through fascinating desert landscape. Four-wheel drive is required.
9. A self-guided nature trail that contains some of the plants of the Colorado desert.
10. Cottonwood Spring, a planted palm oasis noted for its birdlife.
11. A trail (7½ miles round-trip) that leads to the park's largest group of palms.

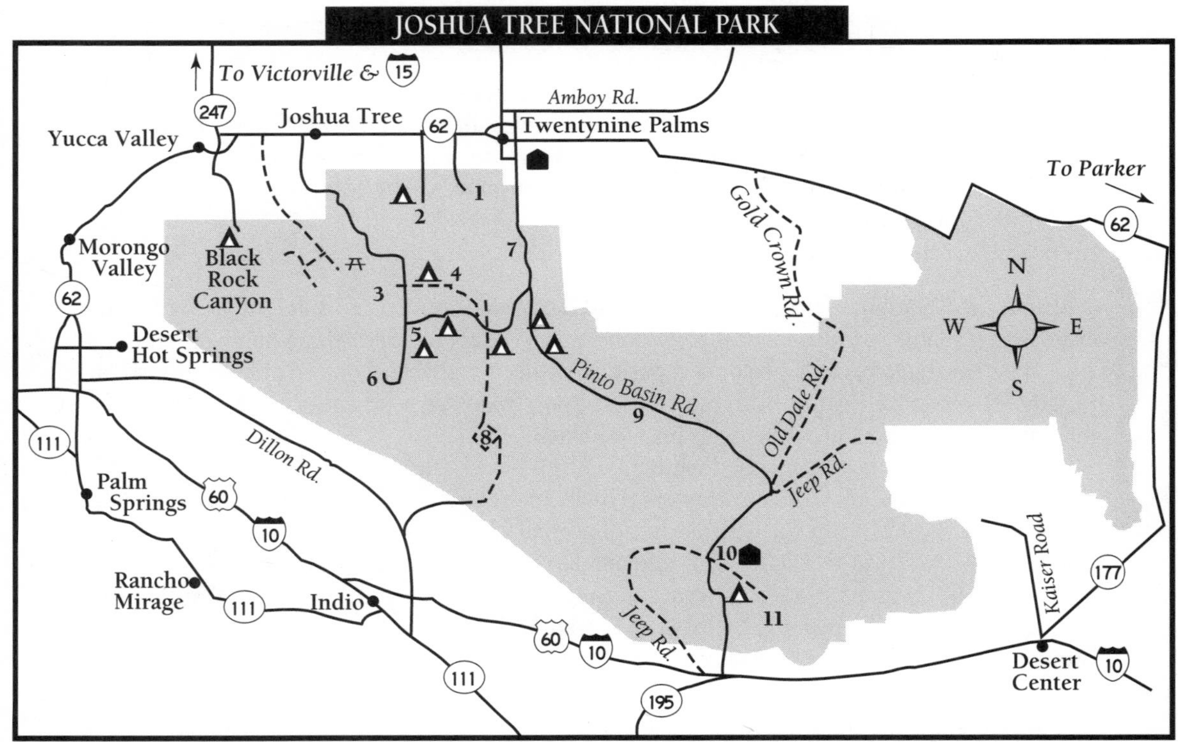

FACILITIES: Overnight accommodations and food service are available in nearby towns but not in the park. Water and flush toilets are available at the visitor center and at the campgrounds at Black Rock Canyon and Cottonwood Spring.

CAMPING: Nine campgrounds are available in the park. The only locations with water and flush toilets are Black Rock Canyon (one hundred spaces) and Cottonwood Spring (sixty-two spaces), near the park's south entrance. Reservations are recommended for Black Rock Canyon campground (800–365–2267). Those with vault toilets and no water include Belle (twenty spaces), Hidden Valley (thirty-nine spaces), Indian Cove (101 spaces and thirteen group sites), Jumbo Rocks (125 spaces), Ryan (thirty-one spaces), Sheep Pass (six group sites, reservations only), and White Tank (fifteen spaces).

FISHING: No fishing is available in Joshua Tree National Park.

KINGS CANYON NATIONAL PARK; SEQUOIA NATIONAL PARK

Three Rivers, CA 93271-9700
(559) 565–3341
www.nps.gov/seki

General Grant and Sequoia National Parks were established in 1890. Kings Canyon National Park was established separately in 1940 and incorporated General Grant National Park. Today, the parks' combined 1,300 square miles are administered as a single unit. The parks are especially noted for groves of giant sequoias growing in canyons surrounded by the High Sierra. Sequoia and Kings Canyon are located in central California, between Yosemite and Death Valley. Access is from the west, with State Highway 180 from Fresno leading into Kings Canyon and Route 198 from Visalia entering Sequoia. No road crosses the Sierra Nevada range in either park.

The Sierra Nevada is the result of an uplifting of the earth's crust millions of years ago. Later, during the great ice age, glaciers quarried canyons and scooped basins, giving the mountains their present shape. Once the glaciers began melting, the basins turned into lakes and plant life returned to the region. The sequoias dominating the park were once widespread but now grow only on the western slope of the Sierra. Although not as tall as the related coastal redwoods, the sequoias are immense, with trunk sizes that are simply amazing.

The parks' three major developed areas are Lodgepole, Grant Grove, and Cedar Grove. Generals Highway connects Ash Mountain, Lodgepole, and Grant Grove. Entering at Ash Mountain, the road passes through Giant Forest, which contains some of the finest groups of giant sequoias, including the General Sherman tree—the world's largest living thing. The area is covered with trails, and short walks to Moro Rock, Beetle Rock, and Sunset Rock provide excellent viewpoints. A visitor center is located at Lodgepole.

After leaving the park at Lost Grove, the road wanders in a northwesterly direction to Grant Grove, an isolated section of Kings Canyon. Here, the visitor can see the General Grant—the nation's Christmas tree. Nearby are other large sequoias, and a visitor center with exhibits and a slide presentation is about a mile away. Be sure to visit this area of giant trees. Big Stump Basin, where large trees were cut during the logging era before the basin became part of Kings Canyon National Park, is reached via a self-guided trail near the south entrance. The Grant

KINGS CANYON NATIONAL PARK

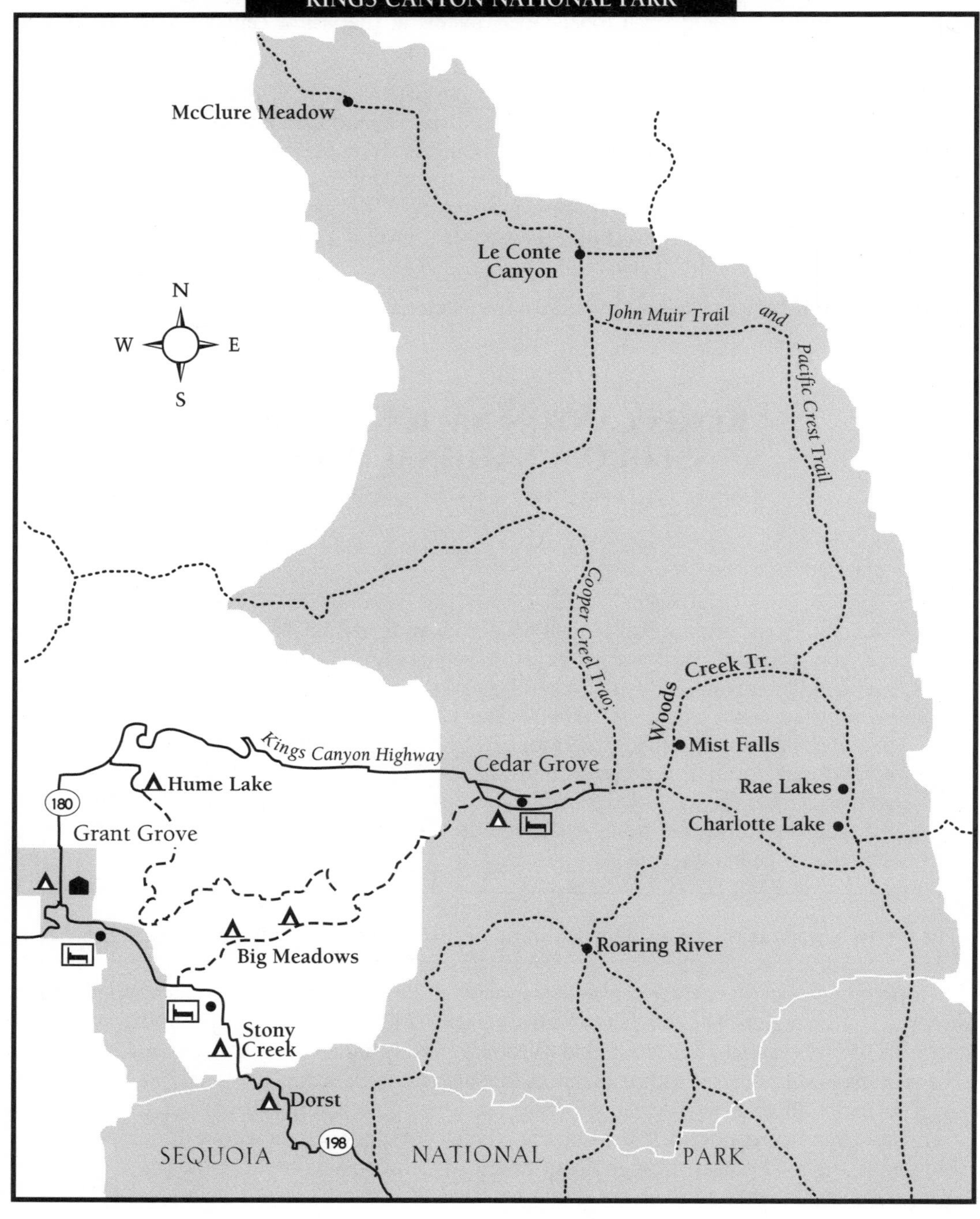

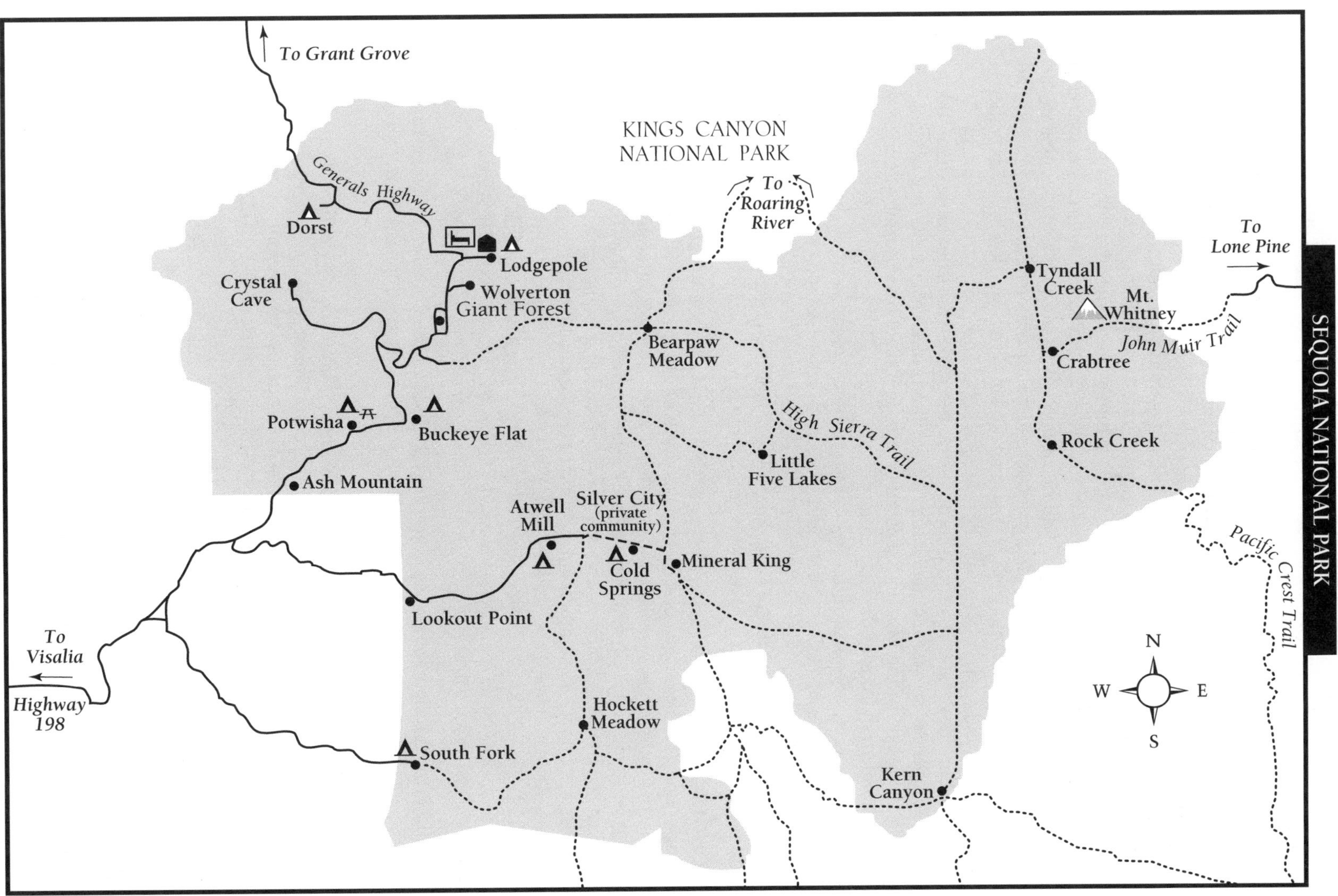

SEQUOIA NATIONAL PARK
To Grant Grove
Generals Highway
Dorst
Lodgepole
Wolverton
Giant Forest
Crystal Cave
KINGS CANYON NATIONAL PARK
To Roaring River
Bearpaw Meadow
To Lone Pine
Tyndall Creek
Mt. Whitney
Crabtree
John Muir Trail
High Sierra Trail
Little Five Lakes
Rock Creek
Potwisha
Buckeye Flat
Ash Mountain
Atwell Mill
Silver City (private community)
Mineral King
Cold Springs
Lookout Point
Pacific Crest Trail
To Visalia
Highway 198
N
W
E
S
Hockett Meadow
South Fork
Kern Canyon

Grove area is convenient to both Cedar Grove and Giant Forest (about 30 miles to each), which makes it a good place to stay if you have only limited time. The road from Grant Grove to Cedar Grove (30 miles) is open from about mid-April to mid-November, and the view of the canyon is something not to be missed. Cedar Grove is one of the centers of activity in Kings Canyon. Visitors will find it considerably warmer than Grant Grove. Here peaks rise to a mile or more above the south fork of the Kings River. The river is fair for fishing, but because of the swift current and very cold water, it is not suitable for swimming or rafting. The end of the road is the site of major trailheads to the high country (long-term parking is available). A self-guided nature trail is nearby. The trailhead to Mount Whitney, the highest mountain in the continental United States, is reached along a paved road from Lone Pine on the park's east side.

Ranger-guided walks to areas of interest in both parks are provided throughout the year. Schedules are posted in lodges, campgrounds, and visitor centers. Campfire programs are presented at Lodgepole, Grant Grove, Dorst, and Cedar Grove and less often at Mineral King. Saddle horses and pack animals may be rented at corrals near Wolverton, Mineral King, Grant Grove, Cedar Grove, and at various locations on the park's east side. More than 700 miles of trails are open to horses. Limited tours (fee required) of Crystal Cave are scheduled Friday through Monday during May and September and on a daily basis during summer months. A steep ½-mile trail leads to the cave entrance.

Winter season at Sequoia and Kings Canyon is from December through March. Cross-country ski tour centers are at Grant Grove and Wolverton, where ski and snowshoe rentals are available. Many miles of marked trails are in the Grant Grove and Giant Forest areas. A 3-mile marked trail from Wolverton to Giant Forest is available for cross-country skiing. Sleds, tubes, and platters are permitted at Wolverton and Grant Grove.

LODGING: Lodging is available all year at Grant Grove Lodge, which offers hotel rooms and cabins. Stony Creek Lodge, located 15 miles north of Giant Forest Village in Sequoia National Forest, has rooms in a two-story building that is open from May through Labor Day, depending on weather. Cedar Grove Lodge, in the Cedar Grove area of Kings Canyon National Park, has eighteen rooms in a modern two-story wooden building that is open from mid-May to mid-October, depending on weather. For information on reservations in any of these facilities write Sequoia–Kings Canyon Park Services, P.O. Box 909, Kings Canyon National Park, CA 93633. Call (559) 335–5500. A new lodging facility north of the Lodgepole was completed in 1999. For reservations write Wuksachi Village, P.O. Box 89, Sequoia NP, CA 93262. Phone (559) 565–3435 or (888) 252–5757.

FACILITIES: A restaurant is open year-round at Grant Grove. Food service is available at Stony Creek and Cedar Grove from late May to October. General supplies are available at Cedar Creek, Lodgepole, Grant Grove, and Stony Creek.

CAMPING: A variety of campgrounds are located within the two parks. Most offer tables, grills, water, and flush toilets. In Sequoia, the Giant Forest area has Lodgepole (218 spaces, dump station, pay showers, store) and Dorst (209 spaces, seven group sites, dump station). Lodgepole fills first, and reservations are available by calling 800–365–2267. In the Mineral King area, Atwell Mill (twenty-one spaces) and Cold Springs (forty spaces) have pit toilets. No trailers are permitted in either campground. At lower elevations in Sequoia are Buckeye Flat (twenty-eight spaces, no trailers or recreation vehicles), Potwisha (forty-two spaces, dump station, swimming), and South Fork (ten spaces, pit toilet, trailers not recommended).

In Kings Canyon, the Grant Grove area has Azalea (114 spaces, dump station), Crystal Springs (sixty-six spaces), and Sunset (119 spaces, limited trailer space). A market and pay showers are located within walking distance of these campgrounds. In the Cedar Grove area are Canyon View (thirty-seven spaces, four group sites), Moraine (120 spaces), Sentinel (eighty-three spaces), and Sheep Creek (111 spaces, dump station). Of these, Sentinel generally fills first and is the most crowded, while Moraine has somewhat less shade and is the least crowded. The amphitheater and ranger station are at Sentinel Campground.

FISHING: Many wilderness lakes and streams contain golden, rainbow, brook, and brown trout. The most popular fishing spots are along the Kings River and the forks of the Kaweah River. A California fishing license is required and may be purchased at the stores.

LASSEN VOLCANIC NATIONAL PARK

P.O. Box 100
Mineral, CA 96063-0100
(530) 595–4444
www.nps.gov/lavo/

Lassen Volcanic National Park comprises 106,000 acres and was established in 1916 to protect hot springs, fumaroles, mud pots, and sulfurous vents surrounding a volcano last active around 1921. The park is located in north-central California, about 42 miles east of Redding off State Highway 44.

Lassen is a beautiful and relatively uncrowded mountainous area of forests, lakes, and extinct and inactive volcanoes. Centered toward the west side of the park is Lassen Peak, a 10,457-foot plug-dome volcano that last erupted during a seven-year period beginning in 1914. In addition to Lassen Peak, an inactive cinder cone and active boiling springs are in evidence.

A single main paved road, Lassen Park Road (summer only), winds in a north-south direction through the west side of the park. The southwest entrance has an entrance station, a chalet, a nature trail, and a seasonal winter-sports center. The northern entrance at Manzanita Lake includes a nature trail and a museum. Between these two entrances, visitors will find a variety of things to do and see.

Many of the park's 150 miles of trails begin from the roadside. A self-guided trail (3 miles round-trip) to Bumpass Hell begins 7 miles inside of the southwest boundary. This leads to the park's best area in which to observe thermal activity. In addition to the trail to the Lassen Peak summit, there is also the 4-mile (round-trip) Cinder Cone Trail, which climbs to the top of a 700-foot cinder cone. This latter trail begins at Butte Lake, at the northeast corner of the park. Daily interpretive programs take place throughout the summer. Most of these begin from various points along the main road. The walk around Manzanita Lake is delightful and relatively easy. The winter sports area is near the southwest entrance.

FACILITIES: Only minimal accommodations are present in Lassen. A general store operating near the Manzanita Lake campground during summer months provides fast food, groceries, and gasoline. Limited food service is available at Lassen Chalet, near the southwest entrance station, during the summer months. Overnight accommodations are available at Drakesbad Guest Ranch between June and September. Write California Guest Services, 2150 Main Street, Suite 5, Red Bluff, CA 96080 (530–529–1512). Ranger stations are located at Manzanita Lake, Summit Lake, Juniper Lake, and Warner Valley.

CAMPING: Improved campgrounds are located at Manzanita Lake (179 spaces, pay showers), Summit Lake (ninety-four spaces), and Southwest (twenty-one spaces). The latter has campsites located approximately 100 yards from parking facilities, but the first can accommodate trailers and motorhomes. All of these camps have fire grates, picnic tables, water, and toilets. Summit Lake usually fills earlier than the other two. Less-improved campsites (pit toilets, tables, fireplaces) are found at Crags (forty-five spaces), Warner Valley (eighteen spaces), and Juniper Lake (eighteen spaces). Juniper Lake and Warner Valley are not recommended for trailers.

FISHING: Fishing is permitted anywhere except Emerald Lake, Manzanita Creek, and within 150 feet of the inlet to Manzanita Lake. A California fishing license is required, and possibilities include brown, brook, and rainbow trout. Grassy Creek, connecting Horseshoe and Snag lakes, is closed from October 1 to June 15. Manzanita Lake is catch and release only. Only artificial lures and single barbless hooks can be used.

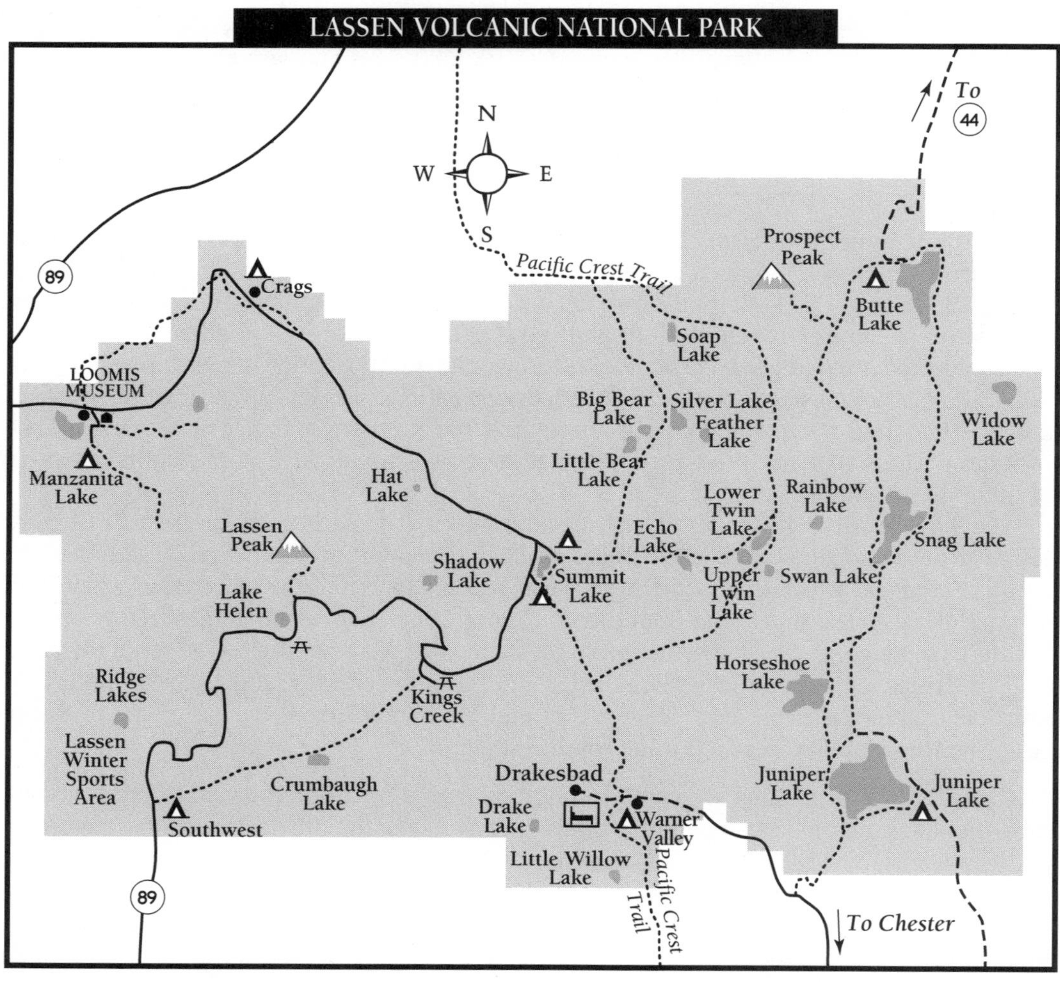

LAVA BEDS NATIONAL MONUMENT

P.O. Box 867
Tulelake, CA 96134-0867
(530) 667–2282
www.nps.gov/labe/

Lava Beds comprises 46,500 acres, and it was established as a national monument in 1925 to preserve a rugged landscape formed by volcanic activity and the historic battlefields of the Modoc War. The monument is located in extreme north-central California, 45 miles southeast of Klamath Falls, Oregon.

Centuries ago, a group of vents spewed great masses of molten basaltic lava over this region of the country. As the rivers of liquid rock cooled and hardened, the landscape of Lava Beds National Monument was born. Cinder cones are scattered throughout the area, and both smooth and rough (such as Devil's Homestead and Schonchin Flow) lava flows cover the monument. A number of these lava flows created lava-tube caves that are found throughout the area. Twenty-one caves are developed for visitors.

The only major Indian war to be fought in California took place in the lava beds. In November 1872, a group of 150 Modocs took refuge in the lava beds after skirmishes with settlers and the U.S. Army. Over the next 4½ months, fifty Modoc warriors used their knowledge of the local terrain to stand off a siege by nearly 600 troops. After peace negotiations stalled, some warriors convinced Captain Jack, the Modoc leader, to attack the peace commissioners during negotiations. Two members of the commission were killed. The Modocs were forced to abandon their stronghold a week later. After additional battles, the war ended with Captain Jack's capture on June 1, 1873. Jack and three other Modoc leaders were executed, while the survivors were sent to Oklahoma. Modoc War sites in the monument include Captain Jacks Stronghold (self-guiding trail), Hospital Rock and Gillems Camp (army campsites), Canby Cross (the site of the attack on the peace commission), and the Thomas-Wright battlefield (site of a battle after the Modocs left the Stronghold).

A visitor center is located 3 to 4 miles inside of the southeast entrance; a small museum explains the history and geology of the area. During summer months, park rangers give guided walks, cave tours, and campfire programs. A loop road south of headquarters provides access to many of the developed lava-tube caves. Numerous trails are located throughout the monument. Schonchin Butte, one of the largest cinder cones, can be climbed, and a trail leads to Black Crater.

Near the visitor center, Mushpot Cave is lighted for an easy self-guided tour that takes about twenty minutes. The tour is worthwhile and should be a visitor's first order of business after viewing the visitor-center exhibits. The remainder of the caves are without lighting, so flashlights must be used. These may be borrowed at the visitor center. For those with even a mild interest in caves, a trip through one or more of these is a must. It is a unique experience that by itself makes a trip to the monument memorable.

FACILITIES: Food and lodging are not available within the monument, but both can be found in either Tulelake or Klamath Falls. Water and modern rest rooms are located at headquarters and at the campground. The picnic areas at Fleener Chimneys and Captain Jacks Stronghold have no water.

CAMPING: Indian Well Campground (forty-three spaces) is open all year, and grills, tables, water, and flush toilets are provided. The campground is located a short distance from the visitor center, with sites interspersed among juniper trees that provide some shade for campers but not much for their vehicles.

FISHING: No fishing is available at Lava Beds National Monument. Thirty-six miles south of the park on U.S. Forest Service land, Medicine Lake provides excellent trout fishing. A California fishing license is required and an area map showing the location of the lake is available in the Lava Beds visitor center.

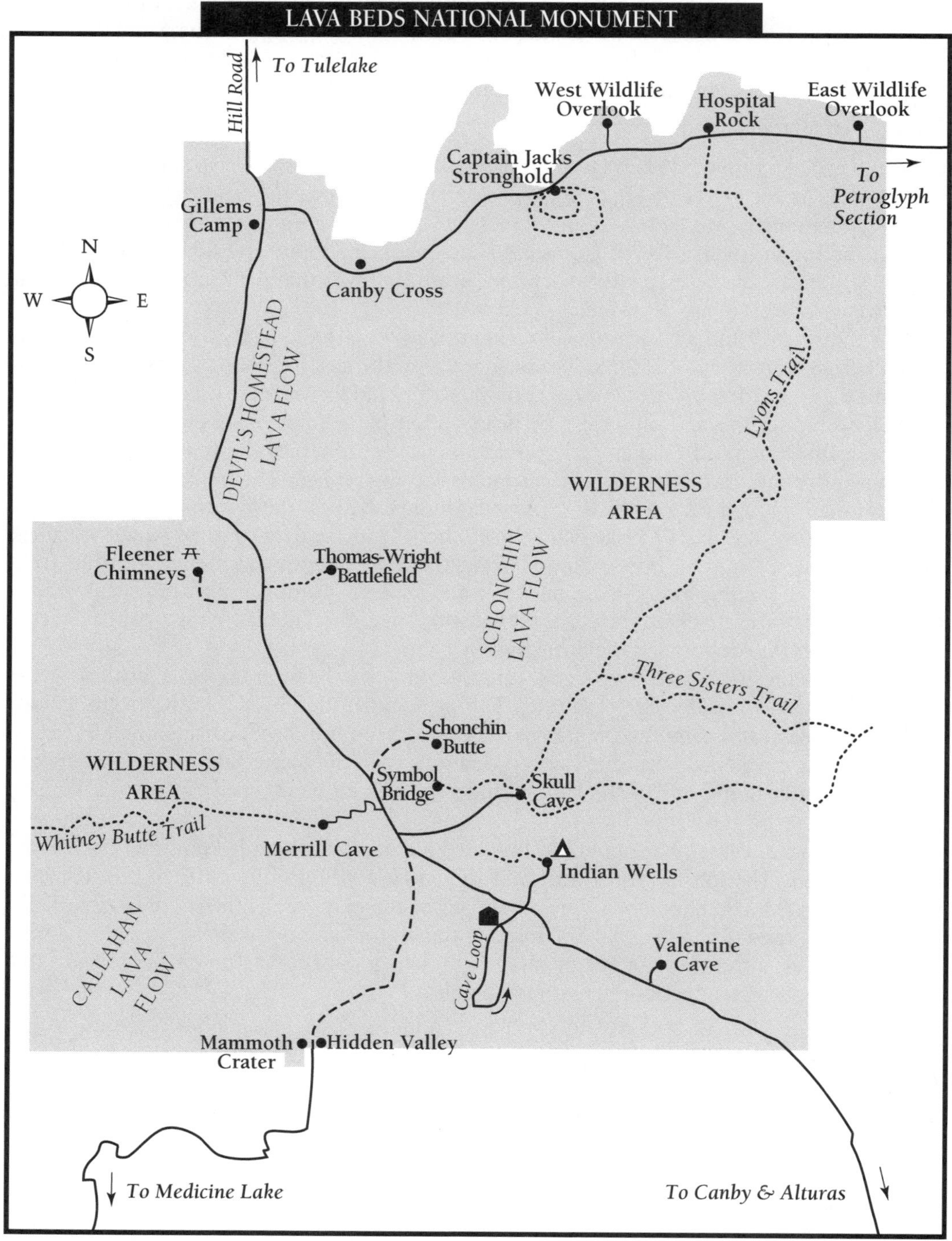

MANZANAR NATIONAL HISTORIC SITE

P.O. Box 426
Independence, CA 93526
(760) 878–2932
www.nps.gov/manz/

Manzanar National Historic Site comprises 813 acres and was authorized in 1992 to preserve the Manzanar War Relocation Center and commemorate the World War II internment of Japanese-Americans. The site also interprets the area's history with respect to American Indians and agricultural settlement. The historic site is located in southeastern California, 12 miles north of Lone Pine, just off U.S. Highway 395.

Two months after the Japanese attack on Pearl Harbor, President Franklin Roosevelt signed an executive order that called for all people of Japanese ancestry residing on the West Coast of the United States to be placed in relocation camps. Manzanar became the first permanent detention camp, eventually holding approximately 10,000 people. The facility comprised nearly 6,000 acres and included an agricultural area, a cemetery, a reservoir, and a sewage treatment plant, in addition to the detention area of approximately 550 acres that forms most of the historic site. Manzanar was in operation from 1942 to late 1945.

Most of the facility's wooden buildings were sold and removed from the site following decommissioning. Still visible are concrete building foundations, stonework shells of the police post and sentry house, portions of the water and sewer systems, and the remains of the large wooden auditorium. Photos, drawings, paintings, and artifacts associated with Manzanar can be seen in the Eastern California Museum, 5 miles north in the town of Independence.

FACILITIES: No facilities, including drinking water or rest rooms, are available at the site. Food and lodging are available in Independence, 5 miles north, and Lone Pine, 12 miles south.

CAMPING: No camping is permitted at the site. Numerous public campgrounds operated by the National Forest Service and the county are in the Independence/Lone Pine area.

MOJAVE NATIONAL PRESERVE

222 East Main Street, Suite 202
Barstow, CA 92311
(760) 255–8801
MOJA_Baker_Interp@nps.gov
www.nps.gov/moja/

Mojave National Preserve was created in 1994 to protect 1.4 million acres of fragile desert that includes volcanic cinder cones, sand dunes, desert scrubland, and mountain-top forests. The preserve is located in southeastern California, bounded on the north by Interstate 15 and on the south by Interstate 40. It is accessible from either interstate.

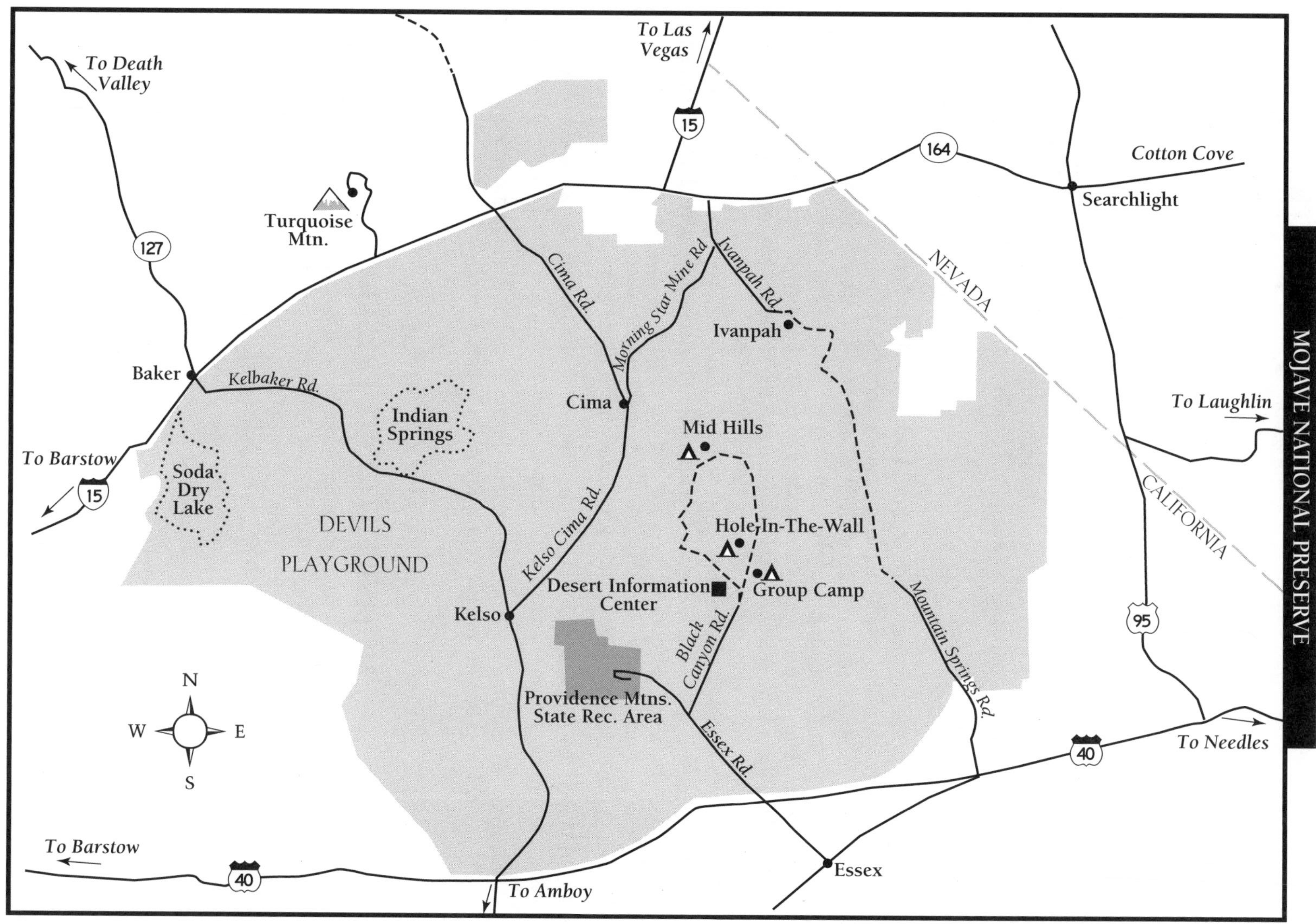

MOJAVE NATIONAL PRESERVE
To Death Valley
127
Turquoise Mtn.
To Las Vegas
15
164
Cotton Cove
Searchlight
NEVADA
CALIFORNIA
Cima Rd.
Morning Star Mine Rd
Ivanpah Rd.
Ivanpah
Baker
Kelbaker Rd.
Cima
Indian Springs
Mid Hills
To Laughlin
To Barstow
15
Soda Dry Lake
DEVILS PLAYGROUND
Hole-In-The-Wall
Kelso Cima Rd.
Desert Information Center
Group Camp
Kelso
Black Canyon Rd.
Mountain Springs Rd.
95
N
W
E
S
Providence Mtns. State Rec. Area
Essex Rd.
40
To Needles
To Barstow
40
To Amboy
Essex

Mojave National Preserve comprises a huge (twice the size of Yosemite National Park) tract of pristine desert that is rich in geology and wildlife. Mojave NP is the third largest national park area in the lower 48 states. Three of North America's deserts, the Mojave, Great Basin, and Sonoran, meet in this preserve which serves as home to a variety of birds and nearly 300 species of animals, including bighorn sheep and desert tortoises. The preserve has rock art from the native desert people who once lived here and old mines and ranches from more recent inhabitants. Nearly half the preserve is designated as wilderness. Providence Mountain State Recreation Area, administered by the California Department of Parks and Recreation, offers 1½-hour guided cavern tours. Call (805) 942–0662 for information or group reservations. The recreation area is within Mojave NP boundaries.

The preserve provides a variety of activities including sightseeing, camping, and hiking. Points of interest include 700-foot Kelso Dunes, an old Union Pacific train depot that is being restored by the National Park Service, numerous volcanic cinder cones, and 7,929-foot Clark Mountain, the highest peak in the preserve. Hunting is permitted in designated areas. Summer temperatures can be extreme, with very hot days and cold nights, so it is important to come prepared with appropriate clothing. Limited water is available seasonally in the campgrounds. Maps and brochures with camping information, hiking trails, and points of interest are available at park headquarters in the Mojave Desert Information Center in Baker (72157 Baker Boulevard; 760–733–4040).

FACILITIES: No overnight accommodations are available in the preserve. Limited food items can be purchased in Baker and Nipton. Gasoline, water, and telephones are in only a few sites around the preserve. Lodging, groceries, and supplies are in surrounding towns.

CAMPING: Developed campgrounds with picnic tables, fire rings (bring your own wood), and pit toilets are at Hole-in-the-Wall and Mid Hills. Mid Hills is at a higher altitude and is generally 10–15 degrees cooler than Hole-in-the-Wall campground. Limited water is available. Camping is also available at Providence Mountain State Recreation Area.

FISHING: No fishing is available in the preserve.

MUIR WOODS NATIONAL MONUMENT

Mill Valley, CA 94941-2696
(415) 388–2595
goga_wk_information@nps.gov
www.nps.gov/muwo/

Muir Woods was established in 1908 and features coastal redwoods among its 550 acres of old growth forest. The park is located 17 miles north of San Francisco via U.S. 101 and California 1.

Millions of years ago at least forty species of giant trees related to today's redwood and sequoia grew throughout the Northern Hemisphere. Today, the coast redwood grows only in a 500-mile-long, 30-mile-wide belt along the Pacific coast, from just south of Monterey to the southwestern corner of Oregon. This is where the Pacific Ocean produces fog and a cool damp climate in protected or sheltered areas such as Muir Woods. In this park some specimens have reached more than 250 feet in height, while farther north in the state, trees exceed 360 feet.

Redwoods resist fire, insects, and fungi, with their thick, asbestos-like bark which is filled with tanic acid. Although these trees have survived three to five fires per century, the last natural fire in the Muir Woods was in 1845. Recent controlled burns along the Ben Johnson Trail allow visitors and researchers to observe the benefits of low-intensity burns. The tree's root system is surprisingly shallow but may radiate for up to 100 feet.

The park is open from 8:00 A.M. to sunset. An admission fee is charged for anyone 17 or older. The visitor center with exhibits and a bookstore is located in the park's southeast corner. The monument is designed to be seen primarily by hiking. About 2 miles of the main walking trails are paved and therefore accessible to wheelchairs and strollers. Six miles of trails connect with those of Mt. Tamalpais State Park to provide the visitor with many hours of exercise, enjoyment, and quiet. Bridges along Redwood Creek make short loops possible, and trailside exhibits, signs, and markers are placed throughout the monument. A self-guided portion of the trail (with booklet) lies between the second and third bridges. Park rangers, volunteers, and interns give daily programs.

Be warned that the monument is quite crowded during summer months and on winter weekends when the weather is nice. During summer weekends the park is packed. As a result, parking is often difficult and solitude on the loop trails is elusive. It is best to visit early in the morning or later in the afternoon and get off the main walking path onto some of the trails. No bikes, horses, or dogs are permitted.

FACILITIES: The park's only facility is a concession shop near the visitor center that sells snacks and souvenirs. Drinking water and rest rooms are located near the park entrance. The nearest picnic facility is at Muir Beach, about 3 miles south of the park.

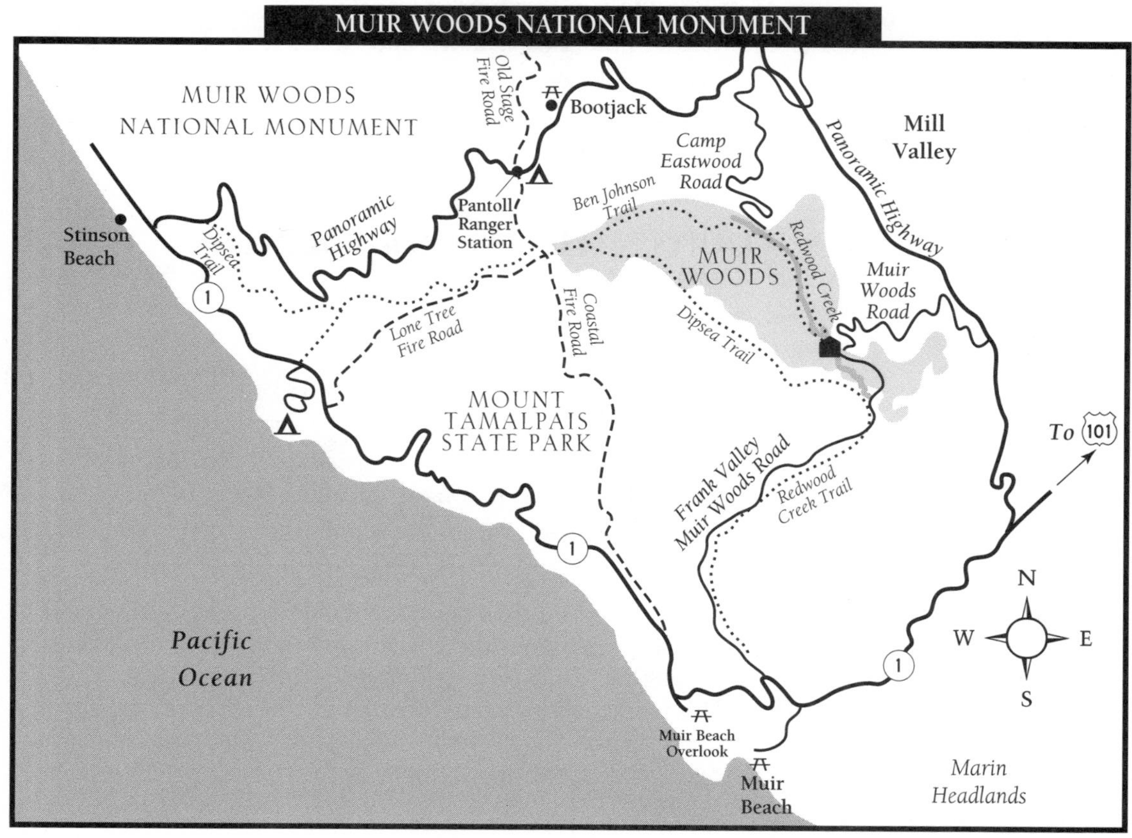

CAMPING: No camping or picnicking facilities are in the monument. Mt. Tamalpais State Park, surrounding Muir Woods, provides walk-in tent-style camping with tables, grills, water, and rest rooms. Automobile parking is about 100 yards from the camping sites. To reach this area at Pantoll, take the Panoramic Highway north after leaving Muir Woods. Another state park is located 26 miles northwest via Highway 1. See the camping section under Point Reyes National Seashore.

FISHING: No fishing is permitted in Muir Woods.

PINNACLES NATIONAL MONUMENT

Paicines, CA 95043-9770
(831) 389–4485
PINN_Visitor_Information@nps.gov
www.nps.gov/pinn/

Pinnacles National Monument was established in 1908 and contains the remains of an ancient volcano that has been eroded by wind, water, and freezing into spectacular pinnacles and spires. The park is located in west-central California, approximately 83 miles southeast of San Jose. The major part of the monument must be approached from the east via California Highways 25 and 146. The entrance to the west side of the monument, from U.S. 101 at Soledad, is not a through road and will not accommodate trailers or campers.

The jagged landscape of Pinnacles National Monument is the result of molten rock that poured over this area twenty-three million years ago. The flow was facilitated by a rift that developed when the Pacific plate collided with and ripped off a portion of the California coast. As the Pacific plate moved northwest, the cone built by the volcanic activity moved nearly 195 miles from its original location. Millions of years of erosion have taken their toll, and the rock formations of today are about one-third the height of the original volcano.

The rugged slopes of Pinnacles are covered by a brushy plant cover known as chaparral. The plants thrive in the hot, dry summers and sparse rainfall (15 inches) found in this area of California. This pygmy forest provides shelter for a variety of wildlife, including black-tailed deer, rabbits, raccoons, bobcats, and gray fox. Frequently seen birds include the acorn woodpecker, brown towhee, California quail, and turkey vulture.

The visitor center, about 2 miles from the east entrance, has changing displays to help interpret the natural history of the area. A park ranger is on duty to help visitors. Although the monument is open all year, its main seasons are spring and fall. Winter months bring the wet season, and summer months are quite hot, with daytime temperatures often exceeding 100 degrees Fahrenheit.

One of the park's main activities is hiking, and a number of trails are located throughout Pinnacles:

•High Peaks Trail (5$^{2}/_{5}$ miles, five to six hours) begins at the Chalone Creek picnic area or at the parking area at the end of Bear Gulch picnic area. The 1,400-foot climb presents viewpoints of the entire park.

•Condor Gulch Trail (1$^{7}/_{10}$ miles, one and a half hours) connects the visitor center with the High Peaks Trail.

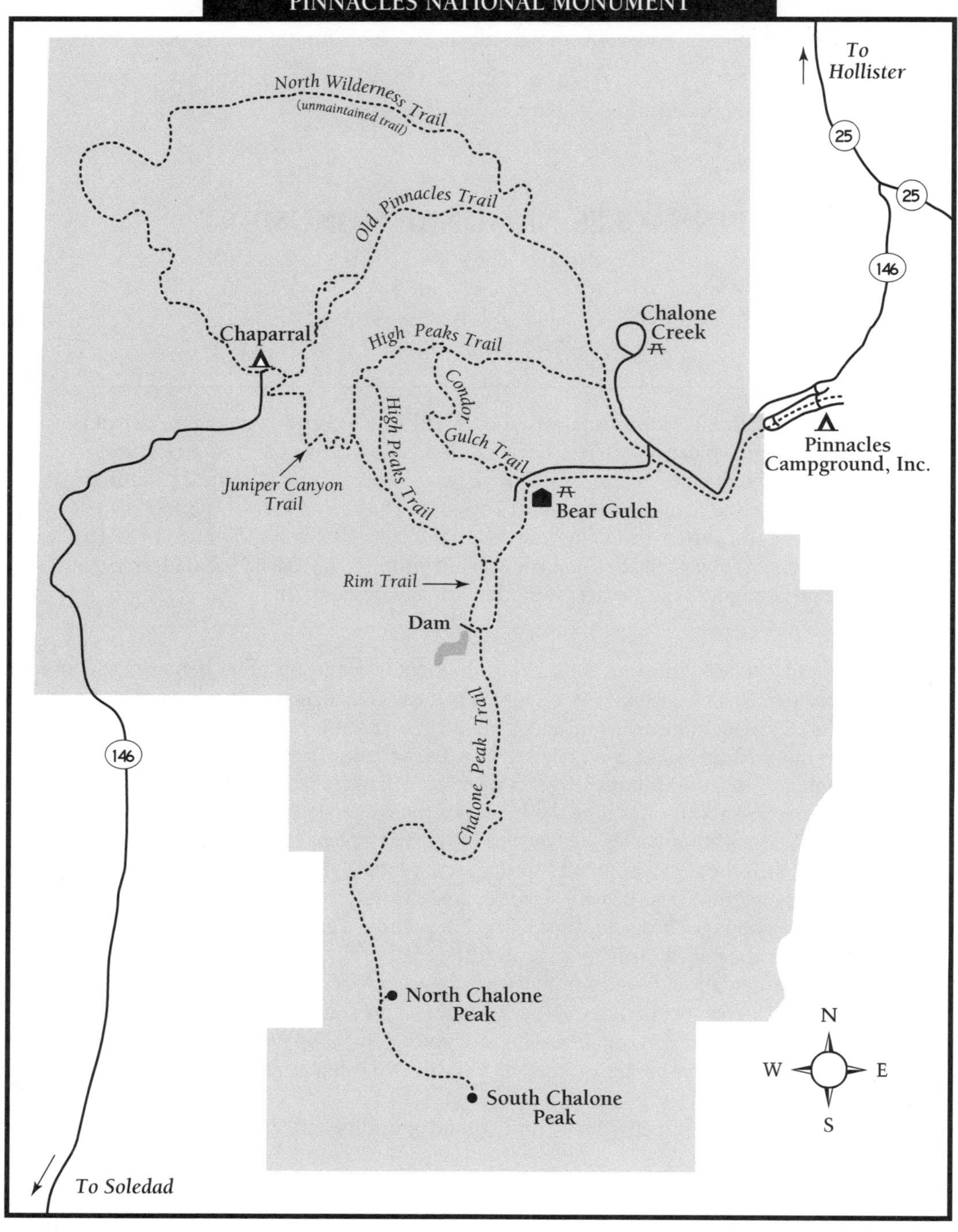
PINNACLES NATIONAL MONUMENT
To Hollister
25
25
146
North Wilderness Trail
(unmaintained trail)
Old Pinnacles Trail
Chalone Creek
Chaparral
High Peaks Trail
Condor Gulch Trail
High Peaks Trail
Juniper Canyon Trail
Pinnacles Campground, Inc.
Bear Gulch
Rim Trail
Dam
Chalone Peak Trail
146
North Chalone Peak
South Chalone Peak
N
W
E
S
To Soledad

•Bear Gulch Trail (1 7/10 miles, one hour) is a self-guided trail connecting the visitor center with the Chalone Creek picnic area.

•Chalone Peak Trail (round-trip: 10 1/2 miles, seven hours) wanders through stands of chapparral on an uphill trip from Bear Gulch to a fire lookout at the top of Chalone Peak.

•Moses Spring Nature Trail (1 3/4 miles, one and a half hours) begins at the parking lot next to the picnic area and leads to the foot of the reservoir dam. The trail is self-guided, and leaflets are available at the visitor center. Return via the Caves Trail, which takes you between and under boulders. (Take a flashlight.)

•Balconies Trail (one way: 1 1/5 miles, two hours) connects Chalone Creek picnic area with Chaparral visitor area on the park's west side. The trail is level and relatively easy to walk.

FACILITIES: No food services or accommodations are available in the monument. A camper store is located just outside the east entrance (short hours during summer weekdays). Drinking water and modern rest rooms are available at the visitor center and in the picnic areas. On the west side, the nearest services are in Soledad.

CAMPING: There are no Park Service campgrounds, although a nice (125 sites) private campground is located just outside the park's east side. The sites offer some shade and are fairly widely spaced. The campground provides tables, grills, hot water, flush toilets, a swimming pool, showers (in poolhouse), and electric hookups. For information or reservations write Pinnacles Campground, Inc., 2400 Highway 146, Paicines, CA 95043 (831–389–4462).

FISHING: No fishing is available in Pinnacles National Monument.

POINT REYES NATIONAL SEASHORE

Point Reyes, CA 94956-9799
(415) 663–1092
www.nps.gov/pore/visit/

Point Reyes was added as a National Park Sevice area in 1962 and has more than 70,000 acres of beaches, lagoons, and forested ridges backed by tall cliffs. The seashore's southern end is located approximately 22 miles northwest of San Francisco via California Highway 1. Park headquarters at Bear Valley is located near the town of Olema, 8 miles from the southern boundary.

Point Reyes National Seashore is a peninsula providing a habitat for more than 400 species of birds, seventy-two species of mammals, many types of other land and marine animals, and a great variety of plant life. The park is an "island" that has been separated from the mainland by the San Andreas Fault. Periodic movement along the fault has resulted in completely different types and ages of rocks on the peninsula as compared with those found on the mainland in the same area. During the 1906 earthquake, land on the west side of the fault moved as much as 21 feet northward. A short self-guided trail (thirty-five minutes) along the fault begins across the parking lot from the Bear Valley Visitor Center.

Park headquarters is located 1/4 mile west of Olema on Bear Valley Road. Here the Bear Valley Visitor Center contains 250 natural history exhibits, an auditorium, 150 plant and animal specimens, and exhibits about the San Andreas Fault. Demonstrations, talks, and nature walks are conducted in the Bear Valley area during summer months. From Bear Valley a paved road heads northwest through Inverness and then splits, with one road going north past Tomales Bay State Park and on to McClures Beach, where tidepools can be seen. The other branch leads to Drakes Beach (a good swimming beach and the point where Sir Francis Drake stopped in 1579 to make repairs to his ship) and Point Reyes. The historic Point Reyes Lighthouse is no longer operating but is open to the public. A visit here is worth the drive, but the long stairway down to the lighthouse requires some effort. Sir Francis Drake Highway is closed at South Beach to Lighthouse and Chimney Rock on weekends and holidays from late December through mid-April. The road to Limantour Beach begins a short distance north of Bear Valley. Watching migrations of the gray whales has become an increasingly popular activity. Peak migrations are in mid-January and mid-March. Whale watching requires a bus ride.

Bear Valley Trailhead, near headquarters, is a gateway to more than 140 miles of trails. The most popular route is the 4 1/10-mile Bear Valley Trail which winds through meadows and forests to the sea. Other trails branch from this main route and ascend into the high country of Inverness Ridge and the southern portion of the seashore. Bicycle use is restricted to designated trails, so riders should check at Bear Valley Visitor Center for specific information. Horses are permitted on most trails. Inquire at the Bear Valley Visitor Center.

FACILITIES: No overnight accommodations or complete food service is available within the park, but both can be found nearby. Drinking water and modern rest rooms are located at park headquarters and at Drakes Beach. Limited food service is available at Drakes Beach.

CAMPING: Four hike-in campgrounds are open year-round. Coast, Sky, Glen Camp, and Wildcat Camp have water, rest rooms, tables, and grills. Sites may be reserved and are always full on weekends and holidays during summer weekends. Reservations can be made up to two months in advance by calling (415) 663–8054, Monday through Friday, 9:00 A.M. to 2:00 P.M. Users must register at Bear Valley Visitor Center and obtain a camping permit. No camping is permitted at Tomales Bay State Park, but a fairly large private campground (415–663–8001) is located on California Highway 1 in Olema. Six miles east of Olema on Sir Francis Drake Highway, Samuel P. Taylor State Park (415–488–9897) provides camping (sixty-eight spaces) with tables, grills, water, flush toilets, and hot showers. The park encompasses a large grove of redwoods.

FISHING: Surf fishing is permitted on all beaches, and a California fishing license is required. No freshwater fishing is available.

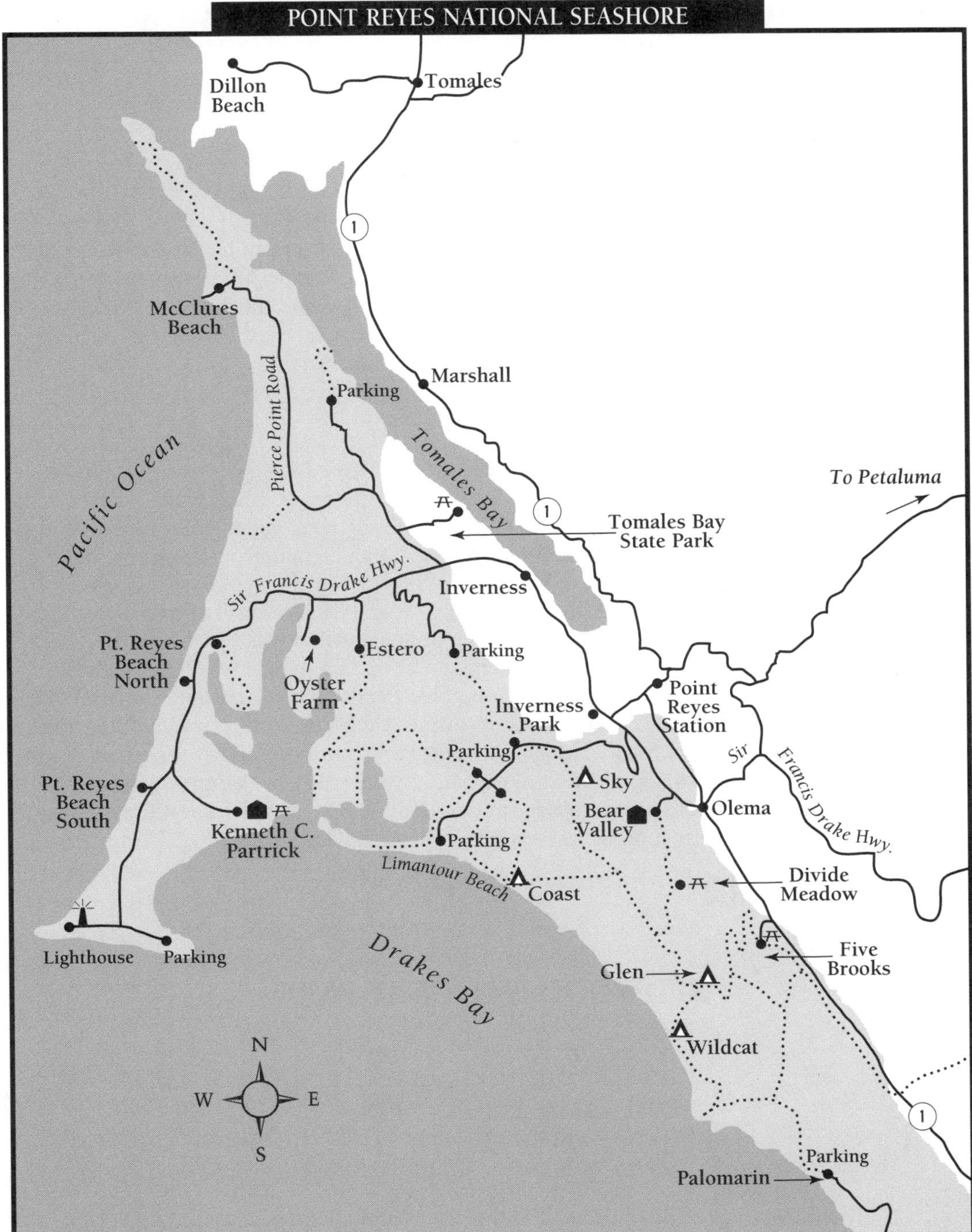
POINT REYES NATIONAL SEASHORE
Dillon Beach
Tomales
1
McClures Beach
Pierce Point Road
Parking
Marshall
Tomales Bay
Pacific Ocean
To Petaluma
1
Tomales Bay State Park
Sir Francis Drake Hwy.
Inverness
Pt. Reyes Beach North
Oyster Farm
Estero
Parking
Inverness Park
Point Reyes Station
Parking
Sky
Pt. Reyes Beach South
Kenneth C. Partrick
Bear Valley
Olema
Sir Francis Drake Hwy.
Parking
Limantour Beach
Coast
Divide Meadow
Lighthouse
Parking
Drakes Bay
Glen
Five Brooks
Wildcat
N
W
E
S
1
Parking
Palomarin

PORT CHICAGO NAVAL MAGAZINE NATIONAL MEMORIAL

c/o Eugene O'Neill National Historic Site
P.O. Box 280
Danville, CA 94526-0280
(925) 838–0249
www.nps.gov/poch/

Port Chicago Naval Magazine National Memorial was authorized in 1992 to recognize the role played by this weapons facility for the Pacific Theater in World War II. It also commemorates the men who worked here and the personnel who lost their lives in a 1944 explosion that occurred here. The memorial is at the Concord Naval Weapons Station near Concord, California.

Construction on Port Chicago commenced in 1942 when the U.S. Navy decided to expand its ability to supply ammunition to the Pacific Theater. By 1944 the facility was being utilized around the clock for loading munitions on ships. African Americans under white officers were assigned to the dangerous duty at Port Chicago. Although the men were members of ordnance battalions, neither they nor their officers had received much training in cargo handling of explosives.

On July 17, 1944, two ships were docked at Port Chicago. One was being prepared for loading while the other was being loaded after returning from its first voyage. Three hundred twenty cargo handlers, crewmen, and sailors were working in the area, which was filled with nearly 5,000 tons of high explosives and incendiary bombs, depth charges, and ammunition. The 10:18 P.M. explosion killed all 320 men on duty, disintegrated one of the ships and the structures around the pier, and damaged every building in Port Chicago. Another 390 people were wounded. Of the 320 men killed in the explosion, 202 were enlisted African Americans.

Access to the site requires a reservation through the United States Navy at Concord Naval Weapons Station. For information or reservations, call (925) 246–5591.

FACILITIES: The National Park Service has no facilities at the memorial.

REDWOOD NATIONAL PARK

1111 Second Street
Crescent City, CA 95531-4198
(707) 464–6101
REDW_management_assistant@nps.gov
www.nps.gov/redw/

Redwood National Park was established in 1968 and comprises nearly 106,000 acres of coastal redwood forests, with ancient groves of trees averaging 500 to 700 years of age and growing to more than 300 feet in height. The park includes 35 miles of rugged and beautiful Pacific shoreline. Redwood National Park lies along U.S. 101 on the extreme northern coast of California. From the east the park is approached on U.S. 199 from Grants Pass, Oregon.

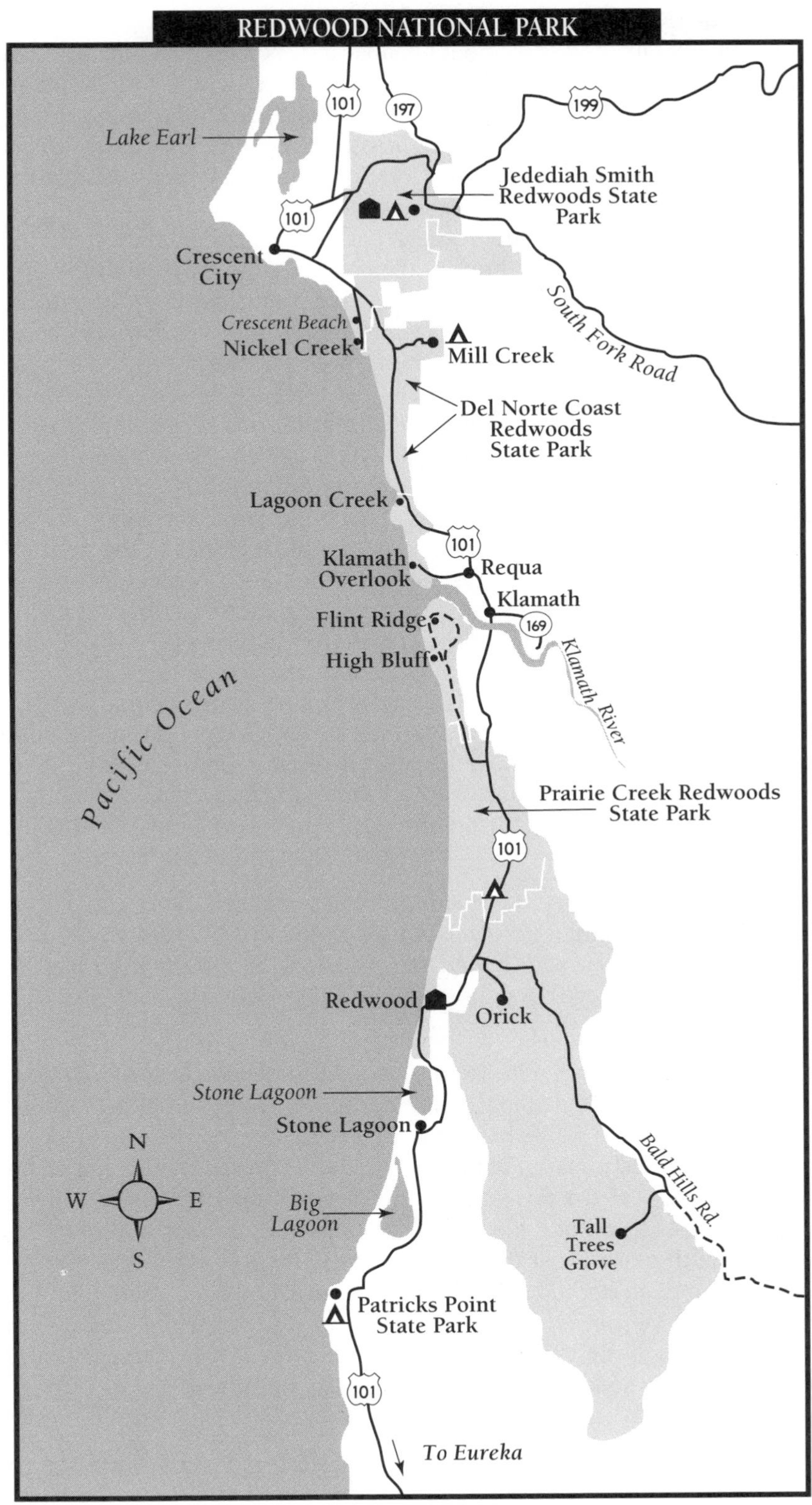
REDWOOD NATIONAL PARK
101
197
199
Lake Earl
Jedediah Smith Redwoods State Park
101
Crescent City
South Fork Road
Crescent Beach
Nickel Creek
Mill Creek
Del Norte Coast Redwoods State Park
Lagoon Creek
101
Klamath Overlook
Requa
Klamath
Flint Ridge
169
High Bluff
Klamath River
Pacific Ocean
Prairie Creek Redwoods State Park
101
Redwood
Orick
Stone Lagoon
Stone Lagoon
N
W
E
S
Bald Hills Rd.
Big Lagoon
Tall Trees Grove
Patricks Point State Park
101
To Eureka

The redwoods of the Pacific Coast are nearly overpowering to someone viewing them for the first time. The world's tallest trees, some individual redwoods live as long as 2,000 years. In addition to the featured redwoods, a visitor will find oak, cedar, and Douglas fir at the higher elevations, cedar, alder, maple, and hemlock along the streams and rivers, and Sitka spruce along the shoreline. Varied wildlife, including Roosevelt elk, fox, bobcat, cougar, black-tailed deer, and black bear, can be found in various locations within the park's boundaries. Birding is a popular activity as well, with both oceangoing and forest birds.

The park encompasses three California state parks (Jedediah Smith, Del Norte Coast, and Prairie Creek Redwoods) established prior to the national park. Approximately 45 miles long, Redwood is only 7 miles wide at its widest point on the south end. U.S. 101 extends the entire length of the park, and additional roads and trails provide access to some of the scenic back-country areas. Bald Hills Road, near the south entrance at Orick, leads to Lady Bird Johnson Grove and the Redwood Creek trailhead. One of the more scenic drives begins near Klamath on Coastal Drive. This 8-mile road along bluffs and headlands is part gravel. Near the park's north entrance, the unpaved Howland Hill Road winds its way through a lush redwood forest and leads to the Stout Grove along the wild and scenic Smith River.

Numerous hiking trails are scattered throughout the park, including the 35-mile-long Coastal Trail System between Crescent Beach in the north and Orick in the south. Viewpoints, exhibits, and beach access are provided as the trail winds along bluffs overlooking the Pacific Ocean. The Redwood Creek Trail, east of Orick, provides an 8½-mile path to the Tall Trees Grove. This grove contains some of the tallest known trees in the world, including a twin-trunk giant towering 366.3 feet in height. The grove is also reached via a 17-mile drive from the Redwood Information Center and a 3-mile round-trip hike. A free permit for the access road can be obtained at the information center. One mile beyond Redwood Creek trailhead, visitors may park and take a slow ½-mile walk to the park's dedication site at Lady Bird Johnson Grove. This includes a self-guided nature trail. Park rangers present evening programs and guided walks in summer throughout the park. Information centers are located at Hiouchi, Crescent City, and Orick.

FACILITIES: A number of motels and food outlets are available along U.S. Highway 101. A hostel is located 17 miles south of Crescent City (707–482–8265). Most modern accommodations are in towns located near park boundaries, Crescent City to the north and Orick to the south. Eureka, a relatively large town, is approximately 45 miles south of the park's south entrance.

CAMPING: Four walk-in campgrounds are provided by Redwood National Park, and four drive-in camping areas are provided in the state parks. Depending on individual taste, a visitor might enjoy camping at Gold Bluffs Beach on the Pacific Ocean. This site is located near the south entrance via a 5-mile unpaved road. The location is breezy and cool in summer. Prairie Creek Campground is located a few miles north of Orick on Highway 101. Two additional campgrounds at the north end of the park can be reserved by calling (800) 444–7275.

Twenty miles south of Orick, at the south entrance, Patricks Point State Park contains an improved campground. In addition, Six Rivers National Forest contains four campgrounds with a total of eighty-seven sites for tents, campers, and small trailers. These are located about thirty minutes east of Highway 101 on U.S. 199. Other, more distant, campgrounds are located in Klamath and Trinity national forests. Camping is also available at private campgrounds and trailer parks along Highway 101.

FISHING: This is an excellent area for salmon and steelhead trout. Surfcasting for red-tail perch is also a popular activity. A California fishing license is mandatory for both ocean and freshwater fishing. California regulations apply throughout the area.

SAN FRANCISCO MARITIME NATIONAL HISTORICAL PARK

Fort Mason
San Francisco, CA 94123
(415) 556–3002
www.nps.gov/safr/

This park of fifty acres was established in 1988 to preserve and celebrate the maritime history of the Pacific Coast. The historical park includes museum exhibits, historic ships, an aquatic park, research collections, and a maritime store. San Francisco Maritime National Historical Park is located just west of Fisherman's Wharf on San Francisco Bay in the city of San Francisco. The park is best reached via public transportation (municipal bus or the Powell and Hyde cable car), as parking is in short supply in this area of the city.

A visit to San Francisco Maritime National Historical Park is a trip to this historic city's past. The heart of the park is the Maritime Museum (415–556–2904) near the terminus of Beach Street across from Ghirardelli Square. Here visitors will find exhibits on the technology of steamships, models of historic ships, and exhibits from the days of the California Gold Rush.

Hyde Street Pier (415–556–3002) is the location of five historic merchant ships, including a vessel that carried lumber from the Pacific Northwest (1895), a sidewheel ferry (1890), an oceangoing tug (1907), a paddle tug (1914), and the last San Francisco Bay scow schooner still afloat (1891). The Maritime Store (415–775–2665) at the entrance of Hyde Street Pier contains books, posters, cards, and gifts appropriate to maritime history.

Within walking distance of the Hyde Street Pier is a World War II submarine (Pier 45, east of Fisherman's Wharf) and the last unaltered survivor of 2,751 World War II Liberty Ships (Pier 3, west of the Municipal Pier). For those with more time, a 3½-mile walk along the shoreline from the museum to Fort Point provides both exercise and relaxation.

Fort Mason Center contains three research collections, which include an extensive maritime library, archives, manuscripts, logbooks, ship plans, and historic photographs. Park personnel schedule numerous activities including talks, guided walks, ship tours, and classes and workshops. Visitors should check at the museum for a current schedule.

FACILITIES: Food and lodging are abundant in the wharf area. Although natives normally stay away from this area, many visitors enjoy trying seafood offered by the many outdoor vendors. An American Youth Hostel at Fort Mason (415–771–7277) provides low-cost lodging for recreational travelers of all ages. Visitors may picnic in Aquatic Park at the terminus of the Powell and Hyde cable car.

CAMPING: See the camping section under Golden Gate National Recreation Area (California).

FISHING: Fishing is permitted along the waterfront.

SANTA MONICA MOUNTAINS NATIONAL RECREATION AREA

401 West Hillcrest Drive
Thousand Oaks, CA 91360
(805) 370–2301
www.nps.gov/samo/

Santa Monica Mountains National Recreation Area was established in 1978 and comprises 150,000 acres of rugged landscape and shoreline within easy reach of millions of nearby residents. The park is located between the cities of Los Angeles and Oxnard in an east–west corridor bordered on the north by U.S. 101 and on the south by the Pacific Ocean.

Santa Monica Mountains NRA is the culmination of years of effort toward the goal of establishing parklands and preserving open spaces in a heavily populated and rapidly growing area. The Santa Monica Mountains are a coastal range stretching 46 miles west of Los Angeles. The area contains mountains, grasslands, oak woodlands, freshwater and saltwater marshes, and plunging waterfalls. Wildlife includes mountain lions, deer, bobcats, red-tailed hawks, and golden eagles. The park visitor center, located at 401 West Hillcrest Drive in Thousand Oaks, offers information on recreation opportunities available in the mountains including maps and guidebooks. Exhibits and film displays are also available. One excellent way of seeing much of the recreation area is to drive 54 winding miles through the park on scenic Mulholland Drive/Highway.

With the widespread nature and diversity of activities available in the park, it is impossible to provide even a short sketch of each point of interest. Some of the more popular locations are listed below. Locations preceded with an asterisk (*) are National Park Service facilities.

**Cheeseboro/Palo Comado Canyon:* Over 20 miles of trails will take you through a valley of oak savanna, rugged rocky canyons, and rolling grasslands.

**Circle X Ranch:* Offers camping for individuals and groups. Spectacular backcountry with trails to mountain peaks.

Point Mugu State Park (818–880–0350): Beaches, cliffs, picnic areas, and campgrounds along 5 miles of ocean shoreline. This park provides 70 miles of hiking and riding trails through canyons and across rugged uplands.

Franklin Canyon Ranch (310–858–3090): A few miles north of Sunset Boulevard; offers trails, picnicking, and an opportunity to observe wildlife in a natural oasis surrounded by the city.

Leo Carrillo State Beach (818–880–0350): More than a mile of ocean beach fronted by cave-riddled bluffs. Three campgrounds for tenters and RV owners.

**Rancho Sierra Vista/Satwiwa:* A 1,151-acre site with hiking trails, a Native American Culture Center, and picnic areas.

**Paramount Ranch:* A 760-acre area that features a western town movie set, opportunities for watching filming, and places for walking, horseback riding, and picnicking.

Malibu Creek State Park (818–880–0350): An area of rugged cliffs and gorges, slopes of chaparral, grasslands, and live oak groves. Fifteen miles of hiking and riding trails wind through the park.

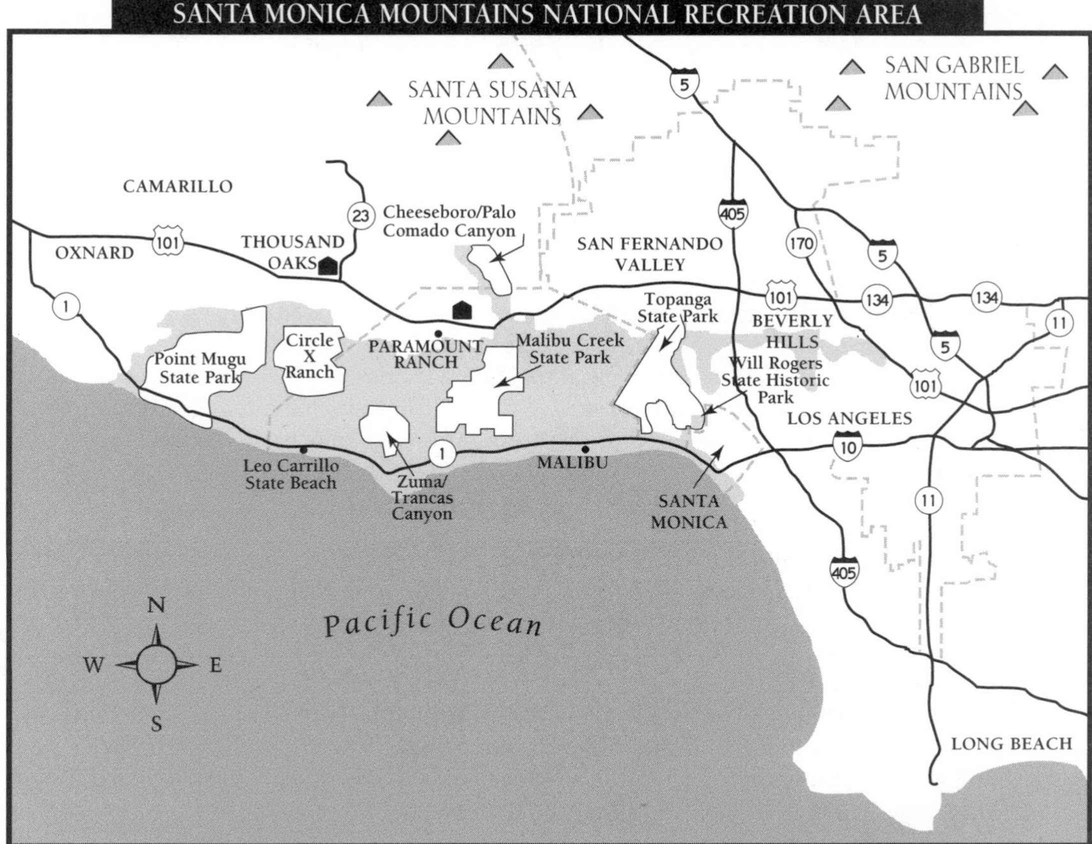

Will Rogers State Historic Park (310–454–8212): Will Rogers' home for the seven years prior to his death in 1935, the park has a visitor center, nature center, and hiking trails in addition to the historic grounds and ranch house.

**Zuma/Trancas Canyon:* A 5,859-acre site offering critical wildlife habitat in the heart of the Santa Monica Mountains. Hiking trails lead through this undeveloped area.

FACILITIES: A variety of facilities, including food and lodging, are available along roads through and bordering the park.

CAMPING: Camping is available in Point Mugu State Park (140 spaces), Malibu Creek State Park (sixty spaces), and Leo Carrillo State Beach (135 spaces). All three parks can accept trailers and campers of up to 31 feet. From March through September, reservations are requested (800–444–7275).

FISHING: Limited fishing is available throughout the park with a California fishing license. The most popular areas are the beaches and the public pier in Santa Monica.

WHISKEYTOWN–SHASTA–TRINITY NATIONAL RECREATION AREA

P.O. Box 188
Whiskeytown, CA 96095-0188
(530) 241–6584
www.nps.gov/whis/

Whiskeytown–Shasta–Trinity NRA was established in 1965 and comprises 403,000 acres of some of the most beautiful scenery in northern California. Whiskeytown Lake, the only one of the three areas operated by the National Park Service, is an excellent source of water-related activities. The lake is located in north-central California, approximately 230 miles from San Francisco. The three-unit area is bisected by Interstate 5, running from Sacramento, California, to Portland, Oregon.

Clair A. Hill Whiskeytown Dam and Whiskeytown Lake are on Clear Creek, a tributary of the Sacramento River, and are designed to store and regulate imported water of the Bureau of Reclamation's Central Valley Project. Water enters the area through pipes to the Judge Francis J. Carr Powerplant at the northwest tip of the lake. Surplus water is either released through another tunnel to the Keswick Powerplant or diverted back into Clear Creek through bilevel outlets in the earthfill dam. The outlets allow the Bureau of Reclamation to regulate temperature for the maximum benefit of the salmon and steelhead trout that use Clear Creek as a spawning ground. Below the dam, on the south side of the lake, Clear Creek winds through steep gorges and rocky hills. Gold was discovered near here in the 1800s.

The Clair Engle and Shasta lake areas extend into Shasta and Trinity national forests and are administered by the U.S. Forest Service. Write Shasta–Trinity National Forest, 2400 Washington Avenue, Redding, CA 96001 or call (530) 246–5112 for information on these areas. Trinity and Shasta dams are north of Redding, approximately 40 miles and 10 miles, respectively.

The five square miles of open water, extensive shoreline, and numerous coves make Whiskeytown Lake an inviting place for nearly any type of water activity. Boat-launching ramps are provided at Whiskey Creek, Brandy Creek, and Oak Bottom, but swimming beaches are available only at the latter two locations. The lake's shallow areas begin to warm by late May or early June, but deeper waters remain cold all year.

About 50 miles of backcountry roads are open for use. These are graded dirt and gravel, although many require four-wheel-drive vehicles. The summit of Shasta Bally (6,209 feet) is 5,000 feet above lake level and may be reached on foot or by four-wheel-drive auto. More detailed information on backcountry road conditions can be obtained at the visitor information center just off Highway 299 on the east side of the lake.

FACILITIES: Snack bars, camper stores, and boat rentals are available at Oak Bottom and Brandy Creek in summer. Restaurants and overnight accommodations are available 8 miles east in Redding. Modern rest rooms are located at both marinas and beaches, the information station, and Oak Bottom Campground.

CAMPING: Brandy Creek (thirty-seven spaces) has no rest rooms and is for self-contained vehicles only. Oak Bottom (22 RV sites, 101 tent sites) has flush toilets, pay showers, water, and a dump station, and tables and grills are provided at tent sites. Cold showers are provided at the beach. The best camping at Oak Bottom is for tenters, because all other camping units are required to stay in a paved parking facility that has no shade, tables, or grills. The dump stations at Brandy Creek and Oak Bottom are open year-round. For groups, Dry Creek has camping with pit toilets. Reservations are required.

FISHING: Fishing is good either from a boat or from shore. The lake is stocked with rainbow and brown trout. Largemouth, smallmouth, and spotted bass, and kokanee are also available in the lake. A California fishing license is required.

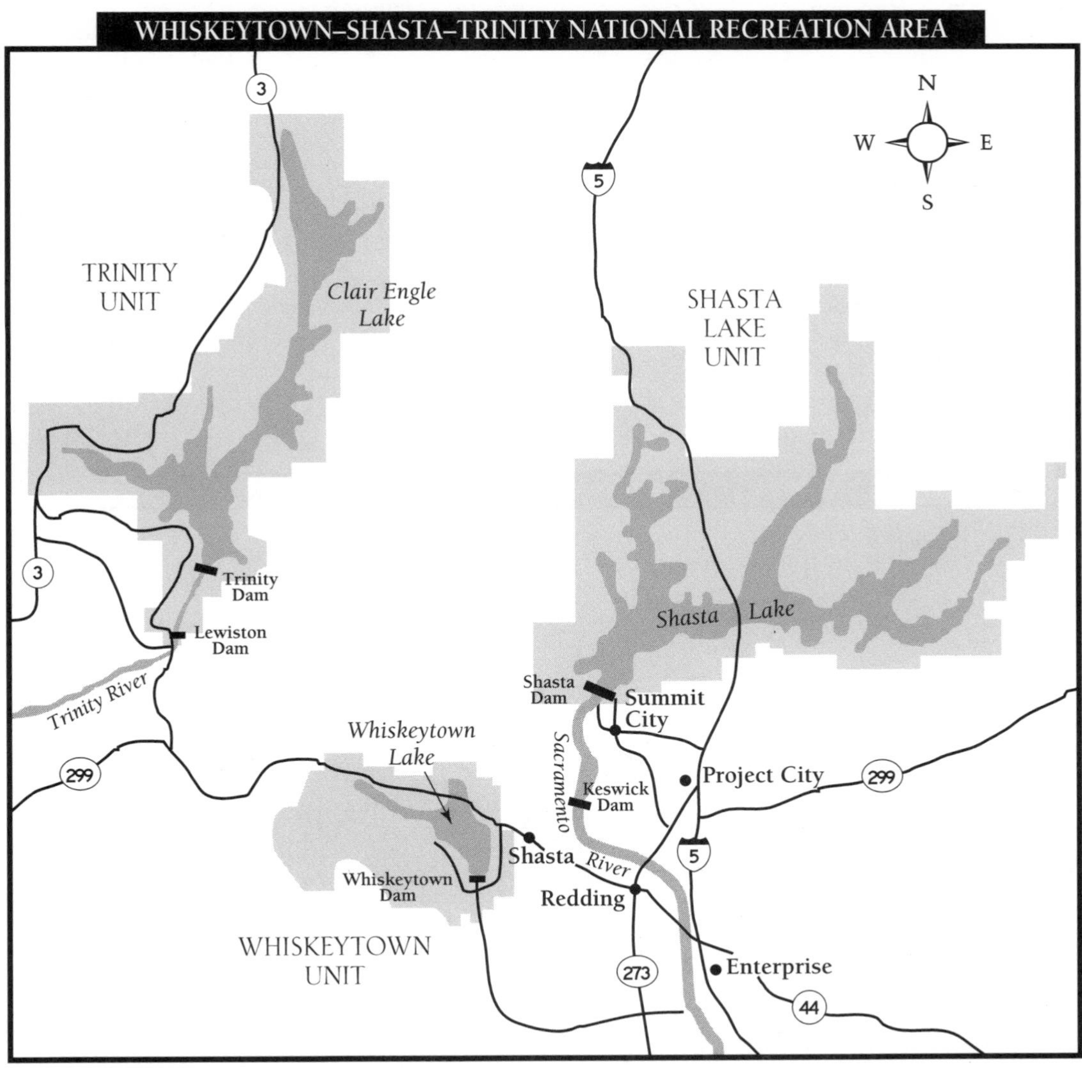

YOSEMITE NATIONAL PARK

P.O. Box 577
Yosemite National Park, CA 95389-0577
(209) 372–0200
www.nps.gov/yose/

Yosemite National Park was established in 1890 and comprises what may be the most beautiful 747,956 acres in the United States. Granite peaks and domes rise above green or snow-covered meadows in the heart of the Sierra Nevada. The park is located in east-central California, approximately 190 miles due east of San Francisco via California Highway 120 east and west, Highway 140 from Merced, and Highway 41 from Fresno. While in the Yosemite area, consider exploring California Highway 49 on the park's west side. Here you will wander through many areas made famous by gold-seekers in 1849. On the park's east side, the ghost town of Bodie, near Mono Lake, is super. Bodie is a state park managed by the California State Department of Parks and Recreation.

Yosemite represents all that is good and most that is bad about the National Park System. The scenery is quite possibly the best of any national park. Yosemite contains beautiful valleys, high-country meadows, sparkling lakes, and spectacular waterfalls. The park's elevations range from 2,000 feet to more than 13,000 feet above sea level, which produces an outstanding variety of both animal and plant life. The bad part is that because of the area's beauty, visitors and campers have loved parts of the park nearly to death. Yosemite Valley is especially heavily used. Bears can be a problem, and visitors are advised to remove food, trash, and odorous items from vehicles. Food storage lockers are available.

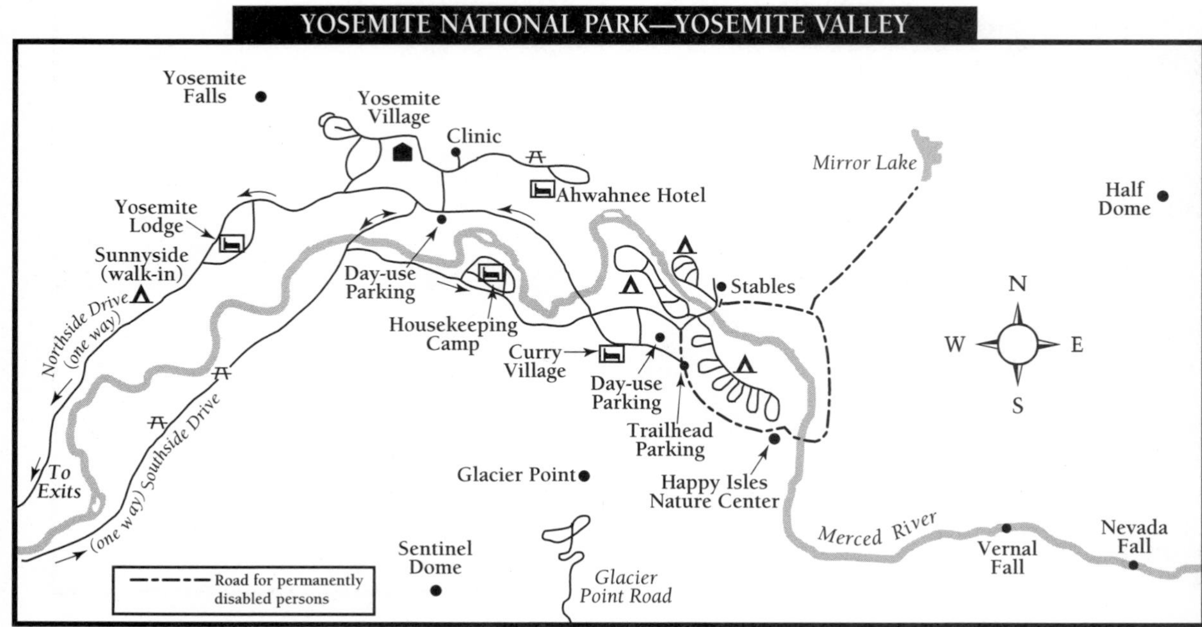

Valley View, Yosemite Valley (opposite page)

There are four major entrances into Yosemite National Park—three from the west and one from the east. A single road—Tioga Road—bisects the park in an east–west direction. To experience the high elevations, it is necessary to use the road because the high country is toward the east side and away from Yosemite Valley. The road is closed from mid-November through early June from Crane Flat to the Tioga Pass entrance..

Most organized activity at Yosemite is in Yosemite Valley. Yosemite Village contains a visitor center and most modern conveniences that can be found in any small town. The entrance road follows the Merced River to all the main buildings and valley campgrounds. A free shuttle-bus service in the east end of the Valley greatly simplifies getting around the congested Valley floor. This service was introduced to reduce auto emissions and congestion. Parking is available at Curry Village and Yosemite Village for day-use visitors. The valley is open all year and contains often-photographed features such as El Capitan, Half Dome, Yosemite Falls, and Bridalveil Fall. The falls are most active in the early summer months.

Although most visitors spend the majority of time in the Valley, Yosemite contains many other worthwhile features. A large grove of giant sequoias is located near the south entrance. Two smaller giant sequoia groves can be found near Crane Flat on the west side of the park. Near the south entrance at Wawona is the Pioneer Yosemite History Center—an exhibit of historic buildings, horse-drawn vehicles, and, during summers, living-history demonstrations.

Fifty-five miles from the Valley across Tioga Road is Tuolumne Meadows. At an elevation of 8,600 feet, this is the largest subalpine meadow in the High Sierra. It is also a center for high-country pack trips and hikes.

Perhaps the best-known activity at Yosemite is rock climbing. A lesser-known but equally exciting activity is hang gliding. This sport is permitted under special regulations. If these are too dangerous, visitors can try some of the 800 miles of hiking trails. Guided horse rides are available at Wawona, Yosemite Valley, and Tuolumne Meadows during summer months. Swimming is available in the park's rivers or at lodge swimming pools. Nightly interpretive programs are available at campgrounds and at concessioner facilities.

Winter activities at Yosemite include downhill skiing at Badger Pass with four lifts, one rope tow, a rental shop, and ski school. Several trails are available for cross-country skiing, and a guide map is available. Other winter activities include snowshoeing, ice skating at Curry Village, and guided trips at Badger Pass. Glacier Park Road from Badger Pass to Glacier Point is closed from late fall to late spring.

LODGING: Seven lodging facilities of varying quality and price are situated within Yosemite. Yosemite Lodge, Curry Village, the Ahwahnee, and Housekeeping Camp are in Yosemite Valley. The Ahwahnee is the most upscale of the four, while Housekeeping Camp offers canvas and cement structures for a relatively inexpensive camping-type experience. The grand Wawona Hotel is outside the Valley, toward the park's south entrance. White Wolf Lodge and Tuolumne Meadows Lodge offer tent cabins and a few regular cabins on Tioga Pass. For reservations at any of these facilities, write Yosemite Reservations, 5410 East Home Avenue, Fresno, CA 93727, or call (559) 252–4848. Yosemite's facilities, especially those in Yosemite Valley, are packed during summer months, so it is necessary to make reservations early.

FACILITIES: Nearly anything can be found somewhere in Yosemite. Lodging, restaurants, and stores are located at Wawona, El Portal, Tuolumne Meadows, White Wolf, and in Yosemite Valley. Reservations are advised for all overnight accommodations. Dental and medical facilities are provided in Yosemite Valley at Yosemite Medical Clinic. A self-service laundry is open year-round at Housekeeping Camp, and pay showers are available at Curry Village. Filling stations can be found summer only at Tuolumne Meadows and at Wawona and Crane Flat all year. The Valley also includes a kennel. Tours are available.

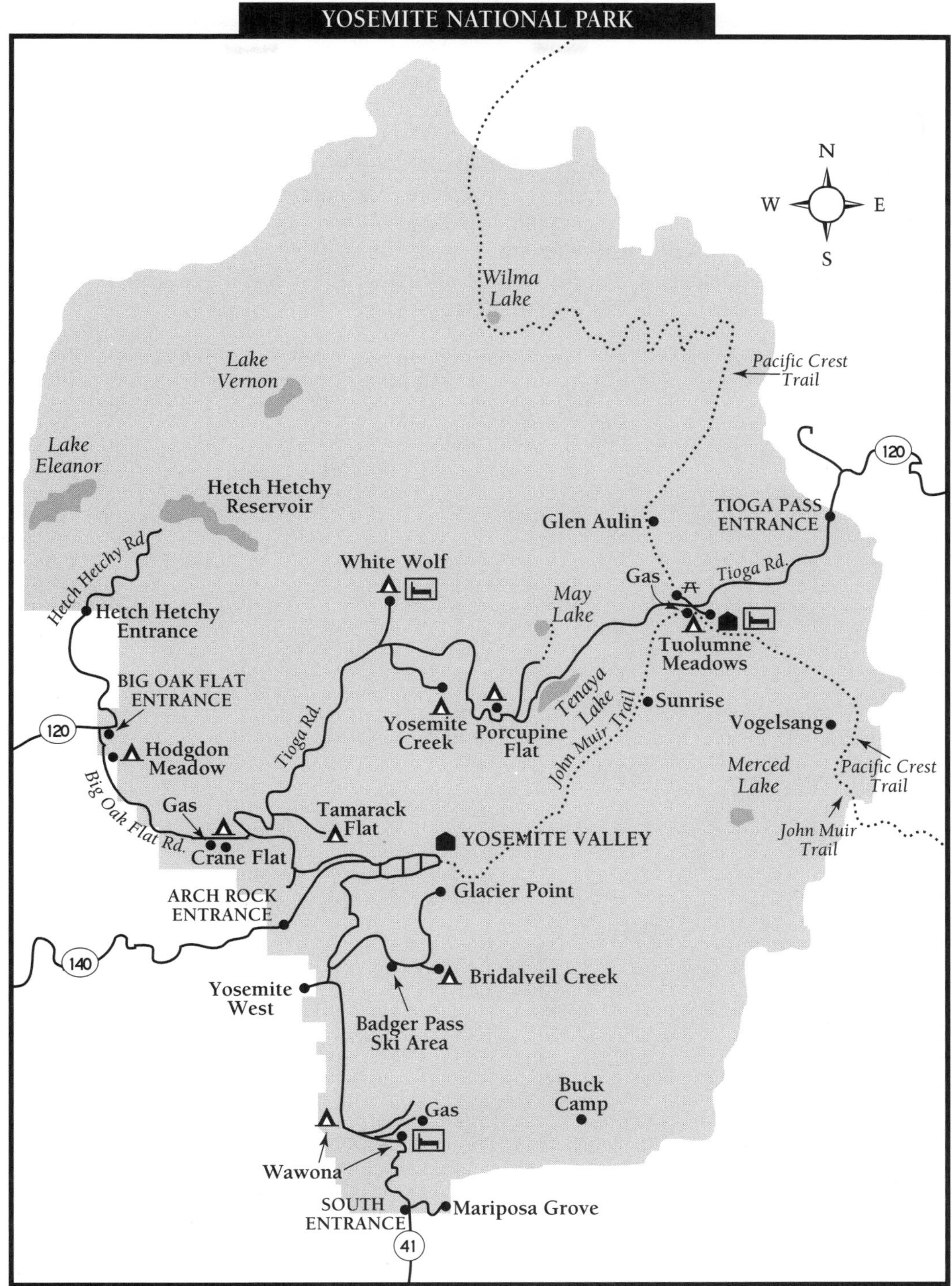
YOSEMITE NATIONAL PARK
N
W
E
S
Wilma Lake
Pacific Crest Trail
Lake Vernon
Lake Eleanor
Hetch Hetchy Reservoir
120
Glen Aulin
TIOGA PASS ENTRANCE
Hetch Hetchy Rd.
White Wolf
Gas
Tioga Rd.
May Lake
Hetch Hetchy Entrance
Tuolumne Meadows
BIG OAK FLAT ENTRANCE
Tenaya Lake
Tioga Rd.
Sunrise
John Muir Trail
120
Yosemite Creek
Porcupine Flat
Vogelsang
Hodgdon Meadow
Merced Lake
Pacific Crest Trail
Big Oak Flat Rd.
Gas
Tamarack Flat
John Muir Trail
Crane Flat
YOSEMITE VALLEY
ARCH ROCK ENTRANCE
Glacier Point
140
Bridalveil Creek
Yosemite West
Badger Pass Ski Area
Buck Camp
Gas
Wawona
SOUTH ENTRANCE
Mariposa Grove
41

CAMPING: Developed campgrounds are located throughout the park, with the four in the Valley usually filling very early. There are nearly 420 spaces in Yosemite Valley, with the largest campgrounds at Upper Pines (240 spaces) and Lower Pines (sixty spaces). Upper Pines is open all year. All of these have picnic tables, fire rings, and flush toilets, and each is near a shuttle-bus stop. Dump stations are located at the Upper Pines campground. The Valley campgrounds are very crowded, sometimes resembling giant parking lots. The park's other improved campgrounds are at Bridalveil Creek (110 spaces), Crane Flat (166 spaces), Hodgdon Meadow (105 spaces), Tuolumne Meadows (314 spaces), Wawona (100 spaces, store, and dump station nearby), and White Wolf (eighty-seven spaces). Unimproved campgrounds are located at Porcupine Flat (fifty-two spaces), Tamarack Flat (fifty-two spaces), and Yosemite Creek (seventy-five spaces). Reservations for Valley campsites are advised. Call (800) 432–7275. A limited number of campsites made available by cancellations are offered on a first-come, first-served basis at a small station in the day-use parking area near Curry Village.

FISHING: Five species of trout—brook, brown, cutthroat, golden, and rainbow—are found in Yosemite waters. Rainbow and brown are most abundant. A state fishing license is required, and the season is from the last Saturday in April to mid-November. Inquire at park visitor centers or information stations for park-specific fishing regulations.

COLORADO

STATE TOURIST INFORMATION
(800) 265–6723

BENT'S OLD FORT NATIONAL HISTORIC SITE

35110 Highway 194 East
La Junta, CO 81050-9523
(719) 383–5010
www.nps.gov/beol/

Bent's Old Fort National Historic Site comprises 800 acres and became part of the National Park Service in 1960 to commemorate a principal Anglo-American outpost on the Southwestern Plains in the early 1800s. The park is in southeastern Colorado, 8 miles east of La Junta and 15 miles west of Las Animas on Colorado Highway 194.

The early 1800s saw an influx of traders into the Santa Fe and Taos area of what is now New Mexico. Caravans from Independence, Missouri, the main staging point, traveled to Santa Fe by two routes. The main trail ran across the Kansas plains to the Cimarron Crossing of the Arkansas River. At this point the trail broke into two branches. The Cimarron Cutoff crossed the Comanche-inhabited Cimarron Desert and offered little water. The Mountain Branch continued along the Arkansas River and turned southwest near Timpas Creek. The second route was longer, but it offered greater safety and more trees and water.

It was on the Mountain Branch that the two Bent brothers and partner Ceran St. Vrain decided in the early 1830s to build a trading establishment. Because of the location, the men knew that a strong fort would be required. The enclosed adobe structure took many men years to construct.

Over a period of years, the merchants became trusted friends of the Indians and built a booming business. Finished goods were brought to the fort from St. Louis, where they were exchanged for buffalo robes and beaver pelts. The men opened additional stores in Santa Fe and Taos. The annexation of Texas in 1845 brought turmoil to the region because U.S. troops

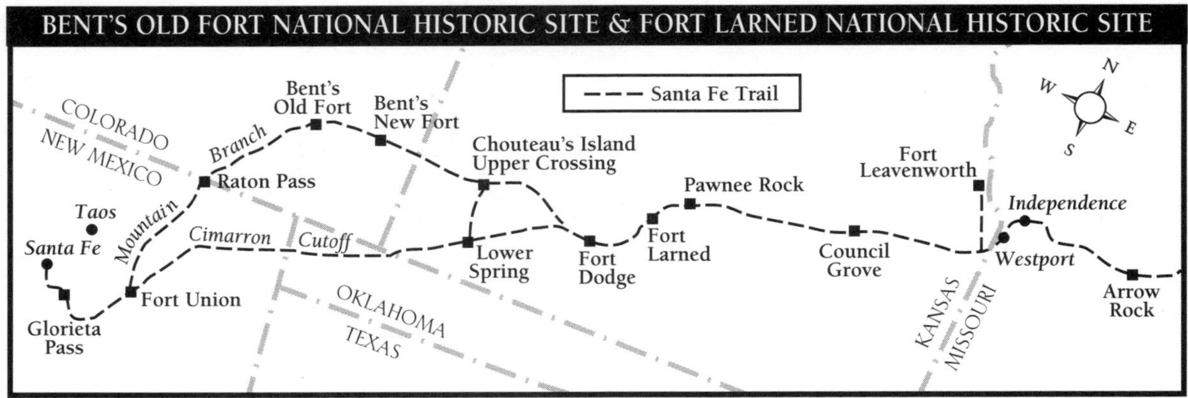

used the fort as a staging area for invasions of New Mexico. The influx of soldiers, settlers, and adventurers resulted in conflict with the once-peaceful Indians, and trade eventually came to a halt. It is thought that reduced trade and a cholera epidemic among the Indians caused William Bent to set fire to the fort and move 38 miles down the Arkansas River. There he built a structure that became known as Bent's New Fort (hence, the present name for the initial structure). Although the old fort was temporarily rehabilitated for use as a stage station, it was once again abandoned so that by the early 1900s, only parts of the old walls were still standing.

During 1975 and 1976, Bent's Old Fort was reconstructed on the original foundation to its 1845–46 appearance. Interpretive Park Service and volunteer personnel are on duty daily inside the fort. Guided walks and a twenty-minute film are offered periodically throughout the day.

FACILITIES: Water and rest rooms are located in the reconstructed fort. Food services and lodging are found in La Junta and Las Animas.

CAMPING: No camping is permitted in the park. Private campgrounds are nearby in La Junta. For travelers on Highway 50, the Corps of Engineers' John Martin Reservoir provides pleasant camping (fifty-one mostly shaded sites, water, flush toilets, no showers, no hookups) 3 miles south of the town of Hasty. Hasty is approximately 32 miles east of Bent's Old Fort.

FISHING: No fishing is available in the park. Fishing is permitted at John Martin Reservoir. (See camping section.)

BLACK CANYON OF THE GUNNISON NATIONAL PARK

102 Elk Creek
Gunnison, CO 81230
(970) 641–2337
cure_vis_mail@nps.gov
www.nps.gov/blca/

Black Canyon of the Gunnison was added to the park system in 1933 to preserve 12 miles of a spectacular and unspoiled canyon that has been cut by the Gunnison River. The park is located in west-central Colorado, with both rims accessible by automobile. The north rim is reached over a 14-mile road (6 miles of gravel) originating from Colorado Highway 92, east of Crawford. The south rim is 5 miles north of U.S. 50 via a paved road beginning 6 miles east of Montrose.

The Black Canyon has been formed over a period of two million years by the continuous erosive forces of the Gunnison River. The river and its seasonal floods have produced a canyon with depths ranging from 1,730 to 2,689 feet and widths of as little as 1,100 feet (at Chasm View). The erosive Gunnison has cut faster than its tributaries, resulting in canyons hanging

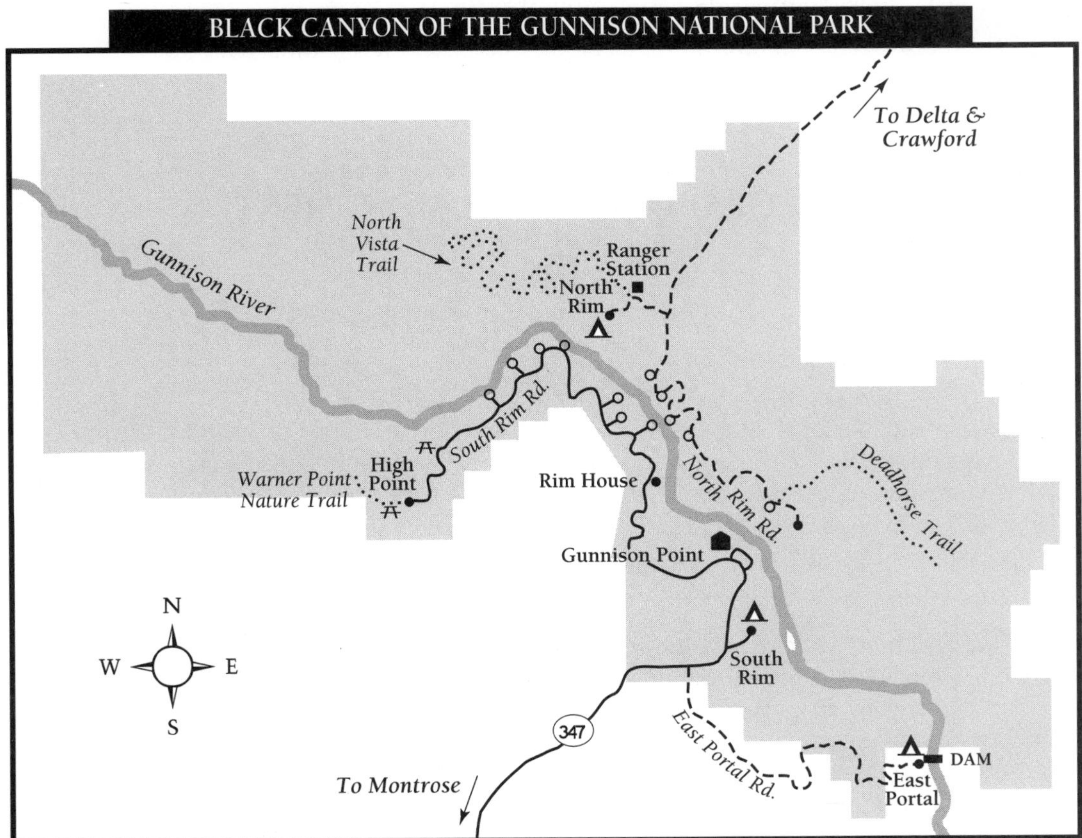

high over the main gorge. The walls are mostly Precambrian rock, from light to dark gray in color—hence, the name. In many places pinkish granite intrusions provide colorful highlights, as can be seen on the "Painted Wall."

The river established its course by cutting through soft volcanic rocks. It then continued to carve into the hard crystalline rocks of the present canyon. Pinnacles in the eastern area of the park have been created with the assistance of the river, as its flow followed the layers of less resistant rock.

Visitors should first stop at the visitor center, where information and exhibits on the life and geology of the park are available. The paved road following the south rim is seldom more than 1/4 mile from the canyon. Spectacular views are available from numerous short foot trails, beginning from parking areas along the road's side. Interpretive signs are generally located at the end of each trail, and a self-guiding trail is located at Cedar Point. Trail booklets are available for the Rim Rock Trail (starting at the South Rim Campground) and the Warner Nature Trail (starting at High Point). During summer months, conducted walks and evening programs take place in the park.

FACILITIES: No overnight accommodations are available at the park, but they can be found in nearby communities. Rim House on the south rim provides lunches, refreshments, souvenirs, and limited camping supplies during summer months. No facilities are available on the north rim.

CAMPING: The park contains two campgrounds. North Rim Campground (thirteen spaces) at Chasm View provides tables, grills, water (trucked in), and pit toilets. South Rim Campground (102 spaces) has similar facilities. Both campgrounds are open from May through October. Commercial campgrounds are located in Montrose.

FISHING: Brown and rainbow trout inhabit the Gunnison River, although access is difficult. A Colorado fishing license is required.

COLORADO NATIONAL MONUMENT

Fruita, CO 81521-9530
(970) 858–3617
COLM_Superintendent@nps.gov
www.nps.gov/colm/

Colorado National Monument was established as part of the National Park System in 1911. The park comprises 20,454 acres of steep-walled canyons and monoliths, in a beautiful sandstone region. The park is located in west-central Colorado, just west of the city of Grand Junction via Interstate 70 or U.S. Highways 6 and 50.

Many western movie scenes shot in Monument Valley, Arizona, could just as easily have been filmed in Colorado National Monument. Water, wind, and freezing have produced some spectacular red canyons. Even though the area's annual 11-inch rainfall is relatively sparse, it generally occurs in concentrated bursts of such intensity as to have a pronounced effect on the landscape. Monument Canyon, in the park's northern end, is one of Colorado National Monument's most impressive areas.

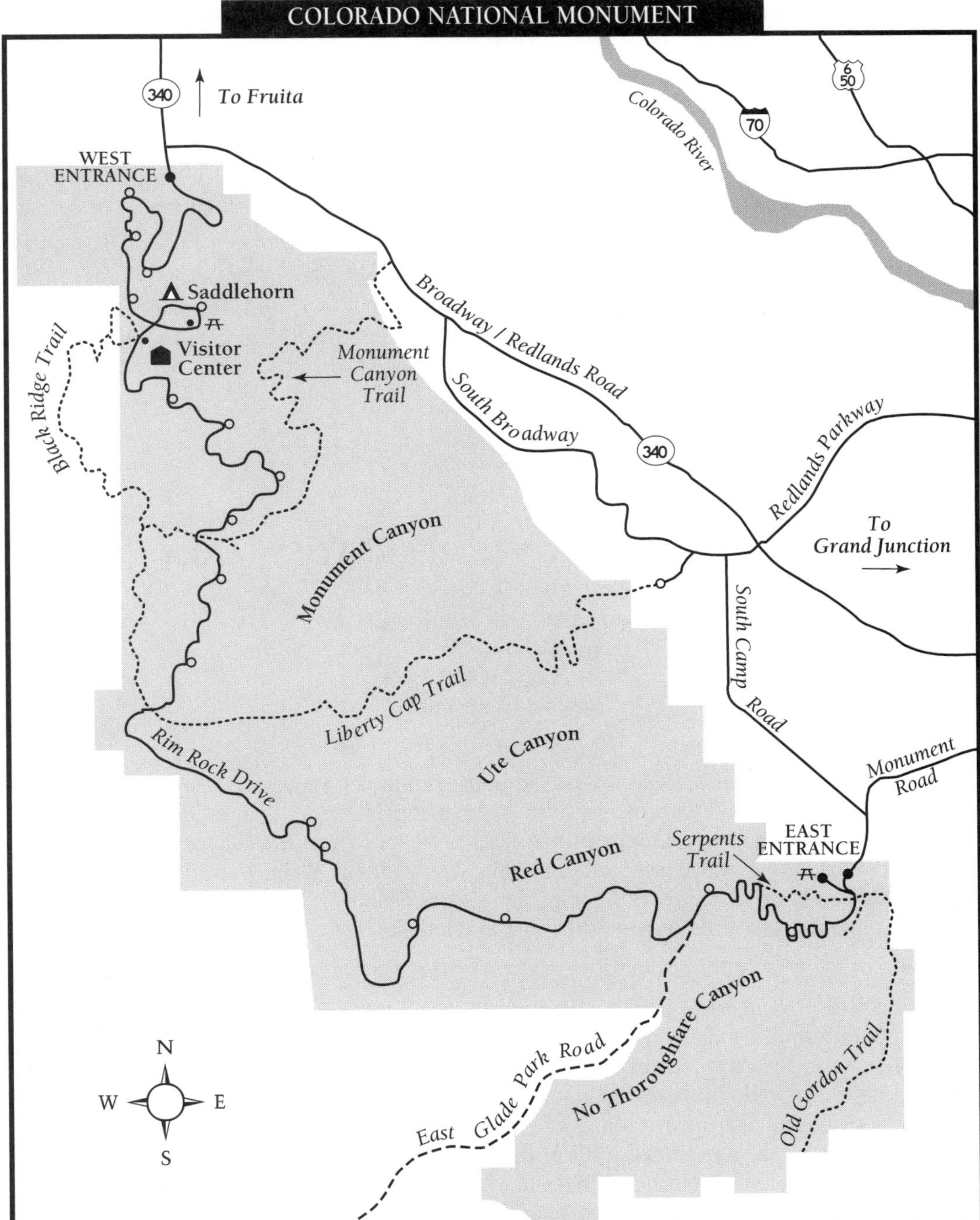

Rim Rock Drive is a 23-mile, narrow, winding, paved road that connects the east and west entrances. The drive is one of the finest offered in any park in the country. Visitors will see many outstanding formations, and a number of parking overlooks are provided. A visitor center near the west entrance is open all year and provides a slide program and exhibits that explain the monument's history and geological formations. It is best to drive the park road from west to east so that the visitor center can be a first stop.

A number of hiking trails provide access to the park's interior. Trails include 2¼-mile Serpents Trail near Devils Kitchen Picnic Area and the longer Monument Canyon (6 miles), Black Ridge (5½ miles), and Liberty Cap (7 miles) trails. There are a number of short trails, including the self-guiding Alcove Trail near the visitor center.

FACILITIES: Picnic areas with tables, grills, water, and flush toilets are located near both the east and west entrances. No food, gasoline, or overnight accommodations are available at the monument, but all three are available at Fruita (3 miles north of the west entrance) or Grand Junction (4 miles east of the east entrance).

CAMPING: Saddlehorn Campground (eighty spaces) is adjacent to the visitor center, 4½ miles south of the west entrance. The campground is open all year and offers tables, charcoal grills, and flush toilets. Juniper and pinyon trees provide some shade. Saddlehorn Campground provides campers with a spectacular view of the Grand Valley. Private campgrounds are in Grand Junction and Fruita.

FISHING: No fishing is available inside the park.

CURECANTI NATIONAL RECREATION AREA

102 Elk Creek
Gunnison, CO 81230-9304
(970) 641–2337
cure_vis_mail@nps.gov
www.nps.gov/cure/

Curecanti National Recreation Area, administered under a cooperative agreement with the Bureau of Reclamation since 1965, comprises more than 40,000 acres. The recreation area consists of three reservoirs, known as the Wayne Aspinall Storage Unit. Two reservoirs are set in the deep canyon of the Gunnison River. The park is paralleled by U.S. 50 in west-central Colorado. The eastern border is approximately 8 miles west of the town of Gunnison.

The reservoirs of Curecanti National Recreation Area, part of the Colorado River Storage Project, result from three dams constructed on the Gunnison River. These three reservoirs provide visitors with a wide variety of water sports and other outdoor activities amid the spectacular scenery of Colorado mesa and canyon country. The land in this region has been shaped by volcanic activity and the erosive forces of nature. Evidence of both is easily seen along the shores of the reservoirs and on the walls of the surrounding cliffs.

Because of the cold winters, the normal visitor season is from mid-May through mid-October. Evening naturalist programs are regularly scheduled during summer months, and activity schedules are posted in visitor-use areas. The park's main visitor center is at Elk Creek, where visitors can view a short video presentation, a fish observation pond, and exhibits. Naturalist activities are available here. In Cimarron, there is an information station with a narrow-gauge railroad exhibit. An 1881 trestle, a steam locomotive (Engine 278 is one of three of this type left in the United States), and several cars, including a caboose from the Denver and Rio Grande Western Railroad, can be seen.

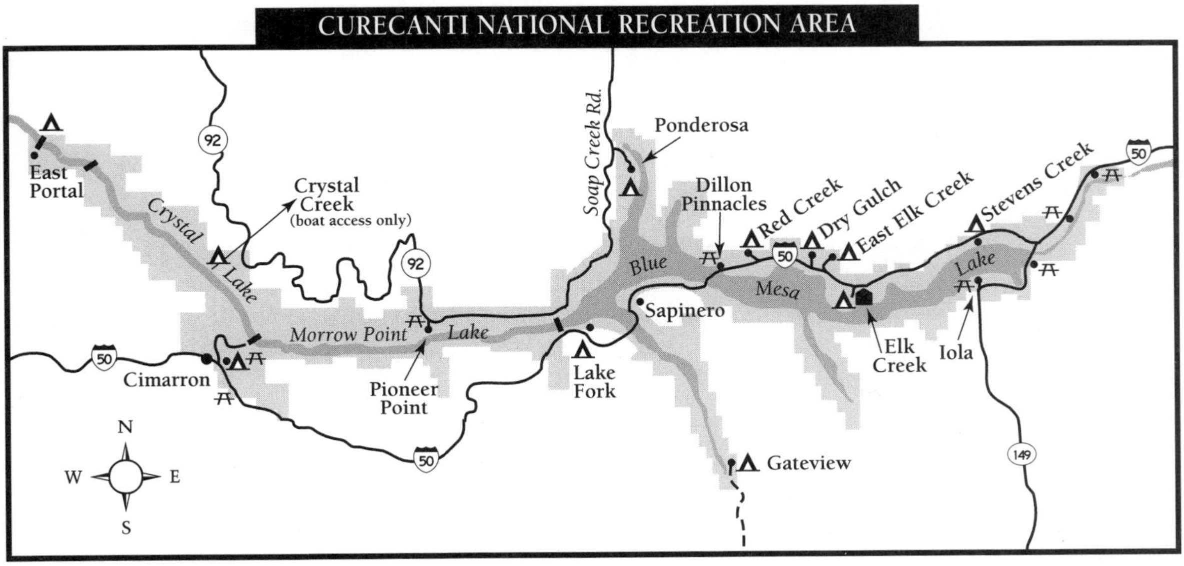

CURECANTI NATIONAL RECREATION AREA

A one-and-one-half-hour, concessioner-operated, naturalist-staffed boat tour of the Upper Black Canyon, a dramatic, fjordlike canyon, begins just below Blue Mesa Dam on Morrow Point Reservoir. The early history of the region, including accounts of the Ute Indians and the Denver and Rio Grande Western Railroad's narrow gauge line, is discussed. The boat tours require reservations, which may be made at Elk Creek Marina (970–641–0402). Reaching the point of departure requires going down 232 steps and walking for half an hour, but the views from the bottom of the 400- to 1,000-foot canyon are outstanding.

FACILITIES: No overnight lodging is available in the park, but accommodations and most services are available in Montrose, Gunnison, and other nearby towns. A nice restaurant is located adjacent to the marina at Elk Creek. Ranger stations and first aid help are available at Cimarron, Lake Fork, and Elk Creek. Marinas at both Elk Creek and Lake Fork offer boat repairs and rentals, gasoline, guided fishing tours on Blue Mesa and Morrow Point, fishing tackle, and groceries.

CAMPING: The most developed campgrounds, with tables, grills, water, flush toilets, and dump stations, are at Cimarron (twenty-two spaces), Elk Creek (179 spaces, pay showers), and Lake Fork (eighty-seven spaces, pay showers). Campgrounds at Dry Gulch (ten spaces), East Portal (fifteen spaces), Gateview (seven spaces), Ponderosa (twenty-nine spaces), Red Creek (seven spaces), and Stevens Creek (fifty-four spaces) have pit toilets. Only Elk Creek is open all year.

FISHING: Federal and state fish hatcheries annually stock nearly two million fish in the lakes. Anglers can enjoy year-round, high-country trout fishing at Curecanti. Ice fishing for rainbow and German brown trout is popular from December through March, and trolling and bank fishing become popular as soon as open water appears in the spring. Trolling fishermen find the rainbow, brown, and lake (mackinaw) trout fishing good throughout the season, with the best kokanee salmon fishing in late June, July, and August. A Colorado fishing license is required and may be purchased at the Elk Creek Marina.

DINOSAUR NATIONAL MONUMENT

4545 E Highway 40
Dinosaur, CO 81610-9724
(970) 374–3000
www.nps.gov/dino/

Dinosaur National Monument, established in 1915, contains fossil remains of dinosaurs and other ancient animals. The 210,000-acre park also includes spectacular canyons cut by the Green and Yampa rivers. The park straddles the border of northeast Utah and northwest Colorado. Access from U.S. 40 is via State Highway 149 at Jensen, which goes north to the Dinosaur Quarry and the main fossil area of the park. Access to the canyons is via Harpers Corner Road at monument headquarters, a few miles east of Dinosaur.

Dinosaur National Monument contains a deposit of fossil bones of crocodiles, turtles, and dinosaurs. Dinosaur Quarry, located 7 miles north of Jensen, Utah, in the southwestern portion of the monument, offers an exposed wall of the quarry. The center is open daily from 8:00 A.M. to 4:30 P.M. during winter, with somewhat longer hours during the busier summer season. It closes on Thanksgiving, Christmas, and New Year's Day.

In addition to the quarry area, Dinosaur offers some spectacularly wild and scenic country. A part of the park is reached by automobile, but most of it is available only to those willing to walk or raft. The 31-mile Harpers Corner Road winds north from monument headquarters, which is located 2 miles east of Dinosaur, Colorado. The road is a self-guided auto tour with interpretive signs at overlooks and three natural trails. This road is paved and is generally open from April through October. The road ends with a 1-mile self-guided nature trail to view numerous canyons cut by the Green and Yampa rivers. Two pit toilets are the only facilities on the road. Visitors should plan to spend from two to four hours for the round-trip.

Backcountry roads are available for the more adventurous motorists, but they are impassable when wet. These are generally rough and dusty and lead to more-remote areas. One of the most spectacular, Echo Park Road, begins just south of the park boundary on Harpers Corner Road. This is a 13-mile dirt road that passes by Indian petroglyphs and Whispering Cave. No trailers, heavy vehicles, or low-clearance vehicles should be driven here because of steep grades and sharp turns. Generally accessible roads are available in the northern and eastern parts of the monument. Self-guiding nature trails are found at Split Mountain Campground, Gates of Lodore, Monument Headquarters, and Harpers Corner Road, and raft trips are available through private concessioners. Information on river running is available at the visitor center. Private river runners are required to have a river permit (fee charged) to navigate Dinosaur's rivers.

FACILITIES: Motels and cafes are available at Dinosaur, Rangely, Craig, and Vernal. Food, gas, and ice are available at these towns and at Jensen. Medical facilities are offered in Craig, Rangely, and Vernal. Ranger stations are located at some public-use areas. Those at Deerlodge Park and Echo Park may be open in summer months.

CAMPING: The only two improved campgrounds are Split Mountain Gorge (group camping only during summer; reservations required) and Green River (ninety-nine spaces, summer only), both located on a paved road east of the Quarry Visitor Center. The campgrounds have picnic tables, fire grates, water, flush toilets, and programs some nights in summer. Green River Campground is shadier. Primitive campgrounds are located at Deerlodge Park (eight spaces, no

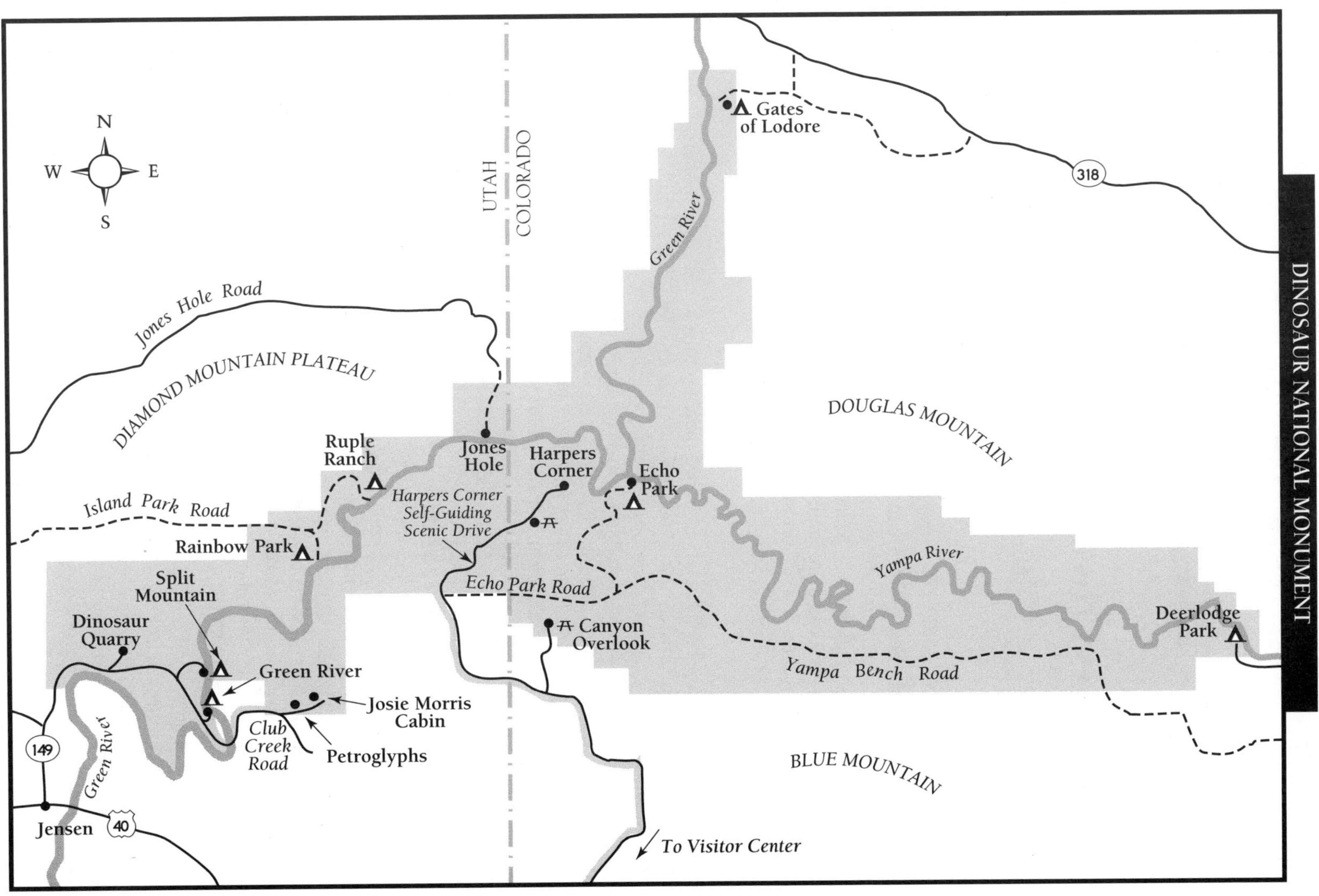
DINOSAUR NATIONAL MONUMENT
N
W
E
S
UTAH
COLORADO
Gates of Lodore
318
Green River
Jones Hole Road
DIAMOND MOUNTAIN PLATEAU
DOUGLAS MOUNTAIN
Ruple Ranch
Jones Hole
Harpers Corner
Echo Park
Harpers Corner Self-Guiding Scenic Drive
Island Park Road
Rainbow Park
Echo Park Road
Yampa River
Split Mountain
Dinosaur Quarry
Canyon Overlook
Deerlodge Park
Green River
Yampa Bench Road
Josie Morris Cabin
Club Creek Road
Petroglyphs
149
Green River
BLUE MOUNTAIN
Jensen
40
To Visitor Center

water), Echo Park (twelve spaces), Gates of Lodore (seventeen spaces), and Rainbow Park (four spaces, no water). These have pit toilets and picnic tables.

FISHING: The Green and Yampa rivers are generally muddy, and fishing for catfish is fair at best. Trout fishing is occasionally good in Jones Creek. Either a Utah or Colorado license must be obtained, depending on where you fish.

FLORISSANT FOSSIL BEDS NATIONAL MONUMENT

P.O. Box 185
Florissant, CO 80816-0185
(719) 748–3253
www.nps.gov/flfo/

Florissant Fossil Beds, which comprises nearly 6,000 acres, was added to the National Park System in 1969 to preserve the fossil insects, seeds, and leaves that are found here in abundance. Standing petrified sequoia stumps are also on display. The park is located in central Colorado, approximately 36 miles west of Colorado Springs on U.S. 24. From the small town of Florissant, turn south on Teller County Road No. 1. Nearby Cripple Creek has limited-stakes gambling.

Fossils in this area have been preserved in sedimentary rock at the bottom of an ancient lake that existed here approximately thirty-four million years ago. Mudflows from a nearby volcanic field buried trees in the ancient forests and later dammed the stream to form the lake. Later, as the volcanic activity showered materials through the air, a large variety of plants and animals died and settled to the lake's bottom. Here they were buried in fine ash and other sediments that eventually compacted to form shale, and the plants and animals became fossilized. Over time Lake Florissant filled with volcanic materials until erosion later exposed the lake bed.

The monument is open from 8:00 A.M. to 7:00 P.M. (until 4:30 P.M. in winter) daily, except Thanksgiving, Christmas, and New Year's Day. The visitor center provides a display of many of the fossils that have been found here. Included are dragonflies, beetles, ants, spiders, fish, mammals, and birds. Also housed here are fossil leaves and blossoms from earlier relatives of birches, maples, willows, beeches, roses, and hickories. Giant petrified sequoia tree stumps have been excavated and can be seen along a ½-mile self-guiding trail behind the visitor center and along a 1-mile trail just north of the center. In the summer, park rangers present hourly interpretive talks and lead guided walks several times each day. A map with descriptions of the 14 miles of trails is available in the visitor center. The Hornbek Homestead, a short distance north of the visitor center, offers an excellent look at a homestead common in this region in the late 1800s and early 1900s. During winter months, visitors can cross-country ski and snowshoe on all the trails. Snowmobiling is prohibited. Dogs are not permitted on any of the trails.

FACILITIES: Neither food services nor overnight accommodations are available in the park. Nearby towns of Woodland Park, Divide, Florissant, Lake George, and Cripple Creek Divide have motels, food, and fuel. The visitor center provides water and modern rest rooms, and a picnic area is nearby. Two other picnic areas are available, one at the Hornbek Homestead and another at an old farm site on Lower Twin Rock Road. Dogs are not permitted in either areas.

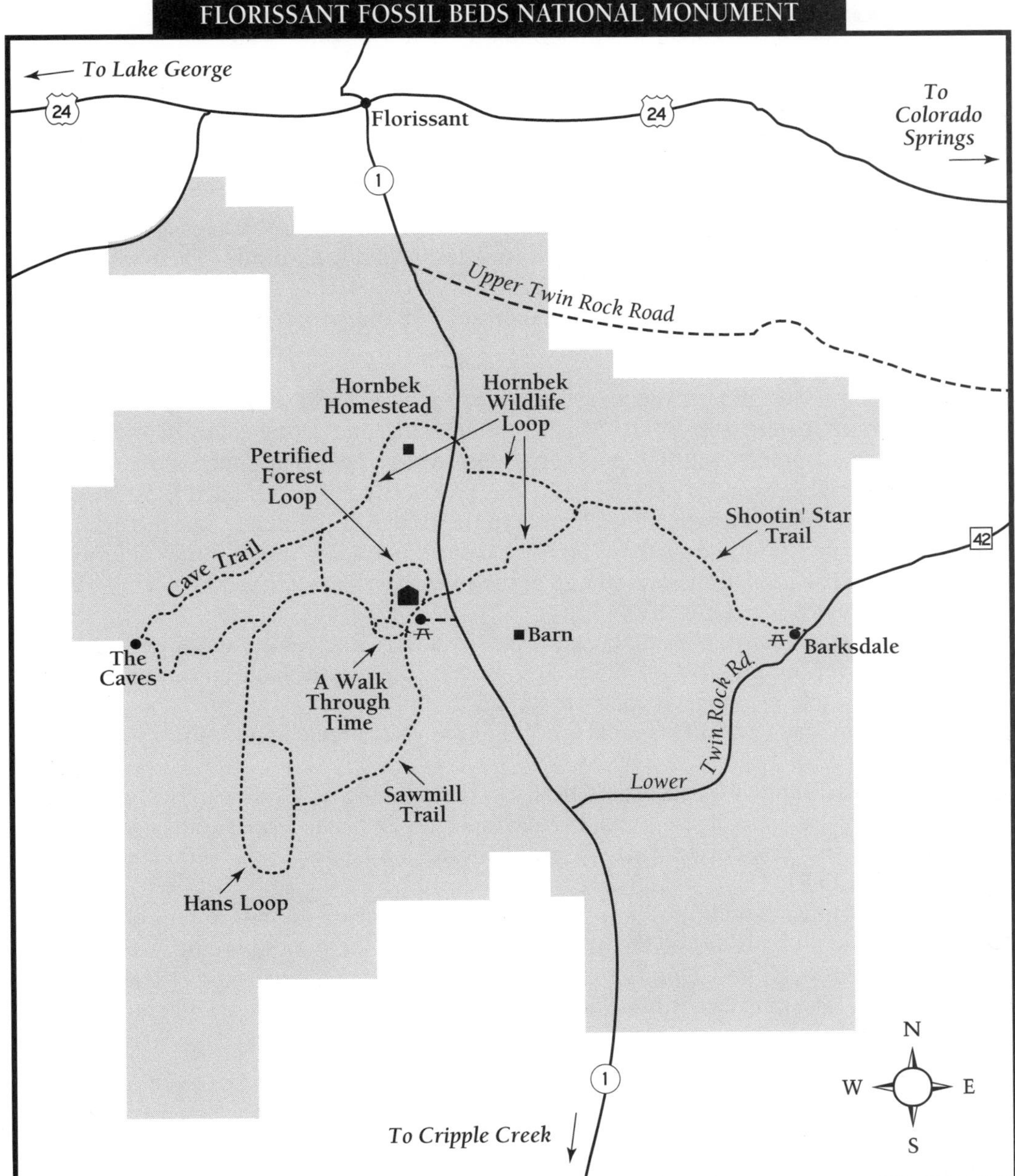

CAMPING: No camping is permitted at the monument. Private campgrounds are located in Cripple Creek and along U.S. 24 toward Colorado Springs. The U.S. Forest Service provides campgrounds near Lake George in Pike National Forest.

GREAT SAND DUNES NATIONAL MONUMENT

11500 Highway 150
Mosca, CO 81146-9798
(719) 378–2312
www.nps.gov/grsa/

Great Sand Dunes National Monument comprises nearly 39,000 acres and was established in 1932 to preserve North America's tallest sand dunes. The park is located in south-central Colorado, 17 miles north of U.S. 160 via Colorado Highway 150. The monument is approximately 38 miles from Alamosa.

The desert floor of the San Luis Valley is surrounded to the east and northeast by the Sangre de Cristo Mountains, to the west by the San Juan Mountains, and to the south by the San Luis Hills. This trap, combined with the prevailing southwesterly winds and the sand and silt that for centuries have been carried into the basin, has produced sand dunes piled to heights of up to 750 feet. The winds produce some changes in the details of the dunes, but the main mass has changed relatively little over the years. The eastern boundary of the dunes is formed by Medano Creek. The small dunes found east of the creek have been formed from sand blowing across the streambed when it is dry.

The visitor center contains exhibits on the history and geology of the area. The visitor center is closed all federal holidays in winter. Pets must be on a leash. Rangers conduct walks to the dunes and give evening campfire programs from Memorial Day to Labor Day. The Montville Nature Trail (1/2 mile) is located north of the visitor center, and leaflets are provided for a nominal fee.

Medano Pass Primitive Road begins near the campground and provides access for four-wheel-drive vehicles. In addition, a concessioner operates four-wheel-drive tours over the road during summer months. For information, write Great Sand Dunes Oasis, 5400 Highway 150 North, Mosca, CO 81146 (719–378–2222).

The most popular activity in the monument is hiking on the dunes. Routes are optional because there are no trails; however, most hikes begin from the dunes parking area. Campers may start at the campground. During summer months, hiking in the morning or late afternoon is most pleasant. The sand can be quite hot; wear shoes when hiking. Watch for lightning. Bring water, a hat, and sunscreen.

FACILITIES: No lodging or food service is provided in the monument, but food, snacks, and gasoline are available just outside the south entrance from May through October. Overnight accommodations can be found nearby and in Alamosa. Water, tables, and fire grates (charcoal only) are provided at the picnic area. Rest rooms with flush toilets are provided at the picnic area and the visitor center.

CAMPING: Pinyon Flats Campground, with forty-four sites, is open year-round. An additional forty-four individual sites and three group sites (by reservation only) are open in summer. The campground provides tables, grills, water, flush toilets, and a dump station. Facilities are limited in the off-season. A private campground near the park has full hookups. Backcountry camping requires a free permit, available at the visitor center.

FISHING: Fishing is generally poor in the monument.

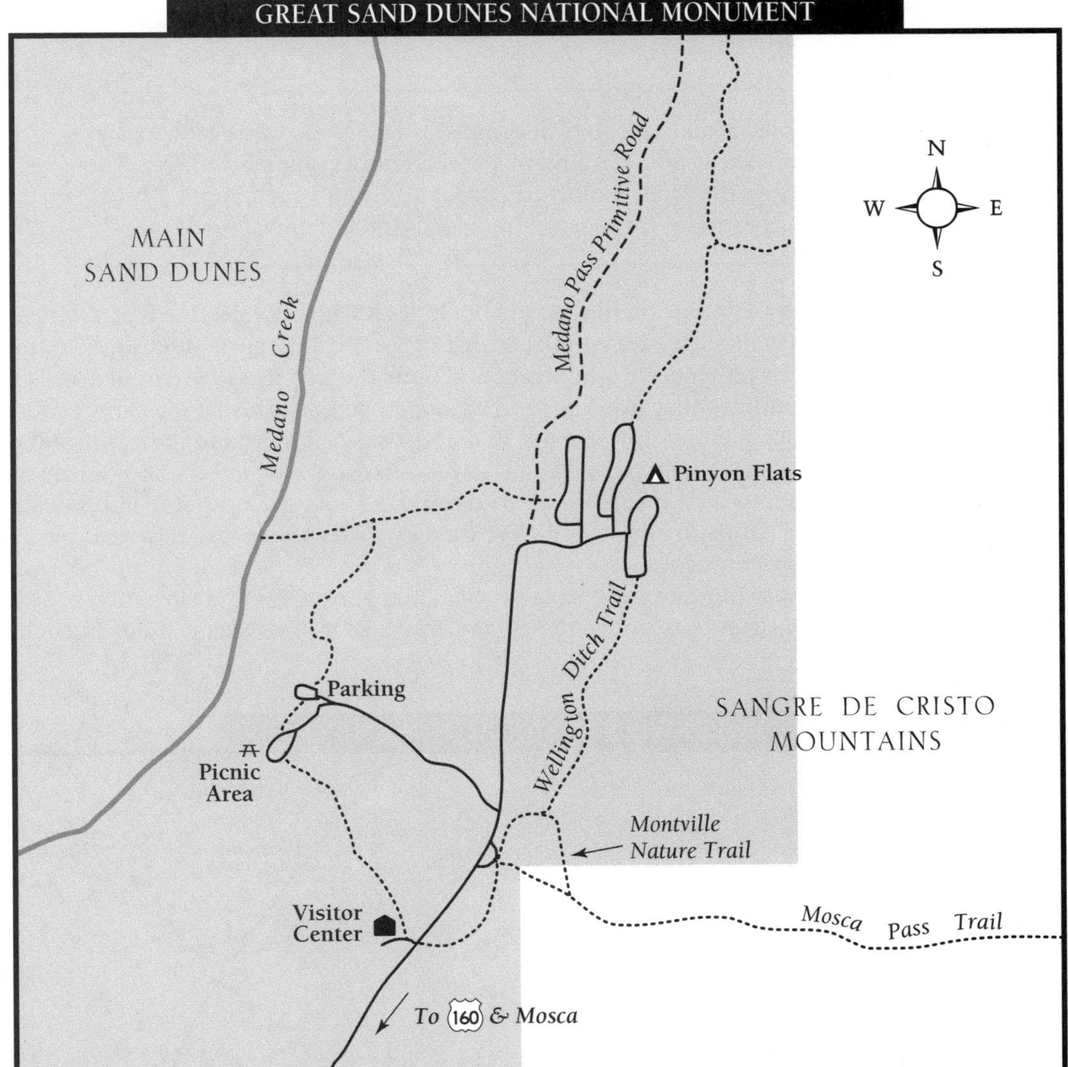
GREAT SAND DUNES NATIONAL MONUMENT
N
W
E
S
MAIN SAND DUNES
Medano Creek
Medano Pass Primitive Road
Pinyon Flats
Wellington Ditch Trail
Parking
Picnic Area
SANGRE DE CRISTO MOUNTAINS
Montville Nature Trail
Mosca Pass Trail
Visitor Center
To 160 & Mosca

HOVENWEEP NATIONAL MONUMENT

McElmo Route
Cortez, CO 81321
(970) 749–0510
NABR_Superintendent@nps.gov
www.nps.gov/hove/

Hovenweep National Monument, which comprises 785 acres, was established in 1923 to preserve six clusters of ruins of pre-Columbian Pueblo Indians. The monument straddles the Utah–Colorado border and is 45 miles from Cortez, Colorado. Approaches range from paved to graded dirt and gravel roads.

The inhabitants of Hovenweep were prehistoric Pueblo Indians who occupied the Four Corners region until A.D. 1300. Their culture was similar to that of the inhabitants of Mesa Verde to the east. The Pueblos raised crops, gathered wild foods, and hunted. They also were excellent artists and craftworkers. For centuries they lived in small, scattered villages. During the early 1100s, however, they began moving into larger pueblos. By 1200, they had moved to the heads of the Hovenweep canyons and had built pueblos and towers, perhaps to protect the permanent springs. The long draws into the canyons could be terraced to hold back the soil and provide sheet-water irrigation for crops. By the late 1200s, the Hovenweep area was deserted, partly because of a long period of drought.

Today's piles of masonry indicate the sizable population that once lived at Hovenweep. The monument consists of six groups of ruins: the Square Tower Ruins and Cajon Ruins in Utah,

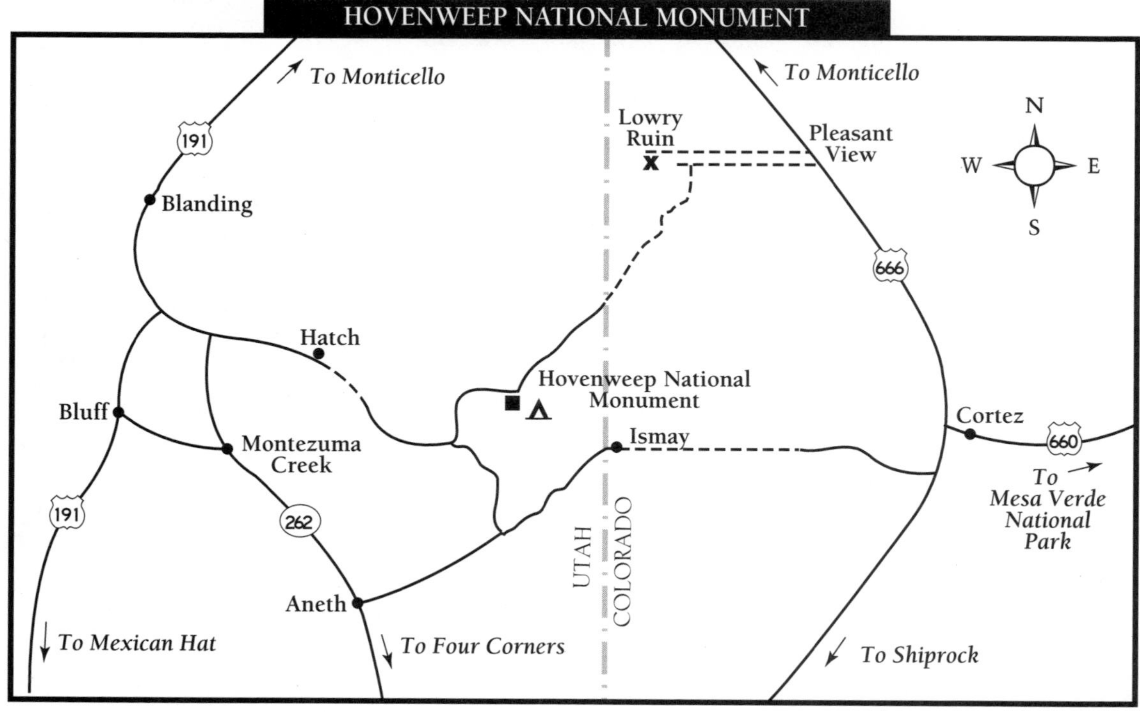

and the Holly, Hackberry, Cutthroat Castle, and Horseshoe ruins in Colorado. These ruins are all notable for their square, oval, circular, and D-shaped towers, many of which are built on boulders or rim edges.

Two self-guided trails are at Square Tower, the monument's best-preserved site. A half-mile loop to Tower Point provides a somewhat–distant view of all the structures in the group. The 1½-mile Square Tower Loop offers a closer view of the same structures. The interior of the canyon has been closed to the public, but daily scheduled ranger-guided walks to the Square Tower and a pictograph panel are available seasonally, generally April through October. The other sites are isolated and difficult to reach. A 4-mile trail from Square Tower leads to Holly Ruin. The Cajon Ruins consist of two large pueblos that have been ravaged by both time and relic hunters. Holly, Hackberry, and Cutthroat Castle sites consist of towers and pueblos.

Temperatures at the monument tend to be moderate, although summer daytime temperatures can exceed 100 degrees Fahrenheit. June is generally a good month to avoid because of the presence of small biting gnats. Fall is probably the best time to visit.

FACILITIES: No lodging or food service is available at the monument. Supplies can be purchased at Hatch Trading Post, 16 miles west, or at Ismay Trading Post, 14 miles southeast. The nearest overnight accommodations are at Blanding and Bluff in Utah and Cortez in Colorado. Water and bathrooms are provided at the ranger station and the campground. Gas is available in Aneth (20 miles to the south), Blanding, and Cortez.

CAMPING: A campground (thirty-one spaces) near the ranger station is open all year and has tables, grills, and flush toilets. Rest rooms are closed during winter months, and pit toilets are available. The campground is rarely filled.

FISHING: No fishing is available at Hovenweep National Monument.

MESA VERDE NATIONAL PARK

P.O. Box 8
Mesa Verde National Park, CO 81330
(970) 529–4465
meve_general_information@nps.gov
www.nps.gov/meve/

Mesa Verde National Park, which comprises more than 52,000 acres, was established in 1906 to protect the most notable and best-preserved pre-Columbian cliff dwellings in the United States. The park is located in the southwestern corner of Colorado, 10 miles east of Cortez and 35 miles west of Durango on U.S. 160.

The ancestral Puebloans of Mesa Verde went through three distinct stages. The earliest people, known as the Basket Makers, lived in clustered dwellings dug into the ground ("pithouses") on mesa tops. Here they grew beans, squash, and corn in the rich soil. By the mid-700s, descendants of the Basket Makers (Pueblos) started building homes above ground by weaving sticks around wooden poles stuck in the ground. The walls and roof were weatherproofed with a thick coating of mud. By A.D. 1000, stone masonry construction began replacing mud mixture between poles. Sometime in the late 1100s, the people of Mesa Verde left their homes on mesa tops and constructed cliff dwellings, for which this park is best known. Exactly what prompted this construction is uncertain, although possible reasons include protection from the elements

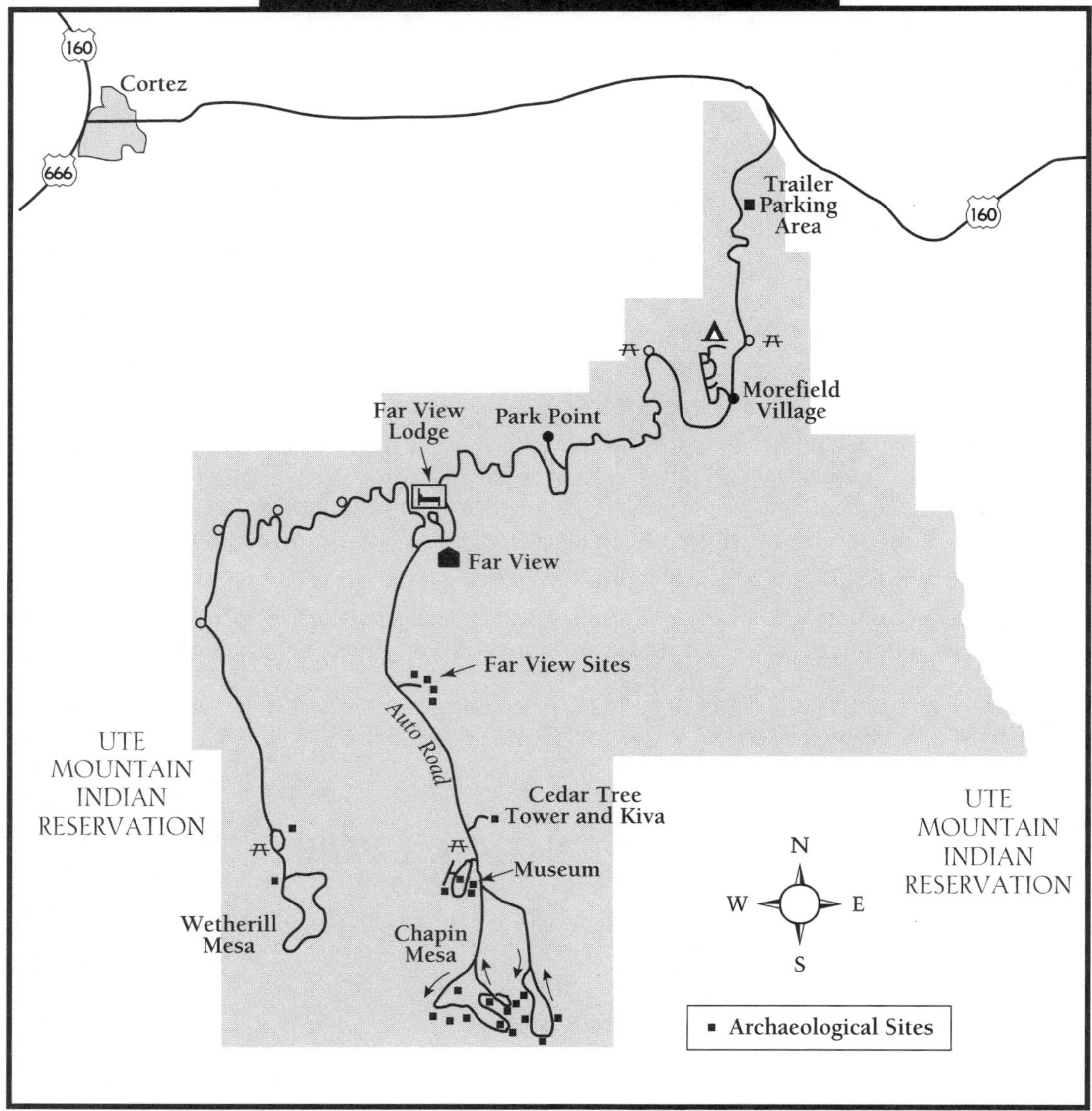

or enemies. The dwellings may also have been constructed for religious or psychological reasons. Less than one hundred years later, for reasons that are still uncertain, the people left Mesa Verde.

Far View Visitor Center, 17 miles from the park entrance, contains displays of contemporary Indian arts and crafts. Approximately halfway from the entrance to Far View is Park Point, which offers a viewpoint of the Four Corners region. The 12-mile drive from Far View to Wetherill Mesa (summer only) offers some excellent views of the park. An archaeological museum at Chapin Mesa contains artifacts and exhibits of life at Mesa Verde. Park personnel are located in each area to answer visitors' questions. During summer months, park rangers conduct trips through some of the sites and present nightly programs at the campground. Schedules are at the visitor center or museum. During winter months, walks are guided only to Spruce Tree House.

Hiking in Mesa Verde is restricted. In the Morefield Area, Prater Ridge Trail (7⁴⁄₅ miles), Knife Edge Trail (1½ miles), and Point Lookout Trail (2³⁄₁₀ miles) require no permit. In the headquarters area, hikers must register for Petroglyph Point Trail (2 4/5 miles) or Spruce Canyon Trail (2 1/10 miles).

FACILITIES: The only overnight lodging inside the park is at Far View Lodge. Meals also are served here. Reservations and information may be obtained by writing ARAMARK Mesa Verde, P.O. Box 277, Mancos, CO 81328 (800–449–2288). Food service is available at Morefield, Spruce Tree Terrace, and Wetherill Mesa, as well as at Far View. Rest rooms are provided at all four locations. Groceries and gasoline may be purchased at Morefield.

CAMPING: Morefield Campground (477 spaces and seventeen group camps) is 4 miles inside the park entrance. It provides tables, grills, water, a dump station, and flush toilets. Pay showers, a laundry, and a grocery are located within easy walking distance. The campground is open from early May until late October.

FISHING: No fishing is available at Mesa Verde National Park.

Cliff Palace, Mesa Verde National Park

ROCKY MOUNTAIN NATIONAL PARK

Estes Park, CO 80517-8397
(970) 586–1206
www.nps.gov/romo.html

Rocky Mountain National Park, established in 1915, comprises 265,727 acres of some of the most beautiful and easily accessible high-mountain country in North America. The park is located in north-central Colorado, with the main entrance near Estes Park, approximately 65 miles from Denver and 91 miles from Cheyenne. Rocky Mountain may also be approached from the town of Grand Lake through Arapaho National Recreation Area on its southwestern boundary.

The area of the present-day Rocky Mountains was once covered by a great sea. More than a hundred million years ago, the sea began to recede, and the ancestral Rockies gradually rose above the old seabed. Over a period of millions of years, the mountains were eroded by the wind and water until only a high rolling plain was left. Approximately sixty million years ago, another gradual uplifting produced today's Rocky Mountains. The range began to erode almost immediately, and then about one million years ago, the ice age created giant glaciers that left U-shaped valleys, lakes, and moraines. Five small glaciers are still in the park today.

The most accessible parts of the park lie along Trail Ridge Road, a 50-mile paved road (open in summer only) connecting Estes Park with Grand Lake, which reaches a height of more than 12,000 feet. Before driving the road, a stop at one of the visitor centers (Estes Park or Grand Lake) will prove worthwhile. Trail Ridge Road stays above timberline for 11 miles and provides numerous viewpoints, and the Alpine Visitor Center at Fall River Pass offers exhibits to help interpret this part of the park. Fall River Road is a section of the original road crossing the mountains and is open from Horseshoe Park Junction to Fall River Pass. West of Endovalley, the gravel road is one way uphill.

The paved road to Bear Lake offers easy but congested access to a high mountain basin. A shuttle-bus service is provided during the summer months. Here, a beautiful lake is combined with a number of the park's trailheads. The parking lots here and at Glacier Gorge Junction often fill early during summer months. Two of the more popular trails beginning here are Dream Lake (2 miles round-trip) and Emerald Lake (3 miles round-trip). The park has more than 360 miles of trails, and horses are allowed on many of them. Cross-country skiing and snowshoeing are popular in winter. Hiking, technical climbing, wildlife watching, and horseback riding are popular in summer months. Ranger-led programs are offered throughout the year.

FACILITIES: No lodging is available inside the park, but accommodations are available in both Estes Park and Grand Lake. For information, write the Chamber Resort Association in Estes Park, CO 80517 (800–443–7837), or the Chamber of Commerce in Grand Lake, CO 80447 (800–531–1019). Food service is provided by a concessioner at the Fall River Pass store (summer only). Water and rest rooms are available at various locations, including the visitor centers and campgrounds. During summer, horses with guides can be hired at two locations inside the park on the east side or from a number of liveries outside both the east and west park boundaries.

CAMPING: Aspenglen (fifty-four spaces), Glacier Basin (150 spaces, twelve group camps, dump station), Longs Peak (twenty-six spaces, tents only), Moraine Park (247 spaces, dump station), and Timber Creek (one hundred spaces, dump station) all provide tables, grills,

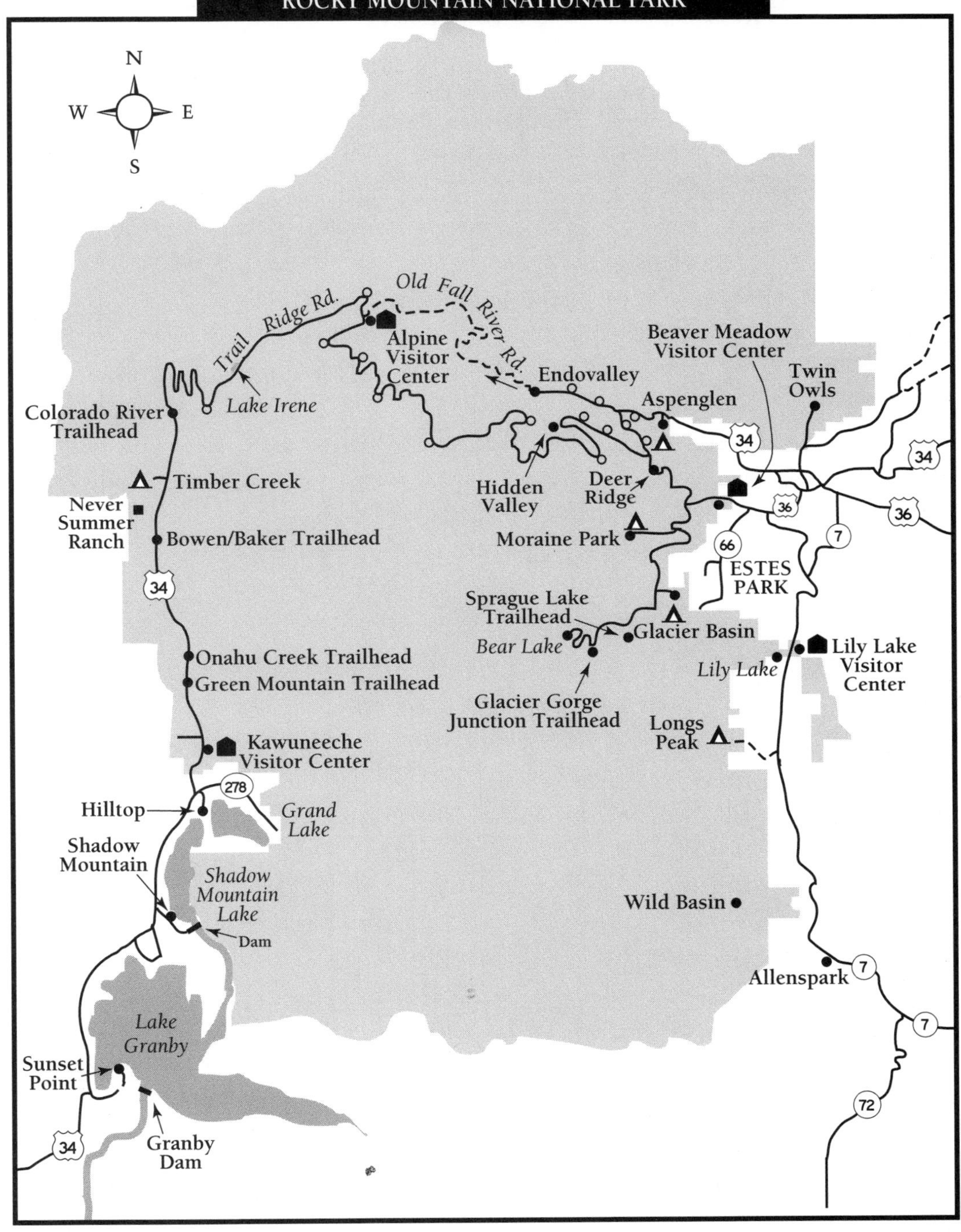

ROCKY MOUNTAIN NATIONAL PARK
N
W
E
S
Old Fall River Rd.
Trail Ridge Rd.
Alpine Visitor Center
Beaver Meadow Visitor Center
Twin Owls
Endovalley
Aspenglen
Lake Irene
Colorado River Trailhead
Timber Creek
Never Summer Ranch
Bowen/Baker Trailhead
Hidden Valley
Deer Ridge
Moraine Park
ESTES PARK
Sprague Lake Trailhead
Bear Lake
Glacier Basin
Lily Lake
Lily Lake Visitor Center
Onahu Creek Trailhead
Green Mountain Trailhead
Glacier Gorge Junction Trailhead
Longs Peak
Kawuneeche Visitor Center
Hilltop
Grand Lake
Shadow Mountain
Shadow Mountain Lake
Dam
Wild Basin
Allenspark
Lake Granby
Sunset Point
Granby Dam
34
36
66
7
72
278

water, and flush toilets. Camping limit is seven days parkwide. At Long's Peak it is three days. Moraine Park, Longs Peak, and Timber Creek are open all year. Campsites at Glacier Basin and Moraine Park may be reserved. Two hundred and sixty-seven backcountry campsites are available once snows have melted by late June. All overnight stays require permits that must be obtained from the Backcountry Office at (970) 586–1242.

FISHING: German brown, brook, rainbow, and cutthroat trout are maintained by natural reproduction in the mountain streams and lakes. The fish are generally not large, and live bait is prohibited except under special circumstances. Fishing is not permitted in Bear Lake. A Colorado fishing license is required.

TOURIST INFORMATION
(800) 873–4826

WAR IN THE PACIFIC NATIONAL HISTORICAL PARK

P.O. Box FA
Agana, GU 96932
(671) 472–7240
www.nps.gov/wapa

War in the Pacific National Historical Park is comprised of nearly 2,000 acres. The park was authorized in 1978 to commemorate the bravery and sacrifices of those involved in the Pacific Theater of World War II. The park includes historic sites associated with the 1944 battle for Guam and consists of seven units on the western and southern shores of Guam.

On December 7, 1941, Pearl Harbor was attacked. A few hours later Japanese dive-bombers attacked the island of Guam. The island remained under Japanese control for two and a half years, until American forces returned on July 21, 1944. After twenty days of bitter fighting, on August 10, 1944, the island was retaken. The recapture of Guam cost more than 7,000 American and 17,500 Japanese casualties.

The T. Stell Newman Visitor Center is located on Marine Drive (Highway 1) in the village of Asan. Here visitors will find audiovisual programs and exhibits depicting the events surrounding the Pacific war and the battle for Guam. A patio on the first floor provides a view of the beach where American troops landed while under attack from Japanese defense positions in the hills above Asan Beach. The park preserves these historic landing beaches, cliffs, and ridges that were significant battle sites in 1944. Park brochures are available at the visitor center, and park rangers can assist with information. Fishing, hiking, picnicking, and (for those with experience) snorkeling and diving are among the recreation opportunities available in the park.

FACILITIES: Food and lodging are available in nearby villages. Drinking water and rest rooms are available at the visitor center, Asan Beach, and Ga'an Point.

CAMPING: No camping is available in the park.

FISHING: Fishing is permitted in units fronting on the Philippine Sea.

HAWAII

STATE TOURIST INFORMATION
(808) 423–1811

HALEAKALĀ NATIONAL PARK

P.O. Box 369
Makawao, Maui, HI 96768-0369
(808) 572–4400
www.nps.gov/hale/

Haleakalā National Park comprises nearly 29,000 acres and was established in 1916 to preserve the outstanding features of Haleakalā Volcano and the unique plants and animals that can be found there. Haleakalā rises 10,023 feet above sea level, and its last volcanic activity occurred about 200 years ago, near sea level. The summit of Haleakalā is a 1½-hour drive from Kahului via Highways 37, 377, and 378. The eastern section of the park (Kīpahulu District) is a three-hour, 55-mile drive from Kahului via Highway 36, a narrow, winding road.

The island of Maui was formed by two volcanoes spewing lava until they merged as one land mass. Haleakalā, the larger of the two, once stood almost 13,000 feet above sea level in addition to 20,000 feet above its base on the ocean floor. During a period of dormancy, rain cut streams down the mountain's slopes and created a large valley, commonly referred to as the "crater," near the summit. Later volcanic activity filled the valley with lava and formed cinder cones in the crater.

Park headquarters visitor center is located 1 mile inside the summit district, on Highway 378. Personnel are available to answer questions and provide permits and publications. Ten miles up the road, Haleakalā visitor center has exhibits and provides an excellent view of the "crater," weather permitting. Interpretive talks are given daily at the summit building, 1 mile farther.

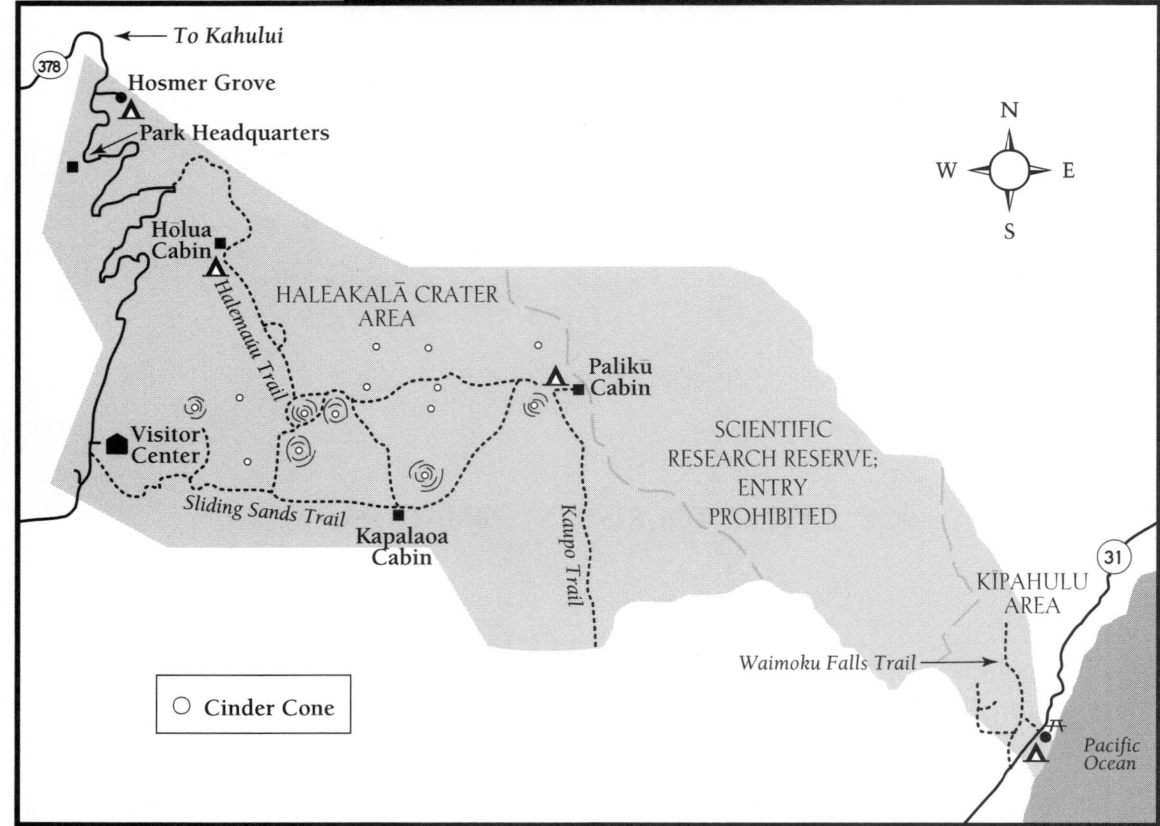

On the east side of the park, the abundant vegetation and tropical nature of the Kīpahulu area stand in vivid contrast to the flows and cinder cones of the "crater" area. Sparkling pools connected by waterfalls are fed by a rain forest receiving more than 250 inches of rain annually.

A variety of trails and guided walks are available in the park. Short, self-guided walks are located in the "crater" area. Halemau'u Trail views Ke'anae Valley and Ko'olau Gap on the 1-mile walk from the highway to the "crater" rim. At the northwest corner of the park, the ½-mile Hosmer Grove Nature Trail displays the interplay between native and exotic plants. A ¼-mile trail to the top of White Hill is located near the visitor center. Self-guided day and overnight hikes through the "crater" are also available. In the Kīpahulu area, self-guided walks include one from the parking area to the lower pools (½ mile round-trip) and to Waimoku Falls on the Pīpīwai Trail (3⁷⁄₁₀ miles round-trip) winding through a bamboo forest. Swimming in the pools at 'Ohe'o is quite popular. Ranger-guided hikes are available in both areas of the park. Call for schedules.

FACILITIES: No overnight motel accommodations, food services, stores, or service stations are located within the park. From Kīpahulu (Route 31 to Hāna), these services are located approximately 10 miles away in Hāna. No drinking water is available at Kīpahulu. From the summit of Haleakalā, a service station is approximately 28 miles away on Route 37, and restaurant and lodge facilities are located within 22 miles on Route 377. The visitor center and Park Headquarters have rest room facilities and drinking water.

CAMPING: Hosmer Grove Campground (total capacity of fifty people) in the northwest corner of the park has tables, drinking water, chemical toilets, and a cooking shelter with barbecue grills. This is a drive-in campground. No permit is required, and space is on a first-come, first-served basis. Camping in the wilderness is permitted in two locations. Each of these is accessible by trail only. A permit is required and can be obtained at park headquarters between 8:00 A.M. and 3:00 P.M. on the day you hike in. Two campgrounds—one near Hōlua cabin (total capacity of twenty-five people) and one near Palikū cabin (twenty-five people)—offer primitive facilities including pit toilets and nonpotable water. Three wilderness cabins are available to winners of a lottery held three months prior to month of the desired stay. Kīpahulu Campground near 'Ohe'o Gulch offers a few tables, grills, and pit toilets, but no drinking water.

FISHING: The Kīpahulu Campground and a picnic area are located near the ocean, and fishing is permitted here.

HAWAII VOLCANOES NATIONAL PARK

Hawaii National Park, HI 96718-0052
(808) 985–6000
Norrie_Judd@nps.gov
www.nps.gov/havo/

Hawaii Volcanoes comprises 230,000 acres and was added to the National Park System in 1916. Active volcanism continues in the park. The most recent activity has been continuing since January 3, 1983, and has built the largest landform on the east rift zone—a 622-foot cinder and spatter cone. Hawaii Volcanoes National Park is located in the southeastern corner of the island of Hawaii. The visitor center is approximately 29 miles southwest of Hilo on Hawaii Highway 11, which bisects the park.

Millions of years ago a hot spot in the earth's mantle in the middle of the Pacific caused lava and gases to spurt from cracks 18,000 feet beneath the ocean's surface. As additional layers of lava were added, the island of Hawaii emerged from the sea. The island is 90 miles across at its base and measures nearly 32,000 feet from ocean floor to summit.

The most recent of the active volcanoes are 13,676-foot Mauna Loa and 4,690-foot Kīlauea. Mauna Loa has been intermittently active during recent times, with large eruptions occurring in 1926, 1942, 1950, and, most recently, in 1984. Kīlauea, one of the most-studied and best-understood volcanoes in the world, has had its summit collapse to form a broad, shallow depression. Its eruptions have generally been characterized by mild and nonexplosive activity, except in 1790 and 1924.

Most of the park's activity centers around Kīlauea Caldera. Crater Rim Drive is an 11-mile paved road passing lush rain forest, raw craters, and areas of devastation. Along the road are trails and overlooks such as Thurston Lava Tube, which has a trail through dense plant growth and part of a tunnel through which once rushed glowing lava (3/10 mile, one quarter of an hour); the paved Devastation Trail (3/5 mile, one half hour); and overlooks at Kīlauea, Kīlauea Iki, Steaming Bluff, and the Jaggar Museum.

The 10-mile paved road from Kīpuka Puaulu to an overlook part way up Mauna Loa is quite narrow but can be worthwhile on a clear day. A loop trail in Kīpuka Puaulu (1 1/10 miles, one

HAWAII VOLCANOES NATIONAL PARK

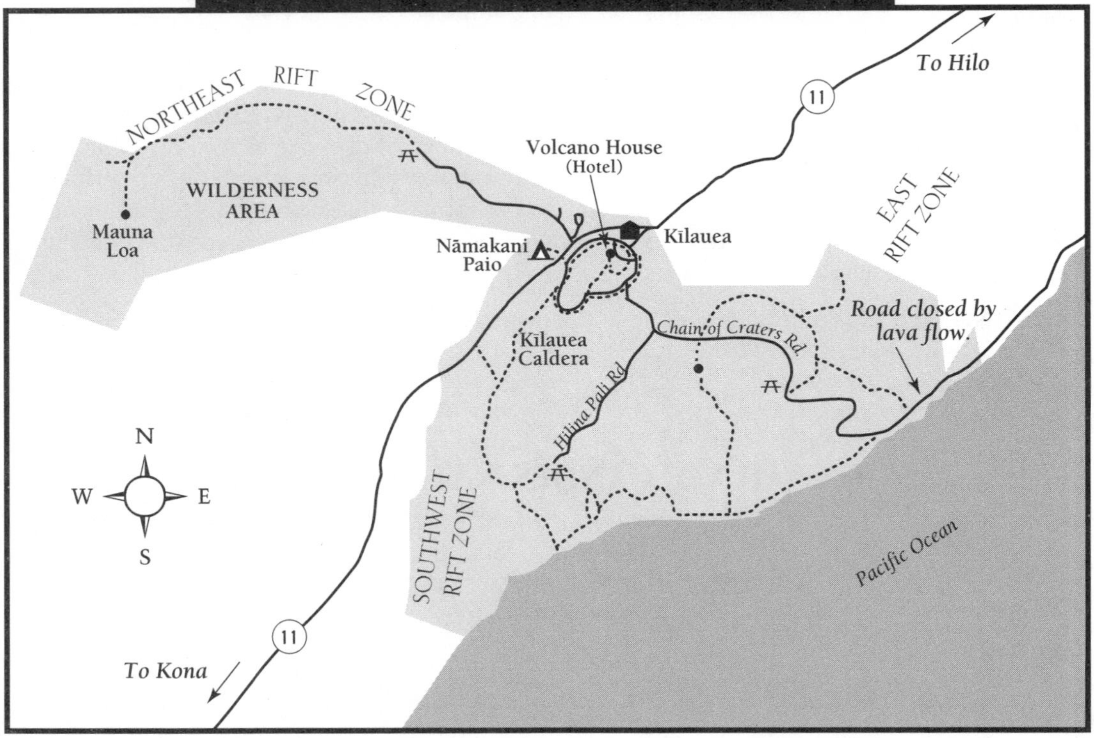

hour) leads into the open forest where many varieties of native trees grow. From a turnoff halfway down the Chain of Craters Road, visitors can drive to the top of Hilina Pali, a series of steep cliffs that provide a spectacular view of the southeast seacoast of the island.

A museum at park headquarters contains exhibits and paintings that help to tell the story of the island. Daily programs include talks by park personnel and a color film of recent volcanic activity.

FACILITIES: Volcano House, on the rim of Kīlauea Caldera, is operated by a concessioner. Information and reservations are available by writing Volcano House, Hawaii National Park, HI 96718 (808–967–7321). Food service is available at the hotel. Groceries, gasoline, and merchandise may be purchased in the town of Volcano, 1 mile outside the park on Highway 11. Automobile repair facilities are 21 miles outside the park at Kea'au.

CAMPING: Camping is limited to seven days annually at the park's developed campground. Namakani Paio (ten spaces, two group camps) offers camper cabins (rented through Volcano House), eating shelters, fireplaces, and flush toilets.

FISHING: Fishing is restricted to native Hawaiians and their guests within the park, except for backcountry at Halape.

KALAUPAPA NATIONAL HISTORICAL PARK

P.O. Box 2222
Kalaupapa, HI 96742-2222
(808) 567–6802
KALA_Interpretation@nps.gov
www.nps.gov/kala/

Kalaupapa National Historical Park comprises 10,779 acres and was authorized in 1980 to preserve and interpret the experiences and memories of the past, especially with regard to Hansen's disease (leprosy). The park is on the central northern coast of the island of Molokai. Access is very limited.

For many years individuals with Hansen's disease were banished to isolated locations, despite the fact that this is one of the least contagious of all communicable diseases. Kalaupapa was a settlement where people in Hawaii with Hansen's disease were sent for "treatment." The first group of patients arrived at the settlement in 1866, one year after King Kamehameha V's signing of an act setting apart land for isolating persons with Hansen's disease. From the fear and hopelessness that surrounded this disease when the settlement was established, medical advancements and changing attitudes have resulted in Hansen's disease being treated on an outpatient basis.

The park is comprised of the Kalaupapa peninsula, adjacent cliffs and valleys, and submerged lands and waters out to ¼ mile from shore. Spectacular cliffs, valleys, a volcanic crater, rain forest, lava tubes and caves, and offshore islands are all in the park. Both geography and regulations make access to the park relatively difficult. All visitors other than guests of patients and staff must tour historic Kalaupapa and Kalawao on a commercial tour guided by Hansen's disease patients who have lived most of their lives at Kalaupapa. For information write Damien Tours, c/o Kalaupapa Settlement, Kalaupapa, HI 96742. For those without the time or energy to arrange a visit to the historical park, Pala'au State Park provides an excellent view of the Kalaupapa peninsula from the edge of steep cliffs. The state park is at the end of highway 470, about 10 miles northwest of Kaunakakai.

FACILITIES: There are no public facilities in the park. Overnight stays are limited to invited guests of residents.

CAMPING: No camping is available in the park. The nearest camping is at Pala'au State Park.

FISHING: Fishing is available for invited guests only.

KALOKO–HONOKŌHAU NATIONAL HISTORICAL PARK

73-4786 Kanalani Street, #14
Kailua-Kona, HI 96740
(808) 329–6881
jerry_case@nps.gov
www.nps.gov/kaho/

Kaloko-Honokōhau NHP was established in 1978 to protect 1,160 acres that served as the site of an important Hawaiian settlement before the arrival of European explorers. The park is located on the west (Kona) coast of the island of Hawaii, a short distance north of the town of Kailua-Kona.

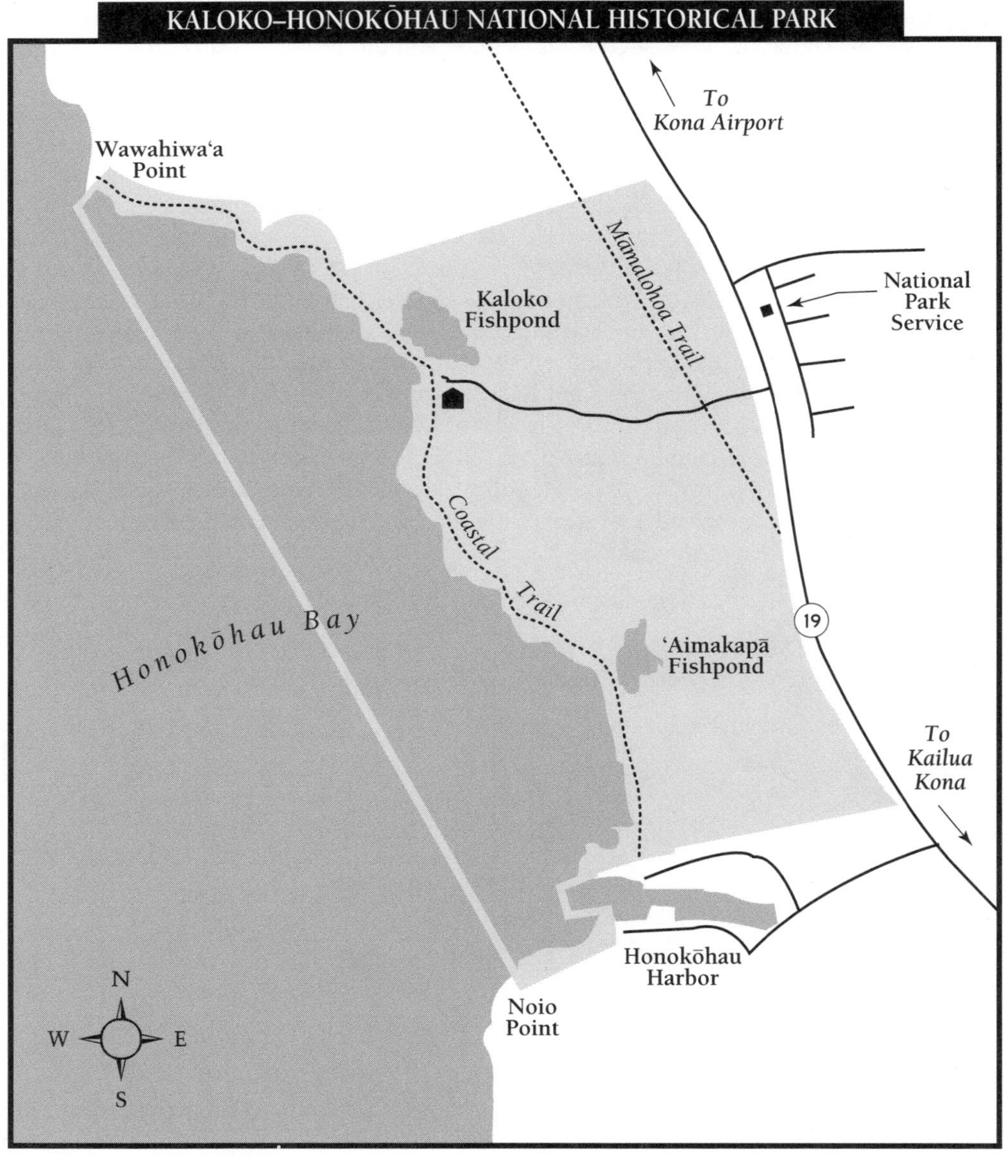

The area forming Kaloko-Honokōhau NHP was once a successful settlement whose inhabitants harvested sea life, cultivated vegetables, and raised chickens, dogs, and pigs. These people actively traded with others who lived farther inland on the island. Remaining evidence of the settlement includes house platforms, rock carvings, trails, canoe landings, and religious sites. The park also contains two fishponds that utilized the tides to trap fish.

The abundant tidal areas and wetlands in the park remain an important home for many waterbirds, including several species that are found nowhere else. The fishponds also serve as a habitat for waterfowl.

The park headquarters (open weekdays, 7:30 A.M. to 4:00 P.M.) is located in the Kaloko Industrial Park, 2 miles south of the Keahole Airport. Turn inland on Hinalani Street and take the first right onto Kanalani Street.

FACILITIES: Drinking water and concessions are not available in the park. Rest rooms are located at Kaloko fishpond and on the trail to Honokōhau beach. Food and lodging are available in Kailua-Kona.

CAMPING: No camping is permitted in the park.

FISHING: No fishing is permitted in the park.

PU'UHONUA O HŌNAUNAU NATIONAL HISTORICAL PARK

P.O. Box 129
Hōnaunau, Kona, HI 96726-0129
(808) 328–2326
www.nps.gov/puho/

Pu'uhonua o Hōnaunau (Place of Refuge of Hōnaunau) comprises 182 acres where, until 1819, vanquished Hawaiian warriors, noncombatants, and taboo breakers could escape death by reaching its sacred grounds ahead of their pursuers. The park is located in the southwestern section of the island of Hawaii, 111 miles from Hilo and 20 miles south of the resort center of Kailua-Kona. From Highway 11, turn west on Route 160, which goes by the park entrance.

The object of war in old Hawaii was to exterminate the enemy, including any members of the opposing side. Vanquished warriors and noncombatants on both sides could receive sanctuary in Hawaii's places of refuge. Although there were at least six refuges on the island of Hawaii at any one time and a number on other inhabited islands of the Hawaiian chain, the one contained in Pu'uhonua o Hōnaunau National Historical Park is historically the most important and the one still nearly intact. The refuge accepted all who sought sanctuary, including those who broke ancient laws. These individuals were absolved by priests before returning home in peace.

The great wall surrounding the place of refuge was constructed around A.D. 1550 in order to provide physical protection to the refugees. Although the seaward end of the south wall has been battered by high surfs, it once probably extended almost to the sea. The wall was built without mortar. An ancient temple that at one time contained the bones of important chiefs and honored males (no females) has been restored by the National Park Service.

The park's visitor center is located beside the parking area. Cultural demonstrations on the grounds vary from day to day and may include canoe carving, thatching a grass hut, and

PU'UHONUA O HŌNAUNAU NATIONAL HISTORICAL PARK

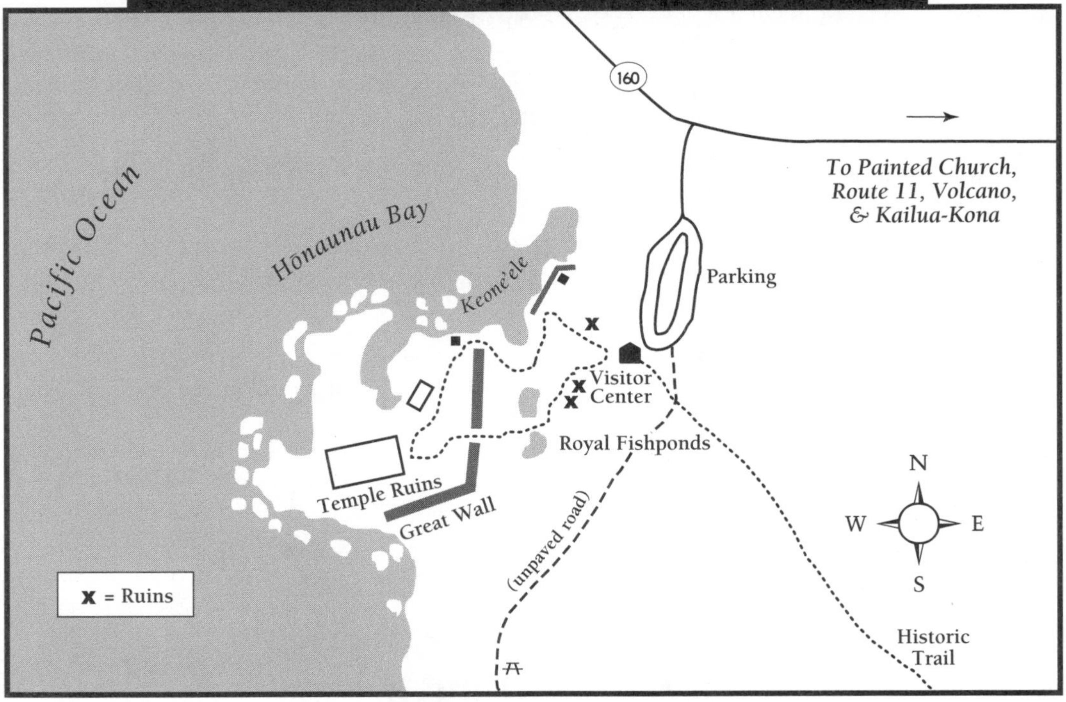

fishing as the ancient Hawaiians did. Coves, cliffs, tidal pools, and associated marine life are easily visited along the shoreline.

FACILITIES: No lodging or food service is available at the site. Both may be found on nearby Highway 11. Water and rest rooms are provided at the visitor center.

CAMPING: No camping is permitted at the site.

FISHING: Saltwater fishing from the shoreline is permitted.

PU'UKOHOLA HEIAU NATIONAL HISTORIC SITE

P.O. Box 44340
Kawaihae, HI 96743-4340
(808) 882–7218
www.nps.gov/puhe/

Pu'ukohola Heiau comprises $85\frac{3}{10}$ acres and was added to the National Park System in 1972 to preserve the historically significant temple associated with Kamehameha the Great, who founded the Historic Kingdom of Hawaii, and the property of John Young, who fought for Kamehameha the Great during the period of his ascendancy to power. The site is located in the northwestern section of the island of Hawaii. It is reached via State Route 270 and is about 12 miles from Waimea.

In 1782, Kamehameha became ruler of the northwest half of the island of Hawaii and unsuccessfully attempted to gain control of the remaining part. After he conquered the islands of Maui, Lanai, and Molokai, Kamehameha's cousin attacked Kamehameha's territory on the Big Island. Before returning to the Big Island, Kamehameha sent his aunt to find the prophet Kāpoūkahi. Kamehameha returned to the Big Island and unsuccessfully fought his cousin. After returning to Kawaihae, Kamehameha received word from his aunt that Kamehameha would control all the islands if he built a large temple to his family war god. The result was a temple atop Pu'ukohola started in 1790 and finished one year later. The prophecy was fulfilled in 1810 after years of war, when Kamehameha became ruler of all the Hawaiian Islands. After Kamehameha's death in 1819, his son abandoned past religious traditions and ordered the temple destroyed.

The temple platform was constructed without the use of mortar by setting lava rocks and boulders together. Three long narrow steps cross the side that faces the sea so the interior could be viewed from canoes floating offshore. For purposes of preservation and safety, the temple site is currently closed to the public.

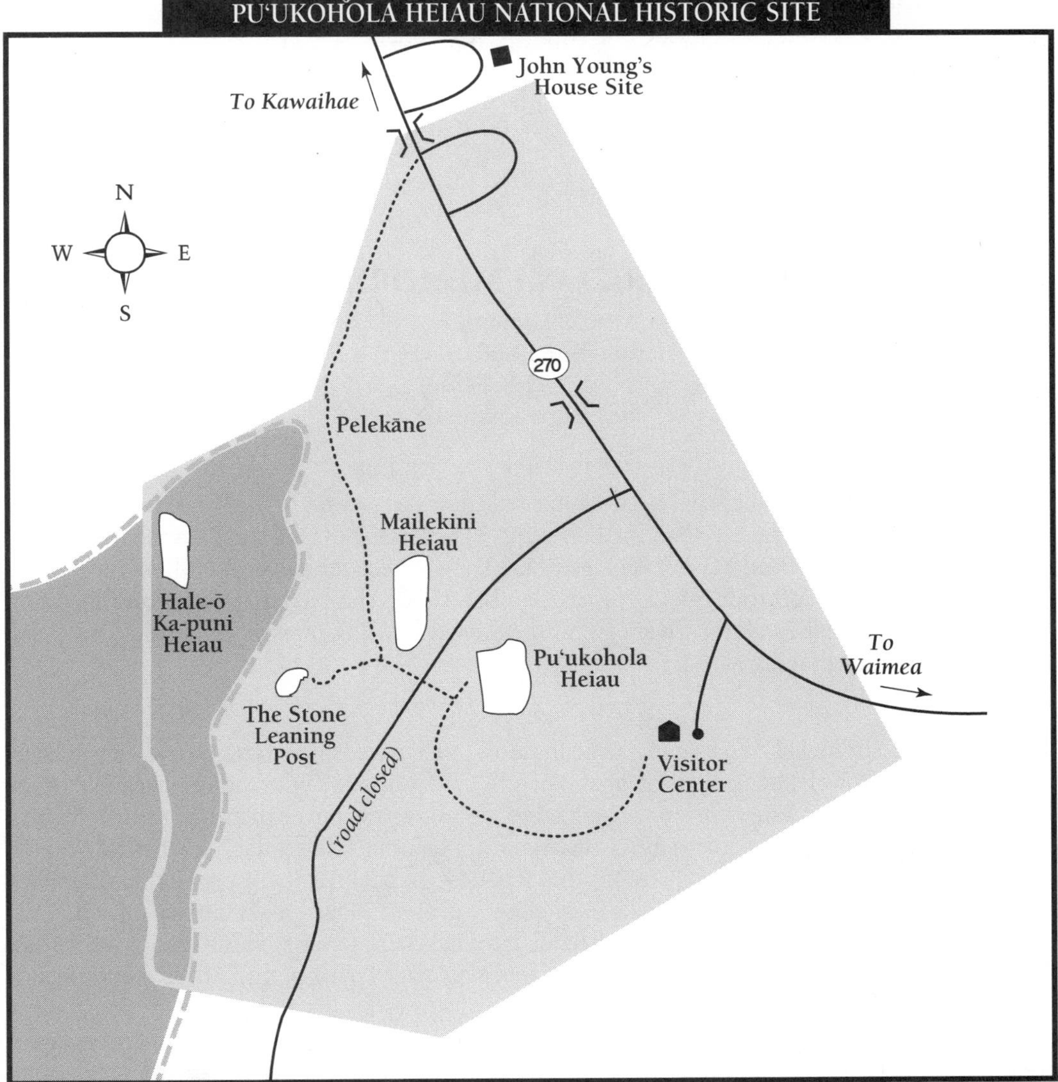

In addition to Pu'ukohola Heiau, the park includes a number of other interesting features. On the hillside between Pu'ukohola Heiau and the sea is the ruin of Mailekini Heiau, a temple used by Kamehameha's ancestors. Just offshore are the ruins of another temple, Hale-ō Ka-puni Heiau, which was dedicated to the shark gods. This temple was last seen in the 1950s, when the rock platform was visible at low tide. The stone leaning post is a rock used by a high chief to lean against as he watched sharks circle about Hale-ō Ka-puni Heiau before devouring the offerings he had placed there. Below Mailekini Heiau is Pelekāne, the site of the king's residence at Kawaihae. In 1790, British sailor John Young was stranded on Hawaii and became a close friend and military adviser of Kamehameha. The site of Young's home is north of Pu'ukohola Heiau across State Road 270.

A small visitor center just off Highway 270 provides information and exhibits on Kamehameha and the park's history. A relatively rugged, steep trail leads from this point to major features of the park.

FACILITIES: No food service or lodging is available at the site. Gasoline and oil and a convenience store for supplies are located 1 mile away. Water and rest rooms are provided at the park's visitor center.

CAMPING: No camping is permitted at the site, but camping and swimming are available nearby at Samuel Spencer County Park. Water and flush toilets are provided.

FISHING: The park's shoreline is a poor location for surf fishing. Better access is available at Samuel Spencer County Park.

USS *ARIZONA* MEMORIAL

1 Arizona Memorial Place
Honolulu, HI 96818-3145
(808) 422–2771
www.nps.gov/usar/

The USS *Arizona* Memorial was established in 1962 as a memorial marking the spot where the Japanese sank the battleship USS *Arizona* during the December 7, 1941, attack on Pearl Harbor. The National Park Service took over the Memorial, visitor center, and tour operations in October 1980. The park is located on the island of Oahu, about twenty minutes west of downtown Honolulu on Kamehameha Highway (Highway 99).

On November 26, 1941, a Japanese task force of thirty-two ships plus twenty-seven submarines set out from Japan to the Hawaiian Islands. The purpose of the mission was to destroy America's Pacific Fleet. The first wave of Japanese aircraft arrived over their targets at 7:55 A.M. on December 7, 1941, and, meeting virtually no opposition, strafed and bombed at will. In addition to the strike at Pearl Harbor, the Japanese attacked other installations such as Wheeler Air Field, Schofield Barracks, Kanehoe Naval Air Station, Hickam Airfield, Ewa Marine Corps Air Station, and Bellows Airfield. The USS *Arizona* sank with a loss of more than 1,100 crew members only nine minutes after being hit by a 1,760-pound armor-piercing aerial bomb shortly after the attack commenced.

The park's visitor center is directly off Highway 99. Visitors should stop at the information desk and obtain tickets for the tour, which includes a film and boat trip to the Memorial.

Tickets are issued on a first-come, first-served basis, and ticket holders enter the theater and ride the boat in groups. The Memorial is often crowded, so long waits can occur. Visitors may browse through exhibits at the visitor center or tour the nearby World War II submarine USS *Bowfin* while waiting for their tour group to be called.

FACILITIES: A snack bar is available. A bookstore with military books and related interpretive material is operated by the nonprofit *Arizona* Memorial Museum Association. Drinking water and rest rooms are available at the visitor center.

CAMPING: No camping is permitted in the park.

FISHING: No fishing is permitted in the park.

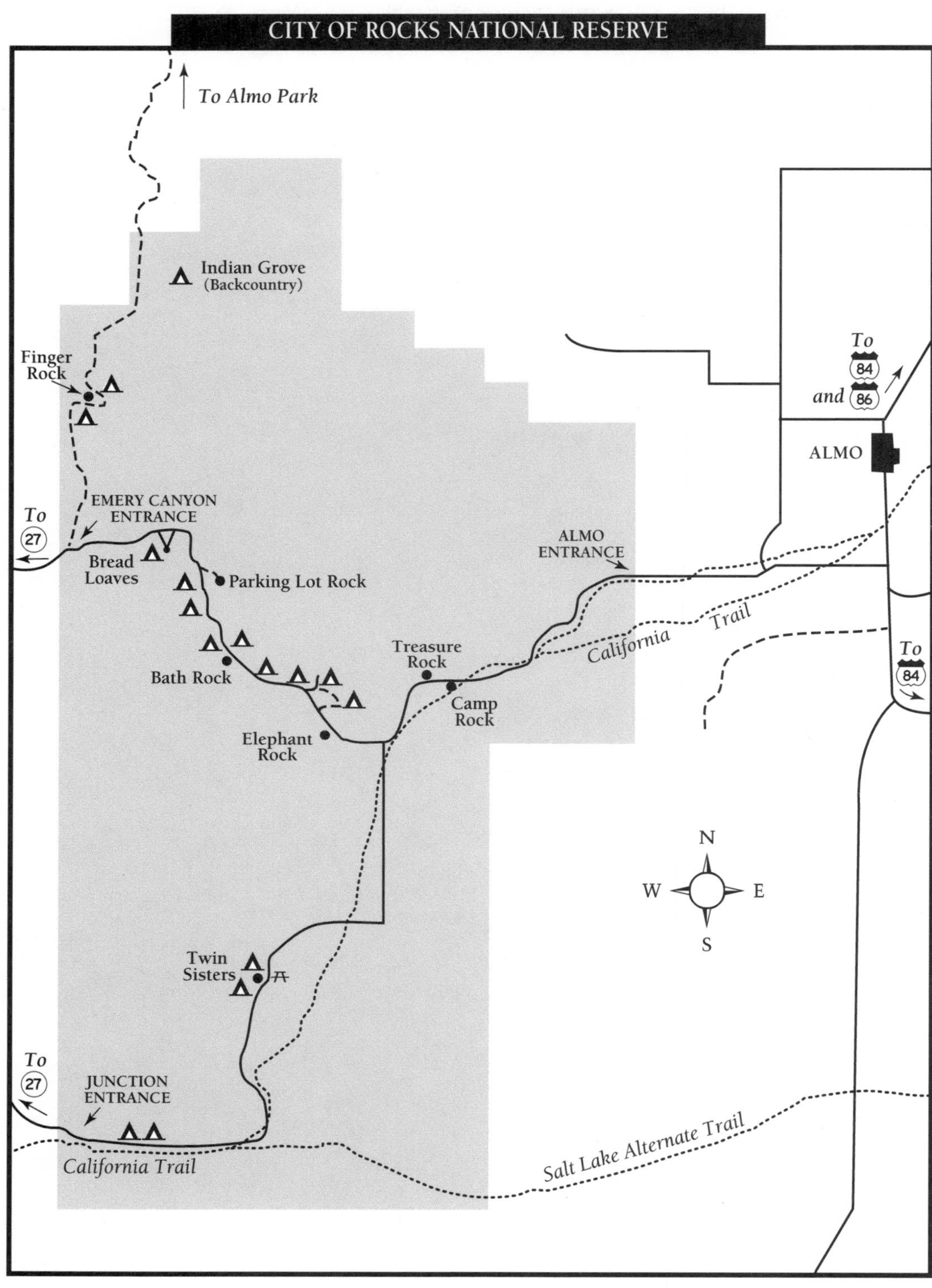
CITY OF ROCKS NATIONAL RESERVE
To Almo Park
Indian Grove
(Backcountry)
Finger Rock
To
27
EMERY CANYON ENTRANCE
Bread Loaves
Parking Lot Rock
Bath Rock
Treasure Rock
Camp Rock
Elephant Rock
ALMO ENTRANCE
California Trail
To
84
and
86
ALMO
To
84
N
W
E
S
Twin Sisters
To
27
JUNCTION ENTRANCE
California Trail
Salt Lake Alternate Trail

STATE TOURIST INFORMATION
(800) 635–7820

CITY OF ROCKS NATIONAL RESERVE

P.O. Box 169
Almo, ID 83312-0169
(208) 824–5519
www.nps.gov/ciro/

City of Rocks National Reserve comprises slightly over 14,000 acres (one-third private, two-thirds public) and was established in 1988 to preserve significant cultural and natural resources, including scenic granite spires, sculptured rock formations, and visible remnants of the California Trail. The reserve is located in south central Idaho, 50 miles south of the town of Burley via Highway 27 from the west and Highway 77 from the east. Reserve headquarters, with a visitor center, is in the town of Almo.

The monoliths, spires, and domes found in City of Rocks National Reserve are the result of millions of years of erosion from wind and water. As overlying rocks and granite cracked and fractured, underlying granite was eroded to form the shapes that can be seen today by visitors. Exposed formations range in age from relatively recent to more than two billion years. The varied rock formations located in the reserve have made this one of the prime areas for climbers from around the world.

This area was once traversed by Shoshone and Bannock Indians. By 1843, settlers traveled through City of Rocks via the California Trail, which linked Sacramento, California, with St. Joseph, Missouri, and the Salt Lake Alternate Trail. It is estimated that 50,000 people passed through in 1852 on their way to the California gold fields. Remnants of the California Trail are still visible.

City of Rocks is in the high desert, 5,000 to 8,000 feet above sea level, where the summer temperature can range from freezing to more than one hundred degrees Fahrenheit. This environment supports aspen, Douglas fir, and lodgepole pine, and, at lower elevations, sagebrush, pinyon pine, and juniper. A variety of wildflowers can be seen in spring and summer. Wildlife includes mule deer, mountain lions, bobcats, porcupines, and coyotes.

FACILITIES: Potable water is available only at a hand pump at the Emery Canyon Road summit, 3/4 mile above Bath Rock. All other water should be boiled or purified. Telephones, gasoline, and food supplies are available at Almo and Oakley, while the nearest full services are in Burley.

CAMPING: Seventy-eight primitive camping sites are scattered along the main road. Each site has a table and fire ring. Two vehicles and eight people are allowed at each site.

FISHING: No fishing is available in City of Rocks National Reserve.

CRATERS OF THE MOON NATIONAL MONUMENT

P.O. Box 29
Arco, ID 83213-0029
(208) 527–3257
www.nps.gov/crmo/

Established in 1924, Craters of the Moon National Monument perserves 83 square miles of the 618-square-mile Craters of the Moon Lava Field. The park contains sixty different lava flows and more than twenty-five cones, including one of the largest basaltic cinder cones in the world. The national monument is located in south-central Idaho, approximately 18 miles southwest of the town of Arco on U.S. 20/26/93.

Craters of the Moon National Monument is a unique unit of the National Park Service. The park is appropriately named and a visit will make you think you actually have arrived on the surface of the moon. Cones and lava flows in the monument range in age from 15,000 to just 2,000 years of age. There are excellent examples of pahoehoe and aa lava as well as rafted blocks, tree molds, and lava tube caves. The north end of the monument contains a portion of Goodale's Cutoff, a part of the Oregon Trail.

Although desolate looking, the park thrives with wildlife and plants. Flowers bloom, birds sing, and mammals scurry about the strange geologic formations. More than 375 species of plants are found in the monument. The flowers are usually at their peak in mid-June. The monument also provides a home for nearly 2,000 insect species, 10 amphibians and reptiles, 162 types of birds, and 43 mammals.

Many interesting points in the park can be reached by means of a 7-mile paved loop drive. Seven trailheads lead from the road or one of its nearby side roads. Two of the longer trails lead into Craters of the Moon Wilderness Area, which contains the largest portion of the monument. The hike to the Tree Molds area will take about two hours, and the trail to Echo Crater will consume considerably more time. The Devils Orchard Nature Trail begins at the end of a side road near the start of the loop. This 1/3-mile self-guided trail takes the hiker through a display of cinder fields and crater-wall fragments and requires approximately twenty minutes to complete. Self-guided and easy-to-walk North Crater Flow Trail begins at a turnout just south of the campground. Two different parking lots provide access to the beginning of a trail to North

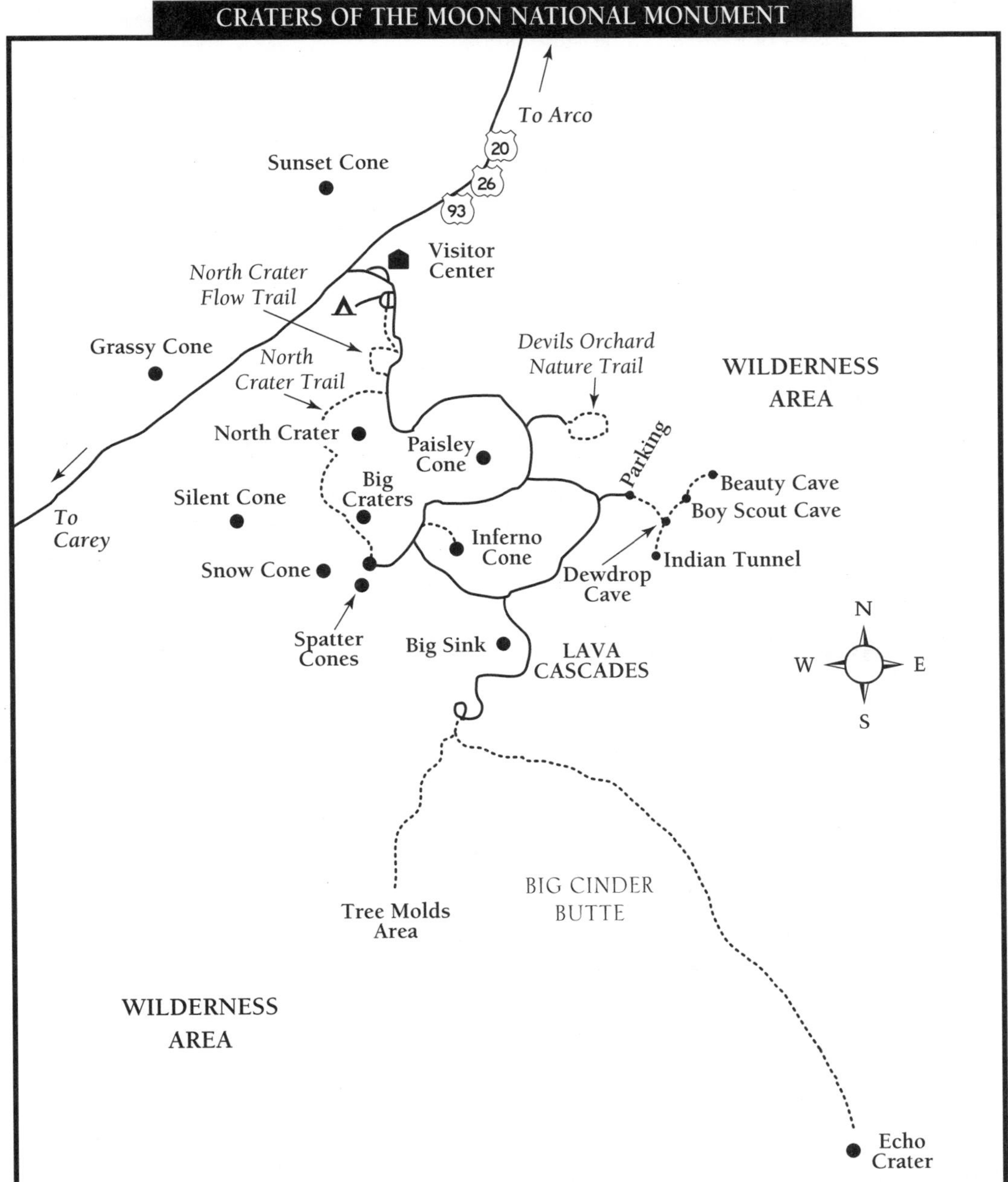

Crater and Big Craters. Although longer (1¾ miles) and quite rigorous, the views into the craters are spectacular.

One fascinating feature of the park is the cave area. These caves are lava tubes and can be reached by hiking a short trail at the end of one of the side roads of the loop drive. The caves were formed when the surface area of lava flows cooled and hardened. This crust formed an insulating barrier so that the still-molten material in the interior could continue to flow. Later, lava drained out of the tubes when the eruption stopped. The largest cave is Indian Tunnel (800 feet). Beauty, Dewdrop, and Boy Scout caves are smaller and more difficult to enter. The latter cave contains a floor of ice that can be quite slippery.

The park is open twenty-four hours daily, year-round. The visitor center, which has a recently remodeled museum with exhibits that explain the natural history of the area, is open daily from 8:00 A.M. to 6:00 P.M. from mid-June to Labor Day, and until 4:30 P.M. the remainder of the year except winter holidays. During summer months, ranger-guided hikes are conducted each day and campfire programs are presented each evening. December, January, and February are usually the best months for skiing and snowshoeing. (Check at visitor center for where to go.) In winter, the 7-mile loop drive is closed and groomed for cross-country skiing.

FACILITIES: Accommodations, food service, and gasoline are not available within the park but can be found in the town of Arco. Modern rest rooms and drinking water are at the visitor center and the campground.

CAMPING: A unique campground (fifty-two spaces) located near the visitor center just off the main highway is set in the volcanic field amid cinders and volcanic rocks. Charcoal grills, tables, drinking water, and flush toilets (summer only) are provided. Little shade is available. No wood fires are permitted. Campsites are not plowed of snow in winter.

FISHING: No fishing is available in Craters of the Moon National Monument.

HAGERMAN FOSSIL BEDS NATIONAL MONUMENT

221 North State Street
P.O. Box 570
Hagerman, ID 83332-0570
(208) 837–4793
www.nps.gov/hafo/

Hagerman Fossil Beds National Monument comprises 4,280 acres and was authorized in 1988 to preserve an area containing extraordinary and abundant fossils. The monument is located in south central Idaho, on the west bank of the Snake River near the small town of Hagerman. From Hagerman, drive 4 7/10 miles south on U.S. 30 over the bridge crossing the Snake River. Turn right on the first road and drive approximately 3 miles to the parking lot and boardwalk overlook, which has several wayside exhibits. Another overlook is at the top of the grade.

Three and a half million years ago, the area that is now the Hagerman Valley was part of a flood plain near a huge lake. Abundant rainfall (twice the annual rainfall of today) produced open grassland and streams. The environment supported vegetation, including pine woodland and hardwood trees, and a variety of wildlife, including camels, four-horned antelope, ducks, egrets, zebralike horses, mastodons, pelicans, storks, and swans. Seasonal flooding buried the skeletons and bones of the plants, birds, and animals under layers of sediment and preserved the fossils that are found in this area today.

The steep bluffs overlooking the Snake River west of Hagerman contain fossils that went largely unnoticed until 1928, when a local rancher showed fossil bones to an employee of the U.S. Geological Survey. Subsequent excavation unearthed the remains of beaver, birds, fish, frog, mastodon, rabbit, turtle, and the largest single deposit ever found of an extinct species of zebralike horse. No fossil collection is permitted.

Hagerman National Monument is a relatively new addition to the National Park Service and has limited facilities and personnel. A temporary visitor center with exhibits and audiovisual programs is located along Highway 30 in the town of Hagerman. The center is open daily from 8:30 A.M. to 5:00 P.M. from June through September, and 10:00 A.M to 4:00 P.M Thursday through Sunday the remainder of the year. Rangers are available to answer questions about the monument and fossils. A trailhead across the road from an overlook provides access to the Emigrant Trail. Parking for horse trailers is at the top of the grade. A more extensive trail system on the north end of the monument is open to hiking, mountain bikes, and horseback riding. Information on the monument's trail system is available at the visitor center.

FACILITIES: The only visitor facilities in the monument are trails. Food and lodging are available in the town of Hagerman and in other nearby towns. Rest rooms and water are available in the visitor center in Hagerman.

CAMPING: Three Island Crossing State Park, approximately 25 miles northwest of Hagerman, near the town of Glenns Ferry, has fifty campsites, water, tables, and flush toilets. There is a dump station here and in Hagerman. Several commercial RV parks are located south of Hagerman along Highway 30, and there is one north of town.

FISHING: Anglers may fish in the Snake River or nearby lakes and creeks. An Idaho fishing license is required.

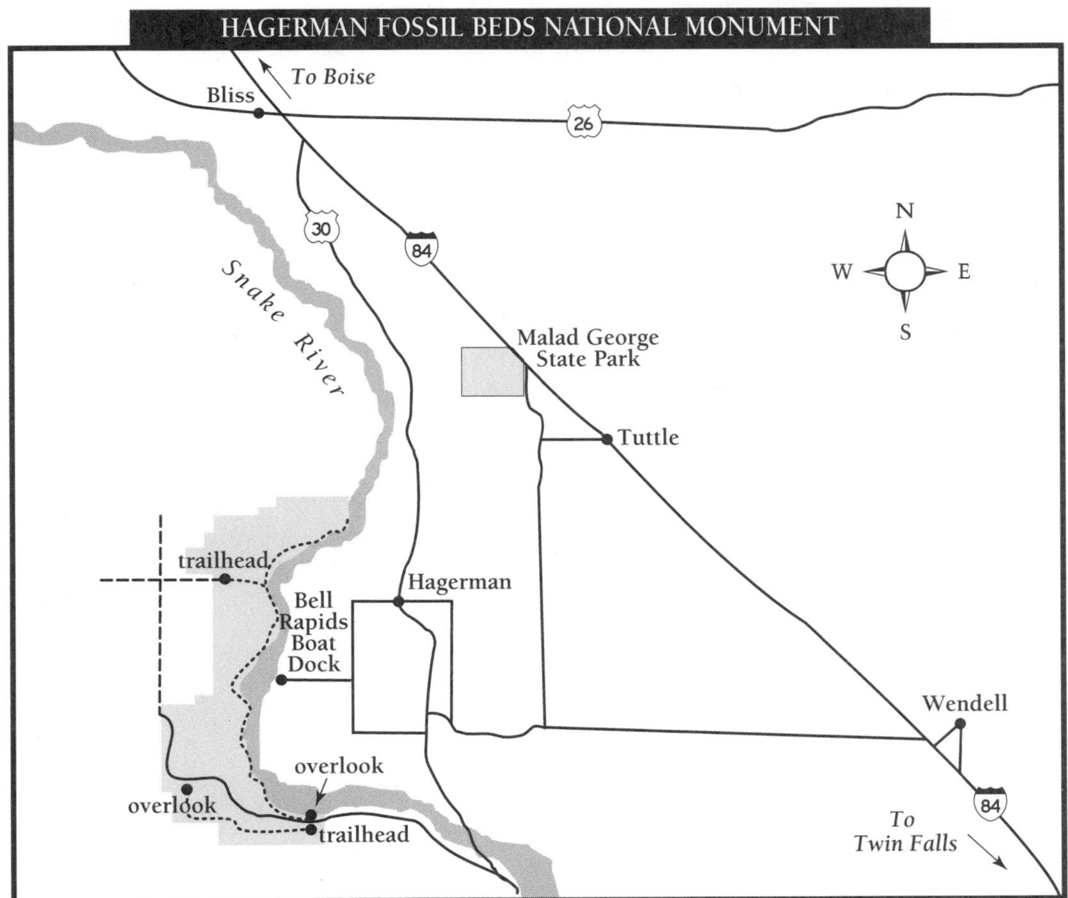

NEZ PERCE NATIONAL HISTORICAL PARK

Route 1, Box 100
Spalding, ID 83540-0093
(208) 843–2261
www.nps.gov/nepe/

Nez Perce National Historical Park was authorized in 1965. It comprises thirty-eight historical sites scattered over a large area of eastern Washington, northeast Oregon, western Montana, and northern Idaho that illustrate a chapter in the history and culture of the American Northwest.

For thousands of years the valleys, prairies, and plateaus of north central Idaho and adjacent Oregon and Washington have been home to the Nez Perce people. In 1965 Nez Perce National Historical Park was established to commemorate the legends and history of the Nez Perce and their interaction with explorers, fur traders, missionaries, soldiers, settlers, gold miners, loggers, and farmers who moved through or into the area. Originally the park comprised twenty-four sites scattered across north central Idaho. In 1992, new legislation was passed adding fourteen sites in Washington, Oregon, Montana, and Idaho. The park headquarters is located at Spalding, Idaho, 11 miles east of Lewiston. Visitor centers are currently located at Spalding and Big Hole National Battlefield near Wisdom, Montana.

In 1805, Meriwether Lewis and William Clark led a small group across the Bitterroot Mountains into Nez Perce country. The Nez Perce received them graciously, gave them supplies, and told them about the river route to the Pacific. Soon fur trappers and traders, both British and American, followed in their wake. By 1855, so many settlers came demanding land that the government was forced to define a reservation for the Nez Perce. Most of their traditional land was inside the new boundaries, but greed for land and gold within the reservation led to the "Steal Treaty" of 1863, in which 90 percent of the original land was taken for white settlement. When Nez Perce bands outside the 1863 treaty area were forced to move, trouble began, resulting in the War of 1877, which lasted four months and covered 1,500 miles, from Wallowa, Oregon, to Bear Paw, Montana, just 40 miles short of the Canadian border.

FACILITIES: Gas, food, and lodging are available in the towns adjacent to the park.

CAMPING: Although no camping is provided by the Park Service, the area offers a diversity of camping opportunities. Clearwater, Nez Perce, and Wallowa-Whitman national forests have campgrounds, as does the Corps of Engineers' Dworshak Reservoir. Winchester, Hellsgate, and Timothy state parks are all within thirty minutes' driving time of Spalding.

FISHING: Major rivers flow throughout the park areas, offering some of the finest sport fishing in the country. Each state requires a fishing license, with an additional steelhead permit required on the Clearwater River in Idaho.

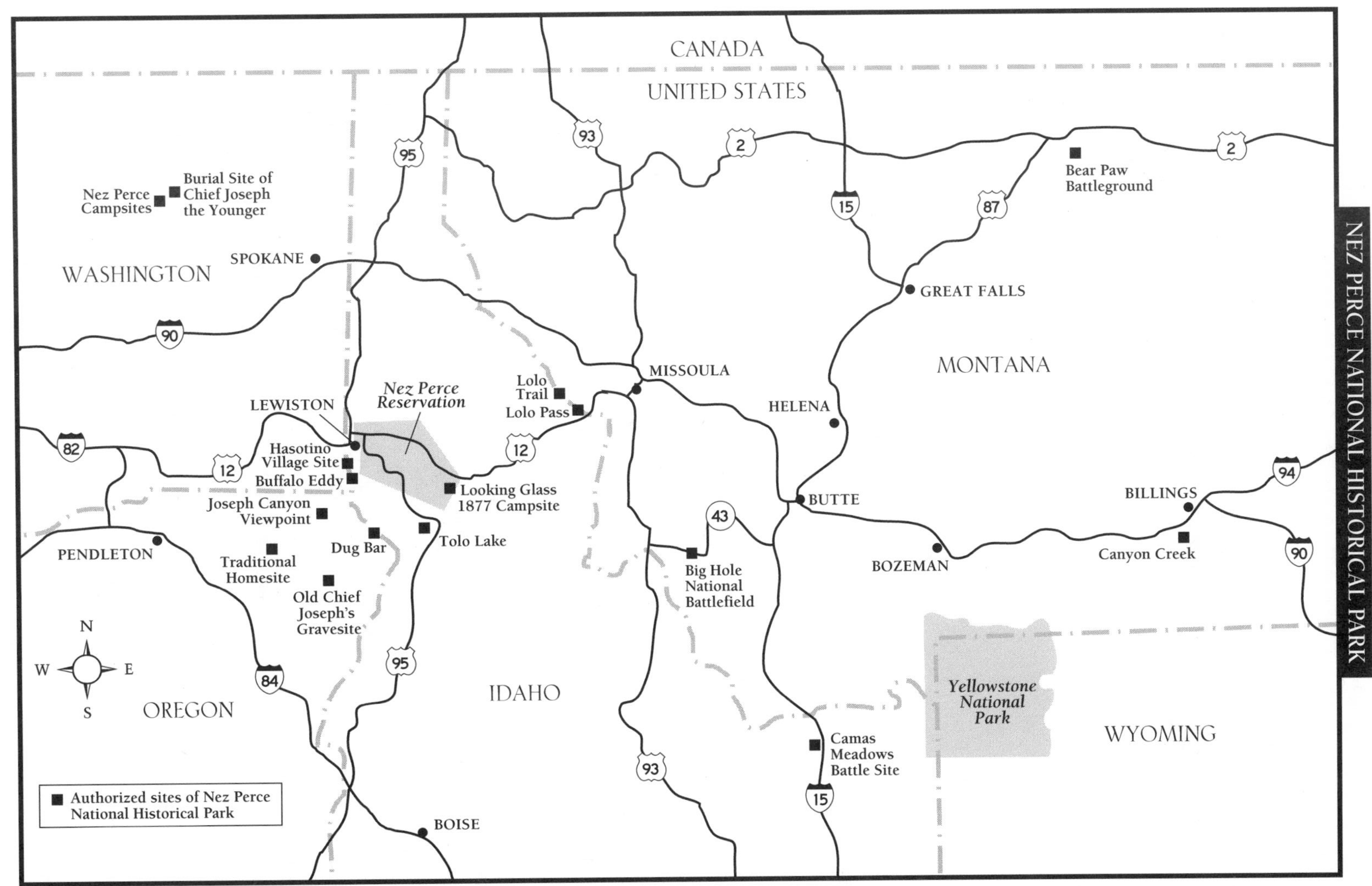
NEZ PERCE NATIONAL HISTORICAL PARK
CANADA
UNITED STATES
WASHINGTON
MONTANA
IDAHO
OREGON
WYOMING
Nez Perce Campsites
Burial Site of Chief Joseph the Younger
SPOKANE
Bear Paw Battleground
GREAT FALLS
MISSOULA
Lolo Trail
Lolo Pass
HELENA
Nez Perce Reservation
LEWISTON
Hasotino Village Site
Buffalo Eddy
Looking Glass 1877 Campsite
Joseph Canyon Viewpoint
Dug Bar
Tolo Lake
BUTTE
BILLINGS
Canyon Creek
BOZEMAN
PENDLETON
Traditional Homesite
Old Chief Joseph's Gravesite
Big Hole National Battlefield
Yellowstone National Park
Camas Meadows Battle Site
BOISE
N
W
E
S
Authorized sites of Nez Perce National Historical Park
95
93
2
15
87
90
82
12
43
94
84
15

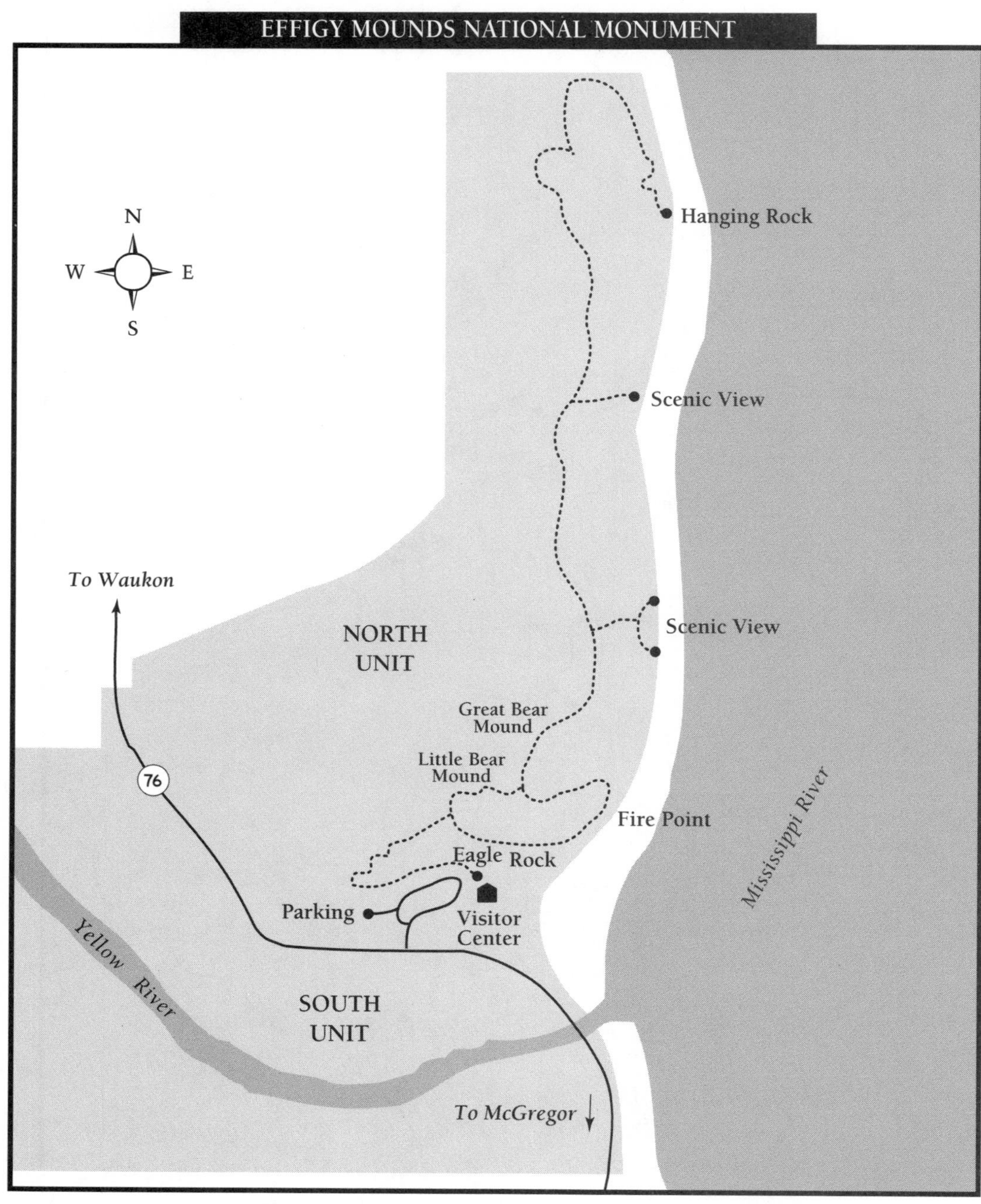
EFFIGY MOUNDS NATIONAL MONUMENT
N
W
E
S
Hanging Rock
Scenic View
To Waukon
Scenic View
NORTH UNIT
Great Bear Mound
Little Bear Mound
76
Fire Point
Mississippi River
Eagle Rock
Parking
Visitor Center
Yellow River
SOUTH UNIT
To McGregor

STATE TOURIST INFORMATION

(800) 345–4692

EFFIGY MOUNDS NATIONAL MONUMENT

151 Highway 76
Harpers Ferry, IA 52146-7519
(319) 873–3491
www.nps.gov/efmo/

Effigy Mounds comprises 1,481 acres. It was established in 1949 to preserve outstanding examples of prehistoric Indian mounds, some of which are in the shapes of birds and bears. The park is located in northeastern Iowa, 3 miles north of Marquette on Iowa Highway 76.

Effigy Mounds National Monument contains 191 known prehistoric mounds, of which twenty-nine are in the form of bear and bird effigies and the remainder are conical or linear shaped. The oldest mound excavated in the park, belonging to the Red Ocher Culture, has been dated to be about 2,500 years old. Burial offerings included large chipped blades, dart points, and spherical copper beads. Other mounds, from a culture dating from 100 B.C. to A.D. 600, have been excavated, revealing pottery and projectile points.

The Effigy Mounds people occupied this land beginning approximately A.D. 700. They differed from the earlier mound builders not only in constructing mounds in effigy forms but also in using copper for tools instead of ornaments and in burying their dead with few lasting offerings. By about 1400, the Effigy Mounds people were replaced by Indians of the Oneota Culture.

The park's visitor center contains museum exhibits and an audiovisual presentation on the geology and history of Effigy Mounds. It is open daily (except winter federal holidays) from 8:00 A.M. until 5:00 P.M. The North Unit contains the self-guiding Fire Point Trail, which provides access to some of the park's major points of interest, including some mounds and viewpoints on 300-foot bluffs along the Mississippi River. Trail markers and exhibits help interpret the walk. Ranger-guided walks are given frequently during summer months. A longer walk along the Hanging Rock Trail takes visitors to other points of interest. The South Unit contains the Marching Bears Mound Group, a spectacular collection of effigy mounds (ten bears, three birds, and two linear mounds). The trail is self-guiding and approximately 2½ miles one way.

FACILITIES: No lodging or food service is available in the park. Rest rooms and drinking water are provided in the visitor center.

CAMPING: No camping is permitted at Effigy Mounds National Monument. Six miles south, on top of a bluff, Pikes Peak State Park offers eighty sites, most of which have electrical and water hookups. Six miles northwest, Yellow River State Forest offers 126 sites, but no showers.

FISHING: No fishing is available at the park. There is a trout stream in Yellow River State Forest, 6 miles northwest of Effigy Mounds.

HERBERT HOOVER NATIONAL HISTORIC SITE

P.O. Box 607
West Branch, IA 52358-0607
(319) 643–2541
heho_interpretations@nps.gov
www.nps.gov/heho/

Herbert Hoover National Historic Site comprises 187 acres and was established in 1965. The park includes the cottage where Hoover was born, his grave site, and his Presidential Library-Museum. The historic site is located in West Branch, Iowa, 10 miles east of Iowa City on Interstate 80.

Herbert Hoover—mining engineer, humanitarian, statesman, and thirty-first president of the United States—was born August 10, 1874 in West Branch, Iowa. His father, a blacksmith, died when Herbert was only six years old. His mother died three years later. Herbert lived with relatives in West Branch until age eleven, when he moved to Oregon to live with an uncle and his family. At the age of seventeen, Hoover enrolled at Stanford University and in 1895 graduated with a degree in geology in the first class of the newly founded Stanford.

Hoover worked in the California gold mines and moved on to mining engineering projects in Australia, China, and England. He became very well known in international mining circles. During World War I, Hoover headed a variety of relief efforts that helped feed millions of people in thirty-three nations. He served as secretary of commerce for eight years and was then elected to the presidency in 1928. Following his unsuccessful effort at reelection, Hoover retired to California, where he devoted much of his time to the Hoover Institute on War, Revolution, and Peace at Stanford. He served on presidential commissions in 1946, 1947, and 1953 to study famine relief and recommend improvements in the executive branch of the federal government. Hoover died on October 20, 1964, and was buried on a hillside overlooking his birthplace.

In addition to the Hoover birthplace and grave site, the park contains a portion of the village of West Branch that is restored as a late-nineteenth-century midwestern neighborhood. A blacksmith shop, schoolhouse, and Friends (Quaker) meetinghouse are open to visitors. A visitor center is located near the park's entrance at Parkside Drive and Main Street. The Presidential Library-

Museum contains a collection of Hoover's presidential papers and exhibits illustrating his distinguished career. The park's buildings are open from 9:00 A.M. to 5:00 P.M. daily except Thanksgiving, Christmas, and New Year's Day. The library-museum and the site charge nominal fees for admission. Children are admitted free.

FACILITIES: No food or lodging is available in the park, but both are found in nearby West Branch. Drinking water and rest rooms are provided in the visitor center and the library-museum.

CAMPING: No camping is permitted in the park. Lake McBride State Park offers camping approximately 25 miles northwest of West Branch. Several private campgrounds also are located nearby.

FISHING: No fishing is available at the historic site.

Herbert Hoover Birthplace Cottage, Herbert Hoover National Historic Site

Fort Scott National Historic Site

STATE TOURIST INFORMATION
(800) 252–6727

BROWN V. BOARD OF EDUCATION NATIONAL HISTORIC SITE

424 South Kansas Avenue, Suite 220
Topeka, KA 66603-3441
(785) 354–4273
www.nps.gov/brvb/

Brown v. Board of Education National Historic Site was established in 1992 to commemorate the 1954 Supreme Court decision that ended legal racial segregation in America's public schools. The historic site is located at the former Monroe Elementary School in the city of Topeka in northeast Kansas.

Before the famous 1954 U.S. Supreme Court decision in Brown v. Board of Education of Topeka, racial segregation was justified in parts of the United States on the basis that separate but equal educational facilities were legally permissible. An 1896 U.S. Supreme Court decision had held that "separate but equal" facilities were permissible in public transportation, a ruling that was subsequently applied to other activities including education. In 1951, the NAACP of Topeka filed suit in U.S. District Court arguing that segregated public schools were not equal and could not be made equal. The case was brought on behalf of twenty African-American children who had been denied access to certain elementary schools reserved for whites. Although the District Court ruled against the plaintiffs, the case was ultimately appealed to the U.S. Supreme Court and argued by NAACP attorney Thurgood Marshall. A court led by Chief Justice Earl Warren delivered the unanimous opinion that "separate but equal educational facilities are inherently unequal."

The site's National Park Service headquarters is housed in the Main Post Office Building at 424 South Kansas Avenue. It is open weekdays from 8:00 A.M. to 5:00 P.M. except federal holidays. Offsite interpretive programs are available by calling park headquarters. Monroe

Elementary School, the segregated school attended by the lead plaintiff's daughter, is in the process of major renovation. When completed, the site will serve as an interpretive and resource center for information about the impact on the civil rights movement of Brown v. Board of Education. The school is not currently open to the public except with tours arranged in advance through site headquarters.

FACILITIES: The National Park Service provides no facilities. Food service and lodging are in and around Topeka.

CAMPING: County-operated Lake Shawnee Campground (913–267–1156), 2 miles south of Topeka off I–70 at East Kansas, offers 179 sites with tables, grills, flush toilets, and a dump station. Electrical and water hookups are available at most sites. Perry State Park (785–246–3449), 16 miles northeast of Topeka via state roads 24 and 237, offers 120 sites with tables, grills, flush toilets, and a dump station.

FORT LARNED NATIONAL HISTORIC SITE

Route 3
Larned, KS 67550-9733
(316) 285–6911
FOLS_Internet@nps.gov
www.nps.gov/fols/

Fort Larned, which comprises 718 acres, was incorporated into the National Park System in 1966 to protect the remains of a key military base along the Santa Fe Trail. The fort is located in southwestern Kansas, 6 miles west of the town of Larned on Kansas Highway 156. Also see the map under Bent's Old Fort National Historic Site (Colorado) in this book.

Named after Army Paymaster-General Benjamin Larned, Fort Larned was built in 1860 to protect travelers and the U.S. mail on the Santa Fe Trail from attacks by the Plains Indians. Seven adobe buildings were constructed at the fort during its first year, and in the winter of 1864–65, a stone blockhouse was added for protection. In 1866, additional appropriations allowed a renewed building program. Sandstone from quarries east of the fort was combined with pine timbers shipped from the East in the construction of nine new stone buildings around a quadrangular parade ground.

Following its use as a source of protection for those traveling the Santa Fe Trail, Fort Larned was used as a base of operations for the U.S. Army during the Indian War of 1867–68. By the end of 1868, organized Indian resistance had been broken in the Fort Larned area. During the early 1870s, the fort housed soldiers who were to protect construction workers on the Santa Fe Railroad. The railroad was completed in 1872, and in July 1878 Fort Larned was abandoned.

The nine surviving original stone buildings are today complemented by a restored parade ground complete with a flagstaff and a reconstructed blockhouse. Several of the buildings are open to visitors, and guided tours and living-history programs are presented during summer months. The visitor center—with a museum, audiovisual program, and exhibits—is housed in the barracks buildings next to the parking lot for the handicapped. A brochure for a self-guiding walk of the historic site is available in the visitor center. Four miles southeast, a detached forty-acre unit of the historic site contains well-preserved wagon ruts of the Santa Fe Trail. A brochure is available in the visitor center at the main unit. The park is open daily from 8:30 A.M. to 5:00 P.M. except Thanksgiving, Christmas, and New Year's Day.

FACILITIES: Drinking water and rest rooms are provided in the visitor center. A shaded picnic area is located at the entrance to the site. Food and lodging are available in the town of Larned.

CAMPING: No camping is permitted at the site, but there is a private campground in the town of Larned.

FISHING: No fishing is available.

See map on page 112.

FORT SCOTT NATIONAL HISTORIC SITE

Old Fort Boulevard
P.O. Box 918
Fort Scott, KS 66701-1471
(316) 223–0310
fosc_interpretation@nps.gov
www.nps.gov/focs/

Fort Scott National Historic Site comprises seventeen acres. It was established as an area of the National Park Service in 1979, although federal planning and financial assistance were authorized in 1965 to help preserve and restore this important fort of the mid-1800s. Fort Scott is located in southeastern Kansas, 90 miles south of Kansas City and 60 miles north of Joplin, Missouri. In the town of Fort Scott, the site is located on Old Fort Boulevard.

Fort Scott was constructed in 1842 as part of a chain of posts designed to provide a frontier buffer zone between Indian Territory to the west and the developing states to the east. It was manned by dragoons and infantry that policed the Indian Territory. After Congress opened more western territory to white settlement in the early 1850s, the frontier moved west and Fort Scott's importance diminished. In 1855, all of the army buildings were sold at a public auction, and they became part of the new town of Fort Scott. Throughout the late 1850s, free states and slavery supporters clashed over whether Kansas would be a free or slave state. Violent turmoil ocurred often at Fort Scott. During the Civil War, the town was occupied by the Union Army, and the fort was reactivated. It was a major federal supply base, communications center, and staging area for campaigns into Confederate territory.

The park's visitor center and bookstore are located in the post hospital, near the parking lot. The fort contains a number of other restored and reconstructed buildings open to visitors. Three areas of the park have been restored to tall-grass prairie. Fort Scott is open daily from 8:00 A.M. to 5:00 P.M. April through October and 9:00.A.M to 5:00 P.M. November through March except Thanksgiving, Christmas, and New Year's Day.

FACILITIES: No lodging or food service is available in the park, but both can be found nearby. Rest rooms and drinking water are located in the visitor center.

CAMPING: No camping is permitted in the park. A city-operated campground is approximately 2 miles from the historic site. Two state parks within 25 miles of the site offer camping facilities.

FISHING: No fishing is available.

NICODEMUS NATIONAL HISTORIC SITE

c/o Fort Larned National Historic Site
Route 3
Larned, KS 67550
(316) 285–6911
www.nps.gov/nico/

Nicodemus National Historic Site was authorized in 1996 to interpret and help preserve the only remaining western town established by African-Americans during the reconstruction period following the Civil War. The national historic site is located in the unincorporated town of Nicodemus in north-central Kansas on U.S. Highway 24, and approximately 37 miles northeast of U.S. Interstate 70 at WaKeeny.

Between 1860 and 1880 the black population of Kansas increased from 627 to 43,107 as African-Americans migrated from the South to the Midwest following the Civil War. The town of Nicodemus is one of several all-black Kansas towns that were settled during this period. Named for a legendary slave, the town was officially founded on September 17, 1877. From a few early arrivals in the summer of 1877, within a decade, the town had a bank, two newspapers, a post office, a livery stable, a literary society, and even an ice-cream parlor. The county's black population grew until it reached a peak of 595 in 1910, but by 1950, only sixteen residents remained.

Nicodemus National Historic Site is a relatively new addition to the system, and the National Park Service is currently working on a management plan for the site. The site includes an A.M.E. church, a limestone and stucco building erected in 1885 and in active use until the 1940s; and four privately owned buildings including the First Baptist Church, which was built in 1907 and continued in use until 1977; the St. Francis Hotel, a two-story limestone structure erected in 1880; Nicodemus School, built in 1918 on the site of an earlier schoolhouse; and Township Hall, built in 1939 by the Works Progress Administration. None of the buildings is open to the public.

FACILITIES: No facilities are available at the national historic site. A picnic area with tables and water is maintained by the State Highway Department. Food and lodging are located along U.S. Highway 24.

CAMPING: Ten miles east of Nicodemus on U.S. Highway 24, Webster State Park offers one hundred camping sites with water, grills, tables, flush toilets, and a dump station. Thirty-six of the sites have electrical and water hookups.

FISHING: Fishing is available in Webster Reservoir at Webster State Park. A Kansas fishing license is required.

TALLGRASS PRAIRIE NATIONAL PRESERVE

Route 1, Box 14
Strong City, KS 66869
(316) 273–8494
tapr_interpretation@nps.gov
www.nps.gov/tapr/

Tallgrass Prairie National Preserve was established in 1996 to preserve, protect, and interpret nearly 11,000 acres of nationally significant tallgrass prairie ecosystem. The preserve also includes the historic buildings and cultural resources of the former Z Bar/Spring Hill Ranch. The national preserve is located in the Flint Hills of east-central Kansas, just north of Strong City, on Highway 177.

This 10,894-acre remnant of tallgrass prairie was purchased in 1994 by the National Park Trust, a private, nonprofit, land conservancy dedicated to protecting America's national parks. The former Z Bar/Spring Hill Ranch is home to nearly 400 species of plants and 150 types of birds. Nearly all this land will continue to be owned by the National Park Trust, with no more than

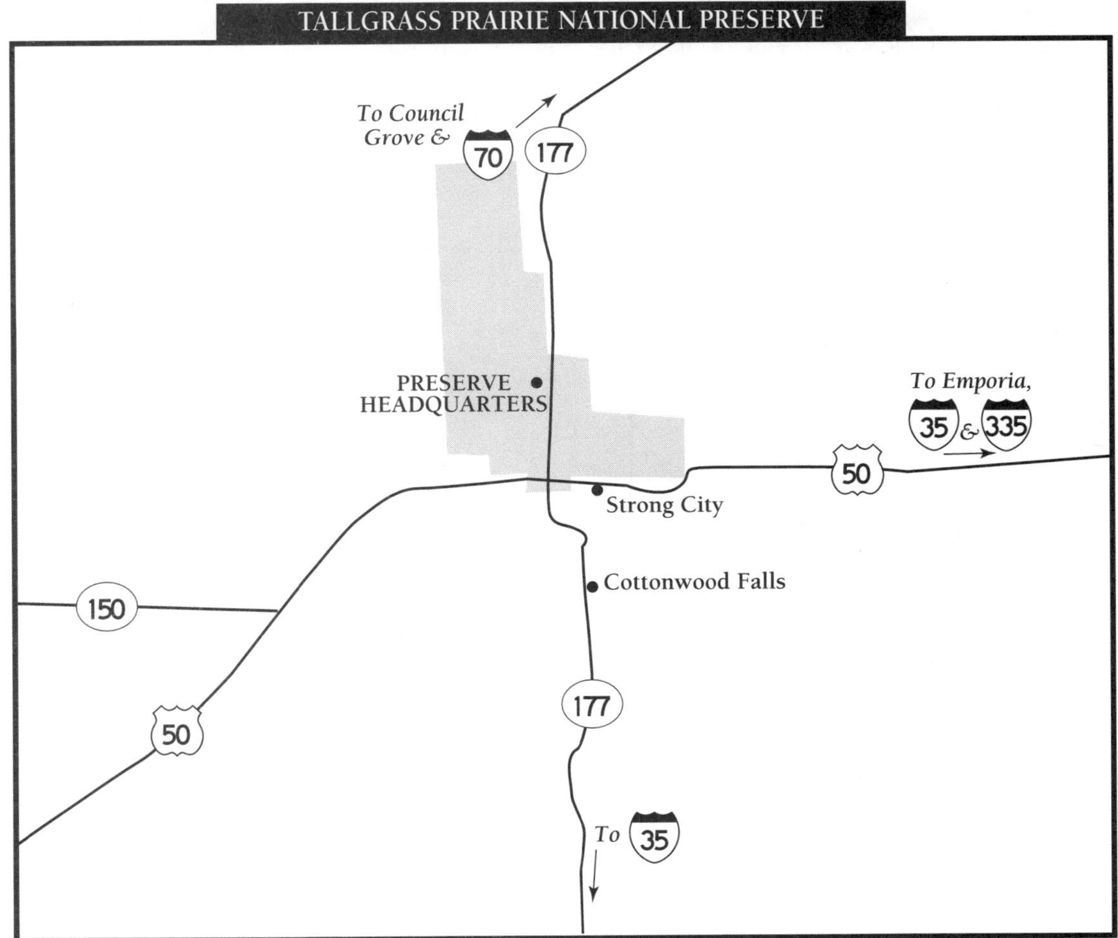

180 acres owned by the federal government. An advisory committee and the general public have been providing input to the National Park Service in developing a General Management Plan for the preserve. The entire preserve will eventually be managed by the National Park Service through a cooperative agreement with the trust.

A complex of ranch buildings is the focal point of the preserve for visitors. Buildings include the main ranch house constructed in 1881, a massive three-story limestone barn, carriage house, chicken house, smoke house, and ice house. An information station offers a ten-minute video presentation, exhibits, and brochures. A bookstore provides visitors with educational materials about the prairie, American Indians, and the rich ranching legacy of the Flint Hills. Visitors can tour the ranch headquarters area on their own with the help of a brochure and wayside exhibits. House tours are available on weekends from mid-April through October. A ranger-led 7-mile, bus tour (fee charged) is offered three times daily, except Tuesdays, from mid-April through October. Tours for groups of fifteen or more are available on a reservation basis (fee charged). The 1¾-mile loop Southwind Nature Trail offers an opportunity for a leisurely stroll through the prairie grassland and by the Lower Fox Creek Schoolhouse. All of the facilities are closed on Thanksgiving, Christmas, New Year's, and during inclement weather.

FACILITIES: Food and lodging are available in Strong City, Cottonwood Falls, Emporia, and Council Grove. At the preserve drinking water is available only at the information station. Portable toilets are across from the barn.

CAMPING: No camping is permitted in the preserve at this time. Two miles west of Cottonwood Falls, Chase State Fishing Lake offers ten campsites with pit toilets. Several Corp of Engineers campgrounds, some with flush toilets, are approximately 20 miles north of the preserve at Council Grove Lake. The park is under development. Contact the preserve for the latest information.

STATE TOURIST INFORMATION
(800) 334–8626

CANE RIVER CREOLE NATIONAL HISTORICAL PARK

4386 Highway 494
Natchez, LA 71456
(318) 352–0383
CARI_Superintendent@nps.gov
www.nps.gov/cari/

Cane River Creole National Historical Park comprises 207 acres and was authorized in 1994 to preserve significant landscapes, sites, and structures associated with the development of Creole culture. The historical park consists of several sections including two plantations and the historic district of the town of Natchitoches. The park is located in west-central Louisiana, southeast of Natchitoches, off Highway 1.

The separate sections of Cane River Creole National Historical Park are situated within Cane River National Heritage Area, a 40,000-acre tract of public and private land that extends 1 mile on either side of the Cane River from the southern boundary of Natchitoches to Monette's Ferry. The National Heritage Area is designed to preserve and interpret the historical and cultural heritage of the region. The historical park is in the planning stage, with various development alternatives being considered. Two plantations that are part of the park are to be stabilized and preserved. The National Park Service tentatively planned to open one of the plantations to visitors in 1999.

Two major segments of the historical park are the Oakland and Magnolia plantations. Oakland Plantation, which dates from the first half of the 19th century, was founded by Pierre Prudhomme, a second-generation native of French descent. The plantation includes the main house, carriage house, stable, carpenter's shop, and cabins, all of which survived the Civil War. Prudhomme's descendants occupied and farmed the plantation until the late-1900s when it was acquired by the National Park Service. Magnolia Plantation was established in 1835 by Ambroise Lecomte and his wife, who were to become the largest slaveholders in the parish. Surviving buildings include the blacksmith shop, eight brick slave cabins, and a gin barn. The main house was burned during the Civil War by retreating Union troops and has been reconstructed outside the park boundaries. Magnolia will be the first of the two plantations open to visitation.

FACILITIES: No facilities are provided by the National Park Service. Food and lodging are available in Natchitoches.

CAMPING: A National Forest Service campground with 10 sites is 3 miles north of Natchitoches on state road 117. Several private campgrounds are near Natchitoches.

JEAN LAFITTE NATIONAL HISTORICAL PARK AND PRESERVE

365 Canal Street, Suite 2400
New Orleans, LA 70130-1142
(504) 589–3882
JELA_Interpretation@nps.gov
www.nps.gov/jela/

Jean Lafitte National Historical Park and Preserve was so designated in 1978 and includes the former Chalmette National Historical Park. The park contains six separate sites in southern Louisiana that preserve significant examples of historical and natural resources of the Mississippi Delta Region. The Acadian sites are 60 to 150 miles west of New Orleans. The other three sites are located in and around the city of New Orleans.

The Mississippi Delta Region is rich in cultural and natural history. The river brought a stream of people and products from all parts of the globe to its point of drainage into the Gulf of Mexico. Jean Lafitte National Historical Park and Preserve, named for a well-known resident of New Orleans during the early 1800s, preserves six sites, showing the diversity of this history. The park is closed Christmas. Some sites may be closed for Mardi Gras.

Acadian Cultural Center: Located at 501 Fisher Road, Lafayette. The center interprets cultural resources of the Acadian people who were relocated to the Mississippi Delta region from Nova Scotia, Canada, over a twenty-year period beginning in 1765. Exhibits allow visitors to interact with and understand traditional and contemporary Acadian culture. The Cultural Center is open daily from 8:00 A.M. to 5:00 P.M. A forty-minute film is shown hourly from 9:00 A.M. to 4:00 P.M. Call (318) 232–0789 for information.

Barataria Preserve: Located on State Highway 45, about 12 miles south of New Orleans, this area of rich coastal wetlands includes bayous, live oak, and alligators. There are about 9 miles of self-guiding trails that provide access to the wetlands. Twelve miles of waterways are available for nonmotorized craft such as canoes. Ranger-guided canoe tours are available on weekends and evenings of a full moon. The visitor center (504–589–2330) offers audiovisual programs and exhibits on the area. It is open from 9:00 A.M. to 5:00 P.M. daily.

Chitimacha Cultural Center: Located off Highway 326 in Charenton. The center features a historical look at the Chitimacha Indians, including their renowned baskets and artwork. The center, administered in partnership by the park and the tribe, is open Tuesday through Friday from 8:00 A.M. to 4:30 P.M. and on Saturday from 9:00 A.M. to 5:00 P.M. Call (318) 923–4830 for information.

Chalmette Battlefield: Located 6 miles east of New Orleans off State Highway 46, this site preserves the battlefield where Andrew Jackson's militia halted a British force of approximately 10,000 soldiers sent to attack New Orleans in 1815. The visitor center (504–589–4430), open daily from 8:30 A.M. to 5:00 P.M., houses a small museum with uniforms and information about the military units that participated in the battle. There is a movie detailing the Battle of New Orleans. Programs about the battle are presented twice daily.

French Quarter Visitor Center: The visitor center, at 419 Decatur Street in downtown New Orleans (504–589–2636), provides exhibits, audiovisual programs, and demonstrations on the cultural diversity of the Mississippi Delta Region. From the visitor center, rangers lead a variety of programs. The center is open daily from 9:00 A.M. to 5:00 P.M.

Prairie Acadian Cultural Center: Located at 250 West Park Avenue in Eunice, the center depicts the heritage of the Prairie Acadians. It includes artifacts, exhibits, and demonstrations that portray this unique culture. In cooperation with the city of Eunice, the National Park Service sponsors a live program in Cajun French every Saturday evening from 6:00 to 8:00 P.M. at the Liberty Theater. The Cultural Center is open Sunday through Friday from 8:00 A.M. to 5:00 P.M., and on Saturday until 6:00 P.M. Call (318) 457–8490 for information.

Trails and Rails: Park rangers and volunteers, in partnership with Amtrak, provide weekly educational/interpretive programs during summer on Amtrak's: "Sunset Limited" between New Orleans and Lafayette, Louisiana; "City of New Orleans" between New Orleans and Jackson, Mississippi; and "Crescent" between New Orleans and Atlanta, Georgia.

Wetlands Acadian Cultural Center: Located at 313 St. Mary Street, Thibodaux, the center explores the water-based life of the Wetlands Acadians. Artifacts and exhibits depict a heritage of fishing, hunting, and trapping in the swamps, marshes, and coastal waters. Various films are shown on request, and music programs are offered on Monday evenings. The center is open Monday from 9:00 A.M. to 5:00 P.M.,Tuesday through Thursday from 9:00 A.M. to 6:00 P.M., Friday from 8:00 A.M. to 5:00 P.M., and Saturday and Sunday from 9:00 A.M. to 5:00 P.M. Call (504) 448–1375 for information.

FACILITIES: No food or lodging is provided by the National Park Service, but both are available near the sites.

CAMPING: No camping is permitted in the park. Public and private campgrounds are available nearby.

FISHING: Fishing is available in the Barataria Preserve with a valid Louisiana fishing license.

POVERTY POINT NATIONAL MONUMENT

c/o Poverty Point State Commemorative Area
P.O. Box 248
Epps, LA 71237
(888) 926–5492

Poverty Point National Monument was authorized in 1988 to commemorate a culture that thrived twelve centuries before Christ and to help preserve some of the largest prehistoric earthworks in North America. The monument is located in northeastern Louisiana, east of the city of Monroe via LA 134 and LA 577. From I–20, take the Delhi exit north on LA 17 to the town of Epps.

Between 1700 and 700 B.C., the inhabitants of Poverty Point built a complex of earthen mounds and ridges that overlook the Mississippi River floodplain. Materials and supplies used in the construction were acquired in trade from various points in the present-day United States. The ridges at Poverty Point form six semicircles, with the outer sections having a diameter of three-fourths of a mile. Evidence from excavations causes scientists to believe the ridges were constructed as foundations for dwellings. Earthen mounds at the site include Poverty Point Mound, a large bird-shaped mound that rises 70 feet from its 700- by 640-foot base. Another 20-foot-high conical mound was constructed over a bed of ash and burnt bone fragments.

The commemorative area that forms the national monument is managed by the Louisiana Department of Culture, Recreation, and Tourism. The area is open daily from 9:00 A.M. to 5:00 P.M. except for Thanksgiving, Christmas, and New Year's. A museum provides visitors with an audio visual presentation and displays artifacts found at the site. The park also includes an archaeological laboratory, observation tower, and self-guiding hiking trails. A guided tram tour operates from Easter through Labor Day.

FACILITIES: Rest rooms, drinking water, and soft drinks are available at the museum. Picnic areas are at the site. The nearest lodging is at Delhi, 16 miles south of the commemorative area.

CAMPING: No camping is permitted in the commemorative area. Chemin-A-Haut State Park, approximately 40 miles northwest, has twenty-six campsites with tables, grills, flush toilets, showers, and a dump station.

FISHING: No fishing is available at Poverty Point.

STATE TOURIST INFORMATION
(800) 657–3700

GRAND PORTAGE NATIONAL MONUMENT

Box 668
Grand Marais, MN 55604-0668
(218) 387–2788
grpo_admin_clerk@nps.gov
www.nps.gov/grpo/

Grand Portage was designated a national historic site in 1951 and was changed to a national monument in 1958. It is comprised of 710 acres that were used as part of a principal route into the Northwest by Indians, explorers, missionaries, and fur traders. An old fur-trading depot is partially reconstructed here. The park is located in the northeastern tip of Minnesota, 151 miles northeast of Duluth on State Highway 61, a beautiful drive.

From approximately 1779 to 1802, Grand Portage served as headquarters for the North West Company, a highly profitable fur-trading enterprise that employed a large number of French-Canadian voyageurs. The North West Company supplied furs to vast European and American markets and also supplied trade goods to American Indians, who acquired a predilection for the trimmings of European society. The North West Company built its posts along the banks of the Pigeon River and at the Lake Superior end of the Grand Portage (the "Great Carrying Place"), an 8½-mile portage that wound its way through the woods, bypassing rapids on the lower end of the Pigeon River and becoming the acknowledged route to Canada's prime fur country.

The Grand Portage post became a convenient meeting place for the voyageurs, who had evolved into two groups based on geography: the north men, or "winterers," and the Montreal men, or "pork eaters." The north men would make their way to Fort Charlotte from the trading posts in the Canadian north each spring, while the pork eaters would journey to Grand

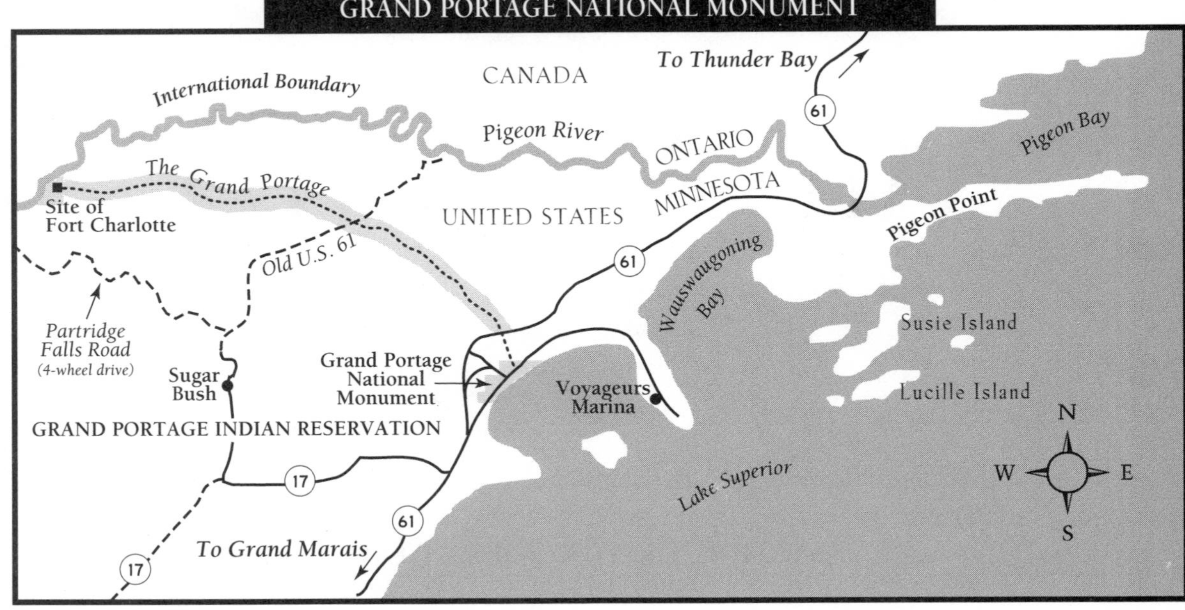

Portage Bay via the French and Ottawa rivers, then north and west across the Great Lakes. Hundreds of voyageurs, company partners, agents, clerks, and American Indians would then gather at Grand Portage in the middle of July for an annual Rendezvous. During this time the company partners held their annual meeting, while the pork-eater voyageurs would portage the canoe cargoes of furs and trade goods across the Grand Portage to Fort Charlotte or to the post at Grand Portage Bay, depending on whether the cargo was trade goods or furs. When the day's work was done, Rendezvous celebrations would commence, with plentiful food and free-flowing liquor—at least for those willing to part with the wages they had just received for the past year's work. On the final night of Rendezvous, the partners and their guests feasted and danced in the Great Hall, while the voyageurs and American Indians staged a celebration of their own outside the palisade walls. Soon after, the voyageurs took up their paddles and headed out for another season of travel and trade. Following Jay's Treaty in 1796, the newly formed United States decreed that it would levy duties on all merchandise and furs passing over the portage. In 1803, the North West Company packed up the buildings, lock, stock, and barrel, and built a new fur-trading post at the mouth of the Kaministiquia River in Ontario, Canada.

Monument lands are open year-round for hiking, cross-country skiing, and snowshoeing. The reconstructed stockade, great hall, kitchen, and canoe warehouse are open 9:00 A.M. to 5:00 P.M. mid-May to mid-October, with guided tours, exhibits, and historical demonstrations available. A passenger ferry leaves the monument daily (summer only) for Isle Royale National Park, 22 miles offshore.

Two hiking trails are available to visitors. The Mount Rose is a ½-mile trail that climbs 300 feet for a spectacular view overlooking the reconstructed fur-trade depot and Lake Superior. An interpretive brochure is available at the trailhead. The Grand Portage (8½ miles) winds through the woods to the site of Fort Charlotte, a way station used for furs en route to Grand Portage.

Interpretive programs and facilities are partially accessible to the handicapped.

FACILITIES: Grand Portage Lodge and Casino provides full food service and overnight accommodations, as does Ryden's Border Store. Other limited services are located nearby. Grand Marais (36 miles southwest) provides a greater variety of alternatives. Drinking water and rest rooms are available at the monument. There are picnic facilities located on-site as well as 6½ miles north at Grand Portage State Park.

CAMPING: Camping is permitted only at two backcountry campsites located at Fort Charlotte. Campers must obtain a free camping permit from one of the rangers stationed at the monument or register at one of three self-registration boxes located along the Portage at Highway 61, old Highway 61, or at Fort Charlotte. Judge Magney State Park, located 20 miles southwest on Highway 61, has camping facilities, as do a few private campgrounds in the Grand Portage area. For those driving north into Canada, Middle Falls Provincial Park, just a few miles past the border, offers campsites as well as scenery.

MISSISSIPPI NATIONAL RIVER AND RECREATION AREA

175 East 5th Street
Suite 418, Box 41
St. Paul, MN 55101-2901
(651) 290–4160
www.nps.gov/miss/

Mississippi NRRA was established in 1988 to preserve and enhance nearly 54,000 acres along a 72-mile corridor of the upper Mississippi River. The corridor runs through five Minnesota counties in the greater Minneapolis/Saint Paul metropolitan area. The north boundary is at the town of Dayton, and the south boundary is just south of the town of Hastings.

The Mississippi River as it passes through the Minneapolis/Saint Paul metropolitan area is characterized by surprising diversity. Shallow and wide at the upper end, the river narrows as it passes through a deep gorge, beginning near downtown Minneapolis and Saint Anthony Falls, the only falls on the entire length of the 2,348-mile Mississippi River. The gorge extends miles downstream to a point below downtown Saint Paul, and by the time the Mississippi reaches its confluence with the St. Croix River, the river has widened to become a vast and powerful part of the largest inland navigation system on earth. During this small fraction of the Mississippi River's length, the character of the waterway changes more rapidly than anywhere else. Emerging from the forests of the north, the river passes through one of America's largest metropolitan areas and the heart of the Upper Midwest's cultural and commercial center before entering agricultural lands to the south.

Trails for biking, walking, in-line skating, and cross-country skiing are found along the river. The Great River Road follows the Mississippi River and provides many opportunities for motorists to stop at points of interests. Canoeing, kayaking, fishing, and boating are popular at sites throughout the river corridor.

FACILITIES: The National Park Service does not operate any interpretive facilities at this time. Information can be obtained by visiting or writing the Mississippi NRRA headquarters at the above address. Within the Mississippi NRRA are numerous parks operated by state, county, and municipal agencies. Visitors may explore and visit interpretive centers and educational facilities operated by these partner parks and other organizations within the river corridor. Food, lodging, and rest rooms are readily available throughout the corridor and the metropolitan area.

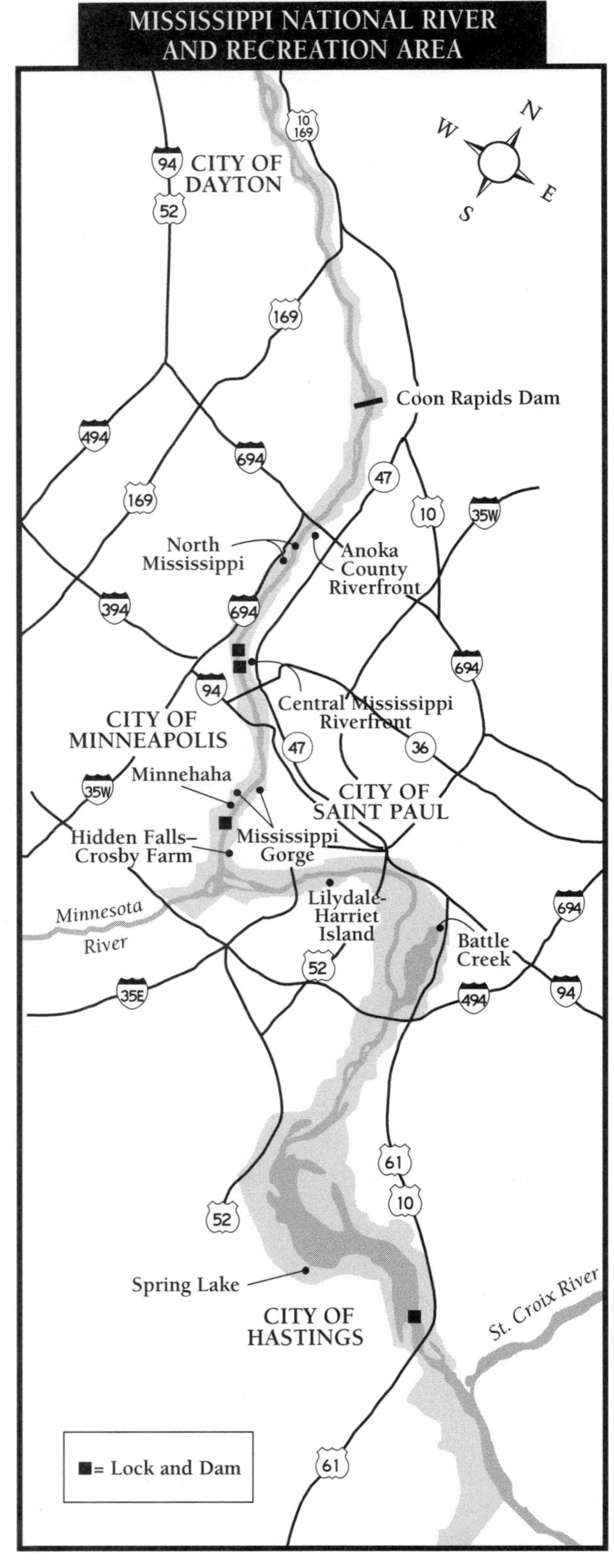
MISSISSIPPI NATIONAL RIVER
AND RECREATION AREA
N
W
E
S
CITY OF
DAYTON
Coon Rapids Dam
North
Mississippi
Anoka
County
Riverfront
Central Mississippi
Riverfront
CITY OF
MINNEAPOLIS
Minnehaha
CITY OF
SAINT PAUL
Hidden Falls–
Crosby Farm
Mississippi
Gorge
Lilydale-
Harriet
Island
Minnesota
River
Battle
Creek
Spring Lake
CITY OF
HASTINGS
St. Croix River
■= Lock and Dam

CAMPING: No National Park Service campgrounds are located within the corridor's boundaries. Private campgrounds can be found throughout the metropolitan area, as well as the adjoining St. Croix National Scenic Riverway.

FISHING: Fishing is permitted with a Minnesota state fishing license.

PIPESTONE NATIONAL MONUMENT

36 Reservation Avenue
Pipestone, MN 56164-1269
(507) 825–5464
PIPE_Interpretation@nps.gov
www.nps.gov/pipe/

Pipestone, which comprises 283 acres, was established in 1937 to preserve quarries where Indians obtained materials used in making peace pipes. The park is located in southwestern Minnesota, adjacent to the north side of the town of Pipestone. It may be reached via State Highways 30 and 23 or U.S. 75.

Millions of years ago, a thin clay layer was sandwiched between layers of sand deposited at the bottom of a sea. Later, additional sediment layers buried these deposits deep beneath the earth's surface, and pressure, heat, and chemical action changed the sand into quartzite and the red clay into stone. As the area was uplifted and eroded, a dense red mineral that today is called pipestone was exposed.

Centuries ago, many Indian tribes traveled thousands of miles to mine the pipestone. Although difficult to quarry, the red stone, once extracted, was easily carved with primitive tools. The rare material was traded over a wide area and was particularly used for ceremonial objects such as peace pipes. Today, only Indians are allowed to excavate the material.

The park's visitor center is open from 8:00 A.M. to 5:00 P.M. (until 8:00 P.M. on summer weekends) and contains exhibits, an audiovisual program, and the Upper Midwest Indian Cultural Center. A 3/4-mile surfaced, self-guiding trail takes visitors past the quarries and through a small section of virgin prairie. Markers are placed along the trail, and guide booklets are available in the visitor center. The monument is closed Christmas and New Year's.

FACILITIES: Food and lodging are available in the town of Pipestone. Drinking water and rest rooms are provided in the visitor center. Rest rooms are also at the picnic grounds on the south end of the monument.

CAMPING: No camping is permitted in the park. Split Rock Creek State Park (seventeen sites, pit toilets) is 8 miles south on Highway 23, and Blue Mounds State Park (seventy-six sites, flush toilets, showers, electricity, swimming beach) is 18 miles south on U.S. 75. A private campground is located just outside the park entrance.

FISHING: No fishing is available at Pipestone National Monument.

See map on the following page.

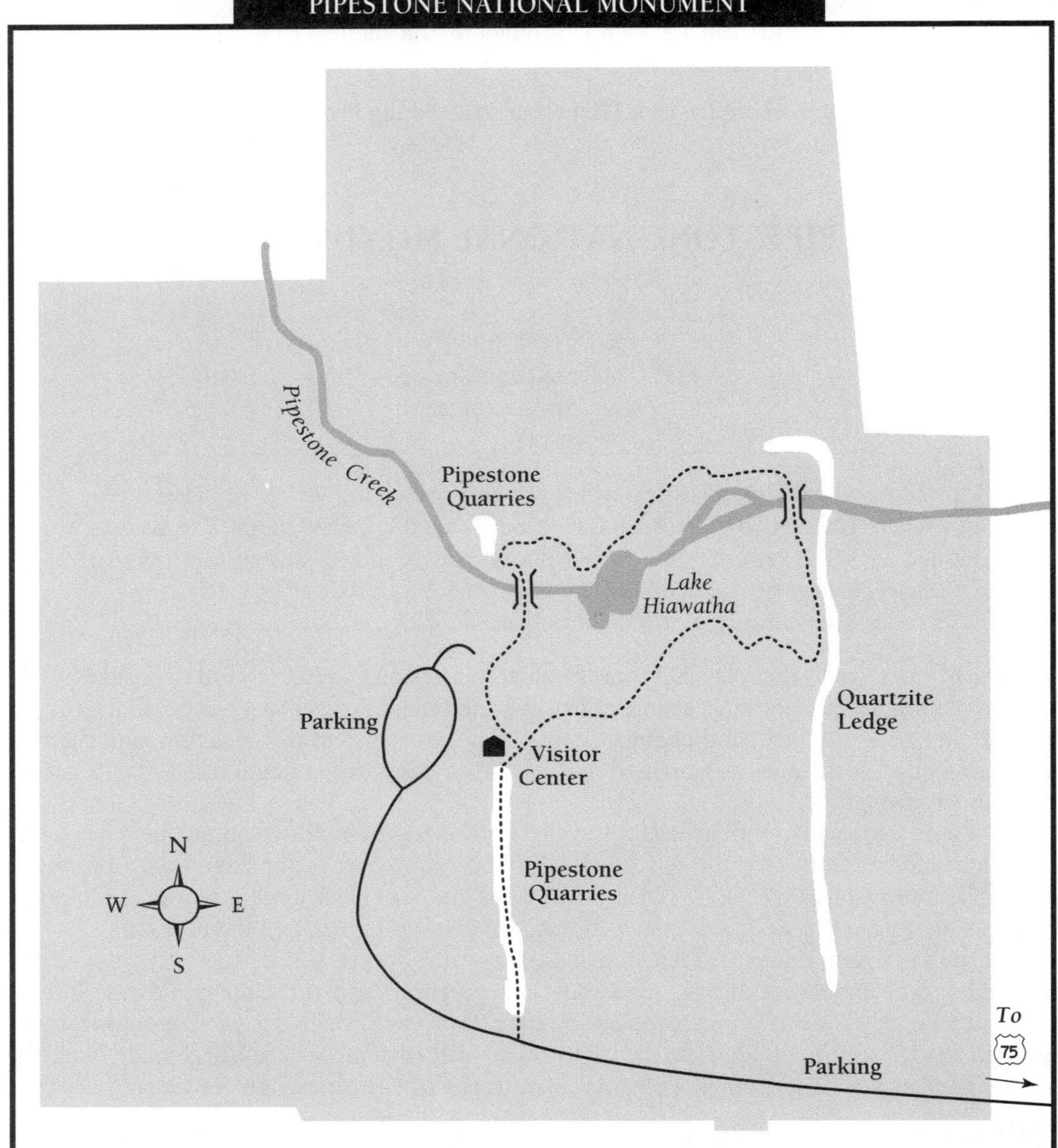
PIPESTONE NATIONAL MONUMENT
Pipestone Creek
Pipestone Quarries
Lake Hiawatha
Quartzite Ledge
Parking
Visitor Center
Pipestone Quarries
N
W
E
S
To
75
Parking

ST. CROIX NATIONAL SCENIC RIVERWAY

P.O. Box 708
St. Croix Falls, WI 54024-0708
(715) 483–3284
www.nps.gov/sacn/

The St. Croix National Scenic Riverway was established in 1968 to preserve approximately 250 miles of rivers that show little evidence of disturbance. The park begins near the sources of the St. Croix and Namekagon Rivers in northern Wisconsin and follows the border between Wisconsin and Minnesota.

Thousands of years ago, this region of the United States was leveled by glacial ice flowing down from the north. As the climate warmed and the glacier melted, much of the resulting water used the St. Croix basin as an escape. The scraping of the advancing ice sheet combined with the later water runoff exposed ancient rocks and volcanic formations that are visible along the rivers.

The French were the first Europeans to venture into this region. Here they found the Dakota and Ojibwa tribes living in an area rich in both plant and wildlife. The St. Croix valley became an abundant source of beaver pelts for Europe until the early 1800s. After that, logging was to be the main industry until the 1920s. Today, much of the riverway cuts through second-growth hardwood forests.

Although the St. Croix and Lower St. Croix were established as two park areas, they actually constitute a single riverway. The St. Croix section consists of 102 miles of the St. Croix River and 98 miles of its Namekagon tributary (see map). The lower St. Croix carries the park an additional 52 miles, from Taylors Falls to the Mississippi. The main visitor centers at St. Croix Falls and Stillwater, Minnesota, are open year-round. Visitor centers are open in the summer near the towns of Grantsburg and Trego, Wisconsin.

Canoeing the rivers is one of the park's most popular activities. During late summer and fall, the water level is generally low, and the lower sections of the river provide the best trips. A listing of the numerous canoe outfitters located along the riverway may be obtained by writing the park superintendent. Most visitors find that 10 to 20 miles of paddling downstream is a full day. The Lower St. Croix is popular for power-boating, waterskiing, and houseboating. State parks along this part of the riverway provide additional camping, picnicking, hiking, and interpretive exhibits.

FACILITIES: No food service or lodging is provided by the Park Service. Overnight accommodations and supplies are available in nearby communities.

CAMPING: A number of primitive campsites are located along the riverway. Campgrounds with vault toilets and water are located at Howell Landing and Earl Park.

FISHING: Bass, muskellunge, walleye pike, and sturgeon are found in the rivers, and the Namekagon is noted for brown trout. A state fishing license is required. Where the river forms a boundary between the two states, a license from either is valid while fishing from a boat.

See maps on pages 174 and 175.

ST. CROIX NATIONAL SCENIC RIVERWAY—UPPER SECTION

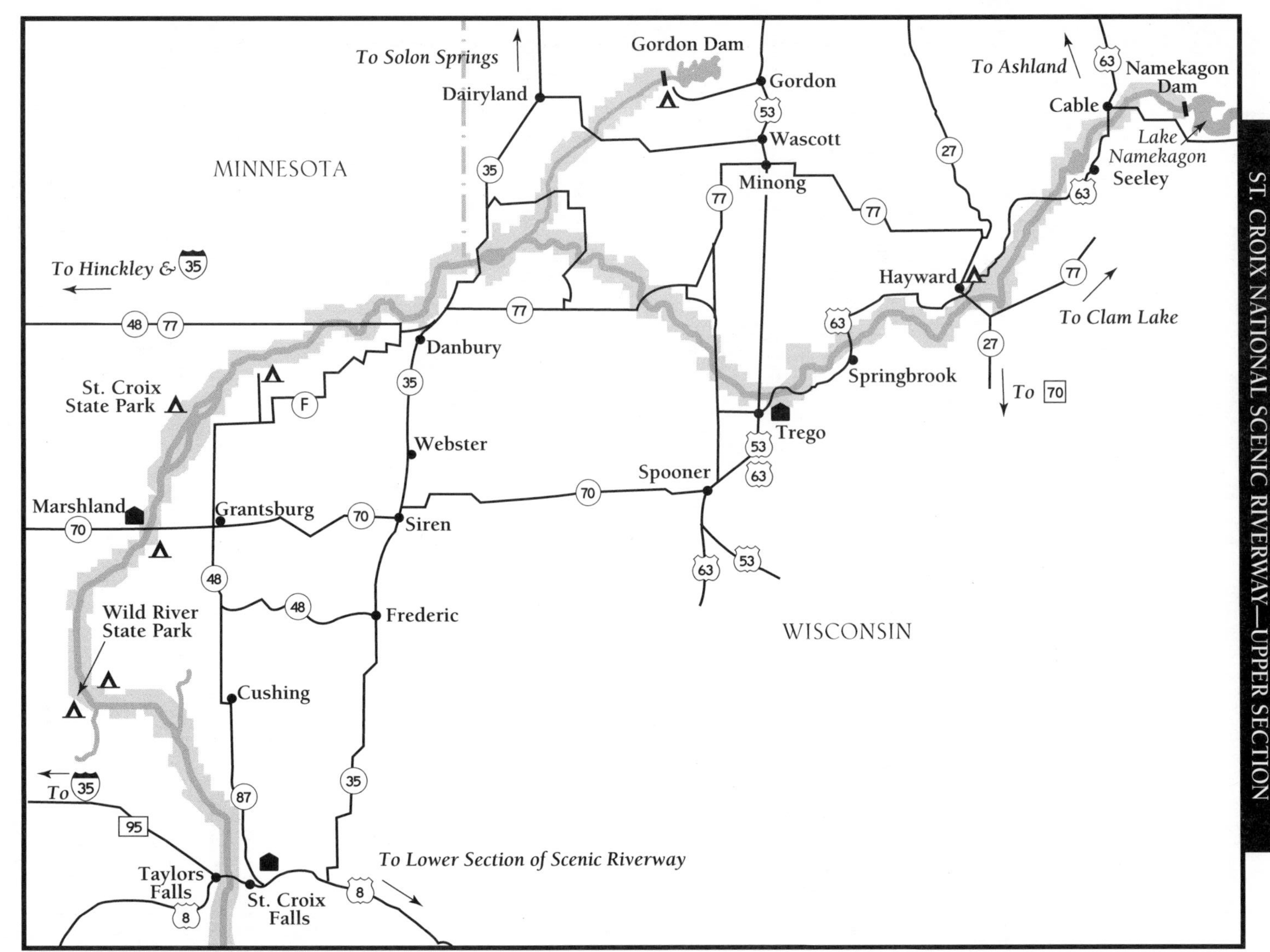

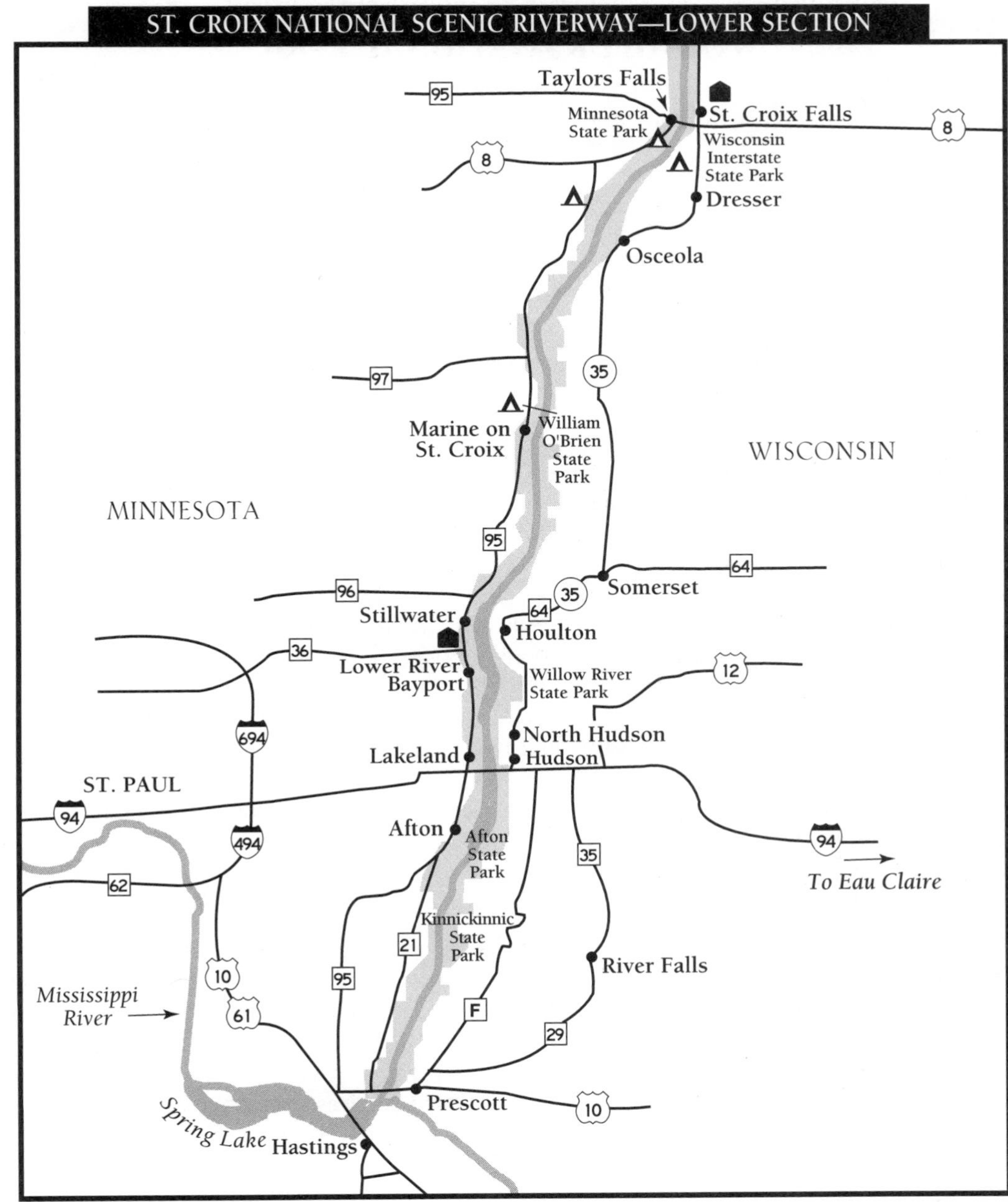

ST. CROIX NATIONAL SCENIC RIVERWAY—LOWER SECTION
95
Taylors Falls
St. Croix Falls
8
Minnesota State Park
Wisconsin Interstate State Park
8
Dresser
Osceola
35
97
Marine on St. Croix
William O'Brien State Park
WISCONSIN
MINNESOTA
95
64
Somerset
35
96
Stillwater
64
Houlton
36
Lower River
Bayport
Willow River State Park
12
694
North Hudson
Lakeland
Hudson
ST. PAUL
94
494
Afton
Afton State Park
94
To Eau Claire
62
35
Kinnickinnic State Park
21
River Falls
10
95
Mississippi River
F
61
29
Prescott
10
Spring Lake
Hastings

VOYAGEURS NATIONAL PARK

3131 Highway 53
International Falls, MN 56649-8904
(218) 283–9821
www.nps.gov/voya/

Voyageurs National Park was authorized in 1971 and established in 1975 to preserve 218,000 acres of beautiful forested lake country that was once inhabited by French-Canadian fur traders. The park is located in northern Minnesota and stretches for 55 miles along the U.S.–Canadian border east of International Falls. Four roads along U.S. 53 provide access, although most summer travel within the park depends on watercraft.

Most of this land, which has been shaped by glaciers into a system of countless waterways, remains as undeveloped and wild as it was when French-Canadian voyageurs made their way through here from Montreal to the Northwest. The pine and hardwoods forests are broken only by lakes and occasional bogs, sand beaches, and cliffs. The south side of the Kabetogama Peninsula is dotted with numerous islands, while the north shore is broken with many coves and small bays. One former fur company trading post was located west of the park, in Fort Frances, north of International Falls.

One of the park's visitor centers is at Kabetogama, approximately 3 miles north of U.S. 53 on Highways 122 and 123. Here visitors will find exhibits and information on the area. The Ash River Visitor Center is 11 miles east of Highway 53 on Highway 129. Both the Kabetogama and Ash River centers are open seasonally. The Rainy Lake Visitor Center is located 11 miles east on Minnesota Highway 11. A variety of interpretive and children's programs are offered on Rainy and Kabetogama lakes, including guided boat tours, Voyageur North Canoe trips, and cross-country ski excursions.

FACILITIES: Lodging, food, and boating services are available at Kettle Falls, inside the park. This lodging complex consists of a historic two-story hotel plus three newer nearby wooden housekeeping villas. Kettle Falls is accessible only by boat, snowmobile, ski, or floatplane. For information, write Kettle Falls Hotel, 10502 Gamma Road, Ray, MN 56669, or call (888) 534–6835. Four resort communities adjacent to the park at Ash River, Crane Lake, Kabetogama Lake, and Rainy Lake provide lodging, food, outfitting services, restaurants, motorboat and canoe rentals, gas, and guide services. Groceries are available in Orr and Ray, and complete facilities can be found at International Falls.

CAMPING: Two hundred twenty campsites/houseboat sites, accessible only by boat, are located throughout the park. Public camping facilities are available nearby in Kabetogama State Forest, and private camping with hookups is available at the four resort communities.

FISHING: Northern Minnesota is noted for sports fishing, especially walleye, northern pike, smallmouth bass, and crappie. A Minnesota license is required.

VOYAGEURS NATIONAL PARK

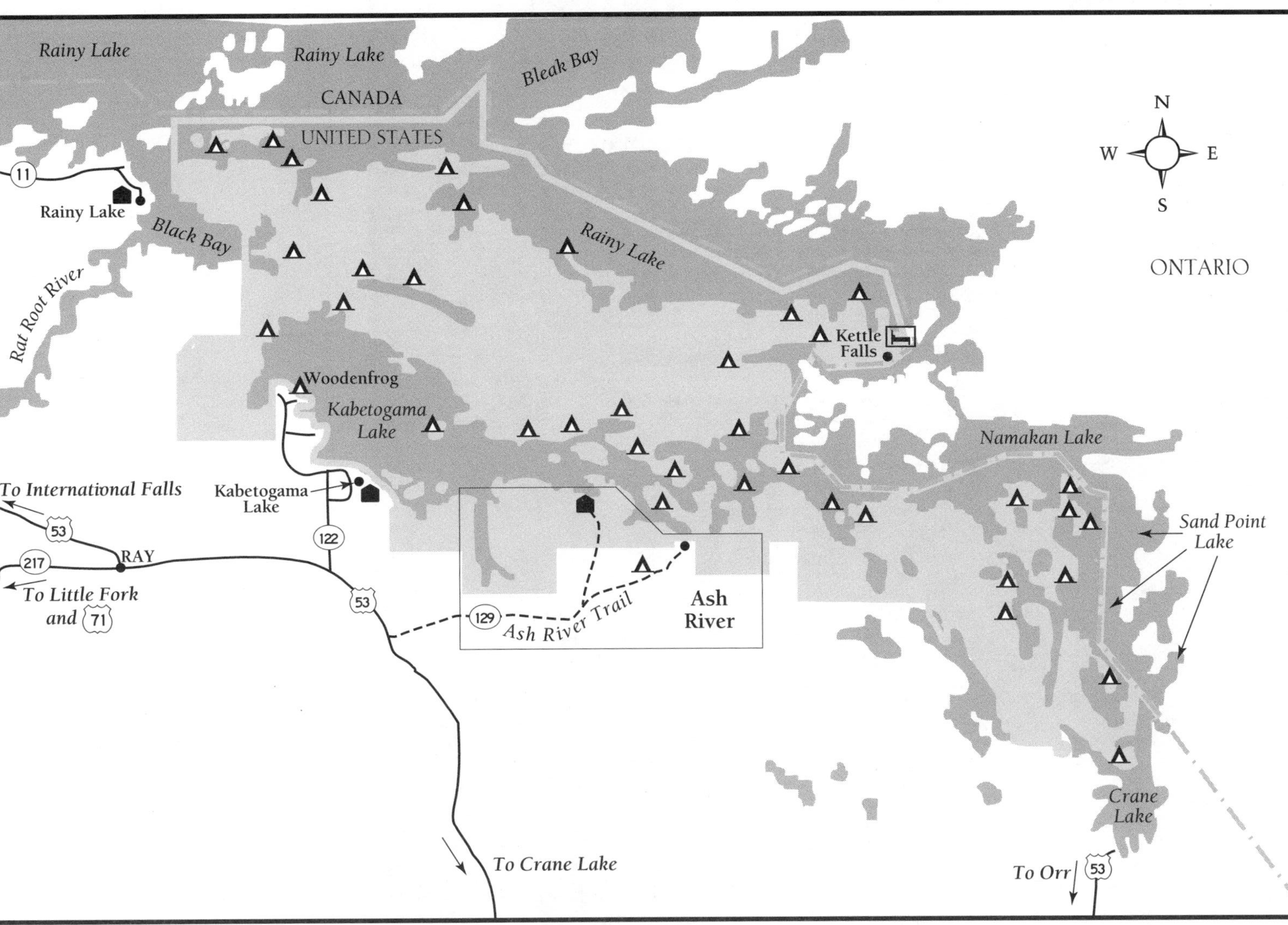

Harry S Truman National Historic Site

STATE TOURIST INFORMATION
(800) 877–1234

GEORGE WASHINGTON CARVER NATIONAL MONUMENT

5646 Carver Road
Diamond, MO 64840-0038
(417) 325–4151
gwca_Superintendent@nps.gov
www.nps.gov/gewa

George Washington Carver National Monument, which is comprised of 210 acres, was established in 1943 to memorialize the birthplace and childhood home of this famous educator, artist, scientist, and humanitarian. The monument is located in southwestern Missouri, approximately 10 miles southeast of Joplin. From either Neosho, Carthage, or when traveling west on I–44 from Springfield, Missouri, take U.S. 71 Alternate (Exit 18A) to the town of Diamond. From there, drive 2 miles west on County Highway V and then south ½ mile on Carver Road. When traveling east on I–44 from Tulsa, Oklahoma, take U.S. 71 (Exit 11A) to County Highway V, go 4½ miles east, and then south ½ mile on Carver Road.

In the mid-1850s, Moses Carver and his wife, Susan, purchased a slave named Mary to help with their 240-acre farm in southwestern Missouri. Some time later, probably in 1864 or 1865, Mary gave birth to her second son, whom she named George. During this time, the Civil War was inflicting a period of suffering on the people of Missouri. Mary and George were carried off by a group of raiders, and, although George was eventually recovered by an acquaintance of Moses Carver, his mother was never heard from again. Upon his return to the farm, George and his brother Jim were taken in and raised by Moses and Susan Carver. George worked and learned alongside the Carvers before adopting their name and leaving for a black school in Neosho just prior to reaching his teens.

The remainder of George Washington Carver's life was a testimony to his initiative. After receiving honorable mention for a painting entered in the World's Columbian Exposition in Chicago in 1893, he earned bachelor's and master's degrees in botany from Iowa State University. In 1896 he accepted a position at Tuskegee Normal and Industrial Institute in Alabama, where he served for forty-seven years. During this period, Carver made significant contributions to southern agriculture and received numerous awards.

The monument is open from 9:00 A.M. to 5:00 P.M. daily except Thanksgiving, Christmas, and New Year's. A self-guided, ¾-mile trail begins near the visitor center parking lot. The trail is partially handicapped accessible and winds through the natural setting that influenced Carver during his boyhood. It passes the Carver Birthplace site, the Carver Boyhood Statue, Williams Pond, the relocated 1881 Moses Carver house, and the Carver Family Cemetery. The visitor center contains a museum with exhibits that trace Carver's life and accomplishments. Two films documenting his life are shown continuously in the visitor center. The Carver Discovery Center for children is located in a separate building on the property and contains interactive exhibits related to the life of Dr. George Washington Carver.

FACILITIES: No food or lodging is available in the park. Food can be found in the town of Diamond. Lodging is nearby in Joplin, Carthage, and Neosho. Water and rest rooms are at the visitor center. Picnic tables are available.

CAMPING: No camping is permitted at the monument. Private campgrounds are within approximately 15 miles of the park. Roaring River State Park provides camping approximately 50 miles southeast, near Cassville.

FISHING: No fishing is permitted at the monument.

HARRY S TRUMAN NATIONAL HISTORIC SITE

223 North Main
Independence, MO 64050-2804
(816) 254–2720
www.nps.gov/hstr/

Harry S Truman National Historic Site was established in 1982 to preserve the home and memorialize the life of the thirty-third president of the United States. Truman's home is located in western Missouri in the town of Independence, near Kansas City. An information center with parking is located at Main Street and Truman Road. Truman Farm, a separate area that is part of the site, is in Grandview, 20 miles south of Independence.

Harry Truman was born in Lamar, Missouri, in 1884 and moved to Independence as a six-year-old boy. It was in Independence that he met Bess Wallace, his future wife, and graduated from high school. After working on the family farm, serving in the United States Army during World War I, and attempting a number of business ventures, Truman was elected Jackson County administrative judge in the early 1920s. By 1935, Harry Truman had been elected to the U.S. Senate and had moved to Washington. He was reelected once before successfully running as Franklin Roosevelt's vice president in 1944. Following Roosevelt's death in 1945, Truman assumed the presidency, to which he was elected in 1948. Deciding not to run again in 1952

Harry Truman returned to Independence in 1953, where he purchased the house at 219 North Delaware Street from his mother-in-law's estate. Truman had lived in the house from his marriage in 1919 and continued to live there until his death in 1972 at the age of eighty-eight. Truman's wife, Bess, continued to live at the residence until her death ten years later.

The Truman Home Ticket and Information Center, located at the intersection of Truman Road and Main Street, contains a twelve-minute audiovisual presentation about the home. The center operates daily from 8:30 A.M. to 5:00 P.M. except for Thanksgiving Day, Christmas, and New Year's Day. Guided tours of the Truman home do not take place on Mondays between Labor Day and Memorial Day. Guided-tour tickets are sold at the ticket center on a first-come, first-served basis, so arrive early in the day. Ticket sales are limited to four tickets per person. From the visitor center, the Truman home is five blocks west on Truman Road to Delaware Street. Parking in the Truman home neighborhood is extremely limited. Ask at the Ticket and Information Center about RV and trailer parking.

The family farm where Harry Truman lived and worked from 1906 to 1917, when he left to serve in World War I, is a separate area of the historic site. The farm is 20 miles south of Independence in Grandview, Missouri. This site is open Friday, Saturday, and Sunday from May through August. Tours are offered from 9:00 A.M. to 4:00 P.M. Tour tickets are available at the site. A map showing directions to the farm is available at the visitor center in Independence.

Other Truman-related sites in Independence include the Harry S Truman Library and Museum and the Jackson County Courthouse, where Truman's political career began. The courthouse features a thirty-minute audiovisual program about the president's life. Between Memorial Day and Labor Day, park rangers conduct guided walks (no charge) at 10:00 A.M. and 2 P.M. through the Truman home neighborhood.

FACILITIES: Rest rooms and drinking water are available at the ticket center, library, and railroad station. Food is available nearby on Independence Square, adjacent to the ticket center; lodging is available at the intersection of Interstate 70 and Noland Road. Neither is offered by the National Park Service.

CAMPING: No camping is available at the park.

FISHING: No fishing is available at the park.

JEFFERSON NATIONAL EXPANSION MEMORIAL

11 North Fourth Street
St. Louis, MO 63102-1882
(314) 655–1700
www.nps.gov/jeff/arch-home

Jefferson National Expansion Memorial comprises ninety-one acres and was designated part of the National Park Service in 1935 to memorialize Thomas Jefferson and other American leaders who directed the territorial expansion of the United States, as well as the pioneers who explored and settled the West. This park, highlighted by the famous 630-foot Gateway Arch, is located on the St. Louis riverfront, within easy walking distance of downtown. Parking is available along the riverfront, just east of the memorial, or in a parking garage to the north on Washington Street.

As the people of the United States began moving westward following the Louisiana Purchase in 1803, St. Louis—with a strategic location on a cliff convenient to the Mississippi, Missouri, and other river approaches—became an important center of commerce, transportation, and culture. Along with being the headquarters of the western fur trade, the city was a congregating point for pioneers starting across the plains. Although most of this activity occurred along the riverfront, an 1849 fire destroyed much of the downtown area where the present park is located. Future growth moved uptown, and only two historical structures—the Old Courthouse and the Old Cathedral—still stand within the park boundaries.

The central feature of the park is Eero Saarinen's 630-foot stainless-steel arch, which was built to commemorate the city's historic role as a gateway for the westward pioneers. A passenger tram (fee charged), with eight five-passenger cars built on the order of baskets on a Ferris wheel, climbs each leg of the arch to an observation deck at the top. Beneath the arch, the Museum of Westward Expansion contains exhibits interpreting the westward migration. Films about westward expansion and the building of the arch are shown periodically throughout the day. Waits of an hour or more to take the tram are common, but visitors can make a tram reservation (do this immediately upon your arrival) and spend the waiting time viewing the exhibits and movies. The Old Courthouse, where Dred Scott sued for his freedom, has numerous exhibits on St. Louis history and is open daily.

FACILITIES: Fast-food restaurants are located in paddle-wheel boats along the riverfront, a short walk from the arch. Drinking water, soft-drink machines, and rest rooms are provided in the visitation area beneath the arch and on surrounding city streets. Food and lodging are available a few blocks away in downtown St. Louis.

CAMPING: No camping is permitted at the memorial.

FISHING: Fishing is permitted in the Mississippi River across the road from the arch. Fishing access also is available 1/2 mile south and 1/2 mile north of the memorial.

OZARK NATIONAL SCENIC RIVERWAYS

P.O. Box 490
Van Buren, MO 63965-0490
(573) 323–4236
www.nps.gov/ozar/

Ozark National Scenic Riverways, established in 1964, includes nearly 80,000 acres that contain 134 miles of the beautiful Current and Jacks Fork Rivers. The park is located in southeastern Missouri, 150 miles south of St. Louis.

The mountains of this region are remnants of a large range eroded by wind and water. In addition to surface erosion, underlying limestone has developed large pockets as a consequence of water dissolving the rock. The result is a large number of sinkholes, caverns, and springs for which this region is noted. One of the largest springs in the nation, Big Spring, is located south of Van Buren. Other large springs are Alley Spring on the Jacks Fork and Welch and Ebb & Flow Springs on the Current River. Among the numerous caves along the riverways, Round Spring Cavern is one of the most popular. Many of the caves are large and beautifully decorated.

The major activity center on the Jacks Fork River is at Alley Spring, and major centers on the Current River are located at Akers, Pulltite, Round Spring, and Big Spring. Evening pro-

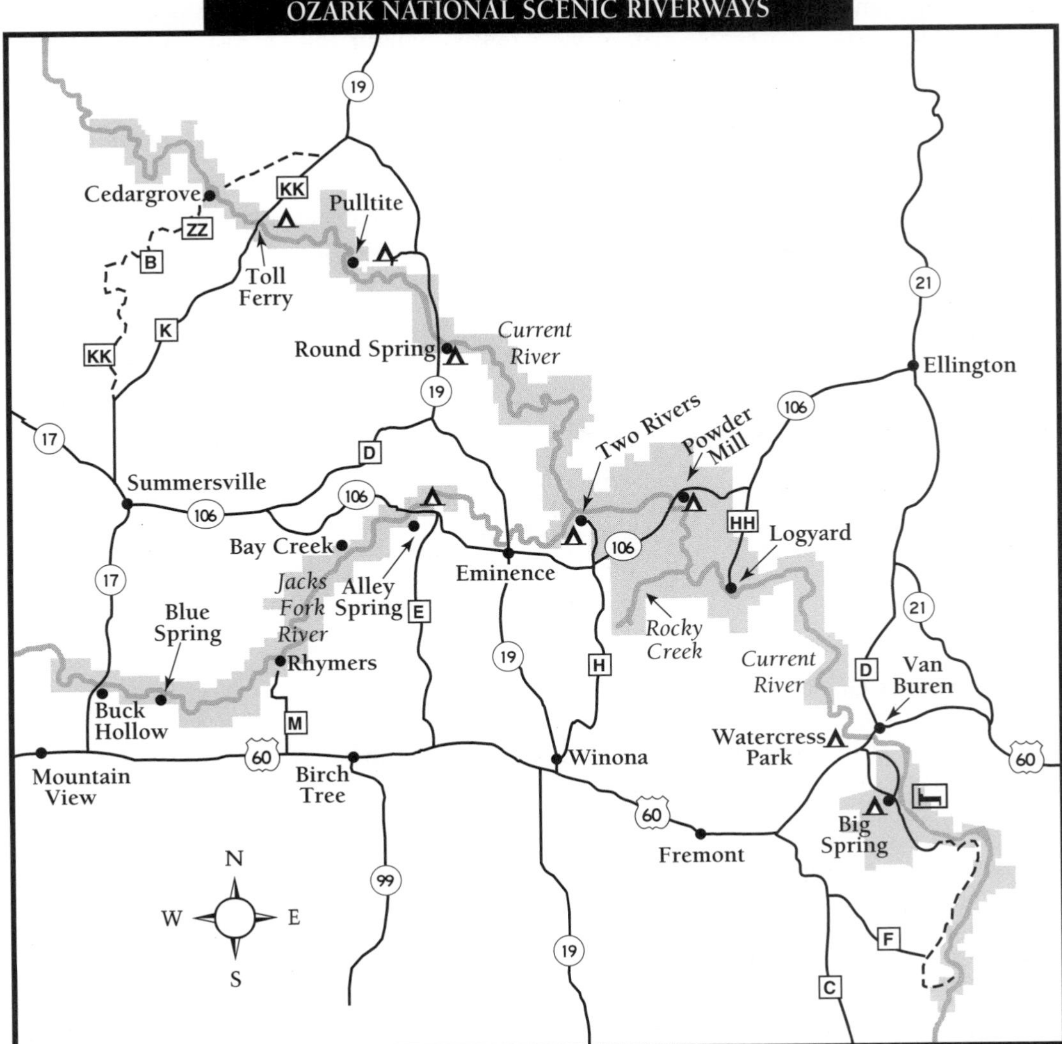

grams on the area's geology and history are conducted during summer. Listings of programs and demonstrations are available at park headquarters and at the activity centers. Tours of Round Spring Cavern are available.

The most popular activity in the park is floating the rivers. Canoes and johnboats (for fishing) may be rented. (A rental agency takes the canoes to launch points and picks up floaters at a scheduled time and place.) The upper stretches of the Jacks Fork River generally are more fun to float during late winter and spring because of low water levels during summer. Maps and guides to both rivers are sold in the park.

FACILITIES: Lodging and food are available in the towns of Van Buren, Eminence, and Mountain View. Big Spring Lodge, the only lodging facility within the riverways' boundary, is located 4 miles south of Van Buren. The lodge offers fourteen wood-and-stone cabins constructed by the Civilian Conservation Corps in the late 1930s. Most cabins have a full kitchen. A dining room in the main lodge building serves three meals a day. Phone (573) 323–4332 or write Big Spring Lodge, P.O. Box 130, Van Buren, MO 63965. Boat rentals are available at Akers Ferry, Pulltite, Round Spring, Two Rivers, Alley Spring, and nearby towns.

CAMPING: Campgrounds with tables, grills, water, and flush toilets are Cedar Grove (six spaces, vault toilets), Hawes (ten spaces, vault toilets), Pulltite (fifty-five spaces, three group sites), Round Spring (sixty spaces, three group sites, dump station, showers, laundry), Two Rivers (twelve spaces, two group sites), Alley Spring (162 spaces, three group sites, dump station, showers), and Big Spring (123 spaces, three group sites, dump station, showers). Floaters may use gravel bars on both the Current and Jacks Fork rivers for camping.

FISHING: Rock bass and smallmouth bass are the most abundant fish caught. Largemouth bass, walleye, and chain pickerel are also fairly common. Trophy trout are found in the Current River from the Montauk State Park boundary to Cedar Grove. A Missouri license is required. Fishing for trout requires a special stamp.

ULYSSES S. GRANT NATIONAL HISTORIC SITE

7400 Grant Road
St. Louis, MO 63123-1801
(314) 842–3298
ulsg_Interpretation@nps.gov
www.nps.gov/ulsg/

Ulysses S. Grant National Historic Site, authorized in 1989, preserves the ten-acre core of the property known as White Haven, where Grant and his wife, Julia, made their home from 1854–58. The site is located in south St. Louis County, adjacent to Grant's Farm on Highway 30.

Following his graduation from West Point in 1843, Lieutenant Ulysses S. Grant was assigned to army duty near St. Louis at Jefferson Barracks, at the time the nation's largest military base. At the suggestion of Fred Dent, his friend and former roommate, Grant became a frequent visitor to White Haven, the Dents' country estate. Here he met and fell in love with Fred's sister, Julia, who became his wife in 1848. Grant's military career sent them to various places around the country, and it was not until 1854, following his resignation from the army, that he and Julia were able to live together at White Haven. They struggled to farm the land for several years, lived in various places on the property, and raised their children, but ultimately the combination of poor weather and a bad economy forced the Grants out of farming. Soon the onset of the Civil War, Grant's resultant fame, and his two-term presidency changed their lives forever. Though the Grants intended to retire to White Haven and over time had purchased the land and made preparations accordingly, they never returned to live at White Haven.

The site contains five historic structures, including the two-story main house, an adjacent stone building, an ice house, a chicken house, and a barn. The latter structure houses a visitor center. The park is open from 9:00 A.M. to 5:00 P.M. seven days a week, with the exception of Thanksgiving, Christmas, and New Year's Day. Ranger programs and self-guided walking tours are available daily, and special interpretive activities are held on the first Saturday of every month. Call the site for more information.

FACILITIES: No food or lodging is available at the site, although both can be found nearby. Rest rooms, a sales center, and a drinking fountain are located in the visitor center, which is also handicapped accessible.

CAMPING: No camping is permitted at the site.

WILSON'S CREEK NATIONAL BATTLEFIELD

6424 West Farm Road 182
Republic, MO 65738-9514
(417) 732–2662
www.nps.gov/wicr/

Wilson's Creek, which comprises 1,750 acres, was authorized in 1960 to commemorate the site of an 1861 Civil War battle for control of Missouri. The park is located in southwestern Missouri, 10 miles southwest of Springfield and 3 miles east of Republic. It is reached from Interstate 44 by going south at Exit 70 on Missouri MM, east on Missouri M to Missouri ZZ, and south on Missouri ZZ to the park.

Missouri's strategic location and resources made its allegiance an important concern following the outbreak of the Civil War. The state was divided in its loyalties, with the governor an active Secessionist and Senator Francis Blair a Unionist.

Hostilities came to a head on August 10, 1861, when 5,400 Union troops attacked a Confederate force of approximately 12,000 camped near Wilson's Creek. The attackers surprised the Confederates and quickly occupied a ridge subsequently named "Bloody Hill." The battle raged for six hours before the Union forces retreated to Springfield. The Union commander, General Nathaniel Lyon, died during the battle, becoming the first Union general to die in battle in the Civil War.

Losses on both sides were heavy, with the North losing 1,317 men and the South losing 1,220. Though the Confederates held the field—and therefore won the battle—the Federals had helped their cause in Missouri. Because of the battle at Wilson's Creek and the Union victory at Pea Ridge seven months later, Missouri remained a Union state.

A visitor center built in 1982 features a thirteen-minute film, a spectacular battle-map display, a museum, and a sales area. A 5-mile self-guiding driving tour features the restored 1852 Ray House and a 3⁄4-mile walking trail at Bloody Hill. Weekend and holiday living-history programs are featured during the summer months.

FACILITIES: No facilities are located in the park, but food and lodging are available in the towns of Republic and Springfield. Drinking water and modern rest rooms are provided in the visitor center.

CAMPING: No camping is permitted in the park. A variety of public campgrounds are available within a 30- to 60-minute range. Private camping is available approximately 5 miles from the park, near Interstate 44.

FISHING: Fishing is available but not recommended.

GEORGE A.
CUSTER
LIEUT. COLONEL
BVT. MAJOR GENERAL
7 U. S. CAV.
FELL HERE
JUNE 25, 1876

STATE TOURIST INFORMATION
(800) 541–1447

BIG HOLE NATIONAL BATTLEFIELD

P.O. Box 237
Wisdom, MT 59761-0237
(406) 689–3155
www.nps.gov/biho/

Big Hole National Battlefield comprises 656 acres. It was authorized in 1910 to preserve the site of an 1877 battle between the U.S. Army and the Nez Perce Indians. The park is located in southwestern Montana, 89 miles southwest of Butte via Interstate 90, Interstate 15, and Montana 43. From Wisdom, drive 10 miles west on State Highway 43.

During the summer of 1877, a group of about 800 Nez Perce Indians began a journey from western Oregon and Idaho, over the Bitterroot Mountains, and into Montana Territory. The reason for the trip was the influx of settlers, miners, and stockmen into the area that had been reserved for the Nez Perce under two separate treaties. Because the Army was charged with returning the Indians to the reservation, the two groups faced each other in battle a number of times during the chase. One such conflict occurred in the Big Hole Valley. Although the Nez Perce were able to hold off the attacking army troops and escape, their losses were large and their spirit was broken. Two months later, after failing to obtain help from the Shoshone and Crow, the Nez Perce surrendered in the Bear Paw Mountains in northern Montana.

A visitor center with exhibits and an audiovisual program is open daily from 8:30 A.M. to 6:00 P.M. from Memorial Day to Labor Day, and 9:00 A.M. to 5:00 P.M. the rest of the year. The battlefield is closed Thanksgiving, Christmas, and New Year's Day. Ranger programs on the Nez Perce and on 1870s military life are presented at the visitor center. A short drive to the lower

Headstone Marker in Little Bighorn Battlefield National Monument (opposite page)

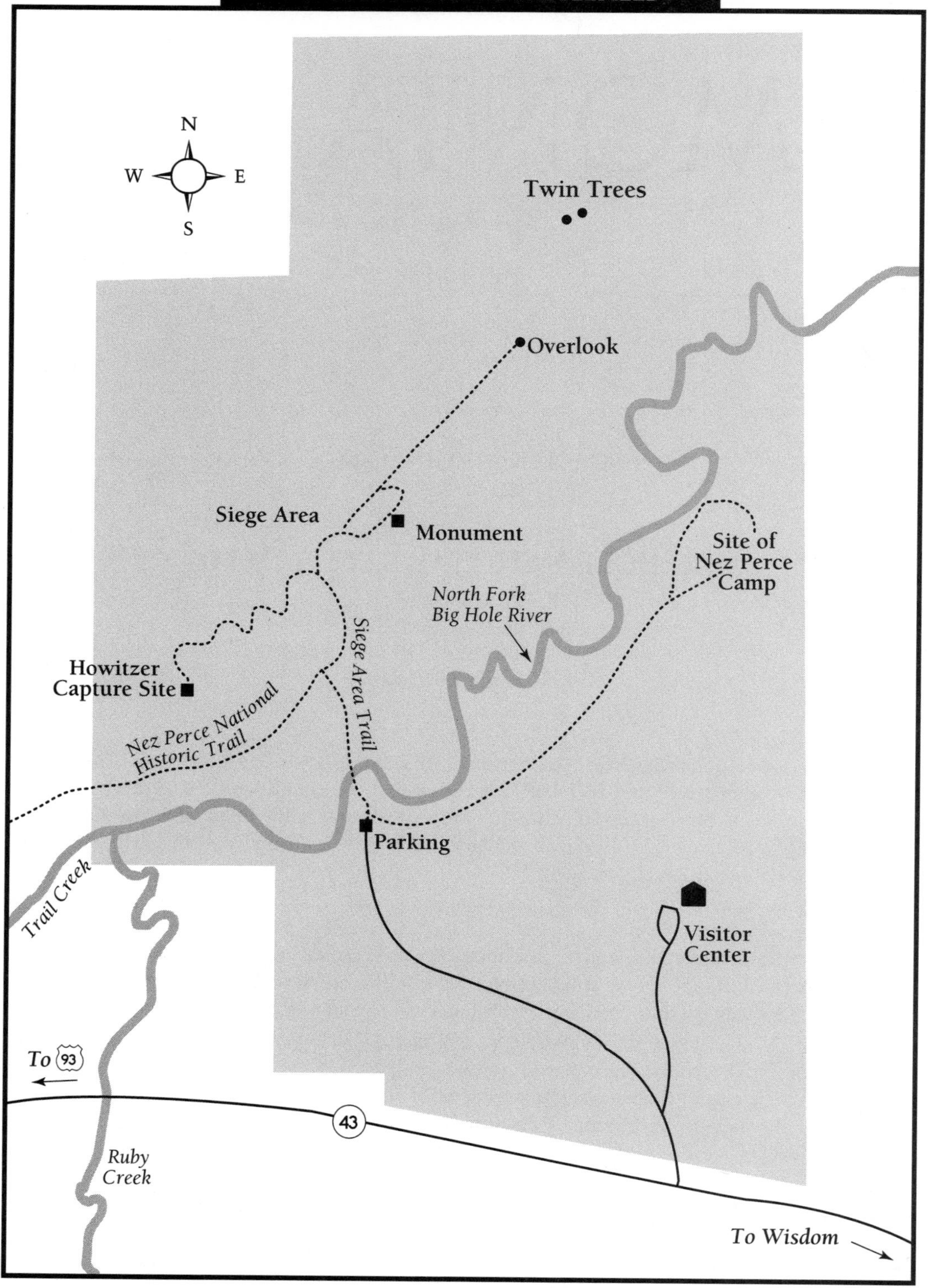
BIG HOLE NATIONAL BATTLEFIELD
N
W
E
S
Twin Trees
Overlook
Siege Area
Monument
Site of Nez Perce Camp
North Fork Big Hole River
Siege Area Trail
Howitzer Capture Site
Nez Perce National Historic Trail
Parking
Trail Creek
Visitor Center
To 93
43
Ruby Creek
To Wisdom

parking area provides access to two foot trails that lead to the battle area. Each trail takes about forty-five minutes to walk. Another trail to the spot where a group of Indians captured an army howitzer takes about thirty minutes. During winter months the battlefield is accessible by snowshoes and cross-country skis. The lower parking area is not plowed, adding an additional ½ mile each way. Allow a minimum of three hours to snowshoe or ski the trails.

FACILITIES: No food or lodging is available in the park. A gasoline station, grocery store, restaurant, and lodging are located in Wisdom. Drinking water and rest rooms are provided in the visitor center.

CAMPING: No camping is permitted in the park. The very nice May Creek U.S. National Forest Service campground is located 7 ¼ miles west on Highway 43. It has twenty-one mostly level sites with grills, fire pits, tables, water, and pit toilets.

FISHING: Trout fishing is permitted in the North Fork of the Big Hole River with a Montana fishing license. Fishing is also available a short walk across the road from the May Creek campground.

BIGHORN CANYON NATIONAL RECREATION AREA

P.O. Box 7458
Fort Smith, MT 59035-7458
(406) 666–2412
www.nps.gov/bica/

Bighorn Canyon was established in 1966. The recreation area comprises more than 70,000 acres, including the 71 miles of Bighorn Lake, which lies within a rugged, steep-walled canyon two thousand feet deep. Bighorn Canyon is located in southeastern Montana and north-central Wyoming. The southern part of the recreation area is reached via U.S. 14A from Sheridan, Wyoming, and via U.S. 310 from Billings, Montana. The northern portion and Yellowtail Dam are reached via Montana Highway 313 from Hardin, Montana.

Bighorn Canyon was cut over a period of millions of years. Yellowtail Dam was completed in 1966 to form 71-mile-long Bighorn Lake. The result is the creation of all types of water-related activities on one of the country's most scenic artificial lakes. In addition to recreation, the reservoir is used for power generation, irrigation, water supply, and flood control.

The canyon cuts across the north end of the Bighorn Mountains in a region where the middle Rocky Mountains border the Great Plains. Upstream from the dam are ½-mile-high limestone cliffs containing fossils that began forming when this region was covered by a shallow sea. Nearby, in the Pryor Mountains, the Bureau of Land Management administers 53,000 acres that have been set aside as a wild-horse range. Visitors may catch a glimpse of some of the 120 wild horses near Sykes or Britton Springs, or from the Sykes Ridge Road or Tillet/Burnt Timber Ridge Road.

Yellowtail Visitor Center, located at the dam in the north end of the park, includes information on Crow Indian history and Yellowtail Dam. Tours of the Yellowtail Dam are available from Memorial Day to Labor Day. About 3 miles below the dam site, traces of the Bozeman Trail may be seen on the right bank of the river. This trail was used for transporting supplies between Fort Laramie, Wyoming, and Virginia City, Montana, after the discovery of gold in Montana.

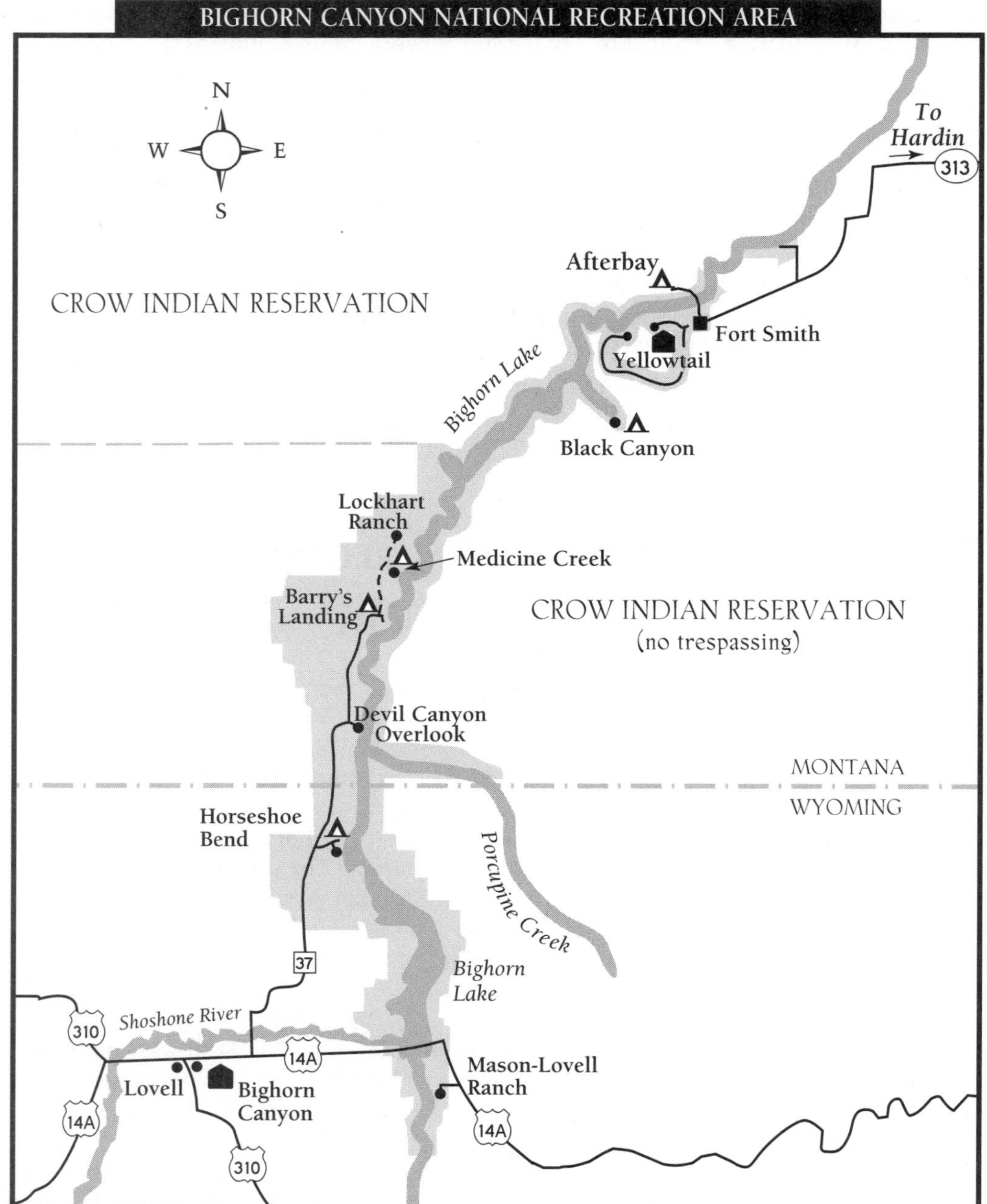

At the park's south end, Bighorn Canyon Visitor Center provides an audiovisual presentation and exhibits. This was the first National Park Service building to be solar-heated. The Mason-Lovell Ranch Site and three other ranch sites can be visited. For those with boats, Barry's Landing, Horseshoe Bend, and Ok-A-Beh all have launching ramps. Gas is available only at the marina at Horseshoe Bend and Ok-A-Beh.

FACILITIES: Horseshoe Bend provides a swimming beach, picnic area, and food and marina provisions. Motels, restaurants, service stations, groceries, and sporting goods are available in Lovell, Wyoming, and Hardin, Montana. Motels, restaurant, grocery, gasoline, and guide service are available in or near Fort Smith, Montana.

CAMPING: Afterbay Campground (twenty-nine spaces) with a nearby twelve-space overflow area offers tables, grills, water, vault toilets, and a dump station. Horseshoe Bend (forty-five spaces) provides tables, grills, water, flush toilets, and a dump station. Trail Creek Campground at Barry's Landing (twelve spaces, with five spaces allocated for tent only) has no drinking water and more primitive facilities, tables, grills, and vault toilets. Black Canyon (five spaces) has a floating comfort station, no drinking water, and is accessible only by boat.

FISHING: Bighorn Lake offers fishing for walleye (about 60 percent of all fish caught), rainbow and brown trout, perch, and black crappie. Bighorn River contains rainbow and brown trout and is a world-class fishing area. A Montana or Wyoming fishing license is required, depending upon the spot selected.

GLACIER NATIONAL PARK

West Glacier, MT 59936-0128
(406) 888–7800
www.nps.gov/glac/

Glacier National Park was established in 1910 and comprises more than one million acres of beautiful wilderness area, including lakes, mountains, and nearly fifty glaciers. Some travelers who have seen much of the United States and many of the areas of the National Park Service consider this to be the most outstanding park in the country. Glacier is located in northwestern Montana, with the west entrance 32 miles from Kalispell via U.S. 2 and the east entrance 62 miles west of Cut Bank via U.S. 2 and U.S. 89.

The landscape of Glacier tells a story that began millions of years ago. Over a long period of time, compacted limestone was covered with sediments which, in turn, were covered with new layers of limestone. Approximately seventy million years ago, pressures within the earth caused the rock to warp and break, until the western section was pushed over the eastern part. This overthrust lasted for millions of years, until a 300-mile section of the earth's crust had been moved more than 37 miles to the east. Much later, the park's surface was shaped by glaciers that formed numerous U-shaped valleys.

Glacier's three visitor centers at St. Mary (mid-May to October), Apgar (late April to late October, weekends other months), and Logan Pass (mid-June to mid-October) provide exhibits and information on the park. Glacier is crossed by the 50-mile Going-to-the-Sun Road. This road, mostly closed in winter, crosses through the heart of the Rockies at the treeline and provides one of America's most spectacular and scenic drives. Another worthwhile drive is along Many Glacier Road, which leaves U.S. 89 nine miles north of St. Mary at Babb.

Numerous outdoor activities are available in Glacier. Guided walks, slide-illustrated presentations, and campfire programs are offered on a daily basis from mid-June through Labor Day. Schedules are posted at ranger stations, visitor centers, and campgrounds. Horseback trips ranging from two hours to all day are operated out of Many Glacier, the Lake McDonald Lodge area, and Apgar. Information on guided backpacking trips and equipment rental may be obtained by writing Glacier Wilderness Guides, Box 535, West Glacier, MT 59936. Call (800) 521–7238 or (406) 387–5555.

Boating on the many lakes found in the park is a popular activity. Motorboats are permitted only on Bowman, Two Medicine Lakes, McDonald, Waterton, Sherburne, and St. Mary.

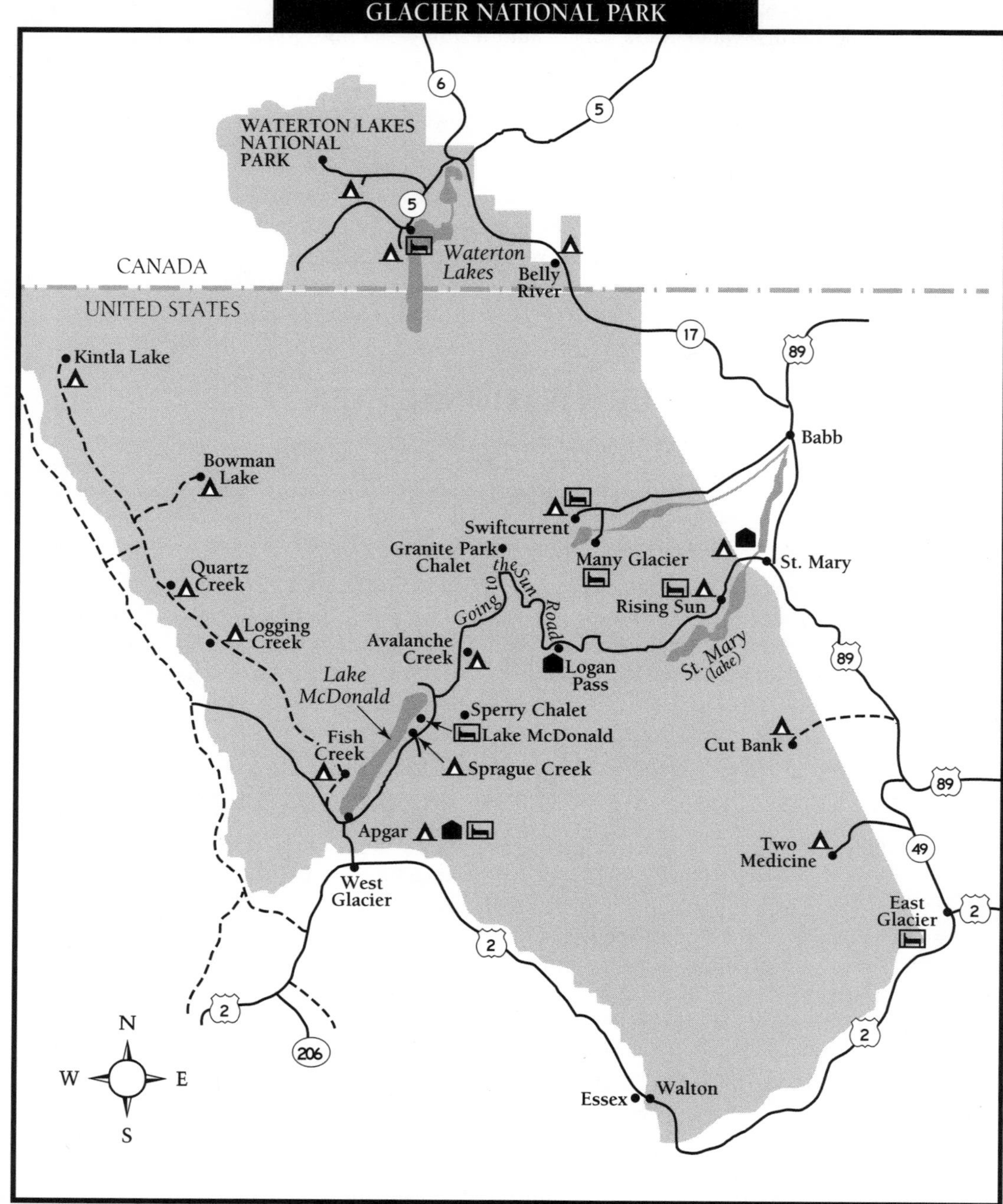

Motors have a limit of ten h.p. on the first two. Boats may be rented at Many Glacier, Apgar, Two Medicine, and Lake McDonald Lodge. Excursion boat cruises, many with a ranger-naturalist on board, are offered at Many Glacier, Rising Sun, Waterton Lake, Two Medicine, and Lake McDonald Lodge.

During winter months, cross-country skiing and snowshoeing have become increasingly popular. There is no downhill ski facility, and snowmobiling is not permitted. Going-to-the-Sun

Road from West Glacier to the head of Lake McDonald (12 miles) is the only road open to automobile traffic in winter.

LODGING: Six lodging facilities with accommodations that range from rustic cabins to a beautiful mountain lodge are within the boundaries of Glacier National Park. Two lodges are on the west side of the park in the small village of Apgar. Lake McDonald Lodge is 10 miles from Apgar along Going-to-the-Sun Road. Rising Sun offers duplex cabins toward the east side of Going-to-the-Sun Road, and two facilities are at Many Glacier on the park's east side. Two lodges outside, but near the park, should also be considered. Glacier Park Lodge is just outside the east boundary in the town of East Glacier. The beautiful Prince of Wales Hotel is in Waterton National Park, Glacier's sister park north of the border. For information or reservations for the lodges noted here, except Apgar Village Lodge, write Glacier Park, Inc., 1850 North Central, Mail Station 928, Phoenix, AZ 85077-0928. Call (602) 207–6000. To reach Apgar Village Lodge, call (406) 888–5484 or write to 200 Going-to-the-Sun Road, Apgar, MT 59336. A wide range of accommodations are in the towns of Kalispell, Whitefish, and Columbia Falls on the park's west side.

Two backcountry chalets are available to hikers and horseback riders. Sperry Chalet is open from early July to mid-September with traditional overnight accommodations and food service. Granite Park Chalet is operated as a hiker shelter with rooms and beds provided. Guests bring and prepare their own meals. For additional information on the chalets, contact the park superintendent.

FACILITIES: Restaurants are located in or near each of the lodges. The village of Apgar offers an ice-cream shop, restaurant, gift shop, and National Park Service visitor center. There are restaurants and a small general store in the Many Glacier area. Full services are in Kalispell, Whitefish, Columbia Falls, and neighboring communities.

CAMPING: Developed campgrounds with tables, grills, water, flush toilets, and dump stations are located at Apgar (196 spaces, ten group camps), Avalanche (eighty-seven spaces), Fish Creek (180 spaces), Many Glacier (110 spaces), Rising Sun (eighty-three spaces), Sprague Creek (twenty-five spaces, no dump station, no towed trailers or units longer than 21 feet), St. Mary Lake (148 spaces), and Two Medicine (ninety-nine spaces). Less-developed campgrounds with pit toilets are at Bowman Lake (forty-eight spaces, no large trailers), Kintla Lake (nineteen spaces, no large trailers), Cutbank (nineteen spaces, RVs not recommended), Logging Creek (eight spaces, RVs not recommended), and Quartz Creek (seven spaces, RVs not recommended). The camping limit at all these sites is seven days. Most campgrounds are available on a first-come, first-served, basis. Fish Creek and St. Mary campgrounds may be reserved through the National Park Service Reservation System by calling (800) 365–CAMP. Campsites are limited to eight people and two vehicles per site. Utility hookups are not available at any of the campsites.

Sixty-six backcountry camps are accessible by trail only. Visitors planning to camp overnight in Glacier's backcountry must stop at a visitor center or ranger station and obtain a Backcountry Use Permit. Backcountry permits may be reserved in advance, in person, or by mail. Permits are limited to six nights, with no more than three nights at each campground. Certain campgrounds have a one-night stay limit. Separate fees are charged for advance reservations and backcountry camping. For information on backcountry camping, contact Glacier National Park, West Glacier, MT 59936, or call (406) 888–7800.

FISHING: Glacier has some good fishing lakes and many miles of streams. Rainbow, brook and cutthroat trout are found in Swiftcurrent, Josephine, and Grinnell lakes, as well as in the lakes of Upper Swiftcurrent Valley in the Many Glacier area and the Middle and North Forks of the

Flathead River on the park's south and west boundaries. Grayling live in a few waters in the Belly River country. A Montana fishing license is not needed to fish in Glacier National Park, but a copy of the regulations should be obtained at visitor centers and ranger stations.

GRANT–KOHRS RANCH NATIONAL HISTORIC SITE

P.O. Box 790
Deer Lodge, MT 59722-0790
(406) 846–2070
www.nps.gov/grko/

Grant–Kohrs Ranch comprises 1,500 acres and was added to the National Park Service in 1972 to preserve the headquarters of one of the country's largest and best-known nineteenth-century open range cattle-ranching empires. The site is located in western Montana, adjacent to the town of Deer Lodge. Exit off Interstate 90 on U.S. 10 until reaching the fairgrounds. For travelers with an interest in the history of the Old West, this stop is a must.

Grant–Kohrs Ranch saw its beginnings in the 1850s, when Canadian trader, Johnny Grant, settled in the Deer Lodge Valley to become one of the area's early ranchers. Within a decade he was running more than 2,000 head of cattle, and in 1862, he constructed one of the largest homes in Montana Territory. In 1866, Grant sold his ranch to Conrad Kohrs, a German-born miner and butcher, for $19,200. From the open ranges of the 1860s and 1870s, Kohrs and his partner and half-brother, John Bielenberg, witnessed the transformation of the range cattle industry to an era of fencing, feed raising, and planted pastures. By 1900 the home ranch had grown to 28,000 acres with an average of 8,000 to 10,000 head shipped annually to Chicago from the partners' extensive Montana landholdings.

Following the deaths of Kohrs and Bielenberg in the early 1920s, the ranch was operated by Kohrs's grandson, who preserved the house, its furnishings and outbuildings, and papers documenting its rich history. Today the site remains a working ranch, with Texas longhorn, shorthorn, and Hereford cattle, Belgian draft horses, and poultry.

The site is open daily except Thanksgiving, Christmas, and New Year's holidays. A small visitor center with exhibits relating the ranch's heritage is located across U.S. 10 from the fairgrounds. From here, a self-guided trail takes visitors to the bunkhouse, blacksmith shop, and many other outbuildings. In addition, rangers conduct free tours of the Kohrs ranch house with its outstanding original furnishings. Reservations are made at the visitor center on a first-come, first-served basis. A living history program from May through September depicts traditional cowboy and ranch life.

FACILITIES: No food or lodging is available in the park, but restaurants, motels, grocery stores, and gasoline stations are available within 1 mile in Deer Lodge. Water and rest rooms are provided near the visitor center and at the ranch.

CAMPING: No camping is permitted at the site. Lost Creek State Park is approximately 25 miles away (northwest of Anaconda) and offers primitive camping facilities. Two private campgrounds are in the town of Deer Lodge. For those traveling on Interstate 90, a nice campground (sixteen spaces, flush toilets, grills, water, and tables) in Montana's Beavertail Hill Recreation Area is 53 miles west of Deer Lodge.

FISHING: There is good fishing at the Clark Fork River. The river is a ½-mile walk, and a Montana fishing license is required.

LITTLE BIGHORN BATTLEFIELD NATIONAL MONUMENT

P.O. Box 39
Crow Agency, MT 59022-0039
(406) 638–2622
www.nps.gov/libi/

Little Bighorn Battlefield (formerly Custer Battlefield) comprises 765 acres and was established as a national cemetery in 1879 (changed to a national monument in 1946) to commemorate the site of the famous Battle of the Little Bighorn. The park is in southeastern Montana, approximately 1 mile from the intersection of Interstate 90 and U.S. 212.

Two years after the discovery of gold in the Black Hills in 1874, the areas reserved for the Cheyenne and Lakota were swarming with gold seekers. When the Indians left the reservation, the army was called upon to force their return. Lt. Col. George Custer was part of one of three separate expeditions sent to converge on the main body of Indians in southeastern Montana. He and the Seventh Cavalry were ordered to approach the Indian concentration on the Little Bighorn. Custer divided his regiment into three battalions and attacked. When the battle ended, Custer and the 209 men of his battalion were dead. An additional fifty-three men from the other two battalions were also killed. Indians removed most of their dead from the battlefield, but their casualties are estimated at less than 100.

The monument's visitor center, which opens at 8:00 A.M. daily, contains historical exhibits and literature to help interpret the area. The visitor center closes at 7:30 P.M. from Memorial Day to Labor Day, 6:00 P.M. in spring and fall, and 4:30 P.M. during the winter. Veterans from Indian battles and more recent wars are buried in a national cemetery just west of the visitor center. (Custer is buried at West Point.) At Custer Hill, where a monument has been erected over the mass grave of soldiers killed in the battle, visitors have a view of most of the battlefield. The national monument also includes a memorial to Native American participation in the battle. Five miles beyond the main part of the monument is a detached section where two other battalions fought the Indians. Guided walks, lectures, and audiovisual presentations are given daily during summer months. Self-guiding tours are available. Bus tours are offered during summer months.

FACILITIES: No lodging or food service is available in the monument. Rest rooms and drinking water are provided at the visitor center. A motel, restaurant, and gas station are located a short distance from the park entrance at the intersection of Interstate 90 and U.S. Highway 212.

CAMPING: No camping is permitted in the monument. A small private campground is located at the intersection of 90 and 212, about a mile from the park entrance. Larger private campgrounds are located in Hardin, 15 miles north. Public camping facilities are available at Bighorn Canyon National Recreation Area, approximately 40 miles away.

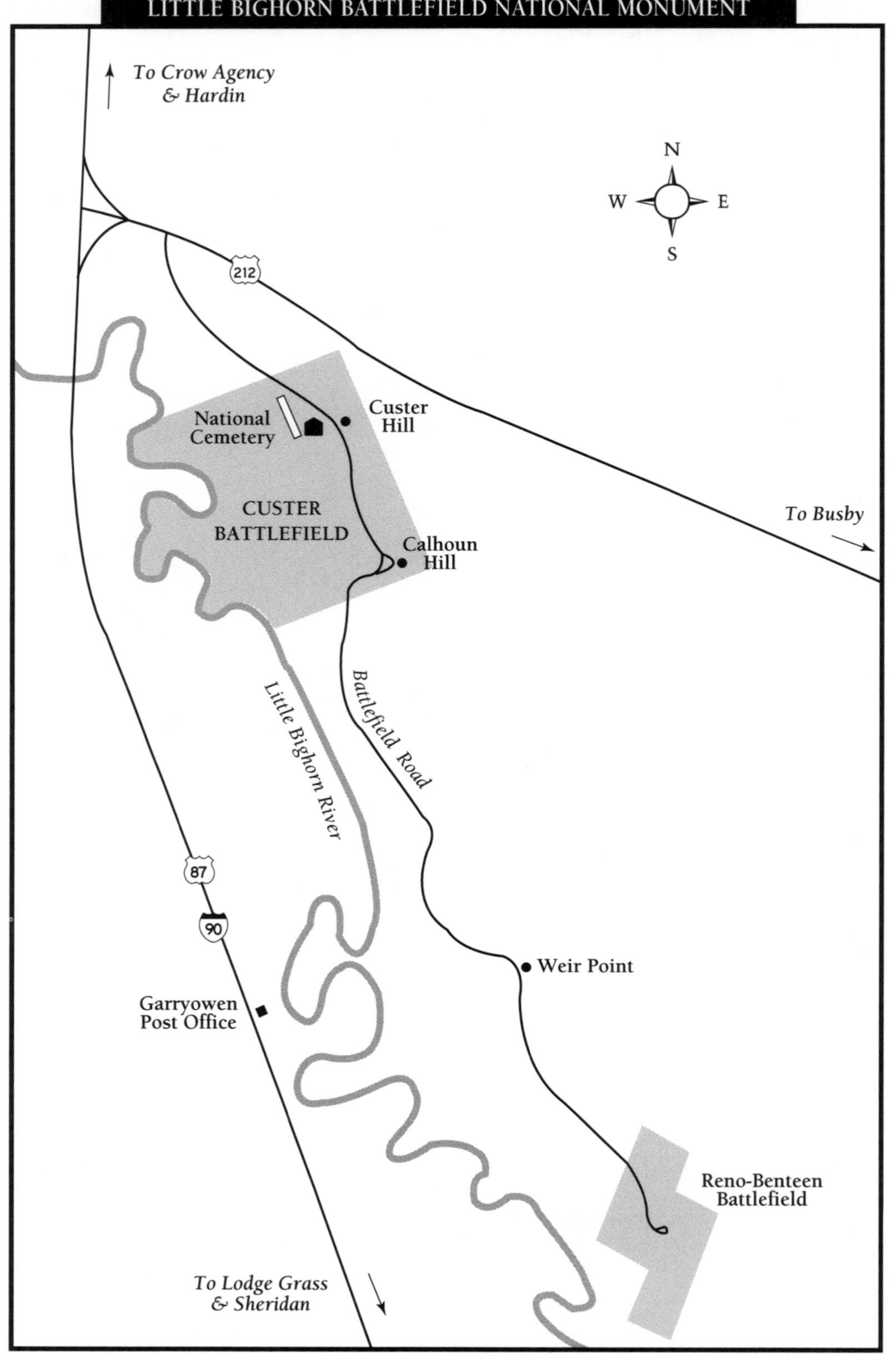
LITTLE BIGHORN BATTLEFIELD NATIONAL MONUMENT
To Crow Agency
& Hardin
N
W
E
S
212
National
Cemetery
Custer
Hill
CUSTER
BATTLEFIELD
Calhoun
Hill
To Busby
Little Bighorn River
Battlefield Road
87
90
Weir Point
Garryowen
Post Office
Reno-Benteen
Battlefield
To Lodge Grass
& Sheridan

FISHING: Non-Indians are not permitted to fish in the Little Bighorn River, which is no longer stocked and supports only catfish. Nearby, the Bighorn River (also on the Crow Reservation) offers some of the finest trout fishing in the Northwest. Outfitters are available in the Fort Smith area of Bighorn Canyon National Recreation Area.

Homestead National Monument (courtesy Homestead National Monument)

NEBRASKA

STATE TOURIST INFORMATION
(800) 228–4307

AGATE FOSSIL BEDS NATIONAL MONUMENT

P.O. Box 27
Gering, NE 69341-0027
(308) 436–4340
agfo_ranger_activities@nps.gov
www.nps.gov/agfo/

Agate Fossil Beds National Monument, which comprises approximately 2,700 acres, was established in 1965 to preserve three renowned quarries that contain numerous well-preserved mammal fossils. The park is located in extreme western Nebraska on State Highway 29, approximately 23 miles south of the town of Harrison.

Agate Fossil Beds contains a concentration of fossils that were deposited as bones nineteen million years ago, during the Age of Mammals. The beds contain a variety of fossilized bones, the most common of which are those from a small two-horned rhinoceros that roamed the plains in huge numbers.

Initial excavation at Agate Fossil Beds occurred in 1904, when two scientists from the Carnegie Museum in Pittsburgh came here. One year later, a professor and four students from the University of Nebraska opened a quarry at University Hill. Subsequent excavations have occurred periodically since that time.

A visitor center with personnel, exhibits, and an audiovisual presentation is located about 3 miles east of Highway 29, between the River Road and the Niobrara River. A self-guiding trail to an area of exposed fossils is nearby. A brochure is available.

FACILITIES: Although lodging and food are not available at the monument, they are in both Harrison and Mitchell. Drinking water is provided in the visitor center, and rest rooms with flush toilets are available.

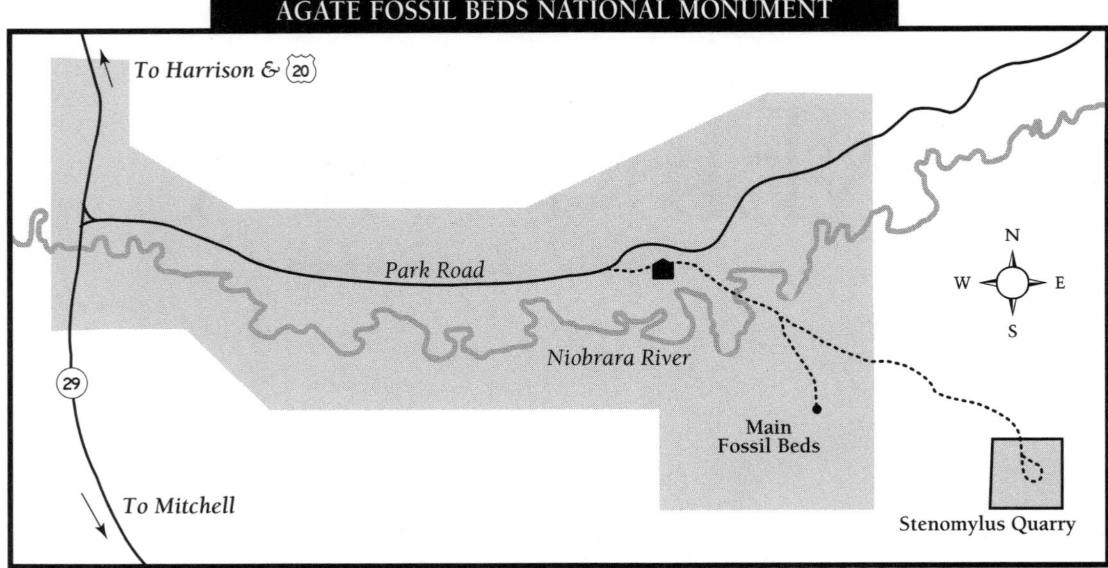

CAMPING: No camping facilities are available within the monument. A nice campground is located at Fort Robinson State Park, 23 miles east of Harrison on U.S. 20. For those heading south, city parks in Scottsbluff and Gering provide campsites.

FISHING: The Niobrara River flows through the monument, and trout may be taken with a Nebraska fishing license.

CHIMNEY ROCK NATIONAL HISTORIC SITE

P.O. Box 27
Gering, NE 69341-0027
(308) 436–4340
www.nps.gov/chro/

Chimney Rock National Historic Site, which comprises eighty-three acres, was designated an affiliated area of the National Park Service in 1956 to preserve the most famous landmark for pioneers traveling along the Oregon Trail. The site is located in western Nebraska, 3½ miles south of the town of Bayard. From near the intersection of U.S. 26 and State Highway 92, a 1½-mile gravel road leads to within ½ mile of the site.

Chimney Rock is one of the best-known natural landmarks in the United States. Located a little more than a mile south of the North Platte River, the 500-foot-high rock formation was used by settlers as a point of reference as far back as the early 1800s. It is most famous, however, as a landmark for westward travelers along the Oregon Trail. The plains to the east of Chimney Rock made it visible to the pioneers for many miles, and it warned them of the mountains ahead.

A small visitor center, operated by the Nebraska State Historical Society, is located on State Road 92, near the site. The center is open from Memorial Day to Labor Day and contains exhibits on the history of Chimney Rock. Other exhibits on this park and on the passage along the Oregon Trail are presented in the visitor center at Scotts Bluff National Monument, 23 miles to the west. Visitors wishing to hike to the spire are advised to wear hiking boots and to watch for rattlesnakes. Information on possible routes may be obtained at the visitor center.

FACILITIES: There are no facilities at the site. Lodging and food are available along U.S. 26 and State Highway 92.

CAMPING: No camping is permitted at the site. Camping is available approximately 10 miles southeast in Bridgeport State Recreation Area.

FISHING: No fishing is available at the site.

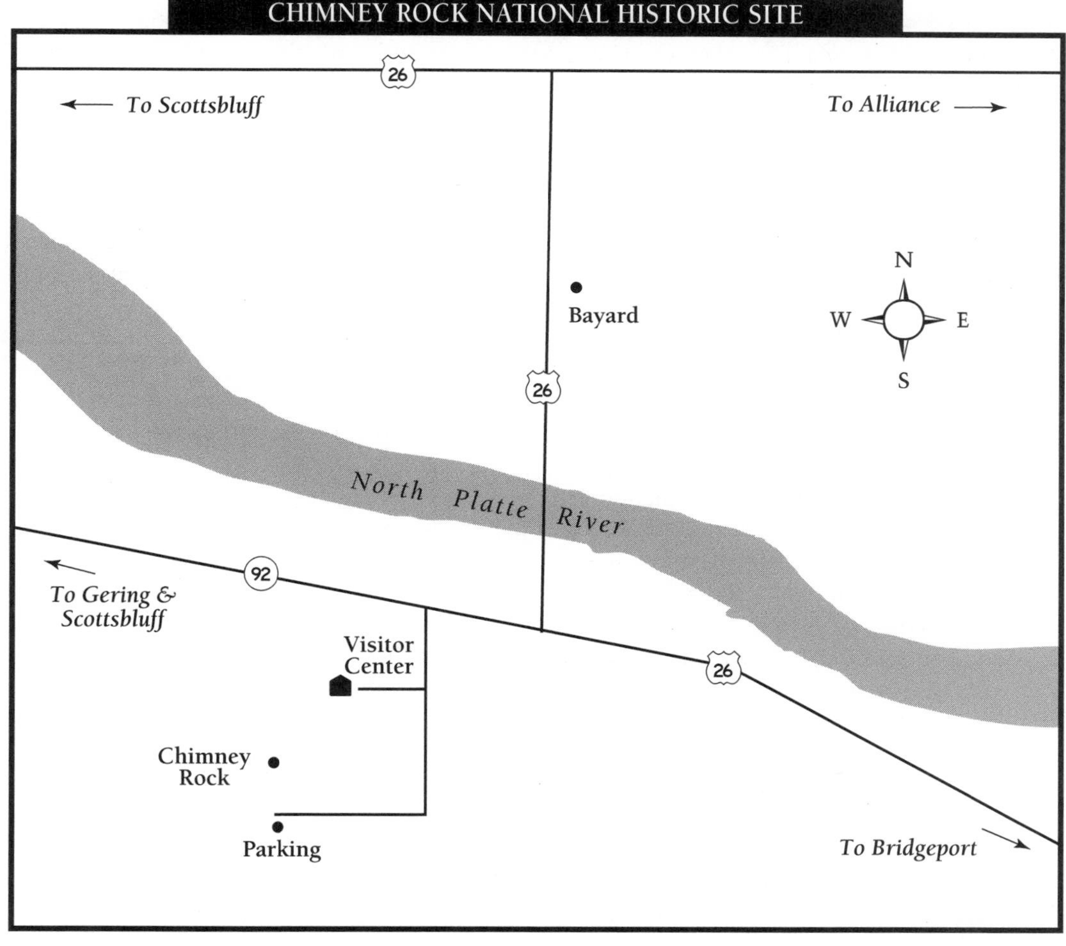

HOMESTEAD NATIONAL MONUMENT OF AMERICA

Route 3
Beatrice, NE 68310-9146
(402) 223–3514
www.nps.gov/home

Homestead National Monument of America was authorized in 1936 to commemorate the homesteading movement and the impact the movement had on the people and the land. It contains close to 200 acres of prairie and woodland on the site of one of the first claims filed under the Homestead Act of 1862. The park is located in southeastern Nebraska, 40 miles southwest of Lincoln via U.S. 77 to Beatrice and 4½ miles west on Nebraska Highway 4.

After decades of pressure to donate public land to settlers, on May 20, 1862, President Abraham Lincoln signed into law the Homestead Act of 1862, which permitted citizens who came West to stake a claim to 160 acres of unappropriated government land. To receive full title, the claimants were required to pay a small filing fee, live on the land, build and live in a house, cultivate 10 acres of crops, and make improvements over a five-year period. Subsequent land acts increased the amount of land that homesteaders could claim as settlers moved westward to more arid land. These later acts also changed the time and other requirements to obtain title to government lands. By the 1930s most of the land in the lower forty-eight states had been claimed, although a few places could still be homesteaded until 1976, when the act was repealed. Alaska was the last area to be homesteaded.

Although it is impossible to prove who the nation's first homesteader was, the claim to Daniel Freeman's homestead, on which the monument is located, was filed early during the first day (January 1, 1863) on which claims were permitted. Freeman and his wife are buried near the monument's eastern boundary. A trail to the grave site provides a panoramic view of the quarter-section homestead.

A visitor center near the monument entrance provides an eighteen-minute video presentation along with displays of historic objects and pictures showing life during the homesteading years. The park buildings are open daily from 8:30 A.M. to 5:00 P.M. Memorial Day through Labor Day, and from 9:00 A.M. to 5:00 P.M. the remainder of the year. The monument is closed on Thanksgiving, Christmas, and New Year's Day. An 1867 homestead cabin from a neighboring township was moved near the visitor center to show how typical homesteaders lived. A 2½-mile trail system winds from the visitor center through the second oldest tallgrass prairie restoration in the United States to the original Freeman cabin site, other Freeman building sites, the Freeman graves, and the squatters cabin site near Cub Creek. The trail is a worthwhile walk.

The Freeman School, a furnished, one-room schoolhouse that served students from 1872 to 1967, is located on Highway 4, ¼ mile west of the visitor center. At the time it closed, the school was the oldest, continuously used one-room school in the state of Nebraska. It is also the site of teaching that was the basis for the first court battle over the use of religion in the classroom. The Freeman School is open to visitors upon request, depending on staff availability.

FACILITIES: Water and rest rooms are provided in the visitor center. A small picnic area is available. Restaurants, motels, and supermarkets are located in Beatrice, 4 miles to the east.

CAMPING: No camping is permitted at the monument. The city of Beatrice (4 miles east) has two city parks with camping facilities. Chatauqua Park—on the south side of town, 3½ blocks east off Highway 77 on Grable Street—has tables, water, electrical hookups, a dump station, and hot showers. Riverside Park—on the west side of Beatrice, 4 blocks north off Court on Sumner—has tables, water, electrical hookups, and a swimming pool.

FISHING: Although permitted in Cub Creek, which flows through the monument, fishing is pretty much a losing proposition. Your luck will be better in the Big Blue River. A Nebraska fishing license is required.

MISSOURI NATIONAL RECREATIONAL RIVER

P.O. Box 591
O'Neill, Nebraska 68763
(402) 336–3970
mnrr_administration@nps.gov
www.nps.gov/mnrr/

Missouri National Recreational River was authorized in 1978 to protect a 59-mile stretch of the Missouri River. A second 39-mile upper stretch and two tributaries were added in 1991. The two sections of the river are located in northeastern Nebraska at the South Dakota border.

The original segment of the recreational river begins at the Gavins Point Dam near Yankton, South Dakota, and ends 59 miles downriver at the southern end of Ponca State Park. This section is prized for the islands, bars, and chutes formed by the river. The second stretch, flowing through landscape from pre-settlement days, was added over a decade later. It includes 39 miles of the Missouri, 20 miles of the lower Niobrara River, and 8 miles of Verdigre Creek. The Missouri River segment begins at the Fort Randall Dam near Pickstown, South Dakota, and ends near Running Water, South Dakota.

The National Park Service has no information facilities. Wayside exhibits interpreting the river's features are at most access sites, overlooks, and parks. The Corps of Engineers operates visitor centers at the Gavins Point Dam and the Fort Randall Dam. Information is also available at Niobrara and Ponca state parks. A variety of outdoor activities are available including camping, fishing, canoeing, boating, swimming, and bird watching. Canoeing is best on the upper reach of the Missouri.

FACILITIES: No National Park Service facilities are available. Food and lodging are in nearby towns. Rental cabins are in Niobrara and Ponca state parks. Public rest rooms are in the visitor centers mentioned above and the state parks.

CAMPING: Niobrara State Park (402–857–3373), ½-mile west of the town of Niobrara, offers 119 sites with tables, grills, flush toilets, showers, and a dump station. Some sites have electrical hookups. Ponca State Park (402–755–2987), 2 miles north of the town of Ponca, has 164 sites with similar facilities. A Corps of Engineers facility is at the Fort Randall Dam.

FISHING: Fishing is popular on both stretches of the Missouri. A Nebraska or South Dakota license is required.

See the map on the following page.

MISSOURI NATIONAL RECREATIONAL RIVER
SOUTH DAKOTA
NEBRASKA
To Sioux Falls
To Sioux City
N
S
E
W
Pickstown
Bitte
O'Neill
Running Water
Santee
Lewis & Clark Lake
Gavins Point Dam
Yankton
Niobrara
Crofton
Vermillion
Ponca State Park
Ponca
Missouri River
Niobrara River
SOUTH DAKOTA
NEBRASKA
281
46
37
50
52
81
12
14
20
29
Missouri National Recreational River

NIOBRARA NATIONAL SCENIC RIVERWAY

P.O. Box 591
O'Neill, NE 68763
(402) 336–3970
niob_Administration@nps.gov
www.nps.gov/niob/

Niobrara National Scenic Riverway comprises 21,074 acres and was authorized in 1991 to protect a 76-mile stretch of a Great Plains river and preserve an ecological crossroads between eastern woodlands and western grasslands. The riverway is located in north-central Nebraska, with the upper portion beginning at Borman Bridge, southeast of the town of Valentine, and the lower portion ending at Nebraska Highway 137, north of the town of Newport.

The Niobrara is a 300-mile river that begins in the Wyoming plains and disappears when it merges with the Missouri River in northeastern Nebraska. Over its course, it has cut into the plains as much as 300 feet, allowing water from the Ogallala aquifer to seep out of the valley walls and add to the river's flow. The western half of the scenic river includes more than 90 waterfalls, the highest of which drops nearly 70 feet.

This area of Nebraska serves as the meeting ground of humid eastern and dry western air masses that cause many species of plant and animal life to reach the limits of their range. Eastern forest species such as American elm and black walnut reach their western limits here. Likewise, western species such as ponderosa pine and horizontal jupiter terminate in this area. Even northern forest species including paper birch and quaking aspen reach their southernmost limits in the Niobrara Valley.

One of the riverway's major activities is canoeing and tubing along the western section of the river. The Fort Niobrara launch area near the Cornell Bridge on Highway 12 east of Valentine is a popular location to begin a trip. A number of firms in Valentine can supply canoes and tubes. A list of outfitters is available from the National Park Service or the Valentine Chamber of Commerce. Phone (800) 658–4024 for information. Hiking and sightseeing are also popular, especially at Smith Falls State Park through which the river flows. Nature trails are at the park and Fort Niobrara National Wildlife Refuge, which offers a driving tour through elk, bison, and longhorn cattle pastures.

FACILITIES: Visitor centers are at the wildlife refuge (operated by the U.S. Fish and Wildlife Service) and at Smith Falls State Park (operated by the Nebraska Game and Parks Commission). Lodging and food service are available in the towns of Valentine and Ainsworth.

CAMPING: Public camping with tables, fire rings, flush toilets, and showers is available at Smith Falls State Park. Reservations are available (402–376–1306). The park may be reached via a 4-mile gravel road from Highway 12. A number of private campgrounds are along the first 30 miles of the river between the wildlife refuge and Norden Bridge. Two commercial campgrounds are near the town of Valentine.

FISHING: Fishing in the river is likely to produce marginal results. A Nebraska fishing license is required.

See the map on the following page.

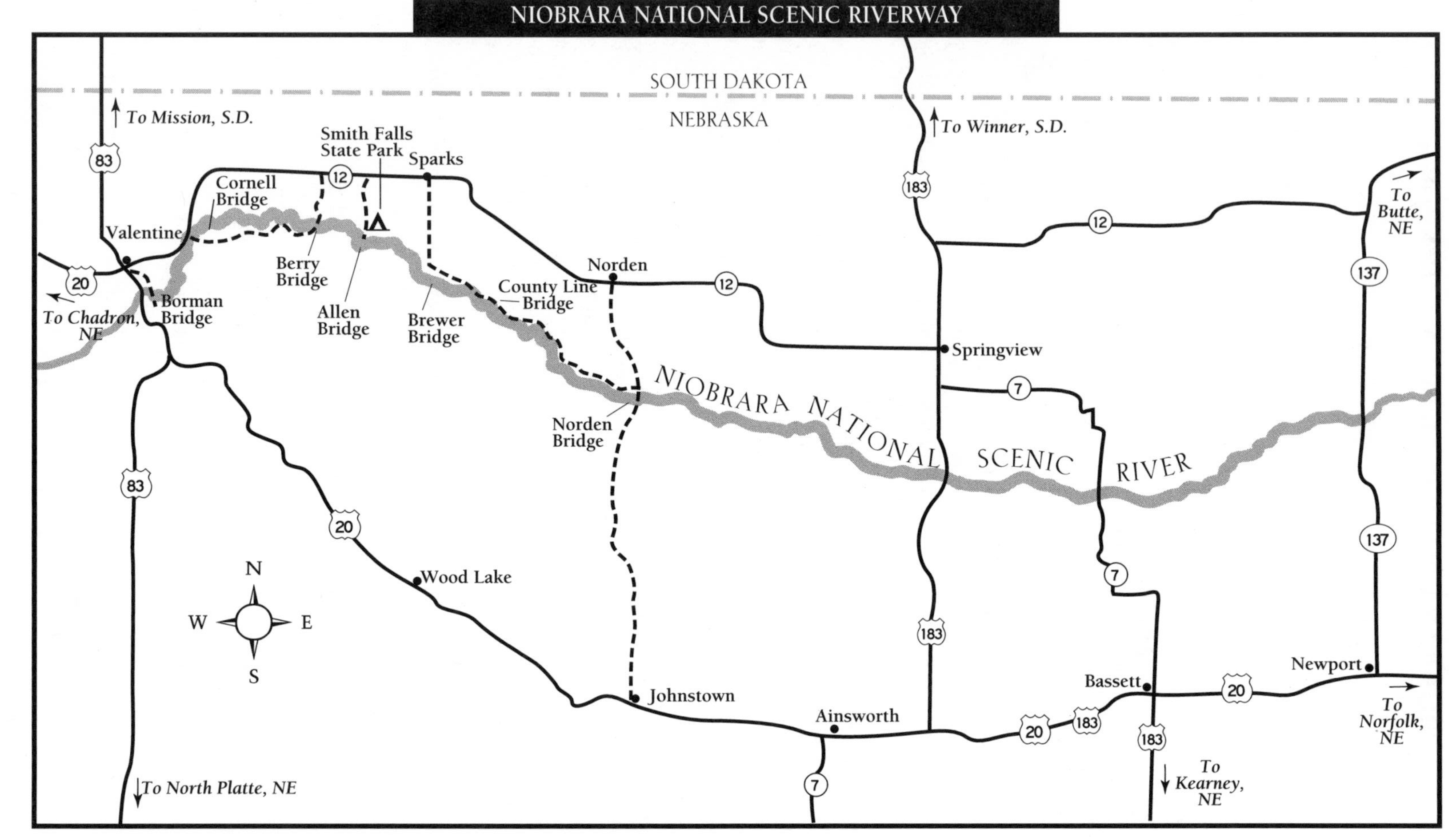
NIOBRARA NATIONAL SCENIC RIVERWAY
SOUTH DAKOTA
NEBRASKA
To Mission, S.D.
To Winner, S.D.
To Butte, NE
To Chadron, NE
To North Platte, NE
To Kearney, NE
To Norfolk, NE
Smith Falls State Park
Sparks
Cornell Bridge
Valentine
Berry Bridge
Borman Bridge
Allen Bridge
Brewer Bridge
County Line Bridge
Norden
Norden Bridge
Springview
NIOBRARA NATIONAL SCENIC RIVER
Wood Lake
Johnstown
Ainsworth
Bassett
Newport
N
W
E
S
83
20
12
183
137
7

SCOTTS BLUFF NATIONAL MONUMENT

P.O. Box 27
Gering, NE 69341-0027
(308) 436–4340
scbl_webmaster@nps.gov
www.nps.gov/scbl/

Scotts Bluff National Monument, which comprises nearly 3,000 acres, was proclaimed a national monument in 1919 to preserve two of a series of massive sandstone and clay bluffs rising 800 feet above the North Platte River. These bluffs became prominent landmarks for travelers bound for Utah, Oregon, and California. The monument is located in western Nebraska, 3 miles west of Gering via Nebraska Highway 92. From Interstate 80, take the Kimball exit and drive north on Nebraska 71 for 42 miles.

Scotts Bluff represents the remains of an ancient plain gradually eroded by wind and water. The dominant features of the bluffs have made them memorable landmarks for thousands of explorers, trappers, traders, and settlers traveling along the North Platte Valley. The first recorded mention of the bluff was in 1812, when fur trappers passed this way on their return to St. Louis.

The series of bluffs was named for Hiram Scott, a fur trader who is believed to have died in this area in 1828. During the mid-1800s thousands of settlers and gold seekers made the bluffs famous by using them for a landmark on the westward trek. In following years the Pony Express, Overland Stage, and Pacific telegraph lines built stations nearby, but completion of the transcontinental railroad in 1869 eliminated the need for most traffic along this route.

A visitor center with a bookstore, museum displays, and paintings by pioneer artist William Henry Jackson is located just off Highway 92. A 1⅗-mile paved road offers automobile access to the summit of the bluff, and a paved hiking trail to the top is also available. Remnants of the old Oregon Trail are still clearly visible within the monument and are accessible via a hiking trail.

FACILITIES: Food and lodging are not available at the monument, but both are found in either Gering or Scottsbluff. Drinking water and modern rest rooms are located at the visitor center.

CAMPING: No camping is permitted at the monument. The town of Gering operates an RV campground along Highway 71, while the town of Scottsbluff maintains the Riverside Park campground southwest of the city. Both sites offer tables, grills, hookups, showers, and a dump station.

FISHING: No fishing is available at the monument.

Great Basin National Park

STATE TOURIST INFORMATION
(800) 237–0774

GREAT BASIN NATIONAL PARK

Baker, NV 89311-9700
(775) 234–7331
www.nps.gov/grba

Great Basin National Park was established in 1986 to protect 77,082 acres of wild and rugged high desert country that includes spectacular mountains and an extensive cave system. The park is located near the Nevada–Utah border. Park headquarters is 10 miles south of U.S. Highways 6 and 50 and 5 miles west of the small town of Baker, Nevada.

The West's Great Basin incorporates western Utah and nearly all of Nevada in a giant panorama of parallel north-south mountain ranges and sagebrush-covered valleys. Great Basin National Park, formerly Lehman Caves National Monument (established 1922) and Wheeler Peak Scenic Area, sits in the middle of this huge desert. The park's three main attractions are Wheeler Peak, which at 13,063 feet is one of the highest mountains in the Great Basin, Lehman Caves, an extensive cavern system of limestone and marble decorated with stalactites and stalagmites, and the ancient bristlecone pines that grow beneath Wheeler Peak.

The park's range of natural environments results from the great variations in elevation. Numerous types of plants and animals may be observed by visitors. Mule deer feed in the higher meadows, and coyotes and cougars are occasionally seen. Plant life depends on the season. Wildflowers begin blooming in the lower country during spring and gradually appear higher on the mountain as the summer progresses. In the fall, slopes are streaked with golden aspen leaves. During years of normal precipitation, the higher peaks are covered with snow for more than six months.

GREAT BASIN NATIONAL PARK

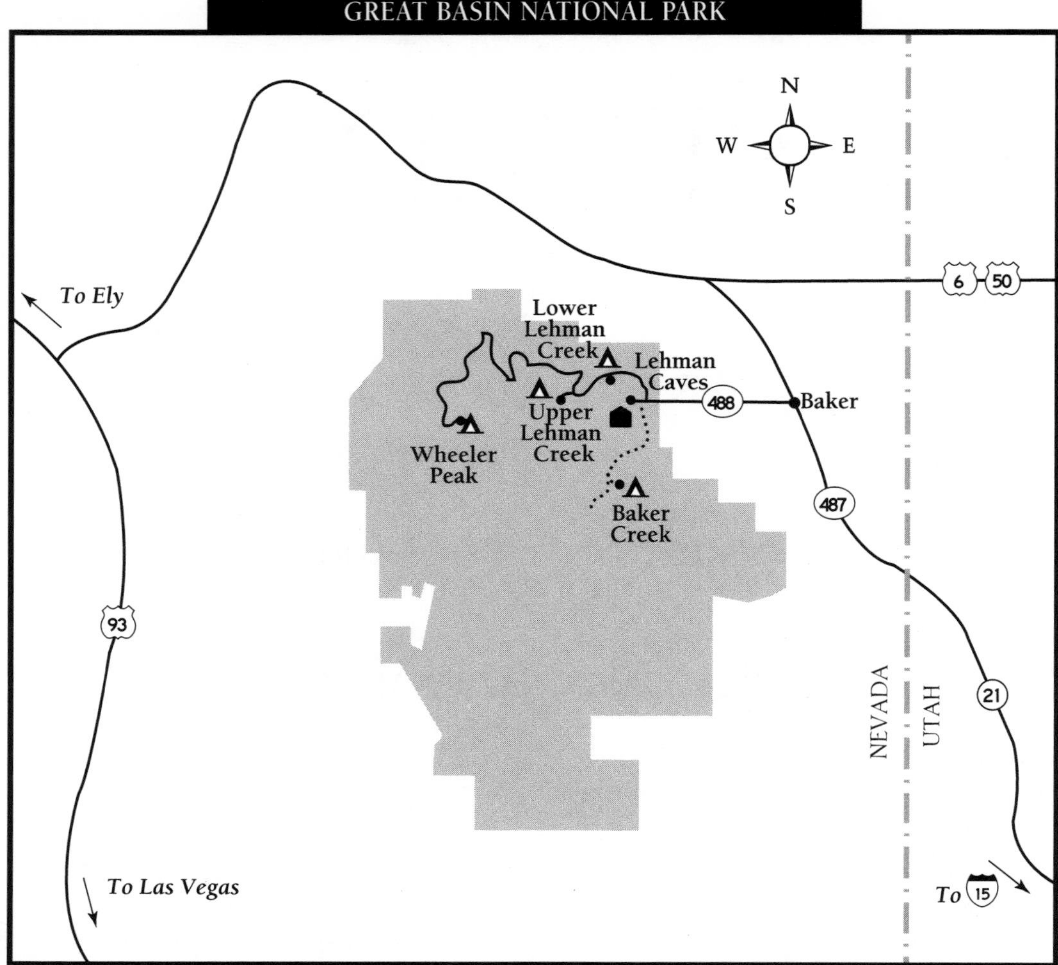

Bristlecone pines live longer than any other earth organism and are one of the outstanding attractions at Great Basin National Park. These ancient trees, which can live for over 3,500 years, are found throughout the Great Basin, generally at elevations between 9,000 and 11,000 feet. In the park, a grove of bristlecones on the northeast flank of Wheeler Peak can be reached via a 2-mile hike, which also passes through an Engelmann spruce and limber pine forest.

The formation of Lehman Caves began millions of years ago, when the water table was higher and the climate was more humid than it is today. Water charged with carbon dioxide widened and enlarged cracks in the mountain's limestone formation. The more soluble rock was dissolved, and as the water table gradually fell, the process of cave decoration began. Stalactites, stalagmites, columns, and shields (round discs of calcite) are all found in abundance throughout the caves. The caves take their name from rancher Absalom Lehman, who was probably the first white man to explore them. Lehman guided parties through the underground rooms from 1885 until his death in 1891.

The park is open daily except Thanksgiving, Christmas, and New Year's Day. Visitors with sufficient time should stop at the visitor center, take the cave tour, and drive the scenic paved road to the base of Wheeler Peak. Conducted tours of the cave (fee charged) require about one and one-half hours and cover approximately half a mile via a paved trail. Tours depart from the visitor center, and warm clothing is suggested because of the cave's 50 degree Fahrenheit temperature. Photography (no tripods) is permitted in the cave.

The paved road to Wheeler Peak climbs approximately 3,000 feet from the visitor center. Large motorhomes and trailers are not recommended beyond Upper Lehman Creek. At the terminus of the road, visitors will find a number of trails to lakes and to a bristlecone pine grove. The Wheeler Peak road is closed in winter.

FACILITIES: Refreshments, meals, and souvenirs are available at the visitor center from April through October. Modern rest rooms and picnic tables are also located here. No overnight accommodations are provided within the park, but restaurants, a small grocery, gasoline, and limited accommodations are available in the town of Baker. Ely, Nevada, 70 miles west, is the nearest major town.

CAMPING: Three campgrounds are located along Wheeler Peak Scenic Drive. Lower Lehman Creek (eleven sites) and Upper Lehman Creek (twenty-four sites) are closest to the visitor center and generally fill first. Wheeler Peak (thirty-seven sites), at an elevation of 9,886 feet, is at the end of the scenic road. Baker Creek (twenty sites) is 4 miles south of the visitor center via a gravel road. All of the campgrounds offer vault toilets, tables, grills, and water, although water in some of the campgrounds must be boiled or purified before drinking.

FISHING: The park offers good fishing opportunities in three creeks and two of the five lakes. Lahonton cutthroat trout are found in Baker Lake, while Johnson Lake has brook trout. Snake, Lehman, and Baker creeks each support rainbow trout. Baker Creek also has brown trout. A Nevada fishing license with a trout stamp is required. Use of live bait is prohibited.

LAKE MEAD NATIONAL RECREATION AREA

601 Nevada Highway
Boulder City, NV 89005
(702) 293–8907
www.nps.gov/lame/

Lake Mead National Recreation Area was established in 1936 and comprises almost 1½ million acres of clear water and desert landscape, making it an attractive area for water-related activities. The park is located in southern Nevada and northwestern Arizona. Main access is via U.S. 93 from Las Vegas to Kingman, Arizona. When approaching on Interstate 15 from the west, take the Highway 146 exit to Henderson, Nevada, and turn south on U.S. 93/95 to Boulder City. Tour buses from Las Vegas make regular trips to the recreation area and Hoover Dam.

Lake Mead and Lake Mohave combine to stretch for more than 180 miles. Both lakes have been formed from the construction of hydroelectric dams on the Colorado River. The most famous of these, Hoover Dam, was completed in 1935.

The park lies astride the Grand Wash Cliffs, which form a transition between two major geographical provinces in North America. To the east, the Colorado has carved a series of canyons (including the Grand Canyon) through high country known as the Colorado Plateau. After leaving the western portal of the Grand Canyon at Grand Wash Cliffs, north-south mountains of the Basin and Range province divert the river southward toward the Gulf of California. Broad enclosed valleys draining toward the river separate the mountain ranges of this region. In the Lake Mead section, the Colorado breached the mountains and provided the local basins with drainage to the south.

The park is open year-round, although daytime temperatures during summer months may rise above 110 degrees Fahrenheit. The main visitor center is a few miles northeast of Boulder City on U.S. 93. Daily tours of Hoover Dam are conducted by the Bureau of Reclamation during fall, winter, and spring. Park personnel present ranger programs and hikes at various locations; schedules are posted at campgrounds and ranger stations. Much of the park's summer activity is water-related. Swimming beaches are open year-round at Boulder Beach and Katherine. Concessioners offer boat trips to various locations, and docking facilities for private boats are located at six marinas on Lake Mead and two marinas on Lake Mohave.

FACILITIES: Most modern facilities, including lodging and food services, are available in Boulder City, Henderson, Las Vegas, North Las Vegas, Searchlight, Overton, Bullhead City, and Kingman. Developed areas in the park are:

Boulder Beach: Ranger station, picnic areas, launching ramp, campground, marina, boat rentals, store, lodging, marine supplies, and restaurant. Write Lake Mead Resort, 322 Lakeshore Road, Boulder City, NV 89005 (702–293–3484). Motel only (702–293–2074); trailer village only (702–293–2540).

Callville Bay: Ranger station, launching ramp, boat rentals, marina, picnic area, campground, store, trailer village, marine supplies, and restaurant. (702–565–8958)

Cottonwood Cove: Ranger station, picnic shelter, launching ramp, boat rentals, campground, marina, store, lodging, marine supplies, trailer village, and restaurant. Write Cottonwood Cove Resort, P.O. Box 1000, Cottonwood Cove, NV 89046 (702–297–1464).

Echo Bay: Ranger station, launching ramp, campground, marina, boat rentals, gasoline, store, lodging, marine supplies, trailer village, and restaurant. Write Echo Bay Resort, Star Route No. 89010, Overton, NV 89040 (702–394–4066).

Katherine: Ranger station, lodging, trailer village, marina, campground, picnic area, launch ramp, restaurant, grocery, gasoline, laundry, houseboat rentals. Write Lake Mohave Resort, Bullhead City, AZ 86430 (602–754–3245).

Las Vegas Bay: Ranger station, marina, campground, launch ramp, restaurant, grocery, gasoline, and laundry (702–565–9111).

Overton Beach: Ranger station, marina, trailer village, snack bar, grocery, marine fuel, and laundry (702–394–4040).

Temple Bar: Ranger station, lodging, trailer village, marina, campground, picnic area, launch ramp, restaurant, and marine fuel. Write Temple Bar Resort, Temple Bar, AZ 86443 (602–767–3211).

Willow Beach: Ranger station, restaurant, grocery, marine supplies, gasoline. Write Willow Beach Resort, P.O. Box 187, Boulder City, NV 89005 (602–767–3311).

CAMPING: The park includes seven campgrounds. All have flush toilets and dump stations. All trailer villages listed below have hookups and are operated by private concessioners. Showers are also concessioner-operated. Stores are located near most campgrounds. Campgrounds in the park are Boulder Beach (154 spaces, five group camps, eighty trailer sites, showers, laundry), Callville Bay (eighty spaces, twenty trailer sites), Cottonwood Cove (149

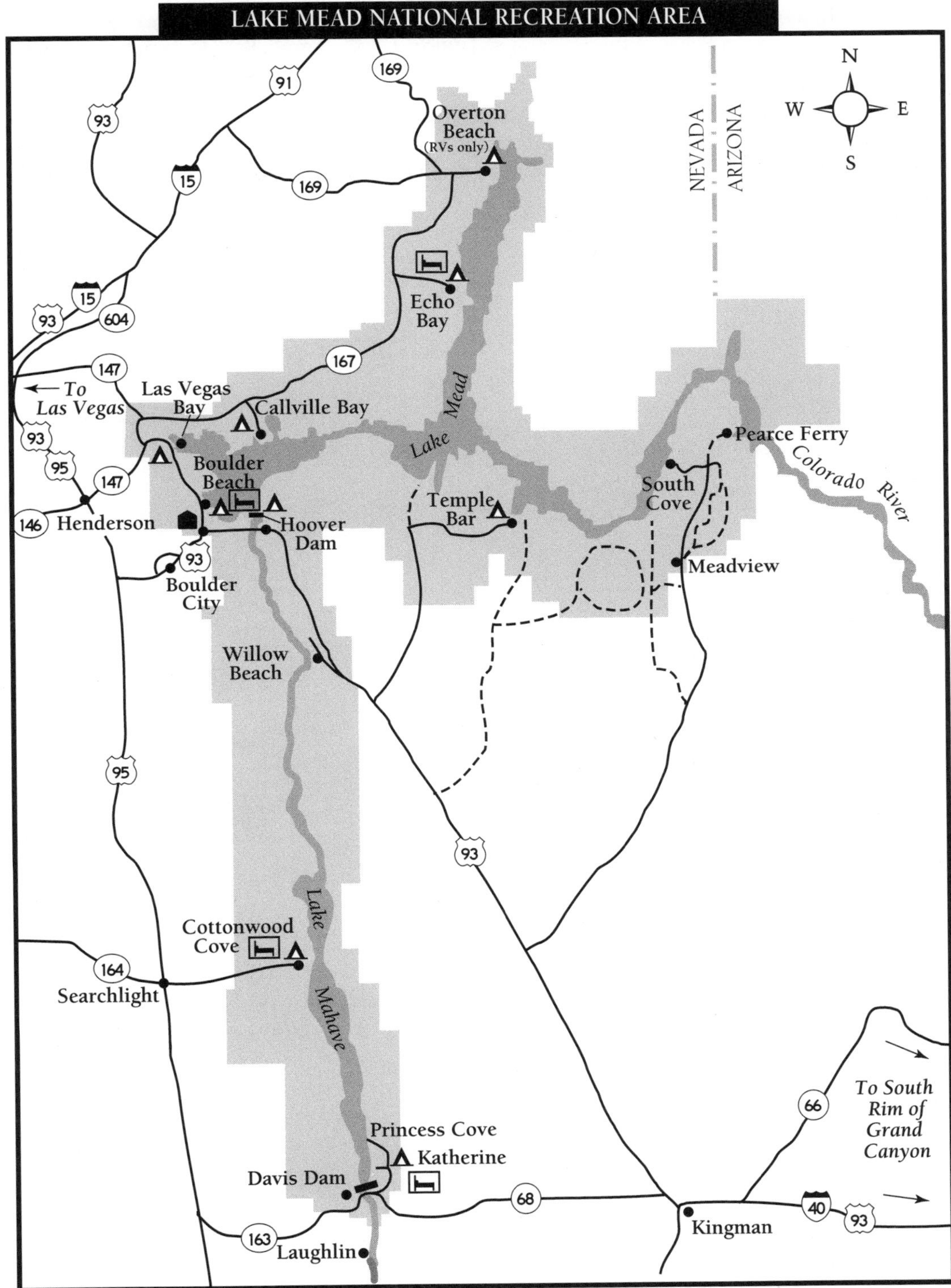
LAKE MEAD NATIONAL RECREATION AREA
N
W
E
S
NEVADA
ARIZONA
169
91
93
15
169
Overton Beach
(RVs only)
Echo Bay
15
93
604
167
147
← To Las Vegas
Las Vegas Bay
Callville Bay
Lake Mead
93
95
147
Boulder Beach
146
Henderson
Hoover Dam
Temple Bar
Pearce Ferry
Colorado River
South Cove
Meadview
93
Boulder City
Willow Beach
95
93
Lake Mahave
Cottonwood Cove
164
Searchlight
To South Rim of Grand Canyon
66
Princess Cove
Katherine
Davis Dam
68
40
93
163
Kingman
Laughlin

spaces, seventy-five trailer sites, laundry), Echo Bay (166 spaces, fifty-eight trailer sites, laundry), Katherine (173 spaces, twenty-seven trailer sites, laundry), Las Vegas Bay (eighty-nine spaces), Overton Beach (fifty trailer sites, laundry), and Temple Bar (153 spaces, fourteen trailer sites, laundry).

FISHING: Lake Mead is especially noted for its largemouth bass, striped bass, and channel catfish. Lake Mohave contains rainbow trout in the upper end and largemouth and striped bass farther down the lake. Sunfish and crappie are also taken in these lakes. A Nevada or Arizona fishing license is required, and a stamp from the other state must be affixed to the license when fishing from a boat.

NEW MEXICO

STATE TOURIST INFORMATION
(800) 545–2040

AZTEC RUINS NATIONAL MONUMENT

P.O. Box 640
Aztec, NM 87410-0640
(505) 334–6174
AZRU_Front_Desk@nps.gov
www.nps.gov/AZRU/

Aztec Ruins, which comprises 319 acres, was established in 1923 to preserve a large Ancestral Pueblo Indian community. The park is located in northwestern New Mexico, north of the town of Aztec, near the junction of U.S. 550 and New Mexico Highway 544.

After the people of the Colorado Plateau region developed farming and a more sedentary lifestyle, the Ancestral Pueblo cultural system now referred to as the Chaco Phenomenon began to grow. The West Ruin at Aztec, open to the public, is a Chaco-style greathouse of more than 400 rooms and kivas built in the early 1100s. Visitors may tour the West Ruin, which is actually only a portion of a larger community consisting of several other unexcavated greathouses, plazas, great kivas, tri-wall kivas, and smaller residential buildings. Prehistoric roadways, now barely visible, link the structures within this community. Short, well-defined road segments suggest a connection to hundreds of smaller residential sites along the Animas River valley and point toward other Chacoan communities in the Four Corners area. Aztec may have served as a major ceremonial, administrative, and trade center for the surrounding population. By the 1200s the Chaco system waned, and a different cultural style emerged that had its roots in the Mesa Verde area to the north. Some remodeling of the pueblo occurred, and the pueblo flourished in Mesa Verde style until the 1300s, when the people left the buildings uninhabited.

The visitor center contains exhibits such as pottery, baskets, and other items made by the Ancestral Pueblo people who lived here. A self-guiding trail leads through the West Ruin and to the Hubbard tri-wall kiva. The great kiva in the West Ruin was reconstructed in 1933–34 by archaeologist Earl Morris. Visitors are cautioned to stay on the trails, since the walls crumble easily. The park is open daily from 8:00 A.M. to 5:00 P.M. (longer during summer) except Thanksgiving, Christmas, and New Year's Day.

FACILITIES: Food and lodging are not available at the monument, but both may be found in Aztec. Drinking water and modern rest rooms accessible to wheelchairs are located in the visitor center.

CAMPING: No camping is permitted at the monument. A city park with camping facilities is located in Aztec.

FISHING: No fishing is available at the monument.

BANDELIER NATIONAL MONUMENT

HCR 1 Box 1 Suite 15
Los Alamos, NM 87544-9701
(505) 672–3861, ext 517
www.nps.gov/band/

Bandelier, which comprises 32,737 acres, was established in 1916 to preserve the ruins of many cliff houses of fifteenth-century Pueblo Indians. The monument is located in north-central New Mexico, 46 miles northwest of Santa Fe. From Santa Fe, drive north on U.S. 285 to Pojoaque and turn west on New Mexico Highway 502 to New Mexico Highway 4. Visitors to Bandelier should make an effort to spend time at the science museum at Los Alamos.

A group of ancestral Pueblo Indians attempting to escape the ravages of drought on the Colorado Plateau during the late thirteenth century sought locations with dependable water supplies. Some of the ruins found today in Bandelier are the result of the Pueblo emigrants who settled here. Some of the plateau that constitutes most of this area is composed of volcanic ash spewed forth over a million years ago by a giant volcano. As the volcano's interior was emptied by eruptions, the summit collapsed and formed a large saucer-shaped depression. Subsequently, the surrounding highland was carved by running water.

The features most accessible to visitors are in Frijoles Canyon. Here, along a stream at the bottom of a deep gorge, lie nearly 2 miles of cliff ruins. The masonry houses of from one to three stories include many cave ruins carved from volcanic ash. Studies indicate that most of the ruins date from the late pre-Spanish period, although a few small ruins are from the twelfth century and earlier. For centuries the Indians honeycombed the cliffs with artificial caves and farmed the valley and the mesa top. During the 1500s, for reasons unknown, the inhabitants left the area and settled in the nearby Rio Grande Valley, leaving the structures and villages unoccupied.

The monument's visitor center provides museum exhibits and an audiovisual presentation, and personnel are on duty to answer visitors' questions. Visitor center hours vary, depending on season and staffing. During summer months, rangers conduct guided walks and present

BANDELIER NATIONAL MONUMENT

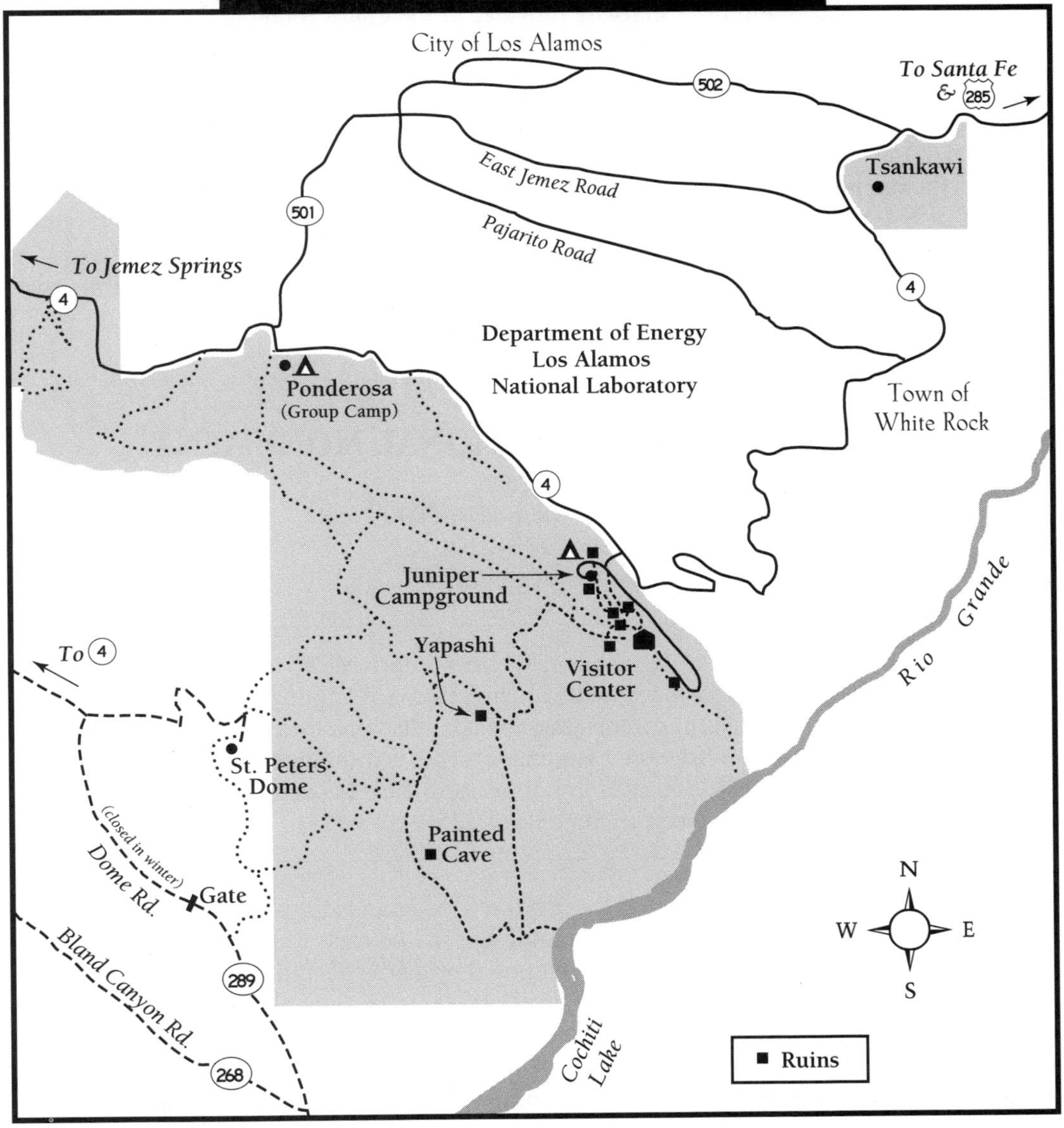

evening campfire talks. A detached section of the park, Tsankawi, is located 11 miles north of Frijoles Canyon on Highway 4. Here a large unexcavated ruin is reached via a 2-mile self-guiding trail (one and a half hours) beginning at the highway. The trail provides access to a number of interesting features, including petroglyphs (rock carvings) and cave structures.Trails are open during daylight hours.

Since most features of the park can be reached only by foot, the 70 miles of trails within Bandelier are well used. The main Frijoles Canyon ruins are accessible by loop trail (one hour) from the visitor center, and most visitors take this walk first. A guide booklet describing the ruins is available. Other trails from the headquarters area, with round-trip distance and time required from each trailhead, are Ceremonial Cave (2 miles, one hour), Lower Waterfall (3 miles, two and a half hours), and Rio Grande (5½ miles, four hours). Trails are open during daylight hours.

FACILITIES: No lodging is available at the park, but motels are located in White Rock and Los Alamos. Drinking water and rest rooms are provided at the visitor center and the campground. A curio store with a snack bar is located near the visitor center. An exceptionally lovely picnic area is a short distance away.

CAMPING: Juniper Campground (ninety-three spaces) provides tables, fireplaces, water, flush toilets, and a dump station. Juniper may be closed from December to March, depending on weather. Ponderosa Campground (two group spaces,) is located 6 miles west of the entrance and has tables, grills, water, and flush toilets. Ponderosa opens April 15 and closes November 1, although the dates are approximate, depending on weather. Reservations are required (505–672–3861, ext 534). A number of wilderness campsites are located throughout the park, and a wilderness permit is required.

CAPULIN VOLCANO NATIONAL MONUMENT

P.O. Box 40
Capulin, NM 88414-0040
(505) 278–2201
www.nps.gov/cavo/

Capulin Volcano National Monument, which comprises 793 acres, was established in 1916 to protect a symmetrical cinder cone rising high above the surrounding plain. The sighting of this prominent cinder cone by travelers some distance away makes it an important landmark today, as it undoubtedly was for the early pioneers. The park is located in northeastern New Mexico, 3 miles north of the town of Capulin, just east off State Road 325.

Capulin Volcano (pronounced cah-poo-leen) is the cone of an extinct volcano that rises more than 1,000 feet above its relatively flat surroundings. The volcano was active between 56,000 and 62,000 years ago, and the mountain is composed primarily of cinders, ash, and rock debris from these explosions, which lasted only a few years. From the highest part of the rim, where the crater drops approximately 415 feet, the visitor can see parts of New Mexico, Colorado, and Oklahoma.

A visitor center containing exhibits explaining volcanoes and the geographical area surrounding Capulin Mountain is located approximately ½ mile inside the park entrance. From here a 2-mile paved road circles and climbs the mountain to a parking area near the rim. At this point, a 1-mile self-guiding hiking trail follows the rim of the crater. The walk is fairly strenuous and takes approximately thirty-five minutes, but the time is well spent. It is probably less strenuous to walk the trail counterclockwise. There is also a ⅕-mile trail from the parking area to the crater's bottom and a short (ten-minute) nature trail by the visitor center. You may want to call ahead to determine hours of operation, which vary seasonally.

The monument contains a surprising variety of plants and wildlife. Porcupines, squirrels, and deer are relatively abundant, and golden eagles are seen on occasion. Extensive plant life is located both at the mountain's base and on Crater Rim Trail.

FACILITIES: Food and lodging are not available in the park. Both are available in nearby Capulin, Des Moines, Clayton, and Raton. Both the visitor center and picnic area contain water and rest rooms with flush toilets.

CAMPING: No camping is permitted at the monument. Camping is available in the towns of Capulin and at Clayton Lake State Park (thirty-three sites, flush toilets, showers), 12 miles northwest of Clayton on Highway 370. Camping is also available at Sugarite State Park (forty-four sites, flush toilets, no showers), 6 miles north of Raton, and 33 miles west of Capulin.

FISHING: No fishing is available within the park.

CARLSBAD CAVERNS NATIONAL PARK

3225 National Parks Highway
Carlsbad, NM 88220-5354
(505) 785–2232
cave_interpretation@nps.gov
www.nps.gov/cave/

Carlsbad Caverns National Park, which comprises 46,775 acres, was established as a national monument in 1923 (changed to a national park in 1930). This series of caverns—one of the largest underground chambers yet discovered—contains many spectacular and strange formations. The park is located in southeastern New Mexico on U.S. 62/180, 20 miles southwest of the town of Carlsbad and 150 miles east of El Paso.

Carlsbad Caverns National Park

CARLSBAD CAVERNS NATIONAL PARK

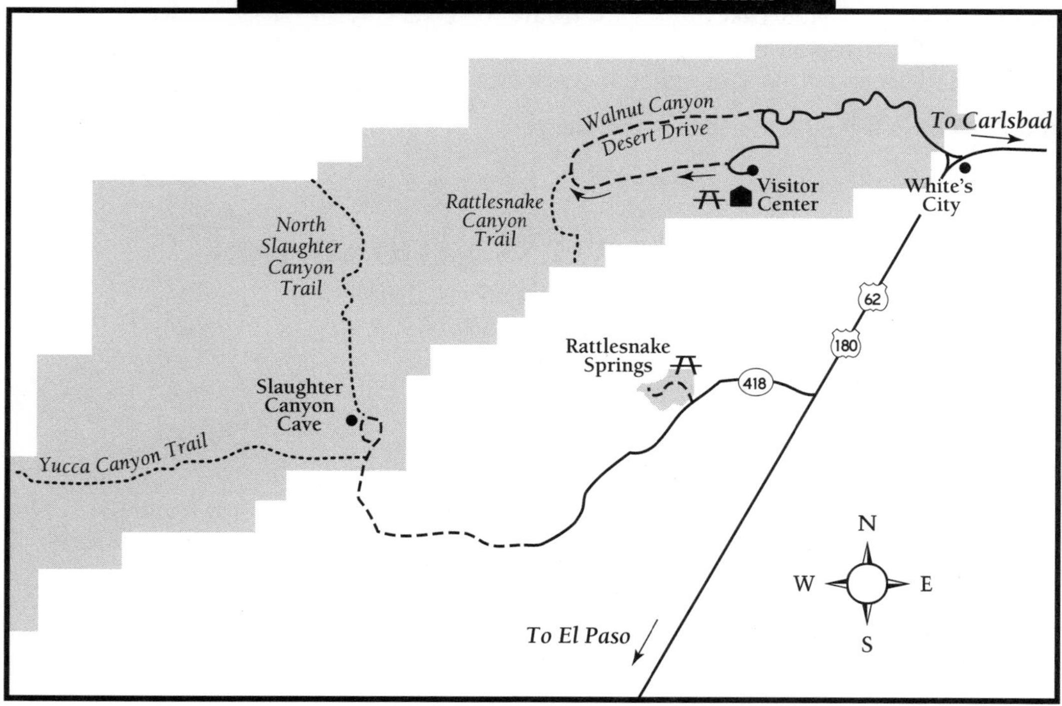

Carlsbad Caverns National Park lies in the Guadalupe Mountains of southeastern New Mexico. These mountains are the exposed remains of a limestone reef that was formed during the Permian Age—about 250 million years ago. Rainwater that became carbonic acid dripped through cracks and dissolved rock, but the main force in creating the caves was hydrogen sulfide from the oil and gas deposits to the east. It mixed with the water in the caves and created a weak sulfuric acid that easily dissolves limestone. This is the process by which Carlsbad Caverns' famous large chambers came to exist. These chambers are also highly decorated with stalactites, stalagmites, helicites, and cave popcorn.

In addition to the eighty-six caves in the park, the rugged landscape of the Chihuahuan Desert offers many interesting features. The range in elevation in the park results in a variety of plants and animals. A total of 740 species of plants, 64 species of mammals, 44 species of reptiles and amphibians, and 331 species of birds have been identified here.

A visitor center is located 7 miles inside the park, near the cavern entrance. Roadside exhibits and panoramic views along the paved road add enjoyment to the drive. The center is open year-round except Christmas Day. It offers exhibits and information services for visitors. Cave entry begins at 8:30 A.M. all year. The last cave entry time is 3:30 P.M. daily and 5:00 P.M. daily in summer. The two 1-mile self-guided tour routes do not require a reservation. The one-and-a-half-hour ranger-guided tour, several off-trail guided tours, and the Slaughter Canyon Cave tours do require a reservation. Call 800–967–2263 for reservations. All cavern tours exit by elevator. Call 505–785–2232 for information. A jacket (56 degrees Fahrenheit inside temperature) and shoes with rubber heels and soles are strongly recommended.

Nature trails are located near the visitor center. Ranger-guided walks into the desert are scheduled during summer months. Permits to hike into the backcountry are free and may be obtained at the visitor center information desk. One of the park's most popular activities in the summer is watching the bats fly from the cavern entrance each evening just before sunset. These bats, which winter in Mexico, feed at night on flying insects.

FACILITIES: A restaurant, gift shop, and kennel are located next to the visitor center. Food service is also provided in the caverns. No lodging is available in the park, but accommodations can be found in nearby communities. Water and rest rooms are located in the visitor center. Picnic facilities are available at the visitor center and at Rattlesnake Springs, 8 miles southwest of the park entrance on Slaughter Canyon Road.

CAMPING: No camping is permitted in the park, but private campgrounds are located in nearby communities. Brantley Lake State Park, 15 miles north of Carlsbad via U.S. 285, has forty-nine sites with water, tables, grills, and electrical hookups.

FISHING: No fishing is available at the park.

CHACO CULTURE NATIONAL HISTORICAL PARK

Box 220
Nageezi, NM 87037
(505) 786–7014
www.nps.gov/chcu/

Chaco Culture National Historical Park comprises nearly 34,000 acres and was established in 1907 to preserve numerous ancestral Pueblo structures, including dozens of monumental buildings called "great houses." In architecture, complexity of community life, social organization, and regional integration, the people of Chaco Canyon attained a unique cultural expression that was not duplicated before or since. The park, located in northwestern New Mexico, is open all year except Christmas Day, Martin Luther King Jr. Day, and Presidents Day. The best access route is from the north. Three miles south of the Nageezi Trading Post on Highway 44, turn south onto CR 7900, which is paved for 5 miles. Continue on the marked dirt road (impassable in wet weather; call ahead for road conditions) for 16 miles to the park entrance. From the south (not recommended): Turn off I–40 at Thoreau and go north on Highway 371 to Crownpoint (24 miles). Four miles north of Crownpoint, turn east on Highway 9 (also marked 57) for 14 miles, then turn north for 20 miles on Highway 57 (unpaved and unmaintained) to the park entrance. **Note: Many maps do not show the current road access from the north.**

From A.D. 850 to 1150, Chaco Canyon was the center of Chaco culture and the economic and ceremonial core of the San Juan Basin. Chacoan ancestral Pueblo people designed and planned the imposing great houses and constructed them over decades and even centuries. These impressive buildings may have been utilized only periodically during times of ceremony, commerce, and trading, when temporary populations arrived in the canyon for these events. The dozens of great houses in Chaco Canyon were connected by "roads" to over 150 great houses built thoughout the region.

These structures were often oriented to solar, lunar, and cardinal directions. Lines of sight between the great houses allowed for communication. Sophisticated astronomical markers, communication features, water control devices, and formal earthen mounds surrounded the great houses. The buildings were placed within a landscape surrounded by sacred mountains, mesas, and shrines that still have deep spiritual meaning for modern Native American descendants.

CHACO CULTURE NATIONAL HISTORICAL PARK

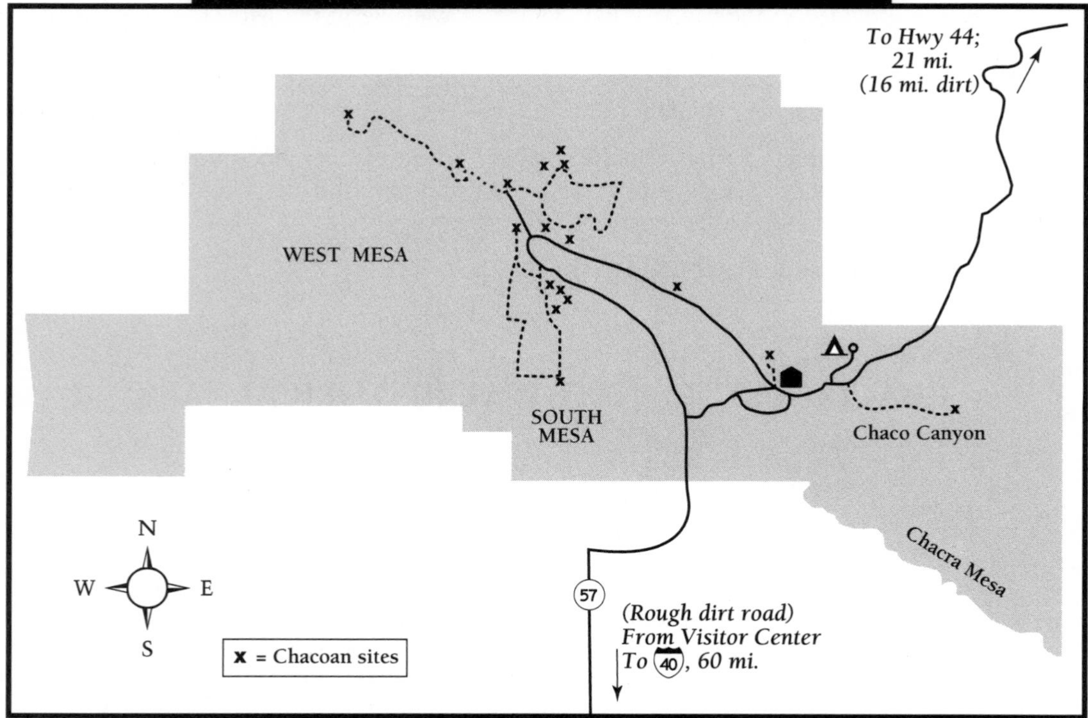

The Chacoans developed an extensive trading network for turquoise. Raw turquoise was imported from distant mines and transformed with exquisite craftsmanship into beads, necklaces, and pendants. Extraordinary quantities were found throughout Chaco Canyon in the form of finished ornaments, worksite debris, and offerings. Great amounts of such jewelry may have been traded to the regional center of Paquimé (Casas Grandes) in northern Mexico and throughout the Southwest.

After prevailing for 300 years, Chaco Canyon declined as a regional center during the mid-1100s, when new construction ceased. Chacoan influence continued on at Aztec Ruins and other centers to the north, south, and west into the late 1100s and 1200s. In time the people shifted away from Chacoan ways, migrated to new areas, reorganized their world, and interacted with foreign cultures. Their descendants are the modern Southwest Indians.

At the park visitor center, museum displays, exhibits, bookstore, and films help explain the history of the Chacoan people. Rangers are available to assist with trip planning, issue backcountry hiking permits, and provide schedules of guided hikes and evening programs. Una Vida, a mostly unexcavated great house, is a short walk from the visitor center parking area. Beyond the visitor center, a paved one-way loop road about 8 miles in length passes near six of the largest great houses, where self-guided trails begin. Parking areas along the drive allow visitors to access the sites of Pueblo Bonito, Chetro Ketl, Hungo Pavi, Pueblo del Arroyo, Kin Kletso, and Casa Rinconada. Each trail takes forty-five minutes to one hour to complete. All trails and the loop drive close between sunset and sunrise. Apart from the self-guided loop tour, you can hike four backcountry trails to see the remote sites or to view the great houses from overlooks on the cliffs above. Free backcountry hiking permits are available at the visitor center.

FACILITIES: No food, lodging, gasoline, repair services, or firewood are available at the park. On weekdays, limited supplies can be purchased at trading posts on Highway 44. The nearest lodging is at the Inn at the Post (bed and breakfast) at Nageezi Trading Post (505–632–3646). Kitchen privileges are available (no restaurant).

CAMPING: The Gallo Campground, 1 mile from the visitor center, is open year-round on a first-come, first-served basis. The sixty-seven spaces and three group sites can fill by noon in the summer. Picnic tables, fireplaces, flush toilets, and a dump station are provided. Water is available at the visitor center parking lot only. Bring your own wood or charcoal. Trailers over 35 feet cannot easily be accommodated. There are no hookups. No overnight camping is permitted in the backcountry.

FISHING: No fishing is available at the park.

EL MALPAIS NATIONAL MONUMENT

123 East Roosevelt, P.O. Box 939
Grants, NM 87020-0939
(505) 783–4774
www.nps.gov/ELMA/

El Malpais National Monument comprises 114,848 acres and was established in 1987 to preserve the geological and archaeological resources of a volcanic area that features ice caves and a 17-mile lava-tube system. This area was also a home for Pueblo Indians. The monument is located in west-central New Mexico, and is accessible via State Highways 53 and 110.

El Malpais (which means "the badlands" in Spanish) National Monument is a lava-filled valley formed by centuries of volcanic activity. Major features of the monument can be accessed via State Highways 53 and 117 and County Road 42. High-clearance, four-wheel-drive vehicles are advised for all roads other than State Highways 53 and 117. The Information Center is 23 miles south of Grants on State Highway 53. Information is also available at the ranger station on Highway 117, near the turnoff to Sandstone Bluffs Overlook. Some activities require permits that should be obtained before your trip.

Along State Highway 53, visitors can hike the Zuni-Acoma Trail, an ancient Indian trade route connecting two pueblos. The rugged 7½-mile hike (one-way) crosses four major lava flows, and a brochure is available. Nearby, El Calderon is a forested area that includes a lava flow, a lava-tube cave, a cinder cone, and a bat cave. Near the monument's west boundary, a privately operated and privately owned area contains a large cinder cone and a lava tube with ice year-round.

Along State Highway 117 visitors will drive up to a ridge of sandstone that offers a view of the lava flows and surrounding countryside. Seven miles south of the bluffs, in El Malpais National Conservation Area, is the largest accessible arch in New Mexico. Just south of the arch, the highway passes through a narrow corridor formed by lava that flowed near the base of 500-foot sandstone cliffs.

Off County Road 42 (which may be impassable during inclement weather), which loops between the two state highways, visitors will find a trail that leads to several lava-tube caves. Farther south are wilderness areas that present spectacular views, including numerous cinder cones.

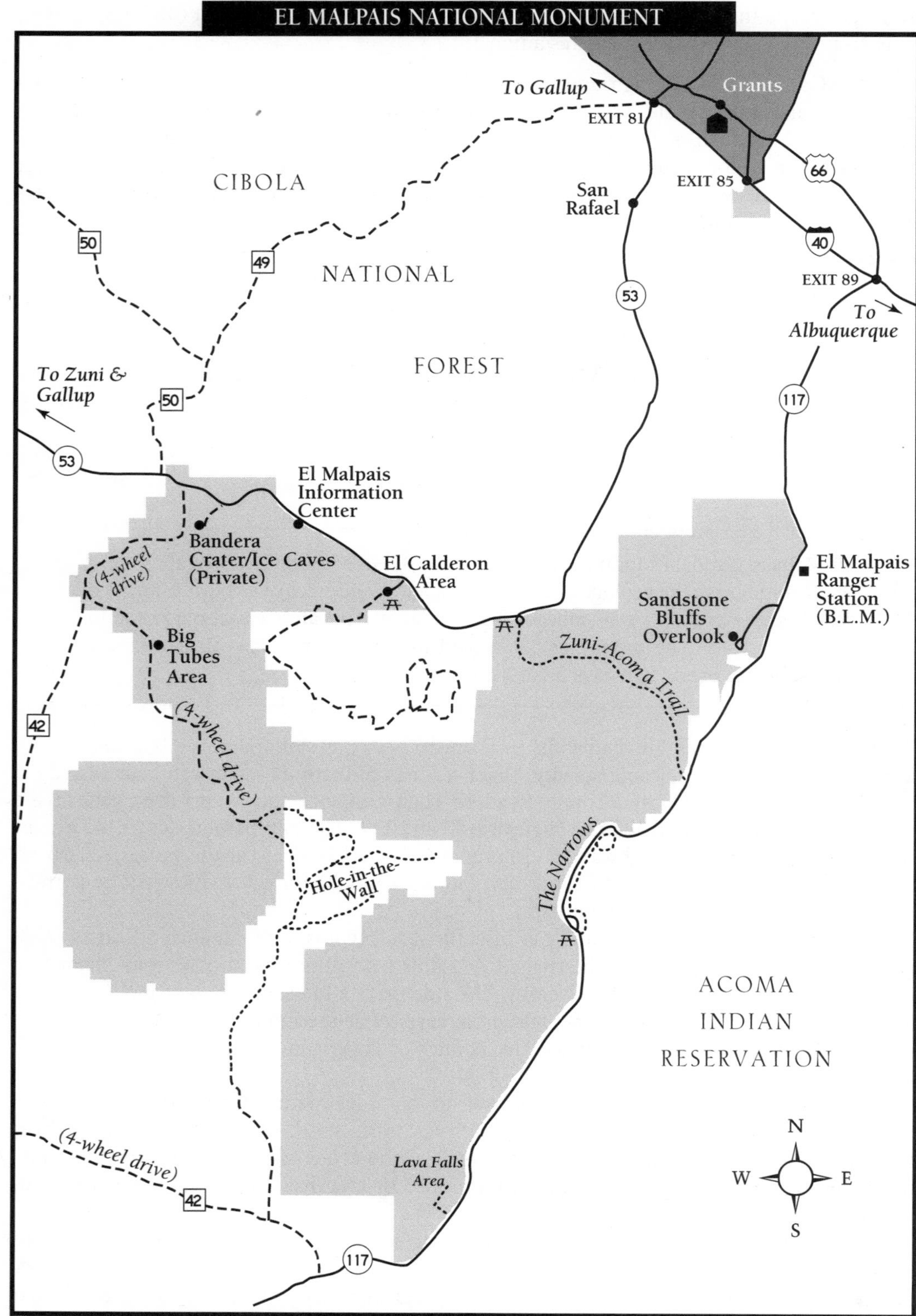
EL MALPAIS NATIONAL MONUMENT
Grants
To Gallup
EXIT 81
66
EXIT 85
San Rafael
CIBOLA
50
49
NATIONAL
40
EXIT 89
53
To Albuquerque
FOREST
To Zuni & Gallup
50
117
53
El Malpais Information Center
Bandera Crater/Ice Caves (Private)
(4-wheel drive)
El Calderon Area
El Malpais Ranger Station (B.L.M.)
Sandstone Bluffs Overlook
Zuni-Acoma Trail
Big Tubes Area
(4-wheel drive)
42
The Narrows
Hole-in-the-Wall
ACOMA INDIAN RESERVATION
N
W
E
S
(4-wheel drive)
Lava Falls Area
42
117

FACILITIES: Along Highway 117 picnic areas are located at The Narrows and Sandstone Bluffs. Along Highway 53 picnic areas are located at the Zuni-Acoma trailhead and the El Calderon area. Full services are available in Grants.

CAMPING: There are no campgrounds in the monument, but primitive camping is permitted. Sixteen miles west of Bandera Crater, El Morro National Monument offers a small but nice campground. For more information, see the camping section under El Morro National Monument. For those traveling on Interstate 40, Bluewater Lake State Park offers water, electrical hookups, showers, fishing, boating, and swimming. The park is 19 miles northwest of Grants via Interstate 40 and State Highway 412.

FISHING: No fishing is available in the monument.

EL MORRO NATIONAL MONUMENT

Rt. 2, Box 43
Ramah, NM 87321-9603
(505) 783–4226
www.nps.gov/elmo/

El Morro National Monument, established in 1906, comprises nearly 1,300 acres, highlighted by "Inscription Rock," a soft sandstone monolith on which thousands of inscriptions have been carved by explorers and settlers. The park is located in western New Mexico, 58 miles southeast of Gallup via State Highways 602 and 53, and 43 miles southwest of Grants via State Highway 53.

El Morro ("The Bluff") rises nearly 200 feet above the valley floor. It was named by the Spanish conquistadors who used this site and its natural water basin, filled by rain and melted snow, as a resting spot from the late sixteenth century through the eighteenth century. Before the Spanish

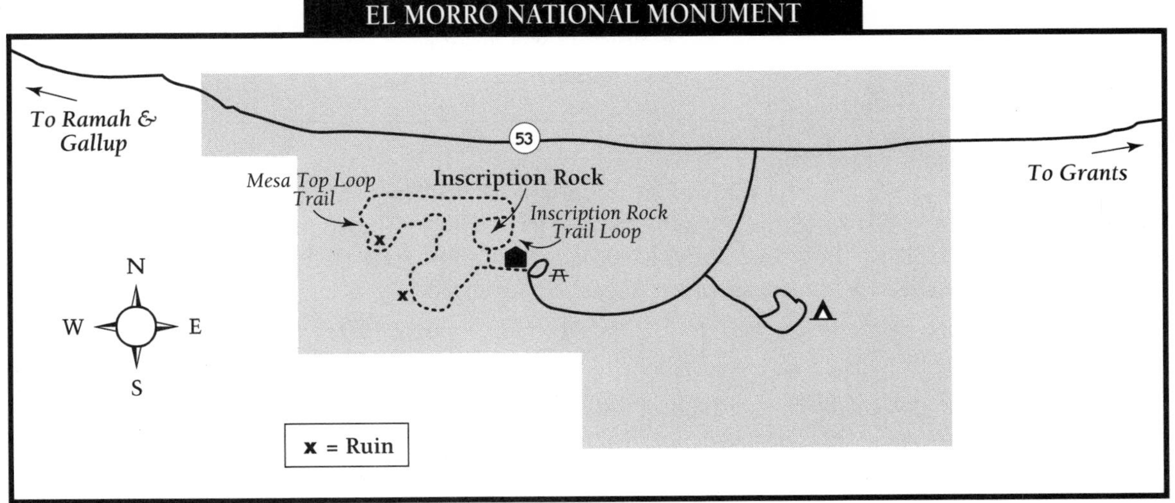

came, Anasazi Indians had abandoned pueblos on the mesa. From the first Spanish inscription in 1605, the sandstone structure has served as a register for people and cultures in this area of the Southwest. The first Anglo-Americans to inscribe their names at El Morro were Lt. J. H. Simpson and artist R. H. Kern. Their inscriptions may still be seen. After their visit in 1849, numerous other individuals—including traders, Indian agents, soldiers, surveyors, and settlers—added their names to the rock. On the top of El Morro are the ruins (mostly unexcavated) of Anasazi Indian pueblos.

A visitor center at the monument (closed Christmas and New Year's Day) contains exhibits about the people and history of this area. Personnel are on duty to answer visitors' questions. A self-guiding trail, which begins in back of the visitor center, leads along the base of the cliff where the inscriptions may be seen and then onto the top of the mesa where the pueblo ruins are located. A guide booklet covering both trails may be picked up in the visitor center. The first portion of the trail along the inscriptions involves a walk of about ½ mile and takes approximately forty-five minutes. If you climb to the top, you will have a total walk of 2 miles and spend about one and one-half hours. The walk to the top requires a 200-foot climb, and the trail on the mesa is difficult. The mesa-top trail may be closed during heavy snowfalls as well as periods of heavy lightning.

FACILITIES: No food service or lodging is available in the park, but both can be obtained at Grants and Gallup. A small cafe is just outside the park. Camping supplies and food service are available at Ramah, 13 miles west of the monument. Picnic tables are located in front of the visitor center, where water and rest rooms (with hot water) are provided.

CAMPING: An attractive small campground (nine spaces) is open from mid-May to mid-October, except for temporary closings forced by snowstorms, and offers tables, grills, water, and pit toilets. The campground is about ⅘ mile from the visitor center. It rarely fills except on weekends. An RV park is located near the monument entrance.

FISHING: No fishing is available at the monument.

FORT UNION NATIONAL MONUMENT

Watrous, NM 87753-0127
(505) 425–8025
foun_administration@nps.gov
www.nps.gov/foun/

Fort Union, which comprises 720 acres, was added to the National Park System in 1954 to preserve the ruins of an important fort on the Santa Fe Trail during the period 1851 to 1891. The monument is located in northeastern New Mexico, 8 miles north of Interstate 25 (exit 366), at the end of State Highway 161. Fort Union is 28 miles northeast of Las Vegas, New Mexico.

Fort Union was established when the U.S. Army decided in 1851 to move its headquarters and depot out of Santa Fe. The log buildings of the first fort served as a station on the Santa Fe Trail and as the principal quartermaster depot of the Southwest. From 1854 until the beginning of the Civil War in 1861, soldiers from Fort Union battled Apaches, Utes, Kiowas, and Comanches. Concern about a Confederate invasion of New Mexico resulted in the construc-

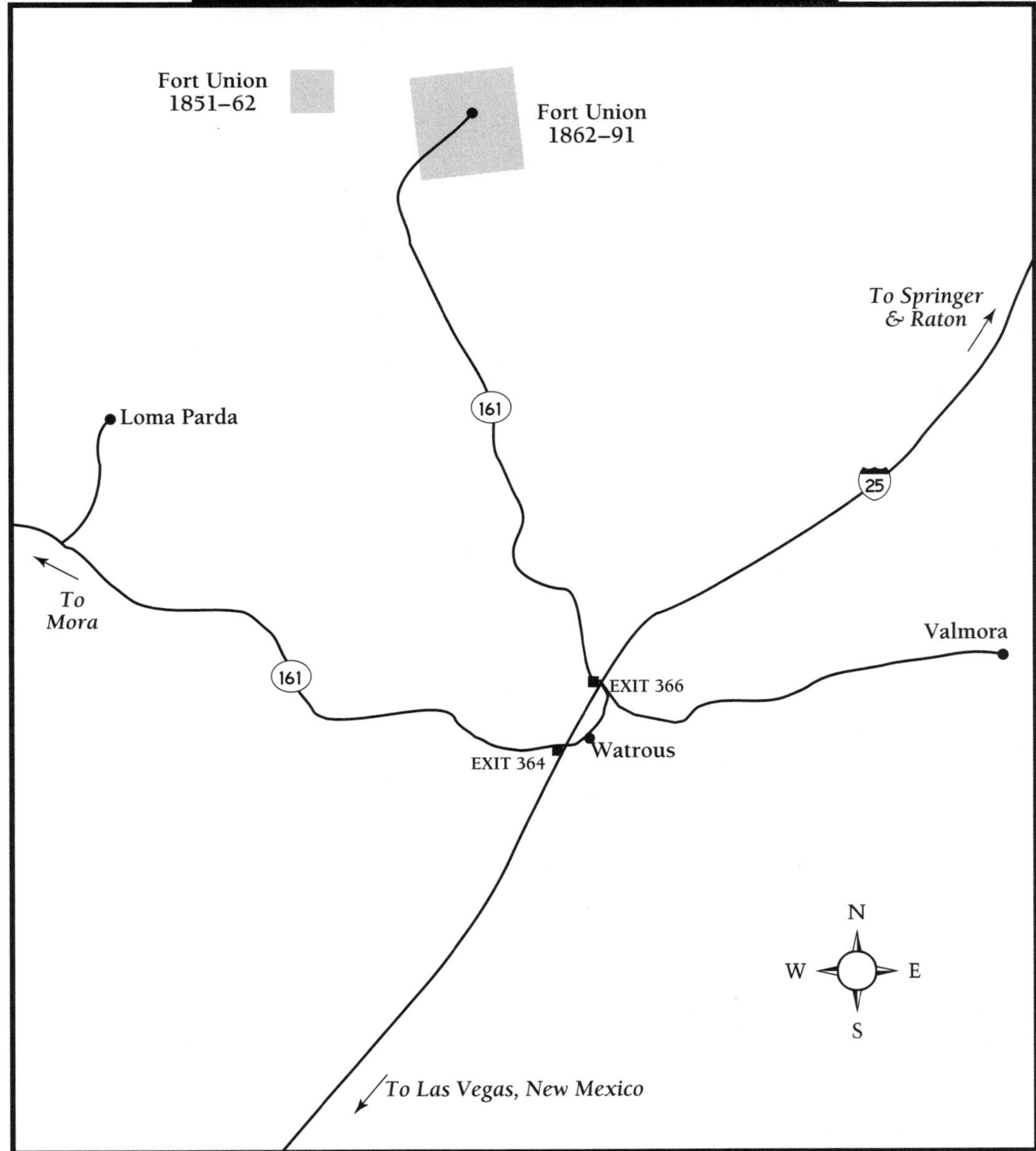

tion of an earthwork fortification in 1861. Although the fort was never attacked, soldiers from the fort were involved in major clashes that secured New Mexico for the Union.

Following the war, Fort Union was again rebuilt, this time with adobe, and continued to serve as the supply depot for the forts throughout the territory. The fort remained as a key outpost in the Southwest until it was abandoned by the military in 1891.

The park is open from 8:00 A.M. to 5:00 P.M. during the winter, except Christmas and New Year's Day, and from 8:00 A.M. to 6:00 P.M. during the summer. While walking among the ruins, keep in mind that the fort consisted of three parts. Military activities were conducted in the post, and the depot was concerned with transportation and supply of other southwestern forts.

The third part of Fort Union, the arsenal, stored and distributed arms and ammunition. As was typical with forts in the Southwest, no stockade or wall surrounded Fort Union. The National Park Service is currently attempting to halt deterioration of the adobe walls of the fort's buildings. A visitor center contains exhibits and artifacts to assist in understanding the fort's history. Recorded messages and pictures are located along foot trails. Ruts of the Santa Fe Trail are visible in numerous places at the fort and its surrounding area. Visitors are welcome to walk in the remains of this famous trail that connected Santa Fe with Independence, Missouri.

FACILITIES: Food and lodging are not available in the park. Las Vegas, New Mexico, has overnight accommodations. Water and rest rooms are provided in the visitor center, and picnic tables are available.

CAMPING: No camping is permitted at Fort Union, but Storrie Lake State Park, on State Road 518 (33 miles from Fort Union), offers thirty-seven campsites with sheltered tables, flush toilets, and showers.

FISHING: No fishing is available at the monument. Storrie Lake State Park offers fishing.

GILA CLIFF DWELLINGS NATIONAL MONUMENT

HC 68, Box 100
Silver City, NM 88061-0100
(505) 536–9461
www.nps.gov/gici/

Gila Cliff Dwellings, which comprises 533 acres, was established in 1907 to preserve some excellent cliff dwellings in natural cavities on the face of a sandstone cliff. The monument is located in southwestern New Mexico, 44 miles north of Silver City via paved State Highway 15. The road is unsafe for trailers more than 20 feet long. An alternative route is New Mexico 35.

Ruins at Gila Cliff Dwellings date back to the second century. At that time, people constructed circular dwellings with floors below ground level. Variations of these pithouses were built in this area until around 1000, when square adobe or twig structures began to be built above ground. During this same period, Pueblo people began constructing cliff dwellings in natural caves. These people farmed the mesa tops and were skilled weavers and potters.

Seven natural caves are located high on the southeast side of one cliff, and five of these contain cliff-dwelling ruins. About forty rooms are contained in these structures, which probably housed eight to ten families at a time. Walls were made from stone and timbers, the latter dating from the 1270s. By the early 1300s, for unknown reasons, the Mogollon had abandoned these dwellings.

A visitor center with exhibits and information to help interpret this historic area is open from 8:00 A.M. until 5:00 P.M. in summer and 8:00 A.M. to 4:30 P.M. in winter. The park is closed on Christmas and New Year's Day. From the visitor center, a short drive to a parking area at the end of the road provides access to the monument's main area. Guide leaflets with numbers keyed to trail markers are available at the trailhead. The 1-mile loop trail is steep in places and takes about one hour to walk (round-trip). The dwellings are accessible 8:00 A.M. to 6:00 P.M. in summer, 9:00 A.M. to 4:00 P.M. the rest of the year.

FACILITIES: Food services and accommodations are not available at the monument, but a store at Gila Hot Springs offers groceries, snacks, soft drinks, gasoline, and ice. Drinking water and rest rooms are located in the visitor center.

CAMPING: The U.S. Forest Service operates Lower Scorpion Campground (seven spaces) and Upper Scorpion Campground (thirteen spaces) between the visitor center and the cliff dwellings. Both are open all year and have tables, grills, water (May–October), and flush toilets. Two less-developed campgrounds with pit toilets and no water are located 5 miles east of the visitor center. A commercial campground is at Gila Hot Springs.

FISHING: Fishing is available in the Gila River with a New Mexico fishing license.

PECOS NATIONAL HISTORICAL PARK

P.O. Box 418
Pecos, NM 87552-0418
(505) 757–6414, ext. 1
www.nps.gov/peco/

Pecos National Historical Park, a National Park Service unit since 1965, was expanded and redefined in 1990 to preserve what remains of six diverse cultural themes and educate the public about these resources. The park is located off I–25 in north-central New Mexico, 25 miles southeast of Santa Fe. Exit I–25 at the Rowe or Pecos interchanges and follow the signs. The park is located 2 miles south of the Village of Pecos on Highway 63.

Native Americans began using the Pecos Valley to make a livelihood by hunting large animals some 12,000 years ago. The Native American lifestyle changed during the years preceding the arrival of the Spaniards. Distinct cultures emerged, sedentary tribes replaced the previously mobile hunters, and new technologies, social organizations, and allegiances were formed to sustain the population.

When the Spanish explorers arrived at the gates of Pecos Pueblo in 1540, they found 2,000 Native Americans living there and conducting a prosperous trading economy that brought many pueblo communities from the Rio Grande Valley together with many Plains tribes to the east. Spanish colonization proceeded, imposing a new government and religion on the entire region, including Pecos Pueblo where the largest seventeenth-century mission church in all of New Spain was built. The church was destroyed in the Pueblo Revolt of 1680. Another was rebuilt over the rubble of the former church. Both the church and ruins of the great Pueblo of Pecos are the main attraction for visitors today.

The park's other resources reflect the several Hispanic families that built homesteads along the Pecos River during the Mexican era, the trade and stage stops along the Santa Fe Trail that spurred on the economic growth of the area and ushered in the U.S. government, the Civil War Battle of Glorieta Pass, and twentieth-century ranching.

The park's visitor center addresses the complex history of the area. A ten-minute film provides an overview and prelude to the 1¼-mile self-guiding trail that leads through the ruins and the ranger-guided tours to the Austin/Fogelson ranch house during the summer months.

FACILITIES: The park's main complex has visitor rest rooms and a picnic area. Food and lodging are not available in the park. Restaurants, drive-ins, a deli, and some small grocery stores operate in Pecos, 2 miles north of the park's visitor center. Lodging is available in Santa Fe.

CAMPING: No camping is permitted at the park; however, there are seven U.S. Forest Service campgrounds and four commercial campgrounds ranging from 5 to 20 miles from the park. For information on Forest Service campgrounds, write Santa Fe National Forest, P.O. Box 1689, Santa Fe, NM 87501.

FISHING: No fishing is authorized in the park.

PETROGLYPH NATIONAL MONUMENT

6001 Unser Boulevard NW
Albuquerque, NM 87120-2033
(505) 899–0205
PETR_Interpretation@nps.gov
www.nps.gov/petr/

Petroglyph National Monument was established in 1990 to protect an area of 7,200 acres that contain more than 15,000 prehistoric and historic Native American and Hispanic images pecked or carved in rock. The monument is located on the west side of Albuquerque. Drive west on Interstate 40 and exit north on Unser Boulevard.

The varied petroglyphs of masks, animal figures, geometric shapes, spirals, and stars found in Petroglyph National Monument were mostly created between A.D. 1300 and 1700, although some may be as much as 3,000 years old. The symbols, most of which reflect the society and religion of the Pueblo peoples, are not well understood. The monument contains more than one hundred archaeological sites to help interpret 12,000 years of human use of this area.

The park is accessible at several locations including the visitor center at 4735 Unser Boulevard NW. The visitor center, with information about the park's features, is open daily from 8:00 A.M. to 5:00 P.M. except Thanksgiving, Christmas, and New Year's Day. A half-mile south of the visitor center on Unser Boulevard, Rinconada Canyon offers a half-mile unpaved trail along the base of the escarpment. This is the location of most of the petroglyphs. The Boca Negra Unit at the north end of the monument is open from 8:00 A.M. to 5:00 P.M. and offers a picnic area and rest rooms. A series of five volcanic cones in the Volcanoes Section of the park's west side is accessed via an unpaved road off Paseo del Volcan (exit 149 off I–40).

FACILITIES: Modern rest rooms, drinking water, and picnic tables are available in the monument. Food and lodging are available on nearby access roads.

CAMPING: No camping is permitted in the monument.

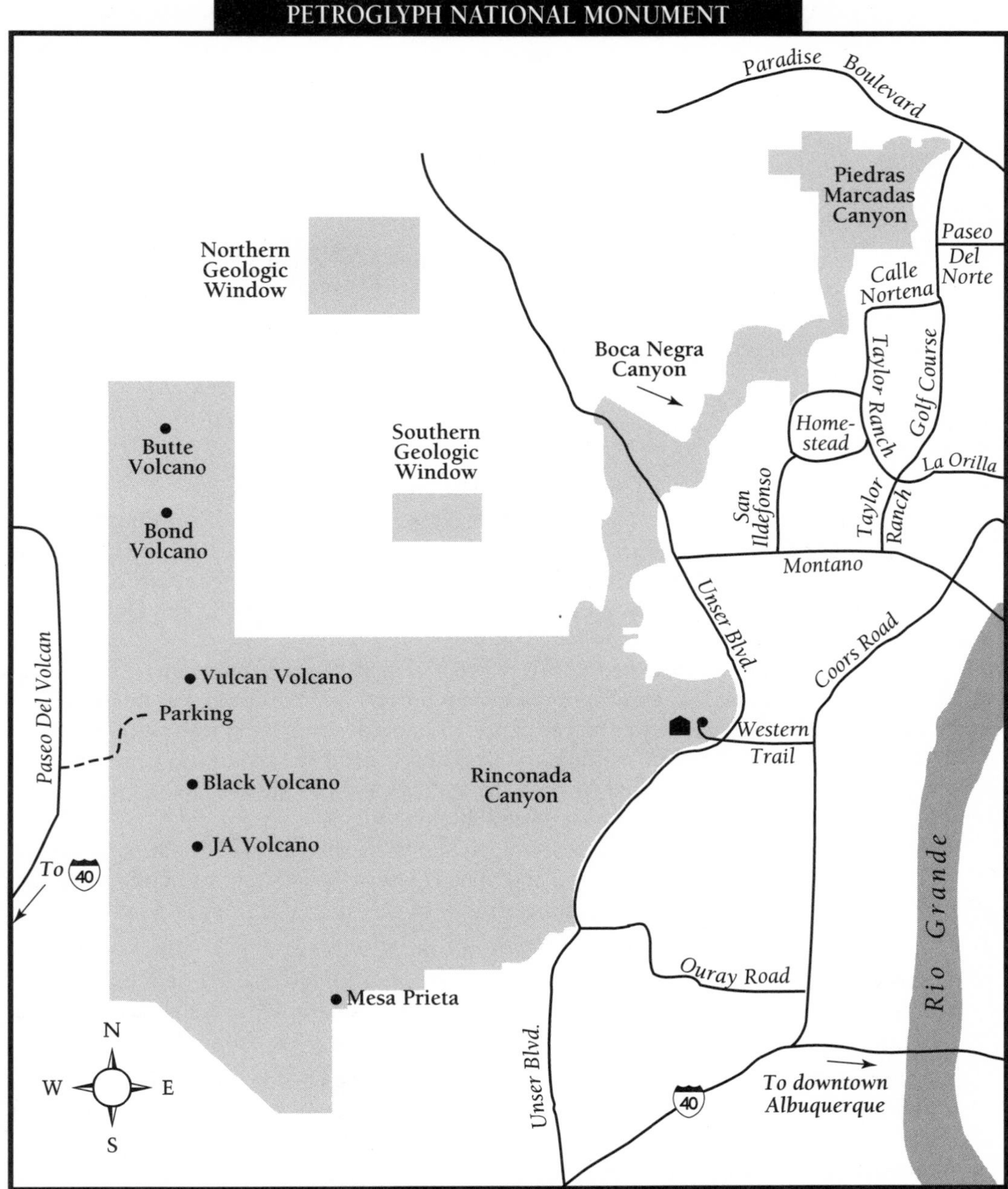
PETROGLYPH NATIONAL MONUMENT
Paradise Boulevard
Piedras Marcadas Canyon
Paseo Del Norte
Calle Nortena
Northern Geologic Window
Boca Negra Canyon
Taylor Ranch
Golf Course
Homestead
Southern Geologic Window
Butte Volcano
Bond Volcano
San Ildefonso
Taylor Ranch
La Orilla
Montano
Unser Blvd.
Coors Road
Paseo Del Volcan
Vulcan Volcano
Parking
Western Trail
Black Volcano
Rinconada Canyon
JA Volcano
To 40
Rio Grande
Ouray Road
Mesa Prieta
N
W
E
S
Unser Blvd.
40
To downtown Albuquerque

SALINAS PUEBLO MISSIONS NATIONAL MONUMENT

Box 496
Mountainair, NM 87036-0496
(505) 847–2585
sapu_ranger_activities@nps.gov
www.nps.gov/sapu

Salinas Pueblo Missions National Monument (formerly Gran Quivira National Monument) was established in 1980. It consists of 1,080 acres, including the ruins of four seventeenth-century Franciscan stone churches and three large Indian villages from an earlier Pueblo culture. The monument is located in central New Mexico in three separate units near the town of Mountainair, at U.S. 60 and New Mexico 55.

In the stones of Salinas Pueblo Missions National Monument are faint echoes of communities that existed there centuries ago. The first Indians began living in this area during the ninth century. As time passed and different cultures were introduced into the area, the inhabitants adapted a successful way of life in this marginal and frequently hostile environment. By the seventeenth century, Salinas had become an important trading center, with Gran Quivira being one of the larger villages in the region.

Although the first Spanish expedition into what is now the southwestern United States occurred in 1540, the first known visit to the Salinas area by any European was in 1598. Even though the Spanish were unable to find the expected mineral riches and crops were difficult to grow, they nevertheless attempted to settle the land and convert the Indians to Christianity. By the early 1670s, the area was vacated by both the Spanish and the Indians. Two of the primary factors that led to the abandonment were severe drought and raids by Apaches.

The monument's headquarters and visitor center is in the town of Mountainair. Here, 1 block west of the intersection of U.S. 60 and State Highway 55, visitors will find exhibits, an audiovisual program, and information on the history of this area. The three areas of ruins are:

Abo Ruins (9 miles west on U.S. 60, ¾ mile north on New Mexico 513). This site contains sophisticated church architecture and a large unexcavated pueblo. A ½-mile handicapped accessible trail winds through unexcavated mounds, visible pueblo walls, and a limited number of excavated pueblo walls. Trail guides are provided. Telephone (505) 847–2400.

Gran Quivira Ruins (26 miles south on New Mexico 55). This site contains two churches and significant excavated pueblo ruins with excavated kivas. A new visitor center has exhibits, and an excellent forty-minute video is shown. A guidebook is available to interpret the trail through the ruins. Telephone (505) 847–2770.

Quarai Ruins (8 miles north on New Mexico 55 and 1 mile west). This area contains the most complete Salinas church and has artifacts on display in a small museum. A trail leads past unexcavated mounds and excavated mission ruins. Trail guides are provided. Telephone (505) 847–2290.

FACILITIES: Food and lodging are available in Mountainair. Drinking water is provided at all sites. Rest rooms are available at the visitor center and at all three sites. A picnic area with tables is provided at each of the three sites.

CAMPING: No camping is permitted in any of the areas of the monument. Manzano State Park (eighteen spaces), with tables (some sheltered), grills, flush toilets, and hot water (no showers),

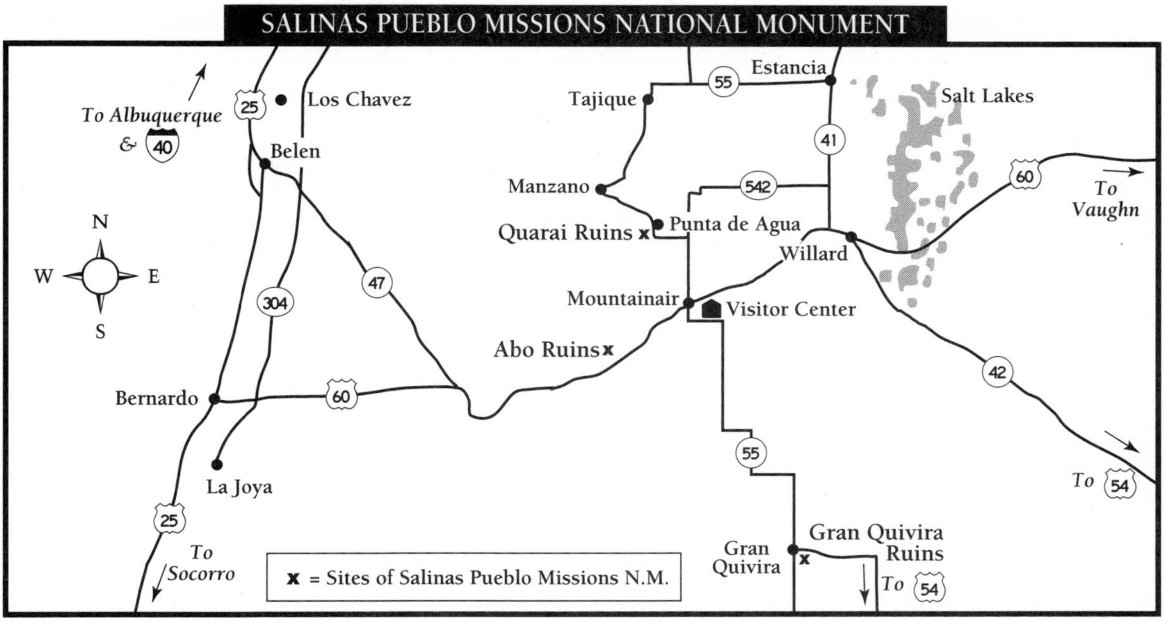

SALINAS PUEBLO MISSIONS NATIONAL MONUMENT

x = Sites of Salinas Pueblo Missions N.M.

is located 15 miles north of Mountainair off Highway 55. Turn west at the south end of the town of Manzano and go 3 miles on a paved road. Open only in the spring and summer. Telephone (505) 847–2820.

FISHING: Fishing is available in Manzano Lake, a small body of water located in the village of Manzano.

WHITE SANDS NATIONAL MONUMENT

P.O. Box 1086
Holloman AFB, NM 88330-1086
(505) 679–2599
whsa_interpretation@nps.gov
www.nps.gov/whsa/

White Sands National Monument, which comprises 145,000 acres, was established in 1933 to preserve dunes of glistening white gypsum sand standing 10 to 60 feet high. The park is located in south-central New Mexico, approximately 54 miles northeast of Las Cruces and 15 miles southwest of Alamogordo via U.S. 70/82.

The features of this area were created millions of years ago (although the current dune field is only about several thousand years old), when a downfaulting of a portion of the earth's crust left surrounding mountains and highlands containing layers of gypsum rock. As rain and melting snow eroded the deposits, the dissolved gypsum washed into Lake Lucero and dried in the wind and sunshine of the basin. The encrusted lake bed is constantly scoured by a southwest wind, and sand-sized gypsum crystals are swept toward the white dunes. As each dune grows and moves farther from the lake, new ones form. Because of the harsh environment in the dunes area, plants and animals have developed unique features that permit their survival.

A visitor center at the park entrance has a seventeen-minute orientation video and exhibits to help visitors interpret this unique area. A paved road leading into the main part of the dunes (16 miles round-trip) has wayside exhibits at pull-out spaces along the right-hand side. The best dunes for climbing are near the end of the Dunes Drive. The monument has a 1-mile self-guided nature trail and a 4½-mile (round-trip) backcountry trail through the heart of the dunes. A quarter-mile wheelchair-accessible boardwalk is available. During summer, ranger-guided walks and evening programs are offered every night. Auto caravans to Lake Lucero are offered every month.

FACILITIES: No lodging or food is offered at the park. The nearest motels and dining are 15 miles east in Alamogordo. Water and modern rest rooms are at the visitor center. Additional rest rooms (no water) are located in the picnic area.

CAMPING: No campground is located at the park. The nearest public camping facilities are in Lincoln National Forest, 35 miles east, and at Aquire Springs, 30 miles west. Oliver Lee Memorial State Park offers camping 10 miles south of Alamogordo on U.S. 54.

FISHING: No fishing is available at White Sands National Monument.

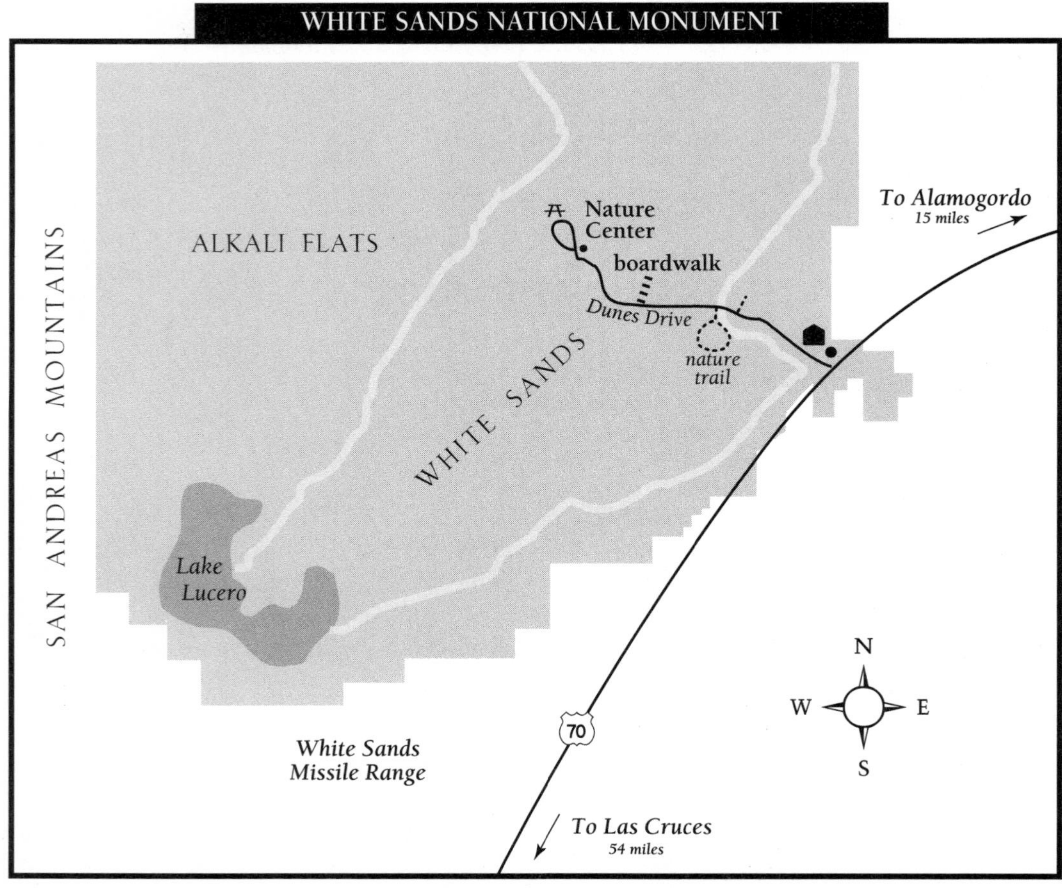

STATE TOURIST INFORMATION
(800) 435–5063

FORT UNION TRADING POST NATIONAL HISTORIC SITE

RR 3, Box 71
Williston, ND 58801-9455
(701) 572–9083
www.nps.gov/fous/

Fort Union Trading Post encompasses 442 acres and was authorized for inclusion into the National Park System in 1966 to preserve the site of the principal fur-trading post in the Upper Missouri River region from 1828 until 1867. The fort is located in western North Dakota, 25 miles southwest of Williston via U.S. 2 and North Dakota 1804.

In 1828, the construction of Fort Union began under Kenneth McKenzie, an executive and trader for the American Fur Company. Four years later the structure was complete, and a lucrative trade with Indian tribes resulted in the fort's being surrounded by tepees as Indian bands would camp a week or two at a time.

The fort's walls were constructed of cottonwood logs 18 feet high, grounded on stone foundations. The walls were 220 feet wide on the north and south sides and 240 feet long on the east and west sides. The imposing post commanded the upper Missouri fur trade and was a mecca for artists and scientists. By the 1860s, conflict overtook the homelands of the Plains Indians. In 1867, Fort Union was sold to the U.S. Army and dismantled for use in building Fort Buford Military Post, a short distance down the Missouri.

The entire site was covered with grass when it was acquired by the National Park Service in 1966. Since then, the foundations of the fort were excavated, and a partial reconstruction of Fort Union was completed in 1991.

A visitor center with exhibits, a bookstore, and a short slide program is open from 8:00 A.M. to 8:00 P.M. (central time) daily in summer and 9:00 A.M. to 5:30 P.M. the remainder of the year.

FORT UNION TRADING POST NATIONAL HISTORIC SITE

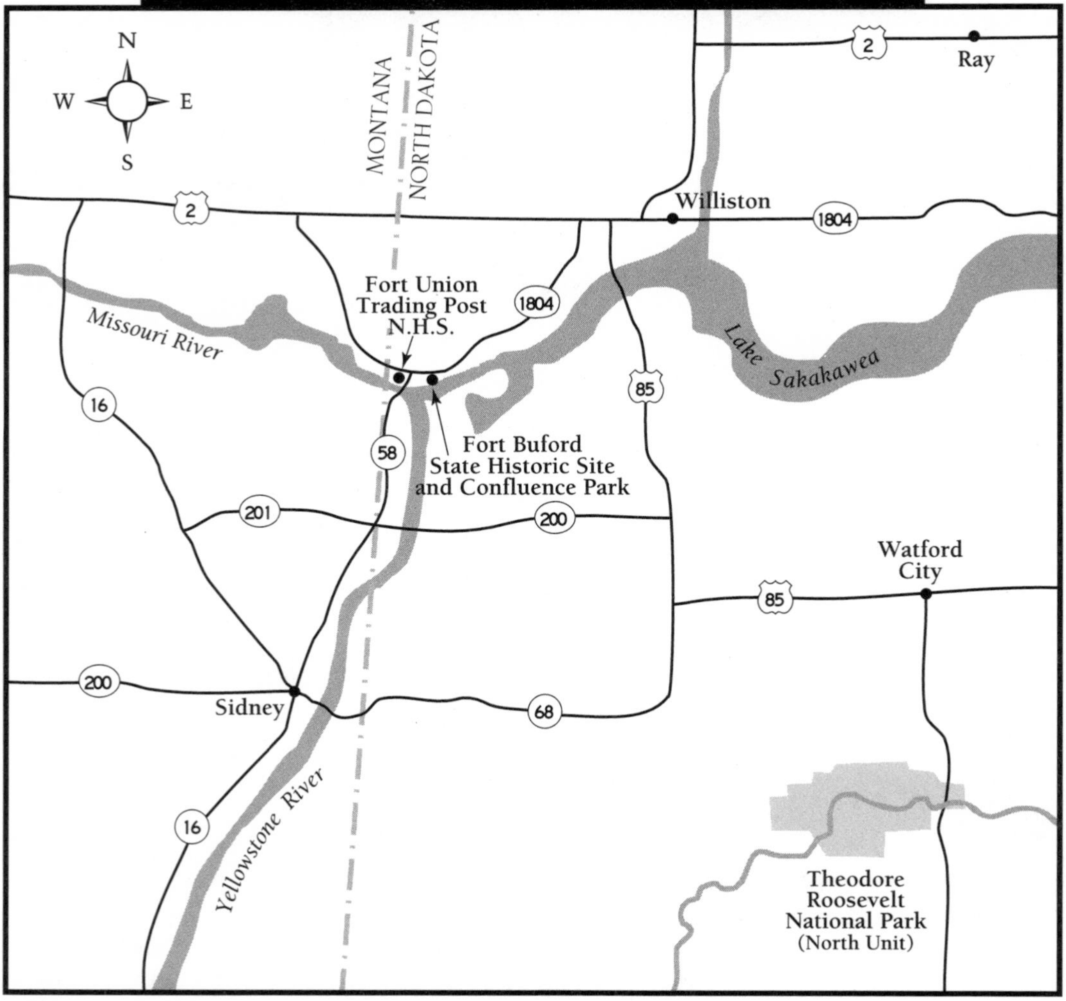

Park rangers offer guided tours and living-history programs during summer months. A four-day fur-trade rendezvous occurs annually during the third weekend in June. Also located in the historic confluence region of the Yellowstone and Missouri are Lewis and Clark sites, the ghost towns of Buford and Mondak, and the Fort Buford State Historic Site.

FACILITIES: A visitor center has drinking water and rest rooms. A picnic area with shelters is at Confluence Park. Food and lodging are available in Williston and Sidney, Montana.

CAMPING: Camping is not permitted at the site but is available at Fort Buford State Historic Site, a short distance to the east.

FISHING: The park is located on the Missouri River, and fishing is permitted with a North Dakota or Montana fishing license.

INTERNATIONAL PEACE GARDEN

Route #1, Box 116
Dunseith, ND 58329
(701) 263–4390, (888) 432–6733
comments@peacegarden.com
www.peacegarden.com

International Peace Garden, an affiliated area of the National Park Service, comprises approximately 2,330 acres. It was dedicated in 1932 to commemorate the peaceful relations between the United States and Canada. The garden is located in north-central North Dakota on U.S. 281 and State Route 3, 15 miles north of Dunseith, North Dakota; and 15 miles south of Boissevain, Manitoba.

The International Peace Garden contains a variety of plant life on its beautifully landscaped grounds, which cross the international border. Wooded areas, floral gardens, and two lakes provide visitors with a peaceful background for leisurely strolls that sometimes include glimpses of white tail deer, moose, and other wildlife. The garden includes an 18-foot working floral clock, a sunken garden, and more than 150,000 annual flowers planted in a different theme each year. The Peace Chapel features quotations from "people of peace" etched in fossil-embellished limestone walls. The 120-foot Peace Towers welcome people from the four hemispheres.

The Interpretive Center features the history of the park and a tribute to Civilian Conservation Corps work at the park in the 1930s. Fun and educational interpretive programs are held daily for visitors of all ages. Other features include a bike path, horse carriage rides, playgrounds, two youth camps, and free concerts on Fridays and Saturdays in June and July.

Driving tours of both units of the park and a walking tour of the formal gardens, chapel, and Interpretive Center take a total of about three hours.

FACILITIES: Food service and gifts are available in the formal area from June to mid-September. An airport with a 3,000-foot paved runway is within walking distance of the park entrance. Rest rooms and picnic areas are in several locations. Overnight accommodations are available in nearby towns.

CAMPING: Approximately 50 camping sites offer tables, grills, rest rooms, and shower facilities. Half have concrete pads, electricity, water, and disposal facilities.

FISHING: No fishing is available at the park. Fishing areas are located nearby.

See the map on the following page.

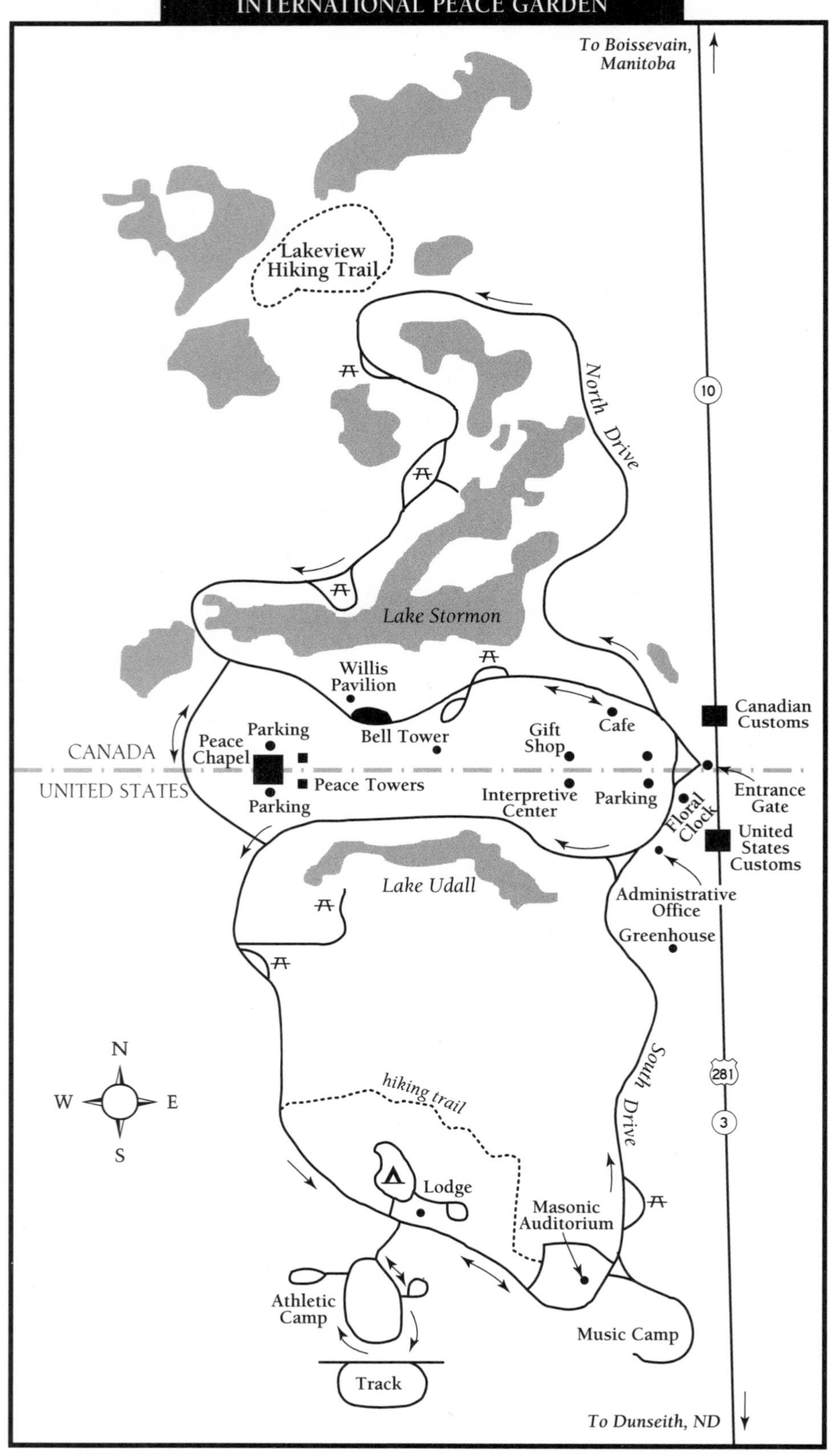

INTERNATIONAL PEACE GARDEN
To Boissevain, Manitoba
Lakeview Hiking Trail
North Drive
10
Lake Stormon
Willis Pavilion
Canadian Customs
Cafe
Gift Shop
Bell Tower
Parking
Peace Chapel
CANADA
UNITED STATES
Peace Towers
Parking
Interpretive Center
Parking
Entrance Gate
Floral Clock
United States Customs
Lake Udall
Administrative Office
Greenhouse
N
W
E
S
South Drive
281
3
hiking trail
Lodge
Masonic Auditorium
Athletic Camp
Music Camp
Track
To Dunseith, ND

KNIFE RIVER INDIAN VILLAGES NATIONAL HISTORIC SITE

P.O. Box 9
Stanton, ND 58571-0009
(701) 745–3309
bill_lutz@nps.gov
www.nps.gov/knri/

Knife River Indian Villages, which comprises 1,758 acres, was authorized as part of the National Park Service in 1974 to preserve remnants of historic and prehistoric Indian villages containing an array of artifacts of Plains Indian culture. The park is located in central North Dakota, ½ mile north of the town of Stanton.

The Indians living along the Knife River were hunters and successful farmers. The Hidatsa, who lived here with their neighbors, the Mandan, built small villages of circular earthlodges. By the early 1800s, the prosperity of this area on the Missouri River was enhanced by Knife River's being at the center of a trade network among various tribes and Euro-Americans.

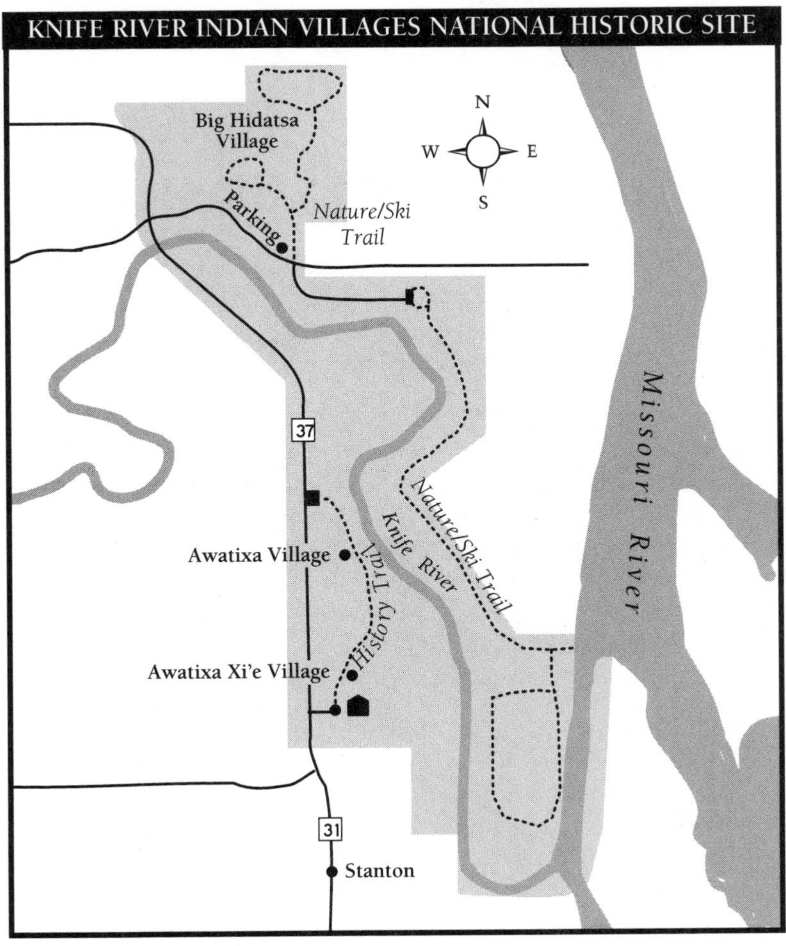

Unfortunately, Europeans brought diseases that decimated the tribes around Knife River, and various smallpox epidemics broke out between the late 1700s and mid-1800s. In 1845, the Mandan and Hidatsa banded together and moved 40 miles up the Missouri River and established Like-a-Fishhook Village. They were joined by the Arikara in 1862 and later became the Three Affiliated Tribes.

The park's visitor center is on County Road 37. Here, visitors will find exhibits, a theater and a full-scale, furnished earthlodge that show the day-to-day life and customs of the Northern Plains Indians. Crafts made by descendants of these Village Indians are sold here. There is hiking access, by trail, to each of the three major village sites. Awatixa Village and Awatixa Xi'e Village are near the visitor center. Big Hidatsa Village is reached via a short trail that begins at a parking area in the north end of the park. Earthlodge tours are offered Memorial Day through Labor Day. The Northern Plains Indian Culture Fest is held the last full weekend of July.

FACILITIES: Limited meals are available in Stanton. Lodging can be found in nearby communities. Drinking water and rest rooms are provided at the park's visitor center.

CAMPING: No camping is available at the site. Approximately 15 miles north of Knife River Indian Villages, Sakakawea State Park provides a large camping area with tables, grills, drinking water, flush toilets, and showers. The state park is 1 mile east of Pick City, off Highway 200. A U.S. Army Corps of Engineers' campground is located 3 miles south of the town of Riverdale, downstream of the Garrison Dam.

FISHING: Fishing is permitted along the Knife and Missouri rivers with a North Dakota fishing license. Both camping areas noted provide opportunities for fishing.

THEODORE ROOSEVELT NATIONAL PARK

P.O. Box 7
Medora, ND 58645-0007
(701) 623–4466
Thro_Interpretation@nps.gov
www.nps.gov/thro/

Theodore Roosevelt National Park, established in 1947, comprises more than 70,000 acres, including scenic badlands along the Little Missouri River and part of Theodore Roosevelt's Elkhorn Ranch. The three separate units of the park are located in western North Dakota. The South Unit is along Interstate 94, west of Belfield, near Medora. The Elkhorn Ranch site is reached via a gravel and dirt road; fording the Little Missouri River is necessary when accessing the site from the east. The North Unit is intersected by U.S. 85, 53 miles north of Interstate 94.

The North Dakota Badlands are the result of erosion through ancient plains where waters had deposited materials from the Rocky Mountains. At one time, the area's lowlands were covered by a jungle whose vegetation decomposed under layers of sediment and eventually turned to coal. Later, volcanoes to the west spewed ash that drifted eastward and either landed in this region or was carried in by ancient streams. Finally, streams cut through the soft land areas and created the badlands.

The park is named for Theodore Roosevelt, who lived and ranched in this area prior to being elected president of the United States. Roosevelt owned an open-range cattle ranch, the Elkhorn, and was a partner in another ranch, the Maltese Cross. The strenuous pioneer life and the rugged beauty of the badlands had a profound effect upon Roosevelt. Although the time he spent here was short, it had a strong influence on his later decisions concerning the nation's natural resources.

At the South Unit, the visitor center near the park's entrance includes a museum, with the restored Maltese Cross Cabin located in the rear. From here, a 36-mile paved loop road provides access to some of this unit's highlights. Scoria Point allows the visitor to see where beds of burning lignite coal baked the surrounding sand and clay to red brick. Farther down the road

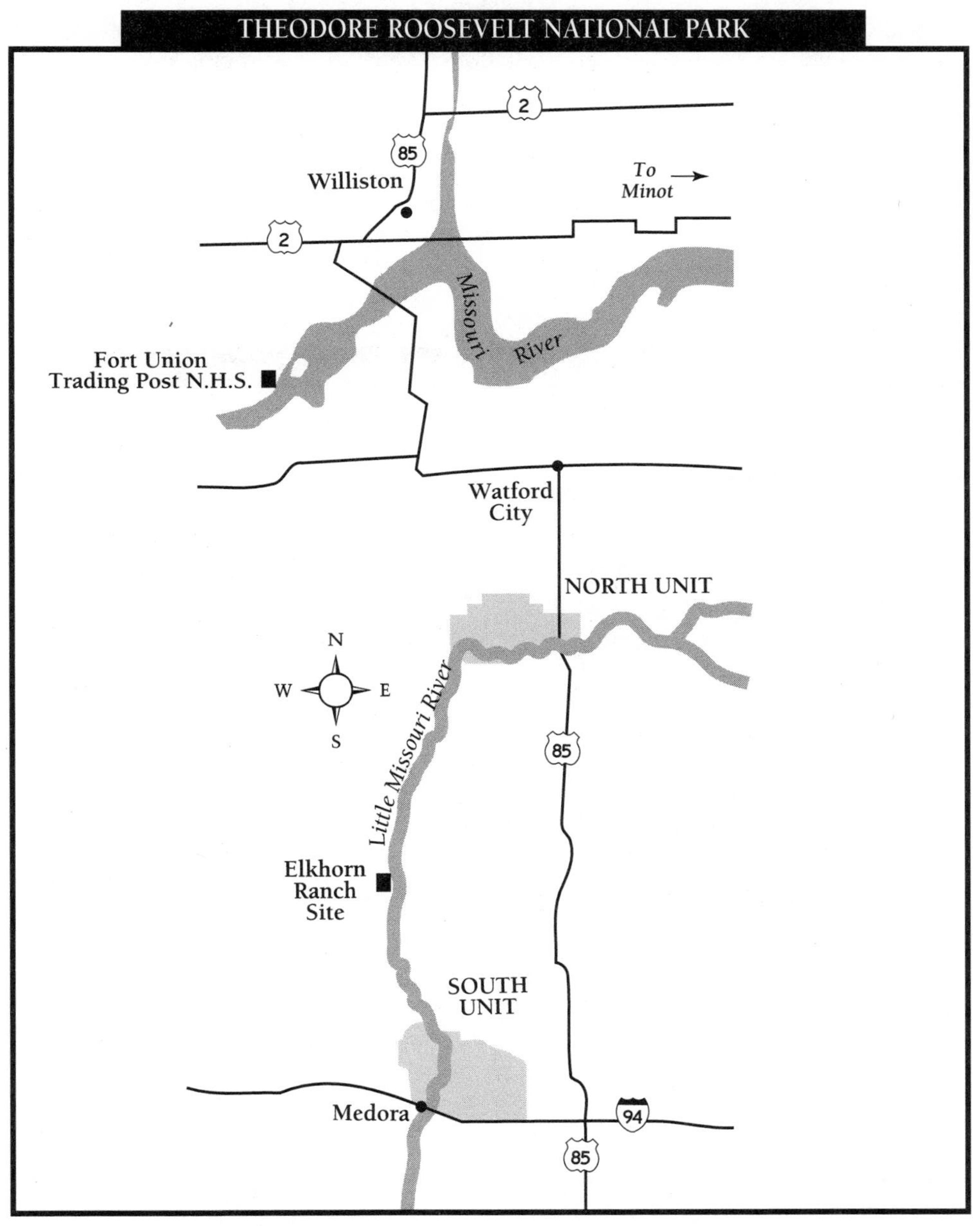

is a lignite seam that burned until 1977 and is thought to have been ignited by a lightning-caused prairie fire in 1951. Visitors may walk to Buck Hill, which at 2,855 feet is one of the highest points in the park. The nature trail at Wind Canyon provides an overlook of the Little Missouri River. Horses may be rented at Peaceful Valley Ranch. Seven miles east of Medora, off Interstate 94, Painted Canyon Overlook provides a view of the badlands.

The park's North Unit is less crowded and more spectacular. It contains a 14-mile scenic paved road to the vicinity of Sperati Point, the narrowest gateway in the badlands. The river once flowed north from here but was blocked during the ice age. Little Mo Nature Trail, a 1⅒-mile self-guiding trail, begins at the southeast corner of Juniper Campground. About 1½ miles west of here is the 1⅗-mile (round-trip) Caprock Coulee Self-Guiding Nature Trail, which is part of a 4-mile-loop hiking trail.

FACILITIES: Lodging and food are not available within the park. Near the South Unit, Medora has restaurants, motels, service stations, and supplies. Painted Canyon Overlook provides rest rooms, picnic shelters, tables, and water. Fifteen miles west of the North Unit, Watford City has motels, restaurants, food stores, and service stations. Water and rest rooms are available at various locations in both units.

CAMPING: Located in cottonwood groves near the Little Missouri River, campgrounds in both units are exceptional. In the South Unit, Cottonwood (eighty spaces) is open all year and has tables, grills, water, and flush toilets (pit toilets, October to May). A group site is available with reservation. Roundup Horse Camp (reservation-only group camp) is open from May through

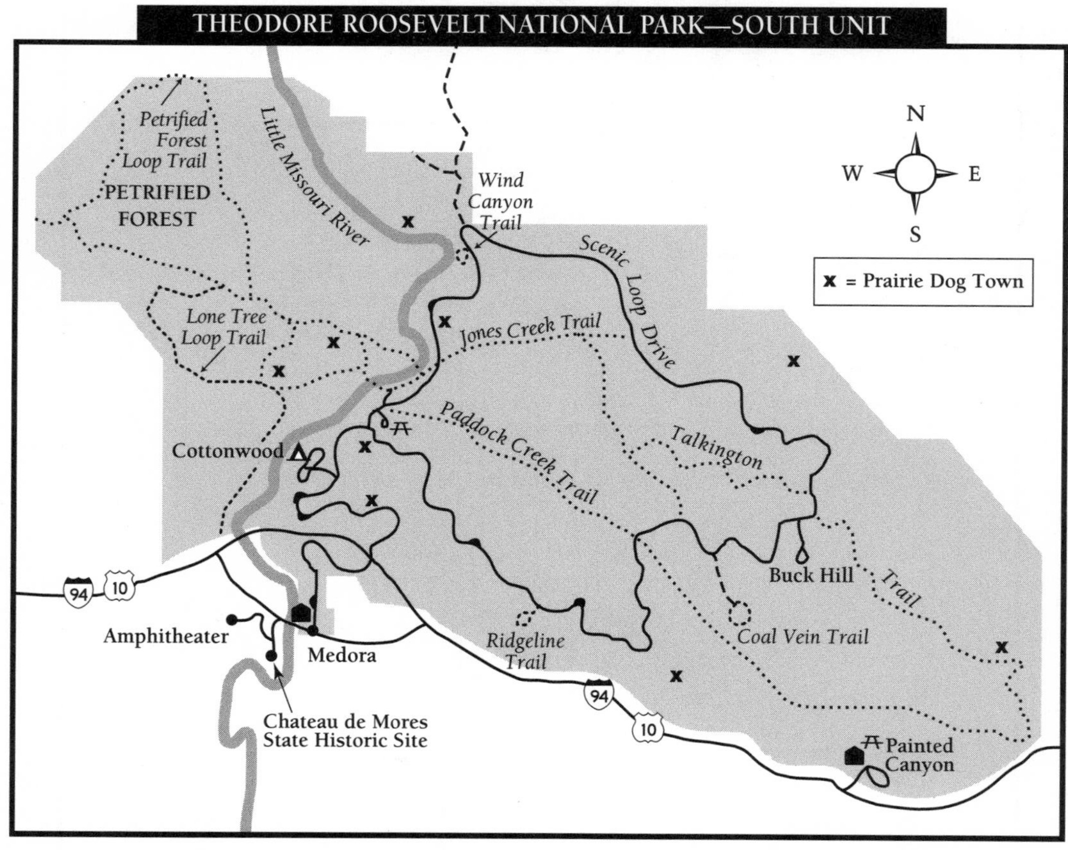

September and has tables, grills, water, and pit toilets. In the North Unit, Juniper (fifty spaces) is open all year and has tables, grills, water, and flush toilets (pit toilets October to May). A group site requires a reservation. No firewood is provided, and the gathering of firewood is prohibited in the park.

FISHING: The Little Missouri River flows through both the North and South units and provides catches of catfish and carp. Fishing requires a North Dakota fishing license.

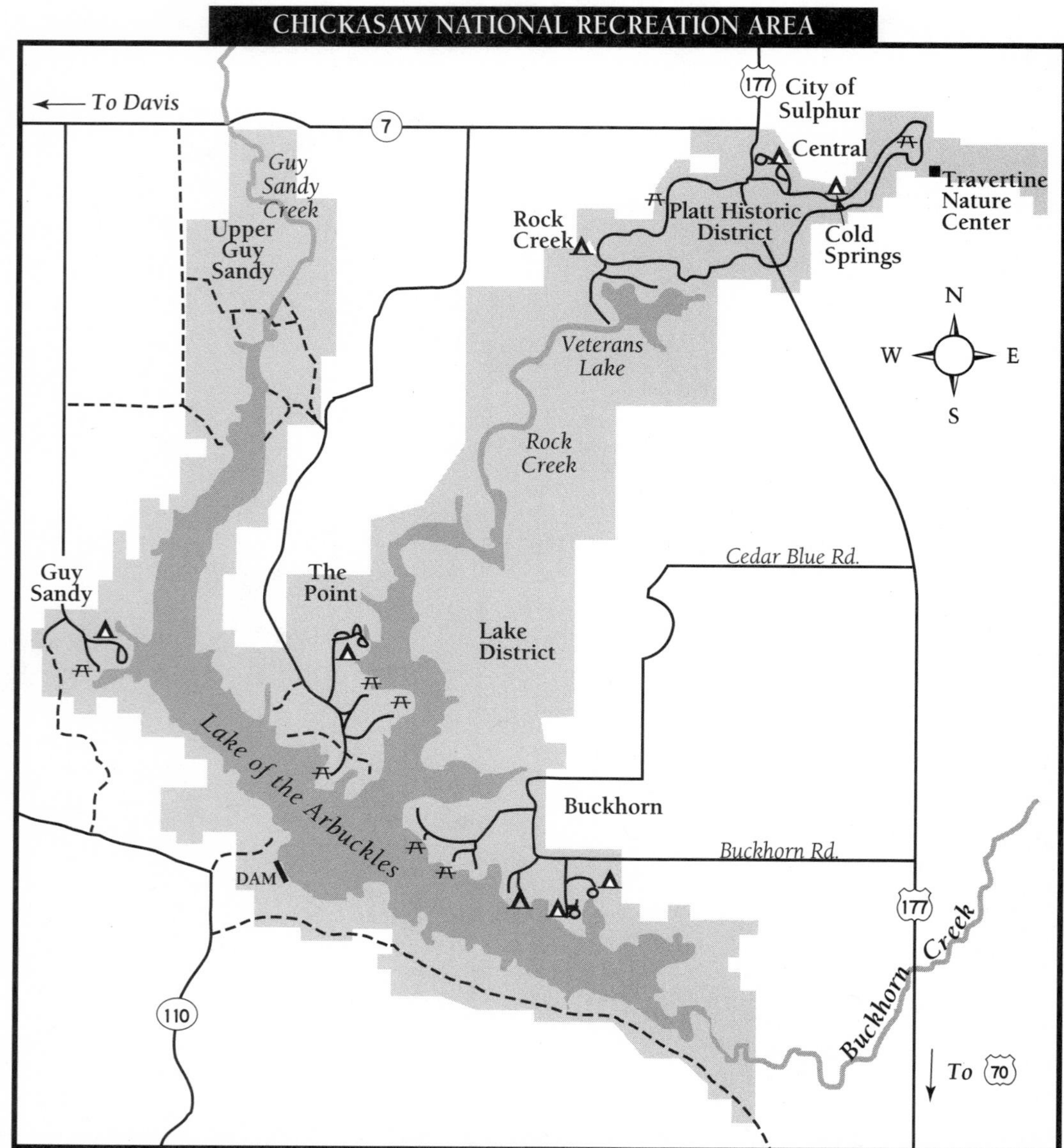

CHICKASAW NATIONAL RECREATION AREA
To Davis
7
177
City of Sulphur
Central
Travertine Nature Center
Platt Historic District
Rock Creek
Cold Springs
Guy Sandy Creek
Upper Guy Sandy
N
W
E
S
Veterans Lake
Rock Creek
Cedar Blue Rd.
Guy Sandy
The Point
Lake District
Lake of the Arbuckles
Buckhorn
Buckhorn Rd.
DAM
177
Buckhorn Creek
110
To 70

STATE TOURIST INFORMATION
(800) 652–6552

CHICKASAW NATIONAL RECREATION AREA

P.O. Box 201
Sulphur, OK 73086-0201
(580) 622–3165
www.nps.gov/chic/

Chickasaw National Recreation Area, which comprises approximately 10,000 acres, was established in 1976 by consolidating Platt National Park, Arbuckle National Recreation Area, and additional lands. The recreation area provides access to numerous outdoor activities. It is located in south-central Oklahoma, just east of Interstate 35, which connects Oklahoma City and Dallas.

Chickasaw National Recreation Area comprises two districts offering very different outdoor experiences. The smaller northeastern area (the former Platt National Park) is noted for its freshwater and mineral springs. The entire 900 acres of this area is a designated historic landscape, which includes cultural structures from the Civilian Conservation Corps of the 1930s and 1940s. On the east side, freshwater Buffalo and Antelope springs are the source of Travertine Creek. A number of cold mineral-water springs are located in the central and western areas of this section. Travertine Nature Center offers exhibits, film of the history of the area, a bookstore, and an environmental study area. During the summer, a daily children's nature program, nature films, and naturalist-conducted nature walks are offered. Various nature trails lead from this area. Over 25 miles of flat to hilly hiking trails are within the recreation area. Most trails are covered with loose gravel. The trail around Veterans Lake is cement surfaced. A 9-mile trail for hikers, mountain bikers, and horses connects Veterans Lake with Lake of the Arbuckles. A trail guide brochure is available at the bookstore.

Eight miles southwest of this wooded area is the park's second unit (the former Arbuckle National Recreation Area). Here, Arbuckle Dam, at the confluence of three creeks, has resulted in the formation of a 2,350-acre lake that provides opportunities for fishing, boating, swimming, waterskiing, and scuba diving (with permit). Boat-launching ramps are located at Guy Sandy, The Point, and Buckhorn. Evening educational programs are held at the Buckhorn amphitheater during the summer months.

FACILITIES: Food and lodging are not available in either unit. Both are provided in nearby towns. Drinking water and rest rooms are located throughout both areas.

CAMPING: In the smaller unit, tables, grills, water, and flush toilets are provided at Central (ten group sites only), Cold Springs (sixty-three spaces), and Rock Creek (106 spaces, dump station). In the southwestern unit, Buckhorn (135 spaces, dump station, electrical and water hookups, showers), Guy Sandy (forty spaces), and The Point (twenty-two spaces) offer tables, fireplaces, drinking water, and flush or chemical toilets. Rock Creek Campground and Buckhorn Campground are open all year.

FISHING: Streams and Veterans Lake in the northeast unit contain sunfish, crappie, largemouth bass, and white bass. In the lake district, there is fishing for channel catfish, largemouth bass, sunfish, and crappie. An Oklahoma fishing license is required to fish at the park.

WASHITA BATTLEFIELD NATIONAL HISTORIC SITE

P.O. Box 890
Cheyenne, OK 73628
(580) 497–2742
www.nps.gov/waba/

Washita Battlefield National Historic Site is comprised of approximately 300 acres and was authorized in 1996 to commemorate an 1868 U.S. Cavalry attack on the southern Cheyenne village of Chief Black Kettle. The controversial attack has been described by some as a battle and others as a massacre. The historic site is located in western Oklahoma, approximately 140 miles west of Oklahoma City, near the small town of Cheyenne. It is approximately 25 miles north of Interstate 40.

The Plains served as the scene for many famous and not-so-famous battles between the U.S. Cavalry and Native Americans. The 1868 battle that took place at Washita was actually precipitated four years earlier by a surprise cavalry attack at Sand Creek that destroyed the camp of Chief Black Kettle and Chief White Antelope. A subsequent peace treaty assigned the Arapahos, Cheyennes, Comanches, and Kiowas to reservations in Indian territory. Restlessness among the Indians caused the U.S. Army to mount a winter campaign that caused Black Kettle and Arapaho Chief Big Mouth to seek protection at Fort Cobb. Turned away by the fort's commander, the Indians made their way to the Washita Valley, where, in November 1868, they were attacked by troopers under the command of Lt. Col. George A. Custer. The attack resulted in the deaths of nearly 60 Indians, including Chief Black Kettle and his wife. The Army captured fifty-three Cheyennes and suffered the loss of twenty-one of its own soldiers.

The historic site is new and relatively undeveloped. An overlook of the battlefield is open daily from dawn to dusk. The Black Kettle museum (donation requested) in the town of

Cheyenne interprets the story of the Cheyenne and the Battle of the Washita. The museum is open 9:00 A.M. to 5:00 P.M. Tuesday through Saturday and 1:00 to 5:00 P.M. Sunday. It is closed on Mondays and state holidays.

FACILITIES: No facilities are available at the site.

CAMPING: No camping is permitted at the historic site. The nearest public camping (ninety-two spaces, tables, grills, dump station) with flush toilets, swimming beach, and fishing is at Foss State Park, on Highway 44, approximately 25 miles southeast of Washita Battlefield National Historic Site.

FISHING: No fishing is permitted at the historic site.

CRATER LAKE NATIONAL PARK

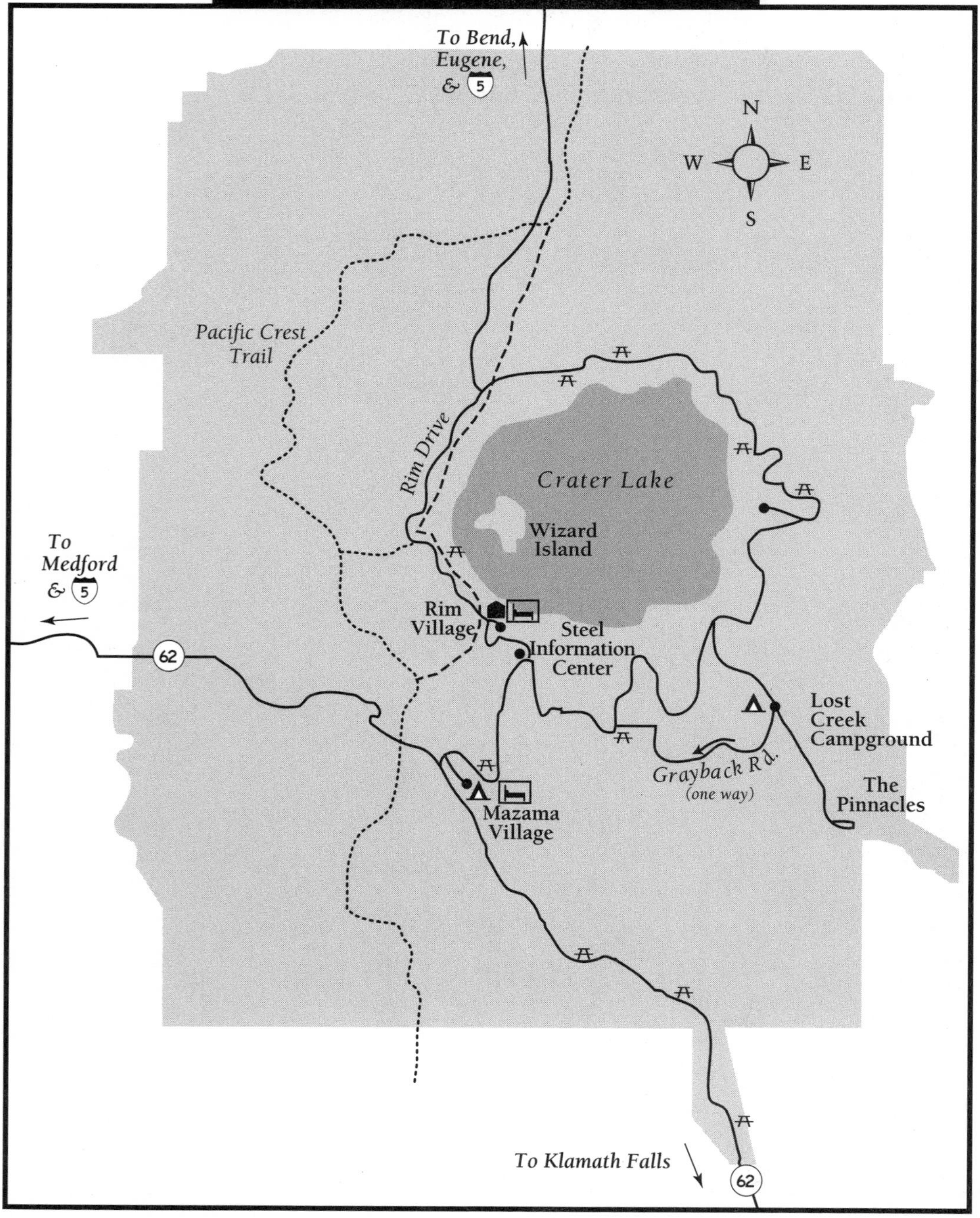

To Bend, Eugene, & 5

N
W
E
S

Pacific Crest Trail

Rim Drive

Crater Lake

Wizard Island

To Medford & 5

Rim Village

Steel Information Center

62

Lost Creek Campground

Grayback Rd.
(one way)

The Pinnacles

Mazama Village

To Klamath Falls

62

STATE TOURIST INFORMATION

(800) 547–7842

CRATER LAKE NATIONAL PARK

P.O. Box 7
Crater Lake, OR 97604-0007
(541) 594–2211, ext. 402
www.nps.gov/crla/home.htm

Crater Lake National Park was established in 1902 to preserve a deep blue lake located in the caldera that resulted from the collapse of an ancient volcano. The lake is surrounded by lava walls 500 to 2,000 feet high. The park comprises 183,000 acres and is located in southern Oregon, 57 miles north of Klamath Falls. The major road into the park is Oregon Highway 62, which runs through the southwest corner. Only the south and west entrance roads to Rim Village are open from October through mid-June.

Crater Lake is located within the remains of the 12,000-foot volcano, Mount Mazama, which collapsed nearly 7,700 years ago after a series of eruptions drained its magma chamber. Additional volcanic activity after the collapse produced a cinder cone now known as Wizard Island. Over a period of centuries, the huge hole accumulated water from rain and snow. Only six lakes in the world are deeper than Crater Lake, which has been measured to a depth of 1,932 feet. Narrated boat tours are offered from June to mid-September by a concessioner. The 1¾-hour trip circles the inside of the caldera and stops at Wizard Island.

A variety of plant life can be found in the park, including mountain hemlock; Shasta and Douglas fir; and lodgepole, whitebark, and ponderosa pine. Wildflowers are abundant in July. Animals inhabiting the area include bears, deer, porcupines, bobcats, elk, coyotes, and many varieties of birds.

Crater Lake National Park receives an average of 533 inches of snow each year, which typically does not melt off until July. Visitors to the park in spring should be prepared for winter conditions. Many high-elevation trails are snow-covered until late July. During summer a variety of activities are available. A 33-mile paved road circles the lake and offers numerous scenic viewpoints. The visitor center at Rim Village provides information. A park ranger is on duty to answer questions. Talks on the origins of Crater Lake are presented throughout the day during summer months. Two nearby trails provide scenic views. Garfield Peak Trail ($1\frac{7}{10}$ miles) begins behind the lodge and ends at a peak 1,900 feet above the lake. Discovery Point Trail ($1\frac{1}{2}$ miles) begins at the opposite end of Rim Village and leads to a point where the lake was discovered in 1853. A number of other trails are located at various points around Rim Drive. Along the lake's north side, Cleetwood Trail ($1\frac{1}{10}$ miles) descends to Cleetwood Cove, the only access to the water. Launch trips around the lake and to Wizard Island originate here. A 6-mile paved road off Rim Drive leads to the Pinnacles. Here spires of pumice and welded tuff rise 200 feet out of Wheeler Creek Canyon.

Winter activities include cross-country ski trips around Crater Lake. Snowmobiling on a designated road is permitted when the snow depth is 3 feet or more. No downhill ski facilities are available.

FACILITIES: Lodging is available in the park from mid-May through mid-October. Crater Lake Lodge offers seventy-one rooms at a completely renovated hotel on the caldera edge. Mazama Village has motel-type units. Information and reservations can be obtained from Crater Lake Lodge, Inc., Crater Lake, OR 97604 (541–830–8700). A variety of food services are available from late May to early October. During winter, only light meals are served. Some groceries may be purchased at Mazama Campground, and a gasoline station is open during summer months. Modern rest rooms are available at Rim Village, Park Headquarters, and the campground.

CAMPING: The park's single major campground, Mazama (198 sites), 7 miles south of Rim Village, is one of the nicest in any of the major national park areas. It provides tables, grills, flush toilets, and a dump station. Sites are generally not squeezed together, and a few front on a canyon. G Loop offers the most secluded sites. A $1\frac{7}{10}$-mile trail behind the campground leads to the bottom of Annie Creek Canyon. Lost Creek Campground (sixteen spaces, tent camping only) is on the road to the Pinnacles and has water and toilets.

FISHING: The lake originally contained no fish but was stocked. Rainbow trout and kokanee salmon still survive in the lake. No fishing license is required.

FORT CLATSOP NATIONAL MEMORIAL

92343 Fort Clatsop Road
Astoria, OR 97103-9803
(503) 861–2471
www.nps.gov/focl/

Fort Clatsop National Memorial became part of the National Park System in 1958. A replica of their fort marks the spot where the Lewis and Clark Expedition wintered in 1805–6 after their historic journey to the Pacific Ocean. The Memorial is located in northwestern Oregon, 5 miles southwest of Astoria off U.S. Highway 101.

After the expedition's party of thirty-three, led by Meriwether Lewis and William Clark, completed the journey from St. Louis to the Pacific, it needed a place to spend the winter before returning home. On December 8, 1805, construction began on a small fort they named Fort Clatsop after a friendly local Indian tribe. During the three and a half months they were here, the men consolidated their journals and maps, traded with the Indians, hunted and trapped, made buckskin clothing, and boiled salt water for salt to flavor and preserve meat for the trip home.

The visitor center at Fort Clatsop contains exhibits, audiovisual programs, and reading material to enhance your understanding of the expedition and the conditions faced by its members. The reconstruction of the fort is nearby, and trails to the spring and canoe landing begin here. National Park Service rangers generally present costumed demonstrations during summer months, which often include flintlock rifle demonstrations, making candles, building canoes, making buckskin clothes, and dressing skins. Hours are 8:00 A.M. to 6:00 P.M. in summer, 8:00 A.M. to 5:00 P.M. the rest of the year. Closed Christmas Day. People planning to visit the Memorial are advised to call for information about summer programs. Entrance fees are charged all year.

FACILITIES: No food or lodging is available in the park. Both may be found nearby. Modern rest rooms, drinking water, and telephones are provided in the visitor center. A day-use picnic area is located nearby.

Daily life at Fort Clatsop

CAMPING: No camping is available in Fort Clatsop National Memorial. Eight miles northwest, Fort Stevens State Park provides camping for both tents (260 spaces) and trailers (343 spaces) with water, grills, tables, and 126 full hookups available. The state park offers fishing, hiking, and ocean beaches. For information call (503) 861–1671. Two private campgrounds, a KOA (503–861–2606) and Campers West (503–861–1814) are also within 7 to 8 miles of the Memorial.

FISHING: Although very few people fish in the Memorial, fishing is permitted near the canoe landing in the Lewis and Clark River with an Oregon fishing license. Fishing conditions are better in nearby streams outside Fort Clatsop National Memorial.

JOHN DAY FOSSIL BEDS NATIONAL MONUMENT

HCR 82 Box 126
Kimberly, OR 97848
(541) 987–2333
joda_Interpretation@nps.gov
www.nps.gov/joda/

John Day Fossil Beds was incorporated into the National Park System in 1975 and comprises 14,000 acres. The monument preserves a fossil record where scientists unearth evidence of land plants and animals extending back 6 million to 54 million years. The park consists of three widely separated units in north-central Oregon. U.S. 26 runs in an east-west direction through the region, while U.S. 395 runs in a north-south direction. The Sheep Rock unit is 5 miles west of the city of Dayville via U.S. 26. To reach the Painted Hills unit, leave U.S. 26 near Mitchell and follow a marked country road for 6 miles. The Clarno unit is on Oregon 218, 20 miles west of Fossil and 15 miles east of Antelope.

The fossil record of John Day was recognized early by the state of Oregon, which began to purchase land in this area during the 1930s. Although rocks of the nearby highlands date from more than 250 million years ago, the record discovered in the monument begins with sea life of approximately 100 million years ago. Various geologic ages since that time have been marked by distinctive earth deposits containing outstanding fossil records. Fossil animals found here include species of ancient horse, oreodonts, tapirs, titanotheres, camels, mastodons, rodents, cats, rhinoceroses, and dogs. In general, the formations are younger toward the south and east, so the oldest formation is in the Clarno unit and the youngest is in the Sheep Rock unit.

Animals inhabiting the park include bobcats, coyotes, badgers, elk, mule deer, jack rabbits, and cottontail rabbits. Birds frequenting the river area and surrounding mountain slopes include Canada geese, ducks, greater blue heron, bluebirds, black-billed magpies, green-tailed towhees, California quail, red-tailed hawks, and bald and golden eagles. Visitors should watch for rattlesnakes in the park's sagebrush and juniper environment.

The park's visitor center and headquarters is in the Sheep Rock unit. This unit includes outstanding examples of geological formations represented in the monument. The historic Cant Ranch includes a visitor center and fossil museum containing exhibits on geology and local ranching history. This location is a nice resting place; a short trail to Sheep Rock Overlook begins here. North of Cant Ranch at Blue Basin, two trails offer spectacular views of the basin

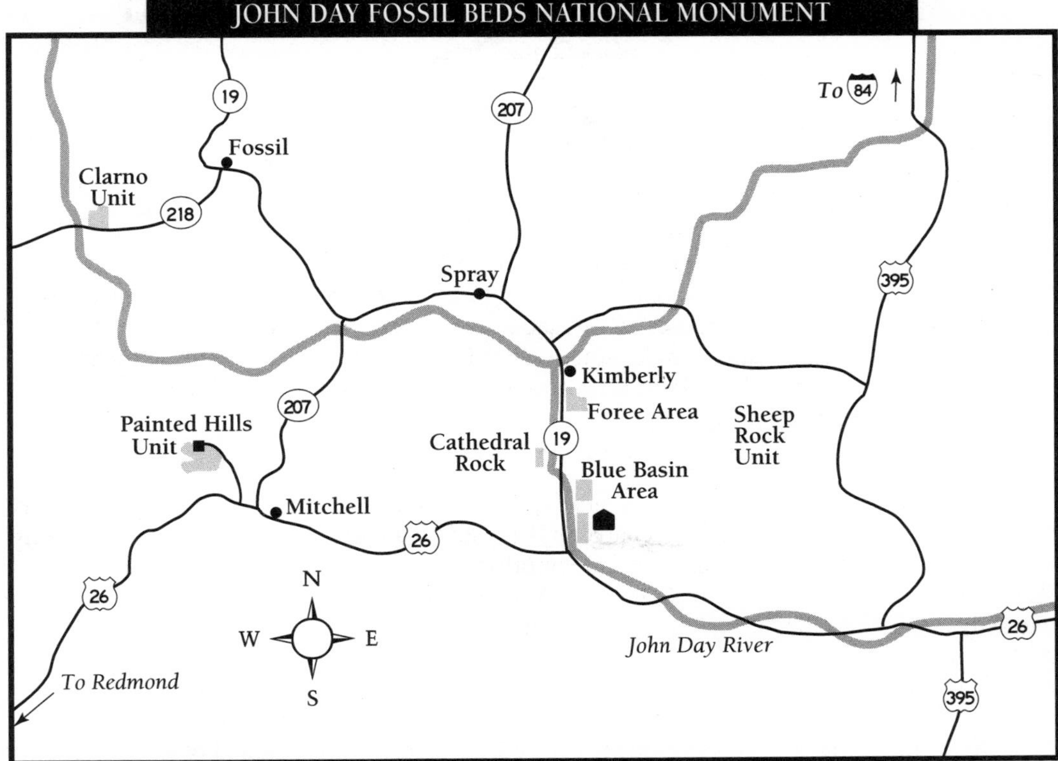

and adjacent river valley. Farther north are a colorful rock formation at Cathedral Rock, and an area of eroded lava flows and impressive outcrops of the John Day Formation, with short self-guiding trails, at the Foree area.

The Painted Hills area consists of an eroded landscape of volcanic ash deposits set within a vast picturesque valley. A ½-mile trail near the overlook, a short ¼-mile loop trail at Painted Cove, and the 1½-mile Carroll Rim Trail provide opportunities to see the colorful formations at close range.

Clarno includes ancient mudslides with two ¼-mile trails to the base of the brown and black palisades that offer views of plant fossils preserved in mudstone.

Scheduled ranger-conducted programs such as guided walks, museum talks, and off-site presentations are offered throughout the year. Wayside exhibits at overlooks along roads interpret outstanding features of each area of the park. In addition, the John Day River offers recreational opportunities. Fossil collecting is prohibited in the monument.

FACILITIES: Lodging, fuel, and food are available in nearby communities but not within the park. Hospitals are located in John Day, Madras, and Prineville. Drinking water and rest rooms can be found at the Cant Ranch, Painted Hills, and Clarno.

CAMPING: No camping is available within any of the three units of the park, but nearby facilities are abundant.

FISHING: The John Day River offers trout fishing in the summer and steelhead fishing in the winter with an Oregon fishing license.

McLOUGHLIN HOUSE NATIONAL HISTORIC SITE

713 Center Street
Oregon City, OR 97045
(503) 656–5146
www.McLoughlinHouse.org

McLoughlin House was designated a national historic site in 1941 to preserve the home of Dr. John McLoughlin, often called the "Father of Oregon." The house is one of the few remaining pioneer dwellings in the region once known as Oregon Country. McLoughlin House, an affiliated area of the National Park System, is located in Oregon City, 13 miles southeast of Portland on Interstate 205. The site is in McLoughlin Park between Seventh and Eighth Streets, less than 4 blocks east of Pacific Highway (U.S. 99).

John McLoughlin was born in Quebec, Canada, in 1784. When he came to the Oregon Country in 1824, McLoughlin was already in charge of the Columbia District of Hudson's Bay Company. From Fort Vancouver, McLoughlin ruled an empire stretching from the Rocky Mountains to the Pacific Ocean and from Alaska to California. Although his primary responsibility was to facilitate activities associated with the fur-trading industry, he also helped to develop other economic pursuits of the Northwest and provided assistance to the increasing numbers of immigrants moving into the region.

In 1829, McLoughlin and Governor George Simpson chose the falls of the Willamette River as a site for development. This eventually evolved into Oregon City, capital of the provisional government and chief town of Oregon Country. In 1845, Dr. McLoughlin resigned from the Hudson's Bay Company. In 1846, he moved to Oregon City and into the house where he lived until his death in 1857.

In 1909, a movement to preserve the house was successful, and the McLoughlin Memorial Association had the house moved from its original site at Third and Main Streets to its present site in McLoughlin Park. Since 1935 the house has been restored as nearly as possible to its original appearance. It contains period furniture, including some pieces that were at Fort Vancouver and many items that were owned by McLoughlin. In 1970, the remains of Dr. and Mrs. McLoughlin were moved next to the house.

The site was established by cooperative agreement among the McLoughlin Memorial Association, the municipality of Oregon City, and the National Park Service. The house sits in a small city park, on a piece of land Dr. McLoughlin set aside for public use. Hours of operation are Tuesday through Saturday (fee charged) from 10:00 A.M. to 4:00 P.M. and Sunday from 1:00 to 4:00 P.M. McLoughlin House is closed on Mondays and holidays and during the month of January. Visitors may take either a self-guided or a conducted tour. National Park Service passes are not accepted. A tourist information center operated by the local chamber of commerce is located on Washington Street on the north edge of town.

FACILITIES: No facilities are available at the site, but food and lodging can be found nearby in Oregon City.

CAMPING: No camping is permitted at the site. For those traveling south, Champoeg State Park (forty-eight spaces), approximately 24 miles southwest, provides full hookups, grills, and tables. From Oregon City take Interstate 205, Interstate 5 (south), and exit west on the Champoeg Park exit. For those traveling north, see the camping section under Fort Vancouver National Historic Site (Washington).

FISHING: No fishing is available at McLoughlin House National Historic Site.

OREGON CAVES NATIONAL MONUMENT

19000 Caves Highway
Cave Junction, OR 97523-9716
(541) 592–2100
roger_brandt@nps.gov
www.nps.gov/orca/index.html

Oregon Caves National Monument was established in 1909 to protect eleven small caves and a 3-mile cave that has rare bats, endemic insects, and all of the earth's six main rock types. Transferred to the National Park Service in 1934, the monument has 480 acres of old growth, including part of the most diverse conifer forest in the world. The monument is located in southwestern Oregon, 20 miles east of Cave Junction via Oregon Highway 46. The last 8 miles are very winding and are not recommended for trailers.

The collision of North America and the Pacific Ocean destroyed an ocean basin and metamorphosed limestone into marble 153 million years ago. Uplift formed faults, joints, and other cracks. Underwater and stream enlargement of cracks dissolved the limestone and formed the caves about 350 thousand years ago. Extensive formations include rimstone, stalagmites, stalactites, coralloids, flowstones, helictites, moonmilk, vermiculations, bell canopies, columns, cave "ghosts," scallops, domepits, pendants, and natural bridges.

After a hunter discovered the main cave in 1874, commercialization damaged the fragile cave. Through airlocks, rubble removal, etc., restoration of the cave to its original state started in 1985. Annual precipitation, mostly snow during winter, is about 55 inches, and the average surface temperature is in the mid-40s. Many plants are at their range limit or are endemic to the Siskiyou/Klamath Mountains.

Most visitors take a seventy-five-minute, concession-guided tour (fee charged) that covers ½ mile of the caves. More than 500 damp steps must be climbed to an exit that was built 240 feet above the entrance. Rubber- or vibram-soled shoes and warm clothing should be worn. Children under 42 inches in height cannot go on the tour. Waits for a summer tour can exceed one and a half hours. Tours are given several times a day during the winter. Cave tours are closed on Thanksgiving and from December through February. Annual visitation is about 100,000, with 75 percent taking place in the summer. Many visitors also stop at the visitor center in Cave Junction. The national monument also has 5 miles of outdoor trails, with scenic views, waterfalls, and meadows. These trails are maintained only in the summer. Dogs are not permitted on the trails.

FACILITIES: There is handicap access to rest rooms, and the first room in the caves. A restaurant and hotel in a historic district are open from mid-May to early September. A snack bar is open year-round. For rates or reservations, write Oregon Caves Company, Box 128, Cave Junction, OR 97523 (541–592–3400).

CAMPING: There is no camping or firebuilding in the monument. The U.S. Forest Service operates two campgrounds in the adjoining Siskiyou National Forest from about the end of May to early September. Cave Creek Campground is 4 miles from the park on Oregon 46. It has tables, grills, water, and pit toilets. Trailers are permitted only in Grayback Campground, located 8 miles down Oregon 46 from the park. Grayback has grills, water, a picnic area, flush toilets, and a phone. Campsites in both areas are secluded, and many are alongside a fishing stream.

FISHING: No fishing is available in the monument.

SAIPAN

AMERICAN MEMORIAL PARK

P.O. Box 5189 CHRB
Saipan, MP 96950
(670) 234–7207
amme_administration@nps.gov
www.nps.gov/amme/

American Memorial Park is an affiliated area of the National Park Service that was authorized in 1978 as a living memorial to honor the sacrifices of the American and Marianas people in the Marianas Campaign of World War II. American Memorial Park is on the island of Saipan in the western Pacific, approximately 6,000 miles southwest of Los Angeles. On Saipan, the park is located immediately north of the town of Garapan.

More than 4,000 U.S. military personnel and local islanders died during the Marianas Campaign in June 1944. This park is a memorial and recreational park to honor their sacrifice. The park's 133 acres (all nonfederal) are primarily utilized as a day-use area for local residents. At the center of the park is the Court of Honor and Flag Circle, in which an American flag is flanked by flags of the U.S. Army, Navy, Marine Corps, and Air Force. A historical society operates a museum with artifacts and photos from the battles that took place in the Marianas. The park contains several historical structures, including the remains of Japanese bunkers and gun emplacements.

Recreational facilities include a 1,200-seat pavilion, four tennis courts, picnic areas, and a recreational field for track, soccer, and football. A bike and walking path connects some of the important sites as it winds throughout the park.

FACILITIES: Complete food and lodging facilities are available nearby.

CAMPING: No camping is permitted in the park.

Mount Rushmore National Memorial

STATE TOURIST INFORMATION
(800) 732–5682

BADLANDS NATIONAL PARK

P.O. Box 6
Interior, SD 57750-0006
(605) 433–5361
www.nps.gov/badl/

Badlands National Monument, established as a National Park Service site in 1939 (changed to a national park in 1978), comprises 244,000 acres of prairie grassland and a scenic eroded landscape, with mammal fossils that are between 23 million and 38 million years old. The park is located in southwestern South Dakota. The Pinnacles entrance is 50 miles east of Rapid City, off Interstate 90 (exit 110), and the entrance at Cactus Flats is off Interstate 90 (exit 131), 71 miles east of Rapid City. Don't miss Wall Drug in the town of Wall. It is unique.

Today's Badlands were once covered by a large inland sea. Millions of years later the land was uplifted and exposed to a humid and warm climate. On this land roamed such animals as a saber-toothed cat and a camel the size of a dog. After dying, they were sometimes buried in mud from rivers and then under additional layers of sediments. Periodically, volcanic activity to the west produced layers of ash, which today appear as gray or white layers in the badlands formations. Today, the White River and its tributaries erode the soft sedimentary layers and leave the strange formations that give the park its name.

Badlands National Park has two visitor centers. Ben Reifel Visitor Center, located 8 miles south of Interstate 90 via the northeast entrance, has exhibits and a slide program to help interpret the badlands. White River Visitor Center (open June through August only), in the south end of the park, has Indian cultural exhibits and a videotape program on the history of the Oglala Sioux. Wayside exhibits are located along the main park road, and self-guiding nature trails are

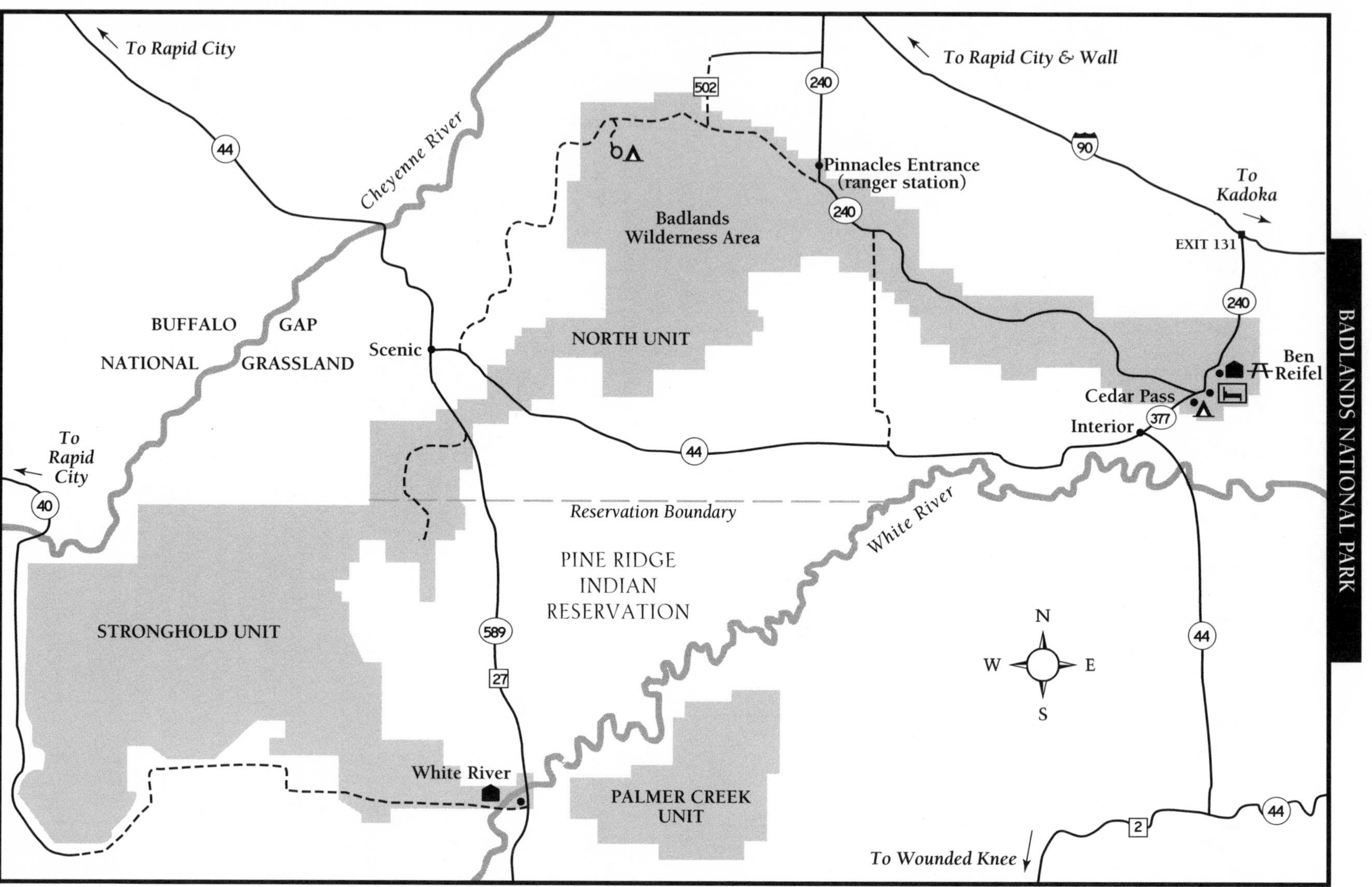

BADLANDS NATIONAL PARK
To Rapid City
44
Cheyenne River
502
240
To Rapid City & Wall
90
Pinnacles Entrance
(ranger station)
240
To
Kadoka
EXIT 131
240
Badlands
Wilderness Area
BUFFALO GAP
NATIONAL GRASSLAND
Scenic
NORTH UNIT
Ben
Reifel
Cedar Pass
377
Interior
44
To
Rapid
City
40
Reservation Boundary
White River
PINE RIDGE
INDIAN
RESERVATION
STRONGHOLD UNIT
589
27
N
W
E
S
44
White River
PALMER CREEK
UNIT
2
44
To Wounded Knee

located near the Ben Reifel Visitor Center and along the park road. Ranger-conducted hikes and evening slide programs are available during summer.

FACILITIES: Cedar Pass Lodge offers twenty-three air-conditioned cabins, as well as full-menu dining from April 15 through October 31. For information and reservations, write Cedar Pass Lodge, P.O. Box 5, Interior, SD 57750 (605–433–5460). Drinking water and rest rooms are located in the visitor center and the lodge.

CAMPING: Cedar Pass Campground (96 spaces, four group sites) provides sheltered tables, water, flush toilets, and a dump station. Sage Creek Campground (no designated spaces) is free and has vault toilets but no water. Both campgrounds are open year-round.

FISHING: No fishing is available at the park.

JEWEL CAVE NATIONAL MONUMENT

RR 1, Box 60AA
Custer, SD 57730-9608
(605) 673–2288
www.nps.gov/jeca/

Jewel Cave National Monument, which comprises 1,275 acres, was established in 1908 to preserve a series of underground chambers, connected by narrow passageways, with many side galleries and fine calcite crystal encrustations in the second longest cave in the United States. The monument is located in southwestern South Dakota, 13 miles west of Custer via U.S. 16. For a map of the Black Hills region, see the map under Mount Rushmore National Memorial.

The caves in this region lie in a limestone layer that was deposited about 350 million years ago in a shallow, ancient sea. Later, after it was covered with layers of sediment, an uplift associated with the formation of the Rocky Mountains formed the Black Hills, and erosion exposed the interior of the Hills. As acidic water seeped into cracks in the limestone, the rock dissolved and caves were formed. The cave was named after the many jewellike calcite crystals that form when calcite crystallizes out of standing water.

Jewel Cave was discovered in 1900 by two prospectors who recorded it as a mining claim. After failing to find valuable minerals, they attempted to turn it into a tourist attraction. In 1908, President Theodore Roosevelt proclaimed the cave a national monument.

The monument's visitor center is open daily year-round. It contains exhibits and an information counter. Naturalist-guided tours (fee charged) are conducted through portions of the cave on a daily basis except Thanksgiving, Christmas, and New Year's Day. Three types of tours are available. The Scenic Tour enters and leaves the cave by elevator in the visitor center; the Candlelight Tour (summer only) uses the historic entrance created by the cave's discoverers. This latter trip is quite strenuous and uses an unimproved trail. For those desiring an even more demanding trip, the Spelunking Tour (reservations required, summer only) is made to order. Individuals planning to visit the monument are advised to call ahead for tour times and availability.

FACILITIES: Lodging is not available in the park. Snacks and soft drink vending machines are available. Motels, restaurants, and service stations are available in Custer, South Dakota, and Newcastle, Wyoming. Drinking water and rest rooms are located in the visitor center.

CAMPING: No camping is permitted in the park. Public camping facilities are available nearby in Wind Cave National Park, Custer State Park, and Black Hills National Forest.

FISHING: No fishing is available at the monument.

MOUNT RUSHMORE NATIONAL MEMORIAL

P.O. Box 268
Keystone, SD 57751-0268
(605) 574–2523
jim_popovich@nps.gov
www.nps.gov/moru/

Mount Rushmore, which comprises 1,278 acres, was dedicated on August 10, 1927, the same day work commenced on sculpting the heads of George Washington, Abraham Lincoln, Thomas Jefferson, and Theodore Roosevelt on the face of this granite mountain. The memorial is located in southwestern South Dakota, 25 miles southwest of Rapid City and 2 miles from the town of Keystone.

The idea of a large sculpture in the Black Hills region was first conceived in 1923. Although the project initially received little public support, opinion gradually changed, and authorization and funding eventually were obtained. In the fall of 1924, Gutzon Borglum, a sculptor then at work on Stone Mountain in Georgia, was invited to study the proposal. Borglum suggested that United States presidents be used as subjects and that the sculpture be on the smooth granite of Mount Rushmore. The original proposal had called for the figures of famous western heroes on another granite formation known as the Needles.

Borglum worked on the project from 1927 until his death in 1941. His son continued the work until funds were exhausted later that year. Although private donations supported the project in its early years, the federal government contributed most of the nearly $1 million the project consumed between 1927 and 1941.

The 60-foot-tall faces are best viewed under morning light. During summer evenings, floodlights illuminate the faces, and programs are presented in the amphitheater. The information center orients visitors to the memorial and Black Hills area. The visitor center/museum has two theaters and exhibits that detail how and why the memorial was carved. The memorial and visitor center are open year-round. A parking fee is charged.

FACILITIES: Meals, souvenirs, and handicrafts are available at the concession. Overnight accommodations are located in nearby communities.

CAMPING: No camping is permitted in the park. Public camping facilities are provided in a number of campgrounds in Black Hills National Forest and in Custer State Park and Wind Cave National Park.

FISHING: No fishing is available at the memorial.

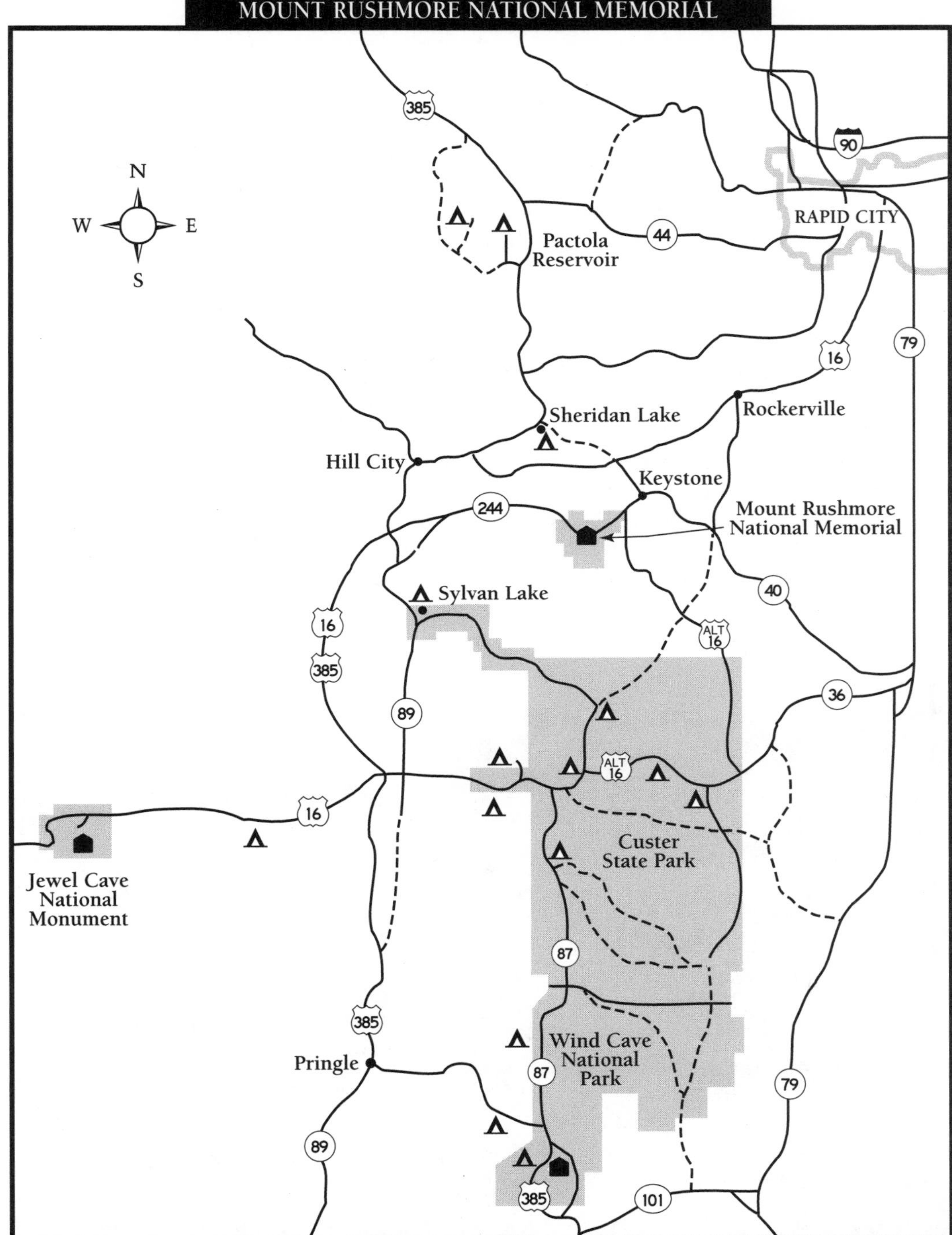
MOUNT RUSHMORE NATIONAL MEMORIAL
N
W
E
S
385
90
RAPID CITY
44
Pactola Reservoir
79
16
Rockerville
Sheridan Lake
Hill City
Keystone
244
Mount Rushmore National Memorial
40
Sylvan Lake
16
385
ALT 16
89
36
ALT 16
16
Jewel Cave National Monument
Custer State Park
87
385
Pringle
Wind Cave National Park
87
79
89
385
101

WIND CAVE NATIONAL PARK

Hot Springs, SD 57747-9430
(605) 745–4600
www.nps.gov/wica/

Wind Cave National Park, which comprises more than 28,000 acres, was established in 1903 to preserve a part of the prairie ecosystem and a unique type of limestone cavern that is one of the longest caves in the United States. The park is located in southwestern South Dakota, approximately 60 miles south of Rapid City via U.S. 16 and 385.

The 300- to 630-foot-thick limestone bed containing Wind Cave was deposited at the bottom of a great sea about 300 million years ago. Later, the region was covered with many layers of sediment before being uplifted approximately sixty million years ago. During the uplift, the limestone was fractured, allowing ground water to dissolve the limestone and deposit the calcite that now decorates the cave.

The cave is most noted for its "boxwork" formations, but other interesting decorations can also be seen. Unlike many caverns, stalactites and stalagmites are uncommon in Wind Cave. The strong winds that blow in and out of the cave (hence, its name) are apparently caused by

Bison Herd, Wind Cave National Park

changes in atmospheric pressure on the outside. Although more than 82 miles of passages have been explored, the regular tours (fee charged) cover only 1½ miles of hard-surfaced trails with stairways and electric lighting. Rubber-soled shoes (low-heeled) and a light jacket (53 degrees Fahrenheit inside) are recommended for visitors desiring to tour the cave.

One of the park's most popular attractions is the bison herd that roams this wildlife sanctuary. A number of prairie-dog towns are located in the park, as are herds of elk, pronghorn, and mule deer, and white-tailed deer. During summer months, park personnel conduct outdoor activities throughout the day. Schedules are posted at the visitor center, which also contains exhibits on prairie and forest resources, the area's history, and cave features.

FACILITIES: No overnight accommodations are available in the park, but motels, hotels, trailer courts, camping supplies, and service stations are located in Custer and Hot Springs. In the visitor center a vending area for snacks and a bookstore are open year-round.

CAMPING: Elk Mountain Campground (seventy-five sites), located 1 mile north of the visitor center, is open May 15 through September 15. Tables, grills, water, and flush toilets are provided. During the off-season (April 1 to May 15 and September 15 to October 30), pit toilets are available, but water is available only at the visitor center. Camping is also available in Custer State Park and Black Hills National Forest to the north and near Hot Springs to the south.

FISHING: Fishing for brown, brook, and rainbow trout is available in the general area.

Mission Concepción, San Antonio Missions National Historical Park

STATE TOURIST INFORMATION
(800) 452–9292

ALIBATES FLINT QUARRIES NATIONAL MONUMENT

Box 1460
Fritch, TX 79036-1460
(806) 857–3151
LAMR_Interpretation@nps.gov
www.nps.gov/alfl/

Alibates Flint Quarries was authorized as a national monument in 1965. It comprises 1,333 acres in an area where, for nearly 12,000 years, pre-Columbian Indians dug agatized dolomite from quarries to make knives, projectile points, scrapers, and other tools. The monument is in northern Texas, 40 miles northeast of Amarillo. From Texas Highway 136, take Alibates Road, 6 miles south of Fritch, and drive 5 miles to the information station.

Tools made from flint dug in the Lake Meredith area of the Texas Panhandle have been found in many places in the Great Plains and the American Southwest. Evidence from archaeological excavations indicates almost continuous use of the flint quarries at Alibates from 10,000 B.C. to the late 1800s. Alibates flint is a hard, sharp-edged rock that, unlike most other flint, has a multitude of bright colors.

Although much of the mining at Alibates was done by nomads, some Indians did settle this area briefly from about A.D. 1200 to A.D. 1450. These Indians farmed in addition to mining and bartering flint.

A small information station at Bates Canyon contains a few exhibits, and park personnel are on duty to answer questions. Free guided walking tours of the quarry pits leave the information station from Memorial Day to Labor Day at 10:00 A.M. and 2:00 P.M. daily. The rest of the year, tours are available with advance reservation.

FACILITIES: The monument is undeveloped, and no visitor facilities other than the information station and comfort station are available. Meals and lodging are available in Fritch and Borger.

CAMPING: No camping is permitted at the monument. Campsites are available in McBride Canyon at nearby Lake Meredith National Recreation Area.

FISHING: No fishing is available in Alibates, but there is quite a lot of good fishing in nearby Lake Meredith.

AMISTAD NATIONAL RECREATION AREA

HCR-3, Box 5J
Del Rio, TX 78840-9350
(830) 775–7491
Amis_Interpretation@nps.gov
www.nps.gov/amis/

Amistad (the name means "friendship") NRA, established in 1965, is comprised of 58,500 acres that provide numerous outdoor recreation opportunities, including boating, fishing, swimming, waterskiing, and hunting. The park is located along the Rio Grande in southwest Texas, near Del Rio. It is accessible via U.S. 90.

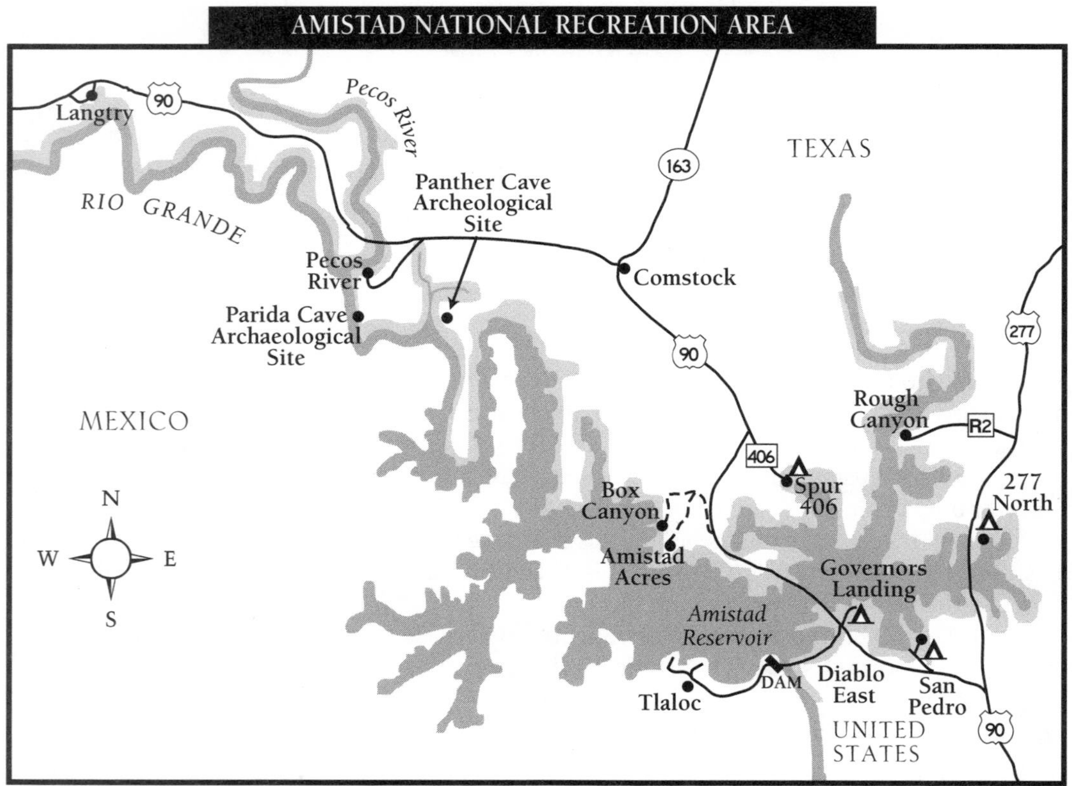

Lake Amistad, the main attraction at Amistad National Recreation Area, is a result of the 1968 completion of Amistad Dam, 12 miles upstream from Del Rio. The dam, a cooperative undertaking between the United States and Mexico, was developed for flood control, water conservation, hydroelectric power, and recreation. It is constructed of a 254-foot-high concrete section in the Rio Grande channel connecting flanking earth embankments. Near the center of the dam is a customs station, an international monument, and the International Boundary and Water Commission/National Park Service Visitor Center.

Rock art in the Lower Pecos River region is considered to be world class and comparable to that found in Europe and Australia. This region also contains some of the oldest-dated and best-preserved archaeological deposits in North America.

The area's most popular activities are boating and fishing, and major boat ramps are found at Pecos River, Diablo East, and Rough Canyon. Boat rentals, rental slips, bait, and gasoline are available at the latter two locations. Boats on Lake Amistad must have a daily or annual permit (fee required). From spring to fall, water in the coves is pleasantly warm for swimming and waterskiing. The beaches are not protected by lifeguards. Swimming is not permitted in the harbor areas. Certain areas of the park are designated for hunting dove, duck, and quail with shotgun; deer, wild turkey, and javelina may be hunted with bow and arrow only. Interested individuals should inquire at the National Park Service headquarters.

FACILITIES: Concessioner-operated stores are located at Diablo East and Rough Canyon. No lodging is available at the park, but motels, travel trailer parks, restaurants, and service stations are available in Del Rio and along U.S. 90 West, near the lake.

CAMPING: There are primitive campsites with chemical toilets but no drinking water in various locations in the park. Several group sites are available by reservation only. Drinking water is available at park headquarters on Highway 90 West and at the Governors Landing campground. Water and dump stations are on the Diablo East entrance road and at the Del Rio Civic Center. Commercial campgrounds are located near the Diablo East, Rough Canyon, and Pecos River facilities.

FISHING: Principal sport fishing is for bass, channel catfish, yellow catfish, striped bass, crappie, and sunfish. There is no closed season, and a Texas fishing license is required. Fishing is not permitted in the harbor and swimming areas. A list of fishing guides is available at park headquarters.

BIG BEND NATIONAL PARK

P.O. Box 129
Big Bend National Park, TX 79834-0129
(915) 477–2251
BIBEINFORMATION@nps.gov
www.nps.gov/bibe/

Big Bend, established in 1944, comprises more than 801,000 acres of desert, mountain ranges, steep-walled canyons, and ribbons of green plant life along the Rio Grande. The park is located in southwestern Texas on the Mexican border. Access from the north is via U.S. 385 from Marathon or State Highway 118 from Alpine. Enter from the west on Texas Ranch Road 170 from Presidio.

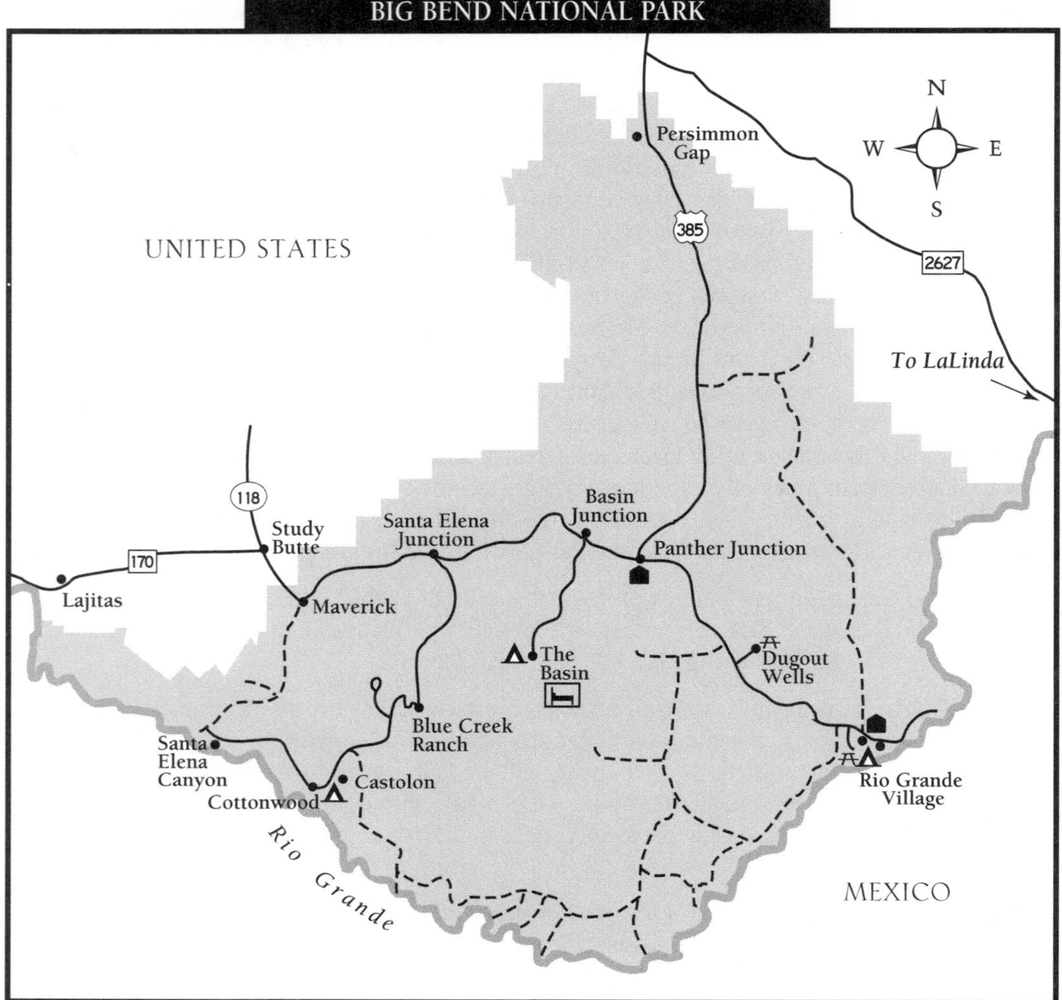

The land of Big Bend is one of vastness and adventure. Its remoteness makes it less heavily used than better-known parks, even though it offers a wide variety of outdoor activities. Big Bend is especially pleasant to visit during the long spring and fall seasons, when the weather is mild.

Visitor centers are located at Panther Junction (park headquarters), Persimmon Gap, The Chisos Basin, Rio Grande Village, and Castolon. These centers provide information and sell publications concerning the park. Entrance fees for private (including motorcycles and bicycles) and commercial vehicles are paid at the entrance stations or at Panther Junction. Park naturalists present evening programs at The Chisos Basin amphitheater all summer and at Rio Grande Village during the fall, winter, and spring. Ranger-conducted hikes and special programs are available, and schedules are posted at various locations. Self-guiding nature trails are provided at Rio Grande Village, Santa Elena Canyon, Panther Junction, Dagger Flat Road, and the Lost Mine Trail and Window View Trail in The Basin.

The 43-mile drive from Panther Junction to Santa Elena Canyon ends at a shaded picnic area, where high cliffs overhang the Rio Grande. A foot trail to the base of the cliff leads upward to a panoramic viewpoint. From there, the trail wanders 3/4 mile along the river. On the other side of the park, Boquillas Canyon is the longest (25 miles) of Big Bend's famous gorges. The path into the canyon descends gently after a short, steep climb.

Primitive roads offer access to scenery not available elsewhere in the park. These roads are patrolled infrequently, so those planning such trips should be well prepared and obtain current road information at park headquarters.

River trips on the Rio Grande are offered by outfitters outside the park. A permit is required to run the river, but no equipment rentals are available inside the park. The visitor centers sell a river guide and can supply a list of river outfitters.

FACILITIES: Chisos Mountains Lodge in The Basin provides a total of seventy-two rooms in motel-type units, stone cottages, and frame cottages, with reservations available from National Park Concessions, Inc., Big Bend National Park, TX 79834 (915–477–2291). The lodge has a dining room and coffee shop. Groceries and camping supplies are available at The Basin, Rio Grande Village, and Castolon. Minor auto repair and gas are available at Panther Junction. Gasoline is also available at Rio Grande Village. Diesel fuel is available at Panther Junction.

CAMPING: Campgrounds with tables, grills, water, and flush toilets are located at The Basin (sixty-two spaces, eight group sites, dump station), Cottonwood (thirty-four spaces, one group site, pit toilets only), and Rio Grande Village (ninety-nine spaces, four group sites, dump station). A concessioner-operated trailer village with hookups is located at Rio Grande Village (twenty-five sites, pay showers). The road into The Basin is steep and winding. Trailers longer than 20 feet are not recommended, and recreational vehicles longer than 24 feet are advised to avoid the road.

FISHING: The Rio Grande provides catches of catfish. A free fishing permit is required.

BIG THICKET NATIONAL PRESERVE

3785 Milam
Beaumont, TX 77701-4724
(409) 839–2689
merle_king@nps.gov
www.nps.gov/bith/

Big Thicket National Preserve comprises 84,550 acres and was authorized in 1974 to preserve a unique ecosystem of great diversity. Plants and animals from southwestern deserts, central plains, eastern forests, the Appalachian Mountains, and southeastern swamps can be found coexisting in close proximity. The preserve comprises twelve widely separated units north, northwest, and northeast of the city of Beaumont, Texas. The Information Station is on FM 420, 2½ miles east of U.S. 69, 7 miles north of Kountze. Big Thicket is also designated a Man and the Biosphere Reserve by the United Nations Educational, Scientific, and Cultural Organization (UNESCO).

Big Thicket is unique because of the abundance of diverse plant life coexisting in a small remnant of what was once a combination of virgin pine and cypress forest, hardwood forest, meadow, and blackwater swamp. The area contains eighty-five tree species, more than sixty species of shrubs, and nearly 1,000 other flowering plants, including twenty orchids and four

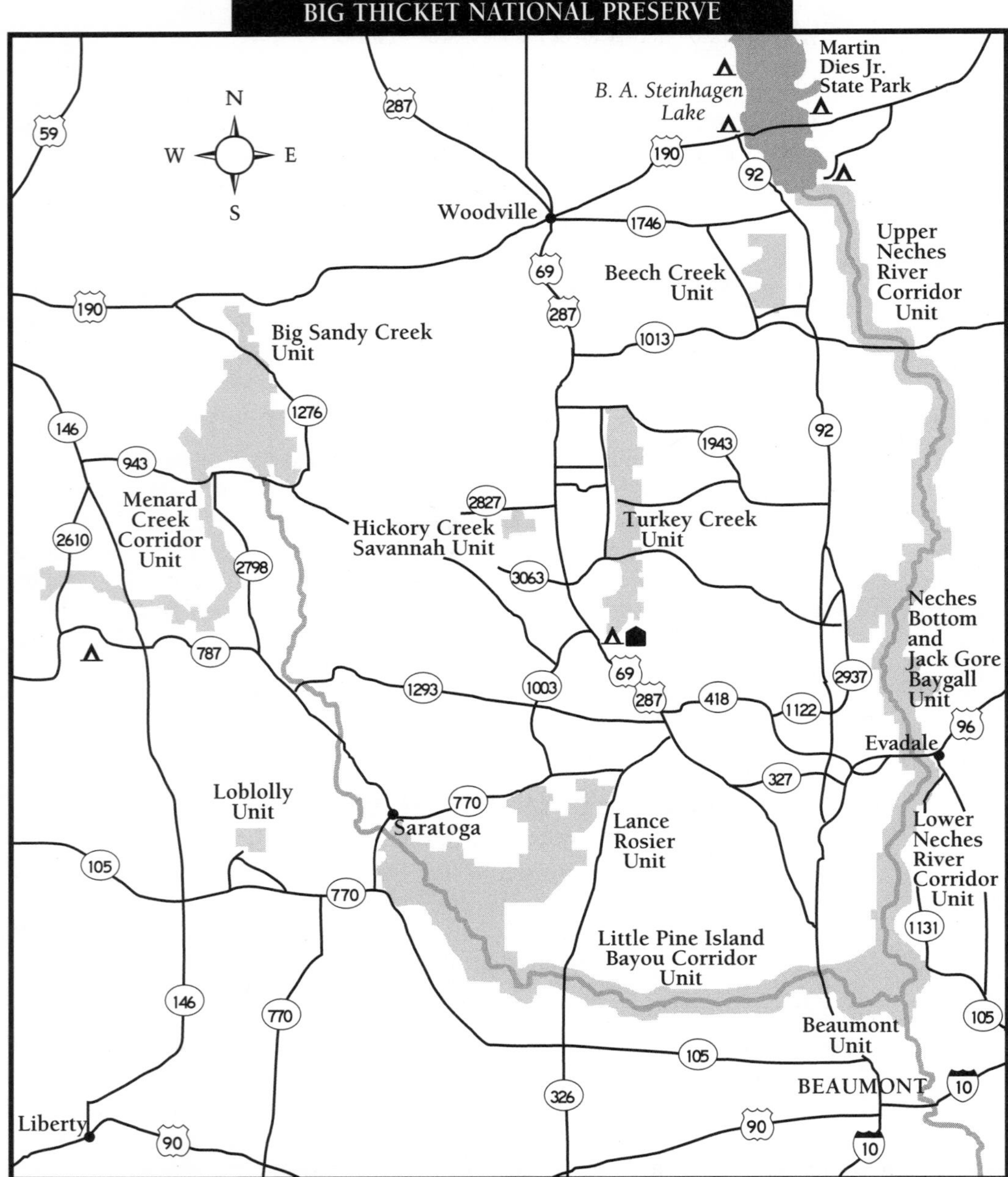

carnivorous plants. Wildlife thrives in the diverse habitats, although many animals come out only at night. During annual migrations nearly 175 kinds of birds have been sighted. Big Thicket is home to a few threatened or endangered species, including the red-cockaded woodpecker, American alligator, and paddlefish.

The Information Station is open daily from 9:00 A.M. to 5:00 P.M. Opening is at 10:30 A.M. on Wednesday. The preserve's twelve units are open to the public, and four have developed hiking trails. Two trails are handicapped accessible. The best way to explore the Big Thicket is to hike a trail or boat or canoe the river corridors and backwater sloughs. Few roads enter the preserve, limiting visitors from seeing the woods from their cars. Ranger-led programs for groups and individuals are available by reservation only. Contact the Information Station at (409) 246–2337 for information and reservations.

FACILITIES: No lodging or food service is available in the park, but both are available in the nearby communities of Woodville, Kountze, Silsbee, and Beaumont. Rest rooms and drinking water are located at the Information Station.

CAMPING: There are no developed camping facilities, although backcountry camping is permitted in designated areas of the preserve. A backcountry permit is required. Campgrounds with flush toilets and showers are located at Martin Dies Jr. State Park, 13 miles west of Jasper on U.S. 190 and at Village Creek State Park, east of Lumberton. Another campground, operated by the U.S. Army Corps of Engineers, is located nearby on B.A. Steinhagen Lake. Contact the preserve for a listing of nearby private campgrounds.

FISHING: Opportunities for bass, catfish, and carp are available in the preserve. A valid Texas fishing license is required.

HUNTING: Hunting is allowed in certain units of the preserve with an annual permit. These free permits are issued during July on a first-come, first-served basis. Contact the preserve for permit information.

CHAMIZAL NATIONAL MEMORIAL

800 South San Marcial Street
El Paso, TX 79905-4123
(915) 532–7273
www.nps.gov/cham/

Chamizal, which comprises fifty-five acres, was authorized in 1966 to memorialize the settlement of a 100-year-old boundary dispute between the United States and Mexico. The park is located in south-central metropolitan El Paso, next to the international border. Entrances to the park are from Paisano Avenue or Delta Drive to South San Marcial Street.

The first commission to survey the international boundary between the United States and Mexico was established in 1849 after the signing of the Treaty of Guadalupe Hidalgo. The survey disclosed that 1,248 miles of the border was formed by the Rio Grande/Bravo, and an additional 23 miles was defined by the Colorado River. These river boundaries created difficulties because they tended to change courses with each flood season. In an 1884 treaty both nations agreed to the principle that if a river changed course by a slow process of erosion, the boundary moved with the deepest channel. Conversely, if the river changed its course suddenly, then the boundary remained in the old channel.

The park, established on a portion of land acquired in the agreement, is open daily except Thanksgiving, Christmas, and New Year's Day from 8:00 A.M. to 5:00 P.M. There is a museum that has exhibits and shows a video to help visitors understand the history of this disputed area. The Los Paisanos Gallery exhibits the finest in national and international visual arts. Special programs in the 500-seat indoor theater and outdoor amphitheater take place throughout the year, with the Siglo de Oro, from late February to early March, recognized as one of the finest existing venues for plays written during Spain's Golden Age, and the ever popular Music Under

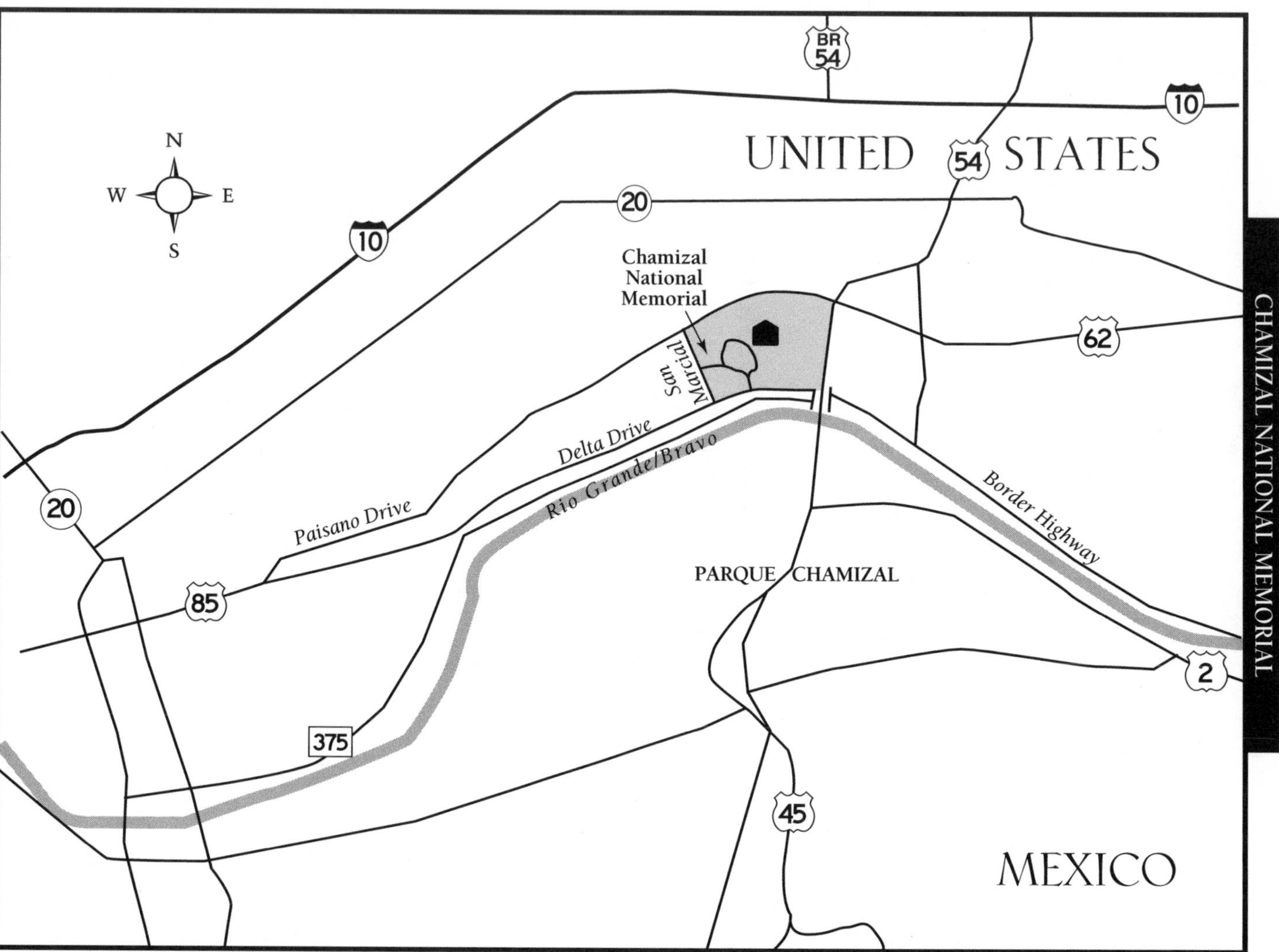
UNITED STATES
MEXICO
Chamizal National Memorial
San Marcial
Delta Drive
Rio Grande/Bravo
Border Highway
Paisano Drive
PARQUE CHAMIZAL
BR 54
10
54
20
62
85
375
45
2
N
W
E
S

the Stars, every Sunday evening June through August, featuring national and international music. The Border Folk Festival in the fall features the very best in traditional music, crafts, demonstrations, dance, and visual art forms.

FACILITIES: No food or lodging is available at the memorial, but both are available nearby.

CAMPING: No camping is permitted. Private campgrounds are located near the park.

FISHING: No fishing is available.

FORT DAVIS NATIONAL HISTORIC SITE

P.O. Box 1456
Fort Davis, TX 79734-1456
(915) 426–3225
www.nps.gov/foda/

Fort Davis, which comprises 460 acres, was authorized in 1961 to preserve the site of an important fort of the late 1800s whose remains are more extensive and impressive than any other of that period in the Southwest. The site is located in western Texas on the northern edge of the town of Fort Davis. It is reached from Interstate 10 via Texas Highways 17 and 118 or from U.S. 90 via Texas Highways 505, 166, and 17.

Fort Davis, named in honor of Secretary of War Jefferson Davis, was constructed in the mid-1850s to protect travelers and settlers in the West Texas region. The first structures consisted of pine-slab *jacales* covered with thatched grass or canvas. By 1856, six stone barracks had been built to house enlisted men. During this period, the soldiers of Fort Davis spent most of their time escorting mail and freight trains and patrolling this sector of the Southwest.

With the beginning of the Civil War, Union troops abandoned the fort, which then became occupied by Confederate forces for nearly a year. After Fort Davis was in turn abandoned by the Southern troops, it was wrecked by Apaches and lay deserted for five years. In 1867, federal troops returned to rebuild the fort, and by the 1880s more than fifty stone and adobe structures housed companies of both cavalry and infantry. As Indian raiding had come to an end, the fort became an unnecessary expense and was finally abandoned in 1891.

Of the more than fifty buildings that formed the second fort, the exteriors of fifteen officer's quarters, two enlisted men's barracks, an officer's kitchen and servant's quarters, a hospital, a commissary, and some of the storehouses have been restored. Five of these (officer's quarters number 2, a commanding officer's quarters, an enlisted men's barracks, a commissary, and an officer's kitchen and servant's quarters) have had interior work and are now restored and refurnished in 1880s' style. These five buildings and the post hospital are open to the public on a self-guiding basis. During the summer months the enlisted men's barracks and commanding officer's quarters are open, with interpreters dressed in period clothing. Stone foundations mark the sites of other buildings. A number of foundations for buildings of the first fort have been uncovered.

The visitor center, located in one of the two restored enlisted men's barracks, is open daily from 8:00 A.M. until 6:00 P.M. (5:00 P.M. from Labor Day through Memorial Day). A slide show may be seen in the auditorium, and audio (bugle call and retreat dress parade) programs can be heard on the parade ground at scheduled times throughout the day.

FACILITIES: Food and lodging are not available at the site but can be found in the town of Fort Davis. Water and rest rooms are located in the visitor center. A picnic area is located on the grounds. Many of the buildings are equipped with ramps for visitors in wheelchairs.

CAMPING: No camping is permitted in the park. Camping facilities are available in Davis Mountains State Park (915–426–3337), 4 miles to the north. The state park offers eighty-eight sites with tables, grills, water, flush toilets, and showers.

FISHING: No fishing is available at the park.

GUADALUPE MOUNTAINS NATIONAL PARK

HC 60, Box 400
Salt Flat, TX 79847-9400
(915) 828–3251
GUMO_Superintendent@nps.gov
www.nps.gov/gumo/

Guadalupe Mountains National Park, established in 1972, comprises 86,416 acres of mountain landscape, including the most extensive exposed fossil reef on Earth. The park is located in western Texas, 55 miles southwest of Carlsbad, New Mexico, and 110 miles east of El Paso via U.S. 62/180. It is 65 miles north of Van Horn, Texas, via SR 54.

The Guadalupe Mountains began to form nearly 250 million years ago, when this region was covered by a great inland sea. Near the shoreline, a reef grew from lime-secreting organisms and precipitates from the water. At the end of the Permian period, the reef died, and layers of sediment buried the entire area. Much later, a general uplifting raised the region several thousand feet and allowed the shaping of today's mountain range through erosion by wind and water. Today, only a small portion of the 350-mile horseshoe-shaped reef is not buried beneath the ground. The most outstanding exposure is included in this park.

A variety of people have passed through and lived in this arid region. Hunter-gatherers, including the Mescalero Apache, made this their homeland. Spanish conquistadors passed the range on their explorations north from Mexico. Don Diego de Vargas, a colonizer of New Mexico, made a trip to the nearby Salt Flats and the Guadalupes in 1692. Military surveyors mapped the pass, and their route was used by settlers and forty-niners headed for the western gold strikes. The route was also used by the Butterfield Overland Mail in the late 1850s. The remains of "The Pinery," a horse-changing stop, are marked and accessed via a trail from the Headquarters Visitor Center.

The Headquarters Visitor Center at Pine Springs is open daily from 8:00 A.M. to 4:30 P.M. (6:00 P.M. during summer). The visitor center offers exhibits, audiovisual programs, a bookstore, and maps. Frijole Ranch, a cultural history site, is 1½ miles north of Pine Springs and features exhibits on Native Americans, Spanish exploration, the Overland Mail, the U.S. Cavalry, and early ranching activities. Visitors may also secure a free permit at the visitor center giving them access to Williams Ranch Historic Site via an 8-mile (four-wheel-drive) road.

McKittrick Canyon Visitor Center is a trailhead for the spectacular canyon, with exhibits on the canyon and the Permian Reef, and to self-guiding trails. The road to the canyon is 7 miles east of Pine Springs on U.S. 62/180. With 80 miles of hiking trails and no road bisecting

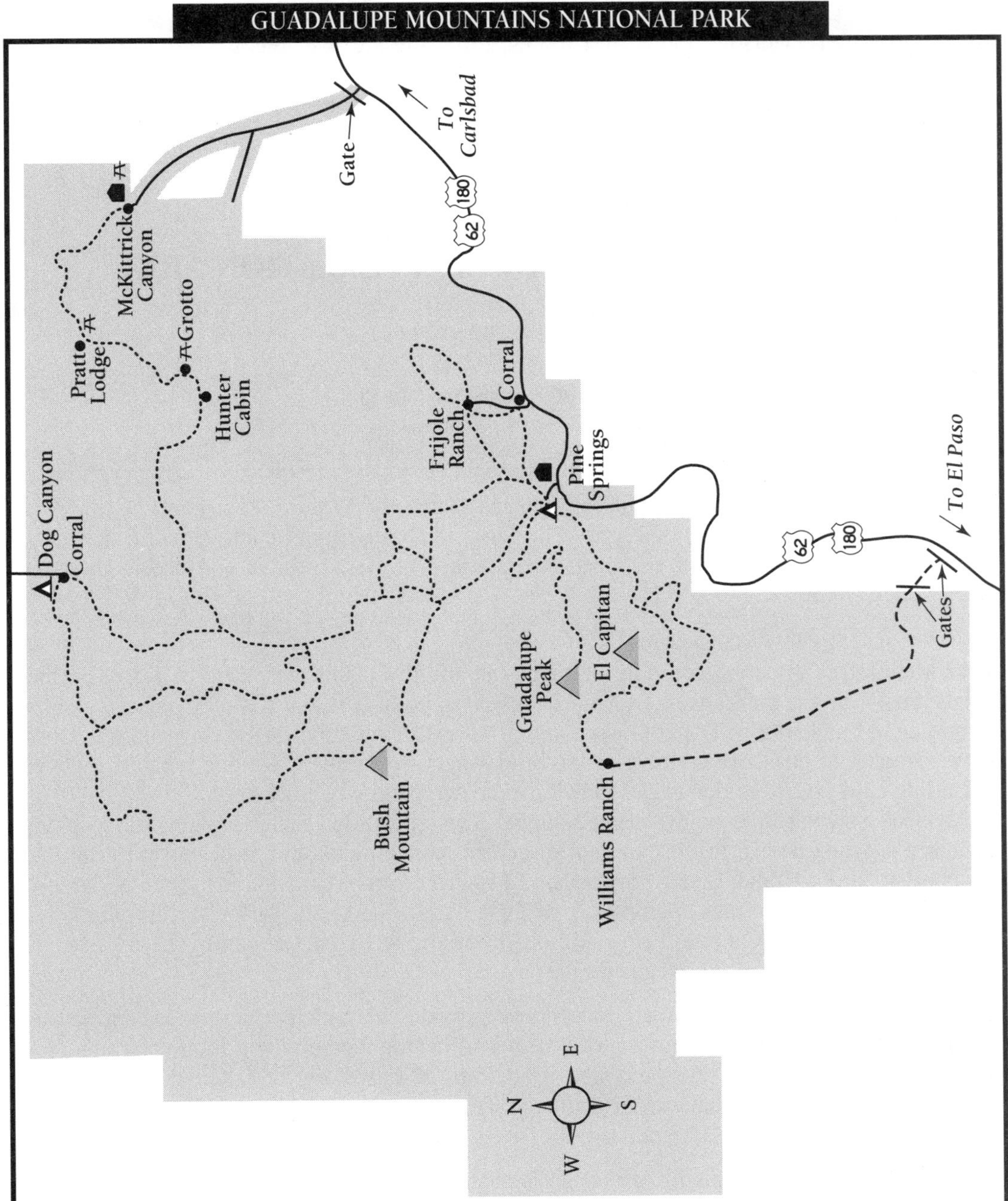

Guadalupe Mountains National Park, backcountry hiking is one of the primary activities. Overnight permits are available at Pine Springs and Dog Canyon.

FACILITIES: Water, rest rooms, and picnic areas are provided at the visitor centers and campgrounds. No food, commercial lodging, or fuel is available at the park.

CAMPING: Pine Springs Campground has twenty tent and nineteen RV sites with tables but no hookups or showers. Two group sites are available. Water, rest rooms, and a service sink are provided. Dog Canyon Campground has nine tent and four RV sites, none with hookups. One group site is available. Tables, rest rooms, and water are available. No fires are permitted at any of the campsites. Dog Canyon is accessed via New Mexico Highway 137 from Carlsbad, New Mexico, or via the state and county road through Dell City, Texas.

FISHING: No fishing is available at the park.

LAKE MEREDITH NATIONAL RECREATION AREA

P.O. Box 1460
Fritch, TX 79036-1460
(806) 857–3151
LAMR_Interpretation@nps.gov
www.nps.gov/lamr/

Lake Meredith National Recreation Area (formerly Sanford Recreation Area) encompasses nearly 45,000 acres. The park is a popular spot for all types of water activities. It is located in the Texas Panhandle, 33 miles northeast of Amarillo via State Highway 136.

Lake Meredith is an oasis located in the high, flat, and dry plains area of north Texas. Formed by Sanford Dam on the Canadian River, the resulting body of water is used by eleven cities as a municipal water supply. The 200-foot canyon walls with white limestone caps and red-brown coves present an attractive contrast to the blue waters. A variety of wildlife inhabits the area, including bald eagles, golden eagles, hawks, mule deer, and white tail deer.

Typical activities at Lake Meredith National Recreation Area include waterskiing, sailing, swimming, scuba-diving, fishing, and hunting. Boat-launching ramps are located at Harbor Bay, Blue West, Sanford-Yake, Cedar Canyon, and Fritch Fortress. A marina is located at Sanford-Yake. Off-road vehicle trails are available at Rosita and Blue Creek Bridge. Swimming is recommended at Spring Canyon, below Sanford Dam and at Cedar Canyon in the lake proper. (Swim at your own risk—no lifeguards.)

FACILITIES: At Sanford-Yake, a concessioner provides a snack bar, a marina, and related services, and an enclosed fish house for year-round fishing. Lodging and food are available in nearby towns. Drinking water and rest rooms are at Fritch Fortress, Cedar Canyon, and Sanford-Yake and are available from April through September. Chemical toilets are also provided at most of the other locations.

CAMPING: Campgrounds with tables, grills, water, and flush toilets are located at Sanford-Yake (fifty-three spaces, dump station) and Fritch Fortress (ten spaces). Campgrounds with chemical toilets but no water are located at Blue West (forty spaces), McBride Canyon (ten spaces), and Plum Creek (fifteen spaces). These sites are open year-round. No camping is permitted at the launching areas or the parking lots.

FISHING: The lake provides opportunities to fish for largemouth, smallmouth, and white bass, four species of catfish, crappie, sunfish, carp, and the only naturally reproducing walleye in Texas. A Texas fishing license is required.

LAKE MEREDITH NATIONAL RECREATION AREA

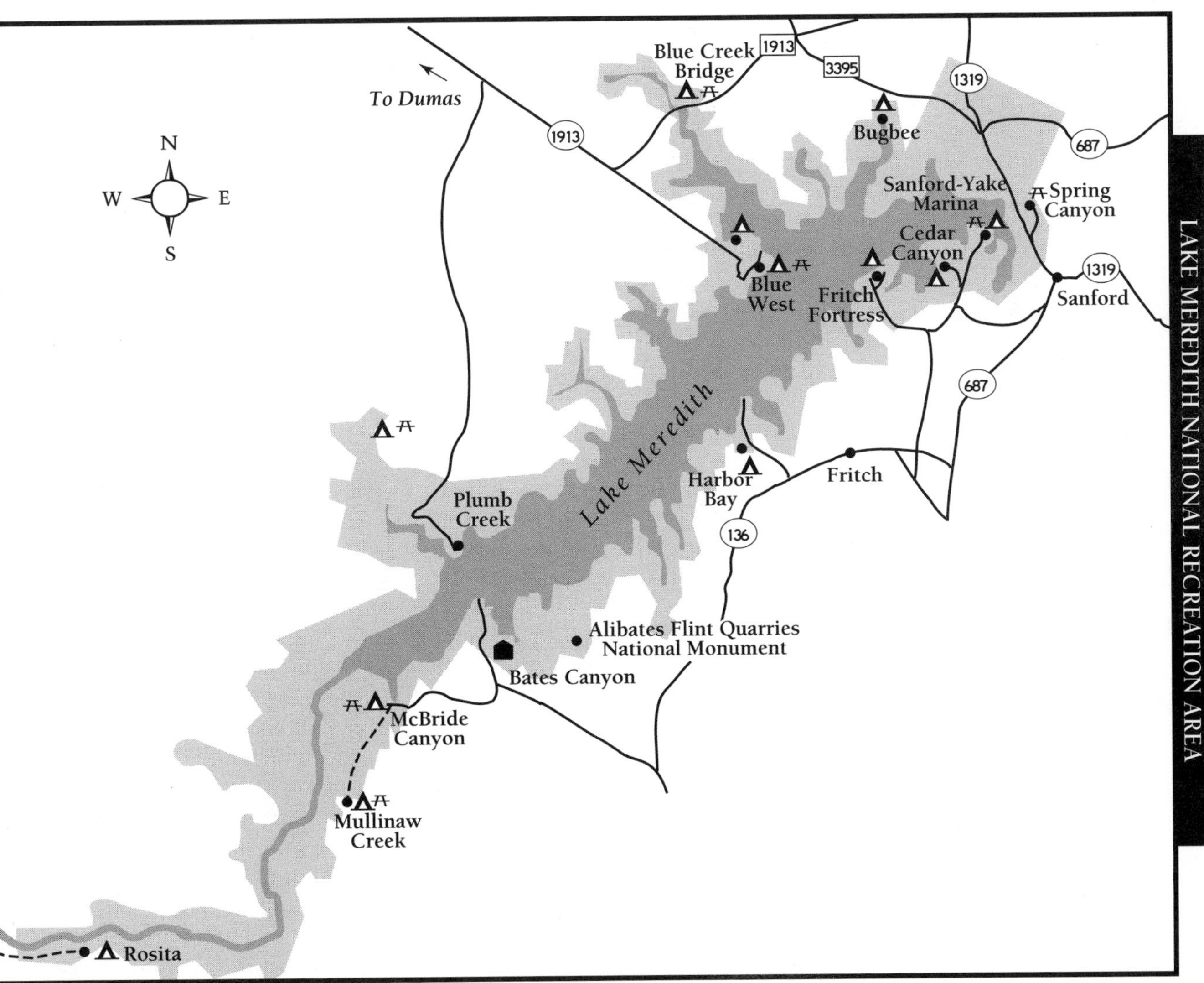

LYNDON B. JOHNSON NATIONAL HISTORICAL PARK

P.O. Box 329
Johnson City, TX 78636-0329
(830) 868–7128
www.nps.gov/lyjo/

Lyndon B. Johnson National Historical Park was authorized in 1969 to preserve the birthplace, boyhood home, and ranch of the thirty-sixth president of the United States. Johnson's grandparents' cattle-droving headquarters is also included in the park. The park is comprised of two areas. One district is located in Johnson City, Texas, 45 miles west of Austin via U.S. 290. The LBJ Ranch district is located 14 miles west of Johnson City, on the same highway.

Lyndon Baines Johnson was born and raised in the Hill Country of Texas. After serving as U.S. congressman from 1937 to 1948, U.S. senator from 1948 to 1960, vice president from 1960 to 1963, and U.S. president from 1963 to 1968, Johnson returned to Texas and lived there from 1969 until his death in 1973. He is buried in the family cemetery near his birthplace on the Pedernales River.

The Johnson City District includes a visitor center, LBJ's Boyhood Home, and the Johnson Settlement. The visitor center staff is available to answer questions and to offer three films covering LBJ's presidency, a biography of Lady Bird Johnson, and a short orientation of the park and the Hill Country. The building provides two exhibit galleries, a bookstore, and visitor facilities, and is accessible to the handicapped. Park staff provide tours of Johnson's boyhood home. A tour of the Johnson Settlement, accessible by a walking trail, begins at the exhibit center, which contains photographs, text, artifacts, graphics, and audiovisuals, to introduce visitors to the history of the Johnson Settlement and the area. The Johnson Settlement area deals with two historical time periods (1867–72 and 1872–1900). Park rangers in period costume demonstrate heritage skills of the Texas frontier on many weekends throughout the year.

Bus tours of the LBJ Ranch depart from the Lyndon B. Johnson State Historical Park Visitor Center, located on Highway 290, 14 miles west of Johnson City. A $3.00 per person fee is collected to offset the operating costs of this program. Children six and under are admitted free. The tours include the Junction School, Birthplace, Johnson Family Cemetery, Sam Ealy Johnson's Farmhouse, Texas White House exterior, LBJ Ranch lands, and the Pedernales River. At the state park's visitor center, visitors are given an orientation to the state and national historical parks. The former serves as a day-use area for picnicking, interpretation of natural and cultural history (Sauer-Beckmann Living History Farmstead), hiking, swimming, and other recreation activities.

FACILITIES: No food or lodging is available in either district of the park. Both can be found nearby. Drinking water and rest rooms are provided in both visitor centers.

CAMPING: No camping is permitted in the Lyndon B. Johnson National and State historical parks. Pedernales Falls State Park provides camping facilities east of Johnson City. Lady Bird Johnson Municipal Park, in the town of Fredericksburg, has an attractive campground. Other commercial sites providing camping facilities are available throughout the area.

FISHING: Fishing is permitted on the south side of the Pedernales River with a Texas fishing license.

PADRE ISLAND NATIONAL SEASHORE

9405 South Padre Island Drive
Corpus Christi, TX 78418-5597
(512) 949–8068
www.nps.gov/pais/

Padre Island National Seashore, authorized in 1962 and established in 1968, comprises 130,434 acres of wide sand beaches on a grass-covered barrier island that stretches for 113 miles. The park is located along the Gulf Coast in southern Texas. It is accessible via State Highway 358 and Park Road 22 from Corpus Christi or by State Highway 361 from Port Aransas.

Padre Island has been built by a combination of wave action and winds off the Gulf of Mexico. This long barrier island, from a few hundred yards to 3 miles in width, is continually changing as grassy interior sections are gradually covered by windblown sand. In some areas the sands have become stabilized by grasses and shrubs that have long, binding roots. Between the island and the mainland lies Laguna Madre, a shallow body of water with a maximum width of 10 miles.

Life on the island is difficult for plant life, which must constantly battle the sand and wind to gain a foothold. Common mammals living here include coyotes, spotted ground squirrels, and white-tailed deer. There are also more than 350 species of birds that are year-round residents or seasonal visitors passing through on their migration routes. Reptiles that may be seen in the area include two species of rattlesnakes.

Visitor information is available at park headquarters in Corpus Christi, at Malaquite Visitor Center, and at the entrance station. A short self-guiding nature trail begins near the entrance station. Nearly all of the beaches are open to hikers and four-wheel-drive vehicles. Conventional cars may be driven 14 miles south of the park's northern boundary. Even four-wheel-drive vehicles cannot be driven the entire length of the island because of the Mansfield Channel. The gradual slope and warm water along the Gulf beach make swimming a popular activity.

FACILITIES: A snack bar, free showers, and rental equipment for beach use are available at Malaquite Beach during summer months. Motels and restaurants are located at both ends of the island and in Corpus Christi and South Padre Island. Boating supplies and launching ramps are available along the John F. Kennedy Memorial Causeway.

CAMPING: Malaquite Beach Campground (forty-six spaces) provides tables, water, flush toilets, cold-water showers, and a dump station. Primitive camping is permitted on the beaches. Public campgrounds with hookups are located in Nueces County Park north of the seashore boundary and in Cameron County Park at the south end of the island near Port Isabel.

FISHING: Fishing is available year-round in Laguna Madre and the Gulf. Some fish that may be caught, with the respective best seasons, are pompano (April and October), redfish (fall), drum (December to April), red snapper (October to March), and tarpon (October and November). Snapper and tarpon are normally deep-water fish rarely caught from the beaches. Sharks and rays are occasionally caught in the surf. A Texas fishing license is required, as well as a saltwater stamp.

See the map on the following page.

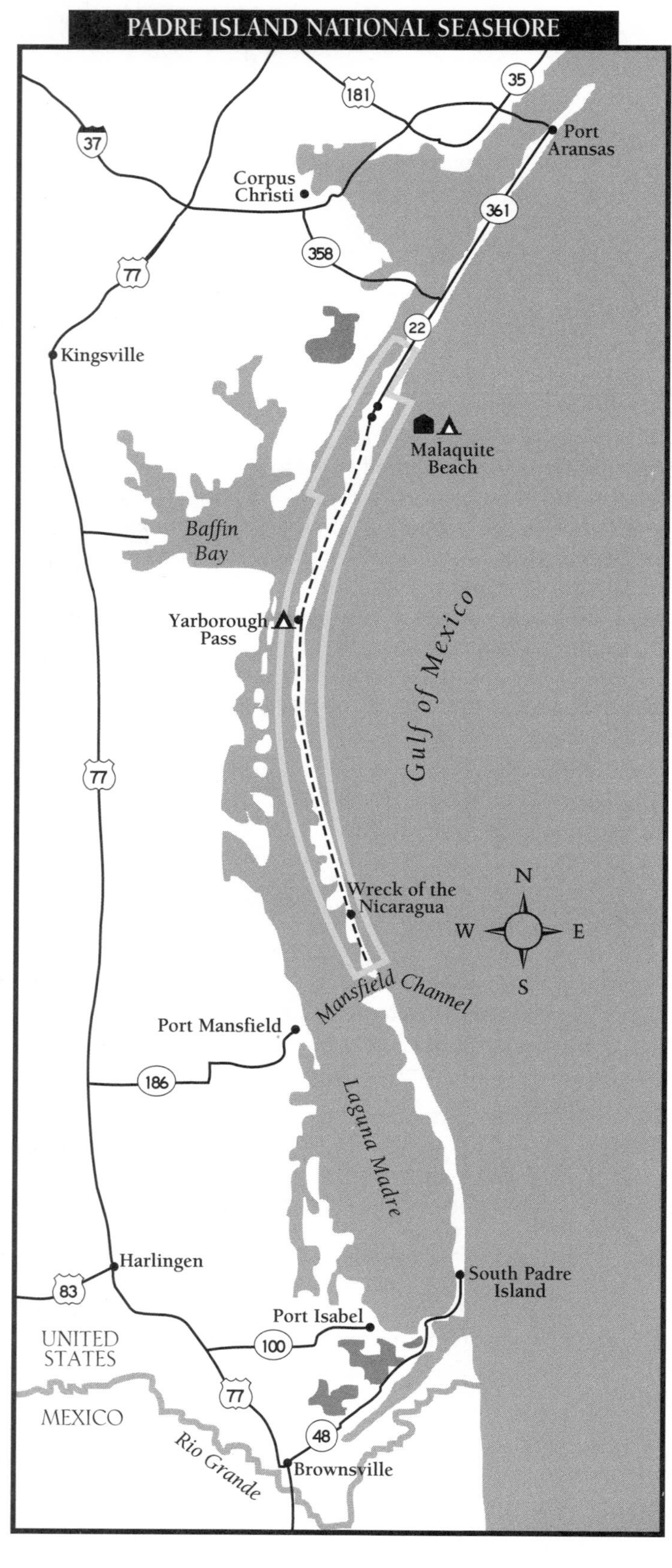
PADRE ISLAND NATIONAL SEASHORE
35
181
37
Port Aransas
Corpus Christi
361
358
77
22
Kingsville
Malaquite Beach
Baffin Bay
Yarborough Pass
Gulf of Mexico
77
Wreck of the Nicaragua
N
W
E
S
Mansfield Channel
Port Mansfield
186
Laguna Madre
Harlingen
South Padre Island
83
Port Isabel
UNITED STATES
100
77
MEXICO
48
Rio Grande
Brownsville

PALO ALTO BATTLEFIELD NATIONAL HISTORIC SITE

1623 Central Boulevard, Suite 213
Brownsville, TX 78520-8326
(956) 541–2785
paal_interpretation@nps.gov
www.nps.gov/paal/

Palo Alto Battlefield National Historic Site is comprised of 3,357 acres and was established in 1991 to preserve a large battlefield on which the initial battle of the 1846–48 Mexican War took place. The historic site also interprets the war and its consequences from the perspectives of both countries. The historic site is located in the southern tip of Texas, approximately 5 miles north of downtown Brownsville. It is at the intersection of FM 1847 and FM 511.

Disputes regarding land ownership and the boundaries of Texas resulted in a two-year war between the United States and Mexico. The Battle of Palo Alto was the first major battle in a series of engagements along the Rio Grande. The Palo Alto battle ensued when Mexican forces decided to overtake Fort Texas, a U.S. base constructed on disputed territory. General Zachary Taylor's 2,300 U.S. troops, sent to stop the bombardment of the fort, encountered 3,400 men under Mexican General Mariano Arista. The resulting cannon battle produced 52 U.S. and 325 Mexican casualties. The battle demonstrated the superior strength of American firepower and the value of academy-educated U.S. military leaders. At the same time, it caused despair among Mexican troops, who had felt they could meet the enemy on even terms.

The historic site is currently under development as the National Park Service works to acquire land and plan facilities. A temporary park headquarters is on the second floor of the International Bank of Commerce building at 1623 Central Boulevard in the city of Brownsville. Here visitors may obtain pamphlets and view displays on the war. A 500-foot trail leading to an overlook of the prairie is 1,000 feet north of the intersection of FM 1847 and FM 511. The remains of the original Fort Texas (later renamed Fort Brown) are on the bank of the Rio Grande near the University of Texas at Brownsville.

FACILITIES: No facilities are currently available at the site.

CAMPING: Numerous private campgrounds are in the Brownsville area.

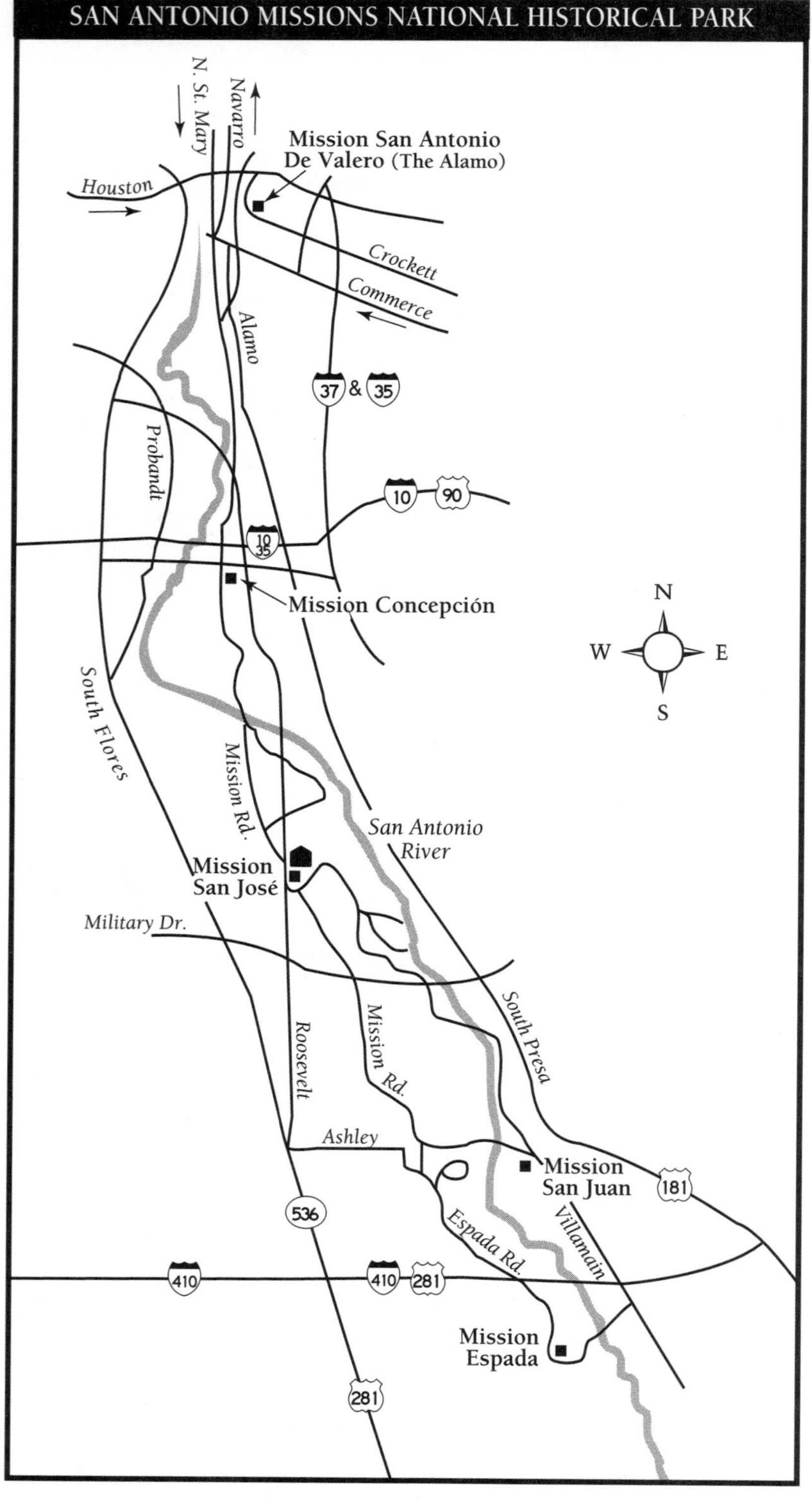

SAN ANTONIO MISSIONS NATIONAL HISTORICAL PARK
N. St. Mary
Navarro
Mission San Antonio
De Valero (The Alamo)
Houston
Crockett
Commerce
Alamo
37 & 35
Probandt
10
90
10
35
Mission Concepción
N
W
E
S
South Flores
Mission Rd.
San Antonio
River
Mission
San José
Military Dr.
South Presa
Roosevelt
Mission Rd.
Ashley
Mission
San Juan
181
536
Espada Rd.
Villamain
410
410
281
Mission
Espada
281

SAN ANTONIO MISSIONS NATIONAL HISTORICAL PARK

2202 Roosevelt Avenue
San Antonio, TX 78210-4919
(210) 534–8833 Headquarters
(210) 932–1001 Visitor Center
www.nps.gov/saan/

San Antonio Missions National Historical Park comprises 835 acres and was authorized in 1978 to preserve four Spanish frontier missions that were part of a colonization system stretching across the Spanish Southwest in the eighteenth century. The park also includes a historic dam and aqueduct, and the ranch associated with Mission Espada (Rancho de las Cabras) near Floresville, Texas. The missions are in south San Antonio along the San Antonio River.

To extend the Spanish culture and propagate the Catholic faith, in the seventeenth, eighteenth, and nineteenth centuries Spain introduced missions from California to Florida. Included in this expansion was a chain of missions established in the eighteenth century along the San Antonio River. These missions provided a link between the missions of east Texas and other Franciscan missions in Mexico. The missions served primarily as religious centers and training grounds for Indians to learn the Spanish culture. Indians who lived at the missions came from a number of hunting and gathering bands. These missions flourished in the mid-1700s, but by the end of the century, the Franciscans had opted to secularize them, turning them over to the local community. The combination of acculturation, intermarriage, and the impact of European diseases had reduced the need for the missions. By 1824, secularization was complete, with mission lands distributed among the mission Indians and the churches transferred to the secular clergy.

The historical park includes four missions along the San Antonio River, south of the city of San Antonio. Except for Mission Espada, which lies just south of Interstate 410, the missions are located between city center and Interstate 410, which loops around San Antonio. A marked driving trail to all of the areas begins in downtown San Antonio at Mission San Antonio de Valero ("the Alamo"). Tour buses with "hop on, hop off" service are available from downtown (near the Alamo) to Missions Concepción and San José. The missions are closed on Thanksgiving, Christmas, and New Year's Day. A wheelchair is available at each mission, but mobility-impaired visitors may have some difficulty with accessibility at Mission San Juan and Mission Espada.

North of Mission Espada is an acequia system that provided irrigation water to crops that were grown at the mission. The system consists of a dam, gravity-flow ditches, and one of the oldest arched Spanish aqueducts in the United States. The system continues to provide water to nearby farms.

FACILITIES: The park visitor center is at Mission San José. Restaurants, lodging, and picnic facilities are available near the historical park. Rest rooms and drinking water are available in the missions.

CAMPING: No camping is available in the park, although commercial camping facilities are located nearby.

FISHING: No fishing is available in the park.

STATE TOURIST INFORMATION

(800) 233–8824

ARCHES NATIONAL PARK

P.O. Box 907
Moab, UT 84532-0907
(435) 259–8161
(435) 259–5279 (TTY)
www.nps.gov/arch/

Arches National Park was established as a national monument in 1929 (changed to a national park in 1971) to preserve 76,489 acres encompassing the country's largest collection of brilliantly colored natural stone arches, spires, windows, and pinnacles. The park is in southeast Utah on U.S. 191, 5 miles northwest of Moab or 28 miles southeast of Interstate 70.

The rock that now presents such beautiful scenery was originally deposited as sand nearly 150 million years ago. This 300-foot layer was eventually formed into rock after being buried by even more sand. Later, the hardened layers of rock were uplifted and cracked. The top stone eroded away, and exposed Entrada Sandstone began to form into shapes that can be seen today. Carved out of red rock by years of rain, frost, and running water, the resulting shapes resemble nearly any fantasy a visitor can imagine. In some areas the stone is softer and the weathering is more rapid. This results in shallow canyons and fins (fin-shaped sandstone rock formations). Arches is particularly spectacular after a summer shower, when streams turn into waterfalls.

The visitor center, located at the main entrance in the southern end of the park, is a recommended stop for the museum and slide program it provides. In addition, visitors may obtain information on activities such as guided walks, sightseeing, and hiking. A road guide is available.

Canyonlands National Park (opposite page)

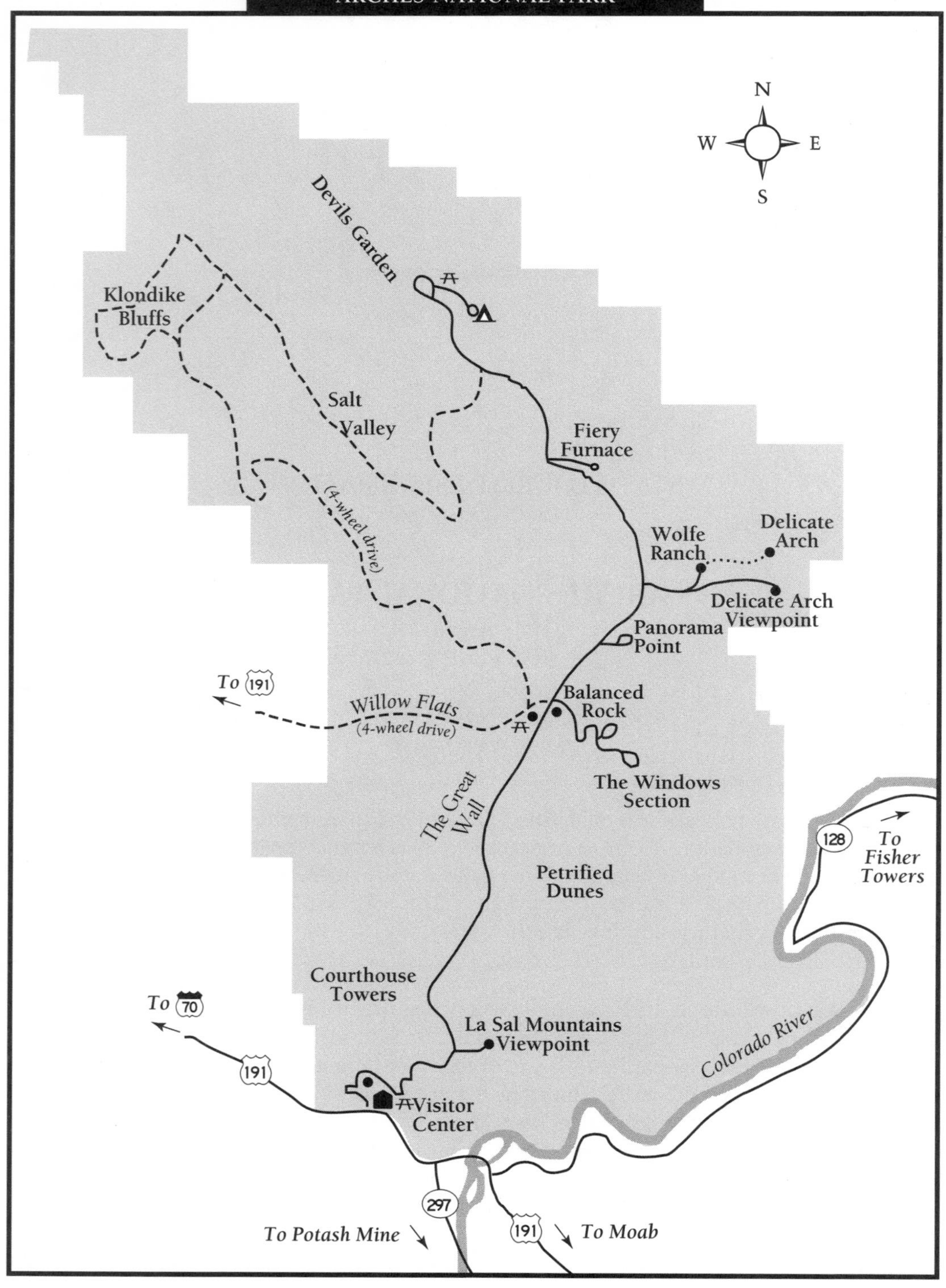
ARCHES NATIONAL PARK
N
W
E
S
Devils Garden
Klondike Bluffs
Salt Valley
Fiery Furnace
(4-wheel drive)
Wolfe Ranch
Delicate Arch
Delicate Arch Viewpoint
Panorama Point
To 191
Balanced Rock
Willow Flats
(4-wheel drive)
The Windows Section
The Great Wall
128
To Fisher Towers
Petrified Dunes
Courthouse Towers
To 70
La Sal Mountains Viewpoint
Colorado River
191
Visitor Center
297
To Potash Mine
191
To Moab

Twenty-three miles of paved roads permit visitors to see much of Arches by car. A paved road begins at the visitor center and ends in the north part of the park. An 8-mile dirt road then continues to Klondike Bluffs in the northwest corner. Klondike Bluffs offers a moderate half-day hike into a remote backcountry area of fins, which contains the massive Tower Arch. Paved roads run to the Windows Section in the east-central part of the park and to Delicate Arch trailhead and viewpoint. The Windows Section is an amazing spectacle of arches, offering close-up views from the road and easy half-mile round-trip walks for closer viewing. A few unimproved roads for four-wheel-drive vehicles are located throughout the park.

Outside the park, State Highway 128, between the park entrance and Moab, takes the motorist in a northeasterly direction along the Colorado River toward Interstate 70. If time permits, be sure to take this drive as it presents some beautiful scenery.

Trails for hiking leave from various points along the main road. The most popular for visitors with only a short time to spare is the leisurely 1-mile walk (each way) through Park Avenue. This worthwhile hike goes through a narrow corridor surrounded by high red-rock walls. Parking lots are located at each end of the trail. The Devils Garden Trail provides access to Landscape Arch, one of the longest natural arches in the world. This trail is a well-maintained gravel path for 1 mile and then becomes primitive for a moderate 5-mile round-trip hike through fins and canyons. Hikers should be aware that daytime temperatures during the summer may reach over 100 degrees Fahrenheit. High temperatures and low humidity make it necessary for hikers to carry a minimum of one gallon of water per person for the full hike.

Perhaps the single most scenic and best-known feature of Arches National Park is Delicate Arch. This isolated formation is located amid bowls and domes. Also within view are the top of canyon walls of the Colorado River and the peaks of the La Sal Mountains. Delicate Arch is reached by means of a 1 1/5-mile paved road and a 1 1/2-mile foot trail. A drive on the paved road to Delicate Arch Viewpoint provides a look across a canyon for a distant view of the arch.

Naturalist-guided walks are made regularly through the Fiery Furnace area (three hours, 2 miles) during summer months when nightly campfire programs are also presented. The Fiery Furnace walk takes hikers through a labyrinth of red-rock fins leading deep into the Furnace, where a surprise arch may wait. On these walks the park naturalists share their knowledge of the wildlife and natural features that make Arches a unique national park. Visitors should also be prepared with good walking shoes, a hat, and water. Reservations and a fee are required for joining the guided walks and must be made at the visitor center.

FACILITIES: No food service or lodging is available within the park. Grocery stores, restaurants, service stations, and motels are available a few miles south of the park in Moab. Modern rest rooms and drinking water are provided at both the visitor center (year-round) and the campground (mid-March through October).

CAMPING: A single improved campground (fifty-two spaces) is located 18 miles north of the park entrance in the Devils Garden area. Tables, grills, and flush toilets (no dump station) are available. Both short and longer hiking trails originate at the campground.

FISHING: No fishing is available within Arches National Park.

BRYCE CANYON NATIONAL PARK

Bryce Canyon, UT 84717-0001
(435) 834–5322
brca_reception_area@nps.gov
www.nps.gov/brca/

Bryce Canyon comprises 35,835 acres. It was authorized as a national monument in 1923 and changed to a national park in 1928. Bryce contains numerous alcoves cut into cliffs along the eastern edge of the Paunsaugunt Plateau. Bordering this winding cliff line is a badlands of vivid colors and fragile forms. The park is located in southwestern Utah and is most easily reached via U.S. 89. Turn east on Utah 12, 7 miles south of Panguitch and drive 17 miles to Utah 63 and the park entrance.

Bryce Canyon is a high section of the Colorado Plateau containing rock strata from the Cretaceous chapter of geologic history. Formed from compacted sediments, this area caps a sequence of rock layers—the most ancient of which are seen in the Grand Canyon. The massive sandstone boulders that represent the middle history may be seen in nearby Zion National Park. At Bryce these earlier rock formations remain buried.

The cliffs in the park are the result of an accumulation of sand, silt, and lime washed into inland lakes and compacted into layers of rock. Later, the lands were uplifted to mountainous heights, and persistent erosion widened gaps and fractures. The resulting color and shapes of the rock formations are Bryce's most outstanding sights.

A visitor center near the entrance provides a slide program and exhibits to help explain the history and geology of the area. A schedule of the park's various programs is posted in the visitor center.

For those with a limited amount of time, a short tour of four excellent viewpoints may be completed within one hour. Sunset Point, Inspiration Point, Bryce Point, and Paria View form a scenic concentration of sculptured red rocks. Trailers should be unhooked and parked at the visitor center parking lot or at your campsite prior to the tour.

A variety of hiking trails is available for visitors. These include the Navajo Loop Trail (1½ miles, one and a half hours) and the Navajo and Peekaboo Loops combined (5 miles, three to four hours) starting at Sunset Point; the Queens Garden Trail (1$\frac{7}{10}$ miles, one and a half hours) beginning at Sunrise Point; Tower Bridge Trail (3 miles, three hours) starting north of Sunrise Point; and the Fairyland Loop Trail (8 miles, four to five hours) beginning at Fairyland or north of Sunrise Point. For the hardy, the Under-the-Rim Trail extends from Bryce Point to Rainbow Point (22 miles). During the summer, ranger-guided programs are offered daily at various points in the park. Activities include geology talks, a Rim Walk near the lodge, and evening campfire programs. A schedule of conducted activities is posted at the visitor center. Morning and afternoon horseback trips are available from a concessioner and begin at the corral near the lodge. For information call (435) 679–8665 or (435) 834–5500.

FACILITIES: Bryce Canyon Lodge, near the rim of Bryce amphitheater, offers three types of sleeping accommodations from April 1 through November 1. Most of the rooms are in cabins or motel-type buildings, with a few suites on the second floor of the attractive main lodge. For information or reservations, write Amfac Parks and Resorts, 14001 East Iliff Avenue, Suite 600, Aurora, CO 80014. Call (303) 297–2757. The main lodge building has a dining room, post office, and gift shop. A store near the Sunrise Point parking area sells groceries and offers pay showers and a laundromat. The nearest hospital is in Panguitch, 26 miles away.

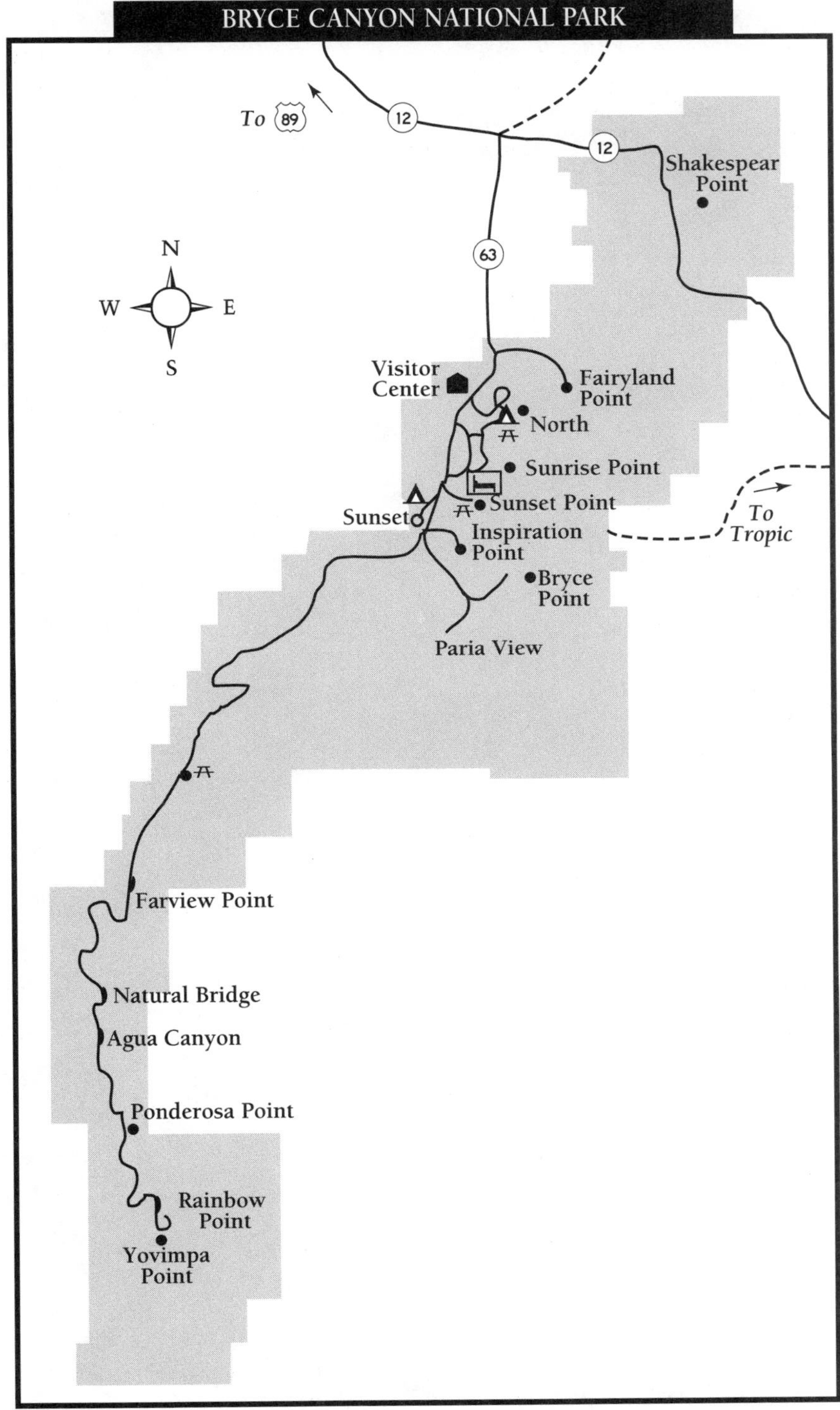
BRYCE CANYON NATIONAL PARK
To 89
12
12
Shakespear Point
63
N
W
E
S
Visitor Center
Fairyland Point
North
Sunrise Point
Sunset
Sunset Point
Inspiration Point
To Tropic
Bryce Point
Paria View
Farview Point
Natural Bridge
Agua Canyon
Ponderosa Point
Rainbow Point
Yovimpa Point

CAMPING: North Campground (109 spaces) is immediately east of the visitor center, and Sunset Campground (109 spaces, one group camp) is 2 miles south. Both provide tables, grills, and flush toilets. The North Campground has a dump station, is closer to the park's developed facilities, and generally fills first.

FISHING: No fishing is available in Bryce Canyon National Park. Trout fishing can be found 22 miles north of the park entrance at Pine Lake and 12 miles west at Tropic Reservoir. The trout are larger and more difficult to catch in Pine Lake.

CANYONLANDS NATIONAL PARK

2282 South West Resource Boulevard
Moab, UT 84532
(435) 259–7164
www.nps.gov/cany/

Canyonlands National Park comprises 337,570 acres and was established in 1964 to protect a geological wonderland of rocks, spires, and mesas. The park is located in east-central Utah and is reached via Utah 191 and its paved extensions.

Canyonlands is an outstanding and unique national park. Its incredible sandstone landscape has been shaped over a period of 300 million years by oceans, winds, and floods. A portion of the park is built on a 1-mile-thick layer of rock and sand covering 3,000 feet of pure salt. The salt was left after the outlet of an inland salt sea was blocked by mountains, and evaporation concentrated the brine into layers of salt. As the salt dissolved and was carried away by underground water, the surface sandstone slowly settled and formed long, narrow, straight canyons (the Needles District).

One of the many spectacular sights in the park is the merging of the Colorado and Green rivers at the confluence. Commercially operated float trips, led by licensed guides, are available down either river. Write the park for a list of available concession trips. Private groups with proper equipment and experience may attempt the trip upon obtaining a permit (fee charged) from the superintendent.

The Needles District in the southern portion of the park contains a "forest" of rock spires. Within the district, Salt Creek and Horse Canyon expose graceful walls and glimpses of past Indian history in the form of rock art and ruins. You must travel 35 miles on a paved road through magnificent canyon country to reach this area. All passenger cars must stop at Elephant Hill, a 40-percent grade traversed only by high-clearance four-wheel-drive vehicles. Tours can be obtained at nearby towns, or jeeps may be rented immediately outside the park at Needles Outpost. Be sure to stop at Newspaper Rock Recreation Site when entering this area on Highway 211.

The Maze District, lying west of the Green and lower Colorado rivers, is the least accessible portion of the park. Two-wheel-drive vehicles can reach the ranger station at Hans Flat most of the time, but the backcountry must be approached by four-wheel-drive vehicles or by foot. The Maze itself is accessible only by foot. This area contains sheer-walled canyons that twist and

View from Inspiration Point, Bryce Canyon National Park (opposite page)

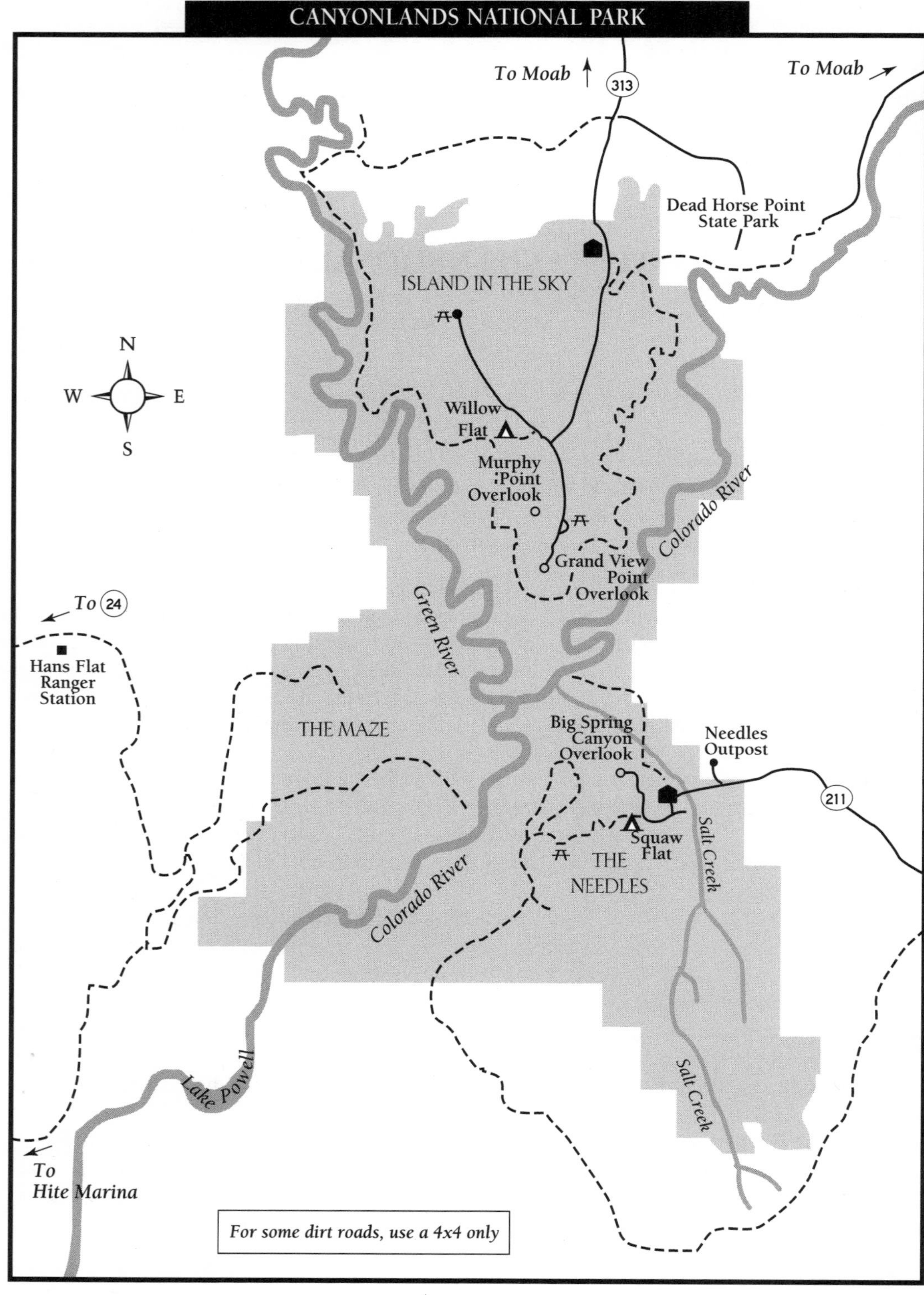
CANYONLANDS NATIONAL PARK
To Moab
313
To Moab
Dead Horse Point
State Park
ISLAND IN THE SKY
N
W
E
S
Willow
Flat
Murphy
Point
Overlook
Colorado River
Grand View
Point
Overlook
To 24
Hans Flat
Ranger
Station
Green River
THE MAZE
Big Spring
Canyon
Overlook
Needles
Outpost
211
Squaw
Flat
THE
NEEDLES
Salt Creek
Colorado River
Lake Powell
Salt Creek
To
Hite Marina
For some dirt roads, use a 4x4 only

wind in a wild manner. Some outstanding pictograph panels are found here. Contact park headquarters for information before visiting the Maze District.

In the north district of the park, Island in the Sky overlooks the remarkable array of landforms to the south that encompass the 40-mile-wide erosional basin of the Green and Colorado rivers. A paved road makes this area completely accessible year-round. From overlooks, visitors can view the White Rim formation, 1,000 feet below, and catch glimpses of the Colorado and Green rivers 1,000 feet below the White Rim. The White Rim Road offers more than 100 miles of four-wheel-drive or mountain bike travel into the backcountry. Shafer Trail Road, for which a four-wheel-drive vehicle is advised, is a thrilling route involving some "testy" driving.

FACILITIES: No overnight accommodations or food services are available within the park. Monticello, Moab, Green River, and Hanksville are the nearest towns providing a full range of services. Needles Outpost, near the Needles entrance, offers fuel, snacks, limited supplies, and scenic flights over the park (March through October). Vault toilets (but no modern rest rooms) are located in the park.

CAMPING: Squaw Flat Campground (twenty-six spaces, three group sites, fee) in the Needles District provides tables, grills, vault toilets, and water. Willow Flat Campground at Island in the Sky (twelve sites) has picnic tables, grills, and toilets, but no water. Primitive campsites without water are located in four-wheel-drive areas.

FISHING: No fishing is available at Canyonlands National Park.

CAPITOL REEF NATIONAL PARK

Torrey, UT 84775-9602
(435) 425–3791
CARE_Interpretation@nps.gov
www.nps.gov/care/

Capitol Reef National Park comprises 241,904 acres and was established to protect one of the largest exposed monoclines in North America. Here narrow high-walled gorges cut through a 100-mile uplift of sandstone cliffs with highly colored sedimentary formations. Capitol Reef remains one of the undiscovered treasures of the National Park System. The park is located in south-central Utah, with the visitor center 37 miles west of Hanksville on Utah 24.

The geology of this high-desert land is derived from millions of years of wind and water erosion. Millions of years ago this part of the country was covered by a shallow sea. As the sea gradually retreated, the land changed to a floodplain and then a desert. The alternation between shallow sea and desert occurred many times during ensuing centuries. Water- and wind-borne sediments deposited during these periods slowly hardened into rock layers of varying color, composition, and thickness. Immense geological forces buckled and tilted the rocks into an upwarp called the Waterpocket Fold. Erosional forces have subsequently dissected and sculptured the Fold. Steeply pitching rock layers spring out of the ground across the breadth of the Fold. The normally horizontal geologic column has been tipped nearly on end, allowing park visitors to drive through 200 million years of geologic history.

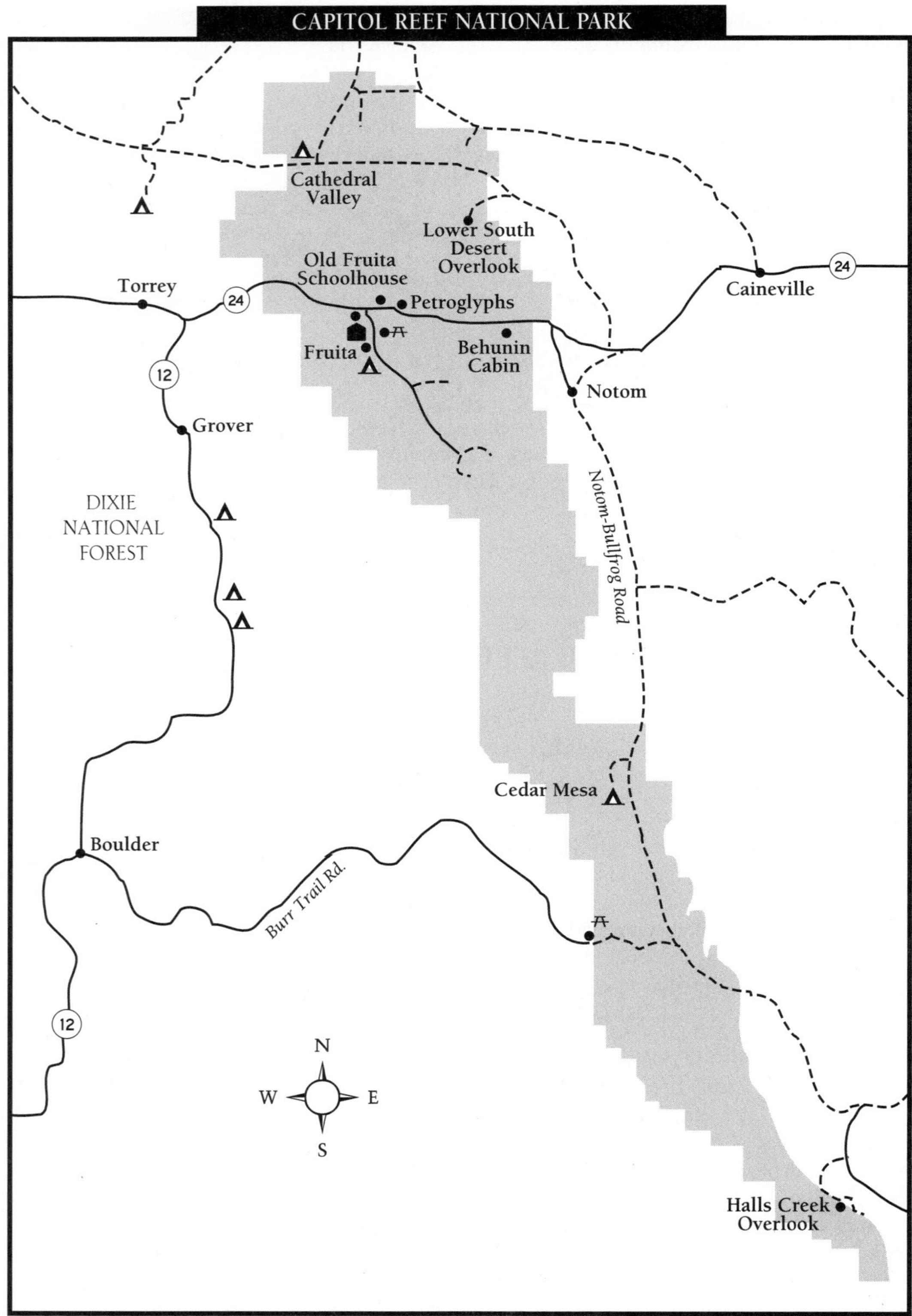

CAPITOL REEF NATIONAL PARK
Cathedral Valley
Lower South Desert Overlook
Old Fruita Schoolhouse
Torrey
24
Petroglyphs
Caineville
24
Fruita
Behunin Cabin
Notom
12
Grover
Notom-Bullfrog Road
DIXIE NATIONAL FOREST
Cedar Mesa
Boulder
Burr Trail Rd.
12
N
W
E
S
Halls Creek Overlook

Perhaps the biggest surprise a visitor will encounter is the oasislike nature of the Fruita District, the park's headquarters area. The sagebrush flats and desert stand in stark contrast to the lush vegetation made possible by irrigation from the Fremont River and Sulphur Creek. Away from the river the land returns to its true desert state.

Capitol Reef National Park was named, in part, because of the resemblance of its rounded white Navajo sandstone to the Capitol Building in Washington. The second half of the name originates from a term used by early prospectors to describe a natural barrier to travel. The area was home to Indians and later to Mormon settlers. The first permanent settlement here occurred at Fruita in 1880. This small community supported up to ten families at one time.

Most of the activity at Capitol Reef is located along or near Highway 24, which cuts through the park in an east-west direction. The visitor center offers a slide program and exhibits to help interpret the area. One mile east is the old Fruita schoolhouse, which has been restored and is open to the public on a limited basis. Ancient Fremont Indian petroglyphs can be found 1/4 mile east of the school and also about 12 miles south of the visitor center in Capitol Gorge. Ranger-guided hikes and interpretive programs take place daily during spring, summer, and fall. Visitors may pick fruit from orchards maintained by the Park Service. Depending upon the season, cherries, apricots, apples, pears, and peaches are available. A paved 10-mile scenic drive heads south from the visitor center. A free pamphlet is provided at the fee station.

FACILITIES: No food or lodging is available in the park. Both may be found in the town of Torrey, 11 miles west of the visitor center on Utah 24. A beautiful, shaded picnic area with picnic tables, grills, and drinking water is located just north of the campground. Modern rest room facilities are available at the visitor center, campground, and picnic area.

CAMPING: The park's developed campground (seventy spaces) is 1 mile south of the visitor center. The campground is surrounded by fruit trees and backs up to the Fremont River. Staying there is one of life's great pleasures. The campsites generally fill every night. Primitive campgrounds (no water) are located approximately 35 miles from the visitor center via dirt roads. Inquire at the visitor center for road conditions and directions.

FISHING: Fishing is available at Capitol Reef National Park. A state fishing license is required and may be purchased locally.

CEDAR BREAKS NATIONAL MONUMENT

2390 West Highway 56 #11
Cedar City, UT 84720-4151
(435) 586–9451
www.nps.gov/cebr/

Cedar Breaks is a 6,155-acre monument that was established in 1933 to preserve a huge multicolored amphitheater that has eroded into the 2,000-foot-thick Pink Cliffs. The park is located in southwestern Utah and can be reached via Utah 14, 27 miles from U.S. 89 at Long Valley Junction, and 23 miles from Interstate 15 at Cedar City. It can also be reached from the north via Utah 143 and Parowan (22 miles) or from U.S. 89 at Panguitch via Utah 143 (36 miles). Zion National Park and Bryce Canyon National Park are 73 and 65 miles away, respectively.

CEDAR BREAKS NATIONAL MONUMENT

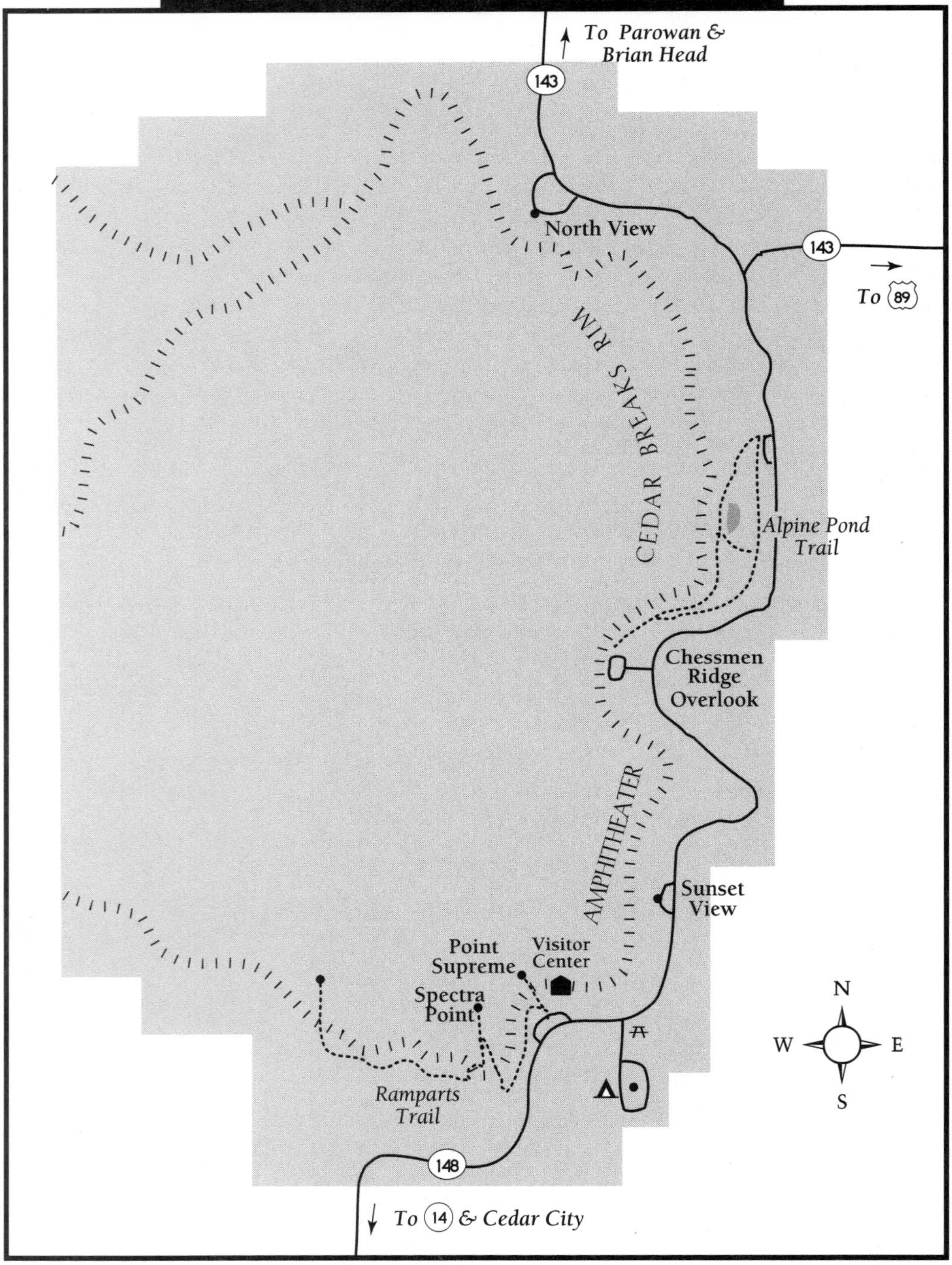

To Parowan & Brian Head
143
North View
143
To 89
CEDAR BREAKS RIM
Alpine Pond Trail
Chessmen Ridge Overlook
AMPHITHEATER
Sunset View
Point Supreme
Visitor Center
Spectra Point
Ramparts Trail
N
W
E
S
148
To 14 & Cedar City

The rock layers that form the amphitheater walls at Cedar Breaks were deposited nearly fifty-five million years ago as a limey ooze in shallow freshwater lakes. Later, as the area was uplifted from near sea level to more than 10,000 feet, the westward-facing limestone wall was exposed to the elements. The softer parts of the limestone have been eroded by centuries of rain, wind, snow, and ice, leaving spires and ridges of spectacular shapes. The period of uplifting was accompanied by volcanic eruptions, and lava may be seen along the road between Cedar Breaks and U.S. 89. The colors of the breaks stem from oxidation of impurities (mainly iron and manganese) contained in the white limestone.

Wildlife in the monument includes mule deer, marmots, pikas, red squirrels, and chipmunks. Birds include the Clark's nutcracker, violet-green swallow, white-throated swift, blue grouse, and golden eagle. Wildflowers begin blooming as the snow melts, and the blooms reach a peak during late July. Bristlecone pines up to 1,650 years old grow within the monument.

Depending upon the weather, the season at Cedar Breaks extends from early June to late October. The visitor center, 1 mile inside the south entrance, contains exhibits on geology and life within the park. The visitor center is open from early June through September and into October, depending on the weather. Much of the monument may be seen from a 5-mile paved road running north and south along Cedar Breaks Rim. Viewpoints with parking areas are located along the road. A number of trails are scattered along 6-mile Rim Drive. Ramparts Trail (2 miles) begins near the visitor center and leads through forests and meadows to a stand of bristlecone pine on Spectra Point (1 mile from the visitor center). Alpine Pond Trail, a self-guided nature trail, leads to an area containing a pond and many wildflowers. Bristlecone Pine Trail is a short walk at Chessmen Ridge Overlook that takes visitors to a stand of bristlecone and limber pine on the rim. Brian Head Peak, 2½ miles north of the north entrance in Dixie National Forest, offers an impressive view of the area. Interpretive presentations are offered daily from late June to Labor Day.

FACILITIES: No food service or overnight lodging is available in the park, but both are found in Cedar City (23 miles southwest), Parowan (19 miles north), and Brian Head (8 miles north). Drinking water and flush toilets are available at the visitor center and the campground.

CAMPING: Point Supreme Campground (thirty spaces) provides tables, grills, water, and flush toilets. The campground is usually open from June 15 to September 15. A number of Forest Service campgrounds are located southeast of Cedar City along Utah Highway 14. There is one Forest Service campground 4 miles south of Parowan off Highway 143.

FISHING: No fishing is available at Cedar Breaks National Monument.

GOLDEN SPIKE NATIONAL HISTORIC SITE

P.O. Box 897
Brigham City, UT 84302-0923
(435) 471–2209
www.nps.gov/gosp/

Golden Spike National Historic Site comprises 2,200 acres and was authorized by Congress in 1965 to commemorate the Union Pacific and Central Pacific railroads' joining on May 10, 1869, to form the first transcontinental railroad. The historic site is located 84 miles northwest of Salt Lake City and 32 miles west of Brigham City.

Although many individuals saw the benefits of a railroad from the Atlantic to the Pacific soon after the development of the steam locomotive, years of debate over the amount of federal financing and the location of an eastern terminus kept the project from commencing. The Pacific Railroad Act, initially signed by President Abraham Lincoln in 1862 and revised two years later, provided that the Union Pacific was to build westward and the Central Pacific eastward. The railroads were given a 400-foot right-of-way through the public domain, twenty sections of land for each mile of completed track, and the loan of government bonds to use as collateral for issuing their own bonds.

The Central Pacific broke ground in January 1863 and the Union Pacific at Omaha in December of the same year. Both railroads experienced manpower shortages until the end of the Civil War, when veterans could be recruited. The Central Pacific helped resolve its labor shortages by hiring Chinese, while the Union Pacific employed European immigrants. It was Congress's intent that the Central Pacific lay track to the California–Nevada border, a point that was later moved 150 miles to the east. Both railroad companies built as fast as possible which resulted in wasteful parallel grades until it was decided in the spring of 1869 that Ogden, Utah, would be the final junction point. On May 10, 1869, the final section of track was laid, and four precious-metal spikes from California, Nevada, and Arizona were symbolically driven with a silver-plated spike maul. Promontory Summit was the temporary junction until early January 1870, when the deal was completed and the junction moved.

By 1904, a shorter route was completed across Great Salt Lake by the Southern Pacific (which had absorbed the Central Pacific), and little traffic was routed through Promontory. In 1942, the rails were pulled and relaid in military depots such as Defense Depot Ogden, Utah, and the Naval Yards in Hawthorne, Nevada.

A visitor center at the park offers exhibits, slide presentations, and films. Nearly 2 miles of track have been relaid on the original roadbed where the rails were joined in 1869. Two operating replica steam locomotives are in operation from the first weekend in May to Columbus Day. Visitor activities include ranger programs, reenactments, the Big Fill Walk, and auto tours. Several special events take place at the historic site, including the annual May 10 anniversary celebration, the Railroaders Festival (second Saturday in August), and the Railroaders Film Festival and Winter Steam Demonstration (weekend after Christmas).

FACILITIES: No overnight accommodations or food services are available in the park, but both are found in Brigham City and Tremonton. The nearest available gasoline is in Corinne, 26 miles from the site. Water and modern rest rooms are located in the visitor center.

CAMPING: No camping is permitted at the site. Hyrum Lake State Park (thirty-five spaces with flush toilets) is located approximately 14 miles northeast of Brigham City on U.S. highways 89 and 91. U.S. Forest Service Box Elder campground (pit toilets) is 1 mile east of Brigham City on U.S. 89. Willard Bay State Park and a private campground are located about 5 miles south of Brigham City, and Crystal Springs Resort is approximately 12 miles to the north.

FISHING: No fishing is available at Golden Spike National Historic Site.

NATURAL BRIDGES NATIONAL MONUMENT

Box 1 Natural Bridges
Lake Powell, UT 84533-0101
(435) 692–1234
nabr_interpretation@nps.gov
www.nps.gov/nabr/

Natural Bridges National Monument comprises approximately 7,500 acres. It was established in 1908 to protect three natural bridges carved from sandstone. The monument is in the southeastern corner of Utah, approximately 4 miles off State Highway 95. Natural Bridges is approached from the east via Highway 95 from Blanding or from the south via Mexican Hat and Highway 261 or from the west via Highway 95 from Hanksville and Hite Crossing.

The making of a natural bridge requires a proper stone with joints or fractures and a desert-type stream with a head of water and sand. In the United States such conditions are most favorable in the Four Corners region of the Southwest. As streams gradually entrench themselves in deep, meandering channels and canyons, they constantly attempt to straighten their courses. During heavy rainstorms, the sand-filled waters batter against the walls in the streambeds. In several places the rock around which a stream winds is so thin that over many centuries a hole is gradually bored through. The result is a natural bridge.

Three natural bridges are highlighted in the monument. Sipapu Bridge (220 feet high, 268-foot span, 31-foot width, 53-foot thickness) has a graceful and symmetrical span with its abutments now far enough from the streambed that the river has little or no cutting effect. Kachina Bridge (210 feet high, 204-foot span, 44-foot width, 93-foot thickness) is the youngest of the three. Its bulk is still being eroded by flood waters in White Canyon. Numerous prehistoric pictographs may be seen on one of its abutments. Owachomo Bridge (106 feet high, 180-foot span, 27-foot width, 9-foot thickness) is the oldest bridge and is no longer eroded by a stream.

A visitor center is located just inside the monument's boundary. A ranger is on duty to answer questions, and a slide program is presented upon request. Ranger talks are given at the campground during the summer when staffing permits. A paved 9-mile loop road links the trailheads to the three bridges.

FACILITIES: No food service or lodging is available at the monument. Drinking water and modern bathrooms are located at the visitor center. The nearest source of gasoline and food is at Blanding, 40 miles away. The nearest overnight accommodations and year-round services are at Blanding and Mexican Hat (45 miles).

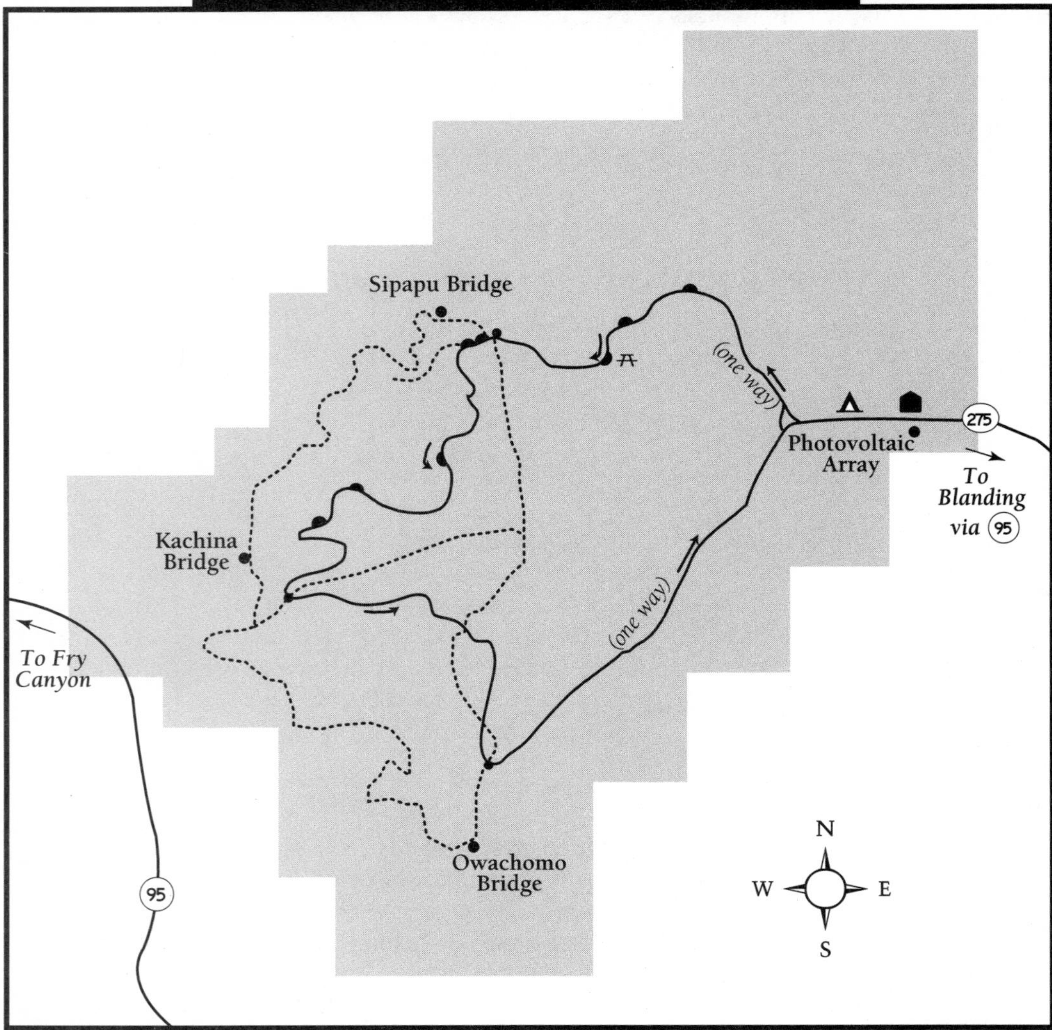

CAMPING: A single campground (thirteen sites) is located near the visitor center. There is a length limit of 26 feet, and only one vehicle per site is permitted. Grills, tables, and pit toilets are available, and modern bathrooms at the visitor center remain unlocked at night. The campground usually fills in the early afternoon during summer months.

FISHING: No fishing is available in the monument.

RAINBOW BRIDGE NATIONAL MONUMENT

c/o Glen Canyon National Recreation Area
Box 1507
Page, AZ 86040-1507
(602) 645–2471
GLCA_CHVC@nps.gov
www.nps.gov/rabr/

Rainbow Bridge National Monument was established in 1910 and comprises 160 acres, including the world's largest known natural bridge. Rainbow Bridge is as high as the nation's Capitol and thicker at the top than a three-story building is tall. The monument is located in south-central Utah on the south edge of Glen Canyon National Recreation Area. It is reached only by a 24-mile trail from Navajo Mountain Trading Post, a 13-mile trail from abandoned Rainbow Lodge, or by boat on Lake Powell. The hiking trails are located on Navajo Reservation land. Permits are required from the Navajo Tribe and may be obtained at P.O. Box 308, Window Rock, AZ 86515.

Millions of years ago slow streams flowed south and west across a broad floodplain in this region. Sand and mud were deposited in thin beds that eventually consolidated to form the reddish-brown layer that is now exposed beneath Rainbow Bridge. Much later, a change in the climate brought winds that deposited great quantities of sand. The resulting pale orange to reddish-brown rock called Navajo sandstone is the material in which Rainbow Bridge and Bridge Canyon have been carved.

Following this period, the next 100 million years saw the area change from desert to swamp to lakes, and the Navajo sandstone was buried under more than 5,000 feet of strata. Approximately 60 million years ago, the region was gradually uplifted, and streams began cutting into the rock layers. Rainbow Bridge was formed during this period by Bridge Creek, which flows today from Navajo Mountain northwest to Lake Powell. For a short description of the formation of a natural bridge, see the narrative on Natural Bridges National Monument.

Water dripping into pools near the bottom of Rainbow Bridge Canyon comes from rainwater seeping through the porous Navajo sandstone. Once it reaches the underlying impervious rock layers, it accumulates and eventually seeps out along the walls of the canyon as springs. Rainwater also causes dark streaks on the side of the arch by washing iron oxide down from the top.

Most visitors to Rainbow Bridge National Monument take the water route of approximately 50 miles from Wahweap, Bullfrog, or Halls Crossing to the landing in Bridge Canyon and then walk about ½ mile (depending on the fluctuating lake level) up the canyon to the bridge. For visitors bringing their own boats, launching ramps are available at Wahweap, Halls Crossing, Bullfrog, and Hite. For visitors interested in the trail trip, inquiry should be made as to trail conditions and availability of water and supplies before beginning. This is a difficult hike, and the roadway leading to the trail is only accessed by high-clearance vehicles.

FACILITIES: There are no facilities within the monument. The nearest town with complete facilities is Page, Arizona, on U.S. 89. Concessioners at Wahweap, Halls Crossing, Bullfrog, Dangling Rope, and Hite sell boating and camping supplies. Tour-boat trips are provided at Halls Crossing, Bullfrog, and Wahweap. A floating complex anchored in Dangling Rope Canyon contains a refueling station, a small store for camping supplies, and a ranger station.

CAMPING: Although picnicking is permitted at Rainbow Bridge, there is no camping within the monument and no picnic area located within the monument boundary. No water is available. Modern National Park Service campgrounds are located at Wahweap, Bullfrog, and Halls Crossing as part of the Glen Canyon National Recreation Area.

FISHING: Fishing is prohibited within the monument. Striped, largemouth, and smallmouth bass, black crappie, and catfish are caught in Lake Powell. A Utah and/or Arizona fishing license is required.

TIMPANOGOS CAVE NATIONAL MONUMENT

RR #3, Box 200
American Fork, UT 84003-9803
(801) 756–5239
www.nps.gov/tlca/

The Timpanogos Cave System was set aside as a national monument in 1922 to preserve a unique limestone cave system. The caves are known for their unusual origin, rare formations, beautiful coloration, and rich human history. The monument is near Utah's two largest population centers—Salt Lake City to the north and Provo/Orem to the south—9 miles east of Interstate 15 on State Route 92.

It is theorized that the caves were dissolved by a weak acid that was created by rising thermal water mixing with the water table. As the Wasatch Mountains rose, the caves drained and calcite formations began to be deposited. The caves are now located more than 1,000 feet above the current water table.

The caves can be reached by hiking on a beautiful 1½-mile paved trail that climbs 1,065 feet. The average round-trip takes about three hours and offers some outstanding views of American Fork Canyon and Utah Valley. The cave system consists of three caves connected by two constructed tunnels. The first, Hansen Cave, was discovered by Martin Hansen in 1887 when he followed cougar tracks to its entrance. Timpanogos Cave was discovered in 1914 by two fourteen-year-old boys, James Gough and Frank Johnson. Finally, Middle Cave was spotted from across the canyon in 1921 by Wayne and Heber Hansen.

The caves are profusely decorated with forty-two different types of cave formations. These formations are highlighted by many natural colors, including purples, greens, and yellows. Small lakes reflect the beauty of these exquisite caves.

A visitor center, located near the parking lot and trailhead, explains the origin and history of the caves. The caves are open from mid-May to November. Visitors can tour the caves with a park ranger after paying a nominal fee. A newly introduced "Introduction to Caving Tour" takes visitors to a section of Hansen Cave that has been closed to the public since 1924. Beginning each May tour tickets can be purchased in advance by calling (801) 756–5238.

FACILITIES: There are two picnic areas with water, tables, grills, and rest rooms. A concession sells lunches and souvenirs.

CAMPING: No camping facilities are available in the monument, but the U.S. Forest Service provides a number of campgrounds nearby in the Uinta National Forest.

FISHING: Fishing is permitted in the American Fork River. A Utah fishing license is required.

ZION NATIONAL PARK

Springdale, UT 84767-1099
(435) 722–3256
www.nps.gov/zion/

Zion National Park contains nearly 147,000 acres of colorful canyons and mesas that create phenomenal shapes and landscapes. Zion is located in southwestern Utah, with the south entrance approximately 150 miles northwest of Las Vegas, Nevada, via Interstate 15 and Utah 9. The southern section of the park is accessed by Utah Highway 9, while access to the northern section is by paved road (exit 40) off Interstate 15.

Zion National Park formed through millions of years of erosion from rain, freezing, and the persistent force of the Virgin River. Scenic drives and trails provide spectacular vistas of

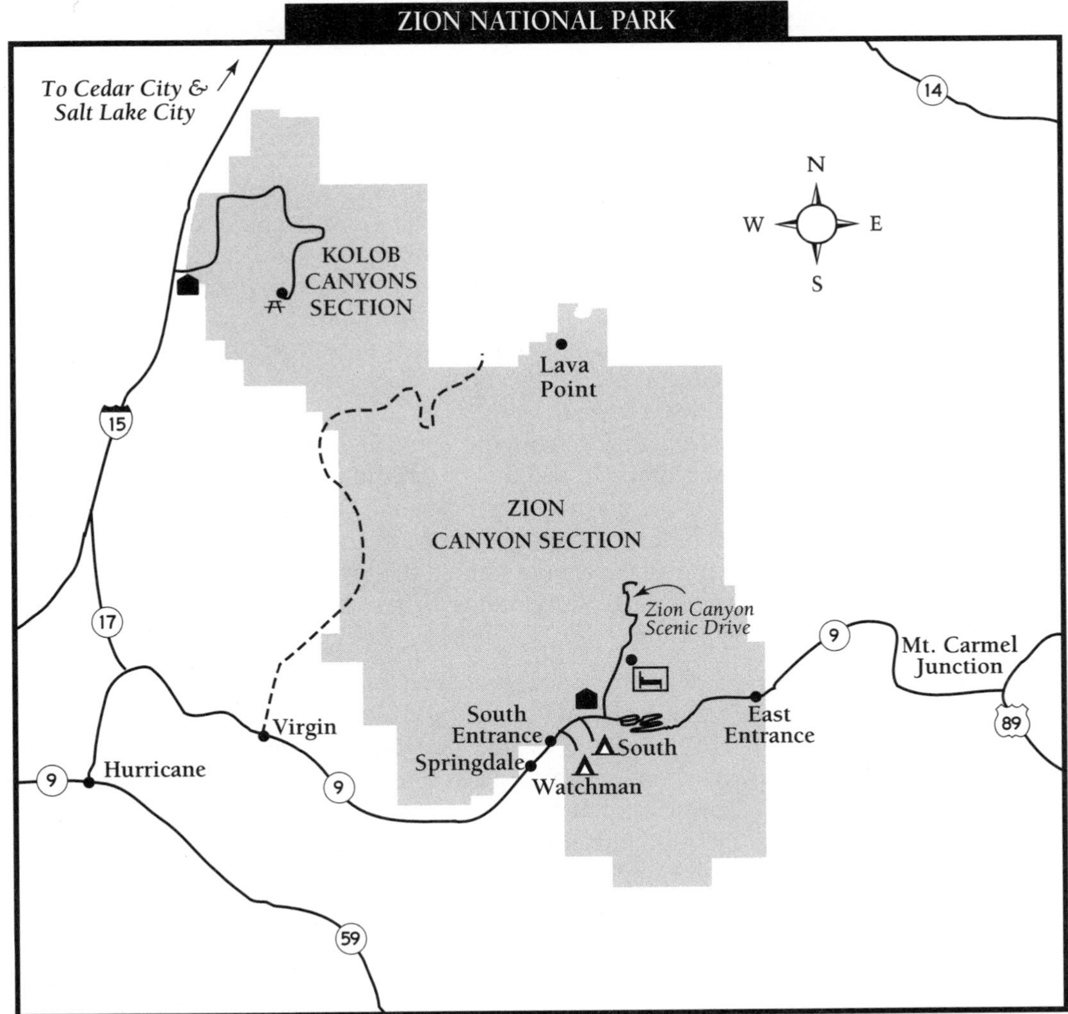

canyons, sculptured rocks, cliffs, and rivers. The park is one of the most beautiful in the National Park System and is Utah's oldest National Park (established in 1909).

In addition to Utah 9, there are three roads in the park. A 7-mile paved road leads from the visitor center through Zion Canyon and past Zion Lodge. Scenic points from the road are The Sentinel, Court of the Patriarchs, Mountain of the Sun, and Great White Throne. A new bus transportation system for the park and the town of Springdale begins in the year 2000 during the busy season of March through October. Visitors not staying at Zion Lodge are required to use the transportation system to enter the park. The system incorporates two loops, one from the south end of Springdale to the park entrance and another from the new Visitor Transit Center at the south end of the park to the end of the scenic drive. Both routes include scheduled stops at various points. The park entrance fee includes use of the transportation system. In the park's northwest section, Kolob Canyons Road is a $5\frac{1}{5}$-mile paved road originating from Interstate 15. This road may be closed by winter snows. A paved road (closed during winter months) connects the town of Virgin with the Kolob Canyons Section to the north. The narrow road leads to Lava Point and includes steep grades.

One of the Zion's most popular visitor activities is hiking, and a great variety of trails wander through this scenic park. The trails range in difficulty from paved loops that can be easily walked in a half-hour to strenuous routes that require a full day to traverse steep grades with sharp dropoffs. It is important to evaluate your physical condition as well as the time available before starting out on a hike. Also remember that summer days are often quite hot. Rangers can recommend trails that are most likely to be compatible with your time and abilities. Two popular paved trails can be walked in an hour or less: One leads to Weeping Rock (round-trip: half-mile, half-hour) and begins at the Weeping Rock parking lot; the other goes to Lower Emerald Pools (round-trip: $1\frac{1}{5}$ mile, one hour) and begins across the road from Zion Lodge. A longer trail (round-trip: 2 miles, two hours) to Middle Emerald Pools begins at the same location. Riverside Walk (round-trip: 2 miles, $1\frac{1}{2}$ hours) is a paved trail that begins at the Temple of Sinawava and follows the Virgin River along the bottom of a narrow canyon. This walk provides views of the Hanging Gardens of Zion, one of the park's most popular attractions. Longer trails begin at the Weeping Rock parking lot and the Grotto picnic area. The park's northwest Kolob Canyons Section also offers trails. All overnight hikes and hikes through Zion Narrows and other narrow canyons require a permit.

The Zion Canyon Visitor Center, near the south entrance, contains exhibits and information on the park's history and geology. In addition, a schedule of events and orientation programs is available. Evening talks are given spring through fall at the lodge and campgrounds. A Junior Ranger Program for children six through twelve years of age operates Memorial Day weekend to Labor Day weekend at the Nature Center. Ranger-guided walks and hikes originate at various points around the park. Reservations for horseback trips within the park may be made at Zion Lodge or by calling (435) 772–3810.

FACILITIES: Zion Lodge has cabin and motel accommodations and is open all year. For information or reservations write Amfac Park and Resorts, 14001 East Iliff Avenue, Suite 300, Aurora, CO 80014. Call (303) 297–2757; fax (303) 297–3175. A dining room and a snack bar are also available at the lodge. Additional food service and accommodations are located in nearby communities. Because of high demand and limited space, reservations are strongly encouraged for facilities within 25 miles of the park. Modern rest rooms and drinking water are available at the lodge, visitor centers, and both campgrounds. Picnic sites are located at the Grotto in Zion Canyon and at the end of the Kolob Canyons Road in the northwest section of the park. A physician is located in Hurricane, 24 miles west of the park. A physician's assistant is sometimes on duty at Zion Canyon Clinic in Springdale during summer.

CAMPING: The two major campgrounds at Zion are near the south entrance. Watchman (156 spaces, some electrical hookups, and seven group campsites) and South (128 spaces) each have tables, grills, flush toilets, and dump stations. Both border the Virgin River. In addition, both are near a private store lying just outside the park. Watchman camping sites can be reserved. Phone (800) 365–2267. Lava Point (six spaces) is a primitive campground off the Kolob Canyons Road and near the West Rim Trail that has pit toilets and no water.

FISHING: Fishing is allowed all year in the Virgin River below Zion Narrows but is poor because of frequent flooding and seasonal fluctuations in water levels. The river is not stocked, and fishing success is very low. A Utah fishing license is required.

STATE TOURIST INFORMATION
(800) 544–1800

EBEY'S LANDING NATIONAL HISTORICAL RESERVE

P.O. Box 774
Coupeville, WA 98239-0774
(360) 678–6084
elba_administration@nps.gov
www.nps.gov/elba/

Ebey's Landing comprises 17,000 acres, including the waters of Penn Cove. It was established as the first national historical reserve in 1978 to preserve a rural community providing a historical record of Puget Sound from its nineteenth-century exploration and settlement to the present. The reserve is located in northwestern Washington on Whidbey Island, about a two-hour drive from Seattle. It is reached from Mount Vernon via the town of Oak Harbor and State Highway 20. The reserve may also be reached by ferry from either Port Townsend or Mukilteo (via Highway 525).

Whidbey Island is the largest of more than 600 islands in Puget Sound. The island was named by Captain George Vancouver who, while exploring this region in 1792, wrote of the beautiful, open, fertile lands. Subsequent years saw the Hudson's Bay Company established near present-day Olympia, but English rule came to an end with the Treaty of 1846, which gave the Oregon Territory to the United States. This treaty opened the Pacific Northwest to settlement. Settlers in wagon trains soon followed the Oregon Trail west and established homesteads, and then farms and communities, around Puget Sound. People also arrived by sailing ship, as did most early settlers of central Whidbey Island.

North Cascades National Park (opposite page)

EBEY'S LANDING NATIONAL HISTORICAL RESERVE

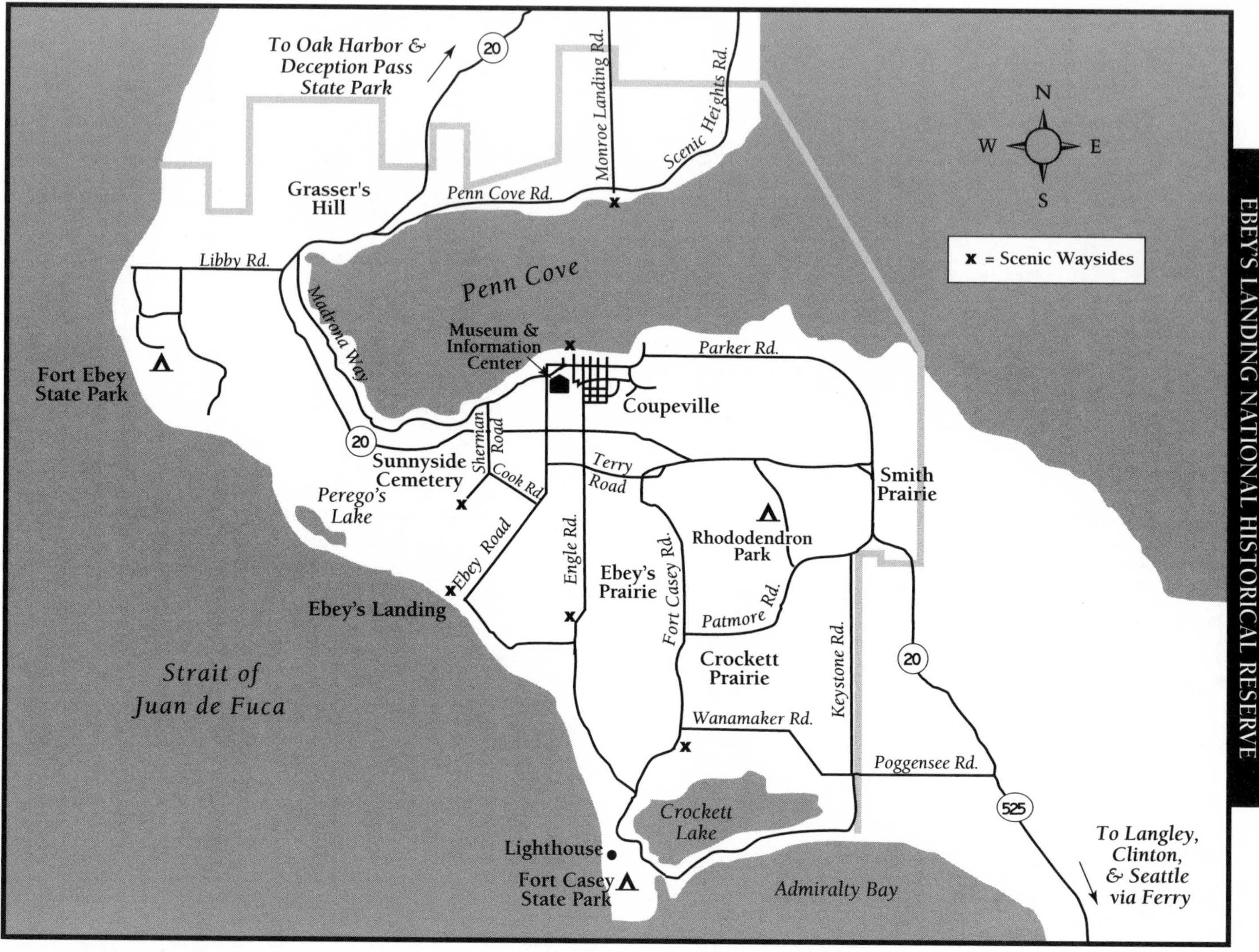

Ebey's Landing National Historical Reserve provides a glimpse of this early settlement. The town of Coupeville was settled by New England sea captains. There are forty-eight historic structures, including many of the sea captains' homes, in the town. An additional fifty structures on the National Register are outside Coupeville but within the reserve. The Historical Society maintains a museum of settler life, and there is National Park Service information in the free museum.

Ebey's Landing, where the island's first American settler landed, is across the island from Coupeville. The beach and a bluff hiking trail are part of the Washington state park system. There are spectacular views of the Olympic Mountains and Puget Sound from the beach and the trail. Several scenic waysides offer beautiful views of open waters, farmland, and historic structures.

The open fields between Coupeville and Ebey's Landing are natural prairies that have been farmed continuously since the 1850s. The farmers who live here today, many themselves descendants of early settlers, continue to plow land claims established by their families in the 1800s. Many of the farmhouses that dot the prairie are the original homes or are built on the foundations of the homes of the first settlers.

There are two state parks within the reserve. Fort Casey, a turn-of-the-century coastal-defense fort, has a lighthouse (with interpretive center), gun emplacements, and a beach to explore. Fort Ebey, established during World War II, offers beach hiking, picnicking, and exploration of World War II gun emplacements.

FACILITIES: Food and lodging are available in Coupeville.

CAMPING: Fort Casey State Park (360–678–4519) has thirty-five sites with tables, grills, and flush toilets, but no showers. Fort Ebey State Park (360–678–4636) has fifty sites with tables, grills, flush toilets, and showers. Both parks offer fishing and swimming. Camping is also available at Rhododendron Park.

FISHING: Surf fishing and a boat ramp are available at Fort Casey State Park. A boat ramp is at Coupeville.

FORT VANCOUVER NATIONAL HISTORIC SITE

612 East Reserve Street
Vancouver, WA 98661-3811
(360) 696–7655
www.nps.gov/fova/

Fort Vancouver National Historic Site was authorized as part of the National Park Service in 1948. It comprises 165 acres commemorating what was the economic, political, social, and cultural hub of the Pacific Northwest. Fort Vancouver is located within the city limits of Vancouver, Washington, and is reached by exiting east off Interstate 5 at the Mill Plain Boulevard interchange and then following signs to the visitor center on East Evergreen. From Interstate 205, exit on Washington 14, drive west 6 miles, take Interstate 5 north and exit at Mill Plain.

After 1800, traders from Canada, England, the United States, and several European countries were competing for the fur resources of the Pacific Northwest. After years of struggle a British firm, Hudson's Bay Company, gained supremacy in the region. In an attempt to strengthen its claim to the territory, in 1824 the company decided to move its western headquarters from a location at the mouth of the Columbia River to a site about 100 miles upstream. It was here that Fort Vancouver was built.

The fort became the center of activity in the Pacific Northwest. Not only did it serve as the headquarters to a huge commercial empire, it was also the center of a farming and manufacturing community and provided much of the cultural and social life for the Oregon Country. At the height of its importance (1844–46), the fort included twenty-two major structures within a palisade of upright logs. In addition, thirty to fifty wooden dwellings were located on the plain to the west and southwest of the stockade.

The Treaty of 1846 between the United States and Great Britain established the forty-ninth parallel as the southern boundary of Canada and placed Fort Vancouver on American soil. A U.S. Army camp was established nearby in 1849, and in 1860 the fort was abandoned by the Hudson's Bay Company. Six years later, the palisade was destroyed by fire.

The historic site is open daily from 9:00 A.M. to 5:00 P.M. (to 4:00 P.M. from November through February) except Thanksgiving Day and December 24 and 25. The visitor center contains a museum, and a small store, and offers a fifteen-minute audiovisual presentation depicting the fort's early history. The National Park Service has reconstructed the palisade and some of its buildings. Guides are available to take visitors through the reconstructed chief factor's house, kitchen, bakehouse, blacksmith shop, Indian trade shop, carpenter shop, fur store, and dispensary.

FACILITIES: No food or lodging is provided by the Park Service, but both are available nearby. Rest rooms and drinking water are available in both the visitor center and the fort. A picnic shelter is next to the visitor center.

CAMPING: No camping is permitted at the site. Battleground Lake State Park (thirty-five regular sites, fifteen walk-in tent sites) provides tables, grills, flush toilets, showers, swimming, and fishing, but no hookups. To reach the state park, drive 20 miles northwest of Vancouver via Interstate 5 and State Highway 502. Directions are available at the Fort Vancouver visitor center.

FISHING: No fishing is available within the park.

KLONDIKE GOLD RUSH NATIONAL HISTORICAL PARK

117 South Main Street
Seattle, WA 98104-2540
(206) 553–7220
KLSE_Ranger_Activities@nps.gov
www.nps.gov/klse/klse_vvc.htm

Klondike Gold Rush was established in 1979 to commemorate the 1898 gold rush to the Yukon. The park is divided into two sections, with the main area located in Skagway, Alaska (see Klondike Gold Rush National Historical Park in the Alaska section of this book), and an interpretive center in Seattle. The Seattle center is in the Union Trust Annex at 117 South Main Street, 2 blocks north of the Kingdome.

The city of Seattle was the focal point through which thousands of goldseekers poured on their way to riches in the Yukon. Seattle advertised itself as the place where miners could outfit themselves before setting off by steamer for the gold fields. It was the people and money brought by the Klondike gold rush that made Seattle the trade and financial center of the Northwest.

The park's visitor center in the Union Trust Annex contains exhibits and a variety of films and slide presentations explaining the gold rush and Seattle's role in the historic event. Films and slide presentations are offered on a request basis from mid-September through mid-June. From mid-June to early September, a walking tour, mining demonstrations, films, slide presentations, and ranger talks are offered on a set basis. Call or write the park for details. The center is open daily from 9:00 A.M. to 5:00 P.M. except on Thanksgiving, Christmas, and New Year's Day. Union Trust Annex is within the Pioneer Square Historic District, an area of the city that has been restored. Pioneer Square contains a number of gold rush–era buildings and many unique shops, restaurants, and antiques dealers.

FACILITIES: Rest rooms and drinking water are available at the visitor center. Restaurants and lodging are available nearby.

CAMPING: No camping is permitted at the park. The nearest public camping is at Saltwater State Park (fifty-two spaces), 2 miles south of Des Moines on Highway 509. The park has hiking trails and a concession stand.

FISHING: No fishing is available at the park.

LAKE ROOSEVELT NATIONAL RECREATION AREA

1008 Crest Drive
Coulee Dam, WA 99116
(509) 633–9441
www.nps.gov/laro/

Lake Roosevelt National Recreation Area (renamed from Coulee Dam NRA in 1997) was added to the National Park System in 1946. The area's principal feature is 151-mile-long Franklin D. Roosevelt Lake, which was formed by Grand Coulee Dam. Approximately 55,000 acres of the lake and its shoreline lie within the NRA. The remainder is within the Colville and Spokane Indian Reservations and is managed by the respective tribes. The park is located in northeastern Washington, and its eastern side is bordered by Washington Highway 25.

Millions of years ago, this region was the scene of successive volcanic lava floods that filled the Columbia Basin and pressed against the granite mountains to the north. As the Columbia River was forced into new channels by each additional flow, it eventually made a large westward bend. During the last ice age, catastrophic floods with ten times the flow of all the rivers on earth raged through this area, carving the spectacular canyon of The Grand Coulee.

Grand Coulee Dam is the largest hydroelectric dam on the Columbia River. Excellent views of the structure may be obtained from the canal headworks, above the west end, or from Crown Point, 2½ miles north on Washington 174. Behind the dam, Franklin D. Roosevelt Lake stretches nearly to the Canadian border.

LAKE ROOSEVELT NATIONAL RECREATION AREA

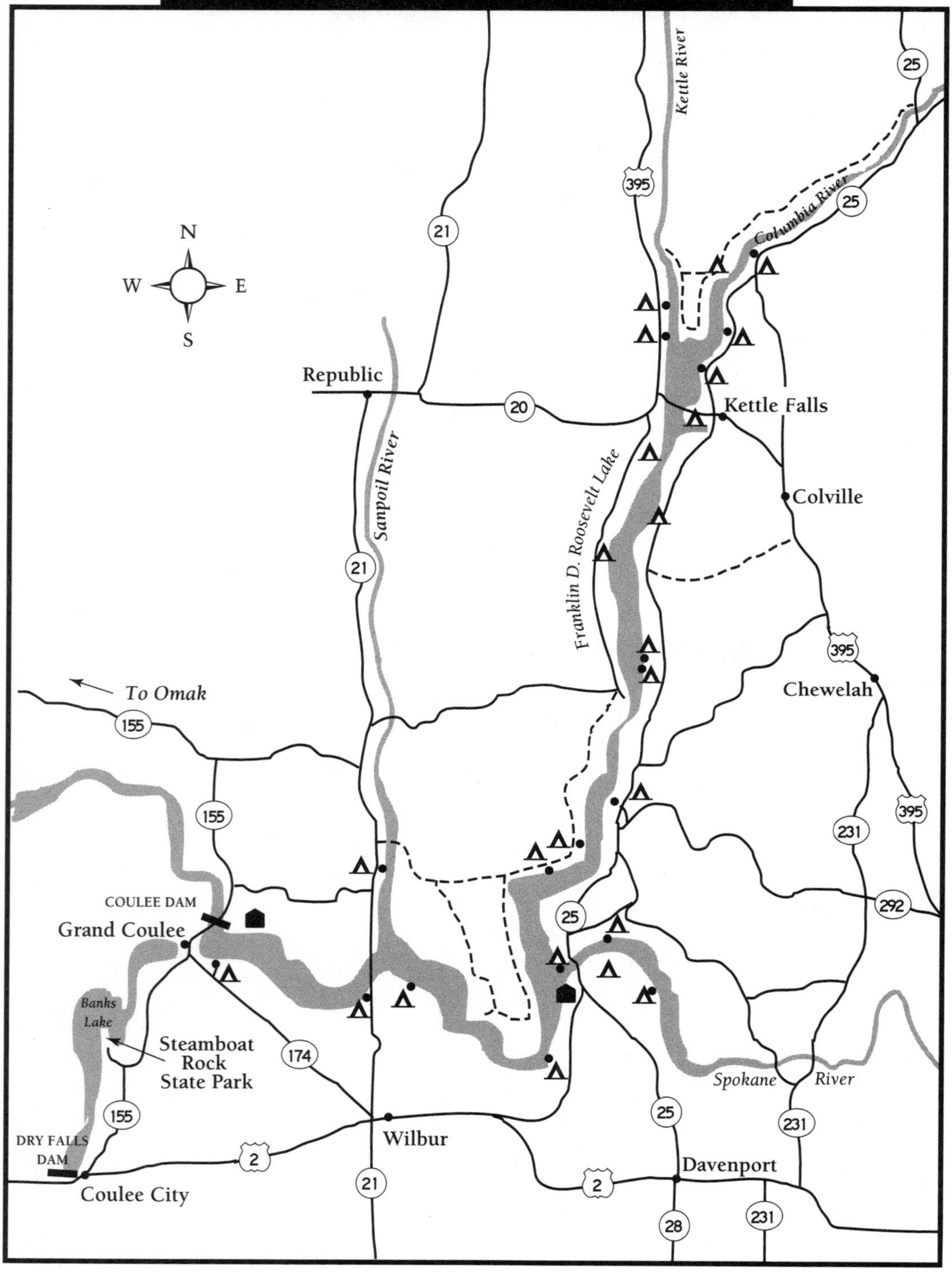

N
W
E
S

Kettle River
Columbia River
Republic
Kettle Falls
Colville
Sanpoil River
Franklin D. Roosevelt Lake
Chewelah
To Omak
COULEE DAM
Grand Coulee
Banks Lake
Steamboat Rock State Park
Spokane River
Wilbur
Davenport
DRY FALLS DAM
Coulee City

25
395
21
20
155
174
2
28
231
292

Driving northward by way of Fort Spokane, the road passes through the rolling wheatlands of eastern Washington before nearing the lake and plunging into evergreen forests. A museum and self-guided trail at Fort Spokane tell the story of the frontier period of the American West. From Fort Spokane, Highway 25 winds northward in the narrow valley between the Huckleberry and Kettle River Mountains. The Gifford ferry provides access to the lake's west side and a different type of scenery. For another scenic drive, cross the lake on the Keller ferry and follow the Sanpoil River north to the old mining town of Republic. From there a drive east over Sherman Pass goes past numerous spots for camping, fishing, picnicking, or relaxing.

Most of the activity in Lake Roosevelt NRA is water-related. Waterskiing is popular within the shelter of larger tributaries such as the Spokane, Kettle, and Colville rivers and Sanpoil Bay. Sailing is excellent because a breeze usually blows on the lake from the surrounding hills.

FACILITIES: Food, lodging, groceries, gasoline, and other services are available in Grand Coulee, Coulee Dam, and other nearby towns. Similar services are provided at Colville, Kettle Falls, and Northport on the northern portion of the lake. Small stores with groceries are located at Seven Bays and McCoys marinas, and at marinas at Keller Ferry, Kettle Falls, Two Rivers, and Daisy. Snack bars are available at Keller Ferry, Kettle Falls, Porcupine Bay, and Spring Canyon. Smaller towns and nearby Indian reservations usually sell gasoline, groceries, and snacks.

CAMPING: Thirty-two campgrounds surround Franklin D. Roosevelt Lake. Those with tables, grills, water, and flush toilets are Spring Canyon (seventy-eight spaces, one group camp, dump station), Keller Ferry (fifty-five spaces, one group camp, dump station), Fort Spokane (sixty-seven spaces, one group camp, dump station), Porcupine Bay (thirty-one spaces, dump station), Hunters (thirty-nine spaces), Kettle Falls (eighty-nine spaces, one group camp, dump station), and Evans (forty-six spaces). Other campgrounds shown on the map are less developed but can be reached by auto. A number of campgrounds have access by boat only and are not included on the map. All campgrounds are open during summer months only, except Hunters and Porcupine Bay, which have a season of May through October. Campgrounds on the west arm of the lake are on open terraces where shade is limited, while those on the north arm are generally in forested areas.

FISHING: More than thirty species of fish make fishing one of the most popular activities in the park. Common catches include walleye (one to four pounds), rainbow trout (one to three pounds), white sturgeon (one hundred to three hundred pounds), yellow perch (three to five pounds), lake whitefish (two to three pounds), and kokanee salmon (one to three pounds). Other fish present are cutthroat trout, bass, carp, pike, white perch, and sunfish. Trolling is a popular method of fishing these waters, with dawn and dusk being the best times.

MOUNT RAINIER NATIONAL PARK

Tahoma Woods Star Route
Ashford, WA 98304
(360) 569–2211
mora_internet_committee@nps.gov
www.nps/mora/

Mount Rainier National Park was established in 1899 and comprises 368 square miles, including the greatest single-peak glacial system in the contiguous United States. The summit and slopes of the ancient volcano are surrounded by glaciers, dense forests, and subalpine flowered meadows. The park is located in southwestern Washington, 80 miles south of Seattle via Interstate 5 and Highways 512, 7, and 706 or Interstate 5 and Highways 161, 7, and 706, and 64 miles west of Yakima via U.S. 12 or 410.

Mount Rainier National Park was named after what has become one of the most-photographed mountains in the United States. The 14,410-foot peak collects snowfall in large quantities as the wet Pacific air flows eastward; it is not unusual to have the three-story Paradise Inn on the park's south side covered up to its roofline during winter. The mountain's two craters and general shape betray its earlier life as an active volcano. Some experts believe Rainier is still a likely candidate for an eruption because steam from within the mountain continues to carve tunnels in the summit ice cap.

Mount Rainier is best known for the numerous glaciers that flow down its slopes. Thirty-five square miles of ice are contained in twenty-six named glaciers. These ice flows have carved deep valleys into the mountain's sides. The huge quantities of ice and snow create dangers that are unique to this type of mountain including mudflows, snow and ice avalanches, and rock slides.

The most popular activities at Rainier are climbing and hiking. The ultimate is a climb to the summit of Mount Rainier. A guide service at Paradise offers one-day snow-and-ice climbing seminars and rents climbing equipment. The summit trip is a two-day affair. Two hundred and forty miles of maintained trails, both short and long, begin at various locations around the mountain. Trail guides and maps are sold at visitor centers. The center at Longmire is open all year; those at Sunrise and Ohanapecosh are open in summer only. Paradise is open year-round but only on weekends from mid-October through April.

Self-guided nature trails are located at Carbon River, Sunrise, Longmire, Ohanapecosh, and Paradise. Naturalist-guided walks and evening programs are available during summer months. Weekly schedules are posted at campgrounds and visitor centers. The Carbon River Road is subject to being washed out for long periods.

During winter, food, lodging, gifts, and recreation equipment are available at Longmire. Inner tubes and platters may be used only in designated runs near the Paradise ranger station. Information about cross-country ski routes and snow conditions is available from rangers. Snowmobiles are permitted on designated roads only. Except for the road from the Nisqually entrance to Paradise, park roads are usually closed from late November to June.

FACILITIES: As one of the country's older and more popular areas administered by the National Park Service, Mount Rainier National Park contains a wide variety of facilities for visitors. Overnight accommodations are available at the National Park Inn at Longmire (year-round) and

Mount Rainier National Park (opposite page)

MOUNT RAINIER NATIONAL PARK

Paradise Inn (late May to early October). For reservations and rates, write Mount Rainier Guest Services, P.O. Box 108, Ashford, WA 94304 (360–569–2275). Outside the park, accommodations are available at Ashford, Packwood, White Pass, Crystal Mountain, and Enumclaw.

Fast-food service is available in the visitor center at Paradise; restaurant service is provided all year at Longmire and at Paradise Inn during its season of operation. A snack bar is available only at Sunrise. Groceries are sold at Sunrise during summer and at Longmire year-round. Gas is not available in the park.

CAMPING: Improved campgrounds with grills, tables, flush toilets, and drinking water are located at Cougar Rock (200 spaces, dump station), Ohanapecosh (205 spaces, dump station), and White River (117 spaces). Campgrounds without flush toilets are located at Ipsut Creek (twenty-nine spaces, no potable water), Mowich Lake (thirty undesignated sites, no potable water, walk-in only), and Sunshine Point (eighteen spaces). The latter is the only campground open all year.

FISHING: Fishing is permitted all year without a license. Most lakes melt by early to mid-July. Fishing through ice is not permitted, but alpine lakes and streams contain cutthroat, rainbow, brown, and brook trout. The Ohanapecosh River and its tributaries are open to fly fishing only.

NORTH CASCADES NATIONAL PARK; LAKE CHELAN NATIONAL RECREATION AREA; ROSS LAKE NATIONAL RECREATION AREA

2105 State Route 20
Sedro-Woolley, WA 98284-9394
(360) 856–5700
noca_interpretation@nps.gov
www.nps.gov/noca/

The North Cascade National Park Service complex, established in 1968, comprises 1,069 square miles of magnificent scenery. Here, high peaks intercept moisture-laden winds, producing glaciers, icefalls, and waterfalls in a wild alpine region where lush forests and meadows thrive. The park is located in northern Washington—the north boundary borders on Canada. Access to the area is gained via Washington State Route 20, which bisects the park through a portion of the Ross Lake section. Hiking access and roadside views of the northwest corner are available from Washington 542 east from Bellingham. Access to Stehekin Valley is by boat, float plane, or trail. Vehicle access to Ross Lake is by graded gravel road from Canada.

The North Cascades complex contains alpine scenery unmatched in the continental United States. Some visitors believe that this is the most beautiful park in the National Park System. The area's heavy precipitation has produced alpine lakes, ice caps, more than 300 glaciers (almost half the glaciers in the contiguous United States), and glacier-carved canyons like Stehekin at the head of Lake Chelan. This lake is 55 miles long, from 1 to 2 miles wide, and occupies a glacial trough exceeding 8,500 feet in depth from lake bottom to valley crest. Ross Lake is 24 miles long and 2 miles across at its widest point, while Diablo Lake and Gorge Lake occupy 910 acres and 210 acres, respectively. Three dams impounding Ross, Diablo, and Gorge lakes provide electrical power for Seattle.

About 386 miles of hiking and horse trails exist throughout the three areas of the North Cascades group. Permits are required for backcountry camping, and are issued on a first-come, first-served basis. Horses and mules are for rent in nearby communities, and professional guide and packtrain services are available. Cross-country skiing is good at Stehekin during winter months, but no developed ski areas are in the park. The park and recreation areas are open year-round but access is limited by snow in winter. State Route 20, the major access to Ross Lake National Recreation Area, is partially closed from approximately mid-November to mid-April depending on weather, snow depths, and avalanche hazards. Scheduled commercial boat service is available on Diablo and Chelan lakes. Three types of boats are available at Chelan, with the first leaving the town of Chelan at about 8:30 A.M. Later boats and daily round-trips are available. Call the Lake Chelan Boat Company (509–682–2224) for schedule information and prices. Interpretive programs are offered at various locations in the park, as staffing permits.

FACILITIES: Guest accommodations are available in the recreation areas and in smaller communities within and near the park. For information or reservations write North Cascades Stehekin Lodge, P.O. Box 457, Chelan, WA 98816 (509–682–4494); Ross Lake Resort, Rockport, WA 98283 (206–386–4437).

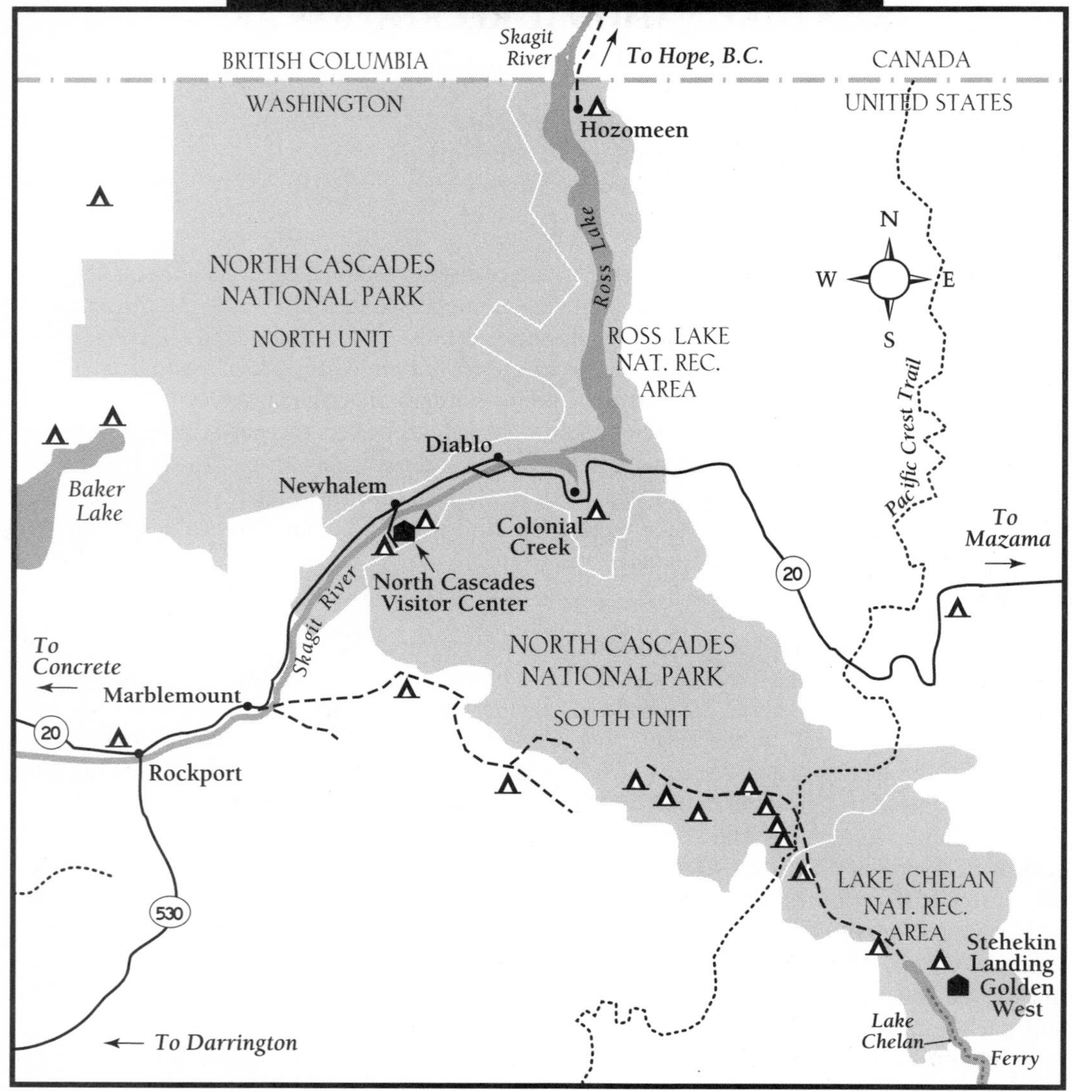

CAMPING: Three developed campgrounds with vehicle access are located along State Route 20 in Ross Lake NRA. Colonial Creek (164 spaces) has tables, grills, flush toilets, and a dump station. Goodell Creek (twenty-two sites and two group camps) provides tables, grills, water, and pit toilets, and is open all year. Only group camps can be reserved. Newhalem Creek (129 spaces) offers flush toilets and a dump station. Hozomeen Campground (122 spaces) in Ross Lake NRA is reached via a 40-mile gravel road from Hope, British Columbia. This campground is less developed but has water and pit toilets.

In the Lake Chelan National Recreation Area, Purple Point (fourteen sites) at Stehekin is within walking distance of the boat landing. It has drinking water and pit toilets. Access to all campgrounds in the Lake Chelan National Recreation Area is by boat, shuttle bus, float plane, or trail only.

FISHING: The principal game fish are trout—rainbow, brook, cutthroat, and Dolly Varden. Lake Chelan offers fishing for kokanee salmon. In addition to the two big lakes, there are many small mountain and valley lakes and countless streams. A Washington state fishing license is required.

OLYMPIC NATIONAL PARK

600 East Park Avenue
Port Angeles, WA 98362-6757
(360) 452–0330
www.nps.gov/olym/

Olympic is a 922,651-acre diverse wilderness that has mountains, active glaciers, Roosevelt elk, more than 60 miles of wild scenic ocean shore, and one of the finest remnants of undisturbed temperate rain forest in North America. The park's two sections are located in the northwestern corner of Washington. Main access is via U.S. 101 and its numerous side roads. Roads penetrate only the perimeter of the park. Information on ferry schedules is available by calling (800) 843–3779 or on the Internet at www.wsdot.wa.gov/ferries/current/.

The Olympic Mountains are composed partially of sedimentary rocks, such as sandstone and shale, formed from sand and silt deposited in the sea that covered this region millions of years ago. These rocks were later uplifted and carved by erosion and glaciers. There are currently 266 glaciers in the Olympic Mountains; the three largest are found on 7,965-foot Mount Olympus. The strip of park along the Pacific contains some of the most primitive coastline to be found in the continental U.S. The rocky shoreline is the home of birds, seals, and other marine wildlife.

The park has three visitor centers—Olympic National Park Visitor Center near Port Angeles (open all year), the Hoh Rain Forest Visitor Center, and Hurricane Ridge Visitor Center. Each contains exhibits, slide programs, and park personnel to answer visitors' questions. Self-guided nature trails are available at Hoh and also at Ozette, Staircase, Elwha, Quinault, Sol Duc, Lake Crescent, and Hurricane Hill. During summer months park rangers lead guided walks and present evening campfire programs. Six hundred miles of trails wander throughout the park.

The west side of the Olympic Peninsula has the wettest winter climate in the continental United States, with annual precipitation of more than 160 inches in some sections. Easy access to the rain forest is available at Hoh and Quinault.

The park's high country is reached from the park's north side at Heart O' The Hills. Hurricane Ridge provides excellent views of Mount Olympus and subalpine meadows. Winter activities at Olympic National Park include cross-country skiing and snowshoe walks along open subalpine ridge tops.

FACILITIES: Four overnight lodging facilities are located within the borders of Olympic National Park. Three lodges are situated on the north end of the park. Lake Crescent Lodge (360–928–3211), on the southeast shore of Lake Crescent, offers a rustic main lodge with a limited number of rooms, cabins, and motor lodge rooms. Log Cabin Resort (360–928–3325) provides lodge rooms, cabins, and chalets on the north side of Lake Crescent. Sol Duc Hot Springs Resort (360–327–3583) has cabins with or without kitchen near a hot mineral spring. Kalaloch Lodge (360–962–2271), with cabins and a limited number of rooms in the main lodge, is directly on the Pacific Ocean. Restaurants are located at each of the four lodges, and

OLYMPIC NATIONAL PARK

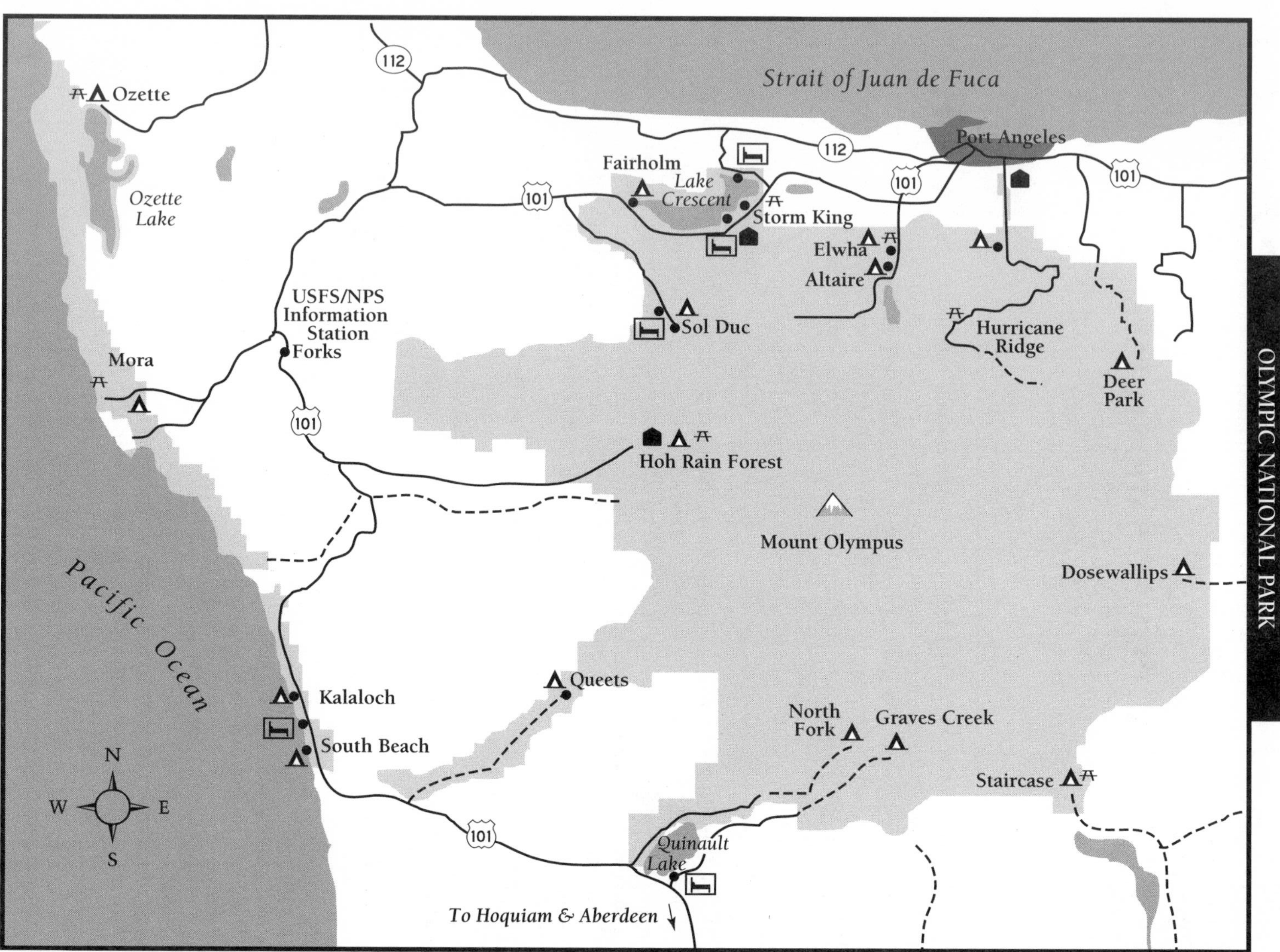

there is a cafeteria at Hurricane Ridge Visitor Center during summer months and on weekends in winter. A snack bar is located at the Fairholm General Store.

Groceries and gasoline are sold at the Fairholm General Store. Groceries only are sold at Sol Duc Hot Springs, Kalaloch Lodge, and Log Cabin Resort. Boat rentals are provided at Fairholm, Lake Crescent Lodge, and Log Cabin Resort.

CAMPING: Campgrounds with tables, grills, water, and flush toilets include Altaire (thirty spaces, summer only, no large trailers), Dosewallips (thirty spaces, summer only, no trailers), Elwha (forty-one spaces, no large trailers), Fairholm (eighty-eight spaces, dump station), Graves Creek (thirty spaces, summer only), Heart O' The Hills (105 spaces), Hoh (eighty-eight spaces, dump station), Kalaloch (175 spaces, dump station), Mora (ninety-four spaces; dump station), Sol Duc (eighty-two spaces, summer only, dump station), and Staircase (fifty-nine spaces). There are limited spaces at each of these campgrounds that will accommodate larger RVs. All other sites are recommended to a maximum of 21 feet.

Campgrounds with tables, grills, and pit toilets include Deer Park (fourteen spaces, summer only, no trailers), Erickson Bay (fifteen spaces, access only by boat or trail), July Creek (twenty-nine spaces, walk-in, water available), North Fork Quinault (seven spaces summer only, no trailers), Ozette (thirteen spaces, dirt road access), and Queets (twenty spaces, no trailers).

FISHING: Olympic's streams and lakes contain cutthroat, rainbow, Dolly Varden, and brook trout, and several species of salmon. Large rivers are noted for steelhead trout. No license is required except when fishing in the Pacific Ocean from shore. Steelhead and salmon punch-cards are required.

SAN JUAN ISLAND NATIONAL HISTORICAL PARK

P.O. Box 429
Friday Harbor, WA 98250-0429
(360) 378–2240
sajh_interpretation@nps.gov
www.nps.gov/sajh/

San Juan Island Historical Park encompasses 1,752 acres on San Juan Island, the second largest island in the San Juan archipelago. The park became part of the National Park System in 1966 to commemorate the peaceful resolution of the boundary dispute of 1859, better known as "The Pig War." English Camp is located on the island's northwest shoreline, while American Camp occupies a windswept prairie on the southern end of the island. San Juan Island is accessible via Washington State Ferries from Anacortes, Washington, about 83 miles north of Seattle, and Sidney, British Columbia, 15 miles north of Victoria on Vancouver Island. Good docking facilities for private craft are available in Friday Harbor and Roche Harbor.

San Juan Island was the scene of a confrontation and then relatively peaceful coexistence between American and British forces during the 1800s. The Oregon Treaty of 1846 between Great Britain and the United States settled the larger land disputes by giving the United States undisputed possession of the Pacific Northwest below the forty-ninth parallel, extending the boundary to the middle of the channel separating the mainland from Vancouver Island. But the treaty's wording left unclear who owned San Juan Island. Both sides declared the island as its possession, and in 1859 an insignificant event caused a confrontation between the two powers. After a series of threats, both sides agreed to withdraw all but token military forces and negotiate a settlement. The Americans remained in place in what is now called American Camp, while the British landed a detachment of royal marines at today's English Camp. San Juan Island remained under peaceful joint military occupation for the next twelve years. In 1871, the two sides signed the Treaty of Washington and submitted the San Juan question to Kaiser Wilhelm I of Germany for settlement. In 1872, the Kaiser ruled in favor of the United States.

Park headquarters at First and Spring Streets in Friday Harbor serves as an information station. It is open from 8:30 A.M. to 4:30 P.M., with extended hours in summer. At English Camp, four historic buildings and a small formal garden have been restored. The buildings are open in summer, and the barracks contains a slide program explaining the territorial dispute. At American Camp, two historic buildings and the remains of an earthwork gun emplacement survive. An exhibit/information center and a self-guided historical walking trail are located here. South and Fourth of July beaches, which flank the Cattle Point peninsula, offer splendid areas for picnicking, walking, and watching wildlife. The Jakle's Lagoon trail network features a variety of woodland and saltwater lagoon hikes.

FACILITIES: A number of motels, lodges, and bed-and-breakfast facilities are available on the island. A listing is at the visitor center. Picnic areas and accessible rest rooms are located at both American Camp and English Camp. Water is only available at American Camp.

CAMPING: No camping is provided by the National Park Service. Limited camping facilities (with flush toilets) are available at San Juan County Park (eighteen sites). For reservations write 380 West Side Road No., Friday Harbor, WA 98250 (360–378–2992). A small commercial trailer park (twenty sites, hookups) is located 1 mile from the ferry landing on Roche Harbor Road (360–378–4717), and three private campgrounds are available on the island.

FISHING: Fishing in bays surrounding the island and in San Juan Channel is available at various locations.

WHITMAN MISSION NATIONAL HISTORIC SITE

Route 2, Box 247
Walla Walla, WA 99362-9699
(509) 522–6360
WHMI_Interpretation@nps.gov
www.nps.gov/whmi/

Whitman Mission was authorized in 1936 to commemorate a landmark on the Oregon Trail where Dr. and Mrs. Marcus Whitman ministered to the spiritual and physical needs of Indians. The site is located in southeastern Washington, 7 miles west of Walla Walla and 4 miles west of College Place. A short connecting road leads south from U.S. 12 to the park.

Marcus Whitman was sent west in 1835 by a Protestant church society to carry out missionary work among the Indians. After returning east to recruit workers, Whitman and his wife crossed the continent in 1836 via steamboat, wagon, two-wheeled cart, and horseback. His mission was established among the Cayuse Indians at Waiilatpu. The Indians remained nomadic and were generally apathetic to spiritual matters, so the society considered closing the mission in 1842. Whitman was able to convince his superiors of the mission's value, and it continued to provide shelter to both the Indians and settlers traveling the Oregon Trail. In 1847, a wagon train brought measles to the area, creating an epidemic that killed half of the Cayuse tribe. In the same year, a small group of Cayuse attacked the mission and killed Marcus Whitman, his wife, and eleven others. The mission buildings were also destroyed. The tragedy spurred Congress to create the Territory of Oregon in August 1848.

The visitor center contains exhibits on Whitman Mission and the Oregon Trail, and a slide show on the establishment of the mission is presented hourly. Self-guided walks lead past the Whitman Memorial and the Great Grave, where the remains of those killed in the massacre are buried. Visitors may also walk around the old mission grounds, where recorded messages and building outlines help interpret the site. A restored section of the old Oregon Trail is available to walk. The mission is open daily except for Thanksgiving, Christmas, and New Year's Day.

FACILITIES: No food service or lodging is available at the site. Water and rest rooms are provided at the visitor center. A shaded picnic area with tables and drinking water (no grills) is located north of the visitor center near the parking area. Full facilities are located 7 miles east in Walla Walla.

CAMPING: No camping is permitted in the park. A county-operated campground with hookups is located 7 miles east in Walla Walla at Fort Walla Walla Park. The park is on Dalles Military Road, and a map showing directions to the campground may be obtained at the visitor center of Whitman Mission National Historic Site.

FISHING: No fishing is available at Whitman Mission National Historic Site.

WYOMING

STATE TOURIST INFORMATION

(800) 225–5996

DEVILS TOWER NATIONAL MONUMENT

P.O. Box 10
Devils Tower, WY 82714
(307) 467–5283
deto_interpretation@nps.gov
www.nps.gov/deto/

Devils Tower comprises nearly 1,350 acres and was established in 1906 as the country's first national monument. The monument contains a spectacular stump-shaped cluster of rock columns rising 867 feet above its base (featured in the movie *Close Encounters of the Third Kind*). Devils Tower is located in extreme northeastern Wyoming, 29 miles northwest of Sundance. The entrance is off Wyoming Highway 24, 7 miles north of U.S. 14. The drive over paved Wyoming Highway 24 (South Dakota Highway 34) connecting Belle Fourche, South Dakota, and the monument is quite scenic.

Devils Tower was formed millions of years ago when molten materials originating from within the earth cooled and crystallized. Joints in the columns were established when the hot rock cooled and contracted. Some of the columns have since fallen as the joints enlarged by the freezing and thawing of water. These broken columns may be seen piled around the base of the tower. The remainder of the monument is composed of rocks formed through the accumulation of materials on the floors of ancient seas. The prominence of Devils Tower is due to the more rapid erosion of the surrounding rock and to the color difference between the tower's core and base.

Devils Tower National Monument (opposite page)

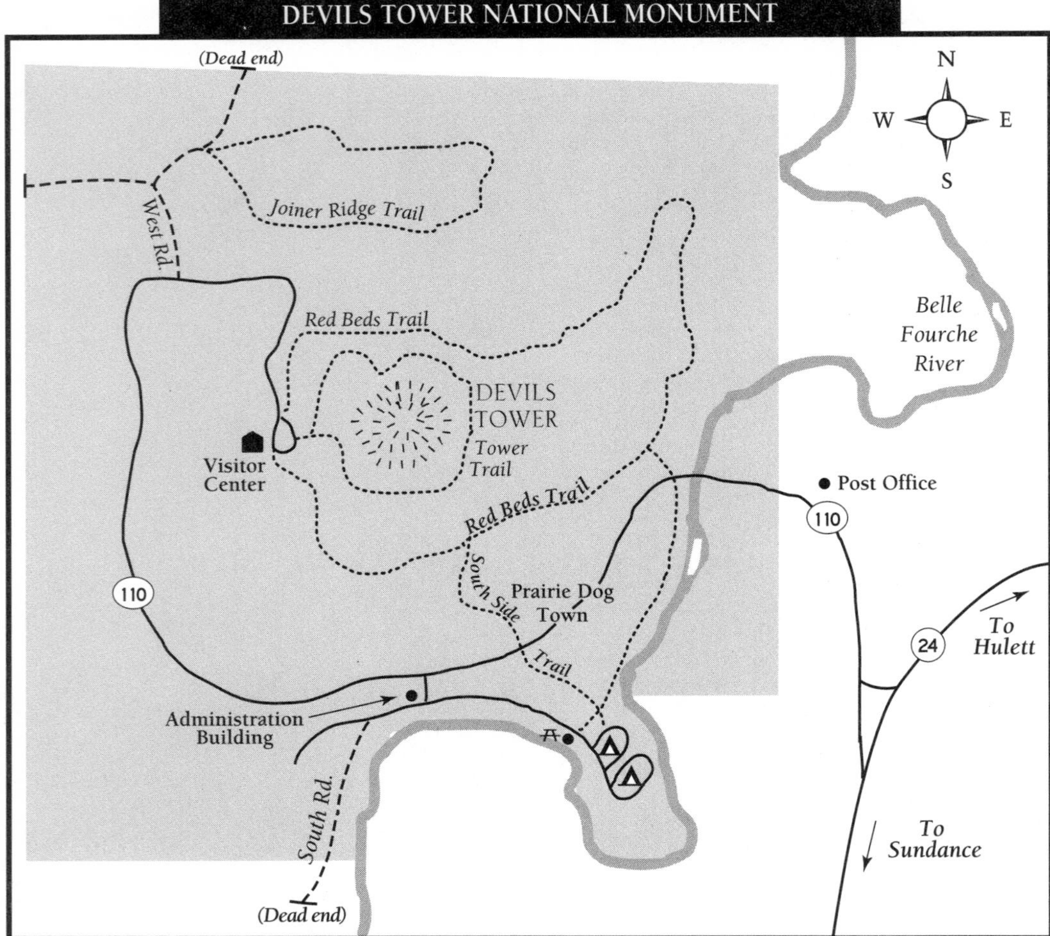

For centuries the butte was an important focus of Indian legends. To this day it is a sacred site of worship to several Plains tribes. As explorers and pioneers moved westward, it became one of their landmarks. The naming of Devils Tower is generally credited to Col. Richard Dodge, who was the commander of a military escort for a U.S. Geological Survey party.

The monument's visitor center contains exhibits explaining the history and geology of the area. Fifteen- to twenty-minute interpretive talks are presented in front of the visitor center. The 3-mile paved road to the visitor center passes through a prairie-dog town approximately ½ mile from the east entrance. The monument has 7 miles of hiking trails, including an easy self-guided nature trail (1¼ miles, one hour) that circles the tower and begins at the visitor center. Here the visitor may see a wide variety of animals and birds. The 2¾-mile Red Beds Trail is quite scenic and is easiest to hike in a clockwise fashion. A picnic area is located near the campground.

FACILITIES: Three general stores, restaurants, and a post office are located just outside the monument, approximately 2 miles from the campground. Modern rest rooms and drinking water are available at the visitor center and at the campground.

CAMPING: A pleasant campground (fifty spaces), located in a grove of cottonwood trees, provides tables, grills, water, and flush toilets. Depending upon the weather, the campground is open, with water and rest rooms available, from approximately May 1 through October. A private campground with hookups and showers is located just outside the park entrance.

FISHING: Fishing is permitted in the Belle Fourche River, which cuts through the park and borders the campground. Catches include catfish, suckers, and carp. A Wyoming fishing license is required.

FORT LARAMIE NATIONAL HISTORIC SITE

HC72, Box 389
Fort Laramie, WY 82212-0001
(307) 837–2221
www.nps.gov/fola/

Fort Laramie comprises 832 acres and was added to the National Park System in 1938 to preserve the site and remaining buildings of an important fur-trading and military post of the 1800s. The park is located in eastern Wyoming, 3 miles southwest of the town of Fort Laramie on County Road 160. It is approximately 95 miles from Cheyenne.

The original stockade, called Fort William, was constructed by fur traders in 1834. Two years later it was purchased by a large fur company and soon became one of the major trading centers in the Rockies. By the 1840s, the fur trade had declined, but the fort's location on one of the main routes west gave it renewed importance.

In 1849, the post was purchased by the U.S. government for use as an army post to protect travelers along the Oregon Trail. Subsequently, Fort Laramie was used as a station for the Pony Express and the Cheyenne–Deadwood Stagecoach and as a staging area for military campaigns against the Plains Indians. By the late 1800s, the importance of the fort had waned, and by 1890, it was abandoned.

The National Park Service has restored a number of the fort's standing buildings—eight have been historically furnished and are open to visitors. The park is open year-round. A visitor center in the commissary storehouse is open from 8:00 A.M. until 7:00 P.M. during summer. Exhibits and a film on the post's history are provided, and park personnel are on hand to answer visitors' questions. Talks and conducted tours are offered daily during June, July, and August. The park presents an excellent living-history program.

FACILITIES: No food service or lodging is available in the park. Both can be found in the town of Fort Laramie. Cold soft drinks are sold during the summer in the soldiers' bar. Water and rest rooms are located in the visitor center.

CAMPING: No camping is permitted in the historic site. The town of Fort Laramie has camping facilities with tables, grills, water, and flush toilets at a small but nice municipal park. Thirteen miles west of Fort Laramie on Highway 26, the town of Gurnsey provides campsites in a city park south of town. Water, electrical hookups, grills, tables, and hot showers are available.

FISHING: Fishing is permitted in the Laramie River outside the fort's historic zone with a Wyoming fishing license. Catches include catfish, carp, and some trout.

FOSSIL BUTTE NATIONAL MONUMENT

P.O. Box 592
Kemmerer, WY 83101-0592
(307) 877–4455
www.nps.gov/fobu/

Fossil Butte comprises nearly 8,200 acres. It was established as part of the National Park System in 1972 to preserve the nation's most extensive concentration of fossilized freshwater fish. Fossil Butte is located in southwestern Wyoming, 11 miles west of Kemmerer via U.S. 30.

For much of geologic time, most of Wyoming was either underwater or beach-front property. Then, seventy million to eighty million years ago, the Rocky Mountains began to form, creating intermountain basins. Fossil Lake, a subtropical freshwater lake, formed in one of these basins.

Fifty-million-year-old fossils found within the butte and surrounding sediments are among the most perfectly preserved remains of ancient plant and animal life in the world. Fish abounded in the lake; palms, ferns, and reeds grew along the shores. Fossils show that flood-

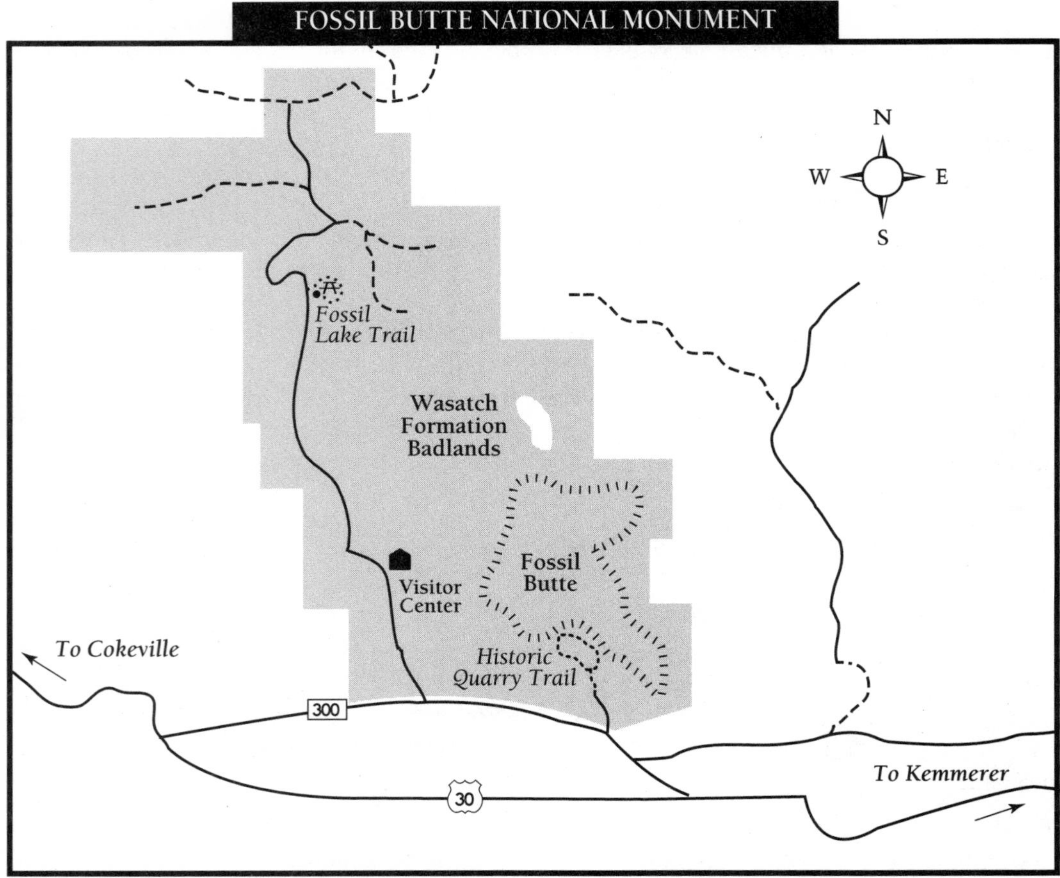

plain forests were inhabited by horses the size of dogs and lemur-like primates, while the streams around the lake contained crocodiles and turtles.

Several theories are advanced for the pristine fossilization conditions over the life of the lake. One theory attributes the abundance of fish fossils, which are actually found in several layers of sediments, to the stratified nature of the large lakes. The temperate climate created surface waters that were warmer and lighter than the deeper waters. Winds blowing across the lakes created well-oxygenated surface layers that acted as seals for the dense bottom waters that became stagnant and void of oxygen. When the fish that thrived in the warm surface water died and sank to the lake bottoms, there were no scavengers to bother their remains, and the fish were rapidly buried by limestone precipitating out of the water.

The new visitor center, located 1 mile north on the park road, provides numerous examples of fossils and information about them. Two videos are offered. One presents an orientation to the Fossil Lake deposits, and a second displays how fossils are quarried and prepared. A preparation lab permits the visitor to observe fossil preparation. A Junior Ranger Program that takes about two hours to complete is offered for children. Personnel in the visitor center provide assistance and hiking information and lead guided walks on weekends. A trail leads to a historic quarry on Fossil Butte. Wayside exhibits describe some of the natural and cultural features of the area. The 1½-mile Fossil Lake Trail begins at the picnic area and winds through aspen groves and meadows.

FACILITIES: No food or lodging is available at the monument, but both are found at Kemmerer and Cokeville. Rest rooms and drinking water are available at the visitor center. Vault toilets are found near the trailheads. A picnic area is located 2½ miles beyond the visitor center.

CAMPING: No camping is permitted in the park.

FISHING: No fishing is available at Fossil Butte.

GRAND TETON NATIONAL PARK; JOHN D. ROCKEFELLER, JR., MEMORIAL PARKWAY

P.O. Drawer 170
Moose, WY 83012-0170
(307) 739–3300
www.nps.gov/grte
www.nps.gov/jodr

Grand Teton National Park was established in 1929 and expanded in 1950. The park is comprised of nearly 310,000 acres of some of America's most impressive mountain landscape. The John D. Rockefeller, Jr., Memorial Parkway contains nearly 24,000 acres and provides a resource link between Grand Teton and Yellowstone. The parks are located in northwestern Wyoming. From Yellowstone and the north, access is via U.S. 89/287/191 and from the south via U.S. 26/89/191. This road parallels the Teton Range. From the east (Casper and Riverton), the park is entered on U.S. 26/287.

GRAND TETON NATIONAL PARK;
JOHN D. ROCKEFELLER, JR., MEMORIAL PARKWAY

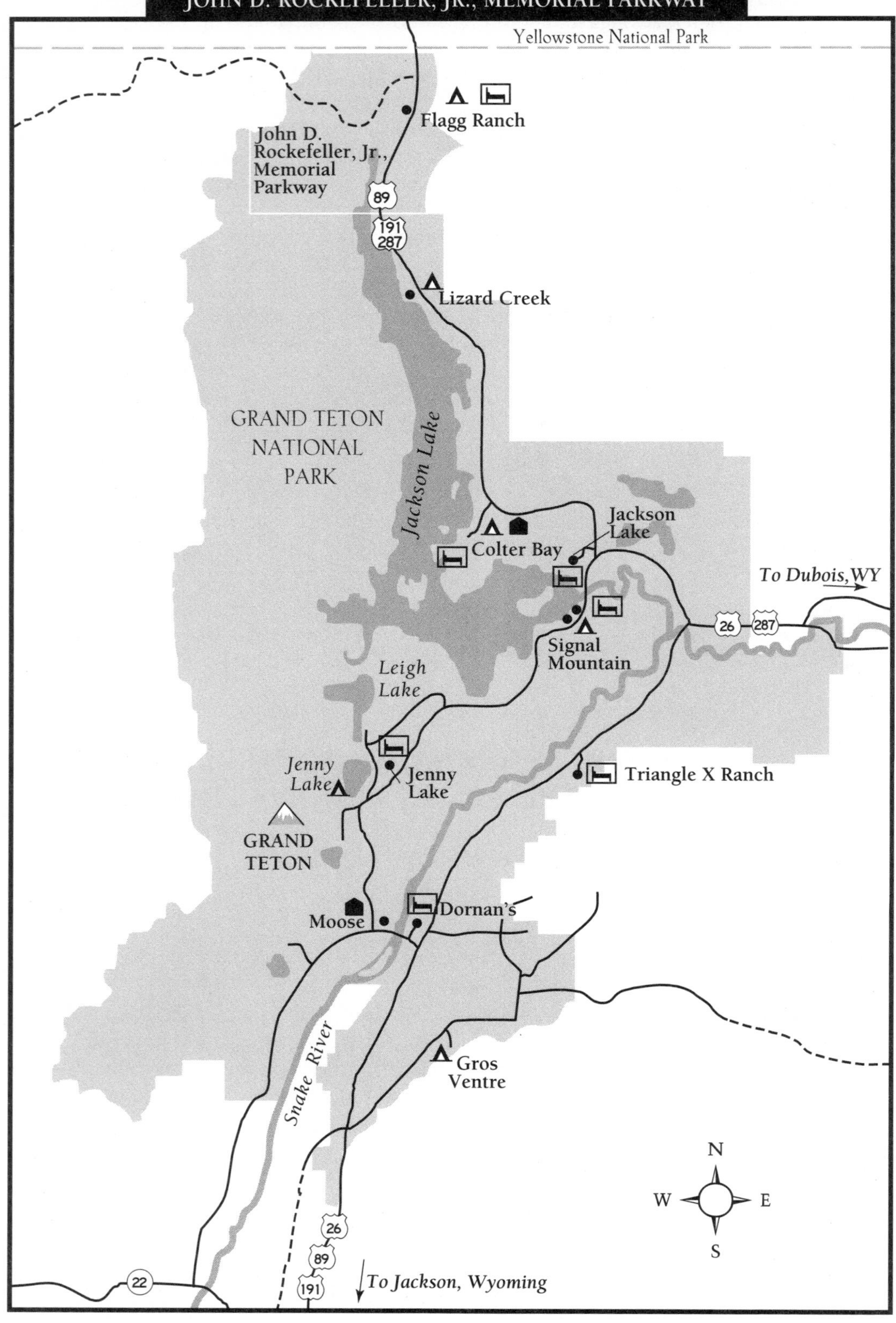

The Teton Range rises nearly 7,000 feet above the valley called Jackson Hole. The steep eastern front is the result of an uplifting that occurred along a fault zone in the earth's crust. As the uplifting progressed, the mountains were eroded by wind and water. Later glaciers carved the gullies into U-shaped valleys. The rock debris carried down by the glaciers (now melted) resulted in natural dams for lakes at the base of the range.

This spectacular park offers visitors a wide variety of outdoor activities. Moose Visitor Center (307–739–3399), at the park's south end, is open all year, and park personnel are on duty to answer questions. At the north end of the park, the Colter Bay Visitor Center (307–739–3594) is open from mid-May through September and offers audiovisual presentations, map and publication sales, and an American Indian art collection.

Some of the more popular activities are boating, fishing, hiking, and mountaineering. The Snake River diagonally bisects the valley portion of the park. A float trip with your own boat (permit required) or on one of the many concessioner-operated rafts is an exciting experience. No motors are allowed on the Snake. Hand-propelled boats are permitted on Emma Matilda, Two Ocean, Bradley, Taggart, Leigh, Bearpaw, and String lakes. Motors of up to 7½ h.p. are allowed on Jenny Lake and Phelps Lake, where boat transportation across the lake is available. All types of boats are permitted on Jackson Lake, and concessioner boat tours operate daily during the summer.

Grand Teton contains more than 200 miles of trails (horses allowed on many miles of these), including access to the high country. One of the more popular hikes near Jenny Lake is a half-day trip to Hidden Falls. Self-guided trails are located at Cascade Canyon, Colter Bay, Cunningham Cabin, and Menors Ferry. Frequent ranger-guided hikes are available in the summer, with schedules posted in the park newspaper. For visitors interested in mountaineering, instruction and guide service are available during summer months.

Two other relatively popular activities are horse riding and swimming. Horses may be rented at Colter Bay and Jackson Lake Lodge. Swimming is possible during late summer in shallow areas of String, Leigh, and Jackson lakes. Most lakes are quite cold, and no lifeguards are on duty.

During winter months, ranger-conducted snowshoe hikes are available (snowshoes provided), and snowmobiles may be operated in designated areas. Although no downhill skiing is available in the park, three private ski developments are located nearby.

LODGING: Seven lodging facilities are in Grand Teton National Park and the John D. Rockefeller, Jr., Memorial Parkway. Accommodations range from cabins at Triangle X Ranch, the only working dude ranch in a national park, to cozy cabins at four-star Jenny Lake Lodge. Other lodging includes panoramic Jackson Lake Lodge, cabins at Signal Mountain, Flagg Ranch, and cabins and tents at Colter Bay. Dornan's Spur Ranch near Moose offers modern log cabins near a gourmet food store.

FACILITIES: A wide assortment of facilities may be found throughout Grand Teton and Rockefeller Parkway. A summary by location is:

Colter Bay: Lodging (cabins, RV park, tent village), food (grill, restaurant, snack bar), laundry, showers, service stations, general store, groceries, and marina. Write Grand Teton Lodge Co., Box 240, Moran, WY 83013 (307–543–2811, 307–543–2855).

Flagg Ranch (Rockefeller Parkway): Lodging (cabins), food (restaurant, deli), package store, service station, gift shop, grocery, float trips, cross-country skiing, and snowmobile rentals. Write Flagg Ranch Village, Box 187, Moran, WY 83013 (800–443–2311, 307–543–2861, or 307–733–8761).

Jackson Lake: Hotel, grill, restaurant, beauty shop, package store, service station, gift shop. Write Grand Teton Lodge Co., Box 240, Moran, WY 83013 (307–543–2811, 307–543–2855).

Jenny Lake: Cabins, dining room, boat rentals and cruises, grocery. Write Grand Teton Lodge Co., Box 240, Moran, WY 83013 (307–543–2811, 307–543–2855).

Moose: Housekeeping cabins, food (restaurant, snack bar), package store, laundry, service station, canoe rental, grocery store, sporting-goods store, float trips. Write Dornan's, Box 39, Moose, WY 83012 (307–733–2415).

Signal Mountain: Lodging (log cabins, motel units, housekeeping apartments), food (coffee shop, restaurant), service station, gift shop, marina, grocery store, float trips. Write Signal Mountain Lodge, Box 50, Moran, WY 83013 (307–543–2831, 307–733–5470).

CAMPING: In Grand Teton, campgrounds with tables, grills, water, and flush toilets are Colter Bay (350 spaces, nine group camps, dump station, a concessioner-operated 111-site trailer village, showers, laundry), Gros Ventre (360 spaces, dump station), Jenny Lake (forty-four spaces for tents only), Lizard Creek (sixty spaces), and Signal Mountain (eighty-six spaces, dump station). Jenny Lake and Signal Mountain generally fill first; Gros Ventre fills last.

In Rockefeller Memorial Parkway, a concessioner campground with 175 spaces is located at Flagg Ranch.

FISHING: Jackson Lake offers cutthroat and lake trout. A number of other lakes and many streams contain whitefish and cutthroat, brook, and rainbow trout. Ice fishing is permitted on Jackson, Leigh, and Jenny lakes, and the Snake River is open only for whitefish in winter. A Wyoming fishing license is required.

YELLOWSTONE NATIONAL PARK

P.O. Box 168
Yellowstone National Park, WY 82190-0168
(307) 344–7381
www.nps.gov/yell/

Yellowstone was established in 1872 as America's first national park. It comprises nearly 3,400 square miles of lakes, waterfalls, and mountains and some 10,000 geysers and hot springs. The majority of the park is located in the northwestern corner of Wyoming, with overlapping areas in Montana and Idaho. Access is available from all four major directions.

The central portion of Yellowstone is a volcanic plateau with an average elevation of approximately 8,000 feet. On the northwest, north, east, and south, this table is surrounded by mountain ranges rising from 2,000 to 4,000 feet above the plateau. The region has been shaped by volcanoes and ice. The volcanic activity began 50 million to 55 million years ago and is still evident in the geysers and hot springs drawing heat from the earth's interior. Ice has moved through the park at least three times. In each case, permanent ice on mountains to the north and east quarried rocks and debris as it flowed into the valleys. As the climate warmed and ice melted, lakes and piles of debris were left.

The park contains nearly 400 miles of public roads leading to a seemingly endless supply of scenic areas. Many major attractions are found near the Grand Loop Road, which makes a figure eight in the park's central area. The road's east side provides access to canyons, moun-

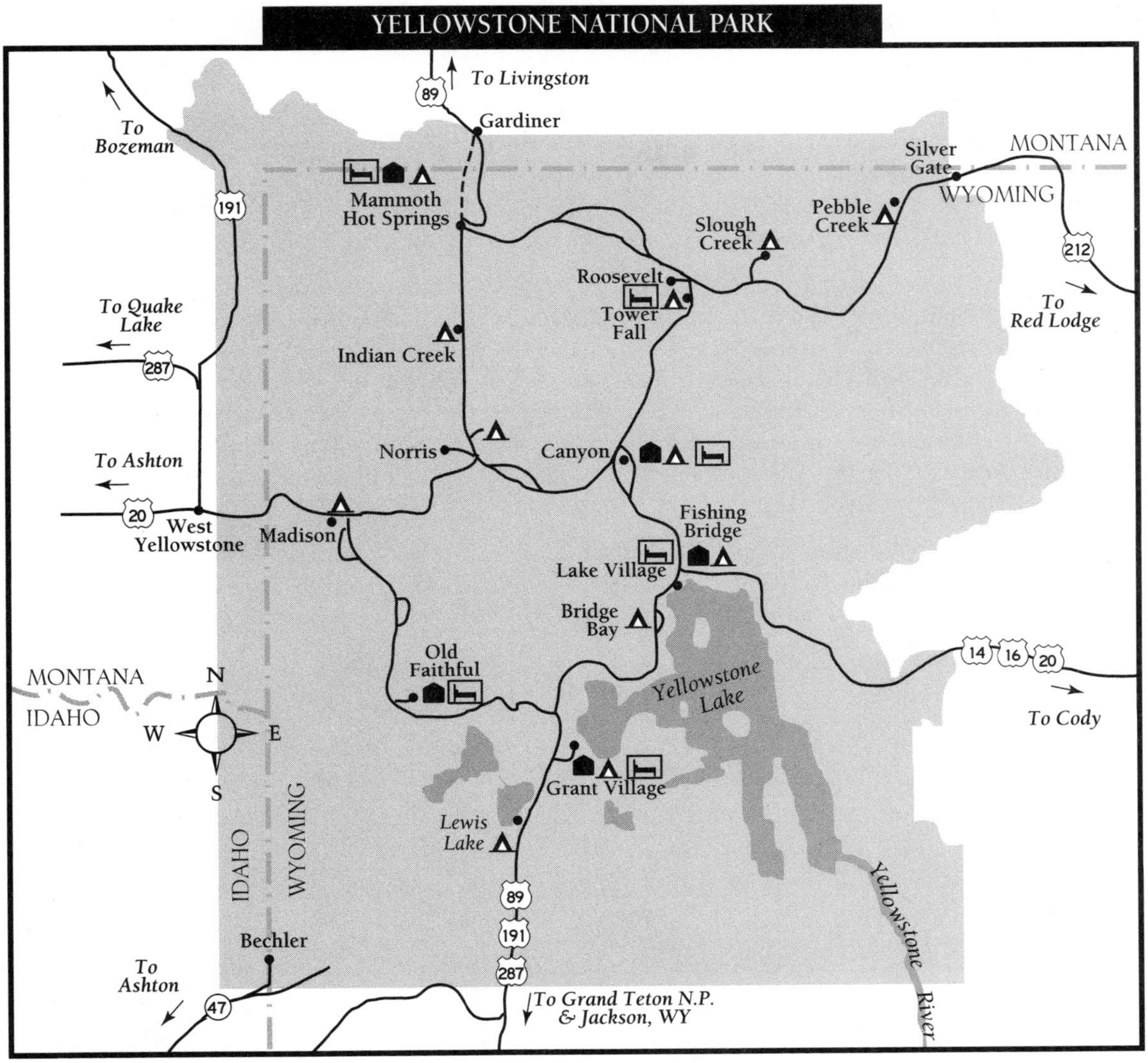

YELLOWSTONE NATIONAL PARK

tains, and waterfalls, while the west side leads to areas of thermal activity. The most popular of these latter attractions is Old Faithful. Numerous other geysers have predictable eruption times that are posted at Old Faithful Visitor Center and Norris Museum. Norris Geyser Basin is the park's most active thermal area—it has numerous steam vents and hot springs. At Mammoth Hot Springs, hot waters cascade over colored limestone pools. In Lower Geyser Basin, Fountain Paint Pots Trail provides access to more varied hot-water phenomena in a concentrated area than any other trail in the park.

Some of Yellowstone's most scenic areas lie along the Yellowstone River. Near Canyon, there are spectacular views of the Grand Canyon of the Yellowstone from Artist Point and Inspiration Point. North of here, a hike to the top of Mt. Washburn ends with a view of the entire park.

Other activities in Yellowstone include horseback trips from Canyon, Tower-Roosevelt, and Mammoth, and stagecoach rides on a regular schedule at Roosevelt. Bus tours leave from hotels and lodges, and boat tours leave regularly from Bridge Bay. Power boating is permitted only on open areas of Yellowstone Lake and on Lewis Lake (includes boat launch). All boaters are required to purchase permits for motorized and nonmotorized boats. For most, swimming is an uncomfortable experience because of Yellowstone's cold lakes and streams.

Winter activities are concentrated at Mammoth and Old Faithful, and U.S. 89 to the north entrance is open year-round for automobiles. Several trails are available for cross-country skiing, and major roadways are open to snowmobiles from mid-December through early March. Snowmobiles may be rented at Mammoth, Gardiner, West Yellowstone, and Flagg Ranch, and tours in enclosed snowcoaches are available via Amfac Parks and Resorts. No downhill skiing is possible in the park, but several ski developments are located nearby.

LODGING: Nine separate lodging facilities are located within Yellowstone National Park. The busy Old Faithful area has three lodging facilities, including famous Old Faithful Inn. Other accommodations are at Grant Village, Mammoth Hot Springs, Roosevelt, Canyon Village, and Lake Village. The facilities range from a wonderful 100-year-old hotel on the banks of Yellowstone Lake to rustic cabins at several locations. Not all rooms or cabins have private bathrooms. All nine lodges are operated by the same firm. For reservations or information write Amfac Parks and Resorts, Reservations Office, P.O. Box 165, Yellowstone National Park, WY 82190. Call (307) 344–7311.

FACILITIES: Yellowstone is one of the more developed parks administered by the National Park Service. As such, visitors can find nearly anything at some location inside its borders.

Bridge Bay: Boat rental.

Canyon: Food service, gasoline station, grocery, laundry, lodging, photo shop, post office, visitor center.

Fishing Bridge/Lake Area: Food service, gasoline station, grocery, hospital (summer only), laundry, lodging, marina, photo shop, post office, propane service, visitor center.

Grant: Food service, gasoline station, laundry, lodging, post office, propane service, visitor center.

Mammoth: Food service, gasoline station, grocery, lodging, medical clinic, photo shop, post office, visitor center.

Old Faithful: Food service, gasoline station, grocery, lodging, photo shop, medical clinic (summer only), post office, propane service, visitor center.

Tower-Roosevelt: Food service, gasoline, grocery, lodging.

CAMPING: Campgrounds with tables, fireplaces, dump stations, and flush toilets are located at Bridge Bay (430 spaces, showers), Canyon (272 spaces, showers), Grant Village (425 spaces, showers), Madison (280 spaces, no showers), Mammoth (eighty-seven spaces, no dump station, no showers), and Norris (116 spaces, no dump station, no showers). Less developed campgrounds are located at Indian Creek (seventy-five spaces), Lewis Lake (eighty-five spaces), Pebble Creek (thirty-two spaces), Slough Creek (twenty-nine spaces), and Tower Falls (thirty-two spaces). Only Mammoth is open all year. Campsites at Bridge Bay, Canyon, Grant Village, and Madison may be reserved through Amfac Parks and Resorts, Box 165, Yellowstone National Park, WY 82190. Call (307) 344–7311. The other campgrounds do not accept reservations.

A concessioner-operated trailer park at Fishing Bridge offers hookups and is open from mid-June to early September.

View from Artist Point in Yellowstone National Park (opposite page)

FISHING: Yellowstone Lake is noted for its native Yellowstone cutthroat trout. Other park streams and lakes contain rainbow, brook, brown, cutthroat, and lake trout, grayling, and whitefish. Fishing regulations vary widely throughout the park—some waters are closed, others are restricted to fly fishing, and some are open only for catch and release. Anglers twelve to fifteen years of age are required to obtain a free park fishing permit that is available at all ranger stations and visitor centers. Individuals over fifteen years old must purchase a permit. No state fishing license is required for fishing in the park.

NATIONAL PARK AREAS FACILITIES AND ACTIVITIES CHART

The following chart presents current information on visitor services in the areas described in this book. Generally, the services listed are those in the parks themselves. Additional services are usually available in nearby cities. Parks permitting activities such as horseback riding or boating do not necessarily rent equipment. Many parks curtail service in their off-seasons. A few park areas are not listed here or their entries are blank because they do not have the visitor services listed here.

	Fees	Visitor Center	Programs/Tours	Self-guided Tour/Trail	Guide for Hire	Picnic Area	Campground	Group Camp Site	Backcountry Permits	Hiking	Mountain Climbing	Horse Trail	Swimming	Bathhouse	Boating	Boat Rental	Boat Ramp	Fishing	Hunting	Bicycle Trail	Snowmobile Route	Crosscountry Ski Trail	Cabin Rental	Hotel, Motel, Lodge	Groceries, Ice	Restaurant, Snacks	Campsites	Handicap Access: Activities/Service	Handicap Access: Visitor Center
ALASKA																													
Aniakchak Natl. Monument and Preserve, P.O. Box 7, King Salmon, AK 99613									●	●	●				●			●	●										
Bering Land Bridge Natl. Preserve, P.O. Box 220, Nome, AK 99762		●	●		●					●								●	●										●
Cape Krusenstern Natl. Monument, P.O. Box 1029, Kotzebue, AK 99752		●	●		●					●					●			●			●								●
Denali Natl. Park and Preserve, P.O. Box 9, Denali National Park, AK 99755	●	●	●	●		●	●	●	●	●	●							●	●					●	●	●	●	●	●
Gates of the Arctic Natl. Park and Preserve, P.O. Box 2630, Battles Field, AK 99726–9999		●	●		●					●	●				●	●		●	●										
Glacier Bay Natl. Park and Preserve, P.O. Box 140, Gustavus, AK 99826		●	●				●	●	●	●	●				●	●		●	●					●		●		●	●
Katmai Natl. Park and Preserve, P.O. Box 7, King Salmon, AK 99613	●	●	●	●		●	●		●	●	●				●	●	●	●	●				●	●		●			●
Kenai Fjords Natl. Park, P.O. Box 1727, Seward, AK 99664	●	●	●	●		●	●			●	●				●			●			●	●	●						●
Klondike Gold Rush Natl. Historical Park, P.O. Box 517, Skagway, AK 99840 (See also Wash.)	●	●	●			●	●	●	●	●														●	●	●		●	●
Kobuk Valley Natl. Park, P.O. Box 1029, Kotzebue, AK 99752		●	●		●					●					●			●			●								●
Lake Clark Natl. Park and Preserve, 4230 University Drive, Anchorage, AK 99508		●	●		●					●	●		●		●	●		●	●		●	●	●	●		●			
Noatak Natl. Preserve, P.O. Box 1029, Kotzebue, AK 99752		●	●		●					●					●			●	●		●								●
Sitka Natl. Historical Park, P.O. Box 738, Sitka, AK 99835	●	●	●	●		●				●								●											●
Wrangell–St. Elias Natl. Park and Preserve, P.O. Box 439, Copper Center, AK 99573		●		●	●	●				●	●	●			●	●		●	●	●	●	●	●	●	●	●			●
Yukon–Charley Rivers Natl. Preserve, P.O. Box 167, Eagle, AK 99738		●			●					●	●				●			●	●										
AMERICAN SAMOA																													
National Park of American Samoa, Pago Pago, AS 96799–0001		●	●	●	●					●			●		●			●											
ARIZONA																													
Canyon de Chelly Natl. Monument, P.O. Box 588, Chinle, AZ 86503		●	●	●	●	●	●	●	●	●		●												●	●	●	●		●
Casa Grande Ruins Natl. Monument, 1100 Ruins Drive, Coolidge, AZ 85228	●	●	●	●		●																							●
Chiricahua Natl. Monument, Dos Cabezas Route, Box 6500, Wilcox, AZ 85643	●	●	●	●		●	●	●		●		●															●	●	●
Coronado Natl. Memorial, 4101 E. Montezuma Canyon Road, Hereford, AZ 85615		●		●		●				●																		●	●
Fort Bowie Natl. Historic Site, P.O. Box 158, Bowie, AZ 85605		●		●		●				●																			●
Glen Canyon Natl. Recreation Area, (Utah, Ariz.) P.O. Box 1507, Page, AZ 86040	●	●	●	●	●	●	●	●	●	●		●	●		●	●	●	●	●	●				●	●	●		●	●
Grand Canyon Natl. Park, P.O. Box 129, Grand Canyon, AZ 86023	●	●	●	●	●	●	●	●	●	●		●						●					●	●	●	●	●	●	●
Hubbell Trading Post Natl. Historic Site, P.O. Box 150, Ganado, AZ 86505		●	●	●		●																			●			●	●
Montezuma Castle Natl. Monument, P.O. Box 219, Camp Verde, AZ 86322	●	●		●		●																						●	●
Navajo Natl. Monument, H.C. 71, Box 3, Tonalea, AZ 86044-9704		●	●	●		●	●	●	●	●		●															●		●

ARIZONA *(continued)*																													
Organ Pipe Cactus Natl. Monument, Rt. 1, Box 100, Ajo, AZ 85321	●	●	●	●		●	●	●	●	●																	●	●	●
Petrified Forest Natl. Park, P.O. Box 2217, Petrified Forest Natl. Park, AZ 86028	●	●	●	●		●			●	●															●	●		●	●
Pipe Spring Natl. Monument, HC 65 Box 5, Fredonia, AZ 86022	●	●	●	●						●																●		●	●
Saguaro Natl. Park, 3693 S. Old Spanish Trail, Tucson, AZ 85730-5699	●	●	●	●		●			●	●		●								●								●	●
Sunset Crater Volcano Natl. Monument, Rt. 3, Box 149, Flagstaff, AZ 86004	●	●	●	●		●	●	●		●																	●	●	
Tonto Natl. Monument, HC 02 Box 4602, Roosevelt, AZ 85545	●	●	●	●		●																						●	●
Tumacacori Natl. Monument, P.O. Box 67, Tumacacori, AZ 85640	●	●	●	●		●				●																			●
Tuzigoot Natl. Monument, P.O. Box 219, Camp Verde, AZ 86322	●	●		●																								●	●
Walnut Canyon Natl. Monument, Walnut Canyon Rd. #3, Box 25, Flagstaff, AZ 86004-9705	●	●	●	●		●																						●	
Wupatki Natl. Monument, H.C. 33, Box 444A, Flagstaff, AZ 86004	●	●	●	●		●			●	●																		●	●
ARKANSAS																													
Arkansas Post Natl. Memorial, 1741 Old Post Road, Gillett, AR 72055		●	●	●		●				●								●										●	●
Buffalo Natl. River, P.O. Box 1173, Harrison, AR 72602	●	●	●	●	●	●	●	●		●		●	●		●	●	●	●	●				●			●	●	●	●
Fort Smith Natl. Historic Site, P.O. Box 1406, Fort Smith, AR 72902	●	●	●	●																									●
Hot Springs Natl. Park, P.O. Box 1860, Hot Springs, AR 71902		●	●	●		●	●			●				●										●	●	●	●	●	●
Pea Ridge Natl. Military Park, P.O. Box 700, Pea Ridge, AR 72751	●	●		●		●				●																			
CALIFORNIA																													
AIDS Memorial Grove National Memorial, 856 Stanyan Street, San Francisco, CA 94117				●																									
Cabrillo Natl. Monument, 1800 Cabrillo Memorial Dr., San Diego, CA 92106	●	●	●	●		●				●								●										●	●
Channel Islands Natl. Park, 1901 Spinnaker Dr., Ventura, CA 93001		●	●	●		●	●	●		●			●		●			●										●	●
Death Valley Natl. Park (Calif., Nev.), P.O. Box 579, Death Valley, CA 92328	●	●	●	●	●	●	●	●		●	●	●	●							●			●	●	●	●	●		●
Devils Postpile Natl. Monument, P.O. Box 501, Mammoth Lakes, CA 93546	●	●	●			●	●		●	●		●						●											●
Eugene O'Neill Natl. Historic Site, P.O. Box 280, Danville, CA 94526		●	●	●																									●
Fort Point Natl. Historic Site, P.O. Box 29333, Presidio of San Francisco, CA 94129		●	●	●														●		●								●	●
Golden Gate Natl. Recreation Area, Fort Mason, Building 201, San Francisco, CA 94123	●	●	●	●		●	●	●		●		●	●	●				●		●						●			●
John Muir Natl. Historic Site, 4202 Alhambra Ave., Martinez, CA 94553	●	●	●	●		●				●																		●	●
Joshua Tree Natl. Park, 74485 National Park Dr., Twentynine Palms, CA 92277	●	●	●	●	●	●	●	●	●	●	●	●															●	●	
Kings Canyon Natl. Park, Three Rivers, CA 93271	●	●	●	●	●	●	●	●	●	●	●	●						●				●	●	●	●	●	●	●	●
Lassen Volcanic Natl. Park, P.O. Box 100, Mineral, CA 96063	●	●	●	●		●	●	●	●	●		●	●		●		●	●				●	●		●	●	●	●	●
Lava Beds Natl. Monument, P.O. Box 867, Tulelake, CA 96134	●	●	●	●		●	●	●		●																	●	●	●
Manzanar Natl. Historic Site, P.O. Box 426, Independence, CA 93526																													
Mojave National Preserve, 222 E. Main St., Suite 202, Barstow, CA 92311–2366	●	●	●	●		●	●	●		●		●							●	●				●	●	●	●	●	●
Muir Woods Natl. Monument, Mill Valley, CA 94941	●	●	●	●						●																●		●	●
Pinnacles Natl. Monument, Paicines, CA 95043	●	●	●	●		●	●	●		●																	●	●	●
Point Reyes Natl. Seashore, Point Reyes, CA 94956	●	●	●	●		●	●	●	●	●		●	●					●		●						●		●	●
Port Chicago Naval Magazine Natl. Memorial, c/o Eugene O'Neill NHS, P.O. Box 28, Danville, CA 94526																													
Redwood Natl. Park, 1111 Second St., Crescent City, CA 95531		●	●	●	●	●	●	●	●	●		●	●		●			●		●							●	●	●
San Francisco Maritime Natl. Historical Park, Fort Mason, San Francisco, CA 94123	●		●	●		●							●							●									

	Fees	Visitor Center	Programs/Tours	Self-guided Tour/Trail	Guide for Hire	Picnic Area	Campground	Group Camp Site	Backcountry Permits	Hiking	Mountain Climbing	Horse Trail	Swimming	Bathhouse	Boating	Boat Rental	Boat Ramp	Fishing	Hunting	Bicycle Trail	Snowmobile Route	Crosscountry Ski Trail	Cabin Rental	Hotel, Motel, Lodge	Groceries, Ice	Restaurant, Snacks	Campsites	Handicap Access: Activities/Service	Handicap Access: Visitor Center
CALIFORNIA *(continued)*																													
Santa Monica Mountains Natl. Recreation Area, 401 W. Hillcrest Dr., Thousand Oaks, CA 91360		●	●	●		●	●	●		●		●	●							●				●	●	●	●	●	●
Sequoia Natl. Park, Three Rivers, CA 93271	●	●	●	●	●	●	●	●	●	●	●	●						●				●	●	●	●	●	●	●	●
Whiskeytown-Shasta-Trinity Natl. Recreation Area, P.O. Box 188, Whiskeytown, CA 96095	●	●	●	●		●	●	●	●	●		●	●	●	●	●	●	●	●	●							●	●	●
Yosemite Natl. Park, P. O. Box 577, Yosemite Natl. Park, CA 95389	●	●	●	●	●	●	●	●	●	●	●	●	●	●	●	●	●	●		●		●	●	●	●	●	●	●	●
COLORADO																													
Bent's Old Fort Natl. Historic Site, 35110 Highway 194 East, La Junta, CO 81050-9523	●		●	●		●																							
Black Canyon of the Gunnison Natl. Park, 102 Elk Creek, Gunnison, CO 81230	●	●	●	●		●	●		●	●	●							●				●				●	●		●
Colorado Natl. Monument, Fruita, CO 81521	●	●	●	●		●	●			●	●	●	●									●					●	●	●
Curecanti Natl. Recreation Area, 102 Elk Creek, Gunnison, CO 81230	●	●	●	●	●	●	●	●		●		●	●	●	●	●	●	●	●		●	●			●	●	●	●	●
Dinosaur Natl. Monument (Colo., Utah), 4545 Highway 40, Dinosaur, CO 81610	●	●	●	●		●	●	●	●	●					●			●			●						●		●
Florissant Fossil Beds Natl. Monument, P.O. Box 185, Florissant, CO 80816	●	●	●	●		●				●												●							●
Great Sand Dunes Natl. Monument, 11500 Highway 150, Mosca, CO 81146	●	●	●	●		●	●	●	●	●												●			●	●	●	●	●
Hovenweep Natl. Monument (Colo., Utah), McElmo Route, Cortez, CO 81321	●	●	●	●		●	●	●		●																	●		●
Mesa Verde Natl. Park, P.O. Box 8, Mesa Verde, CO 81330	●	●	●	●	●	●	●	●		●												●		●	●	●	●	●	●
Rocky Mountain Natl. Park, Estes Park, CO 80517	●	●	●	●	●	●	●	●	●	●	●	●						●			●	●				●	●	●	●
GUAM																													
War in the Pacific Natl. Historical Park, P.O. Box FA, Agana, GU 96932		●	●	●	●	●				●			●		●			●		●									●
HAWAII																													
Haleakala Natl. Park, P.O. Box 369, Makawao, HI 96768	●	●	●	●		●	●	●	●	●		●	●										●				●		●
Hawaii Volcanoes Natl. Park, P.O. Box 52, Hawaii Natl. Park, HI 96718	●	●	●	●		●	●	●	●	●		●								●			●	●		●	●	●	●
Kalaupapa Natl. Historic Park, P.O. Box 2222, Kalaupapa, HI 96742		●			●	●				●																			
Kaloko–Honokohau NHP, 73-4786 Kanalani St. #14, Kailua-Kono, HI 96740-2600		●				●				●			●		●			●											●
Pu'uhonua o Honaunau Natl. Historical Park, P.O. Box 129, Honaunau, Kona, HI 96726	●	●	●	●	●	●				●			●					●										●	●
Pu'ukohola Heiau Natl. Historic Site, P.O. Box 44340, Kawaihae, HI 96743		●	●	●																								●	●
USS *Arizona* Memorial, 1 Arizona Memorial Place, Honolulu, HI 96818		●	●																							●			●
IDAHO																													
City of Rocks Natl. Reserve, P.O. Box 169, Almo, ID 83312	●	●	●			●	●	●	●	●	●	●							●	●	●	●			●		●		●
Craters of the Moon Natl. Monument, P.O. Box 29, Arco, ID 83213	●	●	●	●		●	●	●	●	●												●						●	●
Hagerman Fossil Beds Natl. Monument, 221 North State Street, Hagerman, ID 83332		●	●							●		●			●		●	●	●	●								●	●
Nez Perce Natl. Historical Park, P.O. Box 93, Spalding, ID 83540		●	●	●		●																						●	●
Yellowstone NP, P.O. Box 168, Yellowstone National Park, WY 82190-0168	●	●	●	●	●	●	●	●	●	●		●	●		●	●	●	●		●	●	●	●	●	●	●	●	●	●

IOWA																													
Effigy Mounds Natl. Monument, 151 Highway 76, Harpers Ferry, IA 52146	●	●	●	●						●							●	●				●							●
Herbert Hoover Natl. Historic Site, P.O. Box 607, West Branch, IA 52358	●	●	●	●		●				●												●						●	●
KANSAS																													
Brown v. Board of Education National Historic Site		●																											
Fort Larned Natl. Historic Site, Rte. 3, Larned, KS 67550	●	●	●	●		●																						●	●
Fort Scott Natl. Historic Site, Old Fort Blvd., Fort Scott, KS 66701	●	●	●	●		●																						●	●
Nicodemus NHS, Fort Larned NHS, Route 3, Larned, KS 67550–9733				●		●																							
Tallgrass Prairie N PRES, P.O. Box 585, 226 Broadway, Cottonwood Falls, KS 66845–0585	●		●	●																									
LOUISIANA																													
Cane River Creole National Historical Park		●	●																										
Jean Lafitte Natl. Historical Park and Preserve, 365 Canal St., Suite 2400, New Orleans, LA 70130		●	●	●		●				●					●			●	●									●	●
MINNESOTA																													
Grand Portage Natl. Monument, P.O. Box 668, Grand Marais, MN 55604	●		●	●		●			●	●								●				●						●	
Mississippi Natl. River & Recreation Area, 175 East 5th Street, Suite 418, Box 41, St. Paul, MN 55101	●	●	●	●		●		●		●					●		●	●		●		●		●	●	●		●	●
Pipestone Natl. Monument, 36 Reservation Ave., Pipestone, MN 56164	●	●		●		●				●																			●
St. Croix Natl. Scenic Riverway, P.O. Box 708, St. Croix Falls, WI 54024		●	●	●		●	●	●		●					●		●	●	●			●					●		●
Voyageurs Natl. Park, 3131 Highway 53, International Falls, MN 56649-8804		●	●	●	●	●	●	●		●			●		●	●	●	●			●	●	●	●	●	●	●	●	●
MISSOURI																													
George Washington Carver Natl. Monument, P.O. Box 38, Diamond, MO 64840	●	●	●	●		●																						●	●
Harry S Truman Natl. Historic Site, 223 N. Main St., Independence, MO 64050	●	●	●																									●	●
Jefferson Natl. Expansion Memorial, 11 North 4th St., St. Louis, MO 63102	●	●	●																									●	●
Ozark Natl. Scenic Riverways, P.O. Box 490, Van Buren, MO 63965			●			●	●	●		●			●		●	●	●	●	●				●		●	●	●	●	
Ulysses S. Grant Natl. Historic Site, 7400 Grant Street, St. Louis, MO 63123		●	●	●																									●
Wilson's Creek Natl. Battlefield, 6424 West Farm Rd. 182, Republic, MO 65738	●	●		●		●				●		●																	●
MONTANA																													
Big Hole Natl. Battlefield, P.O. Box 237, Wisdom, MT 59761	●	●	●	●		●												●				●						●	●
Bighorn Canyon Natl. Recreation Area (Mont., Wyo.), P.O. Box 7458, Fort Smith, MT 59035	●	●	●		●	●	●		●	●			●		●	●	●	●	●						●	●		●	●
Glacier Natl. Park, West Glacier, MT 59936	●	●	●	●	●	●	●	●	●	●	●	●	●		●	●	●	●		●		●	●	●	●	●	●	●	●
Grant-Kohrs Ranch Natl. Historic Site, P.O. Box 790, Deer Lodge, MT 59722	●	●	●	●																								●	●
Little Bighorn Natl. Monument, P.O. Box 39, Crow Agency, MT 59022	●	●	●	●																								●	●
Nez Perce NHP, P.O. Box 93, Spalding, ID 83540–9715		●	●	●		●																						●	●
Yellowstone NP, P.O. Box 168, Yellowstone National Park, WY 82190–0168	●	●	●	●	●	●	●	●	●	●		●	●		●	●	●	●		●	●	●	●	●	●	●	●	●	●
NEBRASKA																													
Agate Fossil Beds Natl. Monument, P. O. Box 27, Gering, NE 69341	●	●	●	●		●				●								●										●	●
Chimney Rock Natl. Historic Site, P.O. Box 27, Gering, NE 69341		●																											
Homestead Natl. Monument of America, Rt. 3, Beatrice, NE 68310		●	●	●		●																●						●	●
Missouri National Recreational River										●					●			●											
Niobrara National Scenic River				●		●	●			●					●			●											
Scotts Bluff Natl. Monument, P.O. Box 27, Gering, NE 69341	●	●	●	●		●				●										●								●	●

	Fees	Visitor Center	Programs/Tours	Self-guided Tour/Trail	Guide for Hire	Picnic Area	Campground	Group Camp Site	Backcountry Use Permits	Hiking	Mountain Climbing	Horse Trail	Swimming	Bathhouse	Boating	Boat Rental	Boat Ramp	Fishing	Hunting	Bicycle Trail	Snowmobile Route	Crosscountry Ski Trail	Cabin Rental	Hotel, Motel, Lodge	Groceries, Ice	Restaurant, Snacks	Campsites	Handicap Access: Activities/Service	Handicap Access: Visitor Center
NEVADA																													
Death Valley Natl. Park (Calif., Nev.), P.O. Box 579, Death Valley, CA 92328	●	●	●	●	●	●	●	●		●	●	●	●							●			●	●	●	●	●		●
Great Basin Natl. Park, Baker, NV 89311	●	●	●	●		●	●			●	●	●						●								●	●	●	●
Lake Mead Natl. Recreational Area (Nev., Ariz.), 601 Nevada Highway, Boulder City, NV 89005-2426		●	●	●	●	●	●	●		●		●	●		●	●	●	●	●	●				●	●	●	●	●	●
NEW MEXICO																													
Aztec Ruins Natl. Monument, P.O. Box 640, Aztec, NM 87410	●	●		●		●																						●	●
Bandelier Natl. Monument, HCR I Box 1, Suite 15, Los Alamos, NM 87544	●	●	●	●		●	●	●	●	●																●	●	●	●
Capulin Volcano Natl. Monument, P.O. Box 40, Capulin, NM 88414	●	●	●	●		●				●																		●	●
Carlsbad Caverns Natl. Park, 3225 National Parks Highway, Carlsbad, NM 88220	●	●	●	●		●			●	●																●		●	●
Chaco Culture Natl. Historical Park, Box 220, Nageezi, NM 87037	●	●	●	●		●	●	●	●	●										●							●	●	
El Malpais Natl. Monument, P.O. Box 939, Grants, NM 87020		●	●	●		●			●	●										●								●	●
El Morro Natl. Monument, Rt. 2, Box 43, Ramah, NM 87321	●	●		●		●	●			●																	●		
Fort Union Natl. Monument, Watrous, NM 87753	●	●	●	●		●																						●	●
Gila Cliff Dwellings Natl. Monument, Rt. 11, Box 100, Silver City, NM 88061		●	●	●		●	●	●		●		●						●									●	●	●
Pecos Natl. Historical Park, P.O. Drawer 418, Pecos, NM 87552	●	●	●	●		●																						●	●
Petroglyph Natl. Monument, 6001 Unser Boulevard NW, Albuquerque, NM 87120	●	●	●	●		●				●		●																	●
Salinas Pueblo Missions National Monument, P.O. Box 496, Mountainair, NM 87036		●	●	●		●																						●	●
White Sands Natl. Monument, P.O. Box 1086, Holloman AFB, NM 88330	●	●	●	●		●			●	●		●														●		●	●
NORTH DAKOTA																													
Fort Union Trading Post Natl. Historic Site (N. Dak., Mont.), RR 3, Box 71, Williston, ND 58801		●	●	●		●												●										●	●
International Peace Garden, Route #1, Box 116, Dunseith, ND 58329		●		●		●	●			●																●		●	
Knife River Indian Villages Natl. Historic Site, P.O. Box 9, Stanton, ND 58571		●	●	●		●				●								●				●							●
Theodore Roosevelt Natl. Park, P.O. Box 7, Medora, ND 58645	●	●	●	●		●	●	●	●	●		●			●			●									●	●	●
OKLAHOMA																													
Chickasaw Natl. Recreation Area, P.O. Box 201, Sulphur, OK 73086		●	●	●		●	●	●		●			●		●		●	●	●								●		●
Washita Battlefield NHS, P.O. Box 890, Cheyenne, OK 73628–0890						●																							
OREGON																													
Crater Lake Natl. Park, P.O. Box 7, Crater Lake, OR 97604	●	●	●	●		●	●		●	●		●						●			●	●		●	●	●	●	●	●
Fort Clatsop Nat. Memorial, Rt. 3, Box 604-FC, Astoria, OR 97103	●	●	●	●		●			●																				●
John Day Fossil Beds Natl. Monument, HCR 82 Box 126, Kimberly, OR 97848		●	●	●		●				●								●										●	●
McLoughlin House Natl. Historic Site, 713 Center Street, Oregon City, OR 97045	●	●	●	●																									

OREGON (continued)																													
Nez Perce NHP, P.O. Box 93, Spaulding, ID 83540–9715		●	●	●		●																					●	●
Oregon Caves Natl. Monument, 19000 Caves Highway, Cave Junction, OR 97523	●		●			●				●														●		●		●	
SAIPAN																													
American Memorial Park, P.O. Box 5189 CHRB, Saipan, MP 96950				●		●														●									
SOUTH DAKOTA																													
Badlands Natl. Park, P.O. Box 6, Interior, SD 57750	●	●	●	●		●	●	●		●													●		●	●	●	●	●
Jewel Cave Natl. Monument, R.R. 1, Box 60AA, Custer, SD 57730	●	●	●	●		●				●																		●	●
Mount Rushmore Natl. Memorial, P.O. Box 268, Keystone, SD 57751	●	●	●	●							●															●		●	●
Wind Cave Natl. Park, RR 1 Box 190, Hot Springs, SD 57747	●	●	●	●		●	●	●	●	●																	●	●	●
TEXAS																													
Alibates Flint Quarries Natl. Monument, P.O. Box 1460, Fritch, TX 79036		●	●																										●
Amistad National Recreation Area, HCR-3, Box 5J, Del Rio, TX 78840	●		●	●	●	●	●	●		●			●		●	●	●	●	●						●		●	●	
Big Bend Natl. Park, P.O. Box 129, Big Bend Natl. Park, TX 79834	●	●	●	●		●	●	●	●	●		●			●			●						●	●	●			●
Big Thicket Natl. Preserve, 3785 Milam, Beaumont, TX 77701		●	●	●		●			●	●		●			●		●	●	●	●									●
Chamizal Natl. Memorial, 800 S. San Marcial St., El Paso, TX 79905		●	●	●		●																						●	●
Fort Davis Natl. Historic Site, P.O. Box 1456, Fort Davis, TX 79734	●	●		●		●																						●	●
Guadalupe Mountains Natl. Park, H.C. 60, Box 400, Salt Flat, TX 79847-9400		●	●	●		●	●	●	●	●		●															●		●
Lake Meredith National Recreation Area, P.O. Box 1460, Fritch, TX 79036	●	●				●	●	●		●		●	●		●	●	●	●	●						●		●	●	●
Lyndon B. Johnson Natl. Historical Park, P.O. Box 329, Johnson City, TX 78636	●	●	●	●																								●	●
Padre Island Natl. Seashore, 9405 S. Padre Island Dr., Corpus Christi, TX 78418-5597	●	●	●	●		●	●			●			●	●	●		●	●							●	●	●	●	●
Palo Alto Battlefield NHS, 1623 Central Blvd. Rm 213, Brownsville, TX 78520-8326		●	●																										●
San Antonio Missions Natl. Historical Park, 2202 Roosevelt Ave., San Antonio, TX 78210-4919		●	●	●		●				●										●									●
UTAH																													
Arches Natl. Park, P.O. Box 907, Moab, UT 84532	●	●	●	●		●	●	●	●	●	●																●		●
Bryce Canyon Natl. Park, Bryce Canyon, UT 84717	●	●	●	●	●	●	●	●	●	●		●										●	●	●	●	●	●	●	●
Canyonlands Natl. Park, 2282 S. West Resource Blvd., Moab, UT 84532	●	●	●	●	●	●	●	●	●	●					●														●
Capitol Reef Natl. Park, HC70 Box 15, Torrey, UT 84775	●	●	●	●		●	●	●	●	●		●															●		●
Cedar Breaks Natl. Monument, 2390 W HWY 56, Suite 11, Cedar City, UT 84720	●	●	●	●		●	●			●											●	●					●		●
Dinosaur Natl. Monument (Colo., Utah), 4545 Highway 40, Dinosaur, CO 81610	●	●	●	●		●	●	●	●	●					●			●			●						●		●
Glen Canyon Natl. Recreation Area (Utah, Ariz.), P.O. Box 1507, Page, AZ 86040	●	●	●	●	●	●	●	●	●	●		●	●		●	●	●	●	●	●				●	●	●		●	●
Golden Spike Natl. Historic Site, P.O. Box 897, Brigham City, UT 84302	●	●	●	●		●				●										●									●
Hovenweep Natl. Monument (Colo., Utah), McElmo Route, Cortez, CO 81321	●	●	●	●		●	●	●		●																	●		●
Natural Bridges Natl. Monument, P.O. Box 1, Lake Powell, UT 84533	●	●	●	●		●	●			●																		●	●
Rainbow Bridge Natl. Monument, c/o Glen Canyon Natl. Recreation Area, P.O. Box 1507, Page, AZ 86040			●												●														
Timpanogos Cave Natl. Monument, R.R. 3, Box 200, American Fork, UT 84003	●	●	●	●		●				●								●								●		●	●
Zion Natl. Park, Springdale, UT 84767-1099	●	●	●	●		●	●	●	●	●		●								●			●	●		●	●	●	

	Fees	Visitor Center	Programs/Tours	Self-guided Tour/Trail	Guide for Hire	Picnic Area	Campground	Group Camp Site	Backcountry Permits	Hiking	Mountain Climbing	Horse Trail	Swimming	Bathhouse	Boating	Boat Rental	Boat Ramp	Fishing	Hunting	Bicycle Trail	Snowmobile Route	Crosscountry Ski Trail	Cabin Rental	Hotel, Motel, Lodge	Groceries, Ice	Restaurant, Snacks	Campsites	Handicap Access: Activities/Service	Handicap Access: Visitor Center
	●	●	●	●	●	●	●	●	●	●	●	●	●	●	●	●	●	●	●	●	●	●	●	●	●	●	●	●	●
WASHINGTON																													
Ebey's Landing Natl. Historical Reserve, P.O. Box 774, Coupeville, WA 98239				●		●	●			●					●		●	●						●	●	●		●	●
Fort Vancouver Natl. Historic Site, 612 E. Reserve St., Vancouver, WA 98661-3811	●	●	●			●																							●
Klondike Gold Rush Natl. Historical Park, 117 S. Main St., Seattle, WA 98104 (See also Alaska)		●	●																									●	●
Lake Chelan Natl. Recreation Area, 2105 State Route 20, Sedro-Woolley, WA 98284		●	●	●	●	●	●	●	●	●	●	●	●		●	●	●	●	●			●	●	●	●	●	●	●	●
Lake Roosevelt Natl. Recreation Area, 1008 Crest Dr., Coulee Dam, WA 99116		●	●	●		●	●	●					●	●	●		●	●						●	●	●	●		●
Mount Rainier Natl. Park, Tahoma Woods, Star Route, Ashford, WA 98304	●	●	●	●		●	●	●	●	●	●	●						●				●		●	●	●	●	●	●
Nez Perce NHP, P.O.Box 93, Spaulding, ID 83540-9715		●		●	●		●																					●	●
North Cascades Natl. Park, 2105 State Route 20, Sedro-Woolley, WA 98284		●			●		●		●	●	●	●						●									●		●
Olympic Natl. Park, 600 E. Park Ave., Port Angeles, WA 98362	●	●	●	●		●	●	●	●	●	●	●	●		●	●	●	●		●		●	●	●	●	●	●	●	●
Ross Lake Natl. Recreation Area, 2105 State Route 20, Sedro-Woolley, WA 98284	●	●	●	●	●	●	●	●	●	●	●	●			●	●	●	●	●				●		●		●	●	●
San Juan Island Natl. Historical Park, P.O. Box 429, Friday Harbor, WA 98250		●	●	●		●				●																			●
Whitman Mission Natl. Historic Site, Rt. 2, Box 247, Walla Walla, WA 99362	●	●	●	●		●																						●	●
WYOMING																													
Bighorn Canyon Natl. Recreation Area (Mont., Wyo.), P.O. Box 7458, Fort Smith, MT 59035	●	●	●		●	●	●		●	●			●		●	●	●	●	●						●	●		●	●
Devils Tower Natl. Monument, P.O. Box 10, Devils Tower, WY 82714	●	●	●	●	●	●	●	●		●	●							●									●		●
Fort Laramie Natl. Historic Site, HC72, Box 389, Fort Laramie, WY 82212	●	●	●	●		●												●										●	●
Fossil Butte Natl. Monument, P.O. Box 592, Kemmerer, WY 83101		●	●	●		●				●													●					●	●
Grand Teton Natl. Park, P.O. Drawer 170, Moose, WY 83012	●	●	●	●	●	●	●	●	●	●	●	●	●		●	●	●	●			●	●	●	●	●	●	●		●
John D. Rockefeller, Jr., Memorial Parkway, c/o Grand Teton Natl. Park, P.O. Drawer 170, Moose, WY 83012		●	●	●	●	●	●			●					●			●	●		●	●	●	●	●	●			●
Yellowstone Natl. Park (Wyo., Idaho, Mont.), P.O. Box 168, Yellowstone Natl. Park, WY 82190	●	●	●	●	●	●	●	●	●	●		●	●		●	●	●	●		●	●	●	●	●	●	●	●	●	●

Help Us Keep This Guide Up to Date

Every effort has been made by the authors and editors to make this guide as accurate and useful as possible. However, many changes can occur after a guide is published—establishments close, phone numbers change, facilities come under new management, and so on.

We would love to hear from you concerning your experiences with this guide and how you feel it could be made better and be kept up-to-date. While we may not be able to respond to all comments and suggestions, we'll take them to heart, and we'll make certain to share them with the authors. Please send your comments and suggestions to the following address:

The Globe Pequot Press
Reader Response/Editorial Department
P.O. Box 480
Guilford, CT 06437
Or you may e-mail us at: editorial@globe-pequot.com

Thanks for your input, and happy travels!

ABOUT THE AUTHORS

DAVID AND KAY SCOTT reside in Valdosta, Georgia, where the winters are mild, the humidity is high, and the people are friendly. They have spent twenty-six summers touring the United States and Canada in a series of Volkswagen campers. The first VW bus they owned was a 1967 model that looked like a relic from World War II. During its first cross-country trip, in 1970, the VW was barely able to make headway against the wind blowing across a Wyoming interstate. Their two- and three-month trips have taken the couple through all the states, the Canadian provinces, and to nearly all the areas administered by the National Park Service. The Scotts drove from Georgia to Alaska and back during the summer of 1982. David and Kay have appeared live from Yellowstone Park and Grand Canyon National Park on NBC's *Today* show, offering tips on visiting the national parks. In addition to their domestic travels, the Scotts spent three summers carrying backpacks while riding trains through Europe.

David Scott was born in Rushville, Indiana, attended Purdue University and Florida State University, and received a Ph.D. in economics from the University of Arkansas. During most of the year, he is a professor of accounting and finance at Valdosta State University. He has written numerous books on accounting, finance, and investing, including nine titles in Globe Pequot's Money Smarts series of personal finance books. In addition to travel, he is interested in amateur radio, computers, and the Atlanta Braves. His e-mail address is dlscott@valdosta.edu.

Kay Woelfel Scott was born in Austin, Minnesota, and was raised in Yankton, South Dakota. She graduated from Clearwater (Florida) High School and earned degrees at Florida Southern College and the University of Arkansas. During the academic year, she is assistant principal at an elementary school in Valdosta, Georgia. She is interested in a wide variety of crafts, including making stained glass and designing and painting T-shirts. She drew all the maps that appeared in the earlier editions of this book.